HUMAN RESOURCE DEVELOPMENT

HUMAN RESOURCE DEVELOPMENT

2nd edition

LEARNING & TRAINING for individuals & organizations

Edited by *John P Wilson*

KOGAN PAGE

London and Philadelphia

Publisher's note

Every possible effort has been made to ensure that the information contained in this book is accurate at the time of going to press, and the publisher and authors cannot accept responsibility for any errors or omissions, however caused. No responsibility for loss or damage occasioned to any person acting, or refraining from action, as a result of the material in this publication can be accepted by the editor, the publisher or any of the authors.

First published in 1999
Reprinted 2001
Second edition 2005
Reprinted 2006

Kogan Page Limited
120 Pentonville Road
London N1 9JN

525 South 4th Street, #241
Philadelphia PA 19147
USA

© Kogan Page, 1999, 2005

British Library Cataloguing in Publication Data

A CIP record for this book is available from the British Library

ISBN-10   0 7494 4352 9
ISBN-13   978 0 7494 4352 8

Library of Congress Cataloging-in-Publication Data
Human resource development : learning and training for individuals and organizations /
[edited by] John P. Wilson
    p. cm.
  ISBN 0-7494-4352-9
  1. Personnel management. I. Wilson, John P. (John Peter), 1955 Aug. 11-
HF5549.H7839 2005
658.3'124–dc22   2005000864

Typeset by Saxon Graphics Ltd, Derby
Printed and bound by Bell & Bain, Glasgow

Contents

List of Figures   *xi*
List of Tables   *xiii*
List of Case Studies   *xv*
List of Contributors   *xvii*
Preface   *xxi*
Acknowledgements   *xxv*
Dedication   *xxvii*

Section One: The Role of Learning, Training and Development in Organizations

1. Human Resource Development   *John P Wilson*   3
   Introduction and learning objectives   3
   Defining the terms: training, education, development, learning and HRD   4
   Strategic HRD   10
   The operating environment of the Human Resource department   12
   The Human Resources compass   14
   HRD roles   18
   Conclusion   23

2. Human Resource Management   *John Shipton*   26
   Introduction and learning objectives   26
   Origins and development of HRM   27
   HRM: the search for meaning   28
   Where is HRM 'coming from'?   29
   Hard and soft HRM   30
   Implications for action   34
   High-performance work practices   38
   Conclusion   40

3. Organizational Change   *Bland Tomkinson*   44
   Introduction and learning objectives   44
   The paradox of change   45
   The nature of change   46
   Methods to make the transition   47
   What can go wrong?   52
   The role of HRD in organizational change   55
   Conclusion   56

4. National Economic Development and Human Resource Development
      John P Wilson   58
   Introduction and learning objectives   58
   Developing the human resources of a nation   59
   Human development   73
   Conclusion   78

Section Two: Learning and Competitive Strategy

5. Strategy and Human Resource Development   *Sue Balderson*   83
   Introduction and learning objectives   83
   The case for strategic HRD   84
   Strategy and strategic HRD   86
   The problem with strategy   89
   Strategy and HRD – an historical context   91
   Strategic analysis and HRD   92
   The Balanced Scorecard   96
   Conclusion   97

6. Learning Organizations and Communities of Practice: A Critical Evaluation
      Rob F Poell   99
   Introduction and learning objectives   99
   Definitions and characteristics of the learning organization   100
   Criticism of the concept of the learning organization   106
   Conclusion   108

7. Knowledge Management   *John P Wilson and Alan Cattell*   111
   Introduction and learning objectives   111
   Data, information, knowledge and wisdom   112
   Knowledge management and information technology   115
   Competitive advantage   115
   Explicit and tacit knowledge   118
   Dimensions of knowledge   119
   The knowledge management process   120
   Learning and knowledge management   127
   Implementing knowledge management   128
   Knowledge workers   130
   Conclusion   131

Section Three: The Identification of Learning, Training and Development Needs

8. The Identification of Learning Needs   *Richard Palmer*   137
   Introduction and learning objectives   137
   Defining training and development   138
   Undertaking an LNA   139
   Needs at the organizational level   141
   Needs at departmental level   146
   Needs at occupational levels   148
   Needs at the individual level   150
   Defining the training priorities   153
   Conclusion   154

9. Performance Management and Human Resource Development   *Alan Cattell*   156
   Introduction and learning objectives   156
   What is performance management?   157
   The effectiveness of performance management   162
   Performance appraisal   173
   Conclusion   182

10. Making the Most of Consultancy: Perspectives on Partnership   *David Sawdon*   187
    Introduction and learning objectives   187
    Purpose and meaning   188
    Perceptions and needs   189
    Process and power   192
    Partnership   195

Section Four: The Planning and Designing of Learning, Training and Development

11. Fundamentals of Adult Learning   *Chris Wiltsher*   201
    Introduction and learning objectives   201
    Learning   202
    The learning process   202
    Levels of competence   206
    Adults and adulthood   209
    Styles of adult learning   211
    Why, what, how and practice   217
    Conclusion   218

12. The Adult Learner: Theory into Practice   *Janet Parr*   220
    Introduction and learning objectives   220
    Adult learning   221
    Motivation and learning   222
    Andragogy   223
    Humanist theories   224
    Barriers to learning   229
    Conclusion   232

13. Reflective Practice *Cheryl Hunt*   234
    Introduction and learning objectives 234
    The reflective practitioner: Donald Schön 236
    Models and loops 237
    Reflection-in-action 239
    Social context 242
    Putting reflection into practice 245
    Personal experience 247

14. Workplace Diversity and Training – More than Fine Words *Joan E Keogh*   252
    Introduction and learning objectives 252
    Equal opportunities and managing diversity – what is the difference? 253
    Training for diversity 262
    Is the educational approach enough? 265
    The law 267
    Towards a learning organization? 268
    Conclusion 268
    Appendix: The legal framework 272

15. Multilingual and Multicultural HRD *Toni Ibarz*   276
    Introduction and learning objectives 276
    Multilingual training and development 277
    Language in the communication age 279
    Language training in HRD 280
    English as the lingua franca 282
    Theories of language learning 283
    Teaching and training methods 285
    The management of language training 287
    The good language learner 290
    The new technologies 291
    Multicultural/cross-cultural learning 293
    Conclusion 294

Section Five: Delivering Learning, Training and Development

16. Open, distance and flexible learning *Geoff Chivers*   299
    Introduction and learning objectives 299
    From teaching to learning 300
    Distance learning 302
    Open learning 305
    Flexible learning 308
    Issues for the learner in ODFL 309
    Issues for ODFL providers 311
    The corporate open learning centre 313
    Conclusion 317

17. E-Learning: A Guide to Principles and Practice   *Maggie McPherson*   319
Introduction and learning objectives   319
What is e-learning?   320
Why is e-learning important?   320
Benefits of e-learning   321
Disadvantages of e-learning   322
What is required to make e-learning successful?   322
Course design and development issues   325
Appendix: The A–Z of training methods   331

18. The Design of Effective Group-based Training Methods   *Colin Beard*   342
Introduction and learning objectives   342
Group training methods   344
Selecting methods   346
Emotion and learning   352
Play and fun   359
Using materials creatively   362
Conclusion: the future of training methods   362

19. Problem-Based Learning (PBL)   *John Blewitt*   365
Introduction and learning objectives   365
Origins and principles   366
PBL: a way of professional and lifelong learning   368
Knowledge and PBL   370
PBL: theoretical underpinning   371
Facilitating PBL   374
The effectiveness of PBL   376
Conclusion   377

20. Management Training and Development: Problems, Paradoxes and
    Perspectives   *Colin Beard and Dominic Irvine*   380
Introduction and learning objectives   380
What do we mean by management?   381
What do we mean by development?   385
Perceptions of management training and development   392
Techniques of management training and development   395
Developing the emotionally intelligent manager   397
Evaluating the effectiveness of management training and development   399
Key issues to consider   400
Conclusion   401

Section Six: Assessment and Evaluation of Learning, Training and Development

21. Evaluation and Assessment   *Catherine Edwards Zara*   407
Introduction and learning objectives   407
Key terms   409
Contemporary approaches to evaluation   411
Contemporary approaches to assessment   418
Conclusion   421

22. Accounting for the Human Resource Development Function   *Chris Wiltsher*   423
Introduction and learning objectives   423
The need for formal accounting   424
Costing   427
Auditing   433
Conclusion   438

23. Intellectual Capital   *Alan Cattell*   439
Introduction and learning objectives   439
Main components of intellectual capital   440
Links between the different forms of capital   444
Tangible, intangible and invisible assets   445
Methods of quantification and measurement   446
Implications for HR practitioners   449
Reporting of capital   452
Challenges for HRD   453
Conclusion   453

Section Seven: Managing the Human Resource Function

24. Total Quality Training and Human Resource Development   *John P Wilson
and Ron Chapman*   459
Introduction and learning objectives   459
Quality   460
Best practice benchmarking   464
Quality control and quality assurance   470
Quality awards   473
Total Quality Training and development   476
Conclusion   482

25. Marketing Human Resource Development   *Jennifer Joy-Matthews*   484
Introduction and learning objectives   484
Why market?   485
Who and where are the customers and how do you know what they need?   487
How do you reach the customers?   491
How do we keep the customers?   496
Evaluating the whole marketing process   497
The way forward, or what you can do   500

26. Managing the Human Resource Development Function   *Pete Sayers*   503
Introduction and learning objectives   503
Management and leadership of the HRD function   505
Control and facilitation – coaching and supportiveness   508
Principles and values   511
Strategic vs operational decision-making   513
Further points for managers of a team of HRD professionals   518
Conclusion   519

Bibliography   521
Index   551

List of Figures

1.1	The role of the HRD department within the internal and external environment	13
1.2	The Human Resources compass	15
4.1	The education, training and development economic spiral	65
5.1	The classic training cycle	84
5.2	Business objectives within a training cycle	85
5.3	Strategy and HRD	90
5.4	A strategic HRD approach	94
5.5	Value chain boundaries	94
7.1	Data, information, knowledge	113
7.2	The knowledge management process	121
7.3	The knowledge management supply chain	123
7.4	The knowledge management cycle	128
8.1	Performance gap	143
9.1	A simple model of a performance management system	162
9.2	Cattell's model of permission	167
9.3	Combining HRM and HRD	172
9.4	Competence-based model of performance management	172
9.5	Appraiser preparation	176
9.6	Appraisee preparation	177
10.1	The four roles of a consultant	191
11.1	The process of perception and experiential learning	206
11.2	The Learning Combination Lock	207
11.3	Levels of competence	208
11.4	Kolb's experiential learning cycle	208
11.5	Bloom *et al*'s taxonomy of learning	215
12.1	Maslow's hierarchy of needs	225
12.2	Critically analysing experience	227
12.3	The learning spiral	228

13.1	Single-loop learning	238
13.2	Double-loop learning	239
14.1	The diversity progression	255
14.2	Managing diversity: pressures forcing action by employers	256
15.1	The communication process	280
15.2	Factors that contribute to effective interaction between L1 and L2 speakers	281
16.1	The teaching–learning system continuum	306
17.1	Identification of interested e-learning stakeholders at different levels	323
17.2	The EMAR model	326
18.1	Design and sequencing of training methods: the learner journey	349
19.1	PBL: a model for self-directed learning	373
20.1	The Management Standards Centre Management and Leadership units	386
20.2	MSC Unit 5: Providing direction: provide leadership for your team	387
21.1	The training wheel	411
23.1	Forms of capital contributing to market value	447
23.2	Metrics for sources of capital	450
23.3	An example of an HR scorecard	451
24.1	An example of a flat-line profile	468
24.2	The EFQM/BQF award assessment model: people, processes and results	474
24.3	The Investors in People standard	478
24.4	The TQM process	481
26.1	Management and leadership – two concepts linked in overlapping circles	505
26.2	The relationship between role power and personal power	509
26.3	Blanchard *et al*'s situational leadership with Sayers and Matthew's mapping of role power and personal power	510
26.4	Three tiers of operation for HRD	514

List of Tables

2.1	'Ideal types' of personnel management and HRM	29
2.2	Trends in reward management	37
2.3	A compilation of high-performance working practices	40
5.1	An historical perspective on strategy and HRD	91
5.2	Example of Balanced Scorecard measures which might form the basis of objectives, appraisal and development for a NHS manager	97
7.1	Key elements of tacit and explicit knowledge	119
8.1	Finishing and packaging department – Human Resources SWOT	147
8.2	Skills matrix, Product A cell	148
9.1	Approaches to the determination of reward	170
9.2	Appraisal methods and features	178
10.1	Stages or cycles of intervention	194
16.1	Potential advantages and disadvantages of open and distance learning from the learner's viewpoint	314
17.1	The ASSURE model	326
17.2	A–Z of training/system methods	331
18.1	Methods as a basic teaching process	343
19.1	Defining characteristics of PBL	369
22.1	Costing HRD activity	431
23.1	Notable authors on the various forms of capital	442
23.2	Areas of capital	444
26.1	Covey's (1992) four management paradigms	512

List of Case Studies

Chapter 2
'Managing people' training for oil industry engineers in East Asia/Australia   33

Chapter 3
Human Resource issues, in merger and change in higher education, and the
   need for development   53

Chapter 4
Bahrain model for boosting training and human resources   61
Institutional development of local NGOs in Mali, West Africa   74
Development in Malaysia   76

Chapter 5
Value chain for the Unipart group of companies   93
Unipart case study   95

Chapter 6
Improvement teams   104
Work-based learning projects   105

Chapter 8
Broadening the scope of LNAs in non-governmental organizations in Mali   140
LNA and competences in the Prison Service   144
Ford Motor Company's employee development and assistance programme   151

Chapter 9
The psychological contract operates in both directions   166
Appraisal and training in a private hospital   174

Chapter 10
Consulting in a healthcare environment   190
Post-traumatic stress disorder and bank raids   192

Chapter 11
Negotiation training for an NHS Trust   217

Chapter 12
Personal factors and learning   226

Chapter 14
Fluent Europe's guidelines   257
Training checklist for diversity   266
BT and diversity   269
The difference starts with you   270

Chapter 15
A successful language learning experience   281
Knoll Pharmaceuticals   288

Chapter 16
Television and training – big changes for small firms   303
Offshore open learning   307
Computer-based training in accountancy   315

Chapter 17
Blended learning for a Master's degree in Training and Development   329

Chapter 18
Negotiating public access to the UK countryside: skills practice section of a
   three-day training course   351
Creative training design: research methodology training   354
Play and fun: coffee and Sunday papers – 'playing with the literature'   360
Visualization, reality and simulation in learning – tree-felling indoors!   361

Chapter 19
Work relations and human resource development: a PBL scenario   376

Chapter 20
Outdoor management development programmes   397

Chapter 21
Evaluation of training including use of focus group method using a combination
   of Kirkpatrick's four levels and the CIRO framework   414

Chapter 24
Value stream mapping to meet the 40-day engine target for Rolls-Royce plc, using DMAIC   467
What is Six Sigma?   472

Chapter 25
David Matthews, freelance outdoor pursuits instructor and trainer   486
Pinderfields and Pontefract Hospitals NHS Trust   490
The Biotechnological and Biological Sciences Research Council (BBSRC)   495
International Youth Hostel Federation (IYHF) – Hostel 2000   498
Case study revisited: David Matthews, freelance outdoor pursuits instructor and trainer 501

List of Contributors

Sue Balderson was a principal lecturer at De Montfort University's graduate School of Business until 2001, when she established her own consultancy in the field of personal and management development. Previously an HRD practitioner in the NHS, Sue is now involved with national management education and development programmes in that sector, as well as working with some blue-chip private sector companies.
sjbcor@dmu.ac.uk

Colin Beard is a senior lecturer at Sheffield Hallam University. He has developed and launched the world's first Outdoor Management Development Masters Degree. He specializes in environmental training, management training, creativity and innovation. He is a Fellow of the CIPD and co-authored *The Power of Experiential Learning*
c.m.beard@shu.ac.uk

John Blewitt is head of the Department of Lifelong Learning and academic manager of the Continuing Professional Development unit at the University of Exeter. John has wide experience of adult, further and higher education and is a keen supporter of Education for Sustainability. He is co-editor of *The Sustainability Curriculum: The challenge for higher education* published by Earthscan in 2004.
j.d.blewitt@exeter.ac.uk

Alan Cattell is course director of the MEd in Training and Development at the University of Bradford. He is a Fellow of the Chartered Institute of Personnel and Development and a past CIPD branch chair. He gained his Masters degree in Education Training and Development at Sheffield University.
a.h.cattell@bradford.ac.uk.

Ron Chapman formerly worked in industry in 57 countries worldwide. He is based in the Centre for Hazard and Risk Management at Loughborough University, actively researching in the field of ethnic minority business and lecturing in information management and strategy, having moved from Adult Continuing Education at the University of Sheffield. r.j.chapman3@lboro.ac.uk

Geoff Chivers is emeritus professor of Risk Management and Professional Development at Loughborough University. He has been involved with continuing education and training for over 30 years, and previously held the chair of Continuing Education at the University of Sheffield. His main research interests are within the area of continuing professional development. g.e.chivers@lboro.ac.uk

Cheryl Hunt is senior lecturer in Professional Learning at the University of Exeter. Her research interests are in critical reflective practice, adult and community education, and spirituality as a dimension of lifelong learning. She has a wide range of experience of teaching on academic and professional courses in a variety of settings. c.hunt@exeter.ac.uk

Toni Ibarz lectures in modern languages at the Institute for Lifelong Learning at the University of Sheffield. His research interests include learner autonomy, assessment and the teaching and learning of languages online. He has recently taken part in two projects to evaluate the impact of CD ROM-based ESOL packages for Learndirect. a.ibarz@sheffield.ac.uk

Dominic Irvine is hopeless at repeat delivery of standardized programmes, he thrives on innovative and scary learning and development solutions. Making organizations rock is his thing. He's either damn cheap or good as the companies he works for ask him to zip around the world doing his thing. Dominic Irvine is part of Epiphanies Ltd. www.epiphaniesltd.com; dom@epiphaniesltd.com

Jennifer Joy-Matthews is a learning and management consultant; a project manager and a researcher. She has worked in the public, private and voluntary sector in Europe, Central America and the Pacific Rim. Jennifer designs, delivers and evaluates a range of interventions. She is a Fellow of the CIPD and an NLP practitioner. joymatthews@supanet.com

Joan Keogh is a consultant with particular interests in job evaluation and payment systems, including equal pay. She is an ACAS appointed independent expert and was awarded the OBE for services to industrial tribunals. She lectures in employment law and discrimination and is associated with the Universities of Bradford, Sheffield Hallam and Strathclyde. joan.keogh@btopenworld.com

Maggie McPherson is a lecturer in the University of Sheffield and a member of Council for the Institute of Management of Information Systems (IMIS). Maggie has been involved in IT project management and e-learning research over the last 12 years. Notable among her publications is a 2004 RoutledgeFalmer book, co-authored with Miguel Nunes, entitled *Developing Innovation in Online Learning: An action research framework.*
m.a.mcpherson@sheffield.ac.uk

Richard Palmer has 30 years' experience in HR and has worked extensively in training and continuous improvement. He has published a book on TQM training and also *Training with the Midas Touch*, exploring how organizations can develop their people. He has a degree in Business and a Master's in Training and Development.

Janet Parr has been an associate lecturer with the Open University for the past 15 years. Having begun her studies as a mature student, she is particularly interested in supporting the educational development of adults, with a special interest in dyslexic students. She is also currently working with her local Crime and Disorder Reduction Partnership to establish a programme for the common monitoring of disclosed domestic violence.
aromatics@madasafish.com

Rob F Poell is associate professor of HRD in the department of Human Resource Studies at Tilburg University (Netherlands). His research interests focus on workplace learning and the organizing strategies used by employees, managers and HRD practitioners. Rob publishes regularly in *Management Learning, Human Resource Development Quarterly, Human Resource Development International, Adult Education Quarterly, Applied Psychology International Review*, and other scientific journals.
r.poell@uvt.nl.

David Sawdon is an independent training consultant and mental health social worker. These different employment roles provide complementary perspectives and experience, and he has particular interests in the management of diversity, quality assurance, team development and action learning.

Pete Sayers is Staff Development Adviser at the University of Bradford. He started his career as a teacher of English as a Second Language and helped organizations with intercultural communication and implementing equal opportunities.
petesayers@blueyonder.co.uk

John Shipton, after a career in human resource management as both practitioner and higher education lecturer, is now a freelance consultant and tutor. His work has included assignments in Europe and South East Asia, and distance learning supervisions in North America, Africa, the Caribbean and Ireland. He is a past vice president of the IPM and a Chartered Companion of the CIPD.
johnshipton@onetel.com

Bland Tomkinson held a number of roles in UMIST prior to its merger with the Victoria University of Manchester, including director of the Teaching and Learning Support Centre, director of Staff Development and head of Personnel. Since the merger he has held the post of University Adviser on Pedagogic Development.
bland.tomkinson@manchester.ac.uk

John P Wilson is CPD manager at the University of Oxford. He is co-author of *The Power of Experiential Learning*, which is also published in Mandarin Chinese. He has worked as a consultant with many organizations and spent two years working in Sweden and four years in Saudi Arabia for an oil company.
john.wilson@begbroke.ox.ac.uk

Chris Wiltsher has worked in adult education and training since 1981. He has a background in philosophy and his main interests are in issues of concepts and their application. With qualifications in finance, he is also interested in the problems of financial measurement for developmental processes such as training.

Catherine Edwards Zara is senior tutor in the Centre for Lifelong Learning at the University of Warwick. She is director of the BA (Hons) and Foundation Degrees in Post-Compulsory Education and Training; and the Open Studies Certificate in Philosophy. Her research and teaching interests include assessment and evaluation in post-compulsory, work-based, profession-related learning and human resource development.
catherine.zara@warwick.ac.uk

Preface

Human Resource Development is a growing and influential discipline, which is increasingly critical to the survival and success of all organizations. This is illustrated by the concepts of the Learning Organization and the Knowledge Organization, which demonstrate the essential requirement of developing all people within organizations. Furthermore, with the spread of information and world-wide communications, competitive advantage based on technology may only be maintained for short periods of time before competitors catch up. The only source of sustainable competitive advantage is to learn faster and more creatively than other competing organizations, and that will only be achieved through swift and effective HRD strategies.

The core principle of this book is to integrate both theory and practice within a virtuous circle. Theory may be generally viewed as refined best practice, which is then fed back to the operational level and continually tested and evaluated, thereby enhancing the theoretical underpinnings of the discipline. Theory without practice remains just that – theory. It needs to be applied, which is why this book contains a significant number of case studies to illustrate the application of theory to practice. It was John Ruskin, the Victorian philosopher and naturalist, who stated that, 'What we think, or what we know, or what we believe is, in the end, of little consequence. The only consequence is what we do.'

The objective of this book is to encourage learning in individuals and organizations through a pragmatic consideration of the underlying theories and their practical application. The book is divided into seven sections which are built around the traditional training cycle.

SECTION ONE: THE ROLE OF LEARNING, TRAINING AND DEVELOPMENT

Chapter 1 begins by exploring the meaning of terms, including training, education, development and learning, thus providing the basis for a consideration of the role of HRD. It is followed by a chapter on HRM, which describes the complementary elements of HR. Learning is another word for change, and Chapter 3 discusses how organizational change can be supported. Learning is also being seen in educational, work and social spheres as a means to encourage national economic success, feeding through to improved health and social circumstances (Chapter 4).

SECTION TWO: LEARNING AND COMPETITIVE STRATEGY

Learning, training and development are key ingredients of the strategy toolbox (Chapter 5) and help encourage success for both individuals or learning organizations (Chapter 6). Indeed, learning combined with the speed of application is now recognized as possibly the only source of sustainable competitive advantage. Through the management and transfer of knowledge, organizations can systematically structure and encourage improved performance (Chapter 7).

SECTION THREE: THE IDENTIFICATION OF LEARNING, TRAINING AND DEVELOPMENT NEEDS

The identification of learning and training needs provides information at individual, occupational and organizational levels for learning interventions (Chapter 8). Similarly, performance management may be used as a mechanism for specifying and indicating developmental requirements (Chapter 9). The identification of training and development needs often requires people to operate as internal or external consultants, and this is discussed in Chapter 10.

SECTION FOUR: THE PLANNING AND DESIGNING OF LEARNING, TRAINING AND DEVELOPMENT

In planning and designing learning interventions the central focus should be the learner. How people learn (Chapter 11) and how their environment influences the learning process are fundamental considerations in the design and development of programmes for adults (Chapter 12). Developing the skills of people to become reflective practitioners in their operational areas has proved to be a successful dimension of professional development (Chapter 13). The final chapters in this section investigate the issue of diversity (Chapter 14), an important area not only for multinational organizations but, given the multicultural nature of the workforce, for all organizations (Chapter 15).

SECTION FIVE: DELIVERING LEARNING, TRAINING AND DEVELOPMENT

The days of chalk and talk are mercifully much rarer than they were, and learning at a time, place and pace to suit the learner can be achieved through open, distance and flexible learning (Chapter 16). One means of achieving this flexibility is to use e-learning (Chapter 17), and not only do we need to have an understanding of how people learn, we must also think about how people learn in groups (Chapter 18). In the medical and health sectors, problem-based learning has proved to be very successful, and it is increasingly being used in many other industrial areas (Chapter 19). Managers handle problems on a regular basis, and much training and development is directed at this group (Chapter 20).

SECTION SIX: ASSESSMENT AND EVALUATION OF LEARNING, TRAINING AND DEVELOPMENT

Accurately assessing and evaluating training and development interventions (Chapter 21) is one of the most difficult aspects of HRD, and for this reason is frequently avoided and ignored. However, difficulty is not a justification to ignore the subject, and it should be included within company accounts, thus raising its profile (Chapter 22). The value of learning to organizations is now leading to increased attention, and to methods to assess intellectual capital (Chapter 23).

SECTION SEVEN: MANAGING THE HUMAN RESOURCE FUNCTION

The final section is concerned with addressing the quality of HRD (Chapter 24) and ensuring that it is marketed to its various constituencies (Chapter 25). All of this falls within the broader issue of managing the HRD function and ensuring that it has a central role to play in the organization (Chapter 26).

Acknowledgements

This book represents the cumulative efforts of a great many people. It grew out of the very positive environment and constructive atmosphere between the tutors, students and support staff involved with the MEd in Training and Development programme at the University of Sheffield and which is now based at the University of Bradford. This was the first programme of its type in the UK and its reception led to it also being delivered in Ireland and Singapore. The enthusiasm which it generated led to it receiving a National Training Award; prizes given by Lloyds Quality Register for the best dissertations, and a former student, Graham Murray, winning the Supreme Individual National Training Award. The programme is recognized by the International Federation of Training and Development Organizations. The programme has developed organically with some former students becoming tutors while others have gone on to write books in the training and development field.

Many thanks to all the chapter authors for identifying case studies to provide flesh to the theory and thus reinforcing the theory–practice cycle. In addition, particular thanks to individual contributors of the case studies including: Peter Voon, Training Manager, East Asia/Australia Regional Training, Anglo-Dutch Oil; Majid Al Binali, The Ministry of Labour and Social Affairs, Bahrain; Hub Gielissen, Senior Adviser, SNV, Mali; Mohammed Nasser Abu Hassan, Malaysia; Anita Nijsten, SNV, Mali; Shane Bryans, Head of Management and Specialist Training, HM Prison Service; Ford UK for details of their progressive Employee Development and Assistance Programme; Stephen R Western, Training Manager, Independent Hospital, Sheffield; Carole Hall, Training Consultant, ETC; Brian Harvey, Clamonta Ltd; Stephanie Warren, Rolls-Royce plc; Fluent Europe Ltd; Oxfam; Neil Currant, University of Bradford; Charlotte Burnip, Investors in People; David Weaver, Management Standards Centre; the National Association for the Care and Resettlement of Offenders for their Training Checklist for Diversity; British Telecom Equal Opportunities Policy Unit for the information on diversity; Liverpool John Moores University; John MacMahon, Editor of Educational Programmes, Television, at Radio Telefís Éireann, Dublin; Liverpool Women's Hospital and Interactive Designs Ltd for the THESEUS database case study; Sarah Wilkinson of Dean Associates, and The Employment Service ESCOM team for the details on computer-based training; Mike –

Language training; Knoll Pharmaceuticals; Tom Ryan, Radio Telefís Éireann, Dublin; Wilson–Connelly Associates, Philip O'Gorman, Training and Development Manager, Dairygold Co-operative Society Ltd, Ireland; Investors in People UK for details of the IiP; British Quality Foundation and European Foundation for Quality Management for the EFQM Model; Management Standards Centre for details of the MCI Management and Leadership Standards; Employment NTO for the Training and Development Standards; David Matthews, Outdoor Pursuits Instructor and Trainer; Richard Firth, Learning and Development Manager, Pinderfields and Pontefract Hospitals NHS Trust; John Scott, Training Consultant, The Biotechnological and Biological Sciences Research Council; Terry Rollinson, Personnel Director, Youth Hostel Association and Kay Price, High Peak College, Derbyshire. Thanks too, to Anthony Cropper for his research into the case studies, and Catherine Willens for technical support. Lastly, many thanks to the Kogan Page staff, in particular Helen Kogan and Kim Collins, and editor Philip Mudd, whose persistence and encouragement enabled this book to materialize.

Dedication

Charles Handy in *The Age of Unreason* (1990:63) stated that, 'I am more and more sure that those who are in love with learning are in love with life. For them change is never a problem, never a threat, just another exciting opportunity.' To all those trainers, trainees, delegates, managers, HRD specialists, consultants, advisors, researchers, lecturers and support staff who are involved with learning and change – may you all remain in love with learning and in love with life.

Section One:

The Role of Learning, Training and Development in Organizations

1

Human Resource Development

John P Wilson

INTRODUCTION AND LEARNING OBJECTIVES

Human Resource Development (HRD) is a title which represents the latest evolutionary stage in the long tradition of training, educating and developing people for the purpose of contributing towards the achievement of individual, organizational and societal objectives. Unfortunately, along with its partner Human Resource Management (HRM), it has attracted a certain amount of criticism for its 'insensitive depiction' of people as replacement parts serving the mechanistic requirements of the organization. For many lay people HRD and HRM are visualized in a similar manner to the way in which Charlie Chaplin was swallowed by the giant cogs in the machine and dehumanized in the 1936 film *Modern Times*.

HRD, as with the title HRM, makes individuals sound rather like the nuts and bolts of an organization that can be interchanged and dispensed with at will. To give it a more human face Drucker suggested the term 'biological HRD' to emphasize the living nature of the people within the organization; however, Webster (1990) suggests that this term gives the unfortunate impression of a washing powder.

This apparently clinical approach to the involvement of people within an organization has developed as a result of numerous factors which we will consider shortly. To contextualize this development we will first investigate some of the component elements which constitute HRD. We will begin first with definitions of training, education, development and learning and use these as a basis for a definition of HRD. We will then consider how HRD contributes to strategic issues and how the various elements interrelate with HRM. In conclusion, there is a consideration of the roles and practical competencies required of those in HRD.

Having read this chapter you will:

- understand and be able to differentiate between training, education, learning, development and HRD;
- understand the relationship between HRM and HRD;
- know the elements of the Human Resource Compass; and
- be aware of the competencies (USA) and the competences (UK) associated with training and development.

DEFINING THE TERMS: TRAINING, EDUCATION, DEVELOPMENT, LEARNING AND HRD

Training

The historical antecedents of training have contributed towards the current perception of training. In many crafts and guilds the purpose of training was to enable indentured apprentices to work for a period of years under the supervision of a master craftsperson. Eventually, the apprentices learned the skills required of that occupation and would produce a complex piece of work, a 'masterpiece', incorporating much of what they had learned. This would then enable them to become members of the specific guild. Hence, today, we have the term 'Master's degree' which illustrates that the person is, or should be, fully conversant with that area.

An often referred source of definitions has been the Manpower Services Commission's (1981:62) *Glossary of Training Terms* which defines training as:

> a planned process to modify attitude, knowledge or skill behaviour through learning experience to achieve effective performance in an activity or range of activities. Its purpose, in the work situation, is to develop the abilities of the individual and to satisfy the current and future needs of the organisation.

The term 'learning experience' was used because the compilers of the *Glossary* expressed the view that there was no clear demarcation between education and training and they also wanted to emphasize the integrated nature of the two.

A more recent source of definitions is CEDEFOP's (The European Centre for the Development of Vocational Training) *Glossarium* of educational and training terms in nine European languages. This glossary was developed to encourage understanding and cooperation between countries. The original intention was to standardize the meaning of terms in

Europe, but partly due to linguistic and cultural differences the proposal was not adopted. CEDEFOP (1996:52) defines vocational training as:

> Activity or programme of activities designed to teach the skills and knowledge required for particular kinds of work.
> Training ... usually takes place at working places, whereas education ... takes place at *educational establishments*. (UK)

Both of the definitions above illustrate the application of training to the requirements of the organization and the fact that this training tends to occur in the workplace. They also indicate a relatively narrow limitation to specific skills and operations. Moreover, training normally has an immediate application and is generally completed in a shorter timescale than education (Van Wart *et al*, 1993).

Education

From an historical perspective education was closely linked to the Church in western countries and the number of people receiving education was very limited, as was the case with the guilds. Much of the emphasis was on classics, ie Latin and Greek, and there was minimal consideration of practical applications. However, the educated person was often more highly regarded and thus oversaw the craftsperson; a trend which may still be seen today and which influences recruitment to some disciplines.

Education is defined as:

> activities which aim at developing the knowledge, skills, moral values and understanding required in all aspects of life rather than a knowledge and skill relating to only a limited field of activity. The purpose of education is to provide the conditions essential to young people and adults to develop an understanding of the traditions and ideas influencing the society in which they live and to enable them to make a contribution to it. It involves the study of their own cultures and of the laws of nature, as well as the acquisition of linguistic and other skills which are basic to learning, personal development, creativity and communication. (Manpower Services Commission, 1981:17)

> A programme of learning over an extended period with general objectives relating to the personal development of the pupil/student and/or his/her acquisition of knowledge. In addition education refers to the area of public policy concerned with programmes of learning in a particular jurisdiction taken altogether (e.g. in the context of education expenditure). (Ireland)
> Activities aim at developing the knowledge, skills, moral values and understanding required in all aspects of life rather than knowledge and skill relating to only a limited field of activity. The purpose of education is to provide the conditions essential for young persons and adults to develop an understanding of the traditions and ideas influencing the society in which they live and to enable them to make a contribution to it. It involves the study of their own and other cultures and the laws of nature as well as the acquisition of linguistic and other skills which are basic to learning, personal development, creativity and communication. (UK) (CEDEFOP, 1996:48)

Education is considerably broader in scope than training and this is perhaps illustrated by the considerably longer definitions above. It also has a less immediate and less specific application than training and is often perceived as being delivered in educational institutions. Education is regarded as encompassing knowledge, skills and attitudes (Bloom *et al*, 1956).

There is a continuing tension between the needs of industry and commerce with their immediate requirements for specific skills, and the educational requirements of the individual and of society, which need people who can contribute to the quality of life in a multifaceted way. There is therefore a tension between traditional education and training provision which is illustrated by Dearden (1991:93):

> But training can be, and often is, very illiberally conceived, and then it may not merely be uneducational but even anti-educational. As an example of the uneducational, one might mention the recent controversy over whether trainees in the YTS (Youth Training Scheme) should be given any opportunity to consider the social significance of work as part of their 'off-the-job' provision.

Distinguishing between education and training can be quite problematic. One very illustrative example of the difference between education and training would be a young child coming home and saying, 'We had sex training today!' This is in stark contrast to sex education classes that imply a theoretical rather than a practical application of learning!

Development

Development is:

> the growth or realisation of a person's ability, through conscious or unconscious learning. Development programmes usually include elements of planned study and experience, and are frequently supported by a coaching or counselling facility. (Manpower Services Commission, 1981:15)

This definition was subsequently broadened from 'a person's ability' to 'an individual's or a group's ability' (MSC, 1985:9) thus reflecting the growing concept of organizational learning:

> Development occurs when a gain in experience is effectively combined with the conceptual understanding that can illuminate it, giving increased confidence both to act and to perceive how such action relates to its context. (Bolton, 1995:15)

It can be seen from the definitions that development indicates movement to an improved situation that for the individual means advancing towards the physical and mental potential we all possess. In many respects development indicates growth and movement by the learner rather than learning itself, which we will consider next.

Learning

Although both learning in general and adult learning are considered in greater depth in Chapters 11 and 12 it is necessary here to provide a definition in order to contribute towards the picture of HRD. Handy (1990:63) considered learning as being a natural response to coping with change and stated that, 'I am more and more sure that those who are in love with learning are in love with life. For them change is never a problem, never a threat, just another exciting opportunity.'

Learning can occur in formal settings such as a university or organizational training centres but it can also occur less formally. Nadler (Nadler and Nadler, 1990) distinguished between what he called 'incidental' learning and 'intentional learning'. Incidental learning is considered to be learning which occurs during the course of doing other things such as reading, talking with others, travelling, etc.

Learning and possessing a knowledge of something is one thing but applying the learning is yet another; thus, learning has limited value unless it is put into practice. Nadler (Nadler and Nadler, 1990:1.5) drew attention to the fact that learning is not guaranteed and that it is only the possibility of learning which may happen. He emphasized that:

> HRD cannot and should not promise that as a result of the learning experience performance will change. This might sound like a radical statement until we look at the false promises that some in HRD have made.

Nadler maintained that performance is based on a variety of factors and the majority of these are not the responsibility of those who work in the HRD department. This pragmatic view of the application of learning does not only relate to the recent demands of organizational objectives, it can also apply in a philosophical sense. The Victorian philosopher and naturalist, John Ruskin, remarked that, 'What we know, or what we believe, or what we think, is in the end of little consequence. The only consequence is what we do.'

Drawing from the preceding discussion learning may be defined as a relatively permanent change of knowledge, attitude or behaviour occurring as a result of formal education or training, or as a result of informal experiences.

One common theme that can be found in many of the definitions of training, education and development is that they contain the word 'learning'. Nadler (Nadler and Nadler, 1990:1.18) gathered these terms together and stated that:

> Training = learning related to present job;
> Education = learning to prepare the individual but not related to a specific present or future job;
> Development = learning for growth of the individual but not related to a specific present or future job.

He maintained that we should not be too concerned about these labels and accepted that the definitions above might be ordered training, development and education.

Garavan (1997:42) also investigated the nature of training, education and development and came to the similar conclusion that they all involved learning. He went on to state that, 'It is therefore logical to suggest that all four (education, training, development, and learning) are seen as complementary components of the same process, ie the enhancement of human potential or talent.'

The debate about the meaning of training, education and development is for many lay people rather an academic one; however, the discussion will continue because it provides an interpretation of a complex subject. For this reason it should not be dismissed as mere academic navel-gazing. Instead it should be recognized that numerous perspectives and valuable insights result which further encourage and direct learning activities both for individuals and organizations. The important thing is for learning to occur and be applied both within organizations and to life as a whole.

As a postscript to the discussion on definitions above, a brief mention of indoctrination should be included since it is rarely covered in training and development literature. Indoctrination can be found in a number of areas such as religious cults, political indoctrination, some military training, company culture and company songs, etc. In some ways it may be regarded as a slightly less intensive form of brainwashing in which individuals or groups are encouraged, persuaded, or forced to adopt a particular mental model or approach to specific areas or even whole lifestyles. Rogers (1986) analysed the relationship of indoctrination, training, and learning. Indoctrination was described as having very restricted objectives and provided for one way of thinking. Training, while still having narrow goals, allowed slightly broader thinking, and learning had the least constraints and tolerated diverse ways of thinking.

Human Resource Development

The term 'Human Resource Development' was introduced to the 1969 Miami Conference of the American Society of Training and Development (ASTD) by Leonard Nadler and he subsequently provided a definition in 1970. Nadler (Nadler and Nadler, 1990) emphasized that there had been a significant number of people entering the HRD field and, therefore, they deserved to have a definition of the subject. At the same time he maintained that good HRD specialists see an input into most of the operational areas and therefore delimiting the field can also have adverse consequences for the profession.

The recognition that HRD fed into most organizational areas was also noted by Galagan (1986:4) who described it as:

> an omnivorous discipline, incorporating over the years almost any theory or practice that would serve the goal of learning in the context of work. Like an amoeba, it has ingested and taken nourishment from whatever it deemed expedient in the social and behavioural sciences, in learning theory and business.

Accurately defining HRD can be problematic particularly if an international perspective is taken because its interpretation and roles tend to vary from one country to another (Hansen and Brooks, 1994). Furthermore, following research among the delegates at an international conference, Jones and Mann (1992:xiv) commented that, 'there was a strong insistence that HRD does not equal training'.

If HRD is about learning and that learning is something which occurs within an individual to cause development then, 'The East, with its grace and wisdom, calls this flux "a becoming" and "an unfolding"; the West, with its systems and structures, names it "human resource development"' Ortigas (1994:xii).

In observing the debate about HRD, Jacobs (1990:66) drew parallels with other disciplines and stated:

> HRD is both an area of professional practice and an emerging interdisciplinary body of knowledge. The inter-relatedness of these two aspects makes HRD similar to most other applied professions, most of which have emerged to meet some important social or organisational need. After practice is established, the need arises to formalise the knowledge gained in practice into some logical structure. Such activity helps legitimise the profession and increases the reliability of practice.

Frank (1988) investigated the theoretical base of HRD in order to distinguish it from other fields and identified three assumptions on which it is based:

1. HRD is based on the research and theories drawn from the field of adult education and is different from the learning that occurs in children. Learning is based on creating the appropriate circumstances in which adults can learn and thereby change behaviour.
2. HRD is concerned with improved performance within the work environment. It is not concerned with improving people's health or their personal relations with their family.
3. HRD utilizes the theories of change and how these relate to the organization. Change affects individuals, groups and the organization and HRD is predominantly concerned with the change of individuals.

Garavan *et al* (2000) conducted a detailed investigation of HRD and associated literature, and suggested that there was a philosophical debate about whether HRD should promote performance or learning. Where HRD is considered to be part of HRM it is concerned with performance; and where it is part of adult education the emphasis is learning. They maintained that it was difficult to make a clear statement about what should be included in HRD even though it is maturing as a subject.

There would thus appear to be a professional need to define the territory of HRD, no matter how limited it may be, in order that those involved with it either as deliverers or receivers can have a reasonable understanding of what it encompasses. Below are a number of definitions of HRD:

> organised learning experiences in a definite time period to increase the possibility of improving job performance growth. (Nadler and Nadler, 1990:1.3)

> Human resource development is the study and practice of increasing the learning capacity of individuals, groups, collectives, and organisations through the development and application of learning-based interventions for the purpose of optimising human and organisational growth and effectiveness. (Chalofsky, 1992:179)

> HRD is the integrated use of training and development, career development, and organisation development to improve individual and organisational effectiveness. (McLagan and Suhadolnik, 1989:1)

> The field of study and practice responsible for the fostering of a long-term, work-related learning capacity at the individual, group, and organisational level of organisations. (Watkins, 1989:427)

> Human resource development encompasses activities and processes which are intended to have impact on organisational and individual learning. (Stewart and McGoldrick, 1996:1)

All the above definitions would appear to have been developed from a theoretical perspective, albeit probably based upon observation and practice. From a more applied point of view Ralphs and Stephan (1986) found, from a study of *Fortune 500* companies, that people placed the following subjects under the umbrella of HRD which scored more than 90 per cent: training and development, organizational development, human resource planning, and career planning.

In spite of all the definitions available, 'there are no universally accepted definitive statements of the meaning either of HRM or of HRD' (McGoldrick and Stewart, 1996:9). HRD is still a young discipline and still in the process of developing and finding a clearer identity for itself. What is clear from the definitions of HRD above and the contributory areas of training, education, development and learning, is that HRD refers to learning at the individual, group and organizational levels to enhance the effectiveness of human resources with the purpose of achieving the objectives of the organization.

STRATEGIC HRD

We have analysed the nature of HRD and now we will proceed to consider how it is integrated into the organization. The word *strategy* originates from the Greek word *strategia* meaning 'generalship' and is related to the science and art of warfare. Organizational competition does not fully equate to warfare but when one comes across books with titles such as *The Management Secrets of Genghis Khan*, it would appear that some people take the subject very seriously indeed.

Strategy, according to Johnson and Scholes (1993), is concerned with a number of dimensions:

- the range of an organization's activities;
- the matching of the organization's activities to the environment;
- the matching of the organization's activities to available resources.

Johnson and Scholes (1993:10) state that:

> Strategy is the direction and scope of an organisation over the long term: ideally, which matches its resources to the changing environment, and in particular its markets, customers or clients so as to meet stakeholder expectations.

A number of strategic pressures have contributed to the increasing importance and strategic role of HRD (McLagan and Suhadolnik, 1989; Garavan *et al*, 1995) and these include:

- accelerated rate of change;
- focus on quality;
- globalization of business;
- increased flexibility and responsiveness of organizations;
- increased pressure to demonstrate the contribution of human resources;
- new competitive structures;
- new technology.

With all these pressures it is apparent that HRD contributes in a variety of ways and at all organizational levels to provide support. This critical role of HRD is described by Torraco and Swanson (1995:11) who state that:

> Yet, today's business environment requires that HRD not only supports the business strategies or organisations, but that it assumes a pivotal role in the shaping of business strategy. ... As a primary means of sustaining an organisation's competitive edge, HRD serves a strategic role by assuring the competence of employees to meet the organisation's present performance demands. Along with meeting present organisational needs, HRD also serves a vital role in shaping strategy and enabling organisations to take full advantage of emergent business strategies.

Similarly, Beer and Spector (1989; in Garavan *et al*, 1995:6) also maintain that:

> Strategic HRD can be viewed as a proactive, system-wide intervention, with it linked to strategic planning and cultural change. This contrasts with the traditional view of training and development as consisting of reactive, piecemeal interventions in response to specific problems. HRD can only be strategic if it is incorporated into the overall corporate business strategy. It is in this way that the HRD function attains the status it needs to survive and to have a long term impact on overall business performance and respond to significant competitive and technological pressures.

In the present environment, sources of competitive advantage are quickly overcome by competitors and, thus, the only source of competitive advantage is the ability of an organization to learn more quickly than others. This learning does not occur in an abstract form within the organization but in the minds of individuals and groups. For this reason Drucker (1993) talks about the post-capitalist society and emphasizes the fact that value now resides inside the heads of the employees and much less within the capital assets of the organization.

Building on this understanding of value residing with the employees has been a recognition that, unlike capital assets which can be used up and also depreciate over time, the value of individuals can actually increase. For this reason and from a strategic perspective there is increased emphasis on the investment in human assets through training and development.

Strategic HRD enables:

- the organization to respond to challenges and opportunities through the identification and delivery of HRD interventions;
- individuals, supervisors, line managers and top managers to be informed of their roles and participate in HRD delivery;
- management to have operational guidelines which explain the reasons for investment in HRD;
- information to be disseminated which explains the training, education, development and learning opportunities available for employees;
- a policy statement to explicitly describe the relationship between the objectives of the organization and the HRD function;
- a positive public relations awareness for new and potential employees to know that skills deficiencies will be provided for;
- the continuous assessment of learning and development opportunities for its employees and thereby enabling them to advance their careers and support organizational growth;
- clearly specified objectives and targets that enable the HRD function to be evaluated against strategic requirements;
- policies which relate the HRD function to the other operating functions;
- training, education, development and learning opportunities to have a coordinated role within a systematic process.

Factors discouraging HRD

The business cycle of peaks and troughs tends to have a significant effect on the delivery of training and development because it is sometimes seen as a cost rather than an investment. When there are pressures on budgets, training is often seen as a relatively easy target in that the consequences are not immediately apparent. The value of HRD is that it is more closely aligned to organizational strategy and the achievement of objectives. Therefore, it becomes more difficult to argue that cuts should occur in the training and development budget.

THE OPERATING ENVIRONMENT OF THE HUMAN RESOURCE DEPARTMENT

It is not uncommon to find departments within an organization having a pre-Copernican view about their role; for instance, finance views operating issues through financial lenses and production views matters through production glasses. In like manner, the same accusations can be levelled at Human Resources being predominantly concerned only with the human dimension of the organization.

People, of course, are far and away the most important resource in any company. But they are not more than that. It is very easy to forget when endeavouring to develop people and to care for them, and even to love them, that the needs of the business must come first. Without that, there can be no lasting security. A fool's paradise in which effort is concentrated only on the present well-being of the staff, without regard for the future, will eventually disintegrate and it may well be the staff that suffer most. (Barham *et al*, 1988:28)

The perspectives above are only natural reactions given the responsibility departments hold; however, they can also restrain understanding of the organizational and external environment. Thus it is important to have a broader perspective, which is illustrated in Figure 1.1.

The organizational environment normally consists of approximately six main departments, namely: distribution, finance, human resources, marketing, production, and research and design. They are all symbiotically related to one another, and although some organizations have outsourced some elements such as distribution eg News International, and others do not involve themselves with production eg Nike, these are essential ingredients which are needed to ensure that the customers receive the product or service they require.

At a broader level the organization does not operate in a vacuum but is influenced and affected by the various forces operating in the external environment. These factors include:

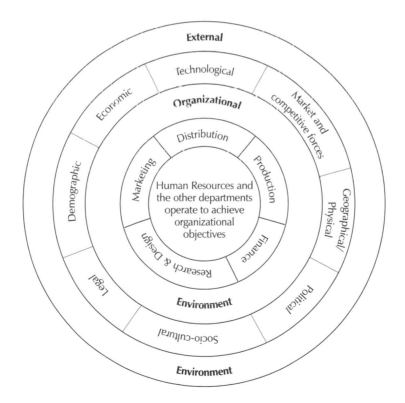

Figure 1.1 The role of the HRD department within the internal and external environment

technology, market and competitive forces, geographical and physical circumstances, political, socio-cultural, legal, demographic and economic factors.

At the organization environment and external environment levels, a department needs to be aware of its role and the forces which affect its operation and success. These are particularly important for the HRD specialist who must have an understanding of operational issues in order to fully contribute throughout the organization. The specific elements affecting the competitive strategy of the organization have been summarized by Porter (1980) who identified the following four factors:

1. *Potential entrants.* In general the more organizations competing in a specific market the greater is the competition. The number of competitors operating in the arena is dependent upon the cost of entering the market and to some degree the cost of exiting the market. Thus, for example, it is very expensive to design and manufacture a car and thus there are a limited number of manufacturers. On the other hand, it can be relatively cheap for people to enter the field of training and development because the set-up costs of providing training are relatively low.
2. *Buyers.* The nature of buyers and consumers in a market and their bargaining power also influences the profitability of the organization. If there are many users of training and development and few providers, demand is likely to be high and vice versa.
3. *Suppliers.* If we can only buy a particular resource from one organization then it is probable that the price of this resource will be quite expensive. Conversely, many suppliers will tend to increase competition and thereby reduce the prices. New areas of training and development normally command higher charges from providers because of limited supply.
4. *Substitutes.* The final force influencing competition in the market place is that of substitutes. If the physical cost of labour in delivering training becomes too expensive there are other forms of delivery, for instance computer-mediated learning, which may be more convenient and cheaper and which may challenge the more traditional forms of delivery.

THE HUMAN RESOURCES COMPASS

The field of Human Resources covers a broad spectrum of human activity, as is apparent in the attempts to define the subject. The Human Resource wheel (McLagan and Suhadolnik, 1989) and the wheel of HRM (Harrison, 1997) provide clearer perspectives of the area. Building on these works the Human Resources compass has been developed because the analogy of a compass indicates an overview of the territory and also gives direction to the various elements in the subject and their interrelationship. It is divided into three main sectors: HRD, HRM and HRD, and HRM; see Figure 1.2.

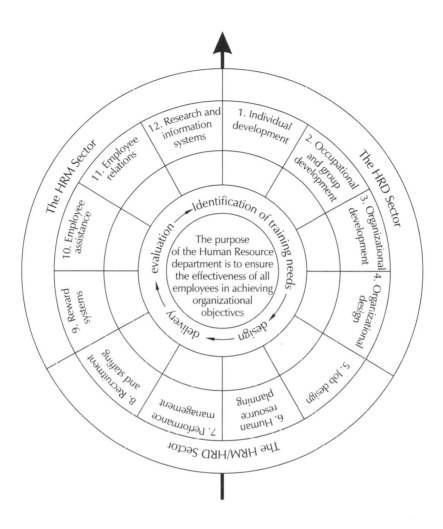

Figure 1.2 The Human Resources compass

The HRD sector

There are three main areas with which human resource development is involved, namely, individual, occupational, and organizational development. These identify the three major areas in which training and development requirements occur within an organization. Boydell (1971), in his work on the identification of training needs, maintained that these were the broad categories in which training and development interventions would occur:

1. **Individual development.** This area can be exceptionally broad and addresses such areas as skill development, interpersonal skills, career development, etc.

2. **Occupational and group development.** Training and development needs frequently occur for groups of workers such as the need to integrate cross-functional workers through a teambuilding programme, or for informing and training employees about new products and services. It also applies to specific occupational groups eg, programmes for childcare workers in new procedures or to implement new legislation.

3. **Organizational development (OD).** This category encompasses the whole organization and may involve the introduction of a new culture or ways of operating. Robbins (1993:685) describes OD as, 'A collection of planned change interventions, built on humanistic-democratic values, that seek to improve organizational effectiveness and employee well-being.' Two examples of OD in operation are the introduction of a customer care programme across the organization; and the introduction of Total Quality Management, which requires all individuals and groups to become involved.

The HRM and HRD sector

The following four areas incorporate elements of both HRD and HRM which tend to have significant degrees of overlap:

4. **Organizational design.** The primary purpose of this area is to integrate the human operations, organizational structure and systems for the delivery of products and services in an effective and economic manner. The planning of the organizational structure is a complex process although many organizations evolve according to their purpose. Minzberg (1983) identified five areas of personnel:

    a. **The operating core.** These are the employees who undertake the delivery of products or services.

    b. **The strategic apex.** This consists of the high-level managers who have organizational responsibility.

    c. **The middle line.** These are middle managers who link the strategic apex and the operating core.

    d. **The technostructure.** This grouping consists of the analysts who provide specialist advice and standardization.

    e. **The support staff.** These people provide indirect support for other elements of the organization.

Each of the five groups of personnel above may require specific forms of training and development. The key role of the HRD specialist is not to design the structure of the organization but to provide advice into the suitability of placing people in certain types of technical systems, and the extent to which people can be trained and developed to operate within that organizational design.

5. **Job design.** Each job should have a clear role within the overall organizational structure. If organizational design is concerned with the macro-factors of integrating different roles and work tasks, job design is the process of identifying the range and scope of a particular job and the degree of output from that job.

6. **Human resource planning.** The purpose of this area is to assess the human resource requirements of the organization. More specifically it concerns the numbers of employees required and the strategies for achieving appropriate staffing levels.

7. **Performance management.** Assessment of personnel performance feeds into career development, compensation and promotion, movement within the organization, and sometimes even termination of employment. Importantly it links the performance of the individual with the objectives of the organization. Assessment of individual performance through mechanisms such as the appraisal system are normally linked to training and development plans which enable people to improve performance and also develop abilities in new areas.

8. **Recruitment and staffing.** The inflow and outflow of people within an organization is a dynamic process and needs to match the requirements of the organization within its operating environment. Training and development support this process by ensuring that staff involved with recruitment and selection have the necessary skills to enable them to successfully recruit and deploy people throughout the organization.

The HRM sector

This final segment of the Human Resource compass is predominantly concerned with the traditional areas of HRM. Yet even here there is potential for HRD to contribute and receive information and direction. The two areas of HRM and HRD are not mutually exclusive and form a close symbiosis to support organizational objectives.

9. **Reward systems.** The value of a person to an organization will to some extent influence the reward they receive. This can be 'both financial and non-financial rewards and embraces the philosophies, strategies, policies, plans and processes used by organizations to develop and maintain reward systems' (Armstrong, 1996:3). HRD policies can operate concurrently with reward systems through improving productivity as a result of training programmes. Moreover, while there are a number of reservations about the practice, some organizations reward employees with training programmes for successful work performance.

10. **Employee assistance.** With some organizations concern for the employee's well-being can result in additional support services such as counselling services designed to alleviate personal problems which can interfere with work performance. At the other end of the scale it can simply involve support services who arrange shopping, or purchase sandwiches to enable core staff to continue working during lunchtime.

11. **Employee relations.** The main factors involved with this area are the interests of the employers and employees; the agreements and regulations by which they operate; the conflict-resolving methods which are utilized; and the external factors which influence the interaction between the buyers and sellers of the labour transaction (Farnham, 1997). While this is predominantly a specialist subject of HRM it does require elements of training and development and many employee relations courses, whether for union or employer representatives, including negotiation exercises.

12. **Research and information systems.** Management information systems are an essential tool for the efficient running of an organization. Not only is general information about an employee held but many organizations incorporate information about the training attended and other development activities with which a person may have been involved.

HRD ROLES

Chalofsky (1992) suggested that the core of the HRD profession should reflect what was essentially HRD in order to separate it from other professions. He said that this core should contain the philosophy, mission, theories, concepts, roles and competences. We have considered the philosophy, mission, theories, and concepts, and will now address HRD roles and subsequently HRD competences.

Arising from the research conducted on behalf of the American Society for Training and Development, McLagan and Suhadolnik (1989:20) identified 11 roles that indicate many of the dimensions carried out by HRD professionals. These are:

1. Researcher
2. Marketer
3. Organizational Change Agent
4. Needs Analyst
5. Programme Designer
6. HRD Materials Developer
7. Instructor/Facilitator
8. Individual Career Development Advisor
9. Administrator
10. Evaluator
11. HRD Manager

Competencies and HRD in the USA

The ASTD research of McLagan and Suhadolnik also identified 35 areas of competence for those involved with HRD:

Technical Competencies

1. Adult Learning Understanding*
2. Career Development Theories and Techniques Understanding
3. Competency Identification Skill*
4. Computer Competence
5. Electronic Systems Skill

6. Facilities Skill
7. Objectives Preparation Skill*
8. Performance Observation Skill
9. Subject Matter Understanding
10. Training and Development Theories and Techniques Understanding
11. Research Skill

Business Competencies

12. Business Understanding*
13. Cost-benefit Analysis Skill
14. Delegation Skill
15. Industry Understanding
16. Organizational Behaviour Understanding*
17. Organizational Development Theories and Techniques Understanding
18. Organization Understanding
19. Project Management Skill
20. Records Management Skill

Interpersonal Competencies

21. Coaching Skill
22. Feedback Skill*
23. Group Process Skill
24. Negotiation Skill
25. Presentation Skill*
26. Questioning Skill*
27. Relationship Building Skill*
28. Writing Skill*

Intellectual Competencies

29. Data Reduction Skill
30. Information Search Skill*
31. Intellectual Versatility*
32. Model Building Skill
33. Observing Skill*
34. Self-knowledge
35. Visioning Skill
*core competency.

Competences in the UK

In Britain the areas of competence for training and development specialists have also been researched, identified, mapped, and linked to National/Scottish Vocational Qualifications. The competences have been structured around the traditional training cycle (Employment National Training Organisation, 2000). The key role of the training and development person is to 'Develop human potential to assist organizations and individuals to achieve their objectives' (Employment NTO, 2000:6). The units and qualifications structure can be seen in Table 1.1.

Standards in Learning and Development

The Standards in Learning and Development are reproduced with permission and developed by Ento (formerly the Employment National Training Organization) (2002). The Standards provide a very useful source of information about the role of learning and development, and below are listed the Units and Elements. Further information can be found at http://www.ento.co.uk.

A1   Assess candidates using a range of methods
A1.1   Develop plans for assessing competence with candidates
A1.2   Judge evidence against criteria to make assessment decisions
A1.3   Provide feedback and support to candidates on assessment decisions
A1.4   Contribute to the internal quality assurance process

A2   Assess candidates performance through observation
A2.1   Agree and review plans for assessing candidates' performance
A2.2   Assess candidates' performance against the agreed standards
A2.3   Assess candidates' knowledge against the agreed standards
A2.4   Make an assessment decision and provide feedback

V1   Conduct internal quality assurance of the assessment process
V1.1   Carry out and evaluate internal assessment and quality assurance systems
V1.2   Support assessors
V1.3   Monitor the quality of assessors' performance
V1.4   Meet external quality assurance requirements

V2   Conduct external quality assurance of the assessment process
V2.1   Monitor the internal quality assurance process
V2.2   Verify the quality of assessment
V2.3   Provide information, advice and support on the internal quality assurance of assessment process
V2.4   Evaluate the effectiveness of external quality assurance of the assessment process

L1   Develop a strategy and plan for learning and development
L1.1   Develop a plan for learning and development
L1.2   Produce a learning and development programme for the organization
L1.3   Evaluate how effective the learning and development process is

L2   Identify the learning and development needs of the organization
L2.1   Review how capable the whole organization is of meeting its development needs
L2.2   Develop a learning and development programme for the organization

L3   Identify individual learning aims and programmes
L3.1   Review learning and development achievements and opportunities
L3.2   Identify and agree learning aims and programmes

L4   Design learning programmes
L4.1   Choose options for meeting learning needs
L4.2   Design learning programmes for learners

L5   Agree learning programmes with learners
L5.1   Negotiate learning programmes with learners
L5.2   Review learning programmes and agree changes with learner

L6   Develop training sessions
L6.1   Identify options for training sessions
L6.2   Deliver training sessions for learners

L7   Prepare and develop resources to support learning
L7.1   Develop learning materials
L7.2   Choose materials to support learning

L8   Manage the contribution of other people to the learning process
L8.1   Agree roles and resources with contributors
L8.2   Co-ordinate the activities of contributors
L8.3   Monitor and review how effective contributors are

L9   Create a climate that promotes learning
L9.1   Develop a good relationship with learners
L9.2   Support learners
L9.3   Promote anti-discriminatory practice

L10   Enable learning through presentations
L10.1   Give presentations to groups
L10.2   Produce follow-up exercises

L11   Enable learning through demonstrations and instruction
L11.1   Demonstrate skills and methods to learners
L11.2   Instruct learners

L12   Enable individual learning through coaching
L12.1   Coach individual learners
L12.2   Assist individual learners to apply their learning

L13   Enable group learning
L13.1   Manage group dynamics
L13.2   Enable the group to learn together

L14   Support learners by mentoring in the workplace
L14.1   Plan the mentoring process
L14.2   Set up and maintain the mentoring relationship
L14.3   Give mentoring support

L15   Support and advise individual learners
L15.1   Give individual learners guidance to help them plan their learning
L15.2   Advise and support individual learners in managing their own learning

L16   Monitor and review progress with learners
16.1   Review progress with learners

L17   Evaluate and improve learning and development programmes
L17.1   Choosing how to evaluate programmes
L17.2   Analyse information to improve learning and development programmes
L17.3   Make improvements to learning and development programmes

L18   Respond to changes in learning and development
L18.1   Respond to changes in learning and development
L18.2   Develop learning and training methods
L18.3   Test and change proposed training and development methods

L19   Provide learning and development in international settings
L19.1   Identify the things that influence international learning and development
L19.2   Design learning and development programmes for international settings
L19.3   Produce learning and development materials and support for international settings
L19.4   Deliver training internationally

L20   Support competence achieved in the workplace
L20.1   Assess performance in the workplace against agreed standards
L20.2   Give staff members support in the workplace and feedback on their performance

L21   Plan how to provide basic skills in the workplace
L21.1   Persuade people that basic skills are important to the organization
L21.2   Identify the needs for basic skills within the organization

L22   Introduce training for basic skills in the workplace
L22.1   Introduce programmes for delivering basic skills in the workplace
L22.2   Introduce learning support for people being trained in basic skills

L23   Support how basic skills are delivered in the workplace
L23.1   Identify the needs and opportunities for learning basic skills in the workplace
L23.2   Help to deliver basic skills in the workplace

L24   Support people learning basic skills in the workplace
L24.1   Help individuals to identify their learning needs
L24.2   Support others in the workplace to develop their basic skills

CONCLUSION

Training and development has had a mixed reception over the years and has frequently had to fight its corner and shout loudly to gain recognition. The acceptance of HRD is altogether much stronger since it has been linked to strategic imperatives and has a much stronger theoretical base in universities which have provided Master's courses to enhance the respect of practitioners.

This progress is clearly apparent in a comparison of the two quotations below. The challenge now is not to become complacent but to build on this appreciation and ensure that HRD continues to contribute to the successful operation of the organization:

> The fact remains that training and development personnel are a motley bunch who by and large service low level needs within the organisation. (Sinclair and Collins, 1992:21)

> During the course of my working life the human resource development (HRD) function in industry has grown from humble 'training officer', a largely peripheral, low status role associated with instructing newcomers in necessary manual skills, to 'human resource development director', a powerful influence in the organisation. (Kilcourse, 1996:3)

Bibliography

Armstrong, M (1996) *Employee Reward*, London, IPD

Barham, K, Fraser, J and Heath, L (1988) *Management of the Future*, Berkhamsted, Ashridge Management College

Beck, A and Jones, T (1988) 'From training manager to human resource manager – not a rose by any other name!', *Industrial and Commercial Training*, May/June, pp 7–12

Beer, M and Spector, B (1989) 'Corporate wide transformations in human resource management', in Walton, R E and Lawrence, P R (eds) *Human Resource Management: Trends and challenges*, Boston, MA, Harvard University School Press

Bloom, B S, Englehart, M D, Hill, W H and Krathwohl, D R (1956) *Taxonomy of Educational Objectives*, London, Longman, Green and Co

Bolton, M (1995) *Assessment and Development in Europe: Adding value to individuals and organisations*, Maidenhead, McGraw-Hill

Boydell, T (1971) *The Identification of Training Needs*, London, BACIE

CEDEFOP (1996) *Glossarium: Vocational training*, Luxembourg, Office for Official Publications of the European Communities

Chalofsky, N (1992) 'A unifying definition for the human resource profession', *Human Resource Development Quarterly*, **3**, 2, pp 175–82

Chalofsky, N and Lincoln, C (1983) *Up the HRD Ladder*, Reading, MA, Addison-Wesley

De Geus, A P (1989) 'Planning as learning', *Harvard Business Review*, March/April, pp 70–74

Dearden, R (1991) 'Education and Training', in Esland, G (ed) *Education, Training and Employment: Vol. 2, The educational response*, Wokingham, Addison-Wesley in association with The Open University, pp 84–95,

Drucker, P (1993) *Post-Capitalist Society*, Oxford, Butterworth-Heinemann

Employment NTO (2000) National Standards for Training and Development: Training and Development: Strategy, Leicester, Employment NTO. (For further details contact: Employment NTO, Kimberley House, 47 Vaughan Way, Leicester LE1 4SG; Tel: 0116 251 7979, website: www.empnto.co.uk)

Farnham, D (1997) *Employee Relations in Context*, London, IPD

Frank, E (1988) 'An attempt at a definition of HRD', *Journal of European Industrial Training*, **12**, 5, pp 4–5

Galagan, P (1986) 'Editorial', *Training and Development Journal*, **40**, 3, p 4

Garavan, T N (1991) 'Strategic human resource development', *Journal of European Industrial Training*, **15**, 1, pp 17–30

Garavan, T N (1997) 'Training, development, education and learning: different or the same?', *Journal of European Industrial Training*, **21**, pp 39–50

Garavan, T N, Costine, P and Heraty, N (1995) 'The emergence of strategic human resource development', *Journal of European Industrial Training*, **19**, 10, pp 4–10

Garavan, T N, Gunnigle, P and Morely, M (2000) 'Contemporary HRD research: a triarchy of theoretical perspectives and their prescriptions for HRD', *Journal of European Industrial Training*, **24**, 2/3/4, pp 65–104

Handy, C (1990) *The Age of Unreason*, London, Arrow

Hansen, C D and Brooks, A K (1994) 'A review of cross-cultural research on human resource development', *Human Resource Development Quarterly*, **5**, 1, pp 55–74

Harrison, R (1997) Employee Development, London, IPD

Jacobs, R (1990) 'Human resource development as an interdisciplinary body of knowledge', *Human Resource Development Quarterly*, **1**, 1, 65–71

Jacobs, R L and Jones, M J (1995) *Structured On-the-Job Training: Unleashing Employee Expertise in the Workplace*, San Francisco, CA, Berrett-Koehler

Johnson, G and Scholes, K (1993) *Exploring Corporate Strategy*, 3rd edn, Hemel Hempstead, Prentice Hall

Jones, M and Mann, P (1992) *International perspectives on development and learning*, West Hartford, CT, Kumarian Press

Kilcourse, T (1996) 'Human resource development – a contingency function? (Whatever happened to theory Y?)', *Journal of European Industrial Training*, **20**, 9, pp 3–8

McGoldrick, J and Stewart, J (1996) 'The HRM-HRD nexus', in J Stewart and J McGoldrick, (eds) *Human Resource Development: Perspectives, Strategies and Practice*, London, Pitman Publishing, pp 9–27

McLagan, P A and Suhadolnik, D (1989) *Models for HRD Practice: The research report*, Alexandria, VA, ASTD Press

Manpower Services Commission (1981) *Glossary of Training Terms*, 3rd edn, London, HMSO

Manpower Services Commission (1985) *A Glossary of Terms Used in Education and Training*, Sheffield, Training Division, MSC

Minzberg, H (1983) *Structure in Fives: Designing Effective Organizations*, Englewood Cliffs, NJ, Prentice Hall

Minzberg, H (1987) 'Crafting strategy', *Harvard Business Review*, July-August, pp 66–75

Nadler, L and Nadler, Z (eds) (1990) *The Handbook of Human Resource Development*, 2nd edn, New York, Wiley

Ortigas, C D (1994) *Human Resource Development: The Philippine experience. Readings for the practitioner*, Manila, Ateneo de Manila University Press

Pettigrew, A, Sparrow, P and Hendry, C (1988) 'The forces that trigger training', *Personnel Management*, December, pp 28–32

Porter, M E (1980) *Competitive Strategy*, New York, Free Press

Ralphs, L and Stephan, E (1986) 'HRD in the Fortune 500', *Training and Development Journal*, **40**, 10, pp 69–76

Robbins, S P (1993) *Organizational Behaviour*, 6th edn, Englewood Cliffs, NJ, Prentice Hall

Rogers, A (1986) *Teaching Adults*, Buckingham, Open University Press

Sinclair, J and Collins, D (1992) 'Viewpoint: training and development's worst enemies – you and management', *Journal of European Industrial Training*, **16**, 5, pp 21–5

Stewart, J and McGoldrick, J (eds) (1996) *Human Resource Development: Perspectives, Strategies and Practice*, London, Pitman Publishing

Torraco, R J and Swanson, R A (1995) 'The strategic roles of human resource development', *Human Resource Planning*, **18**, 4, pp 10–21

Van Wart, M, Cayer, N J and Cork, S (1993) *Handbook of Training and Development for the Public Sector*, San Francisco, CA, Jossey-Bass

Watkins, K (1989) 'Business and industry', in S Merriam and P Cunningham, (eds) *Handbook of Adult and Continuing Education*, San Francisco, CA, Jossey-Bass

Webster, B (1990) 'Beyond the mechanics of HRD', *Personnel Management*, March, pp 44–47

2

Human Resource Management

John Shipton

INTRODUCTION AND LEARNING OBJECTIVES

In many ways, Human Resource Management (HRM) can be seen as a phenomenon of relatively recent times. Coming to the fore during the 1980s, it has dominated the recent literature on the management of people to the extent that it seems to be accepted without question as an ideal for managements in all contexts. HRM developed around the notion that, in circumstances where the liberalization of world markets makes it less easy for organizations to gain even relatively short-term advantage over competitors in areas such as finance, technology, research, etc, the only source of competitive edge is to recruit, retain and develop talented people. The management of people, therefore, becomes of strategic concern for all organizations and the focus moves from an emphasis on control to developing commitment to release that talent for the organization's benefit.

Having read this chapter you will have an understanding of:

- the origins of HRM;
- the debate about the meaning and significance of HRM;
- the different approaches to the practice of HRM; and
- the key components of HRM.

ORIGINS AND DEVELOPMENT OF HRM

Arguably, HRM is not as recent a development as might be supposed. Seeing people as resources for the organization is a central concept for those like Likert (1961) who have campaigned for a more involving approach to management, arguing for a shift in thinking from 'human relations' to 'human resources'. Maslow (1965:262) suggested, 20 years before the popularization of HRM, that treating people as valued resources via what he called 'eupsychian management' provided competitive advantage:

> eupsychian or enlightened management is already beginning to become a competitive factor. That is, old-style management is. . . putting the enterprise in a less and less advantageous position in competition with other enterprises. . . that are under enlightened management and are therefore turning out better products, better service, etc, etc.

Storey (1995), however, reminds us that the first British text on HRM did not appear until 1989. There had, nevertheless, been a debate in the journals before that about the nature of HRM that resembled in some respects the disputation of mediaeval clerics over how many angels could be positioned on the head of a pin (see, for example, Armstrong, 1987). As Storey points out, this debate was carried on without any real data at all. There was a need for empirical work to establish the credentials of HRM and this was provided, among others, by an extensive piece of research from Storey (1992) into long-standing 'standard moderns' which, by definition, were not subject to the special circumstances of ownership and green-field status of the relatively small number of organizations that seemed to be quoted endlessly in the early literature to support the contention that HRM was all around us.

What emerges is evidence that change has, indeed, taken place. In another survey of 560 organizations covered by Leicestershire Training and Enterprise Council, Storey (1995) noted that no less than three-quarters of the organizations studied had adopted a set of management practices associated with HRM within the previous five years. It is customary to explain the change as a shift from old-style personnel management to new-style HRM, although there is some doubt about the clarity, smoothness and universality of the change, which tends to be glossed over by the more normative literature. Various prescriptions of what HRM is (or should be) exist. They differ in detail but tend to have a number of aspects in common:

- Employees provide the organization's principal possibilities for competitive advantage.
- The way in which employees are managed becomes a strategic concern for senior management and involves line managers taking responsibility both for the operation and development of HR policy.
- Competitive advantage will not be realized unless the employees' commitment to organizational goals can be established.
- That commitment is only possible if there exist policies and practices that are designed specifically to promote that end.
- In particular, selection, performance management, training and development, and rewards represent the main areas for attention in creating high commitment strategies.

- An emphasis on communication and the development of a strong culture are necessary to provide the environment in which high commitment initiatives can flourish.

The emergence of HRM is unlikely to be just the result of managers seeing the light. A range of organizational changes has contributed to providing circumstances making the development of HRM both pertinent and possible. The emphasis on customers and the provision of quality service every time mean that organizations must have employees on whose commitment they can rely. Flexible organizations cannot operate without the willing participation of those providing, particularly, functional flexibility. Wide spans of control associated with slimmer and flatter structures require that older ways of (closely) managing can no longer operate. An increasing knowledge content in work together with the need for teamworking and a more educated workforce have produced demands from employees for different styles of supervision. Structural changes in industry and consequently in the makeup of the workforce, with some notable exceptions, have brought about a less confrontational industrial relations atmosphere. The development of HRM has been against this background of considerable change.

HRM: THE SEARCH FOR MEANING

While there seems to be agreement that the dominant approach to the management of people at work has changed, identifying the nature of that change is complicated by the problems associated with seeing personnel management and HRM as single entities. We speak of the two as though they are uniform in all their manifestations – 'personnel management does this, HRM believes that'. (This is an issue closely akin to the tendency we have to reify organizations by treating them as though they are things, or, more likely, persons, and that they can behave like people. 'Bloggs plc values quality, provides a caring atmosphere for its employees, strives for market dominance, etc.' In fact, Bloggs plc cannot **do** anything: only people within Bloggs can, and their behaviour will vary for a range of reasons, from mood to calculated political advantage.) Similarly, personnel management and HRM will vary in practice, maybe considerably, and there will be those who see themselves as personnel managers who practise aspects of what is considered HRM, and HR managers whose behaviour looks indistinguishable from so-called, old-style personnel management. Perhaps the safest way to look at this is to think of a continuum from personnel management at one end to HRM at the other (envisaged as 'ideal types') with most organizational practice strewn out between, rather than an either/or division.

However, so long as we remember that reality is messier than the models in the literature, it is useful to explore the field in simpler terms to enable us to gain some feel for the nature of the personnel management/HRM shift in practice. The characteristics of the two 'ideal types' appear to be those shown in Table 2.1.

Table 2.1 'Ideal types' of personnel management and HRM

Personnel Management	HRM
Emphasis on system and order. Clarity of rules and procedures	Emphasis on business needs. 'Just do it' approaches to work. Beg forgiveness rather than seek permission
Consistency: 'Don't make fish of one and fowl of the other'	Flexibility: 'Do what is necessary to get the task done even if a few feathers are ruffled and noses put out of joint on the way'
Control/monitor	Develop/grow
Some conflict at work seen as inevitable; need is to develop arrangements to manage it	Conflict not seen as inevitable; play down or even ignore differences
Pluralist framework	Unitary framework
Collective bargaining: equity across and between groups	Individual contracts: equity preferable but not first concern
Communicate as necessary via 'proper' channels	Communicate often and directly
Not of concern to business planners	Integrated with business plans
Performed by personnel specialists	Enacted by, and policies developed by, line managers

WHERE IS HRM 'COMING FROM'?

Throughout his pioneering analyses, Storey (1992, 1995) emphasizes that the differences between personnel management and HRM are partly to do with assumptions that underlie their practice. A key area of assumption, as indicated above, is the nature of *perceived* organizational reality – the degree to which organizations are seen as unities (eg, viewed as teams/families) or pluralities (eg, coalitions of conflicting interests). This is not a question of whether organizations *are* one or the other, but rather what the stakeholders in employment (and particularly managers) *believe* them to be.

Those who adhere to the unitary frame argue that organizations are, naturally, like teams or families where what is good for the leaders of those organizations is also good for their members. The emphasis is on shared goals, all pulling in one direction. This, it is argued, is not just a desired way of arranging the work relationship – it is also the natural way of things. Problems arising between manager and managed in the unitary organization are explained as being caused by either ineffective communication or the work of agitators (often seen as the malevolent influence of trade unions). Winning hearts and minds becomes a major goal of selection, development and reward policies. 'Is she or he one of us?' emerges as the critical organizational question.

Pluralists, on the other hand, see organizations as a coming together of people with different backgrounds, experiences and expectations who, legitimately, will not view organizational purpose in the same way. The interests of the managed will not, naturally, be the same as those of managers. Indeed, the interests of different managers will not even converge, and we should not expect them to. As Marchington (1995:60) suggests, 'While first-line managers and supervisors regard themselves as in some sense superior to the people they manage, they still remain estranged from the predominant goals and values of senior management.' The primary managerial activity, therefore, should be to recognize this reality and create mechanisms that will allow differences to be negotiated to achieve enough of a consensus for the organization to function.

(A third view, the radical framework, sees organizations as subsystems of society as a whole; in particular, as a reflection of the power relationships that determine that owners will always have the capacity, under capitalism, to exploit workers. Unitarism is, therefore, a way of whitewashing a system of domination, and pluralism presents an enticing but ultimately false picture of an even playing-field on which differences are settled on equal terms. Radicalists would argue that seeing the personnel management/HRM debate in terms of pluralism vs unitarism misses the central point of organizations as systems of power.)

HARD AND SOFT HRM

Legge (in Storey, 1995) distinguishes between *hard* and *soft* versions of HRM. The hard version places emphasis on the link between HRM and business strategy to the extent that HRM is sometimes called 'strategic HRM'. If, from the characteristics listed above, HRM is of direct concern to senior management, then it follows that it needs to have a strategic effect. As Torrington, Hall and Taylor (2002) point out, it is not enough to identify the need for such a link. The relationship might take any one of four forms:

- The first is where the business strategy is developed and then the HR strategy is designed to be a close fit to it. The business strategy dictates the nature of the HR strategy: arguably, the business strategy causes the HR strategy to be what it is.
- In the second case, the relationship is as above but involves feedback from the HR strategy to the business strategy. HR follows overall, predetermined organizational purposes but provides HR data that might lead to modification of the business strategy. The HR strategy is still subservient to business strategy but the possibility of debate/influence exists.
- A third approach envisages business strategy and HR strategy being developed together, each influencing the other on broadly equal terms. This reflects an organizational realization of the centrality of people to organizational success.
- If, as CEOs are oft given to claim, 'People are the organization's most important assets', the fourth approach provides the ultimate model. Here the HR strategy is developed first and the business strategy is designed to fit, with opportunity for feedback along the lines of the second approach above. In this version, HR policies drive the business strategy. Typically, strategists are asking: 'What are the HR strengths which set us apart from our competitors and how can we design our business strategy to capitalize on those strengths?'

Torrington and Hall, perhaps pessimistically, outline a fifth possibility where no link between HR and business strategy exists. Work by Marginson *et al* (1993:71) indicates that such pessimism may be well placed. They suggest that: 'if one of the defining characteristics of human resource management is the explicit link with business strategies, then this survey has failed to find it for the majority of large companies in the UK'.

This might, however, have more to do with assumptions about the rationality of the strategy-formulation process than about the link itself. Rather than see strategy as a rational, top-down planning activity, it may be more realistic to view it as a more gradual, messy, emergent process. Lewis (2001) applies this idea when suggesting that wholesale changes in HR practices are unlikely to occur in one stage. The more likely position is that incremental changes will emerge over time. The grand plan approach to strategy is rejected in favour of strategy being discovered as it emerges from the interaction of a whole range of stakeholders in an often very political arena. In this context, it may be unrealistic to search for the links in the form suggested by a rational view of strategy formulation, as the study carried out in Hewlett Packard by Truss (2001) confirms.

Hard HRM, associated as it is with business planning, has given new life to human resource planning. Making sure that the staffing of the organization mirrors organizational need and that the right number of people with the right capabilities are in the right place at the right time sits comfortably with 'hard' conceptions of HRM. 'Right', of course, means that it is not just enough to make sure that sufficient employees are in position but also that not too many are there. This has led to the development of flexible staffing policies and, while there is some doubt as to whether flexibility has been thought through in the majority of organizations in anything like a strategic way, flexibility is seen as one of the main distinguishing features of HRM. It has become customary, following Atkinson's (1984) pioneering work, to distinguish between two types of flexibility:

- **Functional flexibility** encompasses the capacity of employees to become multi-skilled and move between functions as business demands dictate. While potentially a characteristic of all employees, this form of flexibility is linked by Atkinson with the organization's core work-force: those who possess organization-specific skills which, by definition, are difficult to buy in from outside.
- **Numerical flexibility** is about managing the headcount to make sure that numbers rise and fall with the exigencies of the business. This is more easily done where the staff concerned have generic skills which can be dispensed with in the knowledge that they can, if necessary, be found in the wider labour market and brought back into the organization with little delay. This is the peripheral workforce, made up largely, but not exclusively, of routine production and administrative staff. The use of contractors, temporaries and the self-employed provides further numerical flexibility (and, maybe, functional flexibility) without the perceived problems of a contract of employment.

Arguably, both functional and numerical flexibilities are ways of achieving financial flexibility. What is being sought is a method of managing more effectively and more efficiently. Further strategies available, particularly with the peripheral workforce, include temporal flexibility where contractual hours of work are varied (including annual hours arrangements and nil hours contracts) to suit business requirements. Building flexibility into HR policies generally, but particularly in the area of remuneration with, for instance, rewards linked to performance or profit, is also a way of increasing the degree of variability in costs associated with employment.

Hard HRM smacks of tight control and, particularly, of an integration of HR policies with business strategy, as discussed above. The emphasis is on a systematic, rational approach. As far as is possible, the human resource is to be managed in the same way as other organizational resources and it is, perhaps, best understood using a production/manufacturing metaphor.

Soft HRM is also framed by business objectives but the emphasis is on those aspects that make employees a unique resource, one that is capable of providing competitive advantage. Stress is, therefore, placed on development, on maximizing human potential: resourceful humans rather than human resources. The metaphor here is agricultural: growing rather than making. However, this valued resource is of little use unless prepared to apply its talent on behalf of the organization. Consequently, soft HRM specifies treating employees as valued contributors to the organization, paying attention to motivation, developing trust, providing development opportunities, keeping them informed so that the commitment necessary for the release of organizationally useful behaviours is developed.

Work on the psychological contract is relevant here. Guest (1996) suggests that a positive psychological contract relates to employee perceptions of fairness, trust and delivery of 'the deal'. It is potentially affected by organizational culture, employee expectations/experience and the degree to which employees have any alternative but to grin and bear it. However, Guest found that, although culture and expectations had some effect, it was the presence or absence of high commitment HR practices that had by far the greatest influence on the nature of the psychological contract. In particular, the organization's attempts to:

- keep employees informed about business issues and performance;
- fill vacancies from within;
- make jobs as interesting and variable as possible;
- deliberately avoid compulsory redundancies and lay-offs;

had the strongest links with a positive psychological contract. Making the effort, then, is not just about being nice to people. There is, potentially, a sound commercial pay-off. Hiltrop (1996) supports this view when she argues that employees actively wish to:

- know more about what is happening in their organizations;
- understand why their managers make the decisions they do (see also TUC initiatives on the 'good boss');
- contribute ideas and participate in decision-making;
- have autonomy and 'meaningful work experiences'; and
- generally feel valued and personally recognized.

HR policies, therefore, need to be aimed at meeting these needs and it is the soft version of HRM that is likely to supply the necessary framework.

While it is important to recognize the different strands in HRM that are the hard and soft approaches, it does not mean that they are incompatible. Organizations can, and do, demonstrate both. The discussion of flexibility above, for example, provides a setting in which this might be illustrated. Core employees are likely to be the knowledge workers of the organization and the potential source of competitive advantage. Soft HRM, with its stress on surfacing competence and developing the necessary organizational commitment, would seem most appropriate as an emphasis in this case. Peripheral workers, on the other hand, are not usually the carriers of organization-specific expertise and the need here is to tightly manage the head-count to keep control of costs via hard HRM techniques. Recent research in the Netherlands lends further support to the possibility, even the necessity, of operating the two together. Boselie et al (2003) identified 'control' HR systems and 'commitment' HR systems and found that practices which aimed at increasing commitment needed to be located in a control system.

Managing this duality is not, of course, without its problems. It may seem very much like elitism and lead to suspicion that messages of unitarism such as '(all) our employees are our greatest assets' ring hollow. Marchington (1995:62–3) points out that:

> The short-termism which is inherent across much of management in Britain is nowhere more apparent than in the way employees are treated, and it is hardly surprising that new initiatives are greeted with scepticism by employees who have 'seen it all before'.

Pascale (1995) sees the process of demands for employee loyalty, without much evidence of reciprocation by employers as 'the sound of one hand clapping'.

'MANAGING PEOPLE' TRAINING FOR OIL INDUSTRY ENGINEERS IN EAST ASIA/AUSTRALIA

A large Anglo-Dutch oil company underwent significant expansion in its Australasia region and recruited a large number of young engineers. Many of these engineers tended to be very logical and 'left-brain'-aligned; they were task-oriented, and they focused on the bottom-line production outputs. The expansion created promotion opportunities within the organization hierarchy. However, the supervisory roles required a different set of competences, ie, the focus was to manage people rather than the 'nuts and bolts' of machines and operating procedures.

Arising from the promotions, a number of managerial and interpersonal problems were noted. These occurred as a result of the engineers directly applying their personal work habits and technical knowledge to the managing of people. These young engineers, apart from their technical training, had never been exposed to management development training, eg, 'people' skills. The higher in the organization hierarchy, the less the demand for 'technical' expertise and the focus shifts towards 'human' and 'conceptual thinking'.

To address the situation a 'Managing People' training programme was developed and delivered to more than 1,500 middle managers from various subsidiary companies in Malaysia, Singapore, Thailand, Hong Kong, Taiwan, Korea, Japan, Australia and New Zealand. This programme emphasized that in order to accomplish a project efficiently and effectively, it is important to strike a balance between focusing on the 'people' and 'process' aspects of working together as a team.

'Thomas' attended the programme and came back with a change in his leadership style in handling his subordinates. In addition, a Team Building workshop was organized which Thomas and his entire team attended. In the workshop, team objectives were thoroughly discussed, debated and consensually agreed, with the participants working towards a single common goal. Ample opportunities were given to individual members to contribute their ideas in coming up with a new set of ground rules for the work norms. Thomas was much more sensitive in attending to his team members' feelings and suggestions. He did not assert his way any more but rather collaborated with the team's efforts to inculcate the members' ownership and commitment.

Learning gains from the Managing People programme included:

- the role of a manager in striking a balance in the three areas of task, people and process;
- a shift from micro-managing 'technicalities' to 'human' and 'conceptual thinking' skills;
- the art of team leadership and the importance of team building, ie, the ability to engage the members' participation, involvement and ownership in the planning and decision-making process; thereby inculcating commitment and accountability (like a flock of geese flying in a V-formation in the same direction).

With acknowledgement to Peter Voon, Training Manager, East Asia/Australia Regional Training, Anglo-Dutch Oil.

IMPLICATIONS FOR ACTION

What does all this mean in practice? The whole gamut of activities associated with the management of people at work, of course, potentially falls within the scope of HRM. However, a few aspects seem to be critical. They are:

- The process of bringing people into the organization – making very sure that new entrants have the potential and willingness to contribute to organizational success.
- The management of performance – making very sure that what employees do is geared to the achievement of relevant goals and that the resources are available to make this happen.
- The reward of performance – on the basis of 'what gets rewarded, gets done', making very sure that rewards are managed rather than merely administered.
- The development of talent – creating the environment in which learning is seen as a way of organizational life.
- The management of culture – developing and communicating a particular vision of what working for this organization means.

All of the above have been the subject of research and comment recently and the following sections will consider each in turn.

Selection

An apparent contradiction of recent years has been the increase in attention paid to selection against the background of historically high levels of unemployment. Even apparently routine shopfloor jobs have been the subject of lengthy selection procedures. Perhaps the most significant pressure producing an interest in selection has been the slimming down of most organizations, which means that it is much less possible to throw people at a problem. It is much more important now to get selection right each time, and if Cook (1990) is right in saying that good employees are twice as valuable in terms of contribution as poor employees, then putting time and resources into selection becomes crucial.

While major developments have taken place in computer-based recruiting – Smethurst and Hardy (2004), for example, report that there appear to be more than 11 million online job seekers in the UK – face-to-face selection methods remain popular in the later stages of selection decision-making, particularly for more senior posts. However, there has been a growing realization that reliance on the interview, as typically performed, is no longer satisfactory. Various meta-analyses of research data have given the traditional interview a poor press. League tables of the effectiveness of selection techniques place the interview towards the bottom, showing little more utility than astrology and chance prediction (see for example Beardwell, Holden and Claydon 2004: 218). However, all is not lost for the interview. Considerable improvement can be made in its effectiveness if three features are emphasized:

1. Typical interviews are relatively unstructured. Using a *structured* approach, in which each candidate faces the same key questions, improves the performance of the interview. To be effective, any selection device needs to be both reliable and valid. Reliability relates to the degree to which the device produces the same results when applied (even by different users) to the same candidates, over and over again. Validity is concerned with the degree to which the selection device does the job (basically, predicts job performance) it purports to do. Because the typical interview is unstructured, it fails the reliability test in that each application tends to be different and, therefore, produces different results from the same candidates when repeatedly applied. If a device is unreliable, it cannot be valid. Structuring the interview goes some way to overcoming this failing and has the added advantage of being demonstrably fairer and, therefore, less likely to be challenged on the grounds of unfair discrimination.
2. Interviews need to include questions that are *situationally based*, which reflect job circumstances known to differentiate between good performers and poor performers. If organizations cannot reliably distinguish between good and poor performers (and this is not as straightforward as some managers believe) then it may be difficult to identify the situations which could form the basis of situational questions. Careful job analysis, which may be outside the resources of some organizations, is also a prerequisite of the approach.
3. Interviewers need to be *trained*. Most interviewers have received little or no training but believe that they are effective selectors. As the introduction to one of the earlier training videos on selection suggested: 'Most people in this country believe that they are good drivers, good lovers and good interviewers.' One of the principal findings of a major study on selection

interviewing indicating that performance improved with training (Mayfield and Carlson, 1966) has been known for some time but the message seems not to have been widely received.

Three selection tools that have seen significant growth in recent years are assessment centres, ability tests and personality questionnaires. The use of all three by the larger UK organizations doubled in the last two decades, although for assessment centres (because of cost) and ability tests (because of fears of adverse impact) there is evidence of a plateauing in take-up. The use of personality questionnaires, however, has shown a steady increase, with over 70 per cent of large organizations now using them for a variety of assessment purposes. All three are an indication of the increased seriousness with which selection is being taken in that they are likely to be more costly to stage than the interview. One reason that interest in the use of more sophisticated selection tools has increased is the tendency for organizations to seek greater flexibility in their employees. In this context, Storey and Wright (2001) argue that selection decisions are likely to be based less on traditional job content criteria but rather on attitudes and cultural fit, in particular the degree to which candidates are likely to support business strategies.

Performance management

A persistent theme of HRM is integration, both internally, in that different HR policies and practices need to send a similar overall message, and in the sense of links with business strategy as discussed above. Bearing in mind Marginson's earlier doubts, some encouragement that this is now taking place comes from a recent piece of research which reports that, in nearly one in three workplaces, a high-performance strategy based on widespread use of HRM practices is evident (White *et al* 2004). Perhaps above all other aspects of HR, performance management emphasizes the need for what individual employees do to be directly relevant to specific objectives of the business. This critical aspect of HRM is considered in detail in Chapter 10.

Reward management

The title of this section signifies the change that has affected the administration of reward systems during recent years. The HRM message is that rewards need to be seen as an important part of the way in which competitive advantage is developed and sustained; in that sense, they are managed rather than administered. Lawler (1995) sees this as so critical that he has identified a need for what he calls 'new pay'. Other commentators have followed Lawler and the new orthodoxy seems to be characterized by the trends shown in Table 2.2.

Armstrong (2002: 20) cautions that new pay 'should be regarded as a conceptual approach to payment rather than a set of prescriptions'.

Perhaps the issue of 'new pay' is best illustrated by the phenomenon of performance-related pay (PRP). Certainly in its individualized form, there is mounting evidence that PRP does not work. Kohn (1993) goes so far as to argue that all forms of incentive are detrimental in that they undermine interest in work itself, encourage employees to play it safe, punish those who do not

Table 2.2 Trends in reward management

From	To
An emphasis on system and order – tightly administered to control drift	Business needs driven – a tool of organizational change which delivers a cultural message
Collectivism: seeing the natural pay constituency in terms of groups of employees	Individualism: to the extent of developing individually 'negotiated' contracts of employment at all levels
Pay structures determined by job evaluation – narrow bands	Paying what is necessary; what the external market requires with less concern for structures as such – broad bands
Rewards for being there – rate for the job	Rewards geared to contribution and/or capability with value added as the key criterion – variable pay
A fair day's pay for a fair day's work	Economic democracy – a share in the prosperity (or otherwise) of the organization
Control	Opportunity

receive, and disrupt (particularly team) relationships. This may be an extreme view, but it is difficult to find hard data in support of PRP. About the best that can be said is that PRP schemes have no effect on performance one way or the other. What gets rewarded may, in fact, not get done – or, at least, may not get done because of the reward on offer. Why then are they so popular? Probably it is because of the cultural message that they send about what is important to the organization, a reinforcement of how the organization's priorities have changed. Hence its importance may lie in its value as a way of thinking, as Armstrong suggests, rather than as a technique.

Training and development

This book is centrally concerned with training and development and, consequently, many of the features associated with this aspect of HRM are reviewed in other chapters. The persistent message contained in the HRM literature is the need to develop an organizational environment in which learning and the desire to learn are second nature to all employees. With new European guidelines aimed at the annual involvement in training of 50 per cent of workers by 2010 (CEDEFOP, 2004), the message has received further endorsement. If competitive advantage lies in the talents of employees, then it is necessary to create the circumstances in which those talents can blossom. The learning organization model is seen as the blueprint and is discussed in Chapter 6.

Culture

Arguably, concern about selection, performance management, reward, and training and development have characterized the literature on management for decades. HRM places a specific gloss on these subjects, but they have been of long-standing interest. The need to develop a strong culture, however, is a relatively recent thought. Underpinning this prescription is a belief that organizations *have* cultures (in the sense that people might have measles) and that it is possible to change cultures, that strong cultures are unifying and motivating, that they can affect business performance and that it is a key responsibility of senior managers to bring about cultural change.

The evidence seems to be that culture change programmes are much more difficult and take longer to complete than the corporate-culture school would lead us to expect. This may be because of a fundamental misdiagnosis of the nature of culture. Could it be, for instance, that culture is not so much something that organizations have but rather something that organizations are (Smircich and Calas, 1987)? This view of culture sees it as much more deep-seated and, therefore, less easily changed than is suggested. Mabey and Salaman (1995) also criticize the corporate-culture school (what they describe as 'this prevalent view') because it implies that an organization has a single culture, ignoring the reality of conflicts of interest and power and the effects of inherent organizational inequalities. It seems, therefore, that cultural change will remain difficult and the examples of organizations that appear to have developed the required strong culture will be over-represented by those that are small or have experienced a recent, significant increase in employees and/or are located on green-field sites.

HIGH-PERFORMANCE WORK PRACTICES

Many of the areas described above are now being recognized as key ingredients in high-performance work practices (HPWP). Furthermore, research into HPWP has provided hard evidence about the importance of HRM on organizational effectiveness. Ashton and Sung (2002:1) stated that 'High performance working practices consist of new ways of organizing work, rewarding performance and involving employees in the decision-making process in the workplace.' The practices include self-directed teams, performance-related pay, 360-degree appraisal, personal development plans, job rotation, employee involvement with decision-making, and support for performance: that is, training and development. Although most of these approaches have existed for some time, their combination is relatively innovative and results in, 'a working environment which not only provides the potential for developing the personality of the worker, but also raises the productivity of the organization'.

A significant body of international research has built up to support the case for HPWP. In North America, research by Betcherman *et al* (1997) in Canada, and in the United States by Kling (1995), Applebaum *et al* (2000), and by Ichniowski et al (1997) into the US steel industry, revealed that the introduction of HPWP increased productivity and financial returns. Similar findings have been made in Taiwan by Tung-Chun Huang (1997), in New Zealand by Guthrie (2001); and by MacDuffie (1995), who investigated 57 auto assembly plants in Australia, Brazil, Japan, Korea, Mexico, the United States and other countries.

In the UK Patterson *et al* (1997) studied 60 manufacturing companies and discovered that the introduction of HPWP resulted in improved performance. Wood (2001) analysed the Workplace Employee Relations Survey in the UK and found that both private and public organizations, and both small and medium-sized organizations, exhibited positive effects. Likewise, Cosh et al (2000) conducted research and found a correlation between an investment in job rotation, performance-related pay, quality circles, TQM and training; and growth in employment.

The economic argument for HPWP is becoming increasingly strong. In the United States Becker and Huselid (1998) suggested that the economic effects consisted of an increase in employee sales of $27,000 and a market value per employee of $18,000. In a 2002 study of the UK aerospace industry, a close correspondence was found between financial performance and companies high on the high-performance work organization index. Sales per employee were £162,000 compared with £62,000, a 161 per cent difference, and value added was £68,000 versus £42,000 (Thompson, 2002).

It would appear that only using one of the practices is unlikely to have a significant effect and may sometimes be detrimental. It is important to bundle the HPWP together because the research indicates that just using one has little impact and may even reduce productivity (Katz et al, 1987; Wood et al 2001). It is perhaps for this reason that Ashton and Sung (2002) argued that business process engineering, quality circles and even the learning organization were fads which came and went. The reason they were introduced was that they contained one 'good idea', and these ideas have tended to remain and have been absorbed by some organizations.

Combining these 'good ideas' has created high-performance work organizations and resulted in increased productivity and profits for the organization. The benefits for the workers are that the practices increase their skills and can raise income. Devolving responsibility means that workers have more challenges and learning opportunities, making their work more satisfying.

However, HPWP are not a quick fix: the practices do not work in isolation and can take years to fully implement. To be successful, Ashton and Sung (2002) suggested that high-performance work organizations need to address four main areas:

- Job design should utilize all the practical and intellectual skills of the workers in self-managed teams and in decision making.
- Knowledge must be disseminated through meetings, briefings and so on so that employees understand the business environment.
- Employees must be provided with learning opportunities through training, mentoring, coaching, appraisals and practice.
- Employees must be rewarded financially, through the learning process and recognition by co-workers and managers.

From the research, there are indications that there may be a divergence occurring within industries, between those organizations that invest in their workforce and those that are less committed. In the aerospace industry, John Rivers, Director of Human Resources at Rolls-Royce, said, 'The risk is the development of a two-tier industry – one investing in people and continually innovating, the other investing less and unable to sustain a competitive edge' (Thompson, 2002:2).

A joint report by the CIPD and Engineering Employers Federation (2003) highlighted that to be successfully introduced, high-performance working required:

- strong and active commitment from senior management;
- commitment from employees to the organization's objectives;

Table 2.3 A compilation of high-performance working practices (Cattell, 2005)

Company vision	Company form/structure	Culture	Learning activity
Differentiation	Flatter	Performance aligned to organizational objectives	Competence definition and development
Customization	Non-hierarchical	Commitment to direction taken by organization	Teamworking
World class	Devolved decision making	Enthusiasm for change	Self-management
Benchmarking	Self-management	Quality recruitment and selection	Multi-skilling
People contribution	Team capabilities	Rewarding performance	Work-based learning
Creativity and innovation	Project based	Trust	Job rotation
Problem-solving capacity	High trust	Harmonization	Project working
Empowerment	High communication and involvement	Engagement with local community	Information sharing

- the opportunity for managers to apply their own discretion at work;
- the pursuit of continuous learning throughout the organization.

The CIPD provides a note of caution, in highlighting the fact that high-performance working is not right for all organizations. It also notes that HRM and HRD practitioners will need to understand what is involved, and need to be ready also to lead the thinking-through of the people management and development implications.

CONCLUSION

Where does this necessarily brief review of HRM leave us? HRM is not universally accepted as a phenomenon with a lasting message for organizational excellence. At its worst, HRM is seen as a confidence trick – perpetrated to whitewash systems of employee exploitation and, particularly, to isolate trade unions – hopefully meeting the requirement for a better story to convince an increasingly knowledgeable workforce, but a story that will eventually be seen through. Another view is that HRM is an 'honest' attempt to bring together the needs of both business and employees but is founded on false assumptions of the nature of organizational reality – ie, that organizations are naturally harmonic so long as nefarious elements can be removed and we communicate better. The more optimistic scenario is that HRM represents the only way we have of releasing the latent talents of our workforces and, in the face of increasing global competition, this is the only way of surviving, both organizationally and nationally. As well as this clear business imperative, HRM offers the best opportunity for some time, maybe ever, to manage organizations in a participative way with empowered employees making major contributions in jobs redesigned both to stretch employee capability and interest and to meet Maslow's earlier vision of better products and better service.

Perhaps the way forward is a partnership which, at first sight, looks unlikely in terms of the HRM model. Analysis of the third Workplace Industrial Relations survey indicates that HRM practices are more likely to be found in unionized firms than in non-unionized (Millward, 1993). Far from providing the opportunity for HRM to grow and develop, the absence of trade unions seems to mean that there is a strong possibility that nothing will develop: Guest's (1995) 'black hole – no HRM and no industrial relations'.

Another view of partnership is evident in the current interest in the role of the HR specialist as a 'business partner'. Popularized by Ulrich (1997), business partnership involves four HR roles: strategic partner, administrative expert, employee champion and change agent. In larger organizations, where the concept has been received more readily, the roles tend to be played by different people, but the critical feature is that all four are seen to have an impact on business performance. General Motors is an example of an organization that has embraced the approach, and Pickard (2004) describes its application in the UK in Vauxhall Motors. Whatever view of partnership is taken – and one does not necessarily preclude the other – the emphasis remains on cooperation rather than conflict, underpinning the unitary flavour of the classic HRM model.

Bibliography

Applebaum, E, Bailey, T, Berg, P and Kallenberg, A L (2000) *Manufacturing Advantage: Why high performance work systems pay off*, London, Cornell University Press

Armstrong, M (1987) 'HRM: a case of the emperor's new clothes?', *Personnel Management*, **19**, 8, pp 30–35

Armstrong, M (2002) *Employee Reward*, London, CIPD

Ashton, D and Sung, J (2002) *Supporting Workplace Learning for High Performance Working*, Geneva, International Labour Organization

Atkinson, J (1984) 'Manpower strategies for flexible organisations', *Personnel Management*, August, pp 28–31

Beardwell, I, Holden L and Claydon T (2004) *Human Resource Management: A contemporary approach*, London, FT/Prentice Hall

Becker, B E and Huselid, M A (1998) 'High performance work systems and firm performance: a synthesis of research and managerial implications', *Research in Personnel and Human Resource Management*, **16**, pp 53–101

Betcherman, G, Leckie, N and McMullen, L (1997) *Developing Skills in the Canadian Workplace*, Ottawa, Canadian Policy Research Networks

Boselie, P, Paauwe, J and Richardson, R (2003) 'HRM, institutionalisation and organisational performance', *International Journal of Human Resource Management*, **14**, 8, pp 1407–29

CEDEFOP (2004) 'Belgium: Conclusions of the 2003 Conference on Employment', *cedefopinfo*, **1**, Luxembourg, Office for Official Publications of the European Communities

CIPD/Engineering Employers Federation (EEF) (2003) *Maximising Employee Potential and Business Performance: The role of high performance working*, London, EEF

Cook, M (1990) *Personnel Selection and Productivity*, Chichester, Wiley

Cosh, A, Hughes, A and Weeks, M (2000) *The Relationship Between Training and Employment Growth in Small and Medium Enterprises*, Nottingham, DfEE Publications

Ento (2002) *Standards in Learning and Development*, London, Ento

Guest, D (1995) 'Human resource management, trade unions and industrial relations' in J Storey (ed), *Human Resource Management: A critical text*, London, Routledge, pp 110–41

Guest, D (1996) 'The psychological contract', paper presented to IPD National Conference, Harrogate

Guthrie, J P (2001) 'High involvement work practices, turnover and productivity: evidence from New Zealand', *Academy of Management Journal*, **44**, 1, pp 180–90

Hiltrop, J (1996) 'Managing the changing psychological contract', *Employee Relations*, **18**, 1, pp 36–49

Huang, Tung-Chun (1997) 'The effect of participative management on organizational performance: the case of Taiwan', *International Journal of Human Resource Management*, **8**, 5, pp 677–89

Ichniowski, C, Shaw, K and Prenushi, G (1997) 'The effects of human resource practices on productivity: a study of steel finishing lines', *American Economic Review*, **87**, 3, pp 291–313

Katz, H C, Kochan, T A and Keefe, J H (1987) 'Industrial relations and productivity in the US automobile industry', *Brookings Papers on Economic Activity*, Vol 3, pp 688–715

Kling, J (1995) 'High performance work systems and firm performance', *Monthly Labour Review*, May, pp 29–36

Kohn, A (1993) 'Challenging behaviourist dogma: myths about money and motivation', *Compensation and Benefits Review*, March–April, pp 35–37

Lawler, E E (1995) 'The new pay: a strategic approach', *Compensation and Benefits Review*, July–August, pp 14–22

Legge, K (1995) 'HRM: rhetoric, reality and hidden agendas', in J Storey (ed), *Human Resource Management: A critical text*, London, Routledge, pp 33–59

Lewis, P (2001) 'Reward management', in T Redman and A Wilkinson (eds), *Contemporary Human Resource Management: Text and cases*, Harlow, FT/Prentice Hall, Pearson Education

Likert, R (1961) *New Patterns of Management*, New York, McGraw-Hill

Mabey, C and Salaman, G (1995) *Strategic Human Resource Management*, Oxford, Blackwell

MacDuffie, J P (1995) 'Human resource bundles and manufacturing performance: organizational logic and flexible production systems in the world auto industry', *Industrial Labour Relations Review*, **48**, pp 197–221

Marchington, M (1995) 'Fairy tales and magic wands: new employment practices in perspective', *Employee Relations*, **17**, 1, pp 51–66

Marginson, P *et al* (1993) *The Control of Industrial Relations in Large Companies*, Research Paper No 45, Industrial Relations Research Unit, University of Warwick

Maslow, A H (1965) *Eupsychian Management*, Homewood, IL, Irwin/Dorsey

Mayfield, E C and Carlson, R E (1966) 'Selection interview decisions: first results from a long-term research project', *Personnel Psychology*, **19**, pp 41–53

Millward, N (1993) 'Industrial relations in transition: the findings of the Third Workplace Industrial Relations Survey', paper presented to BUIRA, York, July

Pascale, R (1995) 'In search of the new 'employment contract', *Human Resources*, November/December, pp 21–26

Patterson, M G, West, M A, Lawthom, R and Nickell, S (1997) 'Impact of people management practices on business performance', *Issues in People Management*, No. 22, London, IPD

Pickard, J (2004) 'One step beyond', *People Management*, 30 June

Smethurst, S and Hardy, R (2004) 'The allure of online', *People Management*, 29 July

Smircich, L and Calas, M (1987) 'Organizational culture: a critical assessment', in F M Jablin, *et al* (eds), *Handbook of Organizational Communication*, Newbury Park, CA, Sage, pp 228–63

Storey, J (1992) *Developments in the Management of Human Resources*, Oxford, Blackwell

Storey, J (1995) *Human Resource Management: A critical text*, London, Routledge

Storey, J and Wright, M (2001) 'Recruitment and selection', in I Beardwell and L Holden (eds), *Human Resource Management: A contemporary approach*, Harlow, Pearson Education

Thompson, M (2002) *High Performance Work Organisation in UK Aerospace, The Society of British Aerospace Companies Human Capital Audit 2002*, London, SBAC

Torrington, D, Hall, L and Taylor, S (2002) *Human Resource Management*, Harlow, FT/Prentice Hall

Truss, C (2001) 'Complexities and controversies in linking HRM with organizational outcomes', *Journal of Management Studies*, **38**, 8, pp 1121–49

Ulrich, D (1997) *Human Resource Champions: The next agenda for adding value and delivering results*, Boston, MA, Harvard Business School Press

White, M, Hill, S, Mills, C and Smeaton, D (2004) *Managing to Change? British Workplaces and the Future of Work*, London, Palgrave Macmillan

Wood, S, de Menezes, L and Lasoasa, A (2001) 'High involvement management and performance', paper delivered at Centre for Labour Market Studies, University of Leicester, May

3

Organizational Change

Bland Tomkinson

INTRODUCTION AND LEARNING OBJECTIVES

If you read the works of whichever management guru takes your fancy, you are likely to find a recipe for prosperity beyond your wildest dreams. 'If you reorganize your enterprise in the way that I tell you,' goes the hype, 'then success is just around the corner.' Seldom does the guru tell you that getting to this management nirvana is a fraught and tricky operation that can lead to bankruptcy, industrial unrest, or, more likely, an 'early bath' for the one who was foolish enough to embark upon such a scheme!

Some consultants, like Ventris (2004), imply a view that by taking a positive approach from the beginning, any senior manager can accomplish major change: but consultants seldom stay around to see the results. And, Argyris (1991) suggests that many consultants and other high-commitment professionals fail to learn because they misunderstand what learning is and how to bring it about. He suggests two sources of misunderstanding. First, the failure to critically reflect on their own behaviour – and how this contributes to problems – leads to too narrow a perception of learning. The second mistake, Argyris believes, is to underestimate the part that defensive reasoning plays in blocking learning. Because consultants infrequently encounter failure they fail to recognize it and attribute blame to external factors. This not only represents a missed opportunity but also reinforces the defensive behaviour. Human resource development is surely the process of moving from one position to another, a process that we would normally count as 'change'.

'Organizational change' has many guises and for some commentators this is limited to the internal restructuring of an organization. In this chapter, however, I shall be using the term to look at any form of change that affects the organization or sections of it, taking it in contradistinction to changes that are individual and personal.

For the HRD professional organizational change provides challenges and chances beyond those faced by the average member of staff. The effects on the developers are picked up before the conclusion of this chapter but, before that, it is important to set down something about the nature of change and also about the theories of how to handle it.

> Having read this chapter you will:
>
> - understand the paradoxical nature of change;
> - be able to describe several methods of implementing change;
> - be aware of what can go wrong in the change process; and
> - understand the roles of the change agent.

THE PARADOX OF CHANGE

Change is full of paradox, including the notion, voiced above, that HRD is itself a change process. But before looking at some of these paradoxes, we need to look at the paradoxical nature of change itself. As an illustration, let us look at a car travelling at a constant speed of 70 mph (or 110 kph, if you prefer) down the outside lane of a motorway. On a straight and level road this is relatively easy to accomplish with a fair degree of accuracy. On the face of it, this could be considered as unchanging. Yet in positional terms the location of the car is constantly changing. Let's take one more step, this time on the brake. Harder to measure perhaps, but let us assume that we brake from 70 mph to a halt at a steady rate. In this case the acceleration (or deceleration if you view it that way) is unchanging but both speed and location are changing.

This leads to the first two paradoxes: change is omnipresent and stopping change is in itself a change!

Taking the first of these, imagine lying on your back on a sunny beach with no one around and your eyes closed. You open your eyes; nothing has changed. But the tide has encroached that little bit further, you have grown a little bit older, the clouds in that otherwise clear blue sky have scudded away. The important thing is the significance of the changes – these small changes have hardly impacted on you so you discount them; but, change is always with us.

Moving on to the second paradox, consider a small stationery shop that principally sells greetings cards, gift-wrapping and similar accoutrements. The business is very seasonal – Christmas cards and tree decorations in September, Easter cards and fluffy chicks in January, birthday cards, anniversary cards, Mother's and Father's Day cards at other times of the year. As proprietor you have to keep up with these seasonal changes, changing your displays and updating your stock. Suppose now that you decide to change the store to one that sells

Christmas items the whole year round; you have eliminated the constant seasonal change of stock but introduced a major disjunction in the business. Which is then more significant: the routine seasonal changes or the change of operation to eliminate them?

The Change Integration Team from Price Waterhouse (now PricewaterhouseCoopers) (Dauphinais *et al*, 1996) has identified other paradoxes relating to the process of change. These are grouped under five *paradox principles:*

1. Positive change requires significant stability. This is predicated on the assumption that individuals can cope with *change* – what they find difficult is *uncertainty*.
2. To build an enterprise, focus on the individual. This paradox focuses on the need to carry all members of staff along with a change decision.
3. Focus directly on culture, indirectly. This emphasizes the role of institutional culture in attitudes to change and the need to tackle culture change circumspectly.
4. True empowerment requires forceful leadership. This paradox emphasizes that empowering workers requires courage at the highest levels.
5. In order to build, you must tear down. Its final paradox principle looks at the disadvantages of disjointed incrementalism as a means of change.

Many of the ideas underlying these principles will be picked up later in this chapter.

THE NATURE OF CHANGE

In looking at the paradox of change we have already begun to look at the nature of organizational change. The first element of change is the locus of the imperative; in some cases this is internal to the organization but often change is a response to changes in the external environment within which the organization operates. A gloss on the internal location is whether the change is top-down or bottom-up (or, as is often the case, from the middle out!).

Second is the degree of compulsion for the change; government regulations may impose change on an organization whether it wishes it or not, but many other changes are taken in response to, for example, perceived market pressures. These latter may be more, or less, voluntary and the outworking of the change within the organization may itself be by mutual consent or by management decree.

The third element is a dichotomy that Burnes (2004) describes as either *radical* or *incremental*. Radical change relates to substantial reworking of an organization's culture and processes over a short period of time; throwing out the old ways and bringing in new. Incremental change is much more subtle and small scale; it can still mean overturning the old ways of doing things but perhaps in only a piecemeal or localized fashion and with a gradual introduction over a lengthy period of time.

Fourth comes the domain or domains of change; a new procedure may be perceived as purely a technical matter or a restructuring as a purely organizational one but in practice these domains will inevitably impact upon one another. In the early 1960s Woodward (1965) pointed to the interrelationship between technology and organization, which echoed similar research at the Tavistock Institute (Trist *et al*, 1963). Homans (1951) took a slightly broader view, embracing the interaction of the cultural, physical and technological environments of the organization. An example of a physical change would be a move to a new building; there may be no intention to change the hierarchy of the organization or its social structures, there may be no attempt to introduce new technology, but the physical change would have considerable impact.

Peters and Waterman (1982) suggest a seven-S framework: Strategy; Structure; Systems; Staff; Style; Shared values; and Skills. All of these domains interact and a change in any one of them is a potential for change in all the others. Handy (1993) suggests that changes are easier in the first three of these domains (the hard Ss) but that the changes may be illusory if no cognisance is taken of the effects in the other four domains (the soft Ss).

Beer and Nohria (2000) suggest two theories of change: an economic approach and an organizational capabilities approach. The first is concerned with short-term economic gain and the second with moving towards a learning organization. In 'Theory E' the emphasis is on a top-down approach, whereas in 'Theory O' the emphasis is on encouraging grassroots participation. They suggest that the two need to be combined in order to achieve success: the Theory E approach can work in the short run but leaves those employees who remain demoralized and disloyal, whereas the Theory O approach may produce organizational change but without any economic benefit to the firm. But a simple intermingling is insufficient and the management of blending the two approaches is seen as yet another paradox.

Higgs and Rowland (2003) attempt to map ideas about change onto a two-dimensional diagram. The dimensions are, first, change as predictable versus change as a complex phenomenon; and second, a uniform approach versus a disseminated and differentiated approach. Their research suggested that treating change as predictable and using a uniform (particularly directive, top-down) approach usually leads to a lack of success.

METHODS TO MAKE THE TRANSITION

A number of different ways have been put forward to tackle the process of change within an organization and the approach taken may vary very much with the nature of the change and the reasons for it.

Lewin

One of the methods advocated is the use of 'Field Theory' (sometimes called 'Field Force Theory'). This emanates from the ideas of Kurt Lewin who brings an analogy of vector mechanics to the psychosocial arena. In the simple form usually adopted by change practitioners this can involve looking at the factors for and against a particular change, listing them and setting out some sort of weighting. Such an approach can have value in, for example, deciding which of two competing technologies to use eg, staying with WordPerfect, for use as a word-processing package, or moving to AmiPro.

Lewin postulated a three-step model of change:

1. unfreezing;
2. moving;
3. re-freezing.

This is dependent on the concepts that the old behaviour has to be discarded (unfrozen) before moving to the new, and that the new behaviour has to be accepted as the norm otherwise there will be a regression to old patterns. Compare this with the fifth of the Price Waterhouse paradoxes. Note, however, that in organizational terms regression would often be difficult to accomplish.

Unfreezing requires analysis and confrontation of the reasons for change and a developmental process to disseminate the need for change. Moving requires the identification of alternative courses of action, evaluation of these and choice of an appropriate route. Re-freezing seeks to rebuild an equilibrium state and may be supported by institutional rewards and benefits or by an educational process, or both.

However, change is usually much more complex than this – as is vector mechanics.

Lupton

A less simplistic view put forward by Tom Lupton (1971) comes as a series of injunctions to managers:

- Set up systematically and in detail the organization alternatives open.
- Map out the present organization as a social system, not forgetting its external links.
- List the groups affected by each organization alternative.
- Examine the issues likely to be raised in each group from the adoption of each alternative.
- Assess likely reactions on each issue and score for acceptability.
- Test economic feasibility against social acceptability and adopt the course that offers the most adaptive and least costly balance.
- Examine the problems this course raises and ask whether existing means of redress of grievance are adequate to cope. If not, take appropriate steps to create such machinery as seems to be required.

This approach broadens the way in which the change is looked at but is still predicated upon the general idea of listing and choosing. Again, this approach has its value in some straightforward cases but a more general model is required if we are to cope with the variety of change that we have so far discussed.

Handy

Charles Handy's (1993) schema for organizational change is:

- Create an awareness of the need for change.
- Select an appropriate initiating person or group.
- Be prepared to allow the recipients to adapt the final strategy.
- Accept the fact that the successful doctor gets no credit but must let the patient boast of his or her sound condition.
- Be prepared to accept a less than optimum strategy in the interests of achieving something rather than nothing.

Handy sees this from the manager's perspective, but sometimes change has to be initiated from the grassroots and the above schema can still hold good in such cases.

Burnes

A more developed version of this schema is the nine-element model developed by Bernard Burnes (2004):

1. *Create a vision.* Why change? The answer must lie in the need to attain some farther goal or realize a distant vision. The first stage, argues Burnes, is to construct this vision. In looking at this process, he suggests four aspects:

   - *mission* – a statement of the organization's strategic purpose;
   - *valued outcomes* – intended performance and human outcomes;
   - *valued conditions* – what the organization should look like to achieve these;
   - *mid-point goals* – intermediate objectives, usually capable of being more clearly stated than the long-term ambitions.

2. *Develop strategies.* Having shaped a future vision, the organization needs to look at the ways of realizing that vision, through a series of strategies. The strategies will relate particularly to those mid-point goals and may be shaped by reference to particular work domains or particular geographical regions. Such strategies are destined to change with time and experience even when the vision remains constant.

3. *Create the conditions for successful change.* In order to create the right conditions for change it is first necessary to create a readiness for change. Burnes suggests three steps to be taken to create this state of readiness:

   - *make people aware of the pressures for change* – the organization not only needs to describe its vision but also to share the vision with its employees. By this means members of the organization come to share common goals and to understand the place of change in safeguarding their future;

- *give regular feedback* – feedback is essential not only on the performance of the individual within the organization but also of the organization itself. This means that employees become aware of deviations from the strategy and hence are prepared for change;
- *publicize successful change* – making people aware of successful programmes of change, either within the organization or outside, helps employees see the benefits of the change process. This can also be an important learning tool.

Burnes further suggests that other steps need to be taken to deal with causes of resistance:

- *understand people's fears and concerns* – employees' fears may well be groundless but to the individuals concerned they are real and important. Change creates uncertainty and failure to get to grips with perceived threats is a major problem in introducing change;
- *encourage communication* – regular open and effective communication is a basic way in which to promote change and to address uncertainty. Transmission of detail helps to overcome the potential for rumour taking hold;
- *involve those affected* – not only does involvement create understanding but it can also alert the change-makers to unforeseen difficulties when those concerned with implementing the change are involved in the detail.

4. *Create the right culture.* Change that is inconsistent with the culture of the organization is doomed to fail, but changing the culture is even more problematic. (Compare this with the third Price Waterhouse paradox.) Desirably, the culture of the organization should foster flexibility and encourage reflection. Encouragement of what Chris Argyris terms 'double-loop learning' – where underlying paradigms are challenged and changed as well as strategies and assumptions – should provide a fertile seed bed for change. He suggests that 'Model II' theory-in-use is the underlying model for fostering this: his 'theory-in-use' is the implicit values exposed by what people actually do as opposed to their 'espoused' theories which describe what they think they do. Senge (1990) suggests that the gap between espoused theory and theory-in-use can present a challenge to the shared vision.

5. *Assess the need for, and type of, change.* Appropriateness of response is also seen as key to the change process – appropriateness not only in the particular change to be undertaken but also in whether to undergo a process of change at all. Burnes suggests a four-phase approach to the assessment:

    a. *The trigger* – organizations should only investigate change for one of the following reasons:

    - one of the organization's strategies highlights the need for change;
    - performance in attainment of the organization's goals appears seriously impaired;
    - opportunities are offered which appear to achieve significant improvement.

    b. *The remit* – a clear remit must be provided for assessing the process of change. This should include the reasons for carrying out the assessment and should cover all relevant domains.
    c. *The assessment team* – the team should be led by a senior manager, preferably one who will go on to champion whatever change is necessary, and should include all relevant disciplines. The first task of the team is to clarify its objectives, reviewing the trigger, the remit and the composition of the team itself.

d. *The assessment* – again, Burnes advocates a four-step approach:

- first, the problem or opportunity should be clarified or redefined;
- second, alternative proposals should be drawn up and tested against criteria founded on the redefined problem specification;
- third, the proposals meeting the criteria, together with the problem or opportunity statement, should be shared with a wider constituency;
- fourth, recommendations for action should be drawn up, including type of change advocated, timetable for implementation and resource implications, and presented to senior management for decision.

6. *Plan and implement change.* Having gone through the assessment process, management needs to commit to the change and to prepare a detailed plan. This should be based on the work of the assessment team but may be implemented by a different, though equally multidisciplinary, team. This team, or sub-groups for a major project, will need to undertake a number of activities:

- *activity planning* – constructing a detailed list of all the tasks to be undertaken, their sequence and the critical path through them;
- *commitment planning* – identifying key people and groups whose commitment to the project is essential to success;
- *management structures* – the team or teams managing the process of change may need new reporting structures with rapid access to top management and to the champions of change;
- *training* – the obvious aspect of training is the acquisition of new technical skills, but training should underpin all aspects of change and target all appropriate individuals and groups, including middle and senior management;
- *review* – Burnes calls this 'post audit'. After the changes have taken place the effects should be audited to see how successful the changes have been in meeting their objectives and to learn how the change process can be improved.

7. *Involve everyone.* Maintaining the commitment, particularly over a long timescale (remember that even the simplest information technology projects can take years to design, build and implement) requires continuing involvement of all parties. (Compare this to the second Price Waterhouse paradox.) Burnes suggests three facets to this:

a. *Information* – letting everyone involved know what is happening right from the beginning and reporting honestly on progress, or lack of it, is the key.
b. *Communication* – providing information is only the start. Communication has to be two-way with employees' responses gathered and listened to.
c. *Actual involvement* – responsibility for detailed aspects of change need to be given to those directly affected; this requires the correct identification of those responsible.

8. *Sustain the momentum.* Particularly in long-term projects, a failure to maintain the momentum of change can lead to regression on the part of those participating and potentially fatal delay. To bolster the momentum, organizations can:

- *provide resources for change* – even where a project is looking for down-sizing, the actual pursuit of change is likely to consume resources (note how finance departments expand during periods of retrenchment) and appropriate resources should be allocated from the beginning of the project;
- *give support to the change agents* – often the change management team is having to boost morale and motivate others. They, in their turn, need support and encouragement lest they become demoralized and pass on their demotivation to others;
- *develop new competences and skills* – training has already been mentioned but the momentum has to be borne on a tide of new styles and approaches. This can involve leadership and teamworking training as well as individual counselling and encouragement;
- *reinforce desired behaviour* – behaviours that are consistent with the change can be reinforced not only in financial ways (for example using suggestion schemes or bonuses) but also symbolically (using praise, changing a job title, or awarding prizes).

9. *Commit to continuous improvement.* Real success should see change as an ongoing process, not a once-and-for-all activity. The prospect of continuing improvement should be built into the project from the outset and a culture of quality enhancement engendered.

Burnes' method arises from his study of what went well (and badly; two-thirds of the changes he surveyed were unsuccessful) in major reorganizations in substantial firms. However, much of what he has to offer is applicable on a smaller scale. His is one of the more comprehensive approaches to the management of change.

WHAT CAN GO WRONG?

Attempts at introducing change can often founder. Some commentators (see above) believe that the majority of major changes fail in substantial ways. But, we can learn from others' experience in trying to facilitate change. Success may be incomplete for a variety of reasons:

- *Unintended consequences.* Unintended consequences are of two types. First there is the under- or over-estimation of the effects of change; typical here is the construction of a new motorway producing more traffic than predicted by the highway engineers. The second type is where there are unexpected consequences, usually in a domain that had not been considered. An example of this is where one section of a department is moved out of a building to a more remote site and social and communication problems arise within the department because people are no longer in informal daily contact.
- *Self-fulfilling fear of failure.* This reflects on the fourth Price Waterhouse paradox – that true empowerment needs a forceful leader. Sometimes change requires a bold leap forward and a half-hearted attempt will lead to a fall into the chasm of failure.
- *Lack of preparation.* The process of change needs to be supported by appropriate human resource development efforts at all stages. Often training and development needs are recognized as an

afterthought so that new technology, for example, may be introduced without operators being given any grounding. More subtly, the less tangible areas of support may be neglected, for example training in leadership or teamwork. Timelines of training are also important.

- *Ill-conceived change process.* Considerable forethought is one of the keys to successful change. Causes of failure can include inadequate attention to any of the stages in the change management process but particularly with regard to inappropriate timescales – going for the quick fix – or to a lack of clear dissemination of ideas and processes.
- *Inadequate consultation.* Nothing can sink a project faster than poorly motivated staff (except, perhaps, a catastrophic computer failure!). An imposed change will only attain grudging acceptance and adherence to the letter rather than the spirit of the transformation. Equally, a pragmatic shopfloor change of practice can induce alarm and antagonism in management if they have not been consulted. Perhaps a special case of this is the:
- *'Not invented here' syndrome.* Sometimes the strongest resistance to change is shown as a response to what is seen as importing the ideas of an alien culture. In university circles we often find this voiced as 'It might work in industry but it's different in a university', or 'The American (Australian, Dutch, Scandinavian, whatever) system is not the same as ours, it would never work here', or even 'Well, that's Mechanical Engineering; in Mathematics we have to do …!'

HUMAN RESOURCE ISSUES, IN MERGER AND CHANGE IN HIGHER EDUCATION, AND THE NEED FOR DEVELOPMENT

As a result of a review of the relationship between them, which considered a range of options for closer collaboration, two major universities in one British city decided to unite. The move was prompted partly by a government imperative that sought wider changes than the merger that evolved. In the event, a joint working party, with an independent chair, recommended a full organic merger as being the best solution for the region, for higher education and for the two universities. The preferred option of the working group was that the two existing universities would be dissolved and a new institution created which would have a new, single management structure, a strategy based on the opportunity to be even more internationally competitive, improved opportunities to bid for research funding, and thus increased stature and reputation.

The concept put forward at the time was one of 'double dissolution', with a new university being created to take their place. The date for the institution of the new university was taken as some two years after the formal decision to go ahead, in order to overcome some of the legal hurdles – an Act of Parliament was required to resolve some of the issues.

Process

As well as a number of project groups, the governing bodies set up a Reference Group – intended to be representative of all the staff involved in the merger (although the word 'merger' was eschewed at the time) – and an External Advisory Group, comprising people at a senior level from outside the two universities whose organizations had been through a process of merger recently.

As a human resource developer, what support would you have sought to give the project groups and the Reference Group?

In addition to compliance with the TUPE regulations, the two universities undertook that there would be no compulsory redundancies and that salaries would be protected for an unstated period – taken to be four years. The latter point is particularly noteworthy because at the same time as the major restructuring brought on by this merger, universities throughout the UK were attempting to introduce a new grading scheme that would apply to all staff. A Human Resources project group was set up, and among its early conclusions was the need to retain and motivate key staff through the period of transition. This was among a number of critical factors that were identified:

- harmonizing terms and conditions of employment for all staff, where appropriate, within a five-year horizon;
- establishing negotiating arrangements;
- moving towards a single pension provision for all staff;
- that key members of staff have a commitment to remain available for the integration process and beyond;
- that sufficient resources be provided to maintain business as usual and at the same time establish the new institution;
- making allowance for any loss of productivity.

With two years to plan for change, what sort of development programme would you set in train?

The human side of the merger was made more complex by the simultaneous change to a new national grading structure for universities. This introduced a 51-point scale of salaries, with individual salary brackets to be decided by job evaluation. Salaries would be protected for up to four years in cases where a lower salary was determined for an existing job. Some jobs in the existing universities were on common national scales but others were on different, locally agreed scales. The intention was that all posts in the new university would be defined on the new scales. But the new scheme was not in place for the process of recruiting to a new structure, so jobs were internally advertised, and offered, initially without any indication of the salary attached!

Given that this scheme proposes two major changes simultaneously, what advice would you give to top management? What development programmes would you initiate to follow this up?

Well over a year into the change process, morale began to sag in many sections and sickness rates rose. The response was to mount a mandatory programme for managers in sickness absence control – delivered by the universities' solicitors.

Was this a necessary and sufficient approach? What might you do differently?

Three months before the vesting day of the merged organization, concerns were growing about morale and the response of staff to the process of change. At this stage a 'Policy on the Management of Stress' was introduced and the joint staff newspaper carried details of counselling and staff support services available. Additional training and development was provided with courses in 'Career Review', 'How to Win at the CVs and Applications Forms Game', 'The Essential Guide to Successful Interviews', 'Starting a Business', 'Pre-retirement' and 'Financial Planning' in the eight weeks leading up to vesting.

What message does this programme give to staff? What do you think about the timing of the programme? What might you do differently? If you were the training manager, what might be your thoughts and feelings about implementing this series of programmes?

Looking at the 'What can go wrong' section of this chapter, what elements of this change have fallen into these categories and what would you have done about it?

THE ROLE OF HRD IN ORGANIZATIONAL CHANGE

By now you should have realized the importance of involving everyone in the change process, but there are those who believe that the human resource developer is the only one fitted to lead organizational change. McCalman and Paton (1992) suggest, however, that change is a multidisciplinary activity; this reflects upon the point made earlier about the domains in which the change is to take place. Luecke (2003) suggests that the HR function should never take responsibility for change. This is a function of line management. However, our case study demonstrates that the HR functions needs to be sensitive to the changes that are taking place and to facilitate this rather than add to the complexity.

Clearly it would be absurd for a human resource developer to take responsibility for a change to a new accounting system; this needs the involvement of those with knowledge of accounting and of information systems. On the other hand, training and development activities can themselves take a long time to design and implement and it is important for the developer to be getting to grips with the training issues in time to design the programmes for implementation. But neither should the design process be seen as beyond the remit of the developer; support for the process itself may be key to success or failure and often the human resource developer will possess appropriate skills to facilitate the process.

Human resource professionals may be employed either as external consultants or 'change agents' or as specialists within their own organization. The role of the developer can embrace both the process of change as well as the associated tasks.

Process roles

Acting as a consultant or change agent is often perceived as a high prestige role but the success of a projected change depends critically upon a number of underpinning aspects, many of which can be ignored by external 'experts'. There is a forceful argument for the developer taking an active role in the change assessment team, and team building and facilitation skills may be needed at the earliest stages. 'Awaydays' or 'Blue Sky weekends' can be the source of ideas for change and the professional developer should be well equipped to facilitate these. Training may need to be given in problem-solving and analysis to help both assessment and implementation teams in the technical aspects of their tasks. Also, interpersonal skills and sensitivity training may need to be developed to handle the 'people' side of the process. Understanding change and educating staff in its processes can also serve to maintain morale. In many cases the developer will be the repository for the learning about how change processes have worked in the organization in the past and will be ideally placed to feed this into new ideas for change.

Task roles

Detailed task roles will vary according to the nature of the change – training in handling new equipment or new software are commonplace consequences as is dealing with new methods of operation – but changes in structure and organization may demand other skills. The trainer will need to familiarize himself or herself thoroughly with the equipment or procedures well before implementation. Individual career, or even outplacement, counselling may be important in some circumstances, particularly where individuals find it difficult to retrain to new ways of working, and changes such as moving from line to group-based working will demand training in the new perspectives. In many cases cascade models of training will be used and the developer will need to ensure that supervisors and shopfloor mentors are appropriately prepared for the task. Above all, if a quality enhancement culture is to be engendered, then considerable effort will need to be devoted not only to communicating the essentials of quality methods but also to group ownership of quality.

CONCLUSION

- Change is a complex and often paradoxical process.
- Even simple technical changes can have social and organizational implications – whatever the expected domain of the change, all domains must be looked at.
- Organizational change needs to be tackled in a systematic way.
- Change is often doomed to failure. It is important to know the causes of failure, to build on previous mistakes and to learn to avoid the principal pitfalls.

- Whatever the change, it has human consequences. It is important for the human resource developer to be involved from the beginning.
- The role of the human resource developer in developing the change process is as important as his or her role in training individuals in new skills – if not more so.

Bibliography

Argyris, C (1991) 'Teaching smart people how to learn', *Harvard Business Review*, May/June, pp 99–109

Argyris, C (1992) *On Organisational Learning*, Oxford, Blackwell

Beer, M and Nohria, N (eds) (2000) *Breaking the Code of Change*, Boston, MA, HBS Press

Burnes, B (2004) *Managing Change*, London, Prentice Hall

Dauphinais, B, Price, C and Pederson, P (The Price Waterhouse Change Integration Team) (1996) *The Paradox Principles*, Chicago, IL, Irwin

Handy C (1993) *Understanding Organisations*, Harmondsworth, Penguin

Higgs, M and Rowland, D (2003) 'Is change changing?', Henley Working Paper HWP 0313, Henley, Henley Management College

Homans, G (1951) *The Human Group*, London, Routledge and Kegan Paul

Lewin, K (1951) *Field Theory in Social Science*, London, Tavistock

Luecke, R (2003) *Managing Change and Transition*, Boston, MA, HBS Press

Lupton, T (1971) *Management and the Social Sciences*, Harmondsworth, Penguin

McCalman, J and Paton, R A (1992) *Change Management: A guide to effective implementation*, London, Paul Chapman

Peters, T and Waterman, R (1982) *In Search of Excellence*, New York, Harper and Row

Senge, P (1990) *The Fifth Discipline: The art and practice of the learning organization*, London, Century

Trist, E L, Higgin, G W, Murray, H and Pollock, A B (1963) *Organizational Choice*, London, Tavistock

Ventris, G (2004) *Successful Change Management: The fifty key facts*, London, Continuum

Walton, J (1999) *Strategic Human Resource Development*, London, Pearson

Woodward, J (1965) *Industrial Organization*, Oxford, Oxford University Press

4

National Economic Development and Human Resource Development

John P Wilson

INTRODUCTION AND LEARNING OBJECTIVES

Since the 1980s, there has been a growing interest at national and international levels in the area of Human Resource Development (HRD) and its impact on economic performance. This interest and concern has been predominantly driven by globalization and the increase in international trade; unemployment levels; national budget deficits; international comparisons of levels of education and training; and the development of new technologies.

Whether a country is in the early stages of development, newly industrialized, fully industrialized or post-industrial, the strategies adopted to bring about further development, in its broadest sense, tend to be of a portfolio nature with a variety of objectives targeted within the political, economic, social and technological areas. These areas are closely interwoven with one another and thus HRD needs to be considered within this broader framework. This chapter will consider the arguments for encouraging education and training at national levels for the purposes of increasing economic output. It will illustrate some of the various strategies adopted by countries, at various stages of development, to enhance their economic well-being and human development.

Having read this chapter you will:

- understand the economic imperative for compulsory education;
- understand the economic imperative for training and developing the workforce;
- be aware of the need for a flexible labour force; and
- understand the role of education in promoting peaceful co-existence and democracy.

DEVELOPING THE HUMAN RESOURCES OF A NATION

There has long been a recognition that education of the individual has been a source of personal advancement and growth, and this rationale has been expanded to apply to the intellectual resources of a nation. In 1776, Adam Smith wrote *An Inquiry into the Nature and Causes of the Wealth of Nations* in which he observed that while people of high status and income had the opportunity to receive an education, the same opportunities were not available for less well-off people who had to begin work in very early childhood. He also maintained that not only would education provide a civilizing effect for the whole population but it would also enable people who had even a rudimentary education to be more productive:

> But though the common people cannot, in any civilized society, be so well instructed as people of some rank and fortune, the most essential parts of education, however, to read, write, and account, can be acquired at so early a period of life that, the greater part even of those who are to be bred to the lowest occupations, have time to acquire them before they can be employed in those occupations. For a very small expence the public can facilitate, can encourage, and can even impose upon almost the whole body of people, the necessity of acquiring those most essential parts of education. (Adam Smith, in Heilbroner, 1986:304)

The education of a country's population has not always been regarded as beneficial; there were believed to be some negative consequences of educating the population. In Britain, during the early 19th century, concerns were expressed that universal education might cause dangers such as subversion, insubordination, and people leaving menial tasks for other jobs. From a national point of view it was felt that education might threaten freedom of thought, and increase the chance of tyranny and the greater control of the populace. Moreover, some people believed it might decrease personal initiative and lead to inefficiency; discourage voluntary charitable schooling; and encourage fecklessness among parents who would not appreciate the benefits if they did not have to pay for education.

Observation of educational practices in other countries alleviated many of the doubts and led Britain to recognize the benefits of universal education. In an ironical twist even some of those against state education were encouraged to support it because 'educated workmen, being able to understand the economic doctrines then current, would appreciate the futility of agitating for better pay and conditions' (Murphy, 1972:9).

During the middle part of the 19th century the pressure for all children to be educated increased in many parts of society. At the same time as the demand for child labour was decreasing an increasing number of parents were recognizing the benefits of sending their children to school. At a national level there was also a growing appreciation that education was necessary to ensure that the economy remained competitive:

> With every year that passed during the 1860s it became more obvious that, however the obstacles were to be overcome, Britain could not long remain without a truly national system of elementary education. Competition from abroad in commerce and industry was becoming ever more keen, yet there did not exist in England and Wales a basis for producing a generally literate labour force, or a foundation on which to erect a comprehensive system of secondary, technical and commercial education. (Murphy, 1972:28–9)

With the passing years the pressure for education increased and there was increasing provision of education through church schools, Sunday schools and private provision. In Britain, the term 'public school' did not, and still does not, mean free state education as it does in many other parts of the world. In Britain, a public school is generally open to the public on the condition that they have the financial resources to pay for the education. The general provision of education is commonly termed 'state education'.

The Education Act of 1871 provided for the education of all children and set the scene over the succeeding years for increased provision. In a number of European Union countries there is compulsory education until the age of 16, with Greece, Ireland, Luxembourg, Austria and Portugal ending this compulsion at 15. In general, full-time compulsory education lasts 9 or 10 years, with Portugal requiring 8 years; Luxembourg and Great Britain (England, Scotland and Wales) 11 years; and the Netherlands and Northern Ireland 12 years (European Commission, 1997a).

There has been a form of inflation in educational qualifications in many countries. The economic success of Japan following the end of World War II, with its large numbers of graduates, has been seen as a model for other countries to increase the volume of people in higher education.

Access and participation in education vary across the world. More than 1 billion young people are receiving formal education now compared with around 300 million in 1953 when the first survey was conducted by UNESCO. Girls are less likely to be enrolled in schools and this imbalance has resulted in different literacy rates for the world's women, at 71.2 per cent against 83.6 per cent for men, although the gap is slowly reducing (UNESCO, 1995).

Compulsory and further and higher education can be considered a long-term investment in the intellectual capital of a country. In some countries more is seen as being better; however, quality assurance and other factors are beginning to challenge open-ended commitments to fully funded publicly provided education. A number of these arguments will be considered later in this chapter.

Demographic factors

In many countries there has been a progressive movement of people from working on the land to living and working in urban areas. This flight from rural areas arose from forces of demand

and supply. There was a growing productivity in agriculture reducing demand for labour, but more particularly there were the pulling forces of regular and higher-paid work in the factories, and improved living conditions in the urban areas.

This movement of people into the secondary industries of textiles, engineering, etc also encouraged an increase in the number of people occupied in tertiary industries, who provided the services required to support these developments, for example, legal and accounting services, distribution and retail. Progressively more and more people have become employed in the tertiary sector as the use of technology with its greater efficiency has resulted in fewer people being employed in secondary occupations. In many earlier industrialized countries more people are now employed in tertiary industries than in secondary ones.

Demographic factors also influence the state of the labour market and the nature of the economic success at micro levels of organizations and macro levels of national economic performance. The baby boom in the 1950s following World War II resulted in a large increase in the supply of labour for the job market some two decades later. It was fortunate that this increase coincided with considerable economic activity and growth that was able to soak up the supply of human resources.

The 1950s and 1960s were a period of low unemployment and such were the shortages being experienced in many countries that large numbers of immigrant workers were encouraged to migrate to the booming economies. The USA and Canada encouraged large-scale immigration during these periods, while Oceania, Australia and New Zealand were also encouraging immigration in order to maintain economic growth levels. Britain and France encouraged large numbers of Commonwealth and former territories people to emigrate and work in the lower-paid sectors, such as public transport and hospitals, which were proving to be unattractive to the incumbent population. In Germany a large number of immigrant workers, particularly from Turkey, were invited to come and were called *'gastarbeiters'* or guest workers. In the Far East, Japan too was encouraging guest workers. In other countries such as the former Soviet Union, large-scale movements of people were encouraged together with inducements and awards for high birth rates.

The growth period of the 'baby boom' years has changed to one of 'baby bust' in some countries, which has resulted in a significant decline in the availability of young people to take up jobs. To some extent this was compensated by the increase in unemployment due to higher productivity and lower levels of economic growth. At a more micro level skills shortages have been addressed by internal training within organizations, and sometimes by local or government initiatives to encourage and develop people within a particular sector.

BAHRAIN MODEL FOR BOOSTING TRAINING AND HUMAN RESOURCES

Bahrain's income, like that of other Arabian Gulf Cooperation Council states, depends on oil sales. Before 1973 the oil price was $5 per barrel and then increased dramatically to reach $34 per barrel by 1978. This rapid increase in oil prices created an economic boom and the government started to establish the modern infrastructure of the nation. The people also started to build houses, buy cars and purchase more household appliances, which led to the establishment of many service and construction companies.

The workforce available in the market at that time was not able to cope with the demand by the new companies, so the government authorized companies to import foreign workers. This imported workforce became an important element for many companies because it was cheap, controllable and easy to repatriate.

The downside of a cheap imported workforce was that Bahraini national job seekers faced difficulties. Moreover, employers claimed that Bahrainis lacked the skills and expertise to fulfil their work requirements. In spite of these obstacles many Bahraini workers/job seekers proved, after proper training, that they were able to perform to the job requirements of the labour market.

The main concern, however, was that the foreign workers suited the employers' intentions more than the locals for the reasons explained above. Therefore, when it was discovered in 1975 that most companies were neither willing to train workers nor to employ local job seekers, the Ministry of Labour and Social Affairs took responsibility for the provision of training services for both company workers and job seekers for those companies that could not provide such services. The High Council for Vocational Training was formed in 1975 to execute this policy and was funded from a levy paid by companies at the rate of 4 per cent of the total wages for the non-Bahraini workers and 2 per cent of the wages of Bahrainis. Companies providing training services were exempted from this levy. Although this levy system encouraged many companies to train their workers through utilizing the levy money, many companies continued importing workers and regarded the money paid as a form of taxation to be forgotten.

Much money was also spent on training for the purpose of localization (replacing expatriate workers with indigenous workers). In 1994 over US$57 million was spent on training but the localization progress was negligible compared with what had been spent. For that reason, in 1995, the Ministry started to take extra measures to monitor the localization process. In addition to intensifying training efforts and adopting modern training systems as a means to better localization, it started to apply a new procedure by asking companies to increase their Bahraini workforce by 5 per cent yearly to reach 50 per cent Bahrainization. Failure to achieve this level meant that work permits for foreign workers would not be issued. Although these procedures were not easy to implement they nevertheless achieved the desired results.

The Ministry of Labour currently motivates companies to undertake localization efforts by providing special treatment or ranking priorities for companies that achieve a higher percentage of localization. For example, the Ministry pays the salaries of the newly recruited employees or part of the salaries for a certain period of time for specific occupations under certain conditions.

Among the efforts to intensify training activities is the development of the Bahrain Training Institute (BTI) that operates under the Ministry of Labour and Social Affairs. The BTI is equipped for vocational and technical training and is recognized within and outside Bahrain. It conducts programmes up to Higher National Diploma (HND) level and follows numerous training approaches including the National Vocational Qualifications (NVQ) framework.

Bahrain is also adopting a strategy to be a regional centre for training and human resources by encouraging international training providers to establish training institutes. Continuous and intensive efforts by the Bahrain government in developing training activities and human resources have significantly increased the level of services provided for most aspects of life. Arising from these efforts the 1998 United Nations Development Programme (UNDP) identified Bahrain as first in the Arab region for developing human resources.

With acknowledgement to Majid Al Binali, The Ministry of Labour and Social Affairs, Bahrain.

National economic competition

We are going to win and the industrialized West is going to lose out. There is nothing you can do about it because the reasons for your failure are within yourselves. With your bosses doing the thinking while the workers wield the screwdrivers, you are convinced deep down that this is the right way to do business. For you the essence of management is getting the ideas out of the heads of the bosses and into the hands of labour. ... For us the core of management is the art of mobilising and putting together the intellectual resources of all employees in the service of the firm. (Konoke Matsushita in conversation with an American businessman, in Abbott, 1994:10)

With the increase in international trade there has been a corresponding growth in competition between nations, as the quotation above indicates. This Darwinian struggle for economic supremacy has become ever more intense and has led to ever greater searches for competitive advantage.

The current concerns in many countries about their standards of training and education are not new. In Britain it would appear that at regular periods there have been major crises about the standards of education and training. Even in the 19th century there was concern, with Lyon Playfair giving a lecture in 1852 on 'Industrial instruction on the Continent' and warning that technical education was necessary in order to maintain superiority over foreign competitors. The Devonshire Commission (1872–5) investigated university provision of scientific and technical education and argued that there were insufficient scientists and engineers, and that this would have a serious impact on the well-being of the country.

People have always tended to look beyond their own particular back yard to find comparisons, and this was demonstrated by the economist Alfred Marshal in 1890 (in Prais, 1995:104) when he stated that:

On the whole we may say that at present England is very much behind hand as regards the provision for the commercial as well as the technical education of the proprietors and principal managers of industrial works.

He also stated that Germany had developed people 'who are better fitted to do the work required of the middle ranks of industry than any the world has ever seen'.

In many countries it was observed that their share of world production and world trade was progressively decreasing and that competition was increasing. The impact of education on economic competitiveness has already been discussed, and similarly the impact of work-related training was also increasingly being recognized. In the USA the Council on Competitiveness (1987) identified that industry training programmes were inadequate and this translated into low productivity. Short-term policies were seen to have resulted in low investment in developing human resources and had led to longer-term economic problems.

During the 1980s the pre-eminence of the USA's economic production was overhauled by Japan, which became the world's leading industrial nation. As a result of this, the competitiveness of the US economy was investigated by the Massachusetts Institute of Technology (MIT, 1989), which identified five key factors necessary for the nation to regain competitiveness. Significantly, the first step identified as a key regenerator of economic success was to invest in human capital.

At a broader international level the Organisation for Economic Co-operation and Development conducted research into economic development and argued that technological advancements would not result in satisfactory economic output without investment elsewhere in the economy (OECD, 1989b). In particular, there needed to be both prior and concurrent institutional and social changes especially in the areas of education and training. The OECD (1990) identified a number of factors that demonstrate the developments that are occurring:

- With new technology there is the potential for new forms of organizational structure and methods of operation.
- There is an increased integration of various technologies which have resulted in the decline and obsolescence of traditional organizations and work structures.
- There is an increasing interest and growth in the recognition that human resources provide a competitive dimension.
- Increased quality, just-in-time practices, and the decreasing lifecycles of services and products have focused attention on the need for integrated planning policies that link technology, work practices and skills more closely together. The traditional Tayloristic approach to work organization has proved to be too inflexible to accommodate rapidly changing markets, and organizational issues of increased local responsibility, flatter organizations, teamwork and decentralization.
- The number of low-skilled and unskilled jobs has decreased dramatically while the areas of job growth require more high-level and broader skills as a result of multiskilling.

The dilemma facing countries is the degree of financial investment to make in the education and training of their populations. The economic educational and training spiral (see Figure 4.1) illustrates how a virtuous circle of investment in education and training can result in increased production and wealth for a country, thus leading to increased resources for further investment. Conversely, a reduction in education and training investment can feed through into reduced output that reduces wealth and leads to a lower capacity to spend on education and training, further exacerbating the crisis.

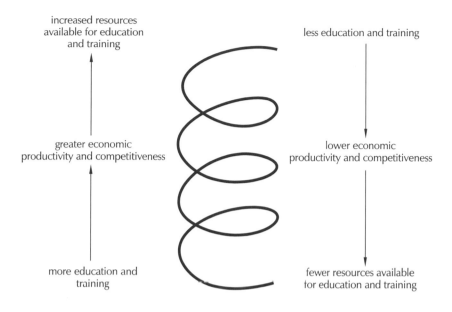

increased resources
available for education
and training

less education and training

greater economic
productivity and competitiveness

lower economic
productivity and competitiveness

more education and
training

fewer resources available
for education and training

Figure 4.1   The education, training and development economic spiral

Many countries are now attempting to position themselves as knowledge-intensive societies. This is illustrated by the situation facing the UK:

> If the national economy is to break out of the prevailing low skills–low quality equilibrium and become the knowledge-based, high technology, highly skilled, high value-added economy purveyed in the political rhetoric it is essential that those factors which are continuing to sustain the low skills equilibrium are addressed. (Esland, 1991:xi)

National strategies

The desire to encourage policies which promote economic growth is central to the work of the Organisation for Economic Co-operation and Development and for this reason a Convention was signed in 1960 by Austria, Belgium, Canada, Denmark, France, Germany, Greece, Iceland, Italy, Luxembourg, the Netherlands, Norway, Portugal, Spain, Sweden, Switzerland, Turkey, the UK and the USA. A number of other countries have since joined the OECD. Its main purpose is enshrined within Article 1, which states:

- to achieve the highest sustainable economic growth and employment and a rising standard of living in Member countries, while maintaining financial stability, and thus contribute to the development of the world economy;
- to contribute to sound economic expansion in Member as well as non-Member countries in the process of economic development; and

- to contribute to the expansion of world trade on a multilateral, non-discriminatory basis in accordance with international obligations. (CERI, 1996: introduction)

There has been a growing recognition that allowing the market forces of companies, public organizations and individuals to determine their own level of skills is an inefficient mechanism for encouraging the development of the overall national economy. For this reason, an increased level of involvement by governmental agencies has been directed at the coordination of strategies and the improvement of standards.

An interventionist or laissez-faire approach to education and training is to some extent a reflection of the prevailing philosophy of the country. In the USA market forces are seen to be the main influence in making it such a strong economic power. To challenge this philosophy has been seen almost as heresy; however, there has been an increasing recognition that the economic advantages it has enjoyed in the past are slowly being eroded. This threat from other nations was deeply felt during the 1980s when Japanese economic output exceeded that of the USA.

Being overtaken in the world economic hierarchy caused much public debate and soul-searching in the USA. This reflection and searching for suitable answers can also be seen in many other countries as their economic performance declines in comparison to other countries. In the USA proponents of market forces maintained there should be little or no intervention while others argued for systematic involvement in training and development.

A middle ground was identified which is illustrated by Porter (1980) who had originally conducted research into the competitive advantages experienced by companies. He transferred this approach to the economic performance of countries in his book, *The Competitive Advantage of Nations*. Porter (1990:620) maintained that, 'Government's most powerful roles are indirect rather than direct ones.' He added that, 'Government's policies that succeed are those that create an environment in which firms can gain competitive advantage.'

The integration of various labour market factors and the awareness of international differences can be seen in the remarks made by Robert Reich, US Labor Secretary, at the 1994 Group of Seven Economic Conference in Detroit. He stated there was a need:

> to combine the kind of investments in education and training and apprenticeship that we find in Europe with the dynamic labour mobility and flexibility we find in the US, all encased within macro-economic policies which encourage growth and jobs. (Graham, 1994:4)

At a broader level Sun (1997:383) analysed the United Nations Development Programme's findings for 173 countries and concluded that government intervention would appear to be significantly related to human development; however, he could not state the ideal level of intervention. He suggested that chaos and restricted levels of goods and services resulted from too little government; while too much government would result in restricted freedom and a stifling of initiative and stagnation. To support his claim he referred to the collapse of the Soviet Union and the market experiments of China. He therefore suggested that, 'a proper degree of government intervention – a *"golden mean"* between central planning and market mechanism – may best promote human development'. Sun (1997:390) concluded that:

for most countries of the world, further human development and fulfilment require more government intervention. The provisions of public goods and services – infrastructure, investment in human capital (education and health), law and order, as well as a certain degree of income redistribution providing an economic safety net – are necessary for continuous human development. Yet, so many Third World countries have not been able to achieve political stability or build consensus for the mobilisation of all the necessary resources so as to render the government a constructive role to play. The realisation that a mean value between central planning and market mechanism may contribute most to human development can certainly help in building the needed consensus and stability.

Integrating education and training

The responsibility for education and training has not always been closely coordinated in terms of governmental departments despite their numerous common objectives. In Britain, the Department of Education and Science was responsible for education in schools, colleges, polytechnics and universities, while the Department of Employment was responsible for vocational training. In order to encourage schooling which was related to the needs of work the Department of Employment provided large levels of financial support through the Technical and Vocational Education Initiative (TVEI). This separation of common purpose has been resolved through an amalgamation of the two departments into the Department for Education and Employment, and a similar formulation can be found in a number of other countries.

During the 1980s there was an increase in the provision of education and training, which was especially noticeable in the area of enterprise training. In addition, many bodies started to provide a variety of programmes designed to ameliorate unemployment. Because of the large number of education and training programmes there was a need for a more coordinated series of measures, which resulted in increased collaboration both within and between training providers, government agencies and employers.

While the approaches to education and training vary according to the labour market conditions that operate within a country, three main strategies have been identified from the CERI research (Frank Press, 1990).

A human resources intensive strategy

This operates where the people entering the job market have received a sound education, up to the ages of 16–19, which allows them to benefit from intensive on-the-job education and training. If the organization has a flexible form of operation then it is possible to encourage job rotation.

The polarization strategy

Some countries do not possess a strong vocational education and training system and this deficiency may sometimes be combined with a high level of failure or drop-out from secondary education. Furthermore, there may well be a relatively inflexible labour market due to the lack of skills and education and low levels of training investment.

In these circumstances organizations tend to adopt a policy of investing in the training of core workers whom they try to retain through various inducements and training contracts. Beyond this group there also exists another group of employees who receive less training and investment and who are more susceptible to the boom and bust of the business cycle. There is thus a polarization of investment and skills, with some being more supported than others.

The mobility strategy

Organizations tend to employ people who have a high level of education, often from universities. Formal education and training is not particularly common; instead learning is very strongly linked with the work in which they are occupied. Mobility between organizations is high and the countries have technologically advanced workforces with a strong service sector. Often the main focus of human resource development within organizations is on effective selection and recruitment and encouraging continuous learning in the work environment.

In order to encourage a closer relationship between education, training and the labour market the OECD (1994) has identified three main factors that encourage integration:

1. initial education and its quality;
2. a smooth transition between initial education and work;
3. investment in adult lifelong learning.

With the development of learning societies and lifelong learning the artificial segregation of education and training has diminished. The two are now closely integrated through a variety of means:

> The barriers between vocational and general education are starting to break down, with the growing recognition that young people need to develop the capacity to learn continuously rather than simply learning a specific set of job-related skills. (CERI, 1996:52)

Demand and supply in the labour market

In many OECD countries there would appear to be a developing skills gap between the labour demand arising from information-based technology and the requirements of knowledge-based industries, and the supply of suitable people within organizations and from educational institutions. The degree of labour shortages in occupational sectors is to a large extent dependent on the country and the differing market conditions and skill levels that exist.

Advances in technology have reduced the demand for and jobs available to unskilled and semi-skilled workers. In particular this is affecting unskilled males with low or non-existent educational qualifications who also lack the interpersonal skills that are more commonly found among females. Findings by CERI (1997:20) demonstrate that 'Higher levels of educational attainment are closely associated, for individuals, with higher earnings, a lower chance of unemployment and more skills that yield social advantage.'

Flexibility in the workplace

Various strategies have been developed by governments to encourage or discourage the availability of labour. For instance, in Britain, the retirement age for women has been increased to 65 in line with that of men, and there is also the option for people to continue working until the age of 70 without compulsory retirement.

Training at apprenticeship levels needs to be flexible and responsive to changing requirements. In some countries apprenticeships have continued for considerable periods after the relevant jobs have largely disappeared. The German apprenticeship system changed to a significant extent during the 1980s and 1990s. In the USA vocational and technical education is focused on the school and there are fewer workplace apprenticeships. In the UK more attention is being given to changing the system.

Bengtsson (1991) identified three main strands emerging from his study into the changes affecting demand and supply in the labour market:

1. Demand changes occur much more swiftly than those on the supply side. The scientific approach of Taylor (1911) seems to be being replaced by a system which is evolving and which incorporates technology, organizations, skills formation, flexibility and human resources.
2. The institutions that deliver formal education and training tend to be less responsive to changes than informal providers and private institutions. These latter organizations would now appear to be developing into a market of their own.
3. The influence of the educational institutions and labour market of a country can be a critical influence on the ability of key organizations to move from a Tayloristic approach to developing more effective strategies. For this reason governmental interventions can have a major impact on the supply of appropriate labour.

It is recognized that the barriers to ensuring an educated and trained workforce are quite considerable. They consist of economic barriers, a blurring of responsibilities between private and public provision, and psychological barriers with regard to the sharing of responsibility and partnership.

Bengtsson (1991) suggests a number of policy considerations that might influence the demand side:

●   Tax systems and inducements should be investigated in order to encourage organizations to provide internal training.
●   Small and medium-sized enterprises should be encouraged to educate and train their workforce where appropriate through the use of alternative delivery methods including information technology.
●   New structures and industrial relations processes and collective bargaining, which move away from Tayloristic methods, should be encouraged.
●   The promotion of strategies that encourage active education and training policies which relate to actual needs, rather than passive subsidy programmes.

Smooth market responses to differences between the demand and supply of labour in the various sectors are rare. There is usually a time lag between the recognition of a labour requirement and the supply of people with the necessary knowledge and skills. Labour market research is increasingly focused on predicting likely future demand so that educators and trainers can plan accordingly.

Benchmarking national performance

We have seen that countries have for centuries been observing the education, training and economic well-being of their competitors in order to benchmark their own performance. This has resulted in regular periods of national anxiety as economic results decline, with criticism being levelled at lack of investment; poor teaching; low levels of skills; ineffectual government, etc.

The figures used to benchmark performance in the area of training and development were for a long time imprecise and often unobtainable. However, as the importance of both has increased there have been greater efforts to provide valid and reliable indicators of outputs and standards. This has often proved to be a very difficult operation and as a result many of the studies tended to be observational and only used crude indicators. Comparisons proved to be of limited value due to the large differences in the educational systems of the various countries. There has been pressure for more transparent data that would allow more direct comparisons, and while the figures which are now available still tend to have limitations, they at least provide indicators as to the impact certain policies have in relation to other countries.

There are two new challenges faced by OECD countries and beyond. The first is to ensure that advanced learning is provided not just to a small elite but to larger numbers. The second is to encourage lifelong learning and not just learning opportunities during the years of formal education. At a meeting in Paris in 1996 Education Ministers' commitment was made to 'lifelong learning for all':

> If IBM were producing results comparable to those of many American schools – that is, if 25% of their computers were falling off the assembly line before they reached the end, and 90% of the completed ones didn't work properly for 80% of the time – the last thing in the world the company would do would be to run that same old assembly line an additional hour each day for an extra month each year. Instead, IBM would re-think the entire system. (Jack Bowsher, former Director of Education, IBM, in Abbott, 1994:44)

One use of internationally comparable figures is to help assess the extent to which the expansion of education has resulted in increased economic performance. Having students sitting in classrooms for longer and longer periods may not necessarily translate into superior performance. The difficulty is finding clear and irrefutable evidence that this is or is not the case. For this reason CERI argued for the need for clearer indicators and a significant sum of money in order to identify and compare more accurately one country with another. It was recognized that, 'Readers. . . should bear in mind that the science of understanding and interpreting international indicators is still in its infancy' (CERI 1996:9–10).

The picture is to some extent becoming further complicated with the increase in lifelong learning: figures are not fully available for other forms of continuing education and training. One thing is certain: Treasury Departments in the member states will not allow high levels of spending on education, training and development without careful thought to the value for money which is spent. For example, identifying the number of teachers/ trainers in initial vocational training has proved problematical and a CEDEFOP (1995a:7) survey explained that 'the production was not easy'. Because the figures were unavailable it was not possible to make comparisons of trainer/trainee ratios.

Figures indicate that educational spending between 1975 and 1993 stagnated, with 5.8 per cent of gross domestic product being spent publicly on education. Private expenditure on education was generally less than 1 per cent, although in Germany, Japan, Spain and the USA it was more than 1 but less that 2 per cent (CERI, 1996:18).

The increased use of international comparisons has made benchmarking of specific skills useful indicators of numeracy. The International Association for the Evaluation of Educational Achievement has carried out a number of international comparisons of the achievement levels of school children. The first, which was carried out in 1963–4, assessed the mathematical abilities of children in 12 countries (Husen, 1967).

'Basic skills' are very necessary because:

> Literacy is a key foundation skill on which the development of other adult competences crucially depends. A well-educated and literate workforce yields national comparative advantage and harnesses forces to counteract polarization and social exclusion. Today, adults need a high level of literacy to function well: society has become more complex and low-skill jobs are disappearing. Therefore, inadequate levels of literacy and numeracy among a broad section of the population potentially threaten the strength of economies and the social cohesion of nations. Yet policy makers in most countries have hitherto lacked any empirical knowledge about the distribution of generic skills such as literacy in the population. (CERI, 1996:31)

It was noted that continuous training and development of the workforce and the upgrading of their skills will benefit those with literacy and numeracy skills and as a result the gap between them and those without such skills will increase.

The complexity of comparing standards is illustrated by the fact that the German employers association (BDA) objected to the comparison of the German apprenticeship with that of a Level 3 National Vocational Qualification in Britain on the grounds of the short period of study and doubts about the levels of qualification.

Numerous forces have affected the competitiveness of nations and the very fact that it is difficult to identify and measure them has resulted in various responses, some more effective than others. Some of the factors affecting the labour market in the USA have been downsizing and the discredited 'business process re-engineering' where large swathes of the workforce have been removed. This has sometimes resulted in acute labour shortages, particularly in areas that require a long period of education and training such as engineering and other technological areas.

Enforcement or encouragement of HRD

Most nations adopt a 'carrot and stick' approach to the development of their human resources. Some countries have introduced mandatory levies, such as France which initially began with 2 per cent of the payroll, but has since reduced it to 1.2 per cent of the total wage bill. This levy, which is a 'national obligation', is strictly devoted to vocational training. People who have been employed for more than approximately two years, and with a minimum of at least six months with their current employer, have the opportunity to receive training to upgrade skills or take a qualification. This can be done under their own initiative (*conge individuel de formation*) or within the employer's training provision (*plan de formation d'enterprise*). During the training these employees will receive at least 80 per cent and sometimes more of their normal salary.

Greece levies 0.45 per cent of the wage bill, which is collected through the social insurance system, and the sum collected is jointly managed by employers and trades unions.

In Belgium there is legislation called the '0.18 rule', in which 0.18 per cent of the wages bill is levied in order to provide training and employment of at-risk groups found among job seekers. This is a cooperative venture between government and industry in an attempt to reduce the levels of long-term unemployment. It is designed to resolve three main problems in the labour market:

1. demand versus supply in the labour market where there is considerable unemployment;
2. low skill levels or lack of qualifications among the unemployed; and
3. the underprivilege experienced by those unemployed for a long period. (Pollet, 1992)

However, although the levies are collected they do not necessarily result in training and development. There is some evidence that some small and medium-sized organizations in France do not send their employees on courses because they are time-consuming and keep them away from their work. Germany does not have mandatory levies but has a tradition of training that has proved very successful and has encouraged a number of countries to imitate the 'dual system'.

For European Union countries training has increasing importance. The European Social Charter states that, 'every EC worker must be able to have access to vocational training throughout their working life'.

The main argument above about the importance of learning is summarized by Wolf (2002:ix), who suggested there is an increasing global consensus: The world's voters think their governments can and should deliver economic prosperity. Their elites agree with them, and even agree with each other on how to do it. Increasingly they sign up to the same package: free trade, market economics, the virtues of entrepreneurship – and education, education, education.

Wolf went on to argue that many countries are aiming to be high-skill, high-earning economies rather than low-skill, low-earning countries. Yet it is not possible for all of them to be top of the league in a world of competition. Furthermore, she emphasized that spending money on education did not always result in guaranteed earning. She maintained that:

> an unquestioning faith in the economic benefits of education has brought with it huge amounts of wasteful government spending, attached to misguided and even pernicious policies. Just

because something is valuable, it does not follow that yet more of it is by definition a good idea: that any addition, any increment, must be welcomed.

(Wolf, 2002:xi)

The role of the HRD specialist is to focus on how learning might be applied to improve organizational performance. However, we should not lose sight of the broader picture of society and the humanizing benefits of education. The role of education is also to encourage values, citizenship, a good society and so on, as Wolf argued, and it is this context that will be considered next.

HUMAN DEVELOPMENT

Education and training for peace

The economic and competitive pressures for the development of a national system of education were quite persuasive, but there have also been other factors that supported this trend. In particular, there were many arguments that an educated society would be more civilized, there would be a reduction in crime, and that democracy would be strengthened. This point is strongly endorsed by Prais (1995:2) who maintained that:

> education has much wider objectives than merely preparing citizens to become more effective 'cogs in the industrial-economic machine'; the history of the horrors of the twentieth century and its totalitarian states should be sufficient warning against that narrow view of the purposes of education.

Education was also viewed as a mechanism for preventing the circumstances in which war might begin. The United Nations Educational, Scientific and Cultural Organization constitution was adopted in 1945 following the end of World War II and stated that:

> the Governments of the States Parties to this Constitution on behalf of their peoples declare: That since wars begin in the minds of men, it is in the minds of men that the defences of peace must be constructed. That a peace based exclusively upon the political and economic arrangements of governments would not be a peace which could secure the unanimous, lasting and sincere support of the peoples of the world, and that peace must therefore be founded, if it is not to fail, upon the intellectual and moral solidarity of mankind. (UNESCO, 1995:16)

As part of this humanitarian movement, the 1948 Universal Declaration of Human Rights states that education 'shall be directed to the full development of the human personality and to the strengthening of respect for human rights and fundamental freedoms'. Thus, in addition to economic reasons for the education of the population, there are also very strong democratic and peaceful ones.

INSTITUTIONAL DEVELOPMENT OF LOCAL NGOs IN MALI, WEST AFRICA

Mali, one of the world's poorest countries, covers an area of 1,240,192 sq km and has a population of almost 10 million people. It is predominantly agricultural with the southern third being dependent on the flooding of the Niger to provide irrigation for crops. The northern third is the arid Sahara desert.

The process of democracy and decentralization in Mali started in 1991 and since that time nearly 1,000 non-governmental organizations (NGOs) have been created. Many of these NGOs contribute significantly to the development of Malian society by means of human resources, activities and goods. These NGOs are active in both rural and urban areas and in all kinds of sectors, for example, healthcare, education, agriculture, and sanitation.

Despite their enthusiasm and motivation, most of the NGOs are rather inexperienced at institutional and organizational levels. Although their personnel are often technically well trained, there is an enormous need for reinforcement of policy development, planning and internal organization of the NGOs. This lack of experience and the need for support and training was not only observed by international organizations, but also by many of the Malian NGOs themselves. In order to improve their managerial and operational performance and be more effective with their target client groups they approached SNV (Dutch Development Agency) for training.

After two years of experimental training and support, SNV has developed several learning experiences linked to a flexible training programme. The differentiated programme provides common training for staff members of NGOs (theory and instruction), together with specific coaching and reflection (practice and exercises) on the same topic at each head office. Moreover, mutual assistance and the exchange of information among these NGOs has been encouraged and supported.

The differentiation also takes place at the level of the trainer. The design and execution of the programme has not been limited to the senior adviser in charge of the programme, but other SNV personnel with a variety of competences. The advice and involvement of external Malian experts in the programme is actively sought. Moreover, SNV contacted other foreign and international development organizations in Mali about their experiences with local NGOs. This has resulted in regular meetings among a group of development organizations from the Netherlands, Canada, Germany, the USA, the UK and the World Bank. The objective is to improve the exchange of information and experiences and to encourage mutual collaboration. A specific example of this is the training, by SNV, of the personnel of other organizations in applying methods for the institutional analysis of NGOs. Financial donor organizations from the Netherlands are also regularly involved in the policy development of Malian NGOs.

This successful intervention has been extended on a regional basis to encourage the various SNV programmes in West Africa to collaborate in supporting the development, training and sharing of information among African NGOs.

With acknowledgement to Hub Gielissen, Senior Adviser, SNV, NGO Programme, Mali.

In focusing on the links between economic performance and training and development it is possible to overlook the human requirements of individuals and society to have not just a quantity of goods and services but also a quality of life. Personal issues such as inner growth and development are highly valued and, indeed, the US Constitution includes the 'pursuit of happiness' as an objective.

Human development has also been considered by the United Nations Development Programme (UNDP, 1996). The Human Development Index is based on a number of factors including gross domestic product per person, educational achievement, life expectancy, and level of literacy. Both Canada and Japan have regularly appeared at the top of this index, indicating a quality of life to which other countries aspire.

This perspective on life is endorsed by the UNDP in a report that also contains a warning based on the experience of human conflict:

> Human development is the end – economic growth a means. So, the purpose of growth should be to enrich people's lives. But far too often it does not. The recent decades show all too clearly that there is no automatic link between growth and human development. And even when links are established, they may be gradually eroded – unless regularly fortified by skilful and intelligent policy management. (UNDP, 1996:1)

In 1976 the World Employment Conference adopted a resolution concerning basic needs and their provision in less developed countries:

> Strategies and national development plans and policies should include explicitly as a priority objective the promotion of employment and the satisfaction of the basic needs of each country's population. ... Basic needs include two elements. First they include certain minimum requirements of a family for private consumption: adequate food, shelter and clothing, as well as certain household equipment and furniture. Second, they include essential services provided by and for the community at large, such as safe drinking water, sanitation, public transport and health, educational and cultural facilities. (ILO, 1977)

While recognizing that investments must occur in agricultural developments, Singh (1979:600–01) concludes that:

> To meet the basic needs of the poor in the Third World in a sustainable way it is essential to raise the rate of economic growth in these countries. This will require a more than proportional expansion of their manufacturing sectors, and therefore an accelerated development of modern industry, including the establishment of appropriate capital goods industries.

The UNDP (1996:iii) has emphasized the reciprocal links between human development and economic development:

> Economic growth and human development thus exhibit a degree of independence, especially in the short term. But there are longer-term links – human development helping economic growth, and economic growth helping human development. Contrary to earlier theories, new theories and evidence suggest that growth and equity need not be contradictory goals. Nor do growth

and participation. And there is strong historical evidence from East Asia that heavy national investment in human development – spreading skills and meeting basic social needs – has been a springboard for sustained economic growth over decades.

In general, most governments provide for human resource development through focusing on specific skills, on more general educational and training policies which can be more broadly targeted, and finally through development issues such as health, education, housing and defence.

Developing countries adopt a number of strategies to encourage economic advancement, one of which is technology transfer that not only includes concrete factors such as plant and equipment but also human resources and the skills and expertise needed to operate the new technology. This can be a very swift and effective means with which to introduce and develop a country's capabilities. However, there can also be a downside in that it can inhibit development unless the local workforce is integrated with the new development. The importation of expatriate labour is insufficient in the long term to provide a satisfactory model (Williams, 1996).

DEVELOPMENT IN MALAYSIA

Malaysia has experienced enviable economic growth and has made a clear exposition of its future objectives linking educational, economic, technological and social objectives. In 1991, the Prime Minister Dato' Seri Dr Mahathir Mohammed (1991: 1–2) announced the nine central strategic challenges of Vision 2020, which described Malaysia's intention to be a fully developed industrialized country by the year 2020:

1. to establish a united Malaysian nation with a sense of common and shared destiny;
2. to create a psychologically liberated, secure and developed Malaysian society with faith and confidence in itself;
3. to foster and develop a mature democratic society;
4. to establish a fully moral and ethical society;
5. to establish a mature, liberal and tolerant society;
6. to establish a scientific and progressive society, a society that is innovative and forward-looking, one that is not only a consumer of technology but also a contributor to the scientific and technological civilization of the future;
7. to establish a fully caring society and a caring culture;
8. to ensure an economically just society;
9. to establish a prosperous society, with an economy that is fully competitive, dynamic, robust and resilient.

The implementation under the 7th Malaysia Plan (1996–2000) (1996:321–22) of Malaysia's integrated education and training programmes to meet the national human resource requirements displays the following objectives:

- to increase participation in education at all levels through expansion of capacity and distance learning;
- to encourage more private sector investment in education and training to complement public sector efforts;
- to increase the capacity of existing institutions and to establish new institutions, particularly in science, engineering and technological fields;
- to improve the quality of education by providing qualified teachers and making better use of computers and information technology;
- to strengthen research and development capacity within existing higher education institutions in collaboration with local and foreign organizations engaged in research and development;
- to develop and exploit commercially the large pool of untapped research funding in public sector research agencies and universities;
- to increase the number of those with scientific and technical skills, especially those working in research and development;
- to provide incentives to increase student enrolment in the science streams;
- to strengthen the use of Bahasa Malaysia as the medium of instruction in all schools and institutions while increasing competency in the English language;
- to improve the management and administration of education and training programmes by improving the performance of managers and the introduction of better monitoring and evaluation systems;
- to improve the financial management of tertiary educational institutions through corporatization and other means;
- to improve the performance of pupils from the rural areas and reduce the dropout rate by improving educational facilities in rural areas;
- to amalgamate small schools in rural and remote areas with fewer than 150 pupil in order to maximize the use of resources, provide a better education and improve hostel facilities for students;
- to improve teacher morale and performance through training, recognition, incentives, awards and better welfare;
- to re-employ retired teachers to make up the shortages in critical subjects;
- to encourage positive values, innovation, communication and analytical skills among students.

While human resource development continued to be a major thrust in Malaysia's development plans, the human resource policy directions under the 7th Malaysia Plan (1996:125) include:

- encouraging greater capital intensity of production in order to save on the use of labour;
- increasing the use of local labour and female labour (including greater utilization of handicapped persons);
- setting up a National Labour Institute to enhance the skill and level of professionalism;
- improving the education and skill delivery system as well as expanding facilities;
- increasing the supply of R&D personnel, including scientists and technologists;

- promoting greater participation of the private sector in human resource development;
- promoting performance-related wage mechanisms that link wages to productivity;
- removing bottlenecks in the labour market through an improved information system;
- reviewing labour laws and legislation that are not consistent with the dynamic changes in the labour market;
- inculcating discipline and other universal positive values among the workforce; and
- re-orienting societal and individual preferences towards skilled and other technical occupations.

With acknowledgement to Mohammed Nassir Abu Hassan, Ministry of Education, Malaysia.

CONCLUSION

There is considerable evidence linking the provision of education and training to the economic well-being of a country. However, there are a number of commentators who are cautious. Ashton and Green (1996:2) state that, 'despite an increasing effort on the part of empirical researchers, there remain enormous gaps in the knowledge of the magnitude of any links between skill formation and economic performance'. This view is supported by Keep and Meyhew (1991:198) who, while accepting that these links are reasonable, state that there is a 'paucity of hard, detailed evidence of direct casual links'.

It is evident that factors such as weak infrastructure, poor design and short-term requirements of returns on the investment of capital by the financial markets can have significant effects on the success or otherwise of an economy. It is clearly not just a question of putting the responsibility on the educational institutions and the training provided by organizations.

In spite of the lack of clear and irrefutable evidence of the positive links between education and training and national performance it would appear that few, if any, governments are prepared to go against perceived wisdom. From a competitive perspective Porter (1990:628) deserves the last word:

> Education and training constitute perhaps the single greatest long-term leverage point available to all levels of government in upgrading industry.

Bibliography

Abbott, J (1994) *Learning Makes Sense: Recreating education for a changing future,* Letchworth, Hertfordshire, Education 2000

Ashton, D and Green, F (1996) *Education and the Global Economy,* Cheltenham, Edward Elgar

Bengtsson, J (1991) 'Human resource development: education, training and labour market development', *Futures,* December, pp 1085–106

British Council (1996) *Education and Training Market Plan,* London, New Leaf Press

CEDEFOP (1995a) *Teachers and Trainers in Vocational Education: Vol. 1: Germany, Spain, France and the United Kingdom,* Luxembourg, Office for Official Publications of the European Communities

CEDEFOP (1995b) *Teachers and Trainers in Vocational Education: Vol. 2: Italy, Ireland and Portugal,* Luxembourg, Office for Official Publications of the European Communities

CEDEFOP (1997) *Teachers and Trainers in Vocational Education: Vol. 3: Austria, Belgium, Greece, Luxembourg, and the Netherlands,* Luxembourg, Office for Official Publications of the European Communities

CEDEFOP (1998) *Teachers and Trainers in Vocational Education: Vol. 4 Denmark, Finland, Iceland, Norway and Sweden,* Luxembourg, Office for Official Publications of the European Communities

CERI (Centre for Educational Research and Innovation) (1996) *Education at a Glance: Analysis,* Paris, OECD

CERI (1997) *Education at a Glance: OECD indicators 1997,* Paris, OECD

Commission of the European Communities (1991) *Structures of the Education and Initial Training Systems, EURIDICE and CEDEFOP project,* Luxembourg, Office for Official Publications of the European Communities

Council on Competitiveness (1987) 'Analysis of US competitiveness problems', *America's Competitive Crisis: Confronting the New Reality,* April, pp 121–26

Dato' Seri Dr Mahathir Mohamed (1991) 'The way forward – Vision 2020', Prime Minister's Department, working paper presented at the Malaysian Business Council

Dearden, R (1991) 'Education and training', in G Esland, (ed) *Education, Training and Employment, Vol. 2, The educational response,* Wokingham, Addison-Wesley, pp 84–95

Esland, G (1991) *Education, Training and Employment, Vol. 1, Educated labour – the changing basis of industrial demand,* Wokingham, Addison-Wesley

European Commission (1996) *Technological learning: Towards the learning society,* White Paper, Luxembourg, Office for Official Publications of the European Communities

European Commission (1997a) *Key Data on Education in the European Union '97,* Luxembourg, Office for Official Publications of the European Communities

European Commission (1997b) *Continuing Vocational Training: Europe, Japan and United States of America,* Luxembourg, Office for Official Publications of the European Communities

European Training Foundation (1997) *Report on the Vocational Education and Training System: Czech Republic,* Luxembourg, Office for Official Publications of the European Communities

Eurydice/CEDEFOP (1991) *Structures of the Educational and Initial Training Systems in the Member States of the European Community,* Luxembourg, Office for Official Publications of the European Communities

Frank Press (1990) 'The role of education in technological competitiveness', *Siemens Review,* February

Graham, G (1994) 'Lack of training shuts out poor', *Financial Times,* 14 March, p 4

Heilbroner, R L (ed) (1986) *The Essential Adam Smith,* Oxford, Oxford University Press

Husen, T (ed) (1967) *International Study of Attainments in Mathematics,* Stockholm, Almqvist & Wiksell

ILO (1977) *Meeting Basic Needs,* Geneva, ILO

Incomes Data Services (1997) *Recruitment, Training and Development,* London, Institute of Personnel and Development

Jones, M and Mann, P (1992) *HRD: International perspectives on development and learning,* West Hartford, CT, Kumarian Press

Keep, E and Mayhew, K (1991) 'The Assessment: Education, training and economic performance', in G Esland, (ed) *Education, Training and Employment, Vol. 1, Educated Labour – The changing basis of industrial demand,* Wokingham, Addison-Wesley, pp 193–213

Malaysia: The Seventh Malaysia Plan 1996–2000 (1996) Prime Minister's Department, May, Percetakan Nasional Malaysia Berhad

MIT (1989) *Made in America,* Cambridge, MA, MIT Press

Mokyr, J (1990) *The Lever of Riches: Technological creativity and economic progress*, New York, Oxford University Press

Murphy, J (1972) *The Education Act 1870: Text and commentary*, Newton Abbot, David and Charles

Nato, T (1988) 'The basis of life-innovator economics', in M A Choudary (ed), *Policy: Theoretical foundations of ethico-economics*, Sydney, Nova Scotia, The Centre of Humanomics, pp 83–96

OECD (Organisation for Economic Co-operation and Development) (1989a) *New Technologies in the 1990s: A socio-economic strategy*, Paris, OECD

OECD (1989b) *Education and the Economy in a Changing Society*, Paris, OECD

OECD (1990) *Human Resource and New Technology: Main trends and issues*, Centre for Educational Research and Innovation, Paris, OECD

OECD (1994) *Jobs Study*, Paris, OECD

Pollet, I (1992) 'Training and employment of the underprivileged: the role of social partners', *Journal of European Industrial Training*, **16**, 9, pp 23–28

Porter, M E (1980) *Competitive Strategy*, New York, Free Press

Porter, M E (1990) *The Competitive Advantage of Nations*, New York, Free Press

Prais, S J (1995) *Productivity, Education and Training: An international perspective*, Cambridge, Cambridge University Press

Ryan, P (1991) *International Comparisons of Vocational Education and Training for Intermediate Skills*, London, Falmer Press

Singh, A (1979) 'The "basic needs" approach to development vs the new international economic order: the significance of Third World industrialisation', *World Development*, **7**, pp 585–606

Sun, Li-Teh (1986) 'Confucianism and the economic order of Taiwan', *International Journal of Social Economics*, **13**, 6, pp 3–53

Sun, Li-Teh (1997) 'Mean value, government and human development', *International Journal of Social Economics*, **24**, 4, pp 383–92

Tan, C H (1989) 'Confucianism and nation building in Singapore', *International Journal of Social Economics*, **16**, 8, pp 5–16

Taylor, F W (1911) *Scientific Management: The principles of scientific management*, New York, Harper and Row, reprinted 1947

UNDP (United Nations Development Programme) (1996) *Human Development Report*, New York, Oxford University Press

UNESCO (1995) *World Education Report*, New York, UNESCO

Williams, T (1996) 'New technology, human resources and competitiveness in developing countries: the role of technology transfer', *The International Journal of Human Resource Management*, **7**, 4, pp 832–45

Wolf, A (2002) *Does Education Matter? Myths about education and economic development*, London, Penguin

Section Two:

Learning and Competitive Strategy

5

Strategy and Human Resource Development

Sue Balderson

INTRODUCTION AND LEARNING OBJECTIVES

In an increasingly competitive world, which is the reality for most organizations today, few would disagree with the view that a link should exist between the training and development that the organization undertakes and the business strategy of that organization. Personnel are now widely regarded as 'human resources' with the implication that, like other resources, they are to be valued and carefully managed. The amount of financial resource available for the training and development of employees is not unlimited, necessitating decisions about where to deploy resources to maximum effect. Such decisions can only be made if those responsible for Human Resource Development (HRD) are clear about the organization's strategy and priorities. An alignment between strategy and HRD is now commonly regarded as good business sense in all corners of the globe (Harrison, 1997; Mabey and Salaman, 1995; Storey, 1991). Despite this there is some evidence from both Europe and the United States (Harrison, 1997; Holden and Livian 1992; Salaman, 1992) that, while at an intellectual level this link is recognized, the practice may be considerably different in many countries. Harrison (1997:25) points out that 'research has failed to reveal any significant connection between HRD and business strategy across UK organisations at large'. Beaumont (1992) reports that studies in the United States found that only 22 per cent of companies had high levels of integration of human resource and business strategy.

This chapter sets out to look at some models of strategic management in relation to models of HRD and to consider why, in many cases, the link between strategy and HRD is not as strong as it might be. Some of the problems with strategy itself are highlighted and approaches to aligning

HRD activity to business goals, based upon Porter's (2004) value chain and Kaplan and Norton's Balanced Scorecard (1996) are suggested as a more workable model for the HRD practitioner today.

Having read this chapter you will:

- understand the need to link HRD to organizational strategy;
- understand how to enable HRD to contribute towards all levels of organizational strategy;
- be aware of the limitations of strategic planning;
- know the elements of strategic management; and
- understand how strategy models can be used to make HRD truly strategic.

THE CASE FOR STRATEGIC HRD

Training and development has traditionally been a functional division of the personnel or human resources department concerned with carrying out the identification of training and development needs, planning and designing training, implementing training and evaluating it, ie the classic 'training cycle' (see Figure 5.1). This notion of a systematic approach to training and development is widely accepted among practitioners.

Although not using the term HRD, Winter (1995:313) talks about 'a systematic approach to developing staff' which has, as its starting point, the business objectives (or strategy); see Figure 5.2. This differs from the classic training cycle only in as much as the identification of training and development needs is now seen to be based on organizational strategy. This is very much the model for the Investors in People standard (see Chapter 24) and symbolizes a more strategic role for training and development.

Definitions of HRD also emphasize a strategic orientation, for example:

> Resourcing is about providing the skills base needed in the organisation. Human resource development (HRD) is about enhancing and widening these skills by training, by helping people to grow within the organisation, and by enabling them to make better use of their skills and abilities. (Armstrong, 1992:152)

Figure 5.1 The classic training cycle

Figure 5.2 Business objectives within a training cycle (adapted from Winter, 1995)

Mabey and Salaman (1995:131) set out 'a strategic approach to training' and present a clear model of strategic training and development. In this:

> The target represents the vision, mission or 'cause' of the organisation. ... From this starting point there are two flows: one into business strategy ... the other into human resource strategies. ... This latter flow will hopefully inform each lever of HRM policy and procedure, providing continuity between recruitment and selection practices, appraisal and assessment, reward systems and career development processes. Critically, training and development provision needs to be mutually supported by each of these human resource levers.

Armstrong (1992) views HRD as focused training and development for all employees which responds to individual and organizational requirements by improving performance and understanding.

A key feature of strategic HRM and HRD is that they are (or should be) activities of management rather than of functional specialists, and are (or should be) aligned to the business strategies of organizations. The parentheses are significant as the descriptions of HRM and HRD can be regarded as 'ideals' rather than actualities – a point made by Mabey and Salaman (1995) in relation to HRM.

The key challenge implicit within all of the models and definitions above is to be able clearly to identify what the organization's strategy and goals are in order that the systematic approach to HRD can be followed. The weakness in them all arises where business strategy is not clearly apparent to those responsible for making decisions about HRD, and, consequently, logical deductions about appropriate training and development interventions are difficult to make. This may be because HRD specialists are not involved adequately at strategic levels of decision-making or because of the dynamic nature of the organization where strategy is constantly on the move. It may be a combination of both of these factors.

Walton (1999) makes a distinction between a strategic approach to training and development and strategic human resource development (SHRD). He differentiates organizations into broadly three types:

- Those that undertake piecemeal training which is typically course based and not explicitly linked to the overall vision and goals of the organization.

- Organizations with a training and development strategy, where training and development provision is derived from the business plans and objectives of the organization, and training and development is very much downstream of strategy (the IiP approach).
- Those that have strategic human resource development, which is more holistic. The belief is that processes of organizational change occur through planned learning to ensure that individuals and the organization are equipped with the skills and knowledge needed to deal with the present and to create the future.

The notion of SHRD is reflected in the concepts of human and intellectual capital and the learning organization, where learning is a deliberate business process. The shift from piecemeal training to SHRD has been driven by growth towards high-tech industries, reliant on highly skilled knowledge workers who are the source of competitive advantage, putting HRD at the top of the strategic agenda.

STRATEGY AND STRATEGIC HRD

An organization's strategy is all about its future orientation. Johnson and Scholes (2002:10) in their authoritative and comprehensive text *Exploring Corporate Strategy*, define strategy as:

> the *direction* and *scope* of an organisation over the *long term:* which achieves *advantage* for the organisation through its configuration of *resources* within a changing *environment*, to meet the needs of *markets* and to fulfil *stakeholder* expectations.

Some key words contained within a number of the definitions of strategy (eg, Andrews, 1994; Ansoff, 1987; Chandler, 1962; Faulkner and Johnson, 1992) are:

1. major objectives, purposes, long-term goals, product-market opportunities, direction, positioning, competitive advantage, long-term perspective, framework;
2. policies, plans, resource allocation/deployment.

It can be seen that these fall into two categories. The first group deals with what Armstrong and Long (1994:16) describe as 'the end'; the second with what they describe as 'the means'. They suggest that *strategic management* deals with both ends and means:

> As an end it describes a vision of what something will look like in a few years' time. As a means, it shows how it is expected that the vision will be realised. Strategic management is therefore visionary management, concerned with creating and conceptualising ideas of where the organisation is going. But it is also empirical management that decides how in practice it is going to get there.

A similar view is suggested by Purcell (1992) who identifies three levels of strategic decision-making and considers how they can interrelate with HRM. These are:

First order: decisions on the long-run goals and the scope of activities.
Second order: decisions on the way the enterprise is structured to achieve its goals.
Third order: functional strategies in the context of levels 1 and 2 (including HRM and HRD strategies).

These are similar to the three levels suggested by Johnson and Scholes (2002) of corporate strategy, business unit strategy and operational strategies. All levels of strategy are influenced by external environmental factors, many of which will have a direct impact upon HRD (eg, technological advances, labour market).

Training and development, if it is to be regarded as a strategic activity aligned to corporate strategy, should as a minimum feature in the second order in the above model whereby it supports the overall strategic direction. Harrison calls this 'business-led HRD'. However, there is also a case to be made that in an ideal situation it should play a role in the first order – termed 'strategic HRD' (Harrison, 1997). Unfortunately, in many cases training and development is relegated to an operational activity, disconnected from or only loosely connected to any of the strategic activities of the organization, or responding to the immediately pressing or a current fad.

Johnson and Scholes (2002) suggest three main elements to strategic management: strategic analysis, strategic choice and strategy implementation, which are not linear events but interlinked. There is a role for HRD (and HRM) considerations in each of these elements:

- The purpose of *strategic analysis* is to form a view of the key influences on the present and future well-being of the organization; what opportunities are afforded by the environment (ie, the opportunities and threats); what are the competences (strengths and weaknesses) of the organization. Considerations for HRD here might include analysis of current skill levels available within and external to the organization which might impinge upon current and future business goals; it would consider the core competences of the organization in terms of human capabilities in existence or which might be developed, and how these might be deployed.
- *Strategic choice* is about identifying the choices open to the organization in terms of, for example, products or services, generating strategic options and evaluating and selecting options. Here again, HRD considerations are important; for instance, against each option can staff be recruited and trained to meet its requirements? Do such considerations render an option viable or not viable? Would some of the core competences held by employees suggest certain choices would be more likely to succeed than others?
- *Strategy implementation* is concerned with the structure and systems needed for chosen strategic options (termed 'the strategic architecture'). The HRD considerations here might be about whether to retrain the existing workforce (in knowledge, skills and/or attitudes) or whether to recruit new people. It may require the management of strategic change and the design and delivery of major training and development programmes to support change.

Strategic analysis will include consideration of external factors relevant to the organization and its strategic direction (the environment). However, the internal resources of the organization (including human resources) are also an important strategic consideration. Here the notion of the 'core competences' is relevant. In considering the strategic direction of the organization, an assessment of the core competences that have been developed over the years may be helpful. These may be associated with particular types of expertise which are special to the organization and differentiate it from others. Some of these core competences may be contained within the systems (eg, the McDonald's fast-food service) for which employees can be readily trained. Others (eg, medical research) may be contained within the people themselves. In considering strategic direction, it is relevant for an organization to identify its core competences and determine how these can best be taken advantage of, given various environmental factors. In training and development terms, this can put the classical training cycle and business planning approach to determining training needs on its head, by suggesting that a starting point might just as well be the existing competences of (certain groups of) employees, and planning the direction of the business around these. This trend is articulated in the emerging literature about knowledge workers (Mayo and Pickard, 1998).

If HRD is, by definition, a strategic activity, it should be possible to assess different strategic scenarios and identify appropriate HRD strategies and policies. Schuler and Jackson (1987) present an interesting model which links strategy to employee role behaviour and HRM policies. For instance, they suggest that in an organization where strategy is primarily to achieve *innovation*, the type of employee behaviour that is desirable is one where creativity can flourish, where people are cooperative and can tolerate unpredictability. Clearly there are implications here for other aspects of human resource strategy such as recruitment and selection. The implication for HRD in this context is that people will need to develop skills that can be used elsewhere in the organization and should be offered broad career paths to reinforce the development of a broad range of skills. By comparison, where an organization's strategy is that of *quality enhancement* the HRD strategy should provide for the extensive and continuous training and development of employees. Where *cost reduction* is a key component of strategy there will be minimal levels of employee training and development targeted to ensure that specialist expertise is maintained.

Practitioners may, at this stage, begin to see some of the pitfalls of *the ideal* of strategic HRD when compared with the reality. Within the UK National Health Service, for example, very often the strategic aims as stated within mission statements highlight all three of these elements of innovation, quality enhancement and cost reduction as priorities. This can lead to a sort of organizational confusion about which HRM and HRD strategies should be pursued. This may be the opportunity for HRD practitioners to play a role in strategy formulation to bring about greater clarity of vision which will help to determine where scarce development resources should be deployed at any point in time to support multiple, and sometimes conflicting, objectives. It is, indeed, why management development is a vital prerequisite of an HRD approach. If managers are the owners and guardians of strategic HRM and HRD, the implications for them in terms of their own development are not inconsiderable.

Another type of analysis links the critical human resource activities to different stages in the business life cycle (Kochan and Barocci, 1985). The suggestion is that a new business should be concerned with determining future skill requirements and establishing career ladders. As the business grows, a priority should be the development of managers and management teams to facilitate organizational development. As the business matures, it should be concerned with maintaining flexibility and skills of the 'ageing' workforce. A business in decline would be involved in retraining and career counselling services.

Within the climate of change in which many organizations find themselves, precise identification of the stage in the life cycle in which the organization resides is not always easy. In large diversified organizations, with mergers, acquisitions and divestments, different parts of the business will be at different stages and may therefore be engaged in all of these activities simultaneously in different divisions. In multinationals, different companies will have different priorities. This raises the question of the extent to which, in such organizations, HRD strategies should be common. Armstrong (1992) draws attention to the problem of achieving a balance between the business unit strategies, tailored to their own circumstances, and the role of the centre in providing policies and a structure which integrate the divisions into a corporate whole.

THE PROBLEM WITH STRATEGY

Models of strategic HRD presuppose, to a large extent, a rational and linear model of strategy formulation and implementation whereby there is a sequence of stages involving objective setting, the analysis of environmental trends and resource capabilities, evaluation of options and ending with careful planning of the strategy's implementation (see Figure 5.3). In such cases the model described in Storey (1991) would apply.

Armstrong and Long (1994) identify a number of problems associated with integrating HRM strategies which stem from the imperfections of the reality of strategic management:

- the diversity of strategic approaches particularly in diversified corporations;
- the complexity of the strategy formulation process which inhibits the flow into functional strategy;
- the evolutionary nature of business strategy which does not fit with the concept of planning and therefore makes it difficult to 'pin down' relevant HRM issues; and
- the absence of articulated business strategies which hinders clarification of strategic issues.

Johnson and Scholes (2002) point out that while many organizations do have formal planning systems, this is not universally the case; similarly, strategies are adopted by organizations without coming through these formal systems. They suggest that strategies typically develop by organizations adapting or building on existing strategies, ie, they are incremental. They distinguish between such incremental strategy and the need which occasionally arises for transformational strategic change where it is important for there to be a clear and compelling vision or strategic intent. Even where strategies are well planned, they are not always realized; alternatively, strategies may be imposed on an organization through, for example, legislation.

> Strategic decisions are characterised by the political hurly-burly of organisational life with a high incidence of bargaining, a trading off of costs and benefits of one interest group against another, all within a notable lack of clarity in terms of environmental influences and objectives. (Johnson, 1987:21)

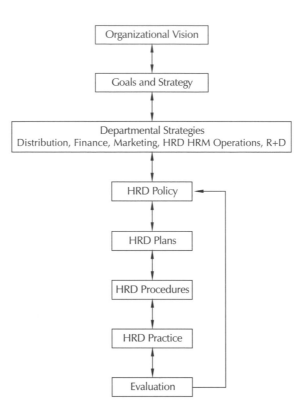

Figure 5.3 Strategy and HRD

Some authors (eg, Stacey 1992) suggest that strategy formulation needs to be radically re-thought, given the turbulent and chaotic environment in which many organizations operate. The suggestion is not that it should be abandoned altogether, but that the myth of the rational planning approach should be replaced with a reality which is about developing organizational structures, processes and styles that enable managers and other employees to draw on their experience, to adopt more questioning approaches, air conflicting ideas and experiment without reproach. This is akin to the *learning organization* concept and will require a significant shift for many organizations still caught up in rituals of strategic and business planning. It requires organizational slack to allow time for managers and other employees to debate and challenge, and a corresponding change in culture and attitude.

This analysis suggests that the *ideal* of HRD may be one where a 'best fit' is sought between the organization's strategic direction and its HRD activities and initiatives. It echoes Hendry's (1995) recommendation that there should be a 'loose coupling' of business and HR strategies. This more pragmatic approach seems sensible given the apparent gap that exists in practice between the ideal and the reality of strategic HRD.

STRATEGY AND HRD – AN HISTORICAL CONTEXT

It is interesting to look at the development of approaches to strategy in an historical context and to align them to thinking about issues of training and development. The model in Table 5.1 attempts to identify key environmental changes, how strategy and orientation have developed correspondingly and how approaches to training and development have rather lagged behind.

This analysis suggests that considerable advancement has occurred in thinking about organizational strategy, with a move away from rational, linear approaches to strategy and planning, and embracing more opportunistic styles. Models of training and development, however, are still often based upon the 'training cycle', and even where 'business objectives' is the starting point, this may be insufficient as the primary tool for developing a strategic approach to HRD in the current environment. This might account for some of the difficulties experienced by organizations attempting to follow an Investors in People type model which demands as the starting point clearly articulated business plans from which HRD priorities will naturally flow.

Table 5.1   An historical perspective on strategy and HRD

Date	Environment	Approaches to Strategy	Focus/ Orientation	Approaches to Training and Development
1960s	static	planned	production/ product	classic training cycle
1970s		incremental	market development	
1980s		emergent	quality management customer service	
1990s	dynamic	chaos theory/ freewheeling opportunism	globalization	training and development strategy based on business plans (IiP) model
2000	virtual		global e-business	strategic HRD learning organization human capital

STRATEGIC ANALYSIS AND HRD

Value chain analysis

An alternative, perhaps more pragmatic approach, to aligning HRD with business strategy is to move away from the rational approach and consider where business planning HRD can contribute in an organization's value chain. Porter (2004) identifies primary activities (inbound logistics, operations, outbound logistics, marketing and sales and service) which, he suggests, are essential to any organization operating in a competitive situation. He points out that the importance of the various primary activities will vary from organization to organization depending upon their core purpose. It is important for any organization to recognize where it creates value in this chain to ensure that it is putting appropriate effort and resource into each element.

HRD (encompassed within HRM in the model) is one of the key support activities that should facilitate the organization's activities along the value chain. Where resources for training and development are limited it can be argued that they should be placed so that they add most value to primary activities.

An earlier stage in the analysis is to consider, given the overall strategic purpose(s) of an organization, what the *critical success factors* are for the strategy to work. Critical success factors are those factors that are essential to the organization achieving its strategic targets. For example, for a fast-food outlet, the critical success factors are fast production of food, standard quality and quick, courteous customer service. There are many implications given these critical success factors for the systems of production but there are also implications for HRD. Using the value chain, it can be seen that HRD effort needs to go into ensuring that managers know procedures for ordering and delivery (inbound logistics). Other staff need to be trained in food handling and preparation and to follow protocols for the quick yet safe production of food (operations). Marketing and sales might be an activity bought with the franchise and not an immediate concern of operations staff other than point-of-sale display and cleanliness. Training and development will need to be designed to be capable of being delivered on a just-in-time basis, given the fairly high turnover of staff in this sector. Using critical success factors and the value chain in this way can provide a framework that enables a fairly quick appraisal of the extent to which investment in training and development is adding value, and HRD strategies can be developed to ensure that this occurs.

Value chain analysis also emphasizes the importance of paying attention to *linkages* between primary activities and between support and primary activities to ensure that value is added along the way. Linkages are seen as the potential source of competitive advantage, as primary and support activities can be replicated relatively easily and may be similar in different organizations.

A further illustration of the application of value chain analysis to developing a strategic approach to HRD is the approach adopted by the Unipart Group of Companies (UGC) Ltd (see the case study below). Given its mission to become the world's best lean enterprise, the critical success factors for the company, which deals with the design and manufacture of original equipment components for the automotive industry, are:

- cost-effectiveness in production and distribution, given the highly competitive nature of the market with downward pressure on prices;
- quality of product;
- quality of customer service.

With reference to these critical success factors, the value chain can be used as a framework for identifying where competence needs to be ensured.

VALUE CHAIN FOR THE UNIPART GROUP OF COMPANIES

Inbound logistics	Buying and negotiating supplies of raw materials
	Building relationships with suppliers
	Just-in-time supply
Operations	Lean production methods
	Team working
	Problem solving
	Change management
	Just-in-time production
Outbound logistics	Lean warehousing and distribution
	Responsiveness to customer needs and wants
	Change management
Marketing and sales	Developing partnerships with customers
	Quality communications
After-sales service	Responsiveness
	Feeding knowledge back into the organization
	Consultancy skills

The linkages are important for a *learning organization* whereby knowledge gained in any primary area is fed through to other parts of the value chain to ensure that the whole system is responsive. It is important for example, that lean production methods give rise to productivity that is in step with customer demand, otherwise warehousing problems will occur. Using this framework, an effective HRD approach might be represented in a linear fashion as shown in Figure 5.4.

In considering the value chain, it is important to note that organizations that interface with one another (whether they be customers, suppliers or other stakeholders) will have their own value chains which may overlap; see Figure 5.5.

core purpose(s) of the organization

|

critical success factors (CSF) for each main purpose

|

competency requirements for each CSF
against primary and support activities on the value chain

|

training and development needs assessment

|

training and development interventions

Figure 5.4   A strategic HRD approach

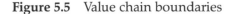

Figure 5.5   Value chain boundaries

The view of the organization as a separate entity which exists by cutting costs at the expense of employees, customers and suppliers is likely to be severely limiting in terms of achieving competitive advantage. If an organization is managing its inbound logistics, that would suggest working in partnership with suppliers to ensure satisfactory long-term arrangements. If the same organization is to satisfy its customers it must link its sales and service activities sensitively to the customers' inbound logistics. This notion of partnership implies that HRD is not restricted to the employees of the organization itself but may be extended to employees of other organizations in the value chain and beyond. Other stakeholders (eg, the local community) may also be brought into the partnership; for example, a skills shortage in a particular area might be alleviated by a pre-employment training scheme.

Using the value chain in this way can assist decision-making about appropriate training and development interventions and where resources are best deployed.

UNIPART CASE STUDY

The Unipart Group (UGC) offers a good example of the application of HRD to the value chain. The group is primarily engaged in distribution and logistics, which includes the marketing, sale and distribution of parts and accessories for the European automotive aftermarket. It employs around 7,500 worldwide with a turnover of over £1 billion.

When Unipart was formed through a management buy-out in 1987, the management team took on a company in which product quality was poor and productivity was dangerously low. The new business had one customer, Rover, which had difficulties of its own.

Within the structure of the buy-out, Unipart gained manufacturing facilities in Oxford and Coventry. Although this was only a small part of the business – less than 10 percent – it became an increasingly important area from which the rest of the group would learn. Unipart adopted the principles of lean production within its manufacturing sites, and set out to abandon traditional ideas in favour of adapting the working practices of world-class companies such as Honda and Toyota. Unipart employees worked in factories in Japan and continually applied new lessons in the process of steady improvement, setting themselves the target of becoming the world's best lean enterprise.

Having begun a journey of learning in manufacturing, the management team recognized the need to spread this knowledge widely across the group. In 1993 UGC opened the Unipart U, one of Europe's first corporate universities and a model for many of today's organizational learning facilities. The Unipart U has a mission 'to develop, train and inspire people to achieve world class performance within UGC and amongst our stakeholders'. The company has learned many principles and practices of continuous improvement from Toyota and Honda, and used the Unipart U and workplace-based learning centres called Faculty on the Floor to engage employees at every level in learning and applying these techniques.

One of its clearly state critical success factors has been to gain competitive advantage through lean thinking, whether in production, distribution or administration. This drive has been codified in The Unipart Way, a philosophy of working underpinned by tools and techniques that form part of the company's knowledge management systems. The Unipart Way enables the company to improve faster than the best alternative on offer to its customers, and has become Unipart's major differentiator in the distribution and logistics arena. In the past two years, the company has won a wide range of new distribution contracts with customers in areas such as retail, information technology, aerospace and telecoms based on the value created through The Unipart Way.

The Unipart Way enables the company to work in partnership with its customers and suppliers to ensure that 'linkages' in the value chain are as lean as possible. Training and development is extended to include customers and suppliers, and representatives of the 'extended enterprise' are invited to contribute the training UGC employees.

All training and development activities are linked precisely to enabling staff to embrace The Unipart Way and to eliminate waste along the value chain. This is not just in the technical aspects of working in a lean enterprise: UGC recognizes that learning to live and work in a constantly change environment and to manage such change at a personal level is as important as learning technical knowledge and skills. Programmes enabling staff to learn and develop 'soft skills' are given equal standing with skills-based training. For those leading change within the organization (called by the Japanese word *sensei*), an innovative degree programme was developed in conjunction with De Montfort University in the UK to provide a formal accreditation of work-based learning.

UGC openly acknowledges that its world-class achievements come from the efficiencies generated from the accumulated knowledge and creative energies of its people. It has capitalized on many of the core competencies that it has developed over the last 10 years. For example, with its strong reputation for workplace-based learning and development, the company established Unipart Advanced Learning Systems, a team of its most experienced learning and change specialists who are focused on adapting Unipart's experience for other companies. This team has worked with organizations in both public and private sectors, with customers as diverse as financial services, design engineering firms, local authorities and ceramic manufacturers. Through Unipart Advanced Learning Systems, UGC has turned its learning, experience and knowledge into a value stream that can extend beyond the group's traditional relationships across a wide spectrum of businesses.

THE BALANCED SCORECARD

Kaplan and Norton's (1996) Balanced Scorecard is being used as a strategic management tool by an increasing number of organizations, and offers potential to those wishing to achieve strategic HRD. The basic tenet of the model is that, to achieve balance, organizations should develop objectives and performance measures in a range of areas which reflect the full scope of the business rather than purely financial aspects. In addition to financial perspectives, the Balanced Scorecard suggests that strategy formulation and evaluation should be undertaken from customer perspectives, internal business perspectives, and innovation and learning perspectives. In each of these four areas, objectives and measures are agreed, based on what must be done to meet stakeholder expectations and requirements.

The category of 'innovation and learning' is indisputably in the realm of SHRD and might contain measures such as:

- percentage of staff aligned to the organization's vision and mission;
- percentage of staff with personal development plans in place and being implemented;
- percentage of staff with required skills and competences.

However this can be taken further, whereby the development needs of individuals and staff groups are met according to an assessment of how equipped they are to meet targets and measures in all four areas. Appraisal systems can be developed which incorporate objectives that reflect the organizational ones.

An example of how Balanced Scorecard measures could be used in the English National Health Service is given in Table 5.2.

Table 5.2 Example of Balanced Scorecard measures which might form the basis of objectives, appraisal and development for a NHS manager

Perspective	Objective	Development need
Financial perspective	Achieve the planned financial position without the need for unplanned financial support	Learn ways of generating income in order to increase available resources
Customer perspective	Achieve standards of hospital cleanliness in accordance with standards agreed by various interest groups	Develop knowledge and skills in ways of engaging meaningfully with user groups to negotiate and agree standards
Internal business perspective	Introduce booking systems which provide convenient choices with guaranteed waiting times	Change management in relation to staff groups that may be resistant to change
Innovation and learning perspective	Use results from clinical audits to develop improved protocols for managing coronary heart disease	Better understand the clinical audit process and current protocols for managing coronary heart disease in order to have informed dialogue with clinicians

CONCLUSION

Part of the cause of the loose connection of HRD to organizational strategy can probably be attributed to the nature of strategy itself and its emergent and sometimes chaotic nature. Exhortations to base HRD strategy upon an organization's business strategy and clearly articulated business goals may be of little help to the HRD specialist struggling to get to grips with how best to focus limited resources. Understanding the strategic framework in which the organization is operating, its vision, mission, goals, critical success factors and performance measures, will enable HRD to take its place as a key player in the strategy process.

Bibliography

Andrews, K A (1994) *The Concept of Corporate Strategy*, Homewood, IL, Irwin/McGraw-Hill

Ansoff, H I (1987) *Corporate Strategy*, Maidenhead, McGraw-Hill

Armstrong, M (1992) *Human Resource Management: Strategy and action*, London, Kogan Page

Armstrong, M and Long, P (1994) *The Reality of Strategic HRM*, London, IPD

Beaumont, P B (1992) 'The US human resource literature: a review', in G Salaman (ed), *Human Resource Strategies*, London, Sage

Chandler, A D (1962) *Strategy and Structure*, Cambridge, MA, MIT Press

Faulkner, D and Johnson, G (1992) *The Challenge of Strategic Management*, London, Kogan Page

Harrison, R (1997) *Employee Development*, London, IPD

Hendry, C (1995) *Human Resource Management: A strategic approach to employment*, Oxford, Butterworth-Heinemann

Holden, L and Livian, Y (1992) 'Does strategic training policy exist? Some evidence from ten European countries', *Personnel Review*, **21**, 1, pp 12–23

Johnson, G (1987) *Strategic Change and the Management Process*, Oxford, Blackwell

Johnson, G and Scholes, K (2002) *Exploring Corporate Strategy*, 6th edn, Hemel Hempstead, Prentice Hall

Kaplan, R S (1996) 'Using the Balanced Scorecard as a strategic management system', *Harvard Business Review*, January–February, pp 75–85

Kaplan, R S and Norton, D P (1996) *Balanced Scorecard: Translating strategy into action*, Harvard MA, Harvard Business School Press

Kochan, T A and Barocci, T A (1985) *Human Resource Management and Industrial Relations*, Boston, MA, Little, Brown

Mabey, C and Salaman, G (1995) *Strategic Human Resource Management*, Oxford, Blackwell

Mayo, A and Pickard, J (1998) 'Memory bankers', *People Management*, 22 January, pp 34–38

Porter, M E (2004) *Competitive Advantage*, New York, Free Press

Purcell, J (1992) 'The impact of corporate strategy', in M Armstrong (ed), *Strategy and Action*, London, Kogan Page

Salaman, G (ed) (1992) *Human Resource Strategies*, London, Sage

Schuler, R S and Jackson, S E (1987) 'Organisational strategy and organisational level as determinants of human resource management practices', *Human Resource Planning*, **10**, 3

Stacey, R (1992) *Managing Chaos*, London, Kogan Page

Stewart, J and McGoldrick, J (1996) *Human Resource Development: Perspectives, strategies and practice*, London, Pitman

Storey, J (ed) (1991) *New Perspectives on Human Resource Management*, London, Routledge

Storey, J (ed) (1995) *HRM: A critical text*, London, Routledge

Walton, J (1999) *Strategic Human Resource Development*, Harlow, Pearson Education

Winter, R (1995) 'An integrated approach to training and development', in S Truelove (ed), *The Handbook of Training and Development*, Oxford, Blackwell

6

Learning Organizations and Communities of Practice: A Critical Evaluation

Rob F Poell

INTRODUCTION AND LEARNING OBJECTIVES

In this chapter the concept of the learning organization is described, critically evaluated, and related to more recently developed ideas concerning communities of practice. The learning organization was one of the most popular concepts in management literature throughout the 1990s, but also one of the most ill-defined, container-type ones. Our intention is to show how core authors have viewed the learning organization and to list the major criticisms it has come to face. It is argued that the traditional emphasis on the development of shared vision encourages a rather one-faceted view of the learning organization concept. The critical approach we advocate informs a more multi-faceted perspective. Two Dutch cases are presented to illustrate how the concept of the learning organization can be elaborated in practice. New theoretical developments around communities of practice are related to the discussion on learning organizations and evaluated accordingly.

Having read this chapter you will:

- understand the nature and characteristics of the learning organization;
- know Senge's five disciplines for learning organizations;
- be able to describe the main elements of a learning organization;
- know questions to ask which identify elements of a learning organization; and
- recognize the role communities of practice play in organizations.

DEFINITION AND CHARACTERISTICS OF THE LEARNING ORGANIZATION

Background of the concept

The concept of the learning organization has been a popular one for quite some time now. According to Garratt (1995), the key ideas about the learning organization were developed immediately after World War II. It took much longer, however, before they were actually applied. The concept came of age under the impact of a rapidly developing world of work and organization. Pedler, Burgoyne and Boydell (1991) trace back the history of the concept (and related ones such as Total Quality Management) as stemming from earlier approaches like organization development, individual self-development, action learning and the excellence movement of the 1970s and 1980s, all of which in turn followed post-war concern for systematic training.

The EC's 1996 *White Paper on Education and Training* highlights the impact of the information society on work and organization, the impact of internationalization on the need for competitiveness, and the impact of scientific and technological knowledge on industry (European Commission, 1996). Growing competition, technological changes, new work methods, financial constraints, globalization, reorganizations, mergers and the like, gave rise to a need for organizations to learn and adapt more quickly to changing circumstances. In the words of McCarthy (1997), these processes necessitated continuous improvement both in people and in organizations. This is a central, if fairly general, feature of the learning organization.

Definitions of the learning organization

There are many more specific definitions of the concept, most of which include notions about continuous learning, innovation, responsiveness, commitment, collaboration, shared vision, openness in communication, shared values, dialogue, the use of IT, empowerment and so forth. Some of these definitions are of a descriptive nature; others are more normatively orientated.

Let us start by looking at how three core thinkers about the concept, Pedler, Burgoyne and Boydell, define it. They describe the learning organization as 'an organization which facilitates the learning of all its members and continuously transforms itself' (1989:2). As indicated above, this definition contains an individual and an organizational change element. Individual learning is necessary but not sufficient for organizations to learn. Interestingly, in a more recent edition the same authors define the concept as 'an organization that facilitates the learning of all its members and consciously transforms itself and its context' (1997: 3). Apparently, organizations now need to be able to impact upon their environment as well as adapt to the changes taking place, a concern that had been raised much earlier by Mintzberg (1979). In fact, Mintzberg showed how (particularly larger) organizations succeed in affecting the circumstances in which they have to operate (for example, their clients and local and government policies).

Individual and organizational learning

Whereas Pedler *et al* stress the importance of organizational learning, Mumford (1995) finds the learning organization literature to focus too much on the structural element. In his opinion, individuals (and teams) must learn before there can be anything like organizational learning. Another core thinker about the learning organization, Senge (1990:3), tries to integrate these two approaches, his definition, however, being quite a normative one: 'an organisation where people continually expand their capacity to create the results they truly desire, where new and expansive patterns of thinking are nurtured, where collective aspiration is set free, and where people are continually learning how to learn together'. He presents his five disciplines for learning organizations:

1. Personal mastery, ensuring individual motivation to learn.
2. Mental models, creating an openness to misconceptions.
3. Shared vision, building long-term commitment in people.
4. Team learning, developing group skills like cooperation, communication and so forth.
5. Systems thinking, which constitutes 'the most important discipline' (1990:12), integrating the other four.

All the disciplines are to be practised alongside each other, and they have an impact on one another as well. As Hodgkinson (2000, 2002) describes, the learning organization is a process rather than a state, something on which all members of an organization have to work all the time, yet which can never be fully realized. Pedler and Aspinwall (1996:182) also stress that the learning company must remain a particular vision, to be realized in the context of a unique organization. Even though this may be the case, they consider it possible to generalize about organizational learning. People in companies learn from the problems, dilemmas and difficulties they encounter, together with their attempts to overcome them. Companies have much to learn from each other, too, but this can only be achieved if the contrasts are raised and the differences between them made explicit. In other words, there is no such thing as *the* learning organization, but a variety of learning organizations that can benefit from each other's experiences.

Knowledge management

Watkins and Marsick (1993) emphasize that systems to capture and share individual learning must be put in place before organizations can learn. Nonaka and Takeuchi (1995) describe such a system of knowledge creation in companies. They distinguish four types of knowledge conversion among people, which can be combined to form processes in time:

1. Socialization, tacit knowledge reproduced as tacit knowledge. People learn from each other by sharing experiences, imitation, trial and error, and so forth.
2. Externalization, tacit knowledge made explicit. People learn by systematizing and codifying their implicit knowledge, making visible what is hidden inside them.
3. Combination, explicit knowledge reproduced as explicit knowledge. People learn by using materials and other resources specifically aimed at teaching people.
4. Internalization, explicit knowledge made tacit. People learn by practising skills, automatizing procedures, acquainting themselves with tasks by doing them.

Nonaka and Takeuchi speak about a hypertext organization rather than a learning organization. According to their ideas, this type of company succeeds in combining the efficiency of a bureaucratic organization with the innovativity of an adhocratic organization (Mintzberg, 1979). This is achieved by involving all layers of the organization in the right kinds of knowledge conversion at the right time, through codification and commodification of individual tacit knowledge (Contu, Grey and Örtenblad, 2003). Every member in the company thus contributes to the creation, management and proliferation of collective knowledge throughout the organization (McDermott, 1999).

Recurring themes in the learning organization literature

In a literature review, Poell, Tijmensen and Van der Krogt (1997) concluded that, although there are many definitions of the concept of a learning organization, a number of issues keep recurring. The definitions describe the elements in a learning system that make for an efficient, flexible and viable company:

- Continuous learning on the individual, group and system level.
- Single and double-loop learning processes. Swieringa and Wierdsma (1994) even conceive of triple-loop learning: not just doing things well, not just doing things better, but also doing better things.
- Creation and distribution of information and knowledge. See Nonaka and Takeuchi (1995).
- Inquiry and dialogue in groups (sharing learning experiences).
- Increasing the learning capacity of members (learning to learn). See Senge (1990).
- Integration of work and learning (informal learning, learning on the job). See Watkins and Marsick (1993).
- Shared vision (theory of action). See Senge (1990) and Hodgkinson (2002).
- Empowerment of individual learners. According to the EU's *White Paper on Education and Training*, 'vocational training in enterprises is increasingly taking place on the basis of a

training plan which the workers themselves and their representatives have been involved in preparing. In the most progressive and most efficient companies, this training is organized less and less around the acquisition of skills for a specific task or even a clearly-defined job' (European Commission, 1996:40).

- Coaching by the manager (in self-managing work teams). See Tjepkema (2003).
- Transformation and innovation.
- Learning tied to business objectives but also for personal development.

Poell and Tijmensen (1998) had already concluded that the literature on learning organizations implicitly proposes a redefinition of the organization of work into team-based structures, so as to allow for an integration of learning and work. Every work activity can also become a learning activity. Work is performed in multifunctional teams, thinking and doing are integrated into jobs, and workers are empowered to participate in team decision-making processes (Tjepkema, 2003).

Communities of practice

As a result of the increasing attention paid to the integration of work and learning, the concept of communities of practice has become very popular in recent years (Wenger, McDermott and Snyder, 2002). The idea was coined by Lave and Wenger (1991) and further elaborated by Wenger (1998). At the core, participation in social contexts is regarded as learning. People gradually increase their knowledge of work (that is, they learn) through participation in the activities that make up that very work. Communities of practice are usually organized around a certain theme or knowledge domain, with which the volunteer participants identify.

On the one hand, communities of practice actively manage organizational knowledge embedded in employees; on the other hand, they are the vehicle for individual learning from work, through real-life problem solving and joint knowledge development. This very much parallels the ideas of the learning organization. Lave and Wenger (1991) introduced the idea of legitimate peripheral participation to understand this connection between individual and social learning. Communities should offer newcomers enough legitimacy to participate in and gain access to the resources of the community. This should then enable the newcomer to proceed gradually from the periphery towards the core of the community, increasingly offering active inputs into the prevailing dialogue and knowledge exchange.

Communities of practice are different from other organizational forms (such as work groups and teams) in their emphasis on learning with and from people other than one's direct colleagues (Wenger, 1998). This is another parallel, however, with the learning organization concept, which also emphasizes strongly the social and boundary-crossing nature of learning. What keeps a community of practice together is a mutual interest in learning and knowledge development within a joint domain. This provides the community and its members with a collective identity, at least as long as all involved see its added value compared with everyday work and learning activities.

Before we return to the learning organization concept and highlight some of its criticisms, two actual examples of the way in which a learning company operates, one from a Dutch electronics firm and one from a Dutch night school for adults may help illustrate the ideas presented in the first part of this chapter.

IMPROVEMENT TEAMS

A Dutch electronics firm wants to become a learning organization by introducing an internal competition between so-called improvement teams. Multifunctional work groups are formed across the company to investigate and try to solve problems. Each of these improvement teams receives guidance from a personal process facilitator, whose task it is to help the team devise a structured problem-solving approach. Each group has a team leader who manages activities on a day-to-day basis. There are several different written guidelines for the groups to follow. Each team has the responsibilities of dividing tasks among its members, presenting its plans and progress to its 'clients' in the organization, getting and using feedback from them, and formally presenting the outcomes of its improvement efforts to the management. Let us take a closer look at how two of these groups have operated.

The first group consists of eight operators representing five work shifts. The management has given it an assignment. The team will work on the problem of extensive waste of materials. They meet for two hours every week to discuss their assignment. It is their initial analysis that work processes that are not transparent are at the core of the waste problem. The group administer a questionnaire to all operators listing elements of the problem. The results enable them to create an initial action plan. The team visit a plant similar to their own to see how they have dealt with the problem. They also invite a number of experts to talk about the problem and possible solutions.

The first small changes in the way the shifts work are introduced. The group members have day-to-day contacts with the operators to monitor progress. A regular newsletter and meeting minutes are distributed among the operators. Because the improvement team consists of operators, feedback from the shifts is immediate, which brings about further incremental changes. The improvement team organize several instruction sessions for the operators. Sub-teams take on special tasks to try out possible improvements, which are then discussed with the whole team. After about six months the workflow has significantly improved and waste amounts are down by a half.

The second group is made up of nine developers, process engineers, product engineers and process technicians. The assignment given to them by the management is to reduce running time for experimental work processes. The team has representatives from every department concerned with the problem, who meet once every fortnight and use a general model for structured problem solving. They initially decide to broaden their assignment to fit what they perceive to be the real problem, namely the communication between the development and production departments. They ask a sub-team to create an ideal picture of operations that they can work towards. Actions for improvement are then derived from this ideal image, tried out by sub-teams and evaluated in the plenary team sessions. There is a constant flow of feedback between the improvement team members and their departments. Gradually, uniform procedures for running experimental work processes are put into place. Checklists are developed accordingly. The two departments together also create contingency plans to handle experimental situations. In regular work meetings, progress is reported and possible sources of resistance are identified at an early stage. When there is sufficient support from both departments, internal trainers are called upon to organize instruction sessions for the operators. After about eight months, the experimental work processes take about the same running time as the standard work processes, which allows new products to be on the market a fair while earlier.

The members of both improvement teams report having gained more insight into the production process as a whole and into the problems experienced by other departments, and being better able to cooperate with colleagues, to delegate tasks to others, and to communicate with them. The atmosphere has improved and people feel their ideas for improvement have been taken seriously. The organization has benefited from solving long-standing problems and from learning to deal with them in a structured approach.

WORK-BASED LEARNING PROJECTS

A Dutch night school for adults wants to become a learning organization by gaining experience with work-related learning projects by teacher groups. The school management wants teachers to work in teams rather than as separate individuals, in order to be able to better serve an increasingly diversified student population. Surveys have shown that teachers express a need for additional training, so there is some common ground to start from. Two experimental project groups are created to gain some initial experiences with team-based learning and work.

The first group consists of teachers of Dutch as a second language (for adult immigrant students). The two coordinators of this group invite an external subject matter expert to run a number of training sessions about Dutch as a second language. This consultant starts the project with a one-day seminar for all teachers, which is well received. Teachers bring lots of questions to the fore, which are addressed in the remainder of the training sessions. Not all teachers participate in the following sessions, but is it agreed that those who do will inform their colleagues during regular work meetings. The coordinators also send minutes of the training sessions to people who cannot attend.

Although individual teachers report having learned a lot of new knowledge and skills within their discipline, they have not benefited much from this group in terms of learning about self-directed project learning. The team has handed over responsibility for the learning process to the external consultant, and its members have not really learned to organize their own learning group.

This is different in the second group, which is made up of liberal arts teachers who want to investigate possibilities for self-directed work with students. They too invoke help from an external consultant, but he is asked to monitor the group learning process rather than transfer any subject matter knowledge. Two participants present the experiences they already have with self-directed student work, one by offering materials from another school and one by discussing a videotaped classroom exercise. The group collects information about self-directed work, and individual participants start experimenting in their own classrooms and in the open learning centre. Sometimes colleagues visit each other's classes for intervision purposes. They discuss their experiences in the group as a whole, and list the consequences of such an approach for school policies. A newly introduced didactic method is adapted to fit the insights gained about self-directed student work. The participants are very enthusiastic about the support they receive from their fellow team members and about the improvements they have implemented in their own classroom practice.

The school management evaluates both projects, which are clearly quite different in terms of self-directed learning by the teams of teachers. Interestingly, the comparison between the two projects teaches them a lot about how (not) to proceed towards becoming a learning organization. These experiences are used in setting up two new learning groups of teachers. Gradually, more and more teachers become enthusiastic about participating in one of the learning groups. On the one hand, they feel they can benefit individually and professionally. On the other hand, they see that the school management is seriously committed to learning from their experiences.

CRITICISM OF THE CONCEPT OF THE LEARNING ORGANIZATION

Neglect of power issues

Various criticisms of the concept have been raised in the learning organization literature. Contu, Grey and Örtenblad (2003) claim that while the learning organization may replace bureaucratic or single-loop learning, in itself it is just as narrowly defined. It is no more than just another form of (self)-control, 'part of the sustained assault on bureaucracy which typifies recent managerial discourse'. What is more, its goals are still primarily tied to business outcomes. The apparently emancipatory ideas about empowerment are more rhetoric than reality. By the same token, Örtenblad (2001, 2004) contends that the learning organization is just another way for a company to become independent of any individual member. According to him, practices like work rotation and information sharing, as well as ideas about shared vision, are aimed primarily at that objective. These issues of power and control are not often addressed in literature about the learning organization. Similarly, the concept of communities of practice seems to avoid the issue of power altogether, focusing as it does on joint interests and egalitarian relationships among members.

A restricted view of learning and work

Poell, Tijmensen and Van der Krogt (1997) express three concerns about the learning organization concept. First, its notion of learning is fairly limited, in that it seems to comprise discussion and reflection aimed at shared values (similar to communities of practice). Second, it is unclear exactly how the work is organized in a learning organization. Implicitly, the work type to which most literature refers seems to be team-based group work. Again, this is a fairly restricted view of work organization. Third, the perspective of a learning organization is appealing, but it remains quite unclear how the concept can be implemented satisfactorily. Poell and Tijmensen (1998) express two more criticisms. For one thing, although workers get more room to organize their own learning, this can also have a negative impact. Not all workers are able or willing to find their own learning route, especially if it means the everyday learning activities they undertake by themselves are ignored or undervalued. The learning organization asks a lot from its workers:

- the willingness to learn continuously;
- the need to be innovative and engaged in double-loop learning on a permanent basis;
- the responsibility for their own development;
- the ability to learn together with colleagues.

The last point of criticism refers to the highly internal orientation of the concept of the learning organization. It is all about the workers, the managers and the training consultants. The external orientation is restricted to market developments and clients. External influences such as government policies, union pressure or advances in the professional field are hardly taken into consideration, even though they have considerable impact on learning issues.

An alternative view of the learning organization

Poell, Tijmensen and Van der Krogt (1997) present an alternative concept of the learning organization in response to the criticisms they have raised. It focuses on multifaceted learning and work arrangements (not only group learning in multi-functional teams) and enabling people to handle tensions they encounter in everyday work life (not only developing shared values). Tensions arise because there are always several actors within and outside the organization who want to impact on the way learning and work are organized. In order to create learning and work arrangements in which all of them can participate effectively, it is important:

- to deal with the autonomy and empowerment of individual employees;
- to provide a clear policy and direction;
- to allow participation and learning in groups, emphasizing shared understanding and reflection;
- to take into account the professional field in which new methods and insights are developed.

A learning organization should explicitly address the relationship between learning and work, and provide people with possibilities to connect the two in multiple ways. Although the two case studies presented offer some examples of how this could be achieved, the organizations involved did not really pay much attention to explicitly relating learning to work. There is still significant room for progress in this area.

CONCLUSION

Although there are many definitions of the learning organization concept in the literature, most of them emphasize notions like shared vision, shared values, collective learning, continuous improvement, making tacit knowledge explicit, and entering into dialogue. As is the case in the popular ideas on communities of practice, issues like conflict, power or interests are less often addressed, even though they should be at the heart of a discussion about learning organizations (Van der Krogt, 1998). The reason why those elements are neglected seems to stem from the managerial perspective that is generally applied. When managers want their company to become a learning organization, it is assumed every member in the organization can be convinced this is needed. But workers can have very different ideas about how to improve their situation, and training consultants may not necessarily agree with the strategy set out by the management. Besides, stressing the idea of a learning organization ignores the wealth of learning that is usually already going on, albeit unrecognized, when people are at work (Poell, 1998).

A model of an organization as an arena in which different actors strive to pursue individual as well as collective interests informs an alternative image of the learning organization. The focus is not on developing shared values, but rather on equipping people to cope with the tensions they experience in everyday organizational life. Tensions and conflicts arise from legitimate differences in interests and power between managers, workers, training consultants and other (also external) actors. People need direction and guidance, but they also need the right amount of autonomy and independence. They need to learn how to cooperate with their colleagues, but they also need to keep up with professional developments. They have their own ideas of what they should learn and how they should learn it, but other people will probably think differently about these issues. These are the tensions people face on a regular basis. A learning organization allows them to resolve these issues satisfactorily.

The following questions can be asked when reasoning from this alternative view of the learning organization. They may help to identify already existing elements of a learning organization on which to base further initiatives.

- What learning is already going on? For instance, how do people solve problems they encounter in their work? Or which individual or private learning efforts may have an organizational spin-off?
- Who organizes learning? Besides trainers and consultants, what learning initiatives have managers and workers already taken? Are there any outside influences on the corporate learning system (such as from government bodies, trade unions or professional associations?
- How do people cope with tensions in organizing learning? How are conflicts resolved? Who is a dominant influence on what learning goes on? How do other organizational members exert their influence?

If organizational learning starts from individual learning, and with most authors I believe it does, all individuals in an organization have a right to be taken seriously in what they learn and how they go about learning it. An awareness of the current situation in the corporate learning system is a starting point from which a true learning organization can arise. As the two case studies show, a learning organization cannot be implemented in one go, it can only grow incrementally out of investigation, experiment and evaluation.

Bibliography

Contu, A, Grey, C and Örtenblad, A (2003) 'Against learning', *Human Relations*, **56**, 8, pp 931–52

European Commission (1996) *White Paper on Education and Training: Teaching and learning: Towards the learning society*, Luxemburg, Office for Official Publications of the European Communities

Garratt, B (1995) 'An old idea that has come of age', *People Management*, **1**, 19, pp 25–29

Hodgkinson, M (2000) 'Managerial perceptions of barriers to becoming a "learning organization"', *The Learning Organization*, **7**, 3–4, pp 156–66

Hodgkinson, M (2002) 'A shared strategic vision: dream or reality?', *The Learning Organization*, **9**, 2, pp 89–95

Lave, J, and Wenger, E (1991) *Situated Learning: Legitimate peripheral participation*, New York, Cambridge University Press

McCarthy, D (1997) 'A critical analysis of the learning organisation concept with a view to establishing a framework for assessment and action', MEd dissertation, University of Sheffield

McDermott, R (1999) 'Knowledge management: why information technology inspired but cannot deliver knowledge management', *California Management Review*, **41**, 4, pp 103–17

Mintzberg, H (1979) *The Structuring of Organizations*, Englewood Cliffs, NJ, Prentice-Hall

Mumford, A (1995) *Learning at the Top*, London, McGraw-Hill

Nonaka, I, and Takeuchi, H (1995) *The Knowledge-Creating Company: How Japanese companies create the dynamics of innovation*, Oxford, Oxford University Press

Örtenblad, A (2001) 'On differences between organizational learning and learning organization', *The Learning Organization*, **8**, 3–4, pp 125–33

Örtenblad, A (2004) 'Toward a contingency model of how to choose the right type of learning organization', *Human Resource Development Quarterly*, **15**, 3, pp 347–50

Pedler, M, and Aspinwall, K (1996) *'Perfect plc'? The purpose and practice of organizational learning*, London. McGraw-Hill

Pedler, M, Burgoyne, J, and Boydell, T (1989) 'Towards the learning company', *Management Education and Development*, **20**, 1, pp 1–8

Pedler, M, Burgoyne, J, and Boydell, T (1991) *The Learning Company: A strategy for sustainable development*, London, McGraw-Hill

Pedler, M, Burgoyne, J, and Boydell, T (1997) *The Learning Company: A strategy for sustainable development*, 2nd edn, London, McGraw-Hill

Poell, R F (1998) 'Organizing work-related learning projects: a network approach', PhD thesis, University of Nijmegen, Netherlands

Poell, R F and Tijmensen, E C M (1998) 'Using learning projects to work towards a learning organisation: two cases from professional work', in R F Poell and G E Chivers (eds), *Continuing Professional Development in Europe: Theoretical views, fields of application, and national policies*, Sheffield, University of Sheffield, pp 43–57

Poell, R F, Tijmensen, E C M and Van der Krogt, F J (1997) 'Can learning projects contribute to develop a learning organisation?', *Lifelong Learning in Europe*, **2**, 2, pp 67–75

Senge, P M (1990) *The Fifth Discipline: The art and practice of the learning organization*, London, Century Business

Swieringa, J and Wierdsma, A (1994) *Becoming a Learning Organization: Beyond the learning curve*, Wokingham, Addison-Wesley

Tjepkema, S (2003) 'The learning infrastructure of self-managing work teams', PhD thesis, Twente University, Netherlands

Van der Krogt, F J (1998) 'Learning network theory: the tension between learning systems and work systems in organizations', *Human Resource Development Quarterly*, **9**, 2, pp 157–77

Watkins, K E and Marsick, V J (1993) *Sculpting the Learning Organisation: Lessons in the art and science of systemic change*, San Francisco, CA, Jossey-Bass

Wenger, E (1998) *Communities of Practice: Learning, meaning, and identity*, Cambridge, Cambridge University Press

Wenger, E, McDermott, R and Snyder, W (2002) *Cultivating Communities of Practice*, Boston, MA, Harvard Business School Press

7

Knowledge Management

John P Wilson and Alan Cattell

INTRODUCTION AND LEARNING OBJECTIVES

To economists there are three main forms of production: land (materials), labour and capital. However, more attention is now being given to a fourth, less tangible form: knowledge. This is increasingly prominent at the centre of the global economy, and understanding what knowledge is and managing it are vital to the success of an organization and the individuals who work within it. This importance was illustrated in 2000 in Lisbon, when European Union leaders declared that by 2010 the EU would be 'the most competitive and dynamic knowledge-based economy in the world, capable of sustaining economic growth with more and better jobs and greater social cohesion'.

The implications of this move away from physical capital to knowledge capital are significant; it may be as revolutionary as the Industrial Revolution. It took a transition of between 50 and 150 years to move from an agricultural to an industrial era. Similarly, we are now in the early stages of moving into a knowledge-based economy which may take from 10 to 50 years (Bertels and Savage, 1998).

The concept of managing knowledge or knowledge management has attracted much attention in recent years. Knowledge is not new, but over the last decade or so the concept has grown from a convergence of ideas and existing practice including:

- core competencies;
- resource-based value;

- dynamic capability;
- high-performance work organizations ;
- strategic advantage;
- the Balanced Scorecard;
- the learning organization;
- total quality management;
- business process re-engineering;
- communities of practice;
- intangible/intellectual assets.

It is the intention of this chapter to explore and provide tangible links between each of these areas. This chapter will also raise the issues of strategic and sustainable competitive advantage, surely the rationale behind the need for knowledge management in the first place.

Having read this chapter you will:

- understand the context of knowledge management and its relationship to organizational strategy and competitive advantage;
- be aware of the role of tacit and explicit knowledge;
- be able to understand the processes that link learning to knowledge creation, acquisition, capture and transfer;
- understand the part that knowledge systems have to play;
- understand the part to be played by HRD professionals in enabling the above.

DATA, INFORMATION, KNOWLEDGE AND WISDOM

A helpful way of understanding knowledge is to distinguish between data, information, knowledge and wisdom, and consider them as a pyramid (see Figure 7.1).

Data consist of images, sounds, digital transmissions and the like, which are generally context-free and difficult to understand. They have little value until they are interpreted by structuring, filtering or summarizing and then they achieve meaning. In other words they become information.

Information is not context-free and is constructed from data. Where once there was often insufficient information with which to make a decision, the world wide web has moved us to an environment with a vast repository of information available. The problem now is that people have too much information, which creates anxiety and information overload and thus impedes the ability to think (Wurman, 2001). Burton-Jones (2001:219) argued that 'Information is not the problem – understanding is. Society is drowning in information but still left thirsty for knowledge.'

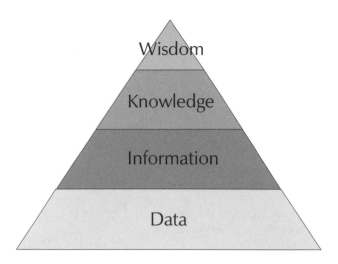

Figure 7.1 Data, information, knowledge

Knowledge differs from information in that it exists within people and is personal to them. Marchand (1998:255) stated that 'Information involves the actions of sensing, collecting, organising, processing, communicating and using expressions and representations of our or others' knowledge, whereas knowledge emphasizes personal interpreting and understanding.'

Wisdom is located at the apex of the pyramid. It is insufficient to know something: the important thing is to understand when to apply that knowledge to best advantage. When knowledge is combined with experience and intuition it is often called wisdom.

Definition

The term 'knowledge management' was first used by Wiig (1990) in a keynote address for the United Nations' International Labour Organization. Yet, although it is now widely used, there are a number of interpretations, and the closer one examines the term, the more elusive it can become. This perspective was shared by von Krogh, Ichijo and Nonaka (2000:6), who stated that 'Knowledge is one of those concepts that is extremely meaningful, positive, promising and hard to pin down.'

A similar view was held by Kluge, Stein and Licht (2001:191), who explained:

> As we have seen, simply divining a definition of the field that is acceptable to academics and practitioners alike is nearly impossible. Scholars worry too much about how many knowledge angels can fit on the head of a pin, and practitioners too often brush the field aside as the soft underbelly of management that either works or does not.

For a term to be adopted and gain common currency it must be understood and have a shared meaning which can be communicated to those who are unfamiliar with the subject. If it cannot be articulated, it cannot be understood, and therefore cannot be effectively applied. A McKinsey survey (Kluge *et al*, 2001) found that the more successful firms had a better understanding of knowledge management and the need for it to be considered holistically throughout the organization.

As a form of production, knowledge is different from land, labour and capital. It is frequently intangible and abstract, and differs in the way it operates and how it can be tracked. The branch of philosophy which deals with knowledge and knowing is called epistemology, and pinning down precisely what it means has been the subject of debates for many hundreds of years if not millennia.

A number of definitions have been offered since the term was first used:

> The focus of knowledge management is to harness and control the organization's expertise to preserve it and to put it to use in the best possible ways.
>
> (Wiig, 1990)

> Knowledge management is the explicit and systematic management of vital knowledge and its associated processes of creation, gathering, organising, diffusion, use and exploitation. It requires turning personal knowledge into corporate knowledge which can be widely shared throughout an organization and appropriately applied.
>
> (Skryme, 1997)

> Knowledge Management is to understand, focus on, and manage systematic, explicit, and deliberate building, renewal, and application ... to maximise the enterprise's knowledge-related effectiveness and returns from its knowledge assets and to renew them constantly.
>
> (Wiig, 1997:2)

> Knowledge management is ultimately about improving the processes of learning, creating and sharing meaning in organisations.
>
> (Gladstone, 2000:148)

> Knowledge is a fluid mix of framed experience, values, contextual information, and expert insight that provides a framework for evaluating and incorporating new experiences and information. It originates and is applied in the minds of knowers. In organisations, it often becomes embedded not only in documents or repositories, but also in organisational routines, processes, practices and norms.
>
> (Davenport and Prusak, 1998:5)

Drawing from the above and a number of other sources, we would suggest the following definition:

> Knowledge management is the systematic process that supports the continuous development of individual, group and organizational learning, and involves the creation, acquisition, gathering, transforming, transfer and application of knowledge to achieve organizational objectives.

KNOWLEDGE MANAGEMENT AND INFORMATION TECHNOLOGY

Early studies and models of knowledge management tended to put forward the notion that capture, codification, storage and retrieval of knowledge were the main drivers for the concept. Such thinking generally infers that information technology (IT) is the key component, and thus makes knowledge management synonymous with data management. These narrower definitions of knowledge management place less emphasis on knowledge creation, product development and incentive systems. Yet organizations that had a narrower definition were found to be less successful (Kluge *et al*, 2001).

The need for knowledge management has spurred the development of software, systems and consulting services. Knowledge databases are becoming more common, and the big consulting firms have introduced numerous related services: Accenture – Knowledge Xchange; Booz Allen and Hamilton – Knowledge on Line; Ernst and Young – Centre for Business Knowledge; KPMG Peat Marwick – Knowledge Manager; and Price Waterhouse – Knowledge View (Brinker, 2000:5).

This emphasis on information and data processing is not only insufficient to achieve a knowledge organization, but is also not new. Drucker stated that 'advanced data-processing technology isn't necessary to create an information-based organization, of course … the British built just such an organization in India when "information technology" meant the quill pen, and barefoot runners were the "telecommunications" systems' (1998:3).

A number of organizations have renamed their information technology managers as chief knowledge officers because they feel that the two roles are similar in scope. However, this ignores the human dimension. Scarborough and Swan (1999) are critical of the emphasis on technology, which can overlook the ways in which people develop, use and communicate knowledge as part of their working activity. In addition, Scarborough and Swan (2001:8) also contend that preoccupation with technology in knowledge management can be at the expense of attention being given to learning in organizations involving 'complex and intangible aspects of human behaviour'. Furthermore, Joy-Matthews, Megginson and Surtees (2004:48) maintain that one of the downsides to knowledge management is that it can be seen as an information-led warehousing approach to accumulating know-how, which often ignores the needs of knowledge workers.

Given the human aspect of knowledge management, the dynamic and potential tension between individual and organizational learning is an important consideration. What ideally is required is an approach that links the individual and the organization with learning processes, systems and technology which will benefit both in a reciprocal partnership.

COMPETITIVE ADVANTAGE

The main impetus for knowledge management is that it is seen as a provider of competitive advantage. Traditional approaches to competing have been to improve by doing things better, cheaper and faster. However, firms can also compete through doing things smarter: by creating or acquiring knowledge and then applying it.

One of the major problems with knowledge is that it has the tendency to leak from the organization. Information and communications technology (ICT) has the ability to transmit information around the world within a few seconds, so that competitive advantage becomes more visible and easier to duplicate because entry barriers in many areas become lower. Arising from globalization there are increased markets in which to sell goods and services but there is also increased competition. The result of this is that business niches may lose their exclusivity, and with increased competition there is increased pressure on prices. Many goods and services are now cheaper than they were a number of years ago.

According to Ichijo, von Krogh and Nonaka (1998) there are two main purposes of strategic management, the first of which is to maintain and support the existing competitive advantages of the organization (D'Aveni, 1995). The second purpose is to construct competitive advantage through the creation of new knowledge which can be used in the future (Hamel and Prahalad, 1994).

Maintaining competitive advantage and protecting knowledge can be secured in a number of ways:

Factors affecting the internal protection of knowledge include:

- complex knowledge;
- employees signing non-disclosure agreements;
- incentives to discourage employees from changing company;
- job design in which employees only contribute to specific sections of the production process;
- products and processes can be designed to prevent core knowledge from being accessed;
- secret recipes and processes (such as for Coca-Cola);
- tacit knowledge.

Factors affecting the external protection of knowledge include:

- copyright;
- international non-proprietary names or generic names for pharmaceutical ingredients;
- legal contracts with customers/suppliers and so on;
- patents;
- protected denomination of origin (used for goods such as Champagne and Parma ham);
- technical standards such as ISO standards;
- time to market;
- trade marks.

Many of the above means of protecting knowledge make use of legal mechanisms. However, over time organizations can partially protect their knowledge by developing strengths and skills that enable them to provide superior goods and services. The competencies that the firm develops result in an improved capability to solve problems (Prahalad and Hamel, 1990).

Other ways of protecting knowledge were suggested by Barney (1991). He proposed that strategic resource required four attributes in order to provide a sustainable competitive advantage:

- *Valuable knowledge* – the organization develops and applies strategies that improve performance, and that capitalize on opportunities or neutralize threats.
- *Rare knowledge* – an organization possesses competitive advantage through a combination of factors rather than one alone, and few competitors are able to implement this approach.
- *Imperfectly imitable knowledge* – this is where the precise content or context of knowledge is unknown to the organization or the potential competitor. Imitability frequently results from historical conditions, knowledge ambiguity and the complex social constitution of the knowledge.
- *No substitution of knowledge* – competitive advantage can also be achieved where there is no competitive substitute for the existing knowledge.

An important dimension of competitive advantage is the speed to market of a product or service, because if it is innovative or novel, there is little competition and premium charges can be used. Then when other competitors are about to come to the market the price is dropped, so competitors find it more difficult to recoup their investment. A prime example of this was the market in hand-held calculators (Ohmae, 1991).

Sharkie stated, 'An organization's success will finally depend on the speed at which it can generate, capture and disseminate knowledge and then use this knowledge to develop capabilities that cannot easily be copied by rivals' (2003:31). He proposed strategic knowledge gap analysis (2003:31) for use in identifying what organizations should do to gain strategic competitive advantage over current and future rivals. He suggested posing the following questions:

- What knowledge must the organization have to be unique and superior to others? How does this compare with the knowledge (particularly embedded tacit knowledge) it actually has?
- What needs to be done to eliminate any gaps? For example, the organization could establish an enabling context to encourage individuals to share their tacit knowledge with others in order to create new knowledge.
- What explicit knowledge appears to be available to rivals but not to the organization? How can the organization acquire it?
- Does the organization have an excess of knowledge in comparison with its knowledge need?
- How does the organization leverage its knowledge to its benefit?

One major source of competitive advantage that it is difficult to imitate is tacit knowledge. This can provide significant benefits as Burton-Jones (2001:31) explained:

> Only tacit knowledge, whether alone or in conjunction with explicit knowledge, can give a firm a sustainable competitive advantage. Such knowledge is always associated with people, whereas explicit knowledge is generally capable of being stored, processed, and communicated using (widely available) technologies.

EXPLICIT AND TACIT KNOWLEDGE

One major perspective for considering knowledge is whether it is explicit or tacit. The word 'explicit' means open, and 'tacit' means 'implied or understood without being stated' (Oxford English Dictionary). It is taken from the Latin *tacitus* meaning silent. The term 'tacit' was initially explored by Polanyi, who emphasized that much of our knowledge is unvoiced and is rarely consciously considered. He stated that:

> …we can know more than we can tell. This fact seems obvious enough; but it is not easy to say exactly what it means. Take an example. We know a person's face, and can recognize it among a thousand indeed a million. Yet we usually cannot tell how we recognize a face we know. So most of this knowledge cannot be put into words.
>
> (Polanyi 1967:4)

The explicit and tacit dimensions were explored in detail by Nonaka and Takeuchi (1995). Nonaka maintained that:

> Tacit knowledge consists partly of technical skills the kind of informal, hard-to-pin-down skills captured in the term 'know-how.' A master craftsman after years of experience develops a wealth of expertise 'at his fingertips'. But he is often unable to articulate the scientific or technical principles behind what he knows.
>
> At the same time, tacit knowledge has an important cognitive dimension. It consists of mental models, beliefs, and perspectives so ingrained that we take them for granted, and therefore cannot easily articulate them. For this very reason, these implicit models profoundly shape how we perceive the world around us.
>
> (Nonaka 1998:28)

A good example of tacit knowledge is the Stradivarius violin, which commands a high price because of its superior sound. Even with all the technology at our disposal it is still difficult to achieve a similar sound.

Nonaka also described the distinction between explicit and tacit:

> Explicit knowledge is formal and systematic. For this reason it can be easily communicated and shared in product specifications, scientific formula or a computer programme.… Tacit knowledge is highly personal, it is hard to formalize and therefore difficult if not impossible to communicate.
>
> (Nonaka 1998: 27)

The distinctions between tacit and explicit knowledge are summarized in Table 7.1.

A firm can be conceptualized as a social community that specializes in the *creation and transfer of knowledge* (Kogal and Zander, 1999). In *The Knowledge Creating Company*, Nonaka and Takeuchi (1995) proposed four ways of creating knowledge in an organization:

- *From tacit to tacit (socialization)* – a master sharing knowledge with an apprentice. Nonaka suggested that this is a form of 'socialization' which is a limited form of knowledge since

Table 7.1 Key elements of tacit and explicit knowledge

Tacit	Explicit
Personal	Codified
Private	Shared
Exists in people's minds	Available to everyone
Unique	Systematic
Hard to formalize	Formal
Difficult to communicate	Articulated and communicable
Generated through experience	Captured
Acquired on the job	
Unarticulated mental models held by an individual	
Specific to particular contexts	
Can develop through social learning and socialization processes	

neither the master nor the apprentice have a full understanding of their craft knowledge. Moreover this knowledge cannot be shared easily throughout the organization.

- *From tacit to explicit (articulation)* – people often internalize what they do and how they operate. When they can articulate their tacit knowledge, it can be communicated to others.
- *From explicit to explicit (combination)* – in this case a person can combine different pieces of explicit knowledge. For example a finance director combines various sources of financial information in a financial report.
- *From explicit to tacit (internalization)* – as explicit knowledge is shared throughout an organization it becomes internalized and so becomes tacit.

These stages from *socialization* to *articulation* to *combination* to *internalization* are in effect a spiral of knowledge, which in a successful learning organization should be a continuous and reinforcing process.

DIMENSIONS OF KNOWLEDGE

The distinction between explicit and tacit knowledge is a useful way of dissecting the subject. However, in reality the different aspects of knowledge are much more complicated than can be summarized with a bipolar division. To provide more insights into the operation of knowledge management, Kluge *et al* (2001) investigated 40 companies and identified six dimensions of knowledge which made it different from the other factors of production. Knowledge is:

- subjective;
- transferable;

- embedded;
- self-reinforcing;
- perishable;
- spontaneous.

Another dimension of knowledge involves economies of scale. Traditionally, in the businesses of agriculture and manufacturing, increases in the scale of operation enabled unit costs to be decreased. For example, small car plants are generally less productive and have higher costs associated with them than do larger ones. The same is not always true for knowledge. ICT has enabled demassification and allowed labour resources to be distributed more widely, so that workers do not always have to be working physically alongside each other. A classic example of people working separately towards a common purpose is Linux operating software. Similarly, an individual student does not always need to attend lectures together with many other students as a result of e-learning (see Chapter 17).

A further categorization of knowledge types was identified by Blackler, Crump and McDonald (1998), who described it as:

- Embodied – this knowledge is action-oriented and is only partly explicit. It is a form of know-how which is illustrated by an expert craftsperson.
- Embedded – this is knowledge that exists within systems and routines. These are the organizational competencies and mechanisms that the organization uses to ensure smooth interaction between individuals and parts of the organization.
- Embrained – this is the knowledge based on cognitive abilities and conceptual skills, which can develop into rules and causations.
- Encultured – this comprises the shared understandings and cultural meanings that people have within the organization.
- Encoded – this is the knowledge captured in books, operating manuals and information systems.

We have considered a number of the many dimensions of knowledge in this section, and these illustrate the complexity involved with managing knowledge. An organization that wishes to be successful needs to give full consideration to these, as Blackler *et al* stated: 'Knowledge is multifaceted. It is both explicit and implicit, abstract and situated, individual and collective, encoded and verbal, mental and physical, and static and developing … all organizations depend upon all forms of knowledge' (1998: 74).

THE KNOWLEDGE MANAGEMENT PROCESS

Knowledge management can be divided into a number of stages, as Figure 7.2 illustrates. These individual elements will now be discussed in further detail:

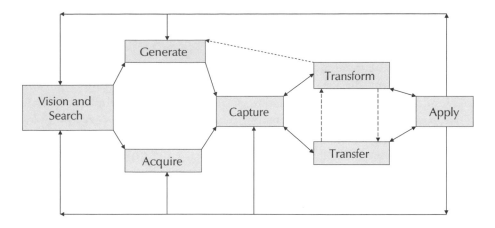

Figure 7.2 The knowledge management process

Vision and search

Probably the main driver for a commercial organization is the desire to earn income and generate profit. Without these the firm would not survive for long, and red ink on the accounts would have the shareholders demanding action. In addition to this very powerful driver of profit, there are also the inner motivations of the owners, managers and employees of the organization. In like manner, public and not-for-profit organizations also have objectives for their services and products, which are based on a vision and values. Bertels and Savage (1998:10) stated that:

> Our aspirations are also very important. Our aspirations are rooted in our deep values. They are the things for which we have passion. They are the energy sources of our actions. They are the drives for innovation, creativity and excellence. They point us to the future and its possibilities.

Generating knowledge

Encouraging the generation or acquisition of knowledge is the lifeblood of a commercial organization, and it can occur in many forms. Arguably, knowledge is created each time employees share their knowledge with others, or a person reads or understands something for the first time. There are numerous approaches to the generation of knowledge, and a range of these will now be considered:

Research and development (R&D)

Much R&D activity is premised on the solution of a particular problem, such as identifying a cure for cancer or solving energy shortages. Of course not all research is targeted at a particular application: some of it is pure science or 'blue sky' research. When breakthroughs occur, there might then be a search for a problem to be solved with the help of the new knowledge. However, it may be many years before a particular discovery finds a suitable application.

Knowledge can also be generated inadvertently. The serendipity element occurs when a person or scientist is searching for one thing and discovers something different. Examples are Alexander Fleming's discovery of penicillin growing in a Petri dish, and Harry Brearley observing that some scrap metal was not rusting, which led to the discovery of stainless steel.

If an organization has an R&D department, this is an obvious area to look for the generation of new knowledge. However, it should not be considered the only place to find innovative capacity. The potential for innovation is high for all employees in their work practices, and it is only through the whole organization seeking alternative ways of working that there can be continuous improvement.

Employees as a source of knowledge

The generation of ideas and knowledge can be encouraged in a wide variety of ways, including laboratory and desk research, think tanks, the Delphi technique, creative friction, devil's advocate, ideas contests, suggestion boxes and brainstorming. The Japanese approach to knowledge creation was described by Nonaka (1998:24). He maintained that it was not just the processing of objective information. More importantly it involved 'tapping the tacit and often highly subjective insights, intuitions, and hunches of individual employees and making those insights available for testing and use by the company as a whole.'

Suppliers and customers

No organization operates in a vacuum, since it is designed to provide a product or service for the benefit of its stakeholders or customers. Moreover it also interacts with its suppliers, and together with customers these constitute the supply chain. If the organization consults with customers, areas for improved performance may be identified, or even new markets. Likewise, interaction with suppliers can provide new ideas, processes, technology and so on, which can raise productivity and effectiveness. The integration of the supply chain increases interaction between individuals and groups, providing the opportunity to share information and knowledge.

Systematic creativity

Systems and processes in an organization are often regarded as the kiss of death to encouraging creativity, but this need not be the case. Without a system, the generation of ideas and applications can be lost or forgotten. Furthermore, creativity is very important in the early stages of product development; however, it can be a hindrance if it occurs too often further down the production process. With systems, ideas can be brought to market more quickly, and they limit the perishable nature of the knowledge.

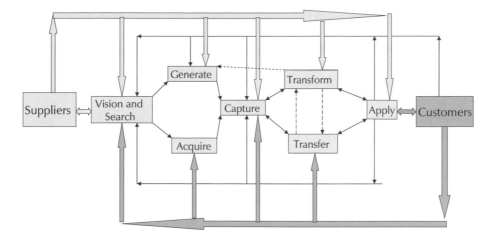

Figure 7.3 The knowledge management supply chain

Diversity

In order to maintain company values and also avoid personal disputes, managers sometimes recruit people with similar dispositions. This may bring short-term harmony but unfortunately it may cause a form of inbreeding which causes people to think in the same way. There is no doubt that having focus is a valuable trait, but it also brings a narrowed vision, which may prevent innovation arising as a result of wider and more encompassing perspectives.

Of course, employing people who think in different ways may cause disputes between, for example, the visionary and the detail person, or the person-oriented employee and the task-oriented person. Yet if it is carefully handled, this creative friction has much potential for encouraging new and innovative ideas and solutions.

Culture

The pursuit of new knowledge and innovation is the essence of organizations (Nonaka, 1998), and for this to be achieved successfully, it requires an environment that is supportive and nurturing. Achieving this is not easy, since it is simpler to manage knowledge of technology or products than to manage knowledge at a human and cultural level, because this latter kind of knowledge is much deeper.

One way of embedding a culture is to have key values that are widely understood and respected within the organization. These need to be communicated regularly and employed by all employees so that they become embodied in creative action. There should be more investigation into the process that supports knowledge and resources for sustainable competitive advantage. This development was termed 'creational knowledge' by Nonaka (1998); however, Ichijo *et al* (1998:175) stated that this knowledge development 'is a highly fragile and subtle process fraught with complexity and uncertainty.'

Knowledge acquisition

There are many examples of organizations that no longer exist, or have failed to anticipate changes in their markets and now hold only a small percentage of their former market share. It could be argued that much of the knowledge that might have prevented these things from happening was already out there; the challenge was to find it.

We do not have to invent new ideas or solutions. It may be possible to purchase, lease, license or share knowledge, or acquire or merge with another organization. Some of these solutions are often much cheaper than generating new knowledge: it is often cheaper to imitate than to innovate.

Another way is to search for other organizations or individuals who have faced the same problem and to copy or, less ethically, steal the idea from them. Michael Milliken, the junk bond king, suggested, 'Steal ideas shamelessly.'

Capture

Knowledge generated in an organization can be lost if it is not captured and stored in some form: for example electronically, in text or in prototypes. This particularly occurs during human interactions, when the solution to a problem might be found but then not acted on for a variety of reasons. Its importance might not be recognized; it might not be timely; or might not be relevant in comparison with other more pressing matters.

As was explained in the section on explicit and tacit knowledge, it is explicit knowledge that is relatively easy to capture and store. Tacit knowledge is much more difficult to identify and codify in order to make it more secure. Storing knowledge also allows its use at some time in the future, assuming that it has not reached its sell-by-date.

Transformation

Knowledge can be generated by compiling or recombining information in new forms. We have already mentioned how an accountant can gather financial data from a number of sources and combine it to provide new and more explanatory facts in financial reports. Other approaches to transforming existing information or knowledge can be through integration, synthesis, fusion and adaptation.

Knowledge transfer

The generation of knowledge in an organization is important, but without transmission its impact can remain minimal. For this reason knowledge and ideas have their greatest value and effect when they are shared and held by a large number of people rather than just a few. Thus knowledge transfer is a necessary component of the knowledge management process, and it can occur in a variety of ways and be dependent on a range of factors for success.

One means of accessing knowledge is to be part of a network. According to Robert Metcalf's principle of networks, the value of a network increases exponentially in proportion to the square of the number of nodes in the network. Yet as the number of points in the network increases, there is also the potential for the reverse to happen, as it becomes too large and unwieldy, thereby inhibiting the transfer of knowledge.

A balance needs to be achieved between connectedness, the number of people involved, and the nature of the knowledge. Increasing the size of a network can be a useful mechanism, but in a global organization using different languages there are added obstacles. In general, people are more likely to share with people local to them, making it better to network regionally than globally. Proximity increases the chances of interaction between employees, which in turn increase the opportunities to share information. Chance encounters around the water cooler, or at coffee or lunch breaks, raise the number of opportunities for information to be shared and new knowledge to be created.

In general there are three levels of knowledge transfer:

- to or from the individual;
- to or from groups;
- to or from the organization.

Thus one of the main purposes of knowledge management is to support the transfer of knowledge between the three levels. Mechanisms for transfer include written reports, oral presentations, site visits, tours, job rotation, education and training programmes, coaching and mentoring, conferences, business plans, cross-functional teams rather than functional teams, databases, intranets, job descriptions, work manuals, meetings, communities of practice and matrix working.

One of Siemens' responses to sharing knowledge was 'ShareNet', a form of groupware which enabled employees to identify sources, share, and also ask for advice and support. In this way local explicit and tacit learning could be transferred at minimal cost throughout its worldwide operations. Gibbert, Jonczyk and Völpel described the competitive dimension of this process: 'This implied identifying best practices quickly, sharing them on a global scale, and ensuring that they were reused for profit in similar settings. The objective was to detect local innovations and leverage them on a global scale' (2000:27).

In Siemens (Gibbert and Krause, 2000:74) six factors were identified as being necessary for the successful sharing of best practice:

- Connecting people: developing employee networks among best-practice owners.
- Exchanging best practice – this was achieved through ICT, and the person who provided the best practice described the problem, its solution, the process of solution, critical success factors, the costs involved and the results.
- Relying on management commitment.
- Mobilizing employees: incentives, rewards and recognition.
- Designing a content structure: drawing a best-practice landscape.
- Energizing support: facilitators and 'best-practice office'.

Knowledge transfer can also be encouraged through 'communities of practice', which develop a shared identity and a base of common knowledge. To develop a community of practice a number of roles were identified in Siemens:

- an initiator;
- sponsor;
- moderator/manager;
- members;
- support;
- external knowledge carriers.

Trust

The benefits of knowledge transfer have been discussed above, but there are also associated dangers. At the individual level there is the fear that if we transfer our knowledge, we might make ourselves dispensable. Zhou and Fink (2003) suggested that people tend to hide knowledge for their own advantage because they are afraid that it diminishes in value if they share it with colleagues. A colleague described how his father worked as an electrician in a major dockyard. When asked if he was worried about the redundancies facing the dockyard, he explained that he had an insurance policy to avoid redundancy; then he produced a little black book. It contained all the details of the wiring systems that had been put into the works over the past 25 years. He was the only one who knew where the wiring went!

In like manner, there is also the danger of outsourcing. Recently, another colleague described how her partner's company had made 75 per cent of the employees redundant because it was offshoring operations to India. The responsibility of most of the remaining staff was to write up all the systems so that they could be used from India. In essence, they were writing their own post-dated letters of resignation, because there would come a day when their knowledge would not be needed.

The motivation to contribute knowledge is an intangible key success factor for any knowledge management activity (Davenport, De Long and Beers, 1998). Yet for this to happen there needs to be a degree of trust between the individual and the organization as part of the psychological contract.

Knowledge transfer can also present dangers at organizational level. Where there is a closely integrated supply chain the suppliers may gain such a good understanding that they become able to cut out the intermediary – their customer – and deal directly with the end user. Similarly, where partnerships and joint ventures are in operation, there can be a fear of losing knowledge to other partners in the supply chain, or to competitors, because of the high degree of integration.

Research by the CIPD and Barron (2004) acknowledged that the first dilemma of knowledge management is between retention and employability. Individuals want employability, and for knowledge workers this means being in possession of up-to-date skills and competencies which will make them attractive to employers. Managers, however, have the dilemma between wanting to retain talent, and offering development and career progression that ties people into a career with the organization, while also being wary of offering development that might make employees too attractive to the opposition.

The second dilemma is between the employer's wish to develop organization-specific skills and the individual's desire for transferable knowledge. A balance needs to be found between the needs of both parties.

The final dilemma relates to appropriation of value. Organizations want to take their employees' knowledge and skills and incorporate them into products and services which can be sold for a profit. On the other hand, knowledge workers want to hold on to as much of their value as possible to ensure that they can trade this at the highest rate on the employment market.

This suggests that organizations would be wise to concentrate on long-term motivational approaches, and incorporate the extent of knowledge contribution as part of the performance management, compensation and rewards structure.

HRM and HRD professionals therefore need to take account of the dynamics of the employment relationship or psychological contract in considering any enabling intervention and strategy to ensure knowledge creation, transfer and retention. Scarborough and Swan (1999) argued that effective knowledge management required supportive human resource management policies, concerning rewards and trust in particular. Francis Bacon (1561–1626), in his *Religious Meditations*, said that, 'Knowledge itself is power.' If this is the case, why should we share it?

Application

Creation of new knowledge is not an end in itself, since it possesses little value unless it is applied. Organizations can tend to hoard this knowledge just in case there is a need for it in the future. However, we could consider knowledge from the perspective of just in time: that is, the knowledge is there at the time it is required. A more significant problem is that less important knowledge can 'drown out' more important knowledge, which then becomes lost to the organization and therefore has little value. Sometimes a number of solutions may be identified for a particular problem, which can lead to their being reviewed and specific ones being selected based on cost, suitability and so on.

Some knowledge can also be stored and used at some future time. Alternatively, if the knowledge does not fit with the direction of the organization it can be licensed, sold or perhaps spun out.

The application of knowledge is everything, as John Ruskin (1819–1900), the naturalist and reformer, said. 'What we think, or what we know, or what we believe is, in the end, of little consequence. The only consequence is what we do.'

LEARNING AND KNOWLEDGE MANAGEMENT

Knowledge can be stored and transferred within an organization, but it is only when it is utilized by individual people that its potential is realized. Providing employees with new information and encouraging them to take responsibility for their own learning creates opportunities for the generation of ideas. Furthermore, the transplanting of information and knowledge through training and guidance from those who know creates new knowledge in the brains of those who don't.

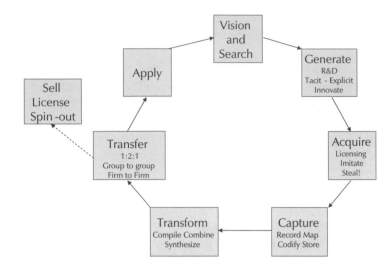

Figure 7.4   The knowledge management cycle

For new ideas to emerge from activities throughout an organization requires a climate and processes where learning is designed into activities and given priority (Mumford, 2001). Inevitably, this means that managers must delve more deeply into the process of how knowledge is produced within local contexts. According to Garvey and Williamson (2002), organizations that learn new ways of doing things become more knowledge-productive.

Learning from corporate history and failure is also an important element in the success of an organization. Kleiner and Roth (1998) suggested that organizations should learn from experience, so that when mistakes are made they should be reviewed rather than quickly moving on. In effect this is reflective practice and action learning. Kleiner and Roth went on to make the salient point that, 'In corporate life, even when experience is a good teacher, it's still only a private tutor. People in organizations act collectively, but they learn individually' (1998:139).

IMPLEMENTING KNOWLEDGE MANAGEMENT

Implementing knowledge management is not always an easy process. Bertels and Savage (1998) refer to Otto Neurath's metaphor of sailors out at sea who are trying to reconstruct their ship from the bottom without putting into harbour. They only have the existing timber and some driftwood, and have to transform the old structure and deal with the associated problems and storms as they happen. Similarly, Siemens have suggested that changing an organization into an e-business is like changing the tyres of a car while driving. Others have described it as like building the car from scratch while driving at full speed.

From research into successful knowledge organizations, Kluge *et al* identified two main development strategies. The first was a push mechanism involving policies such as databases, training and changing organizational structure. The pull strategies involved encouraging employees to seek out knowledge for themselves. Significantly, Kluge *et al*'s (2001:189) survey of knowledge management in companies 'showed that many companies can talk the talk, but few can walk the walk'.

Siemens Business Services (Ramhorst, 2000) identified 10 components in the implementation of a knowledge management framework:

- *Knowledge management and business strategy* – knowledge management needs to be clearly integrated with business strategy. Knowledge was specifically described as a corporate asset.
- *Knowledge culture and organization* – the most important elements in ensuring the successful introduction of knowledge management are the corporate culture and values of the organization. In particular the values of sharing and trust need to be strongly embedded.
- *The market principle* – Siemens constructed an internal market for providers and users of knowledge. Providers were given incentives to share knowledge, such as a frequent flyer scheme.
- *A knowledge broker* – this is the person who is the access point for the organization and who stores and manages the information, coordinates, monitors the findings of expert fora, acts as a change agent, and introduces new functions.
- *Goods available in the marketplace* – both implicit and explicit knowledge are traded, which raises the question of how implicit knowledge can be traded. Implicit knowledge consists of competencies, and these skills are traded by linking the group needing the skill with the individual who possesses it. Knowledge goods include architectures, business frameworks, case studies, checklists, methodologies, practice guides and templates.
- *Knowledge maps* – these are visual displays of knowledge flow and competency networks within the organization which enable the communities of practice to operate.
- *Knowledge measurement and knowledge management metrics* – these measure the return on investment of knowledge management projects and the management of intellectual capital through the use of Balanced Scorecards.
- *Knowledge processes* – knowledge management practices within corporate processes were investigated and expanded in many cases by Siemens. For example, a debriefing stage, initiated by the knowledge broker, was added to the project delivery process in order to capture the learning that had occurred.
- *Knowledge workers* – in addition to the knowledge broker, other roles were developed within the communities of practice. Each community developed a best-practice team of subject matter experts, a community leader and a technical editor. This team assessed the business value and determined the stage in the lifecycle of the knowledge assets.
- *The role of technology*. Changing the culture of an organization can take a long time. However, introducing an intranet-based knowledge instrument can occur much more quickly, and can facilitate interaction between the holders and users of knowledge. Siemens Business Services used knowledge libraries, knowledge mapping and communities of practice, all of which were linked together by knowledge flow applications which included e-mail, newsboards and workflows.

In essence, the implementation of knowledge management systems typically falls into the following broad areas:

- *Knowledge databases and repositories* (explicit knowledge) – storing information and documents that can be shared and reused, such as client presentations, customer data, marketing materials, minutes of meetings, policy documents, price lists, product specifications, project proposals, research reports and training packs.
- *Knowledge routemaps and directories* (tacit and explicit knowledge) – pointing to and identifying people, document collections and datasets that can be consulted, such as 'yellow pages', 'expert locators' containing CVs, competency profiles, research interests and knowledge maps.
- *Knowledge networks* (tacit knowledge) – providing opportunities for face-to-face contacts and electronic interaction, such as established chat facilities/talk rooms, e-learning discussion fora, learning groups, holding best-practice sessions, knowledge brokers and multifunctional project teams.

A quick test to see if knowledge management is working well within the organization was proposed by Kluge *et al* (2001:196), who asked, 'Has your company had a knowledge breakthrough recently, for instance an improved process, better market understanding, or a new product or service? If you have to think about it then the answer is no.'

KNOWLEDGE WORKERS

It is now maintained that we are beginning to live in a post-capitalist society (Drucker, 1993), and that wealth generation is increasingly dependent on knowledge workers who can support competitive advantage as a result of their specialist insights. Although Drucker suggested that there had been a movement from manual and clerical workers to knowledge workers, some writers insist that we are all, in some respects, knowledge workers. Venzin, von Krogh and Roos (1998:72) argued that 'it would be a mistake to assume that only so-called "knowledge workers" or "knowledge-intensive firms" depend on knowledge. Knowledge in its various forms is an integral feature of all individuals and collectives.'

The command and control model used by the military and adopted by business approximately 100 years ago is increasingly resisted by knowledge workers (Drucker, 1998). Indeed, organizations are gradually realizing that knowledge cannot be treated as an organizational asset without the consent and voluntary participation of the owners of that knowledge, namely the employees.

Companies are also recognizing the need to manage their knowledge resources, and many have created knowledge management positions. Accenture, for example, has 'knowledge integrators' who interface with manufacturers but also perform the multiple functions of librarian, intellectual entrepreneur and programme director. Identifying the right people for the job and ensuring that they have the right skills is critical, and this role lies very close to that of the internal organizational development and learning specialist. Indeed, Liebowitz (1999:iv) stated:

Knowledge is information with a process applied to it that may eventually become wisdom or expertise. Many organisations are having their IT (information technology) directors become Chief Knowledge Officers, as top management often feels they are comparable positions. This is a mistake, because knowledge management draws from many disciplines, including IT, and it is broader in scope than the technology functions that an IT director often oversees. A new breed of knowledge officers or knowledge analysts is needed to fill the roles of knowledge managers in organisations.

CONCLUSION

We began by considering the view that we were entering a revolutionary period, moving from physical capital to knowledge capital. Wiig, who coined the term 'knowledge management', looked into the future and suggested that managing knowledge would be unlikely to disappear during the next few decades. Instead he believed that the management of knowledge would become routine, along with the tools and practices needed to support it: 'Management of these assets will have become one of the important but low profile routine activities that are vital for enterprise success' (1997:14).

Knowledge management is indeed an important change in perspective for organizations as well as for learning, organizational development and IT specialists. As with the total quality management philosophy, knowledge management is a journey not a destination, and Kluge *et al* said:

> It is wise to remember that ultimately, knowledge management is a quest for a corporate holy grail. The effort carries its own rewards, but it will obviously never be possible for anyone in the company to know everything all the time.... Just as King Arthur's knights gained personal enlightenment while seeking their Holy Grail, companies striving for knowledge management perfection will discover manifold benefits along the way. (Kluge *et al*, 2001:193)

Bibliography

Barney, J B (1991) 'Firm resources and sustained competitive advantage', *Journal of Management*, **17**, pp 99–120

Barron, A (2004) 'Getting to know those in the know', *People Management*, 15 July, p 25

Bertels, T and Savage, C M (1998) 'Tough questions on knowledge management', in G von Krogh, J Roos and D Kleine (eds), *Knowing in Firms: Understanding, managing and measuring knowledge*, London, Sage, pp 7–25

Blackler, F, Crump, N and McDonald, S (1998) 'Knowledge, organizations and competition', in G von Krogh, J Roos and D Kleine (eds), *Knowing in Firms: Understanding, managing and measuring knowledge*, London, Sage, pp 67–86

Brinker, B (2000) 'Intellectual capital: tomorrow's asset, today's challenge', [Online] http://www.cpavision. org/vision/wpaper05b.cfm

Burton-Jones, A (2001) *Knowledge Capitalism: Business, work, and learning in the new economy*, Oxford, Oxford University Press

D'Aveni, R A (1995) *Hyper-Competitive Rivalries: Competing in highly dynamic environments*, New York, Free Press

Davenport, T, De Long, D and Beers, M (1998) 'Successful knowledge management projects', *Sloan Management Review*, **39**, 2, pp 43–57

Davenport, T H and Probst, G (eds) (2000) *Knowledge Management Casebook: Siemens best practices*, Munich, Publicis MCD Verlag/Wiley

Davenport, T H and Prusak, L (1998:5) *Working Knowledge: How organizations manage what they know*, Boston, MA, Harvard Business School Press

Drucker, P (1993) *Post-Capitalist Society*, Oxford, Butterworth-Heinemann

Drucker, P (1998) 'The coming of the new organization', *Harvard Business Review on Knowledge Management*, Boston, MA, Harvard Business School Press, pp 1–19

Garvey, B and Williamson, B (2002) *Beyond Knowledge Management*, Harlow, Pearson Education

Garvin, D A (1994) 'Building a learning organisation', *Business Credit*, **96**, 1, January, pp 19–28

Gibbert, M, Jonczyk, C and Völpel, S (2000) 'ShareNet – the next generation knowledge management', in T H Davenport and G Probst (eds), *Knowledge Management Casebook: Siemens best practices*, Munich, Publicis MCD Verlag/Wiley, pp 22–39

Gibbert, M and Krause, H (2000) 'Practice exchange in a best practice marketplace', in T H Davenport and G Probst (eds), *Knowledge Management Casebook: Siemens best practices*, Munich, Publicis MCD Verlag/Wiley, pp 68–84

Gladstone, B (2000) *From Know-How to Knowledge*, London, Industrial Society

Hamel, G and Prahalad, C K (1994) *Competing for the Future*, Cambridge, MA, Harvard Business School Press

Ichijo, K, von Krogh, G and Nonaka, I (1998) 'Knowledge enablers', in G von Krogh, J Roos and D Kleine (eds), *Knowing in Firms: Understanding, managing and measuring knowledge*, London, Sage, pp 173–203

Joy-Matthews, J, Megginson, D and Surtees, M (2004) *Human Resource Development*, London, Kogan Page

Kleiner, A and Roth, G (1998) 'How to make experience your company's best teacher', *Harvard Business Review on Knowledge Management*, Boston, MA, Harvard Business School Press, pp 137–51

Kluge, J, Stein, W and Licht, T (2001) *Knowledge Unplugged: The McKinsey & Company global survey on knowledge management*, Basingstoke, Palgrave

Kogal, B and Zander U (1999) 'Knowledge of the firm and the evolutionary theory of the multinational corporation', *Journal of Intellectual Business Studies*, **24**, pp 625–45

Liebowitz, J (1999) *Knowledge Management Handbook*, Boca Raton, FL, CRC Press

Marchand, D A (1998) 'Competing with intellectual capital', in G von Krogh, J Roos and D Kleine (eds), *Knowing in Firms: Understanding, managing and measuring knowledge*, London, Sage, pp 253–68

Mumford, A (2001) 'A learning approach to strategy', *Journal of Workplace Learning*, **12**, 2, pp 265–71

Nonaka, I (1998) 'The knowledge creating company', *Harvard Business Review on Knowledge Management*, Boston, MA, Harvard Business School Press, pp 21–45

Nonaka, I and Takeuchi, H (1995) *The Knowledge Creating Company: How Japanese companies create the dynamics of innovation*, New York, Oxford University Press

Ohmae, K (1991) *The Mind of the Strategist: The art of Japanese business*, New York, McGraw-Hill Educational

Polanyi, M (1967) *The Tacit Dimension*, London, Routledge and Kegan Paul

Prahalad, C K and Hamel, G (1990) 'The competence of the corporation', *Harvard Business Review*, **68**, May/June, pp 79–91

Ramhorst, D (2000) 'A guided tour through the Siemens Business Services knowledge management framework', in T H Davenport and G Probst (eds), *Knowledge Management Casebook: Siemens best practices*, Munich, Publicis MCD Verlag/Wiley, pp 126–40

Scarborough, H and Swan, J (1999) *Case Studies in Knowledge Management*, London, Institute of Personnel and Development

Scarborough, H and Swan, J (2001) 'Explaining the diffusion of knowledge management: the role of fashion', *British Journal of Management*, **12**, 1, pp 3–12

Sharkie, R (2003) 'Knowledge creation and its place in the development of sustainable competitive advantage', *Journal of Knowledge Management*, **7**, 1, pp 20–31

Skryme, D (1997) 'Knowledge management: making sense of oxymoron', *Management Insight*, 2nd Series, No 2 [Online] http://www.skryme.com/insights/22km.htm

Venzin, M, von Krogh, G and Roos, J (1998) 'Future research into knowledge management', in G von Krogh, J Roos and D Kleine (eds), *Knowing in Firms: Understanding, managing and measuring knowledge*, London, Sage, pp 26–66

von Krogh, G, Ichijo, K and Nonaka, I (2000) *Enabling Knowledge Creation: How to unlock the mystery of tacit knowledge and release the power of innovation*, New York, Oxford University Press

von Krogh, G, Roos, J and Kleine, D (1998) *Knowing in Firms: Understanding, managing and measuring knowledge*, London, Sage

Wiig, K (1990) *Expert Systems: A manager's guide*, Geneva, International Labour Organization

Wiig, K (1997) 'Knowledge management: where did it come from and where will it go?', *Journal of Expert Systems with Applications*, **13**, Fall, pp 1–14

Wurman, R S (2001) *Information Anxiety 2*, Berkeley, CA, New Riders

Zhou, S Z and Fink, D (2003) 'Intellectual capital web: a systematic linking of intellectual capital and knowledge management', *Journal of Intellectual Capital*, **4**, 1, pp 34–48

Section Three:

The Identification of Learning, Training and Development Needs

8

The Identification of Learning Needs

Richard Palmer

INTRODUCTION AND LEARNING OBJECTIVES

The third millennium offers fresh challenges to the training professional arising from the dynamic, chaotic, fiercely competitive marketplace which has replaced the relative organizational calm of 25 years ago. Moreover, not only does the leaner organization of today consist of far fewer employees but also the expectations placed upon these individuals in terms of their performance and effectiveness are much higher. This tighter focus upon individual contribution means that the identification of training and development needs has become a far more critical element in determining the organization's success.

It was Mark Twain (in *Pudd'nhead Wilson's Calendar*) who stated that, 'Training is everything. The peach was once a bitter almond; cauliflower is nothing but cabbage with a college education.' There is no doubt that training is important; the question is, what training and to what level of detail? The answer to this question lies in the critical role that learning needs analysis (LNA) plays. In this chapter we shall examine how an organization can identify those training needs which will ensure its continued existence, growth and development through the people it employs.

Having read this chapter you will:

- be able to apply LNA procedures at organizational, departmental, occupational, and individual levels;
- be able to apply various criteria in order to prioritize training and development needs;
- be able to conduct a SWOT analysis; and
- be aware of the application of job analysis techniques to training needs analysis.

DEFINING TRAINING AND DEVELOPMENT

First, we need to define what we mean by training and development. The two terms are often used synonymously. Pepper (1984:9–11) defines training as 'that organized process concerned with the acquisition of capability, or the maintenance of capability'. He goes on to distinguish the meaning of development:

> Where the objective is to acquire a set of capabilities which will equip a person to do a job some time in the predictable future, which is not within his [sic] present ability, that person is often said to undergo a process of development. Of course, straightforward job instruction, or rather job learning, is by this definition a development, but the term has become associated with longer-term and more complex arrangements for learning, often with job moves included in the plan.

For the purposes of this chapter, we shall not be far wrong to consider training as needs against present requirements. Development can be construed as relating to future requirements. For example, this could be preparation for a promotion, or for an organizational development such as the introduction of teamworking. LNA is assumed to include development issues also. As Palmer (2002:76) points out, 'Training and development are certainly not chalk and cheese. They are more Laurel and Hardy, complementary together and feeding off one another.'

The cultural context

It is important to be discerning and take into account the culture of the organization within which LNA will be used. A horticultural analogy may be useful here. Consider the nature of the employees you are tending and growing. The organization may resemble a field of wheat. It has a large number of semi-skilled employees with a limited range of skill requirements. Alternatively, it may be a mature garden with different arrangements of planting, all requiring special and different attention to be at their best. Conversely, it may be a small, chaotic, developing garden where certain plants are emerging to give a structure.

The culture and environment will therefore dictate whether there needs to be more emphasis on the training or on the development aspects, which of the tools are most appropriate, and where the predominant emphases should be laid.

Learning needs and training needs

Before considering the identification of needs, it is important to make the distinction between learning and training needs. The Cabinet Office (1988:4) defines a learning need as arising, 'when an individual or a group are required to do things differently, or to do different things'. These events arise all the time throughout any working environment and can be met informally as a part of the daily round. A training need only arises:

> when a learning need cannot be met within the normal day-to-day processes or when meeting a learning need in this way will take too long, involve too high a risk/cost, not result in the required standard of performance, and when training is the most cost-effective way of meeting the need. (Cabinet Office, 1988:4)

For the purposes of this chapter, we shall use the phrase 'learning needs analysis' to cover the spectrum of learning, training and development needs analysis.

UNDERTAKING AN LNA

It is critical that the training professional, or whoever is carrying out the analysis, has access to the most accurate and relevant information available on the organization's present performance, problems and future plans. As Kenney and Reid (1986:69) point out, 'The quality of the training can be no better than the quality of the analysis permits.' Some sources of data are shown in the subsequent section. Data collection can also take the form of questionnaires, interviews, discussions, brainstorming groups and observation.

For the purposes of this chapter, we shall consider undertaking an LNA throughout a whole organization. The prime difficulty ahead of us is the size and complexity of the task. We therefore need to break the process down into bite-size manageable chunks.

Boydell (1983) has identified three levels of training needs within organizations:

1. organizational;
2. occupational; and
3. individual level.

We shall use these three broad areas as a starting point to break down the process. A fourth area, needs at departmental level, is also a useful consideration when analysing training needs in larger organizations and is included here.

BROADENING THE SCOPE OF LNAs IN NON-GOVERNMENTAL ORGANIZATIONS IN MALI

Activities of non-governmental organizations (NGOs) are playing an important role in the development processes of Mali. These NGOs are often young local organizations without much experience and with small numbers of professionally trained personnel. Many of the NGOs are member organizations of so-called umbrella organizations, eg, CCA-ONG has 110 member NGOs. One of its principal objectives is to improve the competency of its member NGOs by training.

There was a progressive feeling of dissatisfaction among member NGOs and the umbrella organization's staff about the results and services of the training department. The general opinion was that training only partly met needs and it was decided that an evaluation of LNAs would be conducted by an external consultant in order to improve the training services.

Research was done among representatives of the most important stakeholders of the organization, ie, the member NGOs, financial donor organizations, national administrative organizations and partner organizations. The research revealed that the evaluation and improvement of the LNAs was insufficient to improve and adapt the training services to the needs of the member NGOs. Another urgently felt problem was that most of the stakeholders did not believe that the umbrella organization's training policy reflected their own views, ideas and wishes. These opinions were based on a broader analysis of the general context of the Malian social, political and economic situation. LNAs, as executed by the umbrella organization, did not analyse these important factors.

Malian NGOs are operating in a fast-developing social, political and economic context and, consequently, their role in the development process is also swiftly changing. Furthermore, the expectations of professionalism by international partners and donors were increasingly experienced as difficult to meet. Therefore, it was recommended that preceding, and supplementary to, an LNA, the development process and the stakeholders' role should be analysed regularly with all stakeholders and the umbrella organization. This analysis should be followed by a definition of the tasks of the umbrella organization including its role in training. Only after these steps are taken can a regularly executed LNA among member NGOs and other stakeholders be effective.

Research in CCA-ONG has revealed that focusing on the improvement of LNAs without considering external factors is unlikely to resolve the organization's problems, because external developments considerably influence the role of NGOs in the development process. The changing environment has an important impact on training needs. Thus, a regularly performed evaluation of the external circumstances (the development process) and of the different roles of each stakeholder in this process should be executed next to and supplementary to LNAs. These actions should be taken in close consultation with all stakeholders.

With acknowledgement to Anita Nijsten, SNV, Mali.

NEEDS AT THE ORGANIZATIONAL LEVEL

Business objectives

The starting point for an LNA has to be the corporate or business plan. Every organization has a plan. This may be bound in a general strategic statement; couched in precise business objectives; or in broad policy guidelines. In some organizations, it may not be in written form, but to survive and move forward, there is somewhere a plan, even if it is only in the head of the CEO. This is the starting point for examining learning needs.

Most well-run organizations will have a well-defined set of business objectives. Where these exist, they will normally cascade down the organization so that departments, sections and individual managers will have sub-objectives that dovetail into the business plan. These are the prime source of information in developing the LNA at this level, for here are the specific, measurable targets that the organization is committed to pursue.

For example, an organization plans to increase sales of Product A by 10 per cent over the next year. To facilitate this, a further sales manager is being recruited; telesales effort is being redirected to promote this particular product; and manufacturing is gearing up for the anticipated rise in demand. Furthermore, assemblers from a production cell that makes a product with falling demand are to be transferred to Product A cell, and marketing support are preparing new corporate brochures and materials for all field sales personnel. As a part of this, a CD is being prepared as a mailshot.

The planned increase in sales has already thrown up a myriad of learning implications. These include: induction for the new sales manager; training implications for telesales; cross-training of assemblers; briefing of marketing support in the objectives of new promotional materials; and training in the production of PC-based materials. There may also be other training implications to consider; for example, the team leaders of the two affected manufacturing departments may require new skills, and there may be further implications for other areas of the organization. Note that this organizational-level objective is causing learning needs at an organizational, departmental, occupational and individual level.

Organizational-level objectives may contain very large training implications. For example, the redirection of a corporate culture to new beginnings, take-over, or merger, will require careful consideration with regard to the associated learning needs. These will normally require a detailed analysis and a substantial commitment of training resource before they can be implemented.

As an example, consider an organization that has committed itself to move to a culture of continuous improvement. A comprehensive strategy is needed, with a phased implementation plan. Such a strategy will typically include improved communications systems, restructuring of job responsibilities, job redesign for supervisors, empowerment issues, improvements to inter-group interfaces, new alliances with suppliers, and development of group and teamworking capability. Such a major programme will generate a whole suite of training courses that may embrace every employee.

These are complex interventions that will call for an organizational development approach. They will possibly stretch over a number of years and require external consultancy expertise. As such, this scale of programme is an ongoing needs analysis in its own right.

New implementations

Another associated way of considering the objectives of the organization is to consider every-thing new that is proposed in the foreseeable future. Anything that is new will generally have a learning implication. The following is a list of considerations:

- new product;
- new process or method;
- new technology;
- new piece of equipment;
- new legislation;
- new/transferred employee;
- new procedures/standards;
- new customer/market.

All new developments involve change and the facility for mistakes or lost opportunities. The smarter organization will be reviewing the learning implications before rather than during the implementation of anything new. Having said that, the line manager may not always think this way. It is here that the training professional, in keeping an eye open for new implementations, can make a valuable input to ensure the learning need is considered at the right time.

Performance measures

The organization will be measuring itself, not only in terms of traditional financial performance indicators, but also increasingly in other areas. Corporate and departmental metrics such as accident rates, customer complaints, warranty costs and quality costs all give leads to where things are going wrong. Training professionals should ensure they are privy to these measures.

There is a need to look beyond the simple figures. Something going wrong does not neces-sarily indicate a training need. For instance, a shortfall in production in a department may have a training implication. On the other hand, it may simply be down to poor performance of a sub-supplier. In this respect some caution is necessary. A learning needs analysis is perhaps better termed a 'needs analysis'. *The needs of the organization are not necessarily training needs.* Very often, there may be process, systems or procedural issues that need addressing.

The performance gap

While all needs of an organization might not be learning needs, it is true to say that most learning needs can be thought of as arising from a gap between current performance and future desired performance – the performance gap (see Figure 8.1).

The learning needs analysis is most often concerned with this gap between current and future performance. When this occurs in a steady-state situation, it can present a scenario for

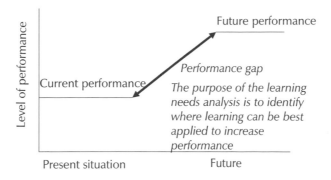

Figure 8.1 Performance gap

which it is not difficult to propose a solution. For instance, an organization is following a new marketing strategy. A comprehensive training package is rolled out to all relevant employees to explain how they will be required to operate this strategy. Everyone now understands what future performance is required of them, and can begin to work towards this. The learning need is solved. But organizational existence is not always so straightforward.

Let us imagine that within a very short space of time a new aggressive competitor enters the market. The proposed marketing strategy is swiftly made redundant. It is not clear how the organization should respond to this market threat. Future performance now becomes an unknown. It is clear that there is a severe performance gap in the market, but the organization does not have a clear solution to fixing this. The need is undefined and hence so is the learning need.

Forming a learning needs analysis will not therefore always be a straightforward process. The owner of the analysis will need to gather intelligence from as broad a range of sources as possible. Forming a strong network of contacts within the organization at different levels and from different functions will help enormously, as will the application of a sensitive thinking and emotionally intelligent view of the current state and likely future scenarios. It is a difficult result to come to because it is more than likely that no one in the organization will know truly what is going to happen.

Ulrich, in discussing strategic partnering of HR, warns of the dangers of quick fixes. 'Diet books, marriage manuals, easy-learning books (foreign language tapes, for example) sell briskly with promises of quick fixes. … Successful weight loss diets, successful marriages, and the acquisition of a foreign language require work. Likewise, HR professionals need to avoid the lure of the quick fix' (1997:60). Learning needs at the organizational level might not be easily identified or solved by simple interventions. An incisive, well-sourced and sensitively intelligent diagnosis is required to get as close as possible to the true needs of the organization.

Problem-solving groups

Many organizations have embraced continuous improvement or Six Sigma philosophies that use quality groups to address operational problems and devise and implement solutions. Such groups can occur at any level within the hierarchy. Such groups can be cross-functional or discreet within a function or department.

These groups are working on critical incidents or failures within organizational processes. As such, they are valuable sources of information on where learning needs may be occurring. Very often, these groups are coordinated in their activity via a steering committee, facilitator, or a quality function. The machinery of the continuous improvement methodology is therefore doing some of the training professional's work in identifying where things are failing within the organization.

LNA AND COMPETENCES IN THE PRISON SERVICE

The Prison Service is an Executive Agency of the Home Office, with an annual budget of £1.3 billion and 36,000 directly employed staff. There are 135 prison establishments in England and Wales, holding 65,000 prisoners. The role of the Service is captured in its Statement of Purpose:

> Her Majesty's Prison Service serves the public by keeping in custody those committed by the courts. Our duty is to look after them with humanity and help them lead law-abiding and useful lives in custody and after release.

The Prison Service is in a period of enormous change. It is expanding rapidly as it faces unprecedented growth in the prison population at the same time as being required to become more effective, both in custodial and rehabilitative work, and more efficient through a demanding cost-reduction programme. An average prison will, for example, have a budget of £20 million and will employ upwards of 500 staff.

The major impact of developments has been on the governor of each prison. Running prisons is becoming an increasingly complex and demanding managerial task. The progressive devolution of responsibility for delivery of services, and the management of resources (money, staff, buildings and plant) to deliver those services, has increased significantly the role of the governor as general manager, in addition to traditional duties.

In light of these changes, a number of high profile prisoner escapes, the White Paper, *Development and Training for Civil Servants*, and a desire to adopt a strategic approach, the Prisons Board commissioned reviews of what competences governors require and what training and development framework would provide those competences.

The Prison Service, like other Executive Agencies, developed a core competency framework (CCF) in 1996. The CCF was intended to inform the recruitment, selection and development processes of staff. Unlike the Home Office, the Prison Service CCF does not have competences identified for each managerial level but rather is a framework of 12 competences applicable to all staff in the Service. Each of the 12 competences has three overarching sentences attached to describe it, and a number of performance indicators.

Using the CCF a 360-degree (line manager, peer, subordinate, self) profiling of the governor's job was undertaken in order to create a model, or benchmark, against which governors could be assessed for promotion, selection and appraisal, and to identify training and development needs. In addition to the behavioural competences, an LNA was undertaken to identify the present and future training and development needs of Governors. This involved questionnaires to all governors and a number of semi-structured interviews.

What emerged from the LNA was that governors required both formal and informal development opportunities. Formal elements included training in: general management; prison operational management; incident command and public sector management. The demand was for classroom-based work, together with distance learning material, thematic seminars, project work and secondments. The informal elements consisted of coaching/mentoring, learning sets, broader development opportunities and personal study.

The Prison Service has, as a result, made a major investment in the training and development of governors. Contracts have been signed with external providers for a Certificate and Diploma in Management, and for a Master's degree in Applied Criminology and Management. A coaching/mentoring scheme has been introduced and thematic seminars have taken place. A Senior Command course has been developed for senior staff, which they attend prior to becoming a governor. The Civil Service College is providing the public sector/civil service modules.

A project is under way to assess the organizational impact of the major investment in training and development for governors. At an individual level, the end-of-training questionnaires indicate that the objectives set have been met, and follow-up questionnaires suggest that people perceive themselves to be more effective having undertaken the activity. Evaluating the impact on the organization continues to be problematic. Directly attributing the improvement in the Prison Service's Key Performance Indicators (such as number of escapes, time out of cell) to the investment in training and development is too simplistic to be defensible. However, the investment in training and development has helped to create a perception that the Prison Service values its senior staff and that in itself is of benefit.

With acknowledgement to Shane Bryans, Head of Management and Specialist Training, HM Prison Service.

Human resource planning

The organization may have a well-developed plan, giving detailed projections on the skill levels required over the next few years. Where such a plan is not available, a lot of valuable information can be garnered from personnel statistics and records. A simple analysis of age profiles, qualification levels and labour turnover will start to give shape to the sorts of people and skills that the organization requires in the foreseeable future and hence their training needs.

Some form of succession plan is also required. This can be in a rough-cut format. Detailed plans are very often difficult to produce, owing to the high degree of future uncertainty. However, some format is needed to highlight those within the organization worthy of development. (See also the section on individual needs, below.)

NEEDS AT THE DEPARTMENTAL LEVEL

In anything but smaller organizations, a detailed LNA becomes too complex and difficult to be generated centrally. This is where the use of LNAs on a departmental basis can be invaluable. It is doubly valuable as it delegates the responsibility for detailed day-to-day learning analysis down to where it should be, with the line manager.

The departmental analysis is performed in exactly the same way as the analysis at organizational level. For instance, reviewing the categories above, the business objectives should have been cascaded down to a departmental level. In the example given above, the manager of Product A cell is already considering the step-up in production. The manager already has more detailed personal objectives relating to the phased increase in production over the next year. He knows the transferees coming into his department and is already planning the reassignment of duties and who will train the transferees.

Likewise, the consideration of anything new can be effective at departmental level. The arrival of a new piece of equipment in the department has a learning need. It is not necessarily a need that could or would be identified or met by a central training facility's analysis of corporate needs.

The department may also have its own set of performance measures. Output, accident rates and absenteeism may all be measured locally and have local training implications. Similarly, there is value in local human resource planning. The manager will know what retirements are forthcoming, absences for maternity or pre-planned medical leave, new entrants, etc.

Departmental problem-solving groups

Where these exist, they can be a useful source of information for training needs at the departmental level. They can provide information on two levels:

1. They will be searching for solutions to departmental problems. Some of these solutions will have learning needs. For example a Six Sigma project team has redesigned a departmental process. Have all users been trained appropriately in the new process?
2. These teams can be directed specifically towards training and people-related issues to identify needs.

An organization may already have trained teams in specific problem-solving techniques. These could be brainstorming, Pareto analysis, fishbone diagrams, forcefield analysis, SWOT analysis, specialist Six Sigma tools or other widely available problem-solving models. These are tools traditionally considered as useful for the solution of operational problems but there is no reason why the majority cannot be applied to training or human resource-related issues and they are particularly valid at departmental level.

An easily applied tool is the SWOT analysis, which asks the team to consider strengths, weaknesses, opportunities and threats relating to a specific situation. The finishing and packing department of a manufacturing organization has asked its problem-solving team to look at the training implications within the department as a starting point for consideration of next year's learning needs. The team has come up with an analysis, shown in Table 8.1.

Table 8.1   Finishing and packaging department – Human Resources SWOT

Strengths	Opportunities
New department manager	Increase in forecast sales
Stable department workforce	Access to PC-based training
Start of multi-skilling	New packaging machine next year
Good morale	'Return to learning' scheme available next year

Weaknesses	Threats
Stock shortages causing too much firefighting	Team leader retires next year
Two trainees recruited	Competition establishing factory nearby
Problem-solving team not fully effective	Wage rates uncompetitive

Such a SWOT analysis provides some useful information to the department. One great value of a SWOT analysis is that it is more than just a snapshot. It is forward-looking in the two right-hand quadrants as well as considering the present situation in the two left-hand quadrants, and it examines both positive and negative aspects of a situation.

The above example raises a number of training issues. The new departmental manager faces a number of changes within his department – likely increase in throughput, new machinery and some staff changes. It is also evident that there are a number of issues relating to the spread of skills within the department that will need to be addressed.

He must also consider the motivation and retention of his staff in the immediate future, since there is likely to be increased competition locally for skills. A further issue, relating to stock shortages, does not necessarily have a training implication but is impacting on the people issues within the department and must be taken into consideration. The SWOT analysis therefore gives some useful raw data that can be further refined to analyse the precise needs of the area.

Much of this departmental activity is too detailed to be identified at a corporate level but can be identified locally, formulated into a departmental plan, then integrated into the corporate training plan.

Using analysis at departmental level does in fact provide an alternative method for organization-wide analysis. The role of the training professional in this method is to coordinate and collate all departmental needs, thereby extracting and meeting any common needs that occur.

The skills matrix

A useful instrument that incorporates much of this information locally is a skills or training matrix. This gives the department a snapshot of the current skills status within the department and, by its very nature, shows where learning needs exist. An example of a very simple matrix, showing broad competence areas, is given in Table 8.2.

Table 8.2 Skills matrix, Product A cell

	Assembly	Drilling	Bending	Fork Lift	Spray	Test	Ship
John Briggs	C	C	C	C	C	C	C
Dal Patel	C	C	C	C	C		C
Jean Phipps	C	C	C	C		C	
Jan Libich	C	C			T	C	
Tony Blitz	C	C	C			T	T
Nadya Smith	C	T					
Ellie Johns		C			C		T

C – Competent; T – Undergoing training

For instance, knowing that a skilled operative, Dal Patel, retires in six months' time, the manager is presently training up a number of operatives in the skills that will be lost. The matrix can be enhanced to give more qualitative information on the level of competences using a categorization such as:

1. Can do job only by reference to job instructions or supervisor.
2. Can do job without reference to instructions/supervisor, but not always to agreed output and quality.
3. Can do job to prescribed output and quality levels.
4. Can do all the above and can train others.

The skills matrix provides an invaluable instant picture of where skills are distributed in a department and provides an excellent visual management tool. The matrices can also be integrated centrally to provide a skills inventory.

NEEDS AT OCCUPATIONAL LEVELS

At this level, learning needs are expressed as the knowledge, skills and attitudes that are needed to carry out specific duties within a job. They are normally defined through the process of job analysis. Gael (1988:xv) discusses more than 40 different approaches to job analysis. He stated that it:

> may be viewed as the hub of virtually all human resources administration and management activities necessary for the successful functioning of organizations. Hardly a program of interest to human resource specialists and other practitioners whose work pertains to organizational personnel does not depend on or cannot benefit from job analysis results. The importance of precise and accurate job information cannot be overemphasized, considering the impact that decisions based upon job information have on individual job applicants and employees and organizations.

Pearn and Kandola (1988) discuss 18 methods of job analysis. These range considerably in their levels of sophistication and the resources required. The spectrum starts with the apparently simple, yet time-consuming technique of observing the job-holder.

Other ways of collecting data are to get the job-holder to record via diaries, logs or self-descriptions the work carried out, or to undertake a job analysis interview with the job-holder. There are also more sophisticated techniques, including the critical incident technique. This method collects information on incidents that are critical or very important in the performance of the job. The range continues through the use of repertory grids, to detailed checklists, inventories, etc. There are, therefore, many techniques available to carry out a job analysis. This chapter does not have the space to discuss all the differing techniques; however, we can review the general principles involved in the process:

- Some common sources of information for a job analysis are the job description, which will list major responsibilities and tasks, and the job specification, which will give indicators on the knowledge, skills and attitudes required by the job.
- The analysis involves breaking down the job into component tasks. The relevant skill and knowledge required to perform each of these tasks are then listed. Attitudes are a difficult area and these are more rarely measured. Analysis will therefore tend to concentrate on knowledge and skills.
- There is now a comprehensive listing of all the skills and knowledge that are required to perform the whole job. Next, the level of competence for the knowledge and skills needs to be defined. This is important, since not all tasks contained within the job will be performed with the same regularity, nor be of equal importance.
- From here the necessary training programmes can be developed to train the job-holder against the required standards. The technique is particularly relevant in defining training needs where new jobs or ranges of jobs are being created. For example, a new factory on a green-field site may find the technique appropriate.

Job analysis is, however, a detailed technique. It therefore lends itself particularly to situations where larger numbers of homogenous jobs exist. To perform a detailed analysis on one-off jobs is a time-consuming process. Indeed, Wellens (1970) points out that job analysis as a means of determining training needs is at its most effective at the lower end of the organization. The discretionary and ever-changing nature of supervisory and managerial jobs means that they cannot be predetermined or prescribed accurately.

Wilson (1997:75) summarizes the debate on the effectiveness of a macro or micro approach to job analysis:

> In order to conduct job analysis, there is the danger of concentrating on the individual elements and details of the job and consequently failing to observe the overall picture i.e. failing to see the wood for the trees. Alternatively, viewing the job as an entity or as purely an outcome may result in a failure to recognize important details.

Job analysis, however, remains a very valid technique for the identification of the skills and knowledge required at the occupational or job level.

NEEDS AT THE INDIVIDUAL LEVEL

There is something rarer than ability. It is the ability to recognise ability.
(Elbert Hubbard)

At this level, the organization is seeking to identify any shortfall in the individual's knowledge, skills and attitudes required to perform his or her job. The difference between the desired level of performance and the current level of performance is *the training gap*.

The analysis of needs at this level has two prerequisites. The first is that the performance parameters of the job have been defined. This can be against a job analysis as defined above. Alternatively there may be individual performance measures identified, particularly at management level, where a manager is measured against personal objectives. However, failure to meet a personal objective does not necessarily indicate a training need; for example, the failure of a production manager to meet output targets where this is a result of serious plant breakdowns.

The second prerequisite is that some form of review takes place against the performance parameters. This is traditionally the performance appraisal or review. Other techniques include self-assessment, assessment centres, 360-degree feedback, etc. Whatever the technique employed, some form of performance measure is required.

Without these two elements – the required and the actual performance – an analysis cannot take place. Where these are in place, there are still difficulties in evaluating individual training needs. For example, a new receptionist is receiving a six-monthly appraisal. The manager has identified a satisfactory match with the functional skills required to perform the job. These include completion of the visitors' book, issuing security passes, answering incoming calls and routing to the relevant extension, notification of visitors to the relevant recipient, etc.

Here the receptionist is utilizing both the required functional skills and required knowledge to perform the job role. No training gap is perceived. The manager is, however, dissatisfied with the job-holder's attitude towards visitors. It appears cold and does not reflect the company's customer-centric values. This leads towards a difficult area of definition. Are the manager's expectations about the receptionist's attitude fair and how can they be measured? And what is a possible training solution? It could be that the job-holder does not possess the warmth the manager expects and the error has been made at the recruitment phase.

ALL I REALLY NEED TO KNOW about how to live and what to do and how to be I learned in kindergarten. Wisdom was not at the top of the graduate school mountain, but there in the sandpile at Sunday School. These are the things I learned:

Share everything.
Play fair.
Don't hit people.
Put things back where you found them.

Clean up your own mess.
Don't take things that aren't yours.
Say sorry when you hurt somebody.
Wash your hands before you eat.
Flush.
Warm cookies and milk are good for you.
Live a balanced life – learn some and think some and draw and paint and sing and dance and play and work every day some.
Take a nap every afternoon.
When you go out into the world, watch out for traffic, hold hands, and stick together.
Be aware of wonder.
(Robert Fulghum, 1989:6)

At the individual level, we also need to review development opportunities. Many appraisal and review systems do build in a forward-looking aspect in which employee and manager can together discuss both the individual's and the organization's view of their future. Other sources of information will be succession plans and human resource plans, where these exist.

Development of individual employees is vital to future organizational growth. Bennis (1989:47) states:

> Our educational system is really better at training than educating. And that's unfortunate. Training is good for dogs because we require obedience from them. In people, all it does is orient them toward the bottom line.

The valid point here is that it is quite feasible for an organization to place too much emphasis on training to meet current performance and business objectives, meeting the short-term bottom line results, at the expense of developing people for the future.

The degree of development activity will depend upon organizational culture and training policy. Some organizations will invest only in the bare minimum of training. Other organizations encourage learning for its own sake and have well-established personal development programmes. Ford's EDAP is a prime example that enables employees to develop themselves.

FORD MOTOR COMPANY'S EMPLOYEE DEVELOPMENT AND ASSISTANCE PROGRAMME

The UK's Ford Motor Company's EDAP was introduced in 1987 as a part of its national pay negotiations with the trade unions. It is run on a tripartite basis with representatives from hourly and salaried unions and management, both at national and at plant level.

The programme offers sponsorship for voluntary activity or study undertaken outside of working hours and all of Ford's UK employees are eligible to apply for assistance.

EDAP offers employees a wide range of opportunities for personal and career development. These can include education, training, retraining or other development activities as well as a variety of services to encourage healthier lifestyles. The programme is not intended to replace the company's job-related training.

The aims of EDAP are:

- to enhance the personal development and well-being of all employees;
- to provide personal educational and training opportunities;
- to provide resources to encourage a healthier lifestyle.

Since its inception, there have been over 300,000 applications for funding. Research shows that at least 70 per cent of employees have participated in the programme at least once. The range of courses available is very broad, encompassing: Open University courses, other academic courses such as BTEC and GCSE qualifications, computer literacy, languages, basic literacy and numeracy programmes, crafts such as plumbing and decorating, music, art, cookery, fitness/health programmes, etc.

Many local committees have developed their own on-site facilities such as classrooms, fitness centres and computer rooms. This offers the flexibility to enable shiftworkers to attend programmes.

The concepts of the Ford EDAP have been copied by many organizations, large and small, since its inception. It is difficult to assign measurable bottom-line benefits to such programmes. But they can have strong motivational aspects and positive employee relations implications as well as the obvious benefits of bringing many employees back into the main body of the church of learning.

Programmes such as EDAP allow many employees back into the learning arena and develop their learning skills and enhance their confidence levels. These philosophies also fit well with continuous improvement programmes whereby organizations seek to enhance all employees' contributions to the business, so that untapped and unseen potential can be harnessed. These programmes, whether they be learning a language at a local college, improving computer skills, or taking a Master's degree, are risky investments. They may have no immediate impact upon company performance nor fulfil any immediate training need. However, issues of leadership, innovation and creativity are becoming more critical to organizational success. Thus, it is these sorts of investments in individual potential which become more valid and sensible.

There is always the danger of assessing learning needs solely from the perspective of the organization. Many individual employees will have their own agendas and plans concerning their educational and developmental needs. And there are sound business and motivational reasons for organizations to assist employees to fulfil these self-development needs.

As human beings, we all have our own personal struggle to find ourselves and our role in life. There are very few that live solely to work, but because work occupies the lion's share of our waking life, each individual usually seeks to gain fulfilment and satisfaction within the working environment. That self-awareness and self-development are, by definition, broader than the pursuit of organizational objectives. As Handy (1997:90) has said:

> We have today the opportunity, which is also the challenge, to shape ourselves, even to reinvent ourselves. Our lives are not completely foreordained, either by science or by our souls. We can make of our lives a masterpiece if we so wish. It is an opportunity that ought to be available to all humans. It could be. It is the fortunate combination of liberal democracy and free market capitalism that gives us this opportunity, as long as we make these two our servants, not our masters.

Developmental training can be more structured, particularly where this is linked into career development programmes. Where succession planning is present, plans may exist for managers to gain experience, for example through secondment to a new function, and to develop themselves educationally. These training needs are identified and budgeted for in agreed development plans.

Development needs, specifically those that are initiated by the individual employee, are hard to quantify in terms of cost benefit to the organization. They therefore become harder to justify and to support as a priority need (see below). For this reason, they should be embedded within a corporate policy, as a percentage figure or money/time investment. Otherwise, they are easily trimmed out as an unquantifiable expenditure.

DEFINING THE TRAINING PRIORITIES

Having undertaken an organization-wide LNA, it is likely that the number of training needs identified are much larger than can be met through current resources. It is therefore imperative to prioritize the needs into some order of importance. The priorities may be self-evident but where this is not the case, the following technique can be applied. It is useful to do this as a group exercise, such as in a training committee:

1. Certain training needs will already be defined through company policy or strategy. For instance, the organization has committed to train three designated managers on an MBA programme. All PC users are to be trained in the new suite of software by the third quarter. Such strategic and policy training decisions are already preordained.
2. A distinction must be made between training needs and training wants, that is, between the essential and the desirable. Where needs are identified against organizational objectives, then the arising needs should be essential to the achievement of those objectives. However, it is probable that in the course of undertaking an LNA, general requests for training will emerge. These may include wants rather than needs. For instance, the financial controller considers that line managers have a poor understanding of the financial measures used in the organization. This may be true. While a properly designed course in finance for non-financial managers may address this issue, will it actually improve the organization's performance? It may be desirable but it is not necessarily essential.

3.   Pareto analysis can be employed as a technique to define the highest priority training needs among the remaining needs. A cost saving resulting from the proposed training is calculated (estimated savings minus estimated training costs). The cost savings are compared and the best savings become the priority needs. Considering the Pareto principle: 20 per cent of the training input is likely to yield 80 per cent of the savings.

For instance, an organization is having broken merchandise returned due to faulty packing. It emerges that staff in the packing department have not been fully trained in the correct packaging methods for a new product range. Returns are costing the organization £3,000 per month. If left unresolved, a substantial cost will accrue. Such a piece of training becomes a high priority against other costed training needs.

Costing of training in softer skills can be trickier. But all that is being attempted here is some rough measure to enable some comparisons to be drawn. Avoid getting drawn into detailed and complex calculations; a rough yardstick is all that may be required.

The three-stage process for prioritizing training needs is summarized below:

1.   Include training needs predetermined at policy level.
2.   Divide remaining needs into essential and desirable.
3.   Cost the essential needs and prioritize via Pareto.

CONCLUSION

We have now reviewed a number of methods for identifying learning needs at four levels throughout the organization and seen that:

- The relevance of the various LNA techniques will depend upon the culture and size of the organization.
- Most literature on the subject infers that the identification of learning needs is the preserve of the training professional, or at least looks at it from this perspective.
- Trends over the last decade have led to the devolution of responsibility into smaller autonomous units within organizations. Smaller business units, self-directed work teams, teamworking, more local empowerment, all lead to the conclusion that LNA must move closer to the coal face.
- As training becomes more highly recognized as a legitimate business investment, the volume of training is likely to rise accordingly.
- With the devolution of responsibility and the rise in the amount of training, training and the identification of learning needs have to become more and more a part of the line manager's and supervisor's people-management responsibility. If they are not, they will become distanced and less relevant to local operating needs.
- The devolution of responsibility for the identification of learning needs raises its own learning need. Have we, as HRD professionals, shown our managers and supervisors how it is done?

Bibliography

Bailey, D (2000) 'Learning needs analysis by another name', *Training Journal*, April, pp 26–29

Bee, F and Bee, R (2003) *Learning Needs Analysis and Evaluation*, London, Chartered Institute of Personnel and Development

Bennis, W (1989) *On Becoming a Leader*, London, Century Business Books

Boydell, T H (1983) *Identification of Training Needs*, London, BACIE

Cabinet Office, Training and Development Division (1988) *A Guide on How to Do a Training Needs Analysis*, London, Cabinet Office (OMCS)

Fulghum, R (1989) *All I Really Need to Know I Learned in Kindergarten*, London, Grafton Books

Gael, S (1988) *The Job Analysis Handbook for Business, Industry and Government*, New York, Wiley

Handy, C (1997) *The Hungry Spirit*, London, Hutchinson

Kenney, J and Reid, M (1986) *Training Interventions*, London, IPM

Palmer, R (2002) *Training with the Midas Touch: Developing your organization's greatest asset*, London, Kogan Page

Pearn, M and Kandola, R (1988) *Job Analysis: A practical guide for managers*, London, IPM

Pepper, A D (1984) *Managing the Training and Development Function*, Aldershot, Gower

Ulrich, D (1997) *Human Resource Champions*, Boston, MA, Harvard Business School Press

Wellens, J (1970) 'An approach to management training', *Industrial and Commercial Training*, 8, 7

Wilson, J P (1997) 'An evaluation of the Management Charter Initiative M11 Standards as the basis for the development of a competence-based language syllabus', unpublished PhD thesis, University of Sheffield

9

Performance Management and Human Resource Development

Alan Cattell

INTRODUCTION AND LEARNING OBJECTIVES

The Chartered Institute of Personnel and Development's report, *Performance through People: The new people management* (2001:3) captures the essence of the importance of people management and performance:

> The new millennium marks a turning point in the history of organisation; for the first time ever it is possible to state with confidence that how organisations manage people has a powerful – perhaps the most powerful – effect on overall performance including the bottom line. ... The bottom line is that the 21st century organisation is one in which people really are the greatest asset, and people management needs to go beyond lip service to become a core competence of every organisation, whether in private, voluntary or public sector, manufacturing or services, new economy or old.

Globalization and the need for companies to gain sustainable competitive advantage require new and different approaches to recruiting, training, developing and retaining employees with key skills. Thus, the need for *integrated* methods of performance management has never been greater when downsizing, de-layering and mergers have become the norm worldwide. Within this competitive and rapidly changing environment, people and people management are seen by a growing number of commentators as being the key to business success. Bassi *et al* (1996:28) observe:

Sustainable competitive advantage is no longer based on technology or machinery. Corporate leaders are saying, 'People are our most important advantage.' Even so, corporate America has undergone massive downsizing, restructuring and reorganization.

Similar findings from two major research projects studying leading multinational companies are reported in the UK by Gratton (1997:25):

The sources of sustained competitive advantage have shifted from financial resources to technological resources and now to human capital. This change has a number of profound implications. It requires a fundamental change in organisational timescales from short term to long term and is predicated by integration and coherence rather than ad-hoc thinking and incoherence. It also means that we must take into account people's aspirations and values and not allow people management to be dominated by tools and techniques.

HR professionals and practitioners have not been exempt from this changing environment. Thus, this chapter provides the opportunity for those involved with HRD to appraise their role within and outside their organizations, and consider their own training and development needs for the future.

Having read this chapter you will:

- understand the role of performance management linked to organizational strategy;
- be able to link appropriate elements of performance management to HRD;
- be aware of some of the approaches to performance management;
- understand the role of trust and the psychological contract; and
- understand the integrated role of appraisal and training.

WHAT IS PERFORMANCE MANAGEMENT?

McBeath (1990:199) suggests that the word 'appraisal' is emotive. Perhaps the phrase 'performance management' is even more emotive, meaning different things to different people, and dependent on which level in the organization they occupy.

Performance management is a broader term than appraisal and, as a concept or philosophy, should ideally be a systematic approach that encompasses:

- motivation of employees to perform;
- vision by employers as to what performance standards they expect of employees;
- ownership of management of performance at a variety of levels within organizations; and
- monitoring and measurement of the performance achieved by employees.

Performance appraisal and derivation of training and development needs at organizational, team and individual levels are an integral part of the performance management process, but there is the potential for conflicting messages as to who plays which part and at what stage.

Edis (1995:1), identifying approaches within the British National Health Service, captures elements of this conflict when he refers to 'a confusing circus display of pay scale acrobatics, trial and error introductions of new performance management systems, and resuscitation of appraisals'.

While there is no single, simple definition of what performance management is, or should be, I will offer a number of 'statements' from which general conclusions can be drawn:

> the practices through which work is defined and reviewed; through which capabilities are developed and through which rewards are distributed in an organization. Performance management may involve goal setting, employee selection and placement, compensation, performance appraisals, training and development and career management. (Mohrman and Mohrman, 1995:2)

> Performance management is the essential bridge between the strategic goals of the organisation and the day-to-day priorities of teams and individuals. It is also the way in which an organisation can gear its people development strategy to the needs of the business – defining the skills and competencies required for excellent performance and then creating PDPs for individuals. (IPD, 1997a:7)

> Performance management is a systematic approach to improving individual and team performance in order to achieve organisational goals. (Hendry *et al*, 1997:20)

> Performance management is the process of trying to bring the rewards which *individuals* desire into line with those required by the *organisation*. (Edis, 1995:10)

> Performance management is creating a shared vision of the purpose and aims of the organisation, helping each individual employee to understand and recognise their part in contributing to them and thereby managing and enhancing the performance of both individuals and the organisation. (Fletcher, 1997:36)

The common elements linking all these statements are:

- the need for well-communicated and commonly understood **strategic goals** within organizations which reflect the needs of the external business and market environment;
- a **shared vision** of the part which each function, team and individual within organizations will play and the benefits to be achieved by doing so;
- a **systematic approach** to performance management which requires a holistic and integrated approach business-wide, rather than one based on functionally driven, short-term and ad hoc 'initiatives'.

Strategic goals: gaining competitive advantage

Whereas previously the notion of competitive advantage may have been mainly centred round market position, an alternative idea, the resource-based view of an organization, has been adopted by an number of organizations. Here strategic advantage is gained by an organization's ability to recognize and mobilize the capabilities and potential offered by its internal resources, particularly people.

Hamel and Prahalad (1994) first suggested that successful companies were those that set ambitious goals and got more out of their resources through the development of particular components of competitor advantage that they called core competencies. These were defined as bundles of skills, capabilities and technologies that enabled a company to provide a particular benefit to customers. Birchall and Tovstiga (1999) propose that building up such a portfolio of capabilities forms the fundamental building block for an organization's core competence.

In support of the resource-based view Sloman contends:

> The emergence of a new strand of strategy analysis, resource based strategy, emphasises what a company can do rather than where a company is positioned in the marketplace. Organisational strengths are identified, developed, stretched and extended for competitive advantage. The aim is to identify and develop distinctive capabilities. These are the factors that can differentiate a company from its competitors; they are built up and sustained over time and cannot be easily reproduced by competitors.
>
> (Sloman 2003:5)

While such an approach may make good sense in strategic and business terms, what effect does it have on perceptions of HR and HR practice in general? Harrison and Kessels state that:

> Over the past two decades, as organisations have come under acute pressures from their competitive environment, HR has been widely criticised for a failure to add value for the business. The resource based view of the firm, one of the most influential bodies of contemporary strategy theory, has a special preoccupation with identifying ways in which a firm's employees can contribute to its competitive advantage.
>
> (Harrison and Kessels 2004:21)

Harrison and Kessels also suggest that in comparison with many traditional HR models which are based primarily on the cutting of costs, resource-based value highlights a firm's HR base as an asset, not a cost to the business, because of its potential to produce valuable organizational capabilities.

Wright, Dunford and Snell (2001) go further by proposing that the increasing importance of resource-based value has done much to promote human resources in general and human capital management in particular, while also bringing about convergence between the fields of strategy and HR.

In terms of HRD, Garavan *et al* (2001:1) cite Losey (1999) and Spangenburg, Schroder and Duvenge (1999), who report that increasingly organizations are seeking to implement sophisticated HRD and workplace learning strategies to develop employee and organizational competencies to enable them to respond quickly and flexibly to business needs.

Research by Easterby-Smith and Graca (2004:37) has identified an organization that has utilized resource-based strategy to identify dynamic capability which will give it competitive advantage. They describe how utilizing expertise and knowledge built up over the years in the chemical sector, Ciba Speciality Chemicals has added selling a range of knowledge-based services globally to its normal business of selling products. The speed of making rapid strategic changes and developing new core competencies in setting up the new business have been the key competitive factors.

Ciba's ability to make these rapid changes is an example of dynamic capability, an extension to the idea of resource-based strategy. Resource-based strategy is based on the notion that competitive advantage depends on how far a firm has unique assets and core competencies that are difficult to imitate. Dynamic capability was first described by Prisano, Teece and Shuen at Harvard Business School in 1997, and concerns the ability of a firm to integrate, develop and reconfigure competencies to address rapidly changing environments.

Easterby-Smith and Graca (2004:38) state that there are a number of implications for HR, and in particular for training and development. The research identified that employees who had previously employed mainly technical skills and scientific innovation in their jobs were required to quickly develop social and customer care skills. In order to achieve this the recognition that technical expertise and behavioural competencies needed to be complementary to each other was key to the ability of individuals and the organization to respond rapidly to changing business needs. The authors of the study call for greater emphasis on managing competencies, as opposed to functions, within organizations.

Such an approach also requires tangible and recognized links between performance management and knowledge management, and a concentration on strategic rather than operational imperatives.

Shared vision

Gratton (1997), reporting on a study of a division of Hewlett Packard, observes links between the highly focused performance management process used by the company, which successfully aligns strategic to individual objectives together with a set of values ('the HP Way'). Among the main features identified by employees surveyed were commitment, pride and trust in the integrity of the company.

A study by the Singapore Institute of Management and Development Dimensions International (1994:61) reports the experiences of five high-performing companies which have won the Singapore National Productivity Award. These companies displayed a number of similarities in their approach to:

- introducing management practices designed to develop self-motivated workers who took pride in their work;
- transferring authority for both tasks and responsibility down the hierarchy to give a sense of ownership;
- regular discussion between managers and employees about performance growth and development.

Included in the benefits highlighted by the companies were lower-than-average turnover rates and employees with strong work values.

Systematic approaches

Within this chapter it is not the intention to examine in detail the myriad performance management approaches. Suffice it to say that there are a profusion (some might say a confusion) of elements that can make up a performance management system. These may include:

- business strategies;
- total quality management strategies;
- human resources strategies;
- organization development strategies;
- reward strategies;
- communications strategies.

Aligned to these there may be a variety of further elements:

- competence-based recruitment;
- skill mix analysis;
- benchmarking;
- job design;
- job evaluation;
- job restructuring;
- performance-related pay;
- competence-based/related pay;
- group/team-related pay;
- merit-based pay;
- gainsharing;
- individual competences and objectives;
- team competences and objectives;
- ongoing performance review – team and individual;
- performance appraisal/feedback;
- team development plans;
- personal development plans;
- continuing professional development;
- succession plans;
- career development plans.

In essence, performance management owes its origins to management by objectives (MBO) first proposed by Drucker (1954). Fowler (1990) suggests as much by the title of his article 'Performance management – the MBO of the 1990s'. While MBO emphasized the linking of individual and managerial objectives to organizational goals through an appraisal process, it was perhaps viewed as an HR-driven exercise and therefore lacked ownership by managers.

Performance management differs in the respect that at its best it should link the strategic elements of a business with key managerial tasks including managing people. As will be outlined in later sections of this chapter, *managerial* responsibility for coaching and support and *individual* ownership of performance improvement are at the heart of performance management. A model of a performance management system is shown in Figure 9.1.

However, put simply there is no one best way. Much depends on the present culture (the way we do things round here) or envisaged future culture of the organization and the type of business which it is in. As Hendry *et al* (1997:20) observe, 'We believe that the approach you take should depend on your organisation, its culture, its relationship with employees and the type of jobs they do.'

In terms of culture, what works in the public sector may not work in the private sector. What works in the UK or the USA might not necessarily work in Asia or Eastern Europe. This is particularly worth bearing in mind in our new 'globalized' marketplace. Trompenaars (1995) notes that much of the management literature and practice has been developed and preached by individuals from the Anglo-Saxon world and is potentially laden with cultural assumptions. As such many purportedly 'universal' ideas, approaches and solutions put forward may have little relevance to a large part of the globe.

Of particular relevance to performance management is Trompenaars' (1995:25–6) statement that:

> In developing pay for performance systems globally, for example, we quickly run into major cultural differences in whether we should recognise and reward individual or group contributions. Individualistic cultures, such as those of the US and Britain, choose the individual and pay the price of impaired teamwork and the tendency to push for personal objectives even when they damage the team as a whole. Collective cultures, such as that of the Japanese, choose the group and often pay the price in a submerging of individual initiative and creativity.

THE EFFECTIVENESS OF PERFORMANCE MANAGEMENT

In opening this chapter I intentionally used the word 'integrated' as a preface to performance management. Any performance management system is only as good as its fit with other key

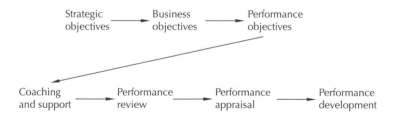

Figure 9.1 A simple model of a performance management system

business systems and strategies. It is not something that is *done* to employees but *with* them. At its best it should *add value* (see also Chapter 2) to the business and to relationships within the business.

Added value

There are two dimensions to added value: that of adding value to the business and that of engaging employees in a way that motivates them to perform to standards where they give added value.

For the organization, added value means establishing performance criteria related to key strategic and business objectives and monitoring its own and its employees' success in performing against these. At managerial level it means alignment to both strategic and business objectives and operationally carrying these out while using time and resources (financial and human) to maximum effect. At team and individual level it means using and developing the skills necessary to secure, retain or enhance employability at an equitable rate of remuneration.

Integrated systems – making the links

In 2003 the Work Foundation (formerly the Industrial Society) interviewed 1,000 UK chief executives about their approaches to strategy and management practices. The report (CIPD and EEF, 2003) identified that the high-performing firms were those that practised and had joined-up systems and integrated approaches and thinking across five categories: customers, markets, shareholders, employees, and creativity and innovation.

This has obvious implications for people management and development, hence the need for integrated systems of managing the business, of which performance appraisal is a part. Hence the need for performance appraisal of which training and development needs analysis is a part. Hence the need for individual self-appraisal of which motivation, ownership and self-reflection should be a part.

If such a system of integration is to be achieved, then how do organizations approach the realignment of often disparate parts of the system into a whole? In the article 'A clear path to peak performance', Egan (1995:35) reviews the elements that make up a comprehensive performance management and appraisal system. He suggests that it is made up of three parts:

1. performance improvement, involving: objective setting, agreement of delegation parameters, work planning, initial training, managerial facilitation and support, feedback, tracking of progress against key objectives, recognition of accomplishment, and development;
2. performance appraisal;
3. discussion of the compensation consequences of the appraisal.

While a chapter cannot detail the full content or implications of Egan's article there are several points of note:

●   Responsibility for performance improvement lies with the line manager in the role of supporting employees to give their best on the assumption that this is what most employees would want to do. The majority of the manager's time should be devoted to the performance improvement stage and if this is done to full effect it requires less time at the appraisal stage.

- If the workings of the day-to-day performance improvement process are good, then the employee being appraised can play a leading and proactive role at the appraisal stage. This is because there are likely to be no new messages and the appraisal therefore becomes a platform for summarizing the messages already heard and building on them. Egan (1995) states, 'Employees who can lead the process should be the rule rather than the exception.'

- The performance management system should be presented as an added value management system and not a human resources system. It is a business system because it focuses on improved performance and business results. As such it is something that can be used by all managers together with their team members to improve both individual, team and unit productivity.

Motivation

It is one thing to have a systematic approach to managing and evaluating performance in order to achieve organizational performance expectations. It is another to have a congruent process that is capable of motivating people to perform to the standards which may be expected of them. This raises the question, whose expectations?

Perhaps the two concepts that have most relevance to modern performance management are expectancy theory and the notion of the psychological contract.

Expectancy theory

Expectancy theory (Vroom, 1965) maintains that people will make an effort to achieve a standard of performance if they perceive that it will be rewarded by a desirable outcome.

Desirable outcome is essentially a product of individual circumstances and perceptions and is therefore subject to change. At one time, lifelong employment and security of tenure at an equitable level of remuneration may have been the driving force for many employees. Those who have suffered the effects of downsizing and redundancy are now likely to view the world in a different manner, where jobs offering short-term and reasonably remunerated employment prospects are more attractive than no job at all. Similarly, those in employment and those seeking employment are likely to have a positive view of work offering the prospect of development of differentiated and transferable skills, as an investment in their future employability. The consultative document, *Opportunity through People* (IPD, 1997c:4) states:

> Outsourcing, downsizing, delayering and the casualisation of jobs are all fashionable. These trends affect employees' explicit or implicit relationships with their employer. Similarly, reduced career opportunities, shorter tenure, the need for transferable skills to assist employability and increased use of fixed term contracts weaken the traditional ties of loyalty to their company's destiny – psychologically as well as formally.

The psychological contract

There are two sets of contracts between employer and employee. The first is the legal contractual relationship which defines who is expected to give what, to whom, and for what. The second, or psychological contract (Schein, 1964) is an unwritten and unstated set of expectations of each other. Within this the organization has expectations of the individual related to results or rewards it will award if outcomes are met. The individual similarly has a vision of the results or rewards expected from the organization which will satisfy his or her needs and in return for which he or she will expend energy at an appropriate level.

Much therefore is unwritten or unspoken and is a perception of the employer on one part and the employee on the other. If there is a mismatch in perceptions this may lead to feelings of lack of cooperation and involvement by one party or exploitation by the other. Herriott and Pemberton describe the psychological contract as 'the perception of both parties to the employment relationship, organisation and individual, of the obligations implied in that relationship'(1997:45–46).

Over the last decade there has been a significant shift in the employment relationship, from length of service and job security, to performance-based, temporary or fixed short-term contracts.

Balance and trust

A balanced/positive contract occurs when both employer and employee feel that the relationship has provided valued outcomes. An imbalanced/negative contract occurs when one party perceives that there are unacceptable disparities which favour the other party.

The key to a successful relationship is therefore one where there is a mutuality of benefit and both parties have something to gain, and where they will work together to ensure a successful result. In a perfect situation, trust is earned through honouring the expectations of the other party and maintaining a positive contract. Otherwise, any breach by either party represents a betrayal of trust, and damage to the relationship in terms of future commitment and effort.

Handy (1985:43–6) proposes that it is possible to categorize organizations according to the type of psychological contract which predominates. These are summarized as follows:

1. *The coercive contract* typified by:

    - the contract is not entered into on a voluntary basis by the individual;
    - organizational philosophy is command and control;
    - power is likely to be in the hands of a small group;
    - the task of the individual is to comply and conform;
    - blame culture – fear of getting it wrong and being punished;
    - stifling of risk-taking, innovation and creativity.

2. *The calculative contract* typified by:

    - the contract is voluntary and is prevalent in many organizations;
    - there is a commonly understood exchange of goods/money given by the organization for services rendered;

- power to reward is in the control of management and is expressed mainly through management's ability to give desired things in return for a high level of performance;
- desired things can include money, promotion, training and development opportunities or work itself;
- the contract is based on the organization's ability to pay. If it cannot do so and seeks more for less, employees will view it as a coercive contract and adjust their side of the contract accordingly.

3. *The cooperative contract* typified by:

- the individual's tendency to identify with organizational goals and become proactive in the pursuit of those goals;
- as well as receiving rewards, individuals are encouraged to voice opinions in selecting goals and given choice on methods of achieving them;
- management relinquishes much day-to-day operational control but retains overall control through its ability to allocate financial resources and to select people.

The cooperative contract may seem to offer a mutually attractive way forward to organizations and individuals. However, what might seem to be an attractive proposition to some employees may not be as attractive to others. This type of contract assumes that individuals will *want* to take shared responsibility for goals and decisions. It also assumes that employees will be committed to the achievement of organizational goals which, while being attractive to managers, mean little or nothing to the lower levels of the organization.

THE PSYCHOLOGICAL CONTRACT OPERATES IN BOTH DIRECTIONS

Working as a training manager in the engineering sector in the early 1980s I was asked by my CEO to facilitate the setting up of quality circles based on the shop floor. Senior management expressed commitment to the idea, which they observed had proved successful in Japan and had also been introduced successfully by Jaguar in the UK. Shop floor employees took readily to the idea and invested their lunch-hour periods and time after normal working hours.

The circles themselves identified a number of production issues that could be improved and suggested solutions to these. Management, however, having first suggested the setting up of quality circles, showed less commitment than the workforce and attended circle meetings on an infrequent basis. This was taken by employees to show a lack of interest. Additionally, when management realized that some of the ideas that showed merit would cost money in the short-term despite long-term savings and improvement, interest in the concept of quality circles dropped dramatically. Commitment and motivation are, after all, a two-way process.

Control or empowerment?

The Egan (1995) model of performance management discussed earlier in this chapter suggests an appropriate framework for empowerment. It requires managers to assume greater responsibility for the softer side of people management as part and parcel of their daily management activity (without relinquishing control). It also requires employees to become more actively involved in the process of performance appraisal, based on a notion of performance improvement related to development outcomes from which they can benefit and are involved in determining.

Such a process also has direct implications for the HRD practitioner at two levels:

1. in helping to create a climate and structure where managers and individuals take ownership of areas for which they have not traditionally regarded themselves as being responsible;
2. in providing appropriate support and training to assist managers in developing facilitation, coaching and feedback skills and to help individuals in developing appraisee skills.

Active involvement in the process by individuals also depends on their level of confidence and their will or ability to take or accept some responsibility. In terms of self-empowerment there would appear to be a number of levels of permission which individuals might either be prepared to accept/not accept or may need. Figure 9.2 demonstrates a model of permission in terms of a continuum from non-empowerment to self-empowerment:

●   *Level 1:* individuals wait to be given permission because either previous life/work experience in terms of control by others has taught them to do so, or conversely they abdicate or are not willing to take responsibility.

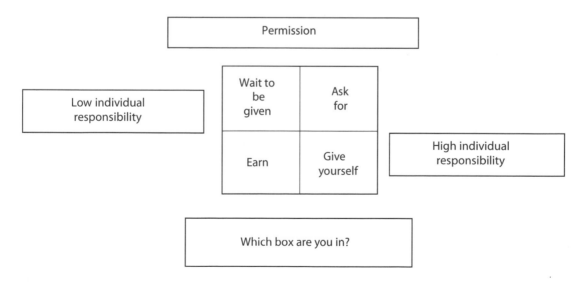

Figure 9.2   Cattell's model of permission
Source: Cattell (2004)

- *Level 2:* in asking for permission, individuals recognize a locus of control or hierarchy and their expected level of discretionary behaviour within this.
- *Level 3:* by volunteering where others don't, or demonstrating expertise/prior knowledge, or, 'going the extra mile', individuals earn the permission to assume a higher level of responsibility that might not otherwise have been granted to them.
- *Level 4:* by giving themselves permission, individuals display a level of confidence, or conversely arrogance, in their ability to take responsibility. The former can represent a plus in an organizational culture where such behaviour is desired and supported. The latter can present obvious problems where the culture espouses hierarchy and control.

HR is not about policing the performance management or appraisal system. It is about *enabling* the process to gain maximum potential for organization and employees, whatever level they work at.

Similarly, identification of training needs and personal development plans does not begin with outputs from the appraisal process. It begins with the identification of the inputs, needs and means by which all the parties involved will gain maximum benefit from the process itself.

Pay and rewards

There has been a long-standing debate over whether discussion of pay and rewards should form part of appraisal discussions. Whether part of the discussion or not, the nature of human psychology is that there is an expectation of reward or benefit by one party wherever there is an expectation of improved or enhanced performance by the other. There may also be different interpretations of what actually constitutes a reward.

Pay in itself does not have to be included within a performance management system but more often than not it is. Common elements of motivation theory would suggest two main types of reward in relation to performance management systems:

1. **Rewards-based systems:** offering incentive/explicit reward. Here the assumption is that individuals work harder if given specific rewards for good performance. Rewards are only provided if desired performance and behaviour are attained.
2. **Development-based systems:** involving implicit/intrinsic reward. Here the assumption is that people work best when given a worthwhile job and are allowed to get on with it. Reward will come from the satisfaction derived from the job itself and the opportunity to develop individual abilities through the encouragement of learning.

In a survey carried out by the IPD in the UK, Armstrong (1996:1) reports two notable trends. The majority of responding companies had introduced performance development plans for their staff which were intended to assist employees in identifying the skills needed for their future careers as well as their current jobs. The survey also showed that companies were emphasizing staff development more than performance-related pay.

Armstrong observes that these trends recognize the need for individuals to develop their future employability and ensure that the workforce has the necessary skills to keep the business competitive as well as helping companies retain valuable staff.

The survey, however, showed staff to be less enthusiastic about the performance management process and its effectiveness, with a number considering it to be time-consuming and bureaucratic. The survey highlights the importance of the need to show individuals how the process will benefit them:

> Companies may not be able to offer people jobs for life or dramatic promotional prospects as incentives to perform better. But by focusing on staff skills and development, both employer and employee can get something out of the process. (Armstrong, 1996:1)

Either/or (or an amalgam of both)

One could argue that discussion of pay/compensation/rewards has little relevance within a book on HRD. Within the context of explicit or implicit reward, it cannot be ignored. Nor can it be assumed that it is a simple choice between either option. There is growing evidence that companies are using a combination of both to reward not only individuals but also teams. The bottom line is that if you do not have adequate means of assessing or appraising performance, how can you reward it?

The decision as to what performance rewards are applicable is still in many organizations either directly or indirectly related to appraisal of performance and essentially shapes the form of appraisal which is carried out.

Table 8.1 shows a variety of approaches to the determination of reward. The contents of the table are intended to be a pointer towards approaches, not an exhaustive list.

Even countries and companies renowned for their high performance practices are having to rethink their approach to performance and reward. Summarizing a report from Arthur Andersen (written by Robert Hodkinson) Walsh (1997:16) cites the example of Japanese companies based in the UK which, despite having previously gained competitive advantage through pioneering practices such as TQM and continuous improvement, are finding that this may no longer be sufficient to beat off competition.

The report identifies that Japanese firms are now having to focus on developing and retaining new employees, moving from seniority-based pay to performance-related and locally set pay, and implementing more effective appraisal and communication systems.

But what of other approaches? Where does the notion of competence/competency fit in?

Competence and competence-related pay

Competence and competency approaches allied to competence-based assessment and related pay are being used by a growing number of companies. Utilization includes applying national frameworks, such as the Management Charter Initiative in the UK, or internally generated organizational core competences, generic and role-specific competences and behaviourally anchored competences.

An important consideration is where the application of competences fits within the performance management process. Roberts (1997) links competences to the initial stages of the

Table 9.1 Approaches to the determination of reward

Type	Features	Advantages	Disadvantages
Merit pay (Also referred to as Performance-related pay)	• Overall pay level is determined by some form of job evaluation • Pay increases are variable and directly related to individual performance ratings • Generally uses some form of comparative performance rating scale • Rating uses either a fixed formula or in some cases is left to local management discretion based on identified targets and a fixed budget	• Based on a premise that those who perform well will gain the greater benefits • Allows the organization to target rewards towards those who are the most effective performers	• Depends on the effectiveness of the comparative rating scale • Depends on the ability of managers across the organization to equitably apply the rating scale • Needs a highly effective performance measurement and appraisal process to make it work
Incremental pay	• Job evaluation determines the salary range • Links with performance appraisal determine how quickly the individual progresses through the salary range • Increment is paid automatically on an annual basis if the individual is judged to have performed satisfactorily	• Individual performance is expected to improve over a period of time • Is easily understood by all • Is perceived as being equitable	• Difficult to recognize significant differences between poor, average and excellent performers • If the increment is automatic it may be seen as being inequitable because poor performers are rewarded on the same basis as more capable individuals
Gainsharing	• Employees and organization share in bonus pool created by added value contribution by employees	• Encourages collective problem solving and performance improvement	• Difficulties in establishing integrated means of assessing where added value has been contributed
Group/team reward	• Based on the achievement of team targets and critical success factors • Reward is collective – group, team or department • Bonuses or pay increases are linked to group, team or departmental performance *or* team and individual performance	• Reflects the interdependency of collective contribution • Acts as a lever for organizational change • Encourages flexible working and multi-skilling • Helps focus priorities on key areas such as customer service, quality, innovation and cooperative work	• Can diminish self-worth • Can compel individuals to conform to oppressive group norms • Can cause difficulties in developing performance measures which are fair • Needs management to effectively audit and monitor costs

recruitment and selection process, which he contends should be ruthlessly streamlined if it is to be effective. Among suggested approaches he includes:

- Definition of key competencies – personal attributes, knowledge, experience, skills and values – to meet the organization's long-term needs.
- Combining a range of selection techniques and methods to obtain reliable data on all core competences.
- Feeding the information gained into the induction, appraisal and development of employees.

Roberts (1997:1) maintains that, 'Neither praise nor pay can motivate people to perform beyond their means, and the best training programme cannot make a silk purse of a sow's ear.' This reminds me of my experience as a young first-time training officer in the late 1970s. My manager introduced me to a model of what he considered HRM and HRD to be all about, and which is still with me today; it is shown in Figure 9.3.

In recruiting, if you are going to invest money in salaries and on-costs you need to get the recruitment decision right. If having recruited the right person you then spend money on training/retraining and developing the individual, the bottom line must surely be in retaining the skills and abilities you have invested in. If not, then you have not realized the full potential of your investment. A statement of the obvious perhaps and a simplistic view, but one which could suggest that performance management is a matter of common sense.

In their pursuit of integrated performance management systems, are organizations perhaps over-concentrating effort on current employees and their performance, rather than concentrating effort also on a vision of recruiting future employees to identified and understood performance standards?

Extending Roberts' competence approach to recruitment, does the competence approach lend itself to a competence-based model of performance management? Such a model is shown in Figure 9.4.

Honey (1997:33) identifies the pros and cons of such an approach:

> Provided that competencies are specific, unambiguous and written down, they are useful in helping everyone know what is expected of their performance. Competencies also have the potential to aid learning and development, *but only if they are integrated into other key processes such as recruitment and selection, feedback and appraisal, coaching and mentoring and (the most contentious) pay. Without this integration there is a real danger that competencies are related to meaningless lists of words with no real impact.*

Competence-based/related pay

Competence-based or -related pay is another area of continuing debate. A report by Towers Perrin looking at European reward systems (1996), identifies that interest in competence-related pay is rising. Brown and Armstrong (1997) examined a number of approaches used by firms in the UK,

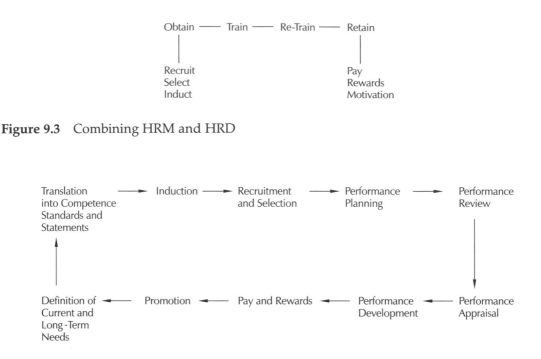

Figure 9.3 Combining HRM and HRD

Figure 9.4 Competence-based model of performance management

including Glaxo Wellcome, Bass, Volkswagen UK, Guinness, ICL, Thomas Cook, Portsmouth Housing Trust, Triplex Safety Glass, Abbey Life, Scottish Equitable, Derby City General Hospital NHS Trust, The Woolwich, and the Royal Bank of Scotland. Brown and Armstrong (1997) conclude that on the basis of their experience, competence-related pay is most appropriate when:

- competence is the key to competitive advantage;
- competence frameworks align with core business requirements;
- there are effective performance management processes;
- it covers knowledge workers for whom conventional performance-related schemes are often ineffective;
- the organization is flat and emphasis is on continuous and lateral development;
- a broadband pay structure is used.

Brown and Armstrong (1997) also point out that, 'An increasing number of organizations are relating salary increases to competence whilst rewarding exceptional achievements with bonuses.' Perhaps *contribution-related* pay would recognize both competence and performance better than either competence- or performance-related pay.

The CIPD *Reward Management Survey* (2004:2) confirms that more firms are using broad bands to organize their pay structures. Additionally the survey (2004:20) shows that most employers are paying for contributions through pay progression linked to individual performance and skills/competence. Variable pay is also used to award cash bonuses for exceptional achievement, linked commonly to either individual performance, or company profit or team performance.

So, the debate continues. Perhaps the only area of agreement by commentators and within organizations is that pay and rewards should ideally be a separate discussion to that of the appraisal discussion itself.

PERFORMANCE APPRAISAL

The purpose of appraisal

The purpose of performance planning, review and appraisal needs to be clearly articulated if individuals at all levels of the organization are going to play an active and productive part in the process.

Research carried out by the UK Institute of Personnel Management (now the Chartered Institute of Personnel and Development) identified a number of key purposes commonly used by organizations (Long, 1986):

- set performance objectives;
- review past performance;
- improve current performance;
- identify training and development needs;
- assist career-planning decisions;
- assess future potential and promotion;
- assess increases/new salary levels.

It is unlikely that the vast majority of organizations will include the full range of purposes within a single appraisal process. The trend would appear to be towards:

- initial planning and agreement of performance objectives;
- interim review of achievement against these (including necessary realignment to take account of changing circumstances);
- full review and appraisal identifying successes and areas of improvement arising from retrospective discussion of performance against objectives;
- planning, discussion and agreement of new objectives;
- identification, discussion and agreement of the support, training and development which will assist performance improvement.

Fletcher (1997:20) suggests that this *results-driven* approach is an extension of the notion of MBO. He also suggests that a growing number of organizations are putting together *results-oriented appraisal* with *competency-based* appraisal. Fletcher (1997:33) states:

This *is* a combination that can work well. It allows the more immediate and legitimate concern for achieving performance targets to co-exist with a focus on developing the appraisee – which in turn is related to the future performance of the organization. It combines the two most motivational elements of appraisal, namely goal setting and personal development. To maximize motivation and performance improvement, this would be the most promising way forward.

It is not the intention of this chapter to explore the aspects of promotion and career development or their relationship to appraisal. For the reader wanting to explore other approaches, Fletcher (1997), Herriot (1992) and Hirsch and Jackson (1995) offer a number of relevant and useful approaches.

APPRAISAL AND TRAINING IN A PRIVATE HOSPITAL

The annual performance appraisal is widely regarded as the platform for identifying training and development needs at the individual level. These needs, once identified, should then be actioned within the forthcoming year and preferably before the next appraisal.

The appraisal system of a medium-sized independent hospital, which is part of a large healthcare group, had been in place for six years and was thought to be functioning well by the management team. However, as a result of feedback from some of the staff, research was undertaken into the effectiveness of the appraisal process. There were five areas that gave rise to doubts about the actioning of training and development plans; these were:

1. The same training and development was identified for individuals for more than three years in succession.
2. Many plans were unrealistic and unachievable.
3. Enthusiasm often waned after the appraisal.
4. The training and development plans were not reviewed once written.
5. Training and development plans bore no relation to the departmental business plans and objectives.

A variety of research methods were used including questionnaire, interviews and a review of training records. The findings were then triangulated to corroborate the conclusions and action was introduced to address the following points:

- Preparation was an issue: only half the responders prepared for the appraisal. This preparation should include reflecting on previous years' work and training, reviewing the previous appraisal notes and preparing bullet point notes to take into the appraisal interview (see Figures 9.5 and 9.6).
- The staff, in some cases, were not given adequate notice of the appraisal date and time. In some instances there was no notice at all. This could affect preparation of both appraiser and appraisee and the formulation of realistic training and development plans.

- The department business plan was ignored, in a lot of cases, when training and development was being identified. The staff were often ignorant of the business goals and there was a lot of opposition to the concept of business planning and its effectiveness in the workplace.
- Training and development interventions were imposed on a significant number of staff. Agreement on any plan formulated between the appraiser and the appraisee is of paramount importance if the appraisee is to be motivated into completing his or her individual plan.
- In most cases the training and development identified was job-related with very little scope for personal development. Personal development is important in a learning environment and often leads to greater willingness to undertake further development.
- Reviews of the plans were very infrequent and lack of time was a major contributor to this issue. Apathy of both appraiser and appraisee was another important reason why the reviews were infrequent.
- The lack of time to perform adequate appraisals and formulate workable and productive training and development plans was seen to be the greatest barrier to achieving a good system. This was noted by both appraisers and appraisees.
- An understanding of business planning and some method of ensuring that all the staff were familiar with the contents of their business plans would greatly improve the situation.
- Lastly, a more participative style of management would certainly solve some of the problems found in the research.

With acknowledgement to Steven R Western, Training Manager, Independent Hospital.
(Western and Wilson, 2001)

Different forms of appraisal

Although different forms of review and appraisal have existed for a number of years, the move towards flexibility, cross-organizational working and self-managed teams has meant that many organizations now use a range of appraisal methods. Traditionally, appraisal has been viewed as a management prerogative in the majority of companies. Additionally, line manager appraisal, rather than being solely manager led, may also include elements of self-appraisal and upward appraisal by the appraisee. The position of team leader has also been increasingly introduced, whereby a member of the team rather than a manager assumes responsibility for the performance of the team.

There is also increasing evidence of the use of 360-degree feedback to combine aspects of line manager, peer, team, upward and self assessment. Competence review is also increasingly being built into appraisal processes.

Saville and Holdsworth (1997:10), reporting on a survey seeking the views of UK HR professionals, highlight the following points:

- The HR area regarded as most likely to impact on appraisals was corporate culture, with competences becoming a popular method of translating culture into individual performance.

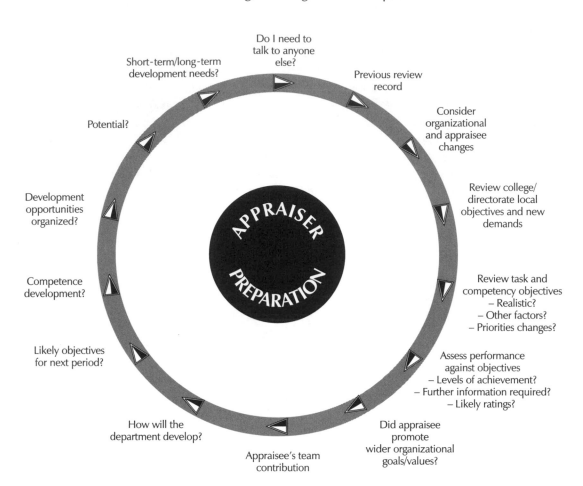

Figure 9.5 Appraiser preparation (from a model originally used by the former Bradford and Airedale College of Health – now the University of Bradford School of Health Studies)

- Even though teamworking was regarded as the second most important initiative impacting on appraisal, less than 40 per cent of responding organizations appeared to set team performance objectives.
- One of the methods regarded as being most useful within performance appraisal was a self-scoreable 360-degree questionnaire providing information on a manager's performance management style.

There are of course a growing range of personality questionnaires and diagnostic instruments that can be used by organizations and individuals to assess personality for self-reflection, assessment and development purposes. Assessment centres and development centres are being used by many organizations for selection and career development purposes. However, this section of the chapter will concentrate on identifying the range of forms of appraisal only.

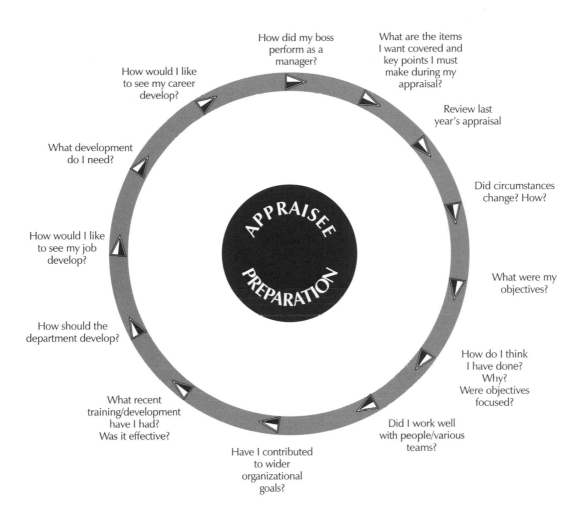

Figure 9.6 Appraisee preparation

Appraisal can be carried out in both *formal* and *informal* settings. Neither should be exclusive of the other. Good practice would seem to suggest that regular informal and formal reviews of performance, for example as part of a manager's normal duties, can mean that the formal yearly appraisal becomes less of a chore and more an extension of an ongoing discussion with the appraisee. Table 9.2 details the range of appraisal methods and identifies the features, advantages and disadvantages of each.

Who owns appraisal?

In all its forms, appraisal should be owned by both appraisers and appraisees as part of the psychological contract. Perhaps this is an ideal, but one that in the context of performance

Table 9.2 Appraisal methods and features

Type	Features	Advantages	Disadvantages
Line Manager appraisal	• Mechanism to link individual goals and strategic direction • Focus on objectives and targets • Can combine regular informal review of performance with formal appraisal to agreed timescales • May include rating scales for comparison purposes	• Clarity about what is expected of the individual and the manager • Identification of performance priorities and agreed actions • Forum for better understanding between manager and employee • Potential to promote better understanding of shared objectives • Can establish appraisal as a two-way process	• Needs the commitment of both manager and subordinate to spend appropriate time on the process • Insufficient preparation by either manager or employee • Failure to follow up on actions agreed • Misuse of comparative rating scales • Lack of support and feedback skills by managers
Self-appraisal	• Often used as preparation for the line manager/subordinate appraisal • Individuals take the lead in reviewing their own performance • Encourages individuals to think about their performance and development needs in a focused way • The combination of involvement and responsibility generates commitment to personally taking action	• Best if individuals compare themselves against their own individual standards rather than others • Works best when geared towards motivation and development • Individuals are most aware of their own performance and are generally critically honest • Less subject to halo effect and is consequently more discriminating	• Lack of objectivity on the part of the individual • Can be prone to either excessive or lenient self-assessment • Individuals may think that they are going to be told about their performance by their manager, so why should they bother
Upward appraisal	• Appropriate in multi-level or source appraisal settings • May take place in the context of the subordinate's appraisal	• Has the potential to establish understanding of shared objectives • Appraisal seen as a two-way process	• Subordinates are likely to be reserved in making meaningful comment • Fear of retaliation if too honest

Table 9.2   *continued*

Type	Features	Advantages	Disadvantages
Peer appraisal	• Individuals nominate their own appraiser • Allows choice of peers who are respected for relevant knowledge or professional specialization • Relevant in a situation where there may be no immediate manager in a position to appraise	• Peers are likely to be members of the same professional specialization or group • Appraiser authority comes from expert power not position power • Peers are knowledgeable about specialist field and the contribution of the individual	• Needs careful control • Appraisee may choose a peer appraiser on the grounds of friendship or as a soft touch
Team review and appraisal	• Establishing team success and areas for improvement • Aids the team-building and objective-setting process • Encourages open and constructive comment among the team • Encourages cooperation among the team	• Complementary to individual performance appraisal • Gives opportunity for the team to discuss issues which may not have been previously debated by boss and subordinate • Establishes commitment from the individual towards team not just individual objectives	• Needs the willingness of all team members to participate • Team may be good at giving positive feedback but less so in giving negative constructive feedback • Team members may be apprehensive about appraising colleagues
Competency-based appraisal	• Setting targets for the roles as specific objectives or other measurable objectives • Behavioural descriptions of the standards expected in fulfilling the role • A development plan specifying training, development and support towards achieving targets and competences • A system of periodic review leading to annual appraisal of performance against targets and achievement of competences	• Developmentally oriented • Directs attention towards improvement of skills • Does not deal with results achievement • Concentrates on the medium to long term rather than the short term	• The nature and quality of the competence statements and their fit with other organizational initiatives • The expectations of employees and the relationship between competence achievement and pay and rewards

Table 9.2 *continued*

Type	Features	Advantages	Disadvantages
360-degree feedback	• The focus is on development of skills and competences which will improve organizational performance • Appraisees may include either direct or other managers, subordinates, peers or customers • Feedback is collected systematically through formally constructed questionnaires • Can include self-assessment for comparison with the views of others • May allow individual to choose who contributes • Is essentially based on ratings which more often than not are aggregated to represent an average score	• Gives a comprehensive indication of the totality of the individuals performance and relationships • Has the potential to overcome the bias of a traditional one person top-down review or appraisal • Peers and subordinates can have an input to the process and can view it as a process which empowers them • Can be incorporated into other appraisal processes • Seems to suit organizations where they need flexibility and teamwork within a less hierarchical structure	• Depends on the design of the questionnaire and how it fits with other organizational performance criteria • Depends on the interpretation and skills of the person giving the final feedback • Depends on the accuracy and quality of the ratings provided by all contributors • Depends on the criteria for choosing contributors. Is the choice free or forced? • Concerns over whether feedback is used exclusively for development or is part of the normal appraisal process and if so whether it is linked to pay and rewards

management needs to be addressed. HRD professionals have a major part to play in influencing this process and in changing negative perceptions into positive contexts for appraisal. Assisting appraisers in developing feedback skills is an end, not a beginning.

A useful starting point in changing perceptions is the following model of active performance management and appraisal which is focused on:

- feedback on *behaviour* instead of *personality;*
- concentration on the *future* instead of the *past;*
- an ethos of *improvement* instead of *punishment;*
- feedback based on *precision* instead of *generalities;*
- comment based on *information* instead of *belief;*
- securing of *commitment* instead of *compliance;*
- active *support* instead of *directive;*
- appraisal that is *person-centred* instead of *form-centred;*
- a process owned by *everyone* instead of *administered by Personnel;*
- a philosophy of *how can **we** benefit* instead of *what can **I** get* from you.

Trust

An overriding consideration for any organization is that it can establish *mutual trust.* The model of active performance management and performance appraisal relies on an open, constructive and trusting relationship between all parties concerned.

I am reminded of a presentation given at the American Society for Training and Development Conference and Exposition in 1996 by Stephen Covey. He argued that if you do not first establish 360-degree trust, then how can you expect to achieve meaningful 360-degree appraisal?

Returning to the theme of the psychological contract, if one party such as the organization is implying that innovation, creativity and risk-taking are the key to organizational success, but then punishing employees for taking risks and making mistakes, trust by employees in their employer has been betrayed. Where downsizing and de-layering have become the rule rather than the exception, trust in their employers by the current or potential workforce has got to be re-established as a key element of business strategy.

Open expression of trust can, however, be espoused by organizations, not by corporate rhetoric but by actions taken and by active and honest communication of business circumstances, whether they be good or bad.

Handy (1997:189–94) notes the importance of organizational trust when he states:

> We manage our young on a loose rein, but the rein is always there, getting looser and looser as we trust them more. It is no different in organisations. By trust, organisations really mean confidence, a confidence in someone's competence and their commitment to meet a goal. Define that goal and the trusted individual or team can be left to get on with it. Control is then exercised after the event by assessing the results, rather than before the event, by granting permission.

This brief quote captures the essence of what good performance management is all about: *confidence; commitment; competence; definition of goals; trust; individual and team effort; support; and finally appraisal or assessment of results.*

Then the cycle starts again based on:

- What did we do well?
- What would we do differently next time?
- What are our areas for improvement?
- How are we going to address these?
- How are we going to evaluate our actions?

It sounds like the classic appraisal and feedback format doesn't it? It is, but it is placed in the context of organizational learning, performance improvement and progress. So what are the implications for the key stakeholders in the process?

CONCLUSION

Implications for organizations, managers and individuals

The clear message arising from research for this chapter is that successful organizations will be the ones which:

1. Explore their current and future markets in a truly strategic sense in order to anticipate trends and prepare for them before they actually happen.
2. Translate the needs of the external business environment into the actualities of the internal organizational environment by sharing and communicating strategic vision and goals. This includes sharing both the good and bad news with employees.
3. Take a systems approach to linking each of their key business strategies together. If long-term strategic planning has taken place, then *strategic systems planning* also needs to take place.
4. Consider the cultural aspects of globalization if they are competing in a worldwide marketplace. The national norms and values of the parent company are not necessarily those of employees in other parts of the world.
5. Consider the effects that ongoing change and reconfiguration will have on the workforce and plan to communicate the rationale behind change to employees rather than impose it on them.
6. Create or at least understand the type of organizational culture/s that will support both the business and its employees.
7. Evaluate their current performance management system on a regular basis and take action to identify gaps and address them.

The common element in each of the above seven points is people and their relationship with and potential to the business. A ten-year longitudinal study (1991 to 2000) entitled 'Impact of people management practices on business performance' (IPD, 1997b:16) reports:

The results reveal that acquisition and development of skills (selection, induction, training and appraisal) and job design (job variety and responsibility, skill flexibility and teamworking) are significant predictors of both change in productivity and change in profitability.

The ideal scenario, suggested by Bassi *et al* (1996:41) includes:

- performance management systems that encourage development, that are highly motivating and that are equitable;
- compensation (pay) systems that reward the best performers appropriately and motivate behaviours critical to business success;
- training and development systems that provide employees with the skills and behaviours for their current and future jobs in the organization.

Implications for HRD professionals and practitioners

There are no easy or simple solutions in the application of performance management, whichever function or discipline within an organization we may belong to. What is evident is that traditional roles and practices are in many cases no longer relevant to the world of today. The reality of the lean organization requires the breaking down of traditional boundaries and barriers.

Modern business requires employees at all levels to be flexible and adaptable. The ability of employees to work across professional disciplines within high performance teams is an oft-quoted example in competence statements and management texts. As Holbeche (1997) states, 'Lean organizations depend on their ability to create and dissolve teams and to enable teamwork uncluttered by functional boundaries or inflexibility.'

If, for example, we extrapolate this into the changing role of the HRD professional, what might this mean? Traditional training officers/managers might consider that the main elements of their role are to identify training needs, design and deliver appropriate training and development courses and initiatives and evaluate them. To do so might involve dialogue with others outside the function but often at an operational level. What will be required of HRD professionals in the future in relation both to performance management and our roles in general, is, where appropriate:

- *To become actively involved at a strategic level within organizations.* Hendry, Bradley and Perkins (1997:20) highlight the fact that if a cross-section of business leaders were to be asked what they understood performance management to be it would result in extremely shallow comment. They state:

  We also lack common understanding of what we mean by integrated performance management. It is unclear as to whether anyone has achieved this. For example, do companies see performance management as part of strategic planning and strategy implementation? The three parties in these processes – HR, finance and strategic planning – do not collaborate at all in the development of their various processes. There is a need to bring these into sync. *One of the things HR professionals can do is to become part and parcel of the strategic planning process at the earliest stage.*

- *To act as change agents and internal consultants in identifying and supporting approaches that are key to the success of the business and which will attract the support and commitment of senior management.*
- *To work in and with project teams across the organization to facilitate the process of change and learning.*

What I am also suggesting is that we cannot expect others to assume new responsibilities or reappraise their roles if we are not modelling the process ourselves. What is evident is that there would appear to be three levels of HRD practice:

1. *Strategic:* influencing, negotiating, planning, organizational development.
2. *Operational*: internal consultant, project team member/leader, facilitator, identifier of training and development interventions, and generalist.
3. *Specialist:* designer, deliverer, subject expert, technician.

We may feel *comfortable* working at one of or across the range of levels. We may however be *required* to work across all three as a result of the downsizing of the HR function in many organizations.

A case in point. My contract over the last eight years has been a continuous one but has involved working for three different 'employers' in five different locations.

Some might call it occupational schizophrenia. I call it survival, but survival with benefits. I entered HRD as a trainer, but after 20 years in the profession I would now regard myself as an educator, trainer and developer. Yes, I receive encouragement and support from my employers, but essentially I see myself as being responsible for my own performance improvement and, to a great extent, my own performance management.

Perhaps that is what performance management is really all about. Integrated systems have a part to play in it but it's about *people* and *mutuality*. Mutual survival through mutual support and progress.

Bibliography

Armstrong, M (1996) *Performance Management Survey*, IPD press release, London

Bassi, L J, Benson, G and Cheney, S (1996) 'Top ten trends', *Training and Development*, November, p 28

Birchall, D and Tovstiga, G (1999) 'The strategic potential of a firms knowledge portfolio', *Journal of Management*, **17**, pp 99–120

Brown, D and Armstrong, M (1997) 'Terms of enrichment', *People Management*, 11 September, pp 36–38

Chartered Institute of Personnel and Development (CIPD) (2001) *Performance through People: The new people management*, London, CIPD

CIPD (2004) *Reward Management Survey*, London, CIPD

CIPD/Engineering Employers Federation (EEF) (2003) *Maximising Employee Potential and Business Performance: The role of high performance working*, London, EEF

Drucker, P (1954) *The Practice of Management*, Maidenhead, McGraw-Hill

Easterby-Smith, M and Graca, M (2004) 'Self service: can your organisation make rapid strategic changes when necessary, even to core competences?' *People Management*, **10**, 3, February, pp 37–38

Edis, M (1995) *Performance Management and Appraisal in Health Services*, London, Kogan Page

Egan, G (1995) 'A clear path to peak performance', *People Management*, 18 May, p 35

Fletcher C (1997) *Appraisal: Routes to improved performance*, 2nd edn, London, IPD

Fowler, A (1990) 'Performance management: the MBO of the 1990s', *Personnel Management*, **22**, 7, pp 47–51

Garavan, T N, Morley, M, Gunnigle, P and Collins, E (2001) 'Human capital accumulation: the role of human resource development', *Industrial Training*, **25**, 2/3/4, pp 48–68

Gratton, L (1997) 'Tomorrow people', *People Management*, 24 July, pp 25–26

Hamel, G and Prahalad, C K (1994) *Competing for the Future*, Cambridge, MA, Harvard Business School Press

Handy, C B (1985) *Understanding Organizations*, 3rd edn, Harmondsworth, Penguin

Handy, C B (1997) *The Hungry Spirit*, London, Hutchinson-Random House

Harrison, R (1997) *Employee Development*, London, IPD

Harrison, R and Kessels, J (2004) *Human Resource Development in a Knowledge Economy: An organisational view*, Basingstoke, Palgrave Macmillan

Hendry, C, Bradley, P and Perkins, S (1997) 'Missed a motivator', *People Management*, 15 May, p 20

Herriot, P (1992) *The Career Management Challenge: Balancing individual and organizational needs*, London, Sage

Herriott, P and Pemberton, C (1997) 'Facilitating new deals', *Human Resources Management*, **7**, 1, pp 45–46

Hirsch, W and Jackson, C (1995) *Careers in Organizations: Issues for the future report*, London, Institute of Employment Studies

Honey, P (1997) *Improve Your People Skills*, 2nd edn, London, IPD

Hodkinson, R (1997) 'Japanese forced into HR strategy rethink', report by Arthur Andersen, London, *People Management*, 23 October, p 16

Holbeche, L (1997) *Motivating People in Lean Organizations*, Oxford, Butterworth-Heinemann

Institute of Personnel and Development (IPD) (1997a) *Reward Management Portfolio*, London, IPD, p 7

IPD (1997b) *Issues in People Management No. 22, Impact of people management practices on business performance*, London, IPD, p 16

IPD (1997c) *Consultative Document: Opportunity through people*, London, IPD

Long, P (1986) *Performance Appraisal Revisited: Third IPM survey*, London, IPM

Losey, M R (1999) 'Mastering the competencies of HR managers', *Human Resource Management*, **38**, 2, pp 99–111

McBeath, G (1990) *Practical Management Development: Strategies for management resourcing and development in the 1990s*, Oxford, Blackwell

Mohrman, A M and Mohrman, S A (1995) *Performance Management is Running the Business: The new pay tool*, New York, American Management Association, p 2

Prisano, G, Teece, D and Shuen, A (1997) 'Dynamic capabilities and strategic management', *Strategic Management Journal*, **18**

Roberts, G (1997) *Recruitment and Selection: A competency approach*, London, IPD

Saville and Holdsworth (1997) '1997 Appraisal survey', *Saville and Holdsworth Newsline*, October

Schein, E (1964) *Organizational Psychology*, 2nd edn, Hemel Hempstead, Prentice Hall

Singapore Institute of Management and Development Dimensions International (1994) *Singapore*, Singapore, SIM/DDI

Sloman, M (2003) *Training in the Age of the Learner*, London, CIPD

Spangenburg, H H, Schroder, H M and Duvenge, A (1999) 'A leadership competence utilisation questionnaire for South African managers', *South African Journal of Psychology*, **29**, 3, pp 117–29

Towers Perrin (1996) *Learning from the Past – Changing for the Future*, London, Towers Perrin

Trompenaars, F (1995) 'Worldwide vision in the workplace', *People Management*, 18 May, pp 25–26

Vroom, V (1965) *Work and Motivation*, Chichester, Wiley

Western, S and Wilson, J P (2001) 'Performance appraisal: An obstacle to training and development; *Career Development International*, vol. 6, No 2, pp 93–99

Wright, P M, Dunford, B B and Snell, S A (2001) 'Human resources and the resource-based view of the firm', *Journal of Management*, **27**, pp 701–21

10

Making the Most of Consultancy: Perspectives on Partnership

David Sawdon

INTRODUCTION AND LEARNING OBJECTIVES

The literature on the use of consultancy, whether internal or external, to enhance individual and/or organizational effectiveness is comparatively sparse. We can, nevertheless, begin to detect different themes, strands and emphases to guide us through the territory. There is, for example, a clear theme of *evolution* and *transition* from trainer to consultant in various guises (Holdaway and Saunders, 1996; Phillips and Shaw, 1996), which recognizes the need for letting go of *performing* as a trainer and acknowledges transferable competences into consultancy. Alternatively, others are more concerned with how organizations might *select* and *use* consultants and become more competent in obtaining value from the endeavour (Bailey and Sproston, 1993; Kubr, 1986, 1993). Each contributor necessarily reflects on *purpose, principles, roles* and *process,* providing comparable three, four, or five stage models, which are often analysed in terms of critical steps, eg, Margerison (1995). Some choose to focus on the *interpersonal skills* and *dynamics* which facilitate the intervention (Heron, 1991; Honey, 1994; Margerison, 1995) and the creation of an 'equal partnership with clients' (Phillips and Shaw, 1996). Others suggest key approaches variously highlighting 'the dynamics of creativity and innovation' (Sonesh-Kedor and Geirland, 1995) or the value of 'dialogue' in promoting organizational learning (Blantern 1997; Senge, 1990).

At this point, depending upon your perspective and need for information, the boundaries of the territory being explored can either expand considerably or, conversely, contract. They can expand in the sense that the literature on central issues to consultancy like managing change, organizational development and interpersonal skills is extensive and, wherever you choose to look, at random or with purpose, you are likely to find some little nugget of value. Alternatively, notions of transferability, core processes, frameworks and skills tend to emerge, whose universality requires discrete application according to context and need. The skills of consultancy may well be perceived as mirroring those of a therapeutic counsellor, for example, and thus we might choose to narrow our focus of study; see, for example, Brown (1984) and Pont (1995). One challenge, therefore, might be to refine and enhance those core skills in the interests of individual and organizational effectiveness, rather than to allow the organizational context to dictate and potentially restrict what is brought into play. A second complementary challenge for the potential traveller is to resist the need to reinvent the wheel. We can acknowledge our available experience, yet still be open in a reflective manner to learning from alternative disciplinary perspectives and how these might be adapted to suit our specific individual and organizational context.

Having taken an initial glance at the terrain, my intention is to give some order or structure to the journey while acknowledging that most journeys of this type have their own elements of unpredictability. A starting point would seem to be to explore *purpose and meaning*; and, bearing in mind the differing contexts where consultancy can have relevance, to take this further into different *perspectives and needs*. Third, analyses of *process* and the *power* issues involved will aim to draw out the roles, characteristics, skills and dynamics. And finally, the culture of the times requires us to examine the notion of *partnership* models, issues and possibilities as a desirable, if not essential, condition for effective outcomes. The use of the alliterative *'p'* is meant to be purposeful, though not excluding, and the reader may well wish to add or amend his or her own terms to accommodate diverse perceptions and problems.

Having read this chapter you will:

- know the four criteria for selecting a consultant;
- be aware of the various roles a consultant can adopt;
- understand the steps involved in a consultancy intervention.

PURPOSE AND MEANING

Steinberg (1989:1), discussing consultation in the context of health and social care practice, cites 85 alternative words to describe the activity. His point is that 'an essentially friendly and user-orientated enterprise' has tended to be hijacked or usurped to meet various specialized purposes. Within his context, it entails one person (the consultant) helping another (the consultee) to do his or her work, 'without taking it over; the consultee retains control of work in hand, the methods used and responsibility for it too'. This unremarkable definition, with its primary emphasis on facilitation or enabling within individualized relationships, may lack weight or direction for some. Equally, the notion that, 'consultants are very much in the business of trying to meet the expectations of their clients' (Holdaway and Saunders, 1996:26) may for others only be seen as stating the obvious. At this point, therefore, caution is required in case we fall into the common negative stereotyping of the consultant as being someone who tells you something you already know. Both the definitions offered above are deceptive; their weight lies within their respective implications.

Margerison (1995:12) might be considered more direct. Consultation, he argues, has always implied giving advice: 'some people having special knowledge which, when required, can be dispensed at a cost to others'. The concept is, however, changing rapidly into: 'a set of activities designed to improve things'. In this sense, consultancy might be applied to a wide range of relationships within an organization just as much as it involves relationships between client organizations and consultants. The role is multifaceted.

What clearly emerges for Kubr (1993) is that the term 'consultant' is generic and can be applied to any person or organization that provides advice to decision-makers: 'Anyone who feels like it can call himself a consultant – if he finds people willing to listen to him.' The risks in such a situation are considerable. Kubr (1993:10–11) thus cites the International Labour Organization's four guiding criteria for selecting a consultant to offer us another insight into the purpose and meaning of consultation:

1. The consultant *offers and provides something that the client is lacking* but wishes to acquire in various areas of business and management knowledge, expertise, experience or know-how (technical competence).
2. The consultant is someone who *knows how to work with clients in helping to identify and solve their problems* (consulting know-how).
3. The consultant is an *independent and objective adviser* (independence).
4. The consultant is someone who has chosen to abide by a *professional code of ethics and conduct* (professional integrity).

If there is any coherence to be obtained from these various attempts at defining purpose, it is that consultancy will be about change, not necessarily from bad to good, but in the interests of improving things. Further, the growing references to the importance of the relationship imply that a sense of partnership can be productive. Some will want a facilitator, others a healer, yet others will want to be authoritatively advised. In reality, we may want and expect a combined package and more, based on trust and absolute honesty, to serve our interests. What transpires will depend considerably on our respective abilities to clarify assumptions, perceptions and needs.

PERCEPTIONS AND NEEDS

Advice is seldom welcome and those who want (or need) it most always like it least. (Earl of Chesterfield, 1774)

It has been suggested that organizational decisions to contract with consultants may often be based on the 'management by rain-dance syndrome' where problems or needs must be seen to be addressed. Cleverley (1971), for example, likens the consultant to a primitive witch doctor called in to perform:

- *exorcism* (diagnosing the causes of the problem and eliminating them);
- *placating demons* (internal morale building by identifying external or structural dysfunction);
- *soothsaying* (forecasting or prescribing the future).

The emphasis is on impact and some cathartic expression of emotional pressures. The efficacy of the consultant's intervention is not subject to rational, empirical test. If recommendations work, then he or she accrues high credibility and power. If they do not work, then the organization has failed to carry out the directives satisfactorily. 'The thought that failure might be due to a flaw in the medicine itself is unacceptable.'

Such a perception of the role and functions of a consultant and the needs to be addressed may indeed be a realistic metaphor in some situations, and not without significant consequences.

CONSULTING IN A HEALTHCARE ENVIRONMENT

A large multidisciplinary health care organization in the UK contracted with external consultants to provide training and consultancy for one of its specialist units in the area of equal opportunities. The expressed objectives were about raising awareness, improving practice, liaison between disciplines and improved service delivery. In effect, the real problem, not articulated, was that some staff were resistant to change and were managing to block structural and procedural development proposals so that an impasse had been reached.

In the course of their intervention, the consultants initially placated the demons by facilitating full expression of emotional pressures about the dysfunctional nature of the situation and, in the process, diagnosed the causes of the problem. Predictions were that, if certain practices did not change, exorcism or elimination of some staff would be inevitable. Although the intervention provided considerable emotional impact, practice did not change in any discernible way and the predicted exorcism took place. In one sense, it could be argued that the consultants were used to manipulate a required change and the only issue was how they helped to achieve it. Alternatively, it was apparent that everyone was stuck and some external force was needed to give the momentum towards change.

Whether or not internal consultants have similar powers is open to debate. Phillips and Shaw (1996:74–5) offer us solid lists of advantages and disadvantages in the internal versus external consultancy discussion, while Margerison (1995) offers a quadrant model highlighting the advisory and the executive role of the consultant; see Figure 10.1.

The potential tensions for the internal consultant lie between having the inside familiarity with the issues and personnel, and yet being insufficiently detached from them to provide freshness and distance. These appear to mirror the tensions for the external consultant, who will need time to discover the internal issues while being seen to be outside the politics of the organization. Thus the tentative conclusions reached by Phillips and Shaw (1996:76) are worth noting:

Figure 10.1   The four roles of a consultant, after Margerison (1995: 5)

- Internal and external consultants working together have the potential to be a highly effective partnership if they make conscious use of the benefits of each other's position and help each other to overcome drawbacks.
- Internal consultants are likely to be more effective if, as far as possible, they manage themselves and their client relationships as though they are external.

It can, therefore, be more helpful to recognize the connections than to exploit the differences. Such positive perceptions allow the possibility of charting the valid transition from trainer to consultant (Holdaway and Saunders, 1996; Phillips and Shaw, 1996) and to acknowledge the 'shamrock organization' described by Handy (1985). Common negative perceptions of the consultant as a failed or redundant practitioner can be re-framed as purposeful career development. Thus, Phillips and Shaw (1996:18) are able to trace three broad developmental paths for trainers:

a.   from training to consulting;
b.   from training to learning;
c.   from individual change to organizational change;

and to arrive at four approaches to training and consultancy:

1   trainer;
2.   training consultant;
3.   learning consultant;
4.   organization change consultant.

These kinds of analyses can give greater clarity to the key questions around the type of consultant being sought or available; what the focus of their work might be; and their likely impact on organizational effectiveness. They also suggest a continuity and valuing of the developing experience of training professionals within and without their employing organization. This raises inevitable questions about credibility, influence and power within organizational development.

PROCESS AND POWER

One of the key underlying themes in the discussion so far has been concerned with how power is exercised by the different parties or stakeholders and, in particular, by consultants. How will change take place and who will decide – the consultant alone, the consultant and clients together, or the clients alone, having consulted? Heron (1991) defines these states as the three political modes of facilitation or the politics of learning:

- *the hierarchical mode* – facilitator/consultant directs the process, takes primary responsibility for diagnosis, proposals for change, exercising authoritative power in the relationship;
- *the cooperative mode* – facilitator/consultant shares his or her power in collaborating, nudging, guiding clients towards greater self-direction through negotiation;
- *the autonomous mode* – facilitator/consultant respects the ability of clients to find their own way and helps to create the conditions whereby full self-determination can operate.

The effective consultant facilitator is someone who can use all of these three modes within the different stages of a consultancy intervention according to the needs and abilities of the parties involved. This construct, and Heron develops this further, has the merit of transcending most situations whether individual, group or organizational and can be applied in therapeutic, advisory and business/management interactions. It also illustrates that consulting is an art where the consultant needs to be able to exercise skill and judgement within each unique assignment, rather than slavishly following a technicist formula.

POST-TRAUMATIC STRESS DISORDER AND BANK RAIDS

An interesting example of consulting can be found in the field of disaster management. A bank wants to ensure that staff can process the trauma of an armed attack in any of its public outlets. It recognizes that post-traumatic stress can lead to sickness/absenteeism, poor work performance, and potential decline in the quality of customer service. It also acknowledges that some form of counselling/debriefing may have individual and organizational benefits.

During the first stages of negotiation/entry/contracting, it is likely that the expertise of the consultant in this specific area of disaster management will give him or her power to propose ways in which matters should be addressed to produce positive outcomes. He or she can take primary responsibility for diagnosis, and exercise authoritative power in the relationship. The bank, whose primary focus is not counselling nor debriefing, may well want some measurable outcome indicators, eg, how soon can they expect 'normal service' to be resumed, but it is unlikely to be able to challenge process and methodology. At the point of delivery of a service (following an incident) traumatized employees may well need the consultant(s) to take charge, to hold the process of debriefing, to provide insights and reassurance. Thus the consultant's capacity to operate in the hierarchical mode comes with the territory, and is expected.

The skilled facilitator in this context, however, will recognize that each individual can present his or her own response to the alleged trauma, and ultimately will need to find his or her own solution. Thus a collaborative approach can acknowledge a gradual shift from potential dependency on the expert through guidance towards greater self-direction. Some may reject any suggestion that they are suffering trauma as a result of the incident. The skilled facilitator consultant respects the ability of each participant to find his or her own way of dealing with what has happened, and helps to create the conditions whereby he or she can exercise that autonomy.

Dilemmas may arise if the healing process takes longer than hoped for in the bank's terms, and is compromised by commercial/organizational considerations. Finding a formula that meets the concerns of each stakeholder will challenge all parties in their exercise of power.

While artistry is, by definition, fluid, subjective and idiosyncratic there would seem to be a large measure of objective agreement among contributors about the requisite stages or cycles of intervention (see Table 10.1).

There are clear differences in language and style and the detail with which each stage is broken down into steps. Moreover, as Margerison (1995) warns, 'Although they are presented in a sequential order, real life consulting projects do not always easily fall into such a pattern.' We can and should expect, however, some coherence in terms of a beginning, middle and end to the process, and be able to explain where we have got to at any point in time.

The artistry and the critical differences will tend to be evident in the way any given consultant exercises power, his or her style and models of intervention. Heron (1991:21) would argue that there are good and bad methods of facilitation, 'but there is no one right and proper method. There are innumerable valid approaches, each bearing the signature of different idiosyncratic facilitators.' Perhaps the most provocative attempt to categorize these alleged idiosyncrasies is that by Margerison (1995), who proposes four role models of consultancy by analogy with four well-known professions. These are:

1. *The Doctor* – client has illness/disease which needs diagnosis and cure.
2. *The Detective* – something is wrong; need to find who is responsible and deal with it or them.
3. *The Salesperson* – has a product to sell which will solve the problem.
4. *The Travel Agent* – finding the best route for where the client wants to go.

Maister (1989) offers a similar quadrant model but refines the medical analogy by comparing the consultancy approach to the following four models:

1. *Psychotherapy/Family Doctor* – interactive skill process.
2. *Nursing* – familiar routine problem, assistance needed.
3. *Surgery* – complex problem, high risk, technical expertise needed.
4. *Pharmacy* – straightforward, routine problem; speedy response at low cost.

Table 10.1 Stages or cycles of intervention

Margerison (1995)	Burke (1982)	Phillips and Shaw (1996)	Holdaway and Saunders (1996)	Heron (1991)
Appraisal (4 steps)	Entry	Gaining entry	Making and securing contact	Planning
Assessment (4 steps)	Contracting Diagnosis	Agreeing a working contract	Data collection	Meaning Confronting
Application (4 steps)	Feedback Planning Change	Data collection, analysis and diagnosis	Identifying problems and agreeing the contract	Feeling Structuring Valuing
	Intervention Evaluation	Formulating proposals	Project management	
		Feedback to clients and decision to act Implementation Follow-up	Learning design and implementing change Disengagement and continuation	

Margerison clearly favours the travel agent model, with the consultant using his or her power in a cooperative mode through providing information about potential 'vehicles' and 'maps' to reach negotiated 'destinations' chosen by the client. One has a sense that the client's autonomy is respected and the consultancy service is about generating and selecting preferred options in partnership.

It is not particularly difficult to propose a list of core and specialist consultancy skills relevant to the stages, roles and approaches described. Such lists, however, often run the danger of describing a paragon and most readers will now be familiar with competency models that can fill huge volumes. Within the space of a brief chapter, my own view tends to reflect the earlier proposal, that consultancy skills will often mirror those of a therapeutic counsellor, coach or mentor (see for example, Carkhuff, 1983; Egan, 1962; Pont, 1995:143). Thus, the active listening skills or behaviours – attending, clarifying, reflecting back data, paraphrasing, summarizing, probing, giving feedback, recognizing and expressing feelings – will have core relevance as underpinning each of the phases of gaining entry, diagnosis, action-planning, implementation and termination (Kubr, 1993). They are also consistent with the 'Five lessons for internal OD consultants' proposed by Geirland and Maniker-Leiter (1996:295):

1. establish your authority;
2. bring added value to the organization;
3. create rapport;
4. avoid misunderstandings; and
5. show courage.

Authority, added value, rapport, avoiding misunderstandings and courage are elements that imply and attract powerful emotions and opinion. They are often less tangible, less measurable than many would like but they tend to constitute the oil that lubricates the consultancy relationship. Any consultant, whether working with an individual in a mentoring context, or with a group of clients with an organizational brief, ignores the feelings and dynamics at his or her peril.

PARTNERSHIP

A collaborative approach involves an attitude of mind and some explicitly negotiated agreements. (Phillips and Shaw, 1996:58)

Partnership, like community, is a term much open to abuse in the sense that it can be attached or sprayed like graffiti on to any issue or situation with a view to making it palatable. That is to say, partnership or collaboration are assumed to be good things. As Ross (1982) has pointed out, however, it depends. Collaboration, in his view, is only one style of managing conflict whereby both parties manage to secure what they want. The necessary conditions are time, energy and a willingness to assert one's own needs while seeking to cooperate or enable the other person(s) to do the same.

Not all conflict situations, however, are best resolved by collaboration alone and access to other styles such as competing, compromising, accommodating and avoiding will enhance our management of such occurrences. A consultant may set out to work in partnership, but along the way may need to question whether a requested shift or new direction, or cut in budget from others outside the original plan represents an unacceptable compromise in relation to key principles and values, for example, or can be accommodated. The next review meeting may reveal that there is minimal choice, or power, to compete with the announced request. The remaining options may be avoidance by pretending nothing has changed – a dangerous course – or to withdraw from the project. Margerison (1995:112–14) paints some graphic pictures of the implications for the external consultant in rejecting assignments; alternatively, Phillips and Shaw (1996:87) encourage the internal consultant to acquire skills in 'the redefinition and re-framing of problems instead of rushing straight into solutions'.

The basic message would again appear to be that effective consultancy requires a certain artistry in the flexible employment of different styles and approaches according to the demands of the situation. Partnership will not necessarily be synonymous with feeling comfortable, nor cosy, but demands hard work on both sides to deliver the agreed objectives, when circumstances conspire to derail the best of intentions. Deadlines, competing stakeholder interests, overwhelming complexities, apathy and general turbulence make uneasy sleeping partners.

Most of us faced with such potential complexity and chaos reach for the security of a unifying theme, which in reality is likely to be an 'attitude of mind', a vision or dream towards which we can strive with varying degrees of success. A core unifying theme figures powerfully in the literature on organizational learning (eg, Argyris and Schon, 1978; Dixon, 1994; Drucker, 1992) and the now familiar concept of the learning company (Harrison, 1995; Pedler *et al*, 1997; Senge, 1990). The focus on learning allows us to embrace some of the core principles of adult education and transformative learning (Mezirow, 1990) and recognizes with Bennis (1993) that 'in complex systems and turbulent times, no one individual or group possesses enough knowledge to do the jobs of everyone else in the organization'. Similarly, Senge (1990:241), quoting Bohm, maintains that through dialogue:

> People are no longer primarily in opposition, nor can they be said to be interacting, rather they are participating in this pool of common meaning, which is capable of constant development and change.

It follows, therefore, that a primary focus on enquiry, learning and understanding means working together with others, based on mutual trust, respect and mutual recognition of the different contributions. The 'explicitly negotiated agreements' with consultants are most likely to be formulated in a working contract. Kubr (1993:141–51) offers us an 'international contract outline', while Phillips and Shaw (1996:54) suggest that, 'There is no single way of writing a contract – it may be informal or formal, a lengthy document, a letter or just a set of points.' Bailey and Sproston (1993) provide us with a range of checklists to inform the process, inviting us to think about day-to-day management, equipping the consultant, managing the information, involving others, managing the finance, time and the unexpected, and ensuring good value. Geirland and Maniker-Leiter (1996) propose six key areas for discussion and defining the contract, 'to avoid misunderstandings'.

Gaining access to this evocative and elusive 'pool of common meaning' will present different challenges to the internal and external consultant. Contracts, promises and agreements are frequently broken without redress, so partnership or collaboration cannot rely on them in isolation. Many of the checklists and outlines offered above often tread a fine line between wanting to control the deviant consultant and giving him or her unlimited power and access to influence the organization.

Let us draw this journey towards some kind of resting place, therefore, with a final reference to what Senge (1990:276–86) describes as 'participative openness' and 'reflective openness'. Although many managers, trainers, consultants and counsellors pride themselves on being 'open', experience suggests that this is frequently restricted or tainted by game-playing. The freedom to speak one's mind (participative openness) within an organization or relationship needs to be complemented by the skills of critical reflection and enquiry (reflective openness). 'It involves not just examining our own ideas but mutually examining others' thinking.' Such skills, however, take time and persistence to develop and many will choose to avoid the task or be ignorant of their existence. They are, however, crucial to making consultancy work.

Given 'the planet wide shift from authoritarian power to collaborative power' (Bourget, 1996), consultants require strong role clarity, a sense of comfort with their own power, and a willingness to 'let go' (Bourget, 1996) in enabling the client autonomy proposed by Heron (1991). Given the comparative absence of 'reflective openness' skills across the different levels of most organizations, human resource professionals, internal and external, would appear to be key figures. They can both demonstrate by personal example and facilitate others in learning the power of Senge's vision to enhance individual and organizational development.

Bibliography

Argyris, C and Schon, D A (1978) *Organizational Learning: A theory of action perspective*, Reading, MA, Addison-Wesley

Argyris, C (1994) 'Good communication that blocks learning', *Harvard Business Review*, July-August, pp 77–85

Bailey, D and Sproston, C (1993) *Choosing and Using a Consultant*, Aldershot, Gower

Bennis, W (1993) *An Invented Life: Reflection on leadership and change*, Reading, MA, Addison-Wesley

Blantern, C (1997) 'Dialogue and organizational learning' in M Pedler, J Burgoyne and T Boydell, (eds) *The Learning Company*, 2nd edn, Maidenhead, McGraw-Hill

Bourget, L (1996) 'The changing face of power: how can consultants prepare to help managers through the power shift?', in J W Pfeiffer, (ed) *The 1996 Annual Vol. 2, Consulting*, San Diego, CA, Pfeiffer

Brown, A (1984) *Consultation*, Oxford, Heinemann

Burke, W W (1982) *Organizational Development: Principles and practices*, Boston, MA, Little, Brown

Carkhuff, R (1983) *The Art of Helping*, Amherst, Human Resources Development

Cleverley, G (1971) *Managers and Magic*, Harmondsworth, Pelican

Dixon, N (1994) *The Organizational Learning Cycle*, Maidenhead, McGraw-Hill

Drucker, P F (1992) 'The new society of organizations', *Harvard Business Review*, September/October, pp 95–104

Egan, G (1962) *The Skilled Helper*, Monterey CA, Brooks/Cole

Geirland, J and Maniker-Leiter, M (1996) 'Five lessons for internal OD consultants', in J W Pfeiffer, (ed) *The 1996 Annual Vol. 2. Consulting*, San Diego, CA, Pfeiffer, pp 295–304

Handy, C (1985) *The Future of Work*, Oxford, Blackwell

Harrison, R (1995) *Consultants Journey*, Maidenhead, McGraw-Hill

Heron, J (1991) *The Facilitators Handbook*, London, Kogan Page

Holdaway, K and Saunders, M (1996) *The In-house Trainer as Consultant*, 2nd edn, London, Kogan Page

Honey, P (1994) *101 Ways to Develop Your People, Without Really Trying*, Maidenhead, Honey

Kubr, M (1986) *Management Consulting: A guide to the profession*, Geneva, ILO

Kubr, M (1993) *How to Select and Use Consultants*, Managing Development Series 31, Geneva, ILO

Maister, D (1989) 'Professional service firm management' in M Kubr, (ed), *How to Select and Use Consultants*, Managing Development Series 31, Geneva, ILO

Margerison, C J (1995) *Managerial Consulting Skills*, Aldershot, Gower

Mezirow, J and associates (1990) *Fostering Critical Reflection in Adulthood*, Albany, State University of New York Press

Pedler, M, Burgoyne, J and Boydell, T (1997) *The Learning Company*, 2nd edn, Maidenhead, McGraw-Hill

Phillips, K and Shaw, P (1996) *A Consultancy Approach for Trainers*, Aldershot, Gower

Pont, T (1995) *Investing in Training and Development*, London, Kogan Page

Ross, M B (1982) 'Coping with conflict', in J W Pfeiffer, (ed) *The 1982 Annual for Facilitators, Trainers and Consultants*, San Diego, CA, Pfeiffer and Co

Senge, P (1990) *The Fifth Discipline*, London, Random Century/Doubleday

Sonesh-Kedor, E and Geirland, J (1995) 'Developing more creative organizations', in J W Pfeiffer, (ed) *The 1995 Annual Vol 2. Consulting*, San Diego, CA, Pfeiffer

Steinberg, D (1989) *Interprofessional Consultation*, Oxford, Blackwell

Swartz, D H (1975) 'Similarities and differences of internal and external consultants', *Journal of European Industrial Training*, **4**, 5

Torrington, D and Hall, L (1995) *Personnel Management: HRM in action*, Hemel Hempstead, Prentice-Hall

Section Four:

The Planning and Designing of Learning, Training and Development

11

Fundamentals of Adult Learning

Chris Wiltsher

INTRODUCTION AND LEARNING OBJECTIVES

Most of those with whom we are involved in human resource training and development are adults. If our programmes are to be successful in helping people to learn, we must understand something of how adults learn.

In this chapter we shall look at some of the features of adult learning and discuss briefly some of the theories that have been developed to help us understand how adults learn.

Since much of the material in this chapter can seem rather abstract, you might find it helpful to ground the material by relating it to your own learning. You might like to pause for a few moments and write down the outlines of two of your own experiences of learning as an adult, one good and one bad. If you keep these outlines close at hand as you read the chapter, you will be able to compare what is being suggested about adult learning with your own experience.

Having read this chapter you should understand:

- the processes of learning;
- some of the features of adulthood relevant to adult learning;
- some of the characteristics of adult learning in particular; and
- the chief features of the main theories of learning.

LEARNING

We are all learning all the time. From day to day, even from minute to minute, we find ourselves faced with the need to adapt in order to survive in different circumstances. We adapt our behaviour and our ways of thinking about the world and interacting with it in order to cope and continue to live. For most of the time the changes required of us are small and hardly noticed; at the other extreme, there are occasions when we have to make major changes very quickly. In between are those occasions when we realize that we have changed, adapted, and now behave differently or see the world differently, or even understand ourselves differently. We realize that we have learned something.

Learning is difficult to define. It is part of the process of change and adaptation to different circumstances. It enables us to draw on the past in order to cope better with the future. It is to do with change.

But what kind of change? Through learning people may change their view of the world, or their understanding of themselves, or their behaviour, or something else. The change may not always be immediately obvious to others, or even to the learner. However, learning eventually produces some observable effect.

What has been said so far implies that learning is a process. There is not one event, but a series of elements that go to make up learning. As with any process, learning is difficult to observe when it is happening; but as with any process, learning can be helped or hindered by many factors which are not themselves part of the process.

It is useful at this point to make a distinction between formal and informal learning:

- *Formal learning* is learning that takes place in a structured and intentional way. Typically, formal learning takes place when we attend some kind of course, often in a particular setting. A good example of formal learning is the learning that takes place in school class-rooms or training rooms.
- *Informal learning* is not structured, though it may occur in a structured setting. Informal learning takes place when we learn something new without intending to. It is the kind of learning that occurs when we pick up tips on doing something from watching an expert at work, or discover a new piece of information through a casual conversation. Much of our learning is informal.

THE LEARNING PROCESS

The process of learning can usefully be split into several stages. To learn we must:

- receive new information or data;
- take the information in;
- assimilate the information;
- store the information;
- use the information.

Exactly how we perform these tasks, by what physical processes they happen, is a matter of great discussion and controversy. For our present purposes, the details are not significant; those interested should refer to books such as Hill (1997), Pinker (1997) and Thompson (1993). However, we must say a little about each stage of learning.

Receiving

We note first that for the purpose of learning we are interested in the new information we receive. Much of the information we receive, especially as we get older and have the benefit of more experience, is not new. We do not ignore it, but it is not part of our learning.

However, we should note that new information is not just pieces of data about the world. New information may include ideas that help us make new connections between pieces of data already stored away in our memories.

Information comes in many forms. Our senses offer us information all the time. We filter the information, selecting what is relevant at the moment, that is, what is significant for the task in hand. Sometimes we make mistakes, and ignore something important; sometimes one piece of information is so overpowering that it blots out everything else. Thus when my sense of touch tells me that I am very cold, this information can blot out everything else, including the words of wisdom of a teacher. This is one reason why the efficiency of our learning is affected by the circumstances in which the learning takes place.

Taking in

Having received information and selected what we wish to take notice of, we have to take the information in. How we do this is not very well understood, but it is clear that human beings vary considerably in their ability to take in information. There are great variations in what we can see, hear, feel and so on. Many of these variations have to do with physical capability, and are affected by circumstances. For example, I see less well in dim light, and hear less distinctly if there is a lot of background noise. Our physical capabilities also change with age. Most people notice a deterioration in their sight and hearing as they grow older, though the speed of change varies enormously.

The effect of all this is that our physical capabilities affect our ability to learn. We learn from what we take in, and it seems that we take in only a fraction of the information we receive through our senses. For our learning to be efficient and productive, we need to maximize the amount of information we take in.

In practical terms this means making sure that we have the best possible chance of taking in as much as possible. The physical setting of our learning is therefore important, as is our own physical state. We can also add to the efficiency of learning by providing more than one means of taking in the same information. Not only do our senses provide information, each can reinforce the others. The old saying, a picture is worth a thousand words, reminds us that what we see has as great an impact as what we hear. For this reason, mind-mapping, developed by Buzan (1995) has become a very effective tool of some people. So too does what we touch, and the combination of sight, sound and touch in doing something is very powerful – which is why we often learn most quickly and easily through doing things.

Assimilating

In order to learn something, we must connect what we have taken in through our senses with information we already have stored away. This helps us first to make sense of the information we have received. Until we can connect the new information in some way with our existing framework of thought and experience, we cannot decide whether the information is significant or worth retaining.

How the processes of assimilation work is again not well understood, but the details do not matter for our present purposes. What is important is the role played by existing frameworks of thought. The more easily we can assimilate information to our existing frameworks, the quicker and more efficient will be our learning. Hence those offering learning must find ways of helping learners to connect new information to old. This is partly expressed in the idea familiar to trainers and teachers, that you must start 'where the students are'.

With adults, starting where they are can be very difficult: in any group of adults there is a variety of experience and a variety of starting points. Even where the group is coming to a task unfamiliar to all of them, the frameworks into which the new information must be assimilated are very varied.

An important aspect of assimilation is the resolution of conflicts between the information we already have and the new information. Generally this is not too difficult, especially if information is presented in units which allow time for the recognition and resolution of conflicts. However, sometimes the conflict is great, for example when a cherished and familiar working practice is described as inefficient or bad practice; then the resolution of the conflict may require a change in the framework of thought as well as the assimilation of new information. Changes in frameworks of thought are difficult, and may have considerable implications – which is why they are often resisted. Sometimes, it has been suggested, the changes are simply rejected. We shall look briefly later at one famous discussion of responses to new information, by Piaget (1950), which suggests this.

Storing

Once information has been assimilated, it must be stored for re-use, if we are to be able to say we have learned it. The processes of memory have been closely studied for many years, but are still a subject of considerable debate and research (see, for example, Shanks, 1997). However, it is now generally agreed that we store things in short- or long-term memory, at least. Many of the items stored in short-term memory will be lost after a period, sometimes of minutes, sometimes of days. Information stored in long-term memory may be there indefinitely, though we may also have difficulty accessing it.

It is often said that memory declines as you grow older. Recent work suggests that it is *use* of memory that declines, rather than memory itself. Other work suggests that older people find it easier to remember some things, because they can assimilate them: what older people may find more difficult is assimilating information that requires changes or extensions in frameworks of thought. Think for example of the difficulties of learning a new language as you get older! A good summary of recent work in this area can be found in the chapter by Boulton-Lewis in Sutherland (1997). See also Chapter 14 on diversity and the dangers of stereotyping certain groups.

One implication of our present understanding of memory is that trainers and teachers have to think about the kind of information being given and what learners are expected to remember. If we want information stored in long-term memory then we must give the learner help in storing.

Using

We cannot say we have learned something until we are able to use it and, usually, use it in contexts different from the context in which we gained it. This implies that we cannot claim to have learned something until we have tried to use it. So learning opportunities should carry with them the opportunity to use what has been learned. This may be as simple as trying to show someone else a skill you have acquired, or explaining to someone else a new idea you have learned.

For the provider of learning, this stage of learning is relevant to assessing learning. In order to know whether students have learned, and what they have learned, we need some form of evaluation. The nature and form of evaluation or assessment will vary according to what is supposed to be learned. For good assessment it is necessary that learners are given the opportunity to show that they can use the information they have gained in different ways. For example, in assessing whether or not someone has learned to use a word-processor, we might need to ask them to produce more than one document, to show that they have learned the skills rather than just a recipe.

Experiential learning

The learning process described above is very similar to that illustrated in Figure 11.1 (Beard and Wilson, 2002). In this model our senses perceive a stimulus which we become aware of at a conscious or subconscious level. The stimulus is then filtered based on previous knowledge, previous experiences and so on, then the stimulus is assimilated, accommodated or rejected according to our mental schema (Piaget, 1950). The next stage in the model allows for cognitive, affective or behavioural responses using Bloom *et al*'s (1956) categories. The final stage in the process is the feedback loop, which allows us to consider the impact of our interaction with the source of the stimulus.

The perception and experiential learning model provides the underpinning framework for the Learning Combination Lock (Beard and Wilson, 2002). This model is a metaphor for the unlocking of individual learning, and consists of six tumblers which provide a systematic approach for considering the learning design process. Beginning on the left, the places and elements tumbler illustrates some of the environmental ingredients which may be incorporated in the learning mix.

The second tumbler addresses the milieu, or in other words, the process of the learning activity, such as a journey or dealing with an obstacle. The third tumbler concerns the senses: the more these can be used, the more stimuli reach our brains, which can lead to enhanced

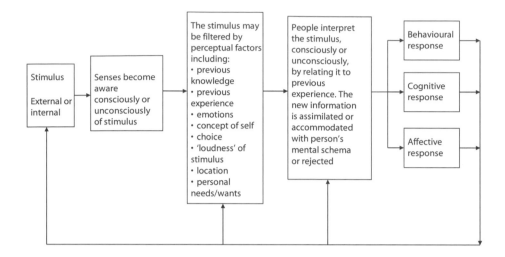

Figure 11.1 The process of perception and experiential learning

learning. Similarly, the fourth tumbler involves the emotions, which can elevate the power of the learning situation and make it a deep and lasting experience.

The fifth tumbler draws upon the work of Gardner (1984) and the notion of intelligences. As trainers and learning specialists we should be aiming to encourage various forms of intelligence within people.

The final tumbler represents some of the various theories of learning that we might take into account as we design the learning event. You are strongly encouraged to use these two models in the design of learning activities. They are described in greater detail in Beard and Wilson (2001).

LEVELS OF COMPETENCE

One of the problems of organizing our learning is that we do not know what we don't know! In other words we are unconsciously incompetent. Through placing ourselves in learning situations or sometimes through serendipity we find ourselves discovering something new but in which we have no ability – conscious incompetence. The next stage of learning and assimilating knowledge and skills is conscious competence, which might be when we are driving a car but have to think about what we are doing. Lastly, there is unconscious competence, which is where we might be thinking about work as we drive home and can't even remember doing the driving, or the journey home! These levels of competence by Dubin (1962) are shown in Figure 11.3.

Next, we must notice three features of learning implicit in what we have discussed so far: learning takes time; learning is an interactive process; and learning is an iterative process.

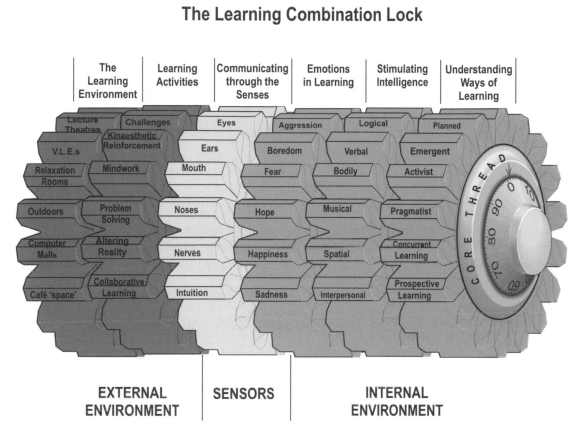

Figure 11.2 A simple diagnostic tool: the Learning Combination Lock

Learning takes time

It is important to notice that the stages we have described take time. We may receive, take in and partially assimilate information in a very short period, but it may take hours or days for us to assimilate the information completely. Learning opportunities must provide time for the necessary reflection to take place.

Learning is an interactive process

Receiving, taking in and using information require us to respond in some way to the world in which we live. Our interaction may be with other people, with objects, or with both: but unless there is interaction, we shall not learn. The interaction may be small, as in so-called 'passive

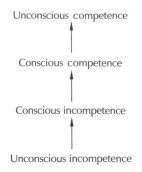

Figure 11.3 Levels of competence

learning', in which we receive information and process it without response (for example, in the traditional lecture to a large audience). However, there is much discussion and some evidence to suggest that the greater our interaction, the quicker and more efficient is our learning: see, for example Brookfield (1991) and Kidd (1983).

Learning is an iterative process

Learning is a process that is never complete. This is partly because neither human beings nor the world we inhabit are static. Changes are always taking place, in us and around us. At any stage of our lives we may find ourselves acquiring new information which makes us change some of the connections we have made, perhaps even discarding old information.

We acknowledge this as the need to revise views and practices. Having learned something, we use it, and we find that it works tolerably well. But we can do better, so we revise our ways of thinking and doing, and try again, and then revise again and so on. A useful way of visualizing this process is given in Kolb's experiential learning cycle (Kolb, 1984), presented in Figure 11.4.

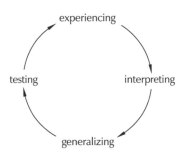

Figure 11.4 Kolb's experiential learning cycle

What Kolb's cycle emphasizes is that learning is a process which involves both noticing things and reflecting on what we have noticed. It is iterative and interactive. Not only does new experience or information become a spur to reflection and action, reflection can lead to testing ideas through experience.

Kolb's cycle is simplified. Just a little thought about our own learning should show that we need to also take account of choices, deliberate decisions to accept or reject particular ways of reflecting, goals and so on. However, the simple picture is sufficient for our present purposes, emphasizing as it does that learning is a process that feeds on itself.

ADULTS AND ADULTHOOD

Having looked very briefly at the processes of learning, we turn to the second part of our task and consider adults and adulthood. Much of our thinking about learning is based on studies of children learning. However, there are significant differences between children and adults, and some of the differences affect learning. This is emphasized by some writers using the distinction between pedagogy and andragogy. Pedagogy is claimed to be a form of teaching and learning appropriate to children in formal settings, which sees them as recipients of instruction; andragogy in contrast is seen as a process of teaching and learning in which the learners are participants. This distinction will be discussed more fully in the next chapter.

What is an adult?

There are many ways in which we normally pick out adults from children, for example, age, size, or occupation. Thus we usually say that someone aged 14 is not an adult; someone aged 41 is an adult. Someone six feet tall is likely to be an adult, someone three feet tall is likely to be a child. Someone in full-time employment is likely to be an adult, someone in full-time compulsory schooling is more likely to be a child.

But already doubts should be creeping in. There are short people who are adults and tall people who are not adults. Whether or not someone in employment or schooling is described as an adult may depend on the laws of the country concerned relating to employment and school attendance. Sometimes we describe people of adult age as behaving like children, and some children are described as behaving like adults. So there are areas of doubt.

The law does not help us either. In many countries there are clear legal rules about when a person may serve in the armed forces, take on debts, vote, marry and so on. All these are taken to be signs of being an adult, yet the variation in age across the world for these significant events is enormous, and in some cases affected by gender.

Clearly then for our purposes none of these ways of characterizing adults is sufficient. Wherever the boundary is drawn there will be people who do not fall into the category of adult but who are nevertheless of interest to us because they are among our adult learners.

Adulthood

It may be more helpful to distinguish between being an adult and adulthood. To be an adult is to fulfil a set of criteria, usually based on age, size, legal status and similar features. Adulthood is a state that is related to age, but not determined by any of the features we have noted so far.

What are the characteristics of adulthood? We can begin to explore these by recalling a remark made above: sometimes we describe people of adult age as behaving like children, and some children are described as behaving like adults. This suggests that we might identify some of the characteristics of adulthood by considering what we expect of adults, for example in their behaviour.

A short list might include words like maturity, experience, responsibility and independence. We expect adults to show maturity in their behaviour for example; we do not expect adults to fly into a rage just because they cannot have exactly what they want immediately. We expect adults to have experience of life, and to draw on that experience in making decisions. We expect adults to take responsibility for their decisions. We expect adults to show independence, making their own decisions.

This does not mean that all adults fulfil these expectations all the time. However, if someone has reached adulthood, we expect him or her to show more of these characteristics rather than less. It is important to recognize that adulthood is a state that is incomplete. Adults are changing and developing all the time, just as children are. But in adults the changes are less dramatic, usually.

We should now note another word of caution: words like maturity and independence are slippery. What counts as maturity in one context will not necessarily count in another, and the same is true of words like independence and responsibility.

Clearly defining adulthood is hard. We can see that adulthood involves a range of attributes, of which we have noted some. Our judgement about whether or not someone has achieved adulthood will involve assessing the extent to which they display appropriate attributes.

The immediate significance of this for adult learning is this: we cannot assume that all adults are the same. They differ markedly, and those differences affect the way they learn. To see this we shall look further at some of the characteristics of adulthood which are of significance for learning.

Adult learners are mature

We have already noted that it is hard to define maturity, but we can recognize it. Among other things, to say that someone is mature is to say that they have a framework of ideas and experience into which everything new must be fitted in order to make sense. The framework has been formed through reflection on a variety of experiences, and may be more or less fixed. Mature people may find it easy to recognize challenges to their frameworks of thought, but hard to adapt those frameworks.

Adult learners are experienced

They have lived through a number of years and a range of experiences, from many of which they have learned. Some of the experiences have been good and positive, others have been bad and negative. Positive or negative, they are part of the baggage brought by adults to learning opportunities and colour the way in which people are able to respond to learning opportunities.

Adult learners are capable of making informed choices

We expect adults to make decisions and choose between courses of action, so it is natural that we should expect them to do so in relation to learning. This means not just that we can expect adults to make choices about courses or whether or not to take up particular learning opportunities; we should also expect adults to make decisions about what they want to learn and how they want to learn. Sometimes it is hard to get adults to make decisions about their own learning, because of their past experience of learning. Sometimes they make decisions which seem wrong, and that raises questions about who controls adult learning, and how.

Adult learners are capable of taking responsibility

This follows on from the last point. We expect adults to take responsibility for their actions, and we should expect adult learners to take responsibility for their own learning. To encourage this to happen, adults need to become actively involved in the design of learning opportunities.

The last two characteristics are very important for the consideration of motivation. It is clear that nobody will learn unless they are motivated to do so. This can be seen in children in school. It is also true of adults. We need to understand something of what motivates those who undertake learning: why they are doing it, what they hope to gain from it, what impediments to learning they carry with them.

This is particularly important in many training programmes. Many of those involved in training and development programmes will be there because they must be there – it is a requirement of the management – and they may not be well-motivated to learn.

One further aspect of adulthood should be noted. Adults are people who have developed an identity, a sense of who they are and how they relate to others. Their identity has many components, but one important element is related to their own particular combination of experience and ideas. In some learning situations new ideas will be presented which require significant changes in their ways of thinking and acting, and those changes may threaten a person's identity. Threats to our identity are always hard to handle, as they have implications for every aspect of life. This aspect of adulthood alone makes the task of offering learning to adults challenging.

STYLES OF ADULT LEARNING

In this section we look at how to engage people in the processes of learning. As we have seen, we need to pay attention to why people want to learn, what they want to learn, and how they want to learn. In practice we shall then need to compromise between the learners' needs and desires and what it is possible to deliver through particular learning opportunities.

Why people want to learn

Usually adult learners will have a mixture of reasons for wanting to learn, and their reasons may change over the course of a learning programme. We can never assume that we know exactly why people have opted to become adult learners. However, it is useful to group the main reasons for learning in ways that relate to the main psychological theories about adult learning. We do not have space for a detailed discussion of these theories, especially as there are many variants within each of the main streams. Books such as Atkinson *et al* (1993) and Hill (1997) provide more detail, and the psychology section of any good library or bookshop will provide a range of detailed discussion for those interested. Here we shall indicate only founding figures and broad strands relevant to our particular concerns.

Behaviourist theories of learning

Some of our learning comes about as a response to a stimulus. We react to something outside ourselves. If the result is good for us, we learn to react in similar fashion in a similar situation, while if the result is bad, we learn not to do that again. This is the basic idea of the behaviourist school of thought, which can be traced back to the work of Pavlov (1927) who taught dogs to salivate at the sound of a bell; and Skinner (1974) who taught pigeons to play table tennis through operant conditioning.

Behaviourists concentrate on modifying behaviour by reinforcement. Behaviour that is seen as positive or good is reinforced by rewards (your car insurance is reduced if you do not make a claim), while unwanted behaviour is treated to negative reinforcement (you are fined if you are caught speeding).

Most people have experienced both positive and negative reinforcement at school, and we can see that behaviourist learning theories have their strengths. At very least they remind us of the importance of the reactions of a teacher to the work of learners. However, this approach to learning has been criticized as mechanistic and tending to focus only on certain behaviour. There is no idea of the exploration of alternatives, and there is evidence to suggest that reinforcement may need constant topping-up to remain effective.

Cognitivist theories of learning

If some of our learning is reactive, some learning can also be described as proactive. That is, we seek out information and try to make sense of it in order to understand better our world and our place in it. This is the basis of cognitivist theories of learning, which make use of the work of researchers such as Kohler (1925) and Piaget (1950). Kohler worked with apes and Piaget concentrated on child development, but their results have been applied more widely.

For the cognitivist, the key feature of human beings for learning is that we are intelligent seekers. According to cognitivist theories, we constantly find that our experience of the world does not quite fit the way we see the world, and we try to do something about the misfit. We seek new information, we adjust our view of the world, we may create a new way of seeing the world. There are clear connections here with some of the elements we noted earlier in the different stages of the learning process.

As we noted earlier, we do not always adjust our view of the world easily; sometimes we resist change. Piaget (1950) claimed that sometimes we reject change. He developed a three-fold classification of responses to new information, suggesting that we may:

- *assimilate* – the new information poses no great challenge to our existing framework of thought and is absorbed;
- *accommodate* – the new information does not fit easily into existing frameworks, but can be taken in with some changes;
- *reject* – the new information is so different from anything we have already that we cannot take it in without great changes in our framework of thinking, and we are not willing to make the changes.

It is questionable whether Piaget's model, developed from work with children, can be applied directly to adults, who have very complex frameworks of thought and considerable experience of accommodation. Nevertheless, we should note that in a cognitivist view, a person's desire to learn may conflict with a reluctance to change established frameworks. I may want to learn information technology skills, but if I am convinced that I cannot cope with 'clever machines', I will struggle.

Cognitivists, we said, see us as intelligent. To some critics, that should read: cognitivists see us as rational. That is, some critics claim that cognitivist theories are biased towards that learning which involves intentional rational thought, in which we are consciously trying to make logical sense of our ideas and bring order to the world as we see it. However, the world is not very orderly, nor are human beings totally rational. Consequently there are aspects of our learning which do not fit the patterns of cognitivist theory.

A development of cognitivist approaches is personal construct theory, due to Kelly (1955). Kelly suggested that we each create our own model of the world and of other people in it, and our relationship to them. Our constructed picture, he suggested, is shaped as much by feelings, beliefs and values, as by our experience. As a result, we all also create our own, individual, way of learning, which is closely related to our beliefs and values.

Humanist theories of learning

Some of our learning is a response to outside stimulus, some of our learning is an attempt to make sense of our world. Some of our learning is the outcome of a natural potential for learning: we learn because in the right circumstances we cannot help it. This is the key idea of the humanist school of thought, exemplified by the work of Rogers (1974). His perspectives on learning are also mirrored by Galileo who stated that, 'You cannot teach anyone anything. You can only help them discover it for themselves.'

This approach recognizes that humans generally respond to warmth, care and understanding. It claims that all human beings are born with a potential for learning. All human beings can learn, and potentially can learn almost anything. What prevents human beings from learning is a combination of external factors and internal fears, associated with a lack of warmth, care and understanding.

The importance of this approach is that it leads to the idea of learner-centred learning, in which the 'teacher' is seen as a facilitator. Responsibility for learning rests mainly with the learner, while the teacher provides resources and encouragement. In learner-centred learning, the learner sets the pace of learning, and the learner's existing knowledge and skills are recognized and used positively.

This approach to learning is very affirmative of learners, especially those who come with very low expectations of themselves. The problem the approach presents is that in many learning situations it is not possible to allow individuals to go at their own pace. Nor, generally, can learners be allowed to determine the content of learning: they do not have the knowledge or experience to do so, and there are frequently constraints imposed by demands for specific outcomes of a learning programme. Finally, this approach can leave learners blaming themselves, or being blamed by others, for their failure to learn.

We can summarize this section by saying that people want to learn because:

- they are responding to a stimulus (which may be the need to upgrade skills in order to keep a job);
- because they want to improve the fit between their perception of the world and their experience (perhaps they need to understand the organization better to make career progress); and
- because they are encouraged to develop their potential (having left compulsory education at the first opportunity, they realize that they are capable of learning a great deal more).

All these reasons for learning can be found expressed in a variety of ways. For those concerned with adult learning, it is important to be aware that behind the many different stated reasons for wanting to learn there lie these different views of human beings and their learning capacities and behaviour. Providers of training and development need to draw on all these theories in order to understand the task before them.

What people want to learn

We engage in learning to acquire skills and knowledge. However, there are several kinds of skills and several forms of knowledge, and the ways in which we learn skills and knowledge reflect this variety.

It is useful first to make a broad distinction between generic knowledge or skills and domain-specific knowledge or skills. Generic knowledge and skills can be used in a variety of situations. The ability to manipulate things with your fingers is a generic skill with applications in feeding and dressing as well as using tools or turning the pages of a book. Knowing that some materials are impervious to water is generic knowledge that has applications in house building and drainage as well as choosing your waterproofs for the rainy season.

Domain-specific knowledge and skills relate to particular areas or domains of our experience. The ability to drive a car is a skill specific to road transport: someone who can drive a car may also be able to drive a bus or truck, but will not automatically be able to steer a boat or fly an aeroplane. Knowledge of the attributes of the particles that make up an atom is domain-specific: it is unlikely to be of use outside specialized fields of particle physics or chemistry.

The significance of this distinction for our purposes lies in the part of the learning process that we called assimilation. Someone who is already knowledgeable or skilful in a specific domain is likely to find it easier to assimilate further knowledge or skills within the same domain, simply because there is already a framework of thought to which to relate the new information. On the other hand, someone who is new to a specific domain may struggle to learn until a suitable framework is established. It is worth noting that expertise in one domain does not guarantee expertise in another, nor does expertise in one domain assure us that learning in a new domain will be quick or easy.

With generic skills and knowledge, we usually find that we learn them once and can then apply them again and again. We may, however, be able to refine our generic knowledge and skills by reflection on our use of them (recall Kolb's learning cycle).

As well as the distinction between generic and domain-specific knowledge and skills, it is worth noting the differences in the types of skills and knowledge we acquire. The best known way of listing these types is Bloom's taxonomy (Bloom *et al*, 1956). Bloom classified skills under three domains: cognitive, psychomotor and affective. His taxonomy is represented in Figure 11.5.

- 'Cognitive' covers knowledge-related skills, knowledge, comprehension, application, analysis, synthesis, and evaluation in ascending order of complexity.
- 'Psychomotor' covers motor skills in the form of abilities, techniques and competences.
- 'Affective' covers feelings and attitudes and activities such as responding, valuing and judging. Krathwold *et al* (1964) identified these as: receiving, responding, valuing, organization and characterization by a value or value complex.

This taxonomy, and other ways of differentiating the skills we learn, are important because they remind us that different skills may be most efficiently learnt in different ways. If we wish to develop psychomotor skills, say the skill of knocking a nail in straight, we may learn best by following the example of an expert and practising until we can do it. If we wish to learn about the political system of a particular country, we may do so most efficiently by reading a book written by an expert.

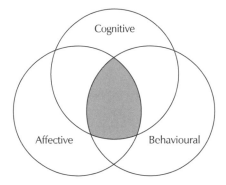

Figure 11.5   Bloom *et al*'s taxonomy of learning

There are other ways of classifying learning skills and knowledge, such as those of Gagné (1967), and Gardner (1984) who proposed seven forms of intelligence:

1. linguistic;
2. logical/mathematical/scientific;
3. visual/spatial;
4. musical;
5. bodily/physical/kinaesthetic;
6. interpersonal;
7. intra-personal.

No one classification is universally accepted. Whichever classification appeals most to us, we should always remember that they are guides only, and that no classification, however complex, can take account of all the differences we find in adults.

How people want to learn

Bloom's taxonomy leads us on to consider how people want to learn. We have noticed that different forms of skill or knowledge may be most efficiently learnt in different ways. However, our concern is with adults learning, and research suggests that adults have their own preferred learning styles, which cut across some of the distinctions made above.

A classification of learning strategies is offered by Honey and Mumford (1986) which is based on the work of Kolb. They isolated four styles of learning:

- *activist* – the style of those who learn by doing things, intentionally or unintentionally;
- *pragmatist* – the style of those who learn by deliberate experimentation;
- *theorist* – the style of those who learn by analysing information and developing models to help them understand;
- *reflector* – the style of those who try to stand back and view events from several angles.

You might like to spend a few moments relating these styles to Kolb's learning cycle, and noting how closely they correspond. This shows how discussion of learning can be a self-reflective process (see Chapter 12). In a work setting have you noticed how you sometimes become frustrated by the fact that some people seem to take a long time before acting; or alternatively act too fast without thinking? Perhaps they are only exhibiting their learning style which is different to yours and which thus creates organizational friction!

It is important to note that most of us use more than one style, without realizing that we are doing so. However, it is claimed that everyone has one or two preferred styles, and it is in using those preferred styles that we learn most efficiently. This is partly because in using our own preferred styles we are doing something with which we feel comfortable; and partly because constant use of one or two styles helps to make us both more comfortable with them and more expert in applying them, thus increasing our potential for learning in these ways.

WHY, WHAT, HOW AND PRACTICE

Our discussion of why people want to learn, what they want to learn and how they want to learn has been very sketchy. Its purpose is to remind us that adults who take up programmes of training or development come with their own ideas about learning, based on past experience, and those ideas have a significant effect on the efficiency with which they learn.

Some of the ideas people have act as barriers to learning, making learning not just inefficient but difficult, perhaps even almost impossible. The next chapter will look in more detail at barriers to learning and overcoming them as the theoretical ideas of this chapter are put into practice.

NEGOTIATION TRAINING FOR AN NHS TRUST

A large NHS Trust in London had found itself increasingly challenged by the contracting aspects of the internal market, which had been introduced into the NHS in 1991. The Trust faced severe competition from nearby hospitals as well as numerous private hospitals and clinics. Traditionally, the hospital's referral area encompassed GPs in all London and Home Counties district health authorities (DHAs). Although the hospital had a well-deserved reputation for its clinical excellence, it was also regarded as expensive and insufficiently responsive to the new market environment.

Each year the number of individual healthcare contracts to be negotiated and secured rose significantly. By 1994 there were over 50 contracts with a value range of £5000 to £30 million. The task also increased in complexity as the market became more sophisticated and competitive. Contracts were negotiated by multi-disciplinary teams from three Directorates lead by the Contracting Director or a Contract Manager.

Relationships and trust between personnel from the different directorates were difficult and fragile, roles and responsibilities were unclear, and there were different behavioural and negotiating style preferences among team members. Some DHA negotiating teams had been able to exploit these difficulties to the detriment of the hospital.

All relevant staff attended a one-day workshop which had been designed to:

- achieve further development of negotiating skills;
- improve trust and understanding;
- enable teams to be configured so that skills and styles were complementary, rather than conflicting.

The workshop was designed and run by a highly experienced facilitator who had previously met each participant. Preparatory work included completing a team styles inventory and the Kiersey Temperament Sorter questionnaire. The pre-workshop one-to-one meetings with the facilitator were particularly valuable. They provided him with knowledge and the opportunity to establish initial trust and confidence.

The workshop was action-learning-based and included:

- negotiation strategies, planning, processes and style preferences;
- personality and behaviour recognition and their implications;
- advanced negotiating skills.

Results were excellent. The next contracting round achieved better outcomes for both sides and was much less arduous:

- the configuration of some teams was changed to ensure a best fit of skills and styles;
- there was improved process planning and preparation with better account taken of DHA interests and negotiating preferences;
- increased understanding and knowledge led to improved trust and relationships that were sustained afterwards. A major contributor to this was the sharing of the outcomes of the various inventories.

With acknowledgement to Carole Hall, Training Consultant, ETC.

CONCLUSION

We have looked very briefly at some of the fundamentals of adult learning. Adult learning emerges from our discussion as a complex process, affected by many factors and discussed in many ways from a variety of perspectives. The provider of training and development for adults is faced with a bewildering array of elements to take into account in constructing learning opportunities. It might be helpful and encouraging to end with some cautionary notes.

First, it is clear that there are many different theories of adult learning, not all of which are totally compatible. We have touched briefly on major strands, but the research work goes on and the discussions grow steadily. No one theory covers everything. We need to be aware of the different ideas, but we also need to recognize that these are ideas. They are ways of helping us to draw in a systematic fashion on the experience of others. They are not prescriptions.

Second, we need to recognize that we cannot do everything. We can be aware of the different styles of learning and of the enormous differences between people on any given training programme or event. But we cannot take account of everything. It is therefore vital to consider what is appropriate and possible in any particular learning situation.

Finally, providers must not be worried by failure. The perfect training event has never happened and probably never will, human beings being what they are. Those professionally involved in training and development can only do their best – and learn from their experiences.

Bibliography

Atkinson, R L, Atkinson, R C, Smith, E E and Benn, D J (1993) *Introduction to Psychology,* 11th edn, New York, Harcourt, Brace, Jovanovich

Beard, C and Wilson, J P (2002) *The Power of Experiential Learning: A handbook for educators and trainers,* London, Kogan Page

Bloom, B S, Engelhart, M D, Furst, E J, Hill, W H and Krathwolh, D R (1956) *Taxonomy of Educational Objectives,* London, Longmans, Green and Co

Brookfield, S (1991) *Understanding and Facilitating Adult Learning,* Buckingham, Open University Press (first published 1986)

Buzan, T (1995) *The MindMap Book,* London, BBC Books

Dubin, P (1962) *Human Relations in Administration,* Englewood Cliffs, NJ, Prentice Hall

Gagné, R M (1967) *Learning and Individual Differences,* Columbus, OH, Merrill

Gardner, H (1984) *Frames of Mind: The theory of multiple intelligences,* London, Fontana

Hill, W (1997) *Learning: A survey of psychological interpretations,* 6th edn, New York, Longman

Honey, P and Mumford, A (1986) *Manual of Learning Styles,* London, Peter Honey

Kelly, G (1955) *The Psychology of Personal Constructs,* New York, Norton

Kidd, J R (1983) *How Adults Learn,* revised edn, New York, Associated Press

Knowles, M (1990) *The Adult Learner: A neglected species,* Houston, TX, Gulf Publishing (first published 1973)

Kohler, W I (1925) *The Mentality of Apes,* New York, Brace and World

Kolb, D (1984) *Experiential Learning,* Englewood Cliffs, NJ, Prentice Hall

Krathwold, D R, Bloom, B S and Masis, B B (1964) *Taxonomy of Educational Objectives: The classification of educational goals, Handbook 2: Affective domain,* London, Longmans, Green

Pavlov, J P (1927) *Conditioned Reflexes,* Oxford, Oxford University Press

Piaget, J (1950) *The Psychology of Intelligence,* London, Routledge and Kegan Paul

Pinker, S (1997) *How the Mind Works,* London, Allen Lane

Rogers, C (1974) *On Becoming a Person,* London, BBC Publications

Shanks, D (ed) (1997) *Human Memory: A reader,* London, Arnold

Skinner, B F (1974) *Adult Behaviour,* London, Jonathan Cape

Stammer, R and Patrick, J (1975) *The Psychology of Training,* London, Methuen

Sutherland, P (ed) (1997) *Adult Learning: A reader,* London, Kogan Page

Thompson, R F (1993) *The Brain: A neuroscience primer,* 2nd edn, New York, W H Freeman

12

The Adult Learner: Theory into Practice

Janet Parr

INTRODUCTION AND LEARNING OBJECTIVES

The whole topic of adult learning has been in the arena for discussion for a number of years, with the current emphasis on both sides of the Atlantic being on lifelong learning. With this increasing awareness, and the emphasis on a changing and flexible workforce, it is important, both for organizations and individuals, not only to encourage adults back into education and training, but to provide a learning environment which ensures that maximum benefit is gained from their return to learning (Longworth and Davies, 1996; Thijssen, 1992).

Adult learners bring with them a range of educational experiences and motivations. They come from a variety of educational backgrounds and a diversity of social experiences, which can be both bonus and impediment. This chapter builds on the previous chapter by revisiting and developing some of the theories outlined therein. It then moves on to examine some of the issues and difficulties which mature students face when they return to education and training. In writing this chapter I have used, in illustration, verbatim material from my recent research into mature students returning to learning on a range of courses, from motor mechanics to Master of Education degrees. Their names have been changed to protect their identity, but their words add depth and reality to the discussion.

Having read this chapter you will:

- know Gagné's five domains of learning;
- understand the distinction between pedagogy and andragogy;
- understand the nature of the learning cycle and learning spiral;
- understand some of the barriers which hinder adult learning; and
- understand how theory can inform practice.

ADULT LEARNING

Learning can be interpreted in three ways:

- To get to know: for example, I learnt last week that certain government White Papers are now published on the internet.
- To learn as in to memorize or learn by heart, as those of us who are old enough learned our multiplication tables at school.
- Learning as change, which can be either reinforcement or alteration of certain ideas or behaviour.

It is this last meaning which is what is usually meant by learning in the sense of education or training and which is the focus of the theories of learning developed and discussed in this chapter.

Learning can be either active or passive. The traditional approach to learning was, by and large, based on passive learning, where the teacher is seen as the expert and fount of all knowledge and the pupil is seen as the recipient of that expertise – what Bowles and Gintis (1976), in a different setting, call the 'mug and jug' theory. The student is the mug – an empty vessel, receiving the knowledge from the teacher – the jugful of knowledge, which is given to the student to fill the deficit.

Many recent theorists of learning though, and particularly those of the humanist school, suggest that people cannot learn simply by being given information – the old saying of 'You can take a horse to water but you cannot make it drink' is central to this argument. The student must have active involvement in the process, either mentally or physically or both, and a desire for knowledge, for learning to occur. To return to the horse metaphor – if the horse is thirsty it will drink, and if it drinks, its thirst will be quenched. The water alone cannot do the job.

One of the long-standing distinctions has, of course, been between practical skills and knowledge, though obviously the division is not as clear-cut as this dichotomy would imply. Certainly, in a modern society, few practical skills do not engage knowledge and understanding in their learning. Gagné (1972) suggested five types (or domains) of learning and Rogers (1996:79) has built on this, making clear links between knowledge and skills:

1.   We may learn new *knowledge* as we collect information that is largely memorized.
2.   Such knowledge may be held uncomprehendingly. We thus need to learn to relate our new material in ways that lead to new *understanding,* that process of organizing and reorganizing knowledge to create new patterns of relationships.
3.   We may learn new *skills* or develop existing skills further; not just physical skills, our ability to do certain things, but also skills of thinking and of learning, skills of coping and solving problems and survival strategies.
4.   Further, since we can learn new knowledge, new understanding and new skills without necessarily changing our attitudes, the learning of *attitudes* is a distinct sphere of learning.
5.   Finally, it is possible for learning changes to be brought about in all four of these areas without accompanying alterations in our way of life, our pattern of behaviour. It is therefore necessary to learn to apply our newly learned material to what we do and how we live, to carry out our new learning into changed ways of *behaving:* what some people would call to learn 'wisdom', in short.

MOTIVATION AND LEARNING

It is generally supposed that adult learners come voluntarily into learning situations and because of this, they will be well motivated. This is not always the case of course, particularly in organizational training situations where there may be an element of compulsion. Motivation then can be both internal and external. Internal motivation comes from the drive within the individual to gain knowledge or a skill. One must remember of course that this internal drive may well have been influenced by external factors. In my research on mature women returners to education (Parr, 1991, 1996) the data revealed a determination by the students to develop new areas of identity which they had some control in shaping. This was influenced greatly by external factors, such as childhood abuse, restrictive and controlling parents, abusive partners, painful divorce and so on. For example, Gerry told me that she had been sexually abused when she was a child and this had had a considerable effect on her self-image. Her intrinsic motivation in returning to education was very much influenced by external factors:

> *Gerry:* My sister and my brother have both got degrees but I hadn't got that kind of qualification and I think probably in the back of my mind I was feeling that I had to prove myself, not just to them but to myself … that spurred me on – perhaps this was a way I could prove to myself, more to myself than anybody else that I wasn't a failure. Even if I didn't actually succeed it was something that I actually got the courage to go and try and have a go at … with everything that happened I felt almost like a failure, well I failed at this; I failed at that.

Grace's internal motivation came from the label which her ex-husband had attached to her:

> *Grace:* Now I know that I've got ability to do things, I'm not an idiot … I'm not a dumb blonde. … nobody can take off me what I've learned. …
> I've found out I can do things that I didn't know I could do before.

I think I've got more confidence now than what I've ever had really.
My ex-husband said, 'Oh you'll never survive on your own.' I thought, 'Well, I'll show him.'

External factors are those which may put pressure on us, but may not necessarily be converted into internal, or psychological pressure. Better pay, promotion, a better job or the potential loss of employment may be issues here. When I interviewed Annabel, she was studying part-time to gain her National Vocational Qualification in Motor Mechanics:

> *Annabel:* I need the qualification really. … I did think I'd learn something as well. Now I'm just here for the qualification. I wanted the practical and the learning, so I have more confidence to go out for jobs.

There are of course situations in which adults participate in education and training unwillingly. This could be the case with employees whose attendance on courses is compulsory rather than voluntary. The external motivator here may well be loss of employment if there is a refusal to attend a course and gain the required updating of necessary skills. Harrison (1993:ch12) discusses the issues extensively and argues the importance of involving individuals in determining their training/education requirements, recognizing that there may be a tension between organizational and individual needs. It behoves the trainer/teacher to remember this and to create a learning environment which recognizes the diversity of motivations and backgrounds from which the participants come.

This necessity to take on board the different needs and learning styles of adults has contributed since the 1950s to the creation of a theory of adult learning termed 'andragogy'. (You may like to refer to Brookfield, 1991, for a discussion of this development.)

ANDRAGOGY

Knowles (1996) maintains that most of what we know about learning has come from studying children and animals. This has been termed 'pedagogy', which literally translated means 'leading the child', but has come to mean the art and science of teaching the child. This approach, he maintains, ignores the wealth of experience which adults bring to their learning. He built on and took forward the thinking on 'andragogy' – the art and science of teaching adults, since he felt that our approach to teaching adults should be substantially different from that of teaching children. Adults, he maintains, bring substantially more experience to the learning arena than children:

> These differences in experience between children and adults have at least three consequences for learning:

1. Adults have more to contribute to the learning of others; for most kinds of learning, they are themselves a rich resource for learning.
2. Adults have a richer foundation of experience to which to relate new experiences (and new learnings tend to take on meaning as we are able to relate them to our past experience).

3. Adults have acquired a larger number of fixed habits and patterns of thought, and therefore tend to be less open-minded. (Knowles, 1996:89–90)

Andragogy is a distinct shift away from 'teaching' to participatory learning in groups, drawing on adult experiences as a resource. This again has implications for the teacher/trainer in that it is necessary to create an environment in which the adult feels safe to perform. It is also necessary for those of us who work with adults to recognize adults' insecurity in being expected to contribute and participate, rather than being told 'the right answer'. There are also issues here for the learners who may have to 'unlearn' some learned behaviour from childhood when experiences may have been negative.

Adult needs from training and education are also different in that there is more immediacy and perceived (or expected) relevance to their everyday lives than there is with children, whether this is voluntary participation or that enforced by a training programme at work. The centrality of the learners, and the recognition of the personal agenda they bring to the learning arena, which is a central tenet of andragogy, clearly has some of its roots in humanist theories of learning, which also focus on the learner rather than on the teacher/trainer.

HUMANIST THEORIES

Humanist theories developed on the one hand as a resistance to the structured, objective and scientific approach of positivism, which assumes stability, the general applicability of scientific laws and universally acceptable values. On the other hand, but clearly linked, there was the emergence of a changing world, with instability, complexity, uncertainty and a range and variety of values. In this more fluid situation, where rapid change was occurring, it was no longer adequate to assume that the teacher was the sole source of learning. Humanist theories thus resisted the passive focus of learning and stressed the active nature of the learner. Carl Rogers (1969) – a leading writer in the humanist school – developed his approach to learning from his concept of client-centred counselling, which is based on the premise that people can generally draw on their own resources to deal with their problems, given a supportive and encouraging environment in which to do so. This led Rogers to the belief that people have a natural desire to learn and the teacher role should be one of encouraging and supporting the learner to learn, rather than the mug-and-jug idea which we discussed earlier. Not only do humanist theories stress the centrality of the learner in the learning process, they also focus on the environment in which learning takes place. As Alan Rogers (1996:99) writes:

> Motivation for learning comes from within; and the material on which the learning drive fastens
> is the whole of life, the cultural and interpersonal relationships that form the social context.

So, according to humanists, there are both motivational and environmental factors brought to bear in the learning process. We have already discussed the fact that there are both intrinsic and extrinsic motivational factors. Extrinsic factors are those incentives that are external to the individual, such as retention of a job, promotion, a new direction, a completely new skill and so on. Intrinsic factors are those which come from within a learner, although they may well have been influenced by extrinsic factors as I suggested above.

Maslow (1968) and Carl Rogers (1974) have put forward strong cases for arguing that motivation comes from within to meet certain needs. Maslow developed a hierarchy of needs that range from biological to psychological (see Figure 12.1). Although attempts to scientifically replicate this have not proved very successful, it is often quoted, and as the examples which follow show, it can contribute to our understanding of factors which influence learning.

The needs at one level must become at least partially satisfied before the individual can move up to the next level. For example, when food and drink become difficult to obtain, the satisfaction of these needs will take priority over all other needs, and only when this need is satisfied, will the individual move on to address other needs. The model also posits an interesting link between the individual and environmental factors. We can relate this directly to learning.

If we move up the hierarchical structure, it is easy to see that the motivational factors in any student can be many and varied. It may be sufficient for some students to be accepted as part of a

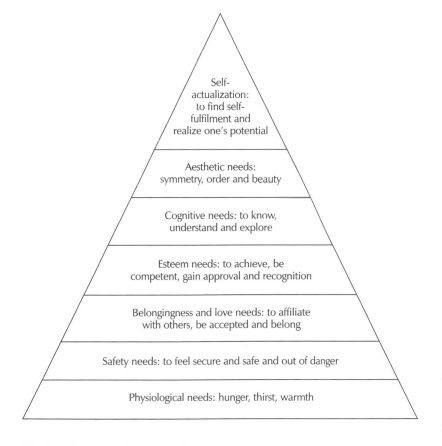

Figure 12.1 Maslow's hierarchy of needs

group and to achieve competency in one small area, whereas others may have an expressed need to know and understand. In addition, threats to lower-order needs may well explain why students become withdrawn and focus on issues other than the immediate learning situation. For the teacher/trainer of adults, these are important points to take on board. We need to recognize that students may have factors that are influencing their decisions, which they may be unwilling or unable to discuss with us at the time. The following case study provides an example.

PERSONAL FACTORS AND LEARNING

Jane arrived late for a residential weekend which was part of her course. She was very distressed and left soon after the start, saying she was very tired, had too much to do and couldn't cope with the work. When I asked her some weeks later whether she was feeling any better, she told me that she had had some negative results from a screening test, and also had problems in a close relationship. She could not over-ride these to concentrate on her work. Within a few months, these were both resolved and she was again able to focus on her course.

When I spoke to Della as part of my research, she clearly illustrated the conflicts between some of her needs. She had returned to learning after separation and subsequent divorce from a very violent relationship. She had taken on a voluntary post in the college which gave her a positive status:

Della: I'm going to do this year ... doing what I do now and doing what I did last year I feel safe ... I want to do a BEd in Special Needs. ... Now I'm scared of nothing, but sometimes I am ... in HE there's not going to be that personal support like I've had here ... I'm not ready ... until I've dealt with everything I need to deal with within me then I don't think I can go. ...

The emphasis with both Rogers and Maslow is that motivation is intrinsic, but there are those who suggests that motivation may well be goal-centred with motivation changing according to the nearness of the goal. For those learners with long-term goals, the motivation to keep going can decline, and it is important for the tutor/trainer to ensure that both long- and short-term goals are given and achievable. Of course students may well have both long- and short-term goals which are linked. Deidre was a student enrolled on a European Union-funded 'Women into Management and Technology' course at a local college, and was part of my research. Her short-term goals were clear, though her long-term ones were more tentative:

Deidre: I can't decide whether I want to go into further, higher education, or just go for employment. It really depends on how well I do on this course. I wanted to know how well I'd done up to Christmas before I applied. From what I can gather, I'm not doing too bad really.

A supportive learning situation was vital for Deidre, as it was for other students I interviewed. It was important both for Deidre and for Della that their tutors recognized *their* short-term goals, and gave them encouragement to achieve those, even though their long-term goals may well have been the completion of the course in preparation for higher education. What we need to remember as trainers and educators is that just as with the learning styles discussed in the last chapter, the 'right learning environment' may well vary from one person to another.

What is clear from both Deidre and Della, and the other students with whom I spoke, is that environmental factors have a central influence on learning/training achievements.

Experiential learning and the learning cycle

For many theorists, and particularly those of the humanist school, the basis of all learning is rooted in experience: the active involvement of the learner in the search for knowledge and meaning is central to the whole activity. Pivotal to the search for meaning is that learners critically reflect on, that is, they critically analyse, their experience. As we have seen in the previous chapter, this has been presented in the form of a cycle (see Figure 12.2).

The learning cycle starts with an experience – this can be something seen, heard, felt, read and so on. This is then reflected on, which leads to action, which then becomes the concrete experience for further reflection, and so on. Action is seen as central to the learning process, rather than as a result of it.

However, I feel that this is rather a simple approach for a very complex process. Reflection is not as simple and straightforward as this implies. If we refer back to the discussion of cognitive theories in the previous chapter, new knowledge (or experience) is set into a prior framework of knowledge which is informed by our own and others' experiences. We draw on this framework to make sense of our experiences. If we cannot, then we may seek further information before taking action.

As has already been discussed, Kolb (1984) argues that in some cases, reflection will lead to generalizations (or in his terms, 'abstract conceptualizations') – identifying a range of possible answers, which then leads to active testing in new situations. The result of this then becomes the new experience (see Figure 10.2, in the previous chapter).

Carl Rogers (1969) however, argues that this cycle does not account for goals, choice and decision-making, which he maintains must occur after reflecting and before generalizing. I would argue also that the cycle does not fully account for extrinsic and environmental influences on those decisions, nor the constraints on the action, which can be taken. The process is therefore much more complex than it would appear to be. For some simple learning, the cycle will stop, and will indeed be a cycle. For more complex learning, the cycle should really be termed a learning 'spiral', as in a coiled spring, which implies forward movement and development; this is

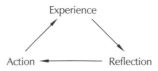

Figure 12.2 Critically analysing experience

shown in Figure 12.3. This spiral may get tighter as a particular topic gets more focused, or may get bigger as the learner seeks to include broader factors into the learning cycle. Other spirals may also be created, as peripheral decisions impinge upon the central focus.

Let's take for example a lone parent who has the opportunity to take up a training programme, which involves being away from his home and children for a number of weekends out of the year. In making the decision, one of the factors he will have to take into account is the welfare of his children. This will set him off on a 'sub-spiral' in which he will need to consider all the alternatives, and take account of the factors shown in the spiral which will impinge on his decision. He may also have to consider when he does his course-work, which sets him off on another 'sub-spiral'. If we also put into the equation his motivation for doing the course, then we begin to realize that the spiral is complex indeed.

At every decision-making point, extrinsic factors will impact on the decision. Individuals will search for explanations within their existing framework, which has been influenced by the culture and socialization processes experienced thus far. The search for new information will involve engagement with others, either directly or indirectly. This will then inform the conceptualization/generalization stage, where a hypothesis or hypotheses may be formed, or 'vague ideas' may begin to take shape. The choice of action will be informed by a range of external issues, such as past experience, the intended goal, other responsibilities such as domestic, caring and work commitments, environmental factors such as access to resources and so on. These

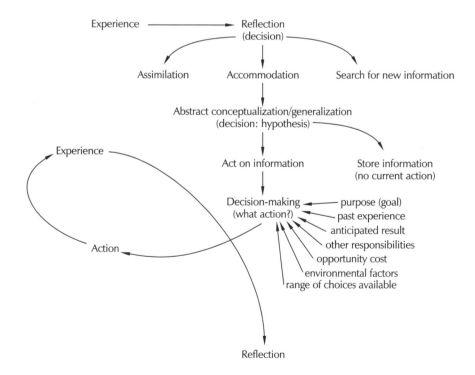

Figure 12.3 The learning spiral

external influences should not be underplayed, since they may have a considerable influence on learning, particularly for adults, and create barriers that will have to be negotiated.

BARRIERS TO LEARNING

Adults may also bring with them considerable personal baggage into the learning setting which may act as barriers to and constraints on their learning. There is a considerable literature that indicates that some adults do meet these barriers to learning, whether that learning is full-time or part-time, vocational or non-vocational, academic or practical, for a wide variety of reasons. See ACACE (1982); *Adults Learning* (special editions in January 1990 and December 1989); Britton and Baxter (1994); Browning (1990); Hughes *et al* (1989); McGivney (1993, 1995); Parr (1991, 1996); Pye (1991); Woodley *et al* (1987); Schutze *et al* (1987).

Both recent and current research in which I am involved indicates that many of these issues exist for students who have returned to learning after a number of years out of the system, regardless of the course they are taking and whether they are full-time or part-time. These barriers may be grouped under five broad headings: psychological, practical, economic, institutional and relationship issues.

Psychological issues

These include the feeling of being too old to learn; of not being bright enough, or as Chris mentioned, the re-emergence of negative feelings from compulsory schooling. Chris left school pregnant with no qualifications at 15, and told me:

> If the classes had been held in a school, I wouldn't have gone, I don't think I could have coped with it.

Dilys talked of the courage it took for her to return to learning:

> When I came on the first day I was nervous as hell and I thought, 'God, what am I doing this for?' I was so scared, and I kept thinking, 'You're going to show yourself up, they're going to ask you all these things, they're going to talk about all these words that you don't know what they're talking about, and they're going to be all these posh people ...' but when I got talking to them, I felt like they're only like me. ...It's made a big difference in me, it's given me a lot more confidence, it's shown me what opportunities there are out there.

The following comments are from two students on a Master's course, which indicate that whatever the level, lack of confidence may still be present:

> Studying at this level is demanding and initially I doubted my ability. I still do at times, but feel that the tutorials and residentials help.
>
> Academically I'm still not sure what standards are required.

Practical issues

Concerns mentioned by the respondents in my research included travel and domestic and caring responsibilities. Frances was enrolled on a European-funded training course close to home:

> It's nearer to come here, you know, when I've took Mark to school, better than actually having to travel – 'cos I haven't got a car or anything and if I went to college … well, I do everything … he (her partner) don't do nothing, except go fishing, so I take Mark, then I come here.

Another student gave his reason for choosing a distance learning course:

> eliminates the problem of transport, travel costs and time wasted travelling.

By far the greatest practical difficulties concerned the juggling of domestic and learning responsibilities, particularly for women. Edwards (1993) talks of the 'two greedy institutions' of home and education and the constant juggling which partnered women with families have to do to satisfy the needs of both. For working women, I have argued that there are 'three greedy institutions' – home, work and education or training. The following vignettes from women are fairly representative of the whole:

> Well, I've got a child and a husband – but it's me mum really, she's the hardest 'cos she's, sort of ill, really, and she's more of a commitment.
> Having a young son (nearly three) and a household of husband, dog, etc, it is often 9 pm before I can settle down to do any work for this course.
> When work and family pressures mount, study becomes of low priority.

And from two male students:

> Neglecting my wife.
> Defending the time to undertake the studying (with) two teenage children and a demanding training role. …

Institutional barriers

Institutional barriers are those concerned with timetabling, choice of courses, availability of information and so on. Timetabling of both training and education is an important issue for many people. The students with whom I spoke often chose courses that fitted in with other commitments. This was particularly so for those with school-aged children:

> *Wanda:* I would have done psychology, but I ended up doing social history instead and although I had to come in five days, I could leave after the children and arrived at the latest about quarter past four which of course is the time they arrive.

For students on the distance learning Master's degree, the flexibility of the timetable was emphasized, particularly as they were in employment:

> Flexibility of being able to choose when to study.
>
> I can study when I can fit it in without committing myself to several hours in the same day/evening which in my job would be difficult.
>
> Because of illness, I have been able to continue my studies whereas if I had been required to attend regular classes/tutorials I would not have.

Financial concerns

The extent to which finance was a problem varied according to the social circumstances and the age of the student. This was dealt with in a variety of ways including choice of course, grants, claiming state benefits and both part-time and full-time work.

One would expect finance to be less of a problem for those students who were working full time. However, while some organizations paid for training and education as part of their staff development programme and gave extra help with travel, books and so on, others did not, and some of the students on the distance learning Master's course had to pay their own fees and meet their own expenses, thus creating a considerable inequity. There is need for serious consideration here when planning and delivering both education and training courses in which all students are assessed using the same criteria.

Personal and social factors

Personal and social influences include relationships with partners, children, relatives and friends. These varied according to the demands of the programme undertaken and the number and type of other commitments. The stresses on relationships with family and friends are implicit in the discussion above on domestic and caring responsibilities. Here, the focus is on partners, albeit briefly.

Some students had partners who were extremely supportive:

> *Heather:* He agreed I should do something I enjoyed doing, so yeah, he backed me up ... but doesn't do anything practically to help.
>
> *Rhona:* He's been very, very supportive, all the time I've been up there ... he's also done a great deal to build up my confidence, teach me how capable I am.

Where partners are not supportive, the situation can be very difficult and can lead to undue stress at the least and course drop-out at the worst.

> *Bryony:* He can't see the point in what I'm doing; he thinks it's just a waste of time. He can't understand why I just don't want to go and get any job ... so I go home, cook the meals, doing the ironing at the same time, as you do ... then I do my homework at night. I get very tired – he says it's my own fault.

Two students put the general situation succinctly:

> Little time for social life/family.
>   Practically speaking, my hobbies and friends have taken second place to study.

Barriers? What barriers?

So where does this leave us? These extracts and issues have been drawn mainly from research into students returning to education, though some are from more practical training programmes in the post-compulsory sector. I have only touched on some of the issues here, but clearly adults' motivation to learn is influenced considerably by extrinsic social and environmental factors. It is interesting that none of the people with whom I spoke used the term 'barrier' and the fact that they are enrolled on education and training programmes means that they are the success story. This is not, however, to underplay the issues, nor the resources which may have had to be used to negotiate the hurdles. Bryant (1995:270) describes the situation for adult returners to formal education, but this can equally apply to training in the workplace:

> For many adult students the return to further or higher education represents an obstacle course of Grand National proportions. Self-confidence has to be developed, writing skills polished up or acquired, academic language demystified and personal and family relations re-ordered.

Clearly, as trainers/educators, we need not only to take on board the learning needs of the adults with whom we are working, we also need to acknowledge the social and environmental factors which impact on their learning.

CONCLUSION

This chapter has ranged across a variety of issues, but the central focus has been on adult learners and the intrinsic and extrinsic influences that impact on their motivation to learn. It has taken some of the learning theories outlined in the previous chapter and expanded and illustrated them with verbatim researched material, moving on to look at some of the issues that adults bring into the learning arena.

What is important to remember for those of us who work with adult learners is that they bring considerable experience, both positive and negative, into the learning arena. These experiences can be both motivators and barriers to adult learning. It is incumbent upon the teacher/trainer to provide a learning environment that maximizes the learning value from those experiences. As Knowles (1996:95–96) says:

> The central dynamic of the learning process is thus perceived to be the experience of the learner, experience being defined as the interaction between an individual and his (sic) environment. ... The critical function of the teacher, therefore, is to create a rich environment from which students can extract learning and then guide their interaction with it so as to maximize their learning from it.

Bibliography

ACACE (1982) *Continuing Education: From policies to practice,* Leicester, ACACE

Bloom, B S (1965) *Taxonomy of Educational Objectives,* Harlow, Longman

Bowles, S and Gintis, H (1976) *Schooling in Capitalist America,* London, Routledge and Kegan Paul

Britton, C and Baxter, A (1994) 'Gender and access to higher education: biographies of mature students', paper presented at the BSA Annual Conference, University of Central Lancashire

Brookfield, S (1991) *Understanding and Facilitating Adult Learning,* Buckingham, Open University Press

Browning, D (1990) 'Beyond GCSE: real choices for adults', *Adults Learning,* **1**, 3, pp 147–48

Bryant, R (1995) 'Why does being a mature student have to be so painful?', *Adults Learning,* May, 270–71

Edwards, R (1993) *Mature Women Students,* London, Taylor & Francis

Gagné, R M (1972) 'Domains of learning', *Interchange,* **3**, 1, pp 1–8

Harris, F R, Johnston, M K, Kelley, C S and Wolf, M M (1965) 'Effects of positive social reinforcement on regressed crawling of a nursery school child', in L Ullmann and L Krasner, (eds) *Case Studies in Behaviour Modification,* New York, Holt, Rinehart and Winston

Harrison, R (1993) *Human Resource Management: Issues and strategies,* Wokingham, Addison-Wesley

Honey, P and Mumford, A (1986) *Manual of Learning Styles,* London, Peter Honey

Hughes, M, Kennedy, M, MacCaffery, J and McGivney, V (1989) 'Editorial', *Adults Learning,* **1**, 4, p 99

Kelly, G A (1955) *The Psychology of Personal Constructs,* New York, McGraw-Hill

Knowles, M (1996) 'Andragogy: an emerging technology for adult learning', in R Edwards, A Hanson and P Raggatt, (eds) *Boundaries of Adult Learning,* London, Routledge and Open University Press

Köhler, W I (1925) *The Mentality of Apes,* New York, Brace and World

Kolb, D A (1984) *Experiential Learning: Experience as the source of learning and development,* New York, Prentice-Hall

Longworth, N and Davies, W K (1996) *Lifelong Learning,* London, Kogan Page

McGivney, V (1993) *Women, Education and Training: Barriers to access, informal starting points and progression routes,* Leicester, NIACE

McGivney, V (1995) 'Women returners' educational needs and aspirations: summary report', unpublished, Oxford, Heart of England TEC

Maslow, A H (1968) *Towards a Psychology of Being,* 2nd edn, New York, Van Nostrand

Parr, J (1991) 'The experience of mature women students in further and higher education', MEd thesis, University of Sheffield

Parr, J (1996) 'Education: what's in it for mature women?', PhD Thesis, University of Sheffield

Pye, J (1991) *Second Chances: Adults returning to education,* Oxford, Oxford University Press

Rogers, A (1996) *Teaching Adults,* 2nd edn, Buckingham, Open University Press

Rogers, C (1969) *Freedom to Learn,* Ohio, Merrill

Rogers, C (1974) *On Becoming a Person,* London, BBC Publications

Schutze, H G (ed), Slowey, M, Wagner, A and Paquet, P (1987) *Adults in Higher Education: Policies and practice in Great Britain and North America,* Stockholm, Almqvist and Wiksell

Thijssen, J (1992) 'A model for adult training in flexible organizations: towards an experience concentration theory', *Journal of Industrial Training,* **16**, 9, pp 5–15

Woodley, A, Wagner, L, Slowey, M, Hamilton, M and Fulton, O (eds) (1987) *Choosing to Learn: Adults in education,* Paris, CERI

13

Reflective Practice

Cheryl Hunt

INTRODUCTION AND LEARNING OBJECTIVES

The real magic of discovery lies not in seeking new landscapes but in having new eyes. (Marcel Proust, 1899)

The term 'reflection' is evocative of a number of images: mirrors, tranquil scenes in still waters, thinking idly about times past, and forms of meditation come immediately to mind. In the context of education and training, though, the term is often used specifically to signify an important stage in the learning cycle where a complex and deliberate process of thinking about and interpreting an experience is undertaken in order to arrive at a new understanding of events and our part in them (Boud *et al*, 1985; Kolb, 1984). I have heard the process jokingly described as, 'What enables someone to have 20 years' experience instead of one year's experience 20 times over'!

The important thing to note about reflection in this context is that it is a conscious act, deliberately engaged in, with the intention of finding out more about our own learning processes and how they affect our professional practice and working relationships. In the final part of this chapter I shall describe how this kind of reflection can be enhanced through writing, and I shall indicate several texts that can be consulted for suggestions and outlines of various reflective techniques and case studies.

First, I shall introduce some of the 'theory' behind the concepts of reflection and reflective practice. Although it is not necessary to know this before trying out the techniques that can enhance reflection, or applying what is learned in this way to professional practice, my own view is that it usually helps to know something about the territory you are going to enter. I should tell you at this point that I read guidebooks in order to find out what I can about local customs and traditions before I visit a country with which I am unfamiliar. I have also worked in a university environment for many years where 'theoretical knowledge' is often privileged over 'practical knowledge' (Schön had something to say about this as we shall see in a moment). Let me explain why I have mentioned these two things about myself.

Part of my own attempt to become a reflective practitioner has been to try to recognize behaviour patterns that I have developed in response to particular situations and to determine where they spill over into other, seemingly unconnected, things that I do, and with what effect. I try, too, to look at how what I do is influenced by the organizational context in which I do it: that way I can begin to identify what I have the power to change, what is a real constraint of my job, and what is merely an habitual response. I believe that an important element in reflective practice is to be able to take ownership of my actions and say, 'This is how it is for me now; and these seem to be some of the reasons that have led me to think/feel/act as I do.' In attempting to facilitate the process for others, I also believe it is essential to try to model it (Hunt, 2001).

I am not sure that I can do that successfully here, but the purpose of alluding to my own background is to indicate how the structure and style of this chapter are essentially the product of my particular experience, of 'baggage' from my past that constantly entwines with pressures in the present to shape how I think and what I do. How you read the chapter – whether you do so from beginning to end, turn to the last part first, look for headings or bullet points, or skip it altogether – and whether you feel comfortable or exasperated with it will similarly be the product of your experience.

So, too, will be your reasons for consulting the chapter: you may be unfamiliar with the term 'reflective practice'; you may be experienced in the practice but wonder if I have anything to add to what you already know; or you may be charged by your employers with doing and/or facilitating reflective practice and want some practical tips. How you approach the task of reading the chapter, as with any other task, will, in turn, affect what you get out of it and what you do afterwards.

The main reason for consciously and systematically engaging with the process of reflection is to learn how to identify, articulate, take ownership of, and begin to control that which constitutes the 'baggage' – habits, ideas, assumptions, preferences, needs and so on – that would itself otherwise control our thoughts and actions; and to consider to what extent, and with what effect, the influences from our past interact with the requirements of the environment in which we now live and work. To be a 'reflective practitioner' is to apply the understanding thus obtained to professional practice so that this can be simultaneously informed by and freed from what we have learnt so far.

Though Aristotle spoke of the need for reflection in developing moral action, Dewey (1933) is generally acknowledged as the first modern educationist to write about the function of reflective thought in learning from experience. However, the notion of the 'reflective practitioner' emanates directly from the work of Schön (1983).

In the next section I shall draw attention to key aspects of this work, to the intellectual and social background against which it was developed, and to some of the major critiques of Schön's ideas.

In keeping with what I believe to be the spirit of reflective practice, I shall continue to use the conversational 'I/you' style where appropriate. This enables me both to indicate and reflect on how I, as writer, am located within the chapter. It also invites you, as reader, not simply to view these pages from 'outside' but to place yourself in the chapter too in order to observe and reflect on the thoughts and feelings that arise during your reading.

Having read this chapter you will:

- understand the nature of reflective practice;
- be able to 'reflect' on thoughts, attitudes and behaviour;
- understand single and double loop learning; and
- understand the role of reflection in professional practice.

THE REFLECTIVE PRACTITIONER: DONALD SCHÖN

Schön wrote his seminal text on the subject of 'the reflective practitioner' because he wanted professionals to recognize the importance of being able to articulate what it is they do. Writing in the early 1980s when, in the USA and the UK in particular, changing political and social attitudes were bringing the purpose and function of the professions increasingly into question, Schön (1983) argued that the lack of clarity about what professionals actually did was one consequence of a widening rift between both research and practice, and thought and action.

Underpinning this was a familiar piece of dualistic 'either-or' thinking in which the 'hard', 'theoretical' knowledge traditionally associated with the universities was seen as separate and different from what Schön (1983:vii) called the 'mystique of practical competence' which allowed professionals to claim that their 'art' could be neither adequately described nor subjected to analysis.

(Interestingly, such thinking seems almost to have come full circle in recent debates about the feasibility of incorporating reflection within the framework of National Vocational Qualifications without divorcing values from techniques. See Ecclestone, 1996, for an examination of this issue in the context of continuing professional development for lecturers in post-compulsory education.)

At the root of Schön's work is an attempt to develop an 'inquiry into the epistemology of practice' (a formal study of the source, nature and limitations of the knowledge which underpins practice) which asks questions like:

> What is the kind of knowing in which competent practitioners engage? How is professional knowing like and unlike the kinds of knowledge presented in academic textbooks, scientific papers, and learned journals? (Schön, 1983:viii)

It is based on the view that the development of a taken-for-granted 'theory of action' in professional practice is an inevitable consequence of the impossibility of developing a new response to every new situation by working through from first principles but that, when asked to articulate their practice, professionals generally do so in terms of 'espoused theories' – usually the 'textbook' theories they were taught as part of their initial professional training. In other words, they fail to address the underlying assumptions they have learned through experience – what, in earlier collaborative work, Argyris and Schön (1974:8) referred to as 'theories-in-use'. Pivotal to the inquiry is the concept of 'reflection-in-action' (Schön, 1983:54–59).

We shall return to this in a moment. It may be useful first to note two other key terms and concepts which were developed during Schön's collaboration with Argyris since they clearly informed his subsequent thinking.

MODELS AND LOOPS

Behaviour patterns: Model I and Model II

Working on extensive case-study material, Argyris and Schön (1974) identified two distinct patterns of behaviour based on the kinds of goals people strive to achieve in their social interactions, especially at work. For the most part, they argued, these goals, or 'governing variables', seem to be built on unquestioned assumptions about the social world and expectations about the behaviour of others. What they called 'Model I' behaviour is governed by the following imperatives:

- *Define and achieve goals.* (People exhibiting this behaviour rarely try to develop a mutual definition of purpose with others, especially subordinates or clients; and they do not seem open to others' perceptions of the task in hand.)
- *Maximize winning, minimize losing.*
- *Minimize generating or expressing negative feelings.* (Because, it is usually felt, this demonstrates incompetence; permitting or helping others to express feelings is regarded as poor strategy.)
- *Be rational.* (ie, objective, intellectual, unemotional.)

Argyris and Schön (1974:83) point out that such behaviour almost inevitably results in 'competitiveness, withholding help from others, conformity, covert antagonism, and mistrust while de-emphasizing cooperation, helping others, individuality and trust'. Nevertheless, most people tend to remain unaware of how such a climate is generated and, especially, of their own contribution to it; it becomes 'self-sealing'.

As Argyris and Schön (1974:86–95) go on to demonstrate, the most significant property of Model II behaviour is its ability not to be 'self-sealing' because it encourages the testing of underpinning assumptions. The governing variables that drive Model II behaviour are:

- *Maximize valid information.* This involves providing others with directly observable data and correct reports about one's thoughts and feelings.
- *Maximize free and informed choice.* A choice is free to the extent that individuals can define their own objectives and how to achieve them, and that they have the capacity to achieve these objectives and relate them to personal needs.

- *Maximize internal commitment to decisions made.* Individuals need to feel that they are responsible for their own choices: to be committed to action because it is intrinsically satisfying, not because someone else is rewarding or penalizing the action (as in Model I).

Where Model II behaviour becomes the norm, Argyris and Schön contend that people are more likely to test publicly their 'theories-in-use' – to examine openly and honestly the assumptions which underpin their actions. Such behaviour is also likely to set learning cycles in motion whereby the climate of trust which such behaviour tends to generate leads to more detailed examination of assumptions, the sharing of more valid information, and the mutual facilitation of learning. (See Radford, 1995, especially pages 196–98 for a practical example of the use of these ideas in creating a learning organization and the responsibilities of the human resource or personnel manager in this context.)

Learning loops

Argyris and Schön also identified two distinct learning patterns. What they termed 'single-loop learning' (see Figure 13.1) helps people to design and select actions which satisfy their governing variables so it is exhibited by people using both Model I and Model II behaviour patterns. It is a form of 'means-ends', task-oriented, non-reflective thinking: it looks, for example, for more effective methods of suppressing conflict.

'Double-loop learning', by contrast, involves reflection and is likely to result in the questioning of, and possible changes in, one's predominant governing variables and underpinning assumptions (see Figure 13.2). Generally associated with Model II behaviour, it asks not only the single-loop question 'Am I doing things right, and if not what can I do to correct my/others' actions?' but also, 'Am I doing the right things, and if not how can I change what I do and/or encourage others to change what they do?' It looks, for example, for ways to articulate and bring conflict to the surface and to resolve, rather than suppress it.

Significantly, as Argyris and Schön (1974:19) point out, 'Double-loop learning does not supersede single-loop learning.' The latter enables us to cope in predictable situations. The former,

Figure 13.1 Single-loop learning

Figure 13.2 Double-loop learning

however, can cause 'ripples of change to fan out over one's whole system of theories-in-use' (ibid). 'Double-loop learning' therefore lies at the heart of reflective practice. Let us now return to Schön's later work in that area, and the concept of reflection-in-action.

REFLECTION-IN-ACTION

Tacit knowledge

The concept of reflection-in-action derives from the idea that, in exhibiting skilful action, people often appear to be drawing on information that they are subsequently unable to put into words. It owes much to the work of Polanyi (1967) on 'tacit knowing', an example of which is how people recognize faces. (Just try to explain how you recognize a face that you know!) Another example is of using a stick or tool to feel the way (simply to walk, or in a craft like sculpting). During this process, which is an essential part of all physical skill acquisition, the nature of the contact between tool and object provides data which are literally 'sensed' in the hand and internalized as tacit (unspoken) knowledge.

The belief that people do know more than they can verbalize probably gave rise to one of the earliest forms of training. Commonly known in the UK as 'sitting next to Nellie', this required a newcomer to sit next to, observe and subsequently try to emulate a skilled operator. In a newer, more sophisticated form, it emerges in the modelling techniques of neuro-linguistic-programming (NLP) and, in sports psychology, in 'playing the inner game' where the sportsperson literally reflects on his or her previous winning performances and mentally 'plays through' the feelings and techniques that will be required in the next race or match. (See Garratt, 1997, for a practical guide to using NLP in training, pages 39–44 in particular for discussion of modelling techniques. Gallwey, 1996, discusses 'inner-game' work.)

The last example is obviously of reflection-on-action with the clear intention of internalizing certain actions for future use. Reflection-in-action occurs when internalized knowledge arises in, and informs, current action. Schön (1983:55), who was an accomplished musician himself, suggests that this is what happens when good jazz musicians improvise together: in the action of playing they 'feel' where the music is going by drawing on past experience and a collective knowledge of musical 'rules'. In essence, they make new sense of what is happening in each moment and adjust their individual performances accordingly.

Points to note

Several aspects of reflection-in-action are important to note from the examples given so far:

- Lacking past experience and being new to the rules of the particular game, novices are usually unable to improvise as well as experienced practitioners (literally, like the jazz musicians, or in complex or emergency situations).
- It is unlikely that the musicians (or other skilled practitioners in other situations) reflect in action through the medium of words.
- So, if asked what they are doing/have just done, skilled practitioners usually find it difficult or impossible to give a detailed verbal analysis (try to describe exactly what you do when riding a bike in traffic – or what the ingredients are that really make a training session buzz). Finally:
- Most of the time, most practitioners do not question what they do.

Some practitioners are understandably wary about the concept of reflection, either in or on action, because they feel that putting what they do into words will either 'break the magic' of what they do well and/or take time that could be better spent actually getting on with their job. To some extent they are right. If you think about how you are doing something as natural as breathing, for example, it will sometimes change the rhythm! And, of course, if every professional stopped to question every decision or event, it would soon bring the wheels of society to a grinding halt

Nevertheless, there are two key issues here. The first is that when our usual performance yields nothing particularly new or unpredictable, it simply reinforces the behaviours/attitudes/values which underpin the performance but which may no longer be appropriate and/or as effective as they might be. The second is that, if professionals are unable to 'speak their own practice', there is a danger that others will do it for them – defining and bounding what is required from a political, academic or managerial perspective.

The requirements laid on teachers, doctors and others in the UK during the years of the so-called 'Thatcher project' when social relationships were drastically redefined are a case in point. Teachers' professional standing and judgement, for example, were called increasingly into question as politicians first defined how teachers should be trained (with more 'practice' in schools and less 'theory' in the universities), how children should be tested, and what the relationship should be between parents and teachers and between the worlds of education and of business – and then set financial and other controlling mechanisms in place to support their own ideas, leaving little room for debate or manoeuvre.

Although Schön's primary impetus came from what he saw as a crisis of confidence in professional knowledge, this crisis was itself part of a more general, and radical, shift in thinking about the nature of knowledge, where it comes from, and what status is attached to different kinds of knowledge. I shall draw attention in a later section to other authors whose ideas you may like to explore further in order to locate Schön's work, the concept of reflective practice, and subsequent developments in the field within this broader context.

Before that I want to do two things: provide a pause for you to reflect on questions that may have emerged from what you have read so far, and draw attention to some of the critiques of Schön's work and its influence.

Several questions are implicit in the foregoing discussion. If you define yourself as an educator or trainer those listed below may be particularly pertinent to your professional practice. However, they probably cannot be answered fully without venturing into the minefield of what constitutes the difference between 'education' and 'training'. (You will find comment on this in Chapters 1 and 2. An interesting perspective is also provided by Clark, 1992:120.)

Here are some questions to reflect on:

- If in 'doing' reflective practice yourself, you begin to expose taken-for-granted assumptions and beliefs in your everyday practices which receive tacit endorsement by your employers but which, when you articulate them fully, suggest a conflict of values between what you thought your job was about and what you are actually required to do, what might you do about it?
- Is reflection only for professionals to incorporate within their practice, or should other 'workers' be encouraged to reflect on what they do, and why and how they do it? (This, of course, leads into another minefield surrounding the concept of 'profession'. Carr, 1995:67–72, includes a useful analysis.) It seems, incidentally, to be a little-reported element of engaging in reflective practice that it will always open up increasingly bigger questions! Does that bother you or not? You may like to set your answer in the context of what you know of your preferred learning style (see Chapter 11).
- What responsibility does the reflective educator or trainer have for encouraging students/ trainees to reflect on their own work (and/or learning processes)?
- If you encourage/facilitate reflective practice for others, what is the extent of your responsibility to them?

Critiques

Although the concept of 'reflective practice' is now commonplace and, in some professions, most notably nurse and teacher education, a systematic approach has been taken to its incorporation into all levels of training, it should be noted that neither Schön's original text nor the practices to which it has given rise are unproblematic. The following authors have provided extensive critiques of both.

Atkins and Murphy (1993) and *Greenwood* (1993) look at reflection in the specific context of nursing where reflective practice has become a statutory requirement. Atkins and Murphy provide a selective review of the literature, focusing in particular on the skills required for reflection but also demonstrating the lack of clarity in definitions and studies of reflection and reflective practice. Greenwood looks specifically at the collaborative work of Argyris and Schön and suggests that there are important inconsistencies between their theorizing and the pedagogical interventions they implemented/recommended.

Gilroy (1993) takes issue with Schön's epistemological stance. His argument is set in the context of teacher education and is a deeply philosophical one based on Plato's *Meno* paradox: 'How will you look for something when you don't in the least know what it is?' In a later work, Schön (1987) refers to, and feels he has successfully resolved, the paradox but Gilroy refutes this and also argues that it was unnecessary for Schön to seek a new epistemology of practice in the first place since one already existed within Wittgenstein's 'Descriptivism'.

Eraut (1995) assesses Schön's contribution to thinking about professional knowledge and expertise. He argues that Schön does not properly demonstrate the difference between reflection-in-action and reflection-on-action, and that none of his examples relates to crowded settings (like a seminar room). He proposes a re-evaluation of Schön's ideas taking into account reflection outside the action, the time dimension involved in different kinds of reflection, and the difference between decision-making and problem-solving processes.

Bright (1996) cautions that although reflective practice has been adopted so rapidly and on such a broad scale by many professional groups, adoption and implementation should not be confused with understanding what it is, the processes and skills it involves, or its implications for practice. He provides a detailed analysis of what seems to constitute reflective practice and its theoretical underpinnings, including among the latter the earlier collaborative work by Argyris and Schön (1974). In Bright's (1996:183) opinion, the present widespread professional acceptance of reflective practice seems 'relatively superficial, and/or is in need of reformulation and review. In other words, we may need to "reflect" on "'reflective practice"'.

Brockbank and McGill (1998, ch 5) identify a number of critiques as well as some practical spin-offs from Schön's work.

SOCIAL CONTEXT

Though the naming and popularizing of reflective practice is largely attributable to Schön, the intellectual and social environment in which the concept took root had inevitably been shaped by other ideas and traditions, most notably those emanating from the Enlightenment and from the critical thinking which underpinned the emergence of the social sciences. This section looks briefly at this broader context and at the way Schön's work has itself become a strand within subsequent developments.

Legacy of the Enlightenment: John Dewey and C Wright Mills

In Western democracies, thinking has long been shaped by the key theme of the Enlightenment period. This holds that, as individuals or as members of social groups, human beings have the capacity to reflect rationally upon their own actions and to use the understanding thus derived as a basis for the personal change which is an important element in social change. John Dewey's work in education was very much a part of this tradition. Dewey (1933:137) argued that all productive thinking and learning has its origins in 'problematic situations' which cannot be resolved simply by the use of prior solutions and, foreshadowing an important technique in reflective practice, noted:

> To grasp the meaning of a thing, an event or a situation is to see it in relation to other 'things', to note how it operates, or functions, what consequences follow from it, what causes it, what uses it can 'be put to'.

Dewey (1939:131) later questioned whether it was any longer enough to hold 'the simple faith of the Enlightenment', that rational thought would automatically precipitate change, especially in society at large. C Wright Mills (Mills, 1967:4–6) subsequently took a similar line, arguing that people could no longer rely on reason alone to sustain them in a society where 'information often dominates their attention and overwhelms their capacities to assimilate it'. What people now needed to develop, according to Mills, was a 'sociological imagination' which would enable them to 'grasp history and biography and the relations between the two within society.' Mills (1967:8) maintained that:

> Perhaps the most fruitful distinction with which the sociological imagination works is between 'the personal troubles of milieu' and 'the public issues of social structure.' This distinction is an essential tool of the sociological imagination and a feature of all classic work in social science.

In Mills' terms, 'troubles' are private matters, usually precipitated by a threat to an individual's values occurring within his or her immediate social setting: it is up to the individual to resolve or deal with them. 'Issues', on the other hand, are of public concern: they include things like unemployment and war which, though they have drastic implications for the individual, can only be resolved at a political/societal level.

In undertaking reflective practice, a useful exercise is to identify the 'level' of a problem in just this way, perhaps also including institutional/organizational levels of management and control: it saves wasting energy and 'worry time' on things that are beyond one's own immediate control! (That does not mean, of course, that managerial or societal 'issues' should be ignored, merely that it is important to locate problems where solutions can most appropriately be found.)

Critical social science: Jurgen Habermas

Writing in the 1970s, Jurgen Habermas expressed some of the same concerns as Mills about the 'limits of reason'. He argued that the very success of reason, as expressed through advances in the natural sciences, had led to an uncritical acceptance of 'the scientific method' which had subsequently clouded thinking about the social world.

Where Mills had highlighted the distinction between the personal and the political and put forward the sociological imagination as a different way of thinking, and of taking forward the newly-developing social sciences, Habermas sought to demonstrate that there are several legitimate forms of scientific inquiry, each geared towards the satisfaction of different human interests/needs and grounded in a different kind of knowledge. His ideas have been extremely influential, particularly in relation to the concept of 'emancipatory knowledge' that empowers people to re-view what they know within a broader social/political framework, which they may subsequently choose to challenge in order to try to effect change in it.

Although Habermas's ideas have given impetus to those of many other people, his own writings do not make easy reading. Carr (1995:114–17) provides a very useful short summary in the context of educational theory; Giddens (1994) gives a general overview and also recommends further reading.

Critical reflective practice: beyond Schön

Though Schön's concern seems primarily to have been with the individual's ability to reflect on, in order to articulate, his or her own practice, the perspective provided by Habermas's work has subsequently led other writers to suggest that reflective practice in Schön's terms is too limited. Brookfield (1995:217) claims, for example, that 'Reflection in and of itself is not enough; it must always be linked to how the world can be changed.' Indeed, Brookfield argues a case for what he calls critical reflective practice that specifically requires the practitioner to take account of, and, where possible, direct action in response to, broader social issues.

Just as earlier intellectual traditions can be identified in Schön's work, so this has itself become a strand in subsequent developments. Brookfield (1995) sees it as one of three that inform the processes of critical reflective practice. Another strand is that of 'critical pedagogy'.

Critical pedagogy is closely associated with the ideas of Habermas and others linked to the so-called Frankfurt School of thought (such as Adorno, 1973, and Horkheimer, 1947) but can be traced back to the writings of Hegel and Marx. The central theme is of the teacher as 'penetrator of false consciousness', as a facilitator who will help his or her students to identify and challenge oppressive ways of thinking and acting which have been imposed by dominant groups and cultures and often sustained by force of habit. The intention is to create change that will result in more democratic and harmonious forms of living and thinking in which people understand and honour their own and others' experiences.

The concept of critical pedagogy is also influenced by the writings of, among others, Gramsci (1978) on hegemony, Freire (1994) on liberation theology and its application in education, and Giroux (1992) on 'oppositional pedagogy', all of which have served to emphasize the political nature of the processes of both teaching and reflection.

Research and theory in and of adult learning constitutes the third strand in Brookfield's view of critical reflective practice. At the base of adult learning theory is the belief that, because adults think and learn in the context of extensive prior experience, the nature of adult learning is qualitatively different from that which characterizes childhood and adolescence.

It would require a separate chapter to discuss in detail the many ideas and investigations that have sought to explain the relationship between experience, reflection and learning. However, the following list indicates some of the authors whose work has been influential in this field and which you may wish to explore further via the bibliography at the end of this chapter.

- Mezirow: One of the most influential theorists. Openly acknowledges influence of Habermas, particularly in relation to 'perspective transformation'. Like Schön, viewed own work as a reaction to forces of 'scientism and technicism' and found support in Polanyi's ideas. Builds on Kelly's (1955) work on personal constructs. Emphasizes the central role of critical reflectivity in adult learning and development as a means by which people can recognize how they are caught in their own history and constantly relive it (see Mezirow 1981). Mezirow (1990) includes advice on how to learn critical reflection and encourage it in others. (NB: Usher and Bryant (1989) also provide useful discussion of critical reflection.)
- Kolb: Identification and acknowledgement of reflection as key stage in the 'learning cycle' helped put reflection on the learning map. Work contemporary with, but independent of, Schön and Mezirow.
- Boyd and Fales: Acknowledge influence of Mezirow (1978) and Kolb *et al* (1974). Work in context of humanistic psychology on concept of reflective learning: 'the process of internally examining and exploring an issue of concern, triggered by an experience, which creates and clarifies meaning in terms of self, and which results in a changed conceptual perspective' (1983:100). (NB: This continues to be one of the most useful and succinct descriptions of the underpinning process of reflective practice. Reviewing the literature on reflection, Atkins and Murphy, 1993:1191, conclude that involvement of 'self' in the reflective process and acquisition of a 'changed perspective' are the 'crucial aspects which distinguish reflection from analysis'.)
- Boud: Notes influence of personal growth movement on his thinking (Boud and Miller, 1996:198–201). Focuses on experiential learning in adulthood. Work conceptualizes reflection and the part it plays in making sense of experience (see Boud *et al*, 1985, 1993). Builds explicitly on Kolb's work.
- Revans: More usually associated with development of management techniques than reflective practice but his work on action learning acted as direct prompt for Kolb and is echoed in Argyris and Schön. Provides a useful bridge between reflection as a tool for self-development and as an essential element of organizational learning. (NB: see McGill and Beaty, 1992, for a guide to action learning as a continuous process of learning. Brockbank and McGill (2004) develop this further.)

PUTTING REFLECTION INTO PRACTICE

Problems and approaches

So, what of practice? How do professionals act on the legacy of traditions and theories and 'do' reflective practice? What do they do? And how can the process best be facilitated for individuals and for the benefit of the organization?

It will probably have become apparent that 'reflective practice' is not one 'thing'. Though the term undoubtedly belongs to Schön, the concept is multifaceted. It incorporates elements of processes and ways of knowing which have been variously referred to as 'tacit knowledge', 'critical thought', 'perspective transformation', 'reflective learning', 'experiential learning' and 'action learning'. Thus, there are no easy answers to the questions above, or to those I posed earlier. The processes of reflection are such that individuals must necessarily arrive at their own answers and preferred techniques, in the light of their own history, values, needs and inclinations.

Wellington and Austin (1996) illustrate this clearly in a useful discussion of 'orientations to reflective practice'. Drawing on work by Van Manen (1977) and Grimmett *et al* (1990) they postulate five different, mutually exclusive, orientations, each of which is closely associated with specific social science paradigms and educational beliefs and values. Orientations are determined by requiring practitioners to follow a decision path based on three questions:

> Does the practitioner engage in reflective practice or not? Does the practitioner believe that education ought to be domesticating or liberating? Is the practitioner systems-orientated or people-orientated? (Wellington and Austin, 1996:313)

It is perhaps because of the apparently fundamental differences between approaches to professional practice and to the place of reflection within it that it is so difficult to determine any 'universals' in reflective practice. Johnston and Badley (1996) have made an attempt to discover 'working definitions, main objectives, processes of reflective practice, perceived difficulties and the main competences needed' but conclude:

> reflective practice at its best is neither just a set of operational techniques nor only a clearly identifiable group of academic skills, but is rather a critical stance. Good reflective practice takes practitioners beyond mere competence towards a willingness and a desire to subject their own taken for granteds and their own activities to serious scrutiny. Competence is not enough. The reflective practitioner has to become, if not an agent provocateur, an educational critic who is willing to pursue self and peer appraisal almost to their limits. (Johnston and Badley, 1996:10)

Given the semantic and operational difficulties with the concept and the nature of individual practice, it is inevitable that there should also be difficulties in pursuing reflective practice with peers, in facilitating it for others and, of course, in assessing it. Hunt (1998, 2001), Knights and Sampson (1995) and Sumison and Fleet (1996) address some of these issues.

Despite the difficulties there are, nevertheless, some tried and trusted techniques to facilitate reflection. The following references will take you to some of them:

- *Critical Incident Technique* (based on Flanagan, 1954). See Pearn and Kandola (1990:25–30) for a description of the technique and of how it can be used specifically in job analysis. Brookfield (1995:ch 6) describes a variation on the technique. Benner (1984:299–302) provides guidelines for recording critical incidents.
- *Good Practices Audit* (Brookfield, 1995 ch 8).
- *Reflective Writing and Journal Keeping* (Holly, 1989; Morrison, 1996; Bolton, 2001).
- *Story-Telling* (McDrury and Alterio, 2003; Parkin, 1998).

In addition, Schön (1991) contains some interesting case studies that indicate how various approaches worked in practice. Mon (1999) also describes a number of useful practical techniques. Brockbank, McGill and Beech (2002) include a series of open-ended case studies to illustrate how organizations have incorporated different approaches to reflective learning.

PERSONAL EXPERIENCE

My own preferred form of reflective practice is through a two-stage process of writing and discussion. The writing may be either structured or unstructured but the crucial thing is that it is for my eyes only – I ignore the niceties of grammar, punctuation, spelling, even of being polite about people! The purpose is to help me to capture and sort out some of the whirling and unfocused thoughts that have occurred throughout the working day and which would otherwise disappear. Once the thoughts have been captured I can then choose from them which ones to share with a 'critical friend' who, as I then do in return for her, provides me with a different perspective and asks questions which help me to explore my thoughts and feelings in ways that I might not have considered had I worked on them on my own.

The importance of writing as opposed to merely 'thinking about' my practice is encapsulated for me in the phrase 'How do I know what I think until I see what I say?' The process of writing helps me not only to see what I say to myself about aspects of my professional practice but also to 'unpack' why I have said it. It helps me, in other words, to find out more about how my mind works. Holly (1989:76) puts it like this:

> Describing how the mind works will help to clarify why journal writing works as a means for reflection: 'Instead of a single intellectual entity that can judge many different kinds of events equally, the mind is diverse and complex. It contains a changeable conglomeration of different kinds of "small minds" – fixed reactions, talents, flexible thinking and these different entities are temporarily employed – wheeled into consciousness – then usually discarded, returned to their place, after use' (Ornstein, 1987:25). Which of the many small minds gets wheeled in depends on many factors, some within our control, others not.

And:

> Writing 'works' because it enables us to come to know ourselves through the multiple voices our experiences take, to describe our contexts and histories as they shape the many minds and selves who define us and others. Through writing we intentionally focus our attention and in so doing assert and affirm both our ideas and the mind itself. (Holly, 1989:78)

Sometimes I take a 'stream of consciousness' approach to what I write. It is not always easy to start writing because, like many educators, I have been 'conditioned' to worry about order and structure. Before I write, therefore, I often find myself dithering over whether I should say A before B and whereabouts C should come – and my brain refuses to release any words at all! By just plunging in – even if the first words I write are, 'I really don't know what I want to say here but …' – I find that thoughts begin to flow, often so fast that my writing hand cannot keep up.

Sometimes I focus on a particular incident which could be:

- a particularly positive experience;
- an occasion when my intervention seemed to have made a real difference to someone's learning;
- a negative experience where things seemed to go badly wrong;
- an experience I found hard to handle;
- something trivial but which made me think, 'What's going on here?'

I then follow the procedure described below.

Structured writing about a practice incident

Process

1. Describe what happened. Be objective. Ask questions like: What did I learn? How did I learn it? In what ways was the experience similar to/different from others I have had?
2. Make judgements. Capture what was good/bad about the experience; its best/worst features; what went well/badly; how did I contribute to all of that?
3. Analyse. Focus on questions like, How did that happen? How can I make sense of that? How can that be explained?

Personalize

Instead of settling for a general statement like, 'It was good/bad', use personal statements like:

- What I understood/enjoyed was …
- What I felt uncertain/uncomfortable/irritable about was …
- What I did well/not so well was …
- What I could have done differently was …

Probe

Instead of settling for a personal statement like, 'What I felt annoyed about was the way X hogged the discussion', use probing questions like:

- Why did it annoy me so much?
- Why didn't I do anything about it?

Make a note of other similar situations; identify any recurring themes eg, particular people, situations, questions that regularly cause you to have the same emotional/behavioural response. Ask:

- Why?
- What can I do?
- Do I want to?

Plan

Out of the above, begin to identify your favoured learning methods, 'hang-ups', responses, etc and make plans for the future, particularly about what you want to change. Focus on one thing at a time, eg:

- personal values;
- working relationships;
- gaining a better understanding of …;
- your role within the organization.

I know from personal experience that trying to understand what reflective practice is can be mind-boggling. 'Doing' reflective practice in any of its many forms can sometimes feel over-whelming, and attempting to facilitate it can be frighteningly complex. However, to return to the quotation with which I began this chapter, there is also some magic to be found in seriously exploring reflective practice – with or without a guidebook! By helping us to discover new meanings and perspectives in ourselves and what we do, it can transform the familiar landscape of professional practice so that we do, indeed, begin to see it through new eyes.

Bibliography

Adorno, T W (1973) *Negative Dialectics*, New York, Seabury Press

Argyris, C and Schön, D A (1974) *Theory in Practice: Increasing professional effectiveness*, San Francisco, CA, Jossey-Bass

Atkins, S and Murphy, K (1993) 'Reflection: a review of the literature', *Journal of Advanced Nursing*, **18**, pp 1188–92

Benner, P (1984) *From Novice to Expert*, London, Addison-Wesley

Bolton, G (2001) *Reflective Practice Writing and Professional Development*, London, Paul Chapman

Boud, D and Miller, N (eds) (1996) *Working With Experience: Animating learning*, London, Routledge

Boud, D, Cohen, R and Walker, D (1993) 'Understanding learning from experience', in D Boud, R Cohen and D Walker (eds), *Using Experience for Learning*, Buckingham, SRHE and Open University Press

Boud, D, Keogh, R and Walker, D (eds) (1985) *Reflection: Turning experience into learning*, London, Kogan Page

Boyd, E M and Fales, A (1983) 'Reflective learning: key to learning from experience', *Journal of Humanistic Psychology*, **23**, 2, pp 99–117

Bright, B (1996) 'Reflecting on "reflective practice"', *Studies in the Education of Adults*, **28**, 2, pp 162–84

Brockbank, A and McGill, I (1998) *Facilitating Reflective Learning in Higher Education*, Buckingham, SRHE and Open University Press

Brockbank, A and McGill, I (2004) *The Action Learning Handbook: Powerful techniques for education, professional development and training*, London, RoutledgeFalmer

Brockbank, A, McGill, I and Beech, N (2002) *Reflective Learning in Practice*, London, Gower

Brookfield, S D (1995) *Becoming a Critically Reflective Teacher*, San Francisco, CA, Jossey-Bass

Brunner, D D (1994) *Inquiry and Reflection: Framing narrative and practice in education*, Albany, State University of New York Press

Carr, W (1995) *For Education: Towards critical educational inquiry*, Buckingham, Open University Press

Clark, D (1992) 'Education for community in the 1990s: a Christian perspective', in G Allen and I Martin, (eds), *Education and Community: The politics of practice*, London, Cassell

Clift, R T, Houston, W R and Pugach, M C (eds) (1990) *Encouraging Reflective Practice in Education: An analysis of issues and programs*, Columbia University, Teachers College Press

Dewey, J (1933) *How We Think*, Boston, MA, Heath

Dewey, J (1939) *Freedom and Culture*, New York, Putnam

Ecclestone, K (1996) 'The reflective practitioner: mantra or a model for emancipation?', *Studies in the Education of Adults*, **28**, 2, pp 146–61

Eraut, M (1995) 'Schön shock: a case for reframing reflection-in-action?', *Teachers and Teaching: Theory and Practice*, **1**, 1, pp 9–22

Flanagan, J C (1954) The critical incident technique', *Psychological Bulletin*, 51, pp 327–58

Freire, P (1994) *Pedagogy of Hope: Reliving pedagogy of the oppressed*, New York, Continuum

Gallwey, W T (1996) *The Inner Game of Tennis*, London, Pan Books (also: *The Inner Game of Golf*)

Garratt, T (1997) *The Effective Delivery of Training Using NLP*, London, Kogan Page

Giddens, A (1994) 'Jürgen Habermas', in Q Skinner (ed), *The Return of Grand Theory in the Human Sciences*, Cambridge, Cambridge University Press, pp 123–39

Gilroy, P (1993) 'Reflections on Schön: an epistemological critique and a practical alternative', in P Gilroy and M Smith (eds), *International Analyses of Teacher Education*, Oxford, Carfax, pp 125–42

Giroux, H A (1992) *Border Crossings: Cultural workers and the politics of education*, New York, Routledge

Gramsci, A (1978) *Selections from the Prison Notebooks*, London, Lawrence and Wishart

Greenwood, J (1993) 'Reflective practice: a critique of the work of Argyris and Schon', *Journal of Advanced Nursing*, **17**, pp 1183–87

Grimmet, P P, Mackinnon, A M, Erickson, G L and Riecken, T J (1990) 'Reflective practice in teacher education', in R T Clift *et al* (eds), *Encouraging Reflective Practice in Education: An analysis of issues and programs*, Columbia University, Teachers College Press, pp 20–38

Heron, J (1996) 'Helping whole people learn', in D Boud and N Miller (eds), *Working With Experience: Animating learning*, London, Routledge, pp 73–91

Holly, M L (1989) 'Reflective writing and the spirit of inquiry', *Cambridge Journal of Education*, **19**, 1, pp 71–80

Horkheimer, M (1947) *Eclipse of Reason*, Oxford, Oxford University Press

Hunt, C (1998) 'Learning from Lerner: reflections on facilitating reflective practice', *Journal of Further and Higher Education*, **22**, 1, pp 25–31

Hunt, C (2001) 'Shifting shadows: metaphors and maps for facilitating reflective practice', *Reflective Practice*, **2**, 3, pp 275–87

Johnston, R and Badley, G (1996) 'The competent reflective practitioner', *Innovation and Learning in Education*, **2**, 1, pp 4–10

Kelly, G A (1955) *The Psychology of Personal Constructs*, New York, Norton

Knights, K and Sampson, J (1995) 'Reflection in the context of team-teaching', *Studies in Education*, **17**, 1, pp 58–69

Kolb, D A (1984) *Experiential Learning*, Englewood Cliffs, NJ, Prentice-Hall

Kolb, D A, Rubin, I M and McIntyre, J M (1974) *Organizational Psychology: An experiential approach*, Englewood Cliffs, NJ, Prentice-Hall

McGill, I and Beaty, L (1992) *Action Learning: A practitioner's guide*, London, Kogan Page

McDrury, J and Alterio, M (2003) *Learning Through Storytelling in Higher Education: Using reflection and experience to improve learning*, London, Kogan Page

Mezirow, J (1978) 'Perspective transformation', *Adult Education*, **28**, 2, pp 100–10

Mezirow, J (1981) 'Critical theory of adult learning and education', *Adult Education*, **32**, 1, pp 3–24

Mezirow, J and Associates (1990) *Fostering Critical Reflection in Adulthood: A guide to transformative and emancipatory learning*, Albany, State University of New York Press

Mills, C W (1967) *The Sociological Imagination*, Oxford, Oxford University Press

Mon, J A (1999) *Reflection in Learning and Professional Development: Theory and practice*, London, Kogan Page

Morrison, K (1996) 'Developing reflective practice in higher degree students through a learning journal', *Studies in Higher Education*, **21**, 3, pp 317–32

Nemiroff, G H (1992) *Reconstructing Education: Toward a pedagogy of critical humanism*, Westport, CT, Bergin and Garvey/Greenwood Press

Parkin, M (1998) *Tales for Trainers*, London, Kogan Page

Pearn, M and Kandola, R (1990) *Job Analysis: A practical guide for managers*, London, Institute of Personnel Management

Polanyi, M (1967) *The Tacit Dimension*, New York, Doubleday

Radford, A (1995) *Managing People in Professional Practices*, London, Institute of Personnel and Development

Revans, R W (1982) *The Origins and Growth of Action Learning*, Bromley, Chartwell-Bratt

Schön, D A (1983) *The Reflective Practitioner: How professionals think in action*, New York, Basic Books

Schön, D A (1987) *Educating the Reflective Practitioner: Toward a new design for teaching and learning in the professions*, San Francisco, CA, Jossey-Bass

Schön, D A (ed) (1991) *The Reflective Turn: Case studies in and on educational practice*, New York, Teachers College Press

Sumison, J and Fleet, A (1996) 'Reflection: can we assess it? Should we assess it?', *Assessment and Evaluation in Higher Education*, **21**, 2, pp 121–29

Usher, R S and Bryant, I P (1989) *Adult Education as Theory, Practice and Research: The captive triangle*, London, Routledge

Van Manen, M (1977) 'Linking ways of knowing with ways of being practical', *Curriculum Inquiry*, **6**, 3, pp 205–08

Wellington, B and Austin, P (1996) 'Orientations to reflective practice', *Educational Research*, **38**, 3, pp 307–16

14

Workplace Diversity and Training – More Than Fine Words

Joan E Keogh

INTRODUCTION AND LEARNING OBJECTIVES

This chapter could have been fashionably titled 'Managing the Mosaic'; at one time it would have more prosaically been an obligatory chapter on equal opportunities; and before that it would have been a discussion on discrimination at the workplace.

Such concerns remain a live issue for organizations, however progressive, but there is more and more emphasis on management's need to recognize and develop the potential of all individuals in their workforce. Some writers argue that people differ in more ways than disability, ethnicity, gender or the like; they regard organizational culture overall as the most important element for effective management, with diversity seen more as added value. However, there has been a significant change of attitude over the past two decades in general acknowledgement that 'people matter' at the workplace, regardless of their differences.

Having read this chapter you will:

- understand the nature of diversity;
- understand the business imperative for diversity in the workplace;
- know the UK legislation that relates to diversity; and
- understand some of the training and development responses that apply to diversity.

EQUAL OPPORTUNITIES AND MANAGING DIVERSITY – WHAT IS THE DIFFERENCE?

Basically, the main differences between the two are as follows (IPD, 1996).

Equal opportunities

- concentration on discrimination/unfairness;
- perceived as an issue for women and ethnic minorities and people with disabilities;
- focuses on boosting proportion of minority groups in employment;
- strategy has to be 'mainstreamed';
- emphasis on positive action rather than corporate vision.

Managing diversity

- aims to ensure that all employees maximize their potential and contribution to the organization;
- concentrates on movement within an organization, its culture and the meeting of business objectives;
- concerns all staff and especially managers;
- does not rely on positive action and provides a vision.

Moody (2003:5) points to another important difference between the two, with equality of opportunities in employment expanded to a legal duty, fairness and human rights in relation to equal access to jobs, training, promotion, and decisions on redundancy.

Diversity defined

One of the problems with words is that they can subtly change in meaning as they become applied to management theories. For example in Handy's (1993:256) seminal work, *Understanding Organizations*, the term diversity occurs more than once in relation to organizational design, and 'management of diversity' is all about distribution of organizational power, match of culture, and structure.

Discussing the wider aspects of organizational culture, Handy (1993:188) suggests that diversity in the organization inclines towards what he categorizes as a 'task culture', with influence based on expert power. Handy describes this as a team culture where 'getting the job done' tends to wipe out 'most status and style differences'. Although it might be unwise to take this parallel too far along the road of organizational theory, in terms of a diverse workforce, it points towards a training ethos which encourages mixed group/team learning as a way forward from the more formalized instruction-type sessions.

But workplace diversity has now taken on a whole new meaning, and Donaldson quotes Dr Judy Rosener from the University of California, author of *Workforce America: Managing employee diversity as a vital resource*, as saying:

> We do not mean just race and gender. We have looked at dimensions of diversity as things that make people different from one another. … Everyone has different dimensions. There are things you cannot change such as age, race, sex and sexual orientation … and others such as marital status, religious beliefs.
>
> (Donaldson 1994:5–6)

Rosener avers that there are 'three steps to diversity – recruiting a diverse workforce, valuing them so that they are not token and managing them [and] you have to have all three'.

From the UK there is Kandola and Fullerton's widely accepted concept of workplace diversity:

> The basic concept of managing diversity accepts that the workforce consists of a diverse population of people. The diversity consists of visible and non visible differences which will include factors such as sex, age, background, race, disability, personality, work style. It is founded on the premise that harnessing these differences will create a productive environment in which everyone feels valued, where their talents are being fully utilised and in which organizational goals are being met.
>
> (Kandola and Fullerton, 1994:8)

In the IPD Position Paper, Bett sees diversity as an evolutionary step in equal opportunities and suggests that:

> The diversity concept expands our horizons beyond equality issues covered by the law and builds on recognized approaches to equal opportunities. It adds new impetus to the development of equal opportunities and the creation of an environment in which enhanced contributions from all employees will work to the advantage of the business, people themselves and society more generally.
>
> (IPD, 1996:1)

Rosener's dimensions are expanded to include a considerably wider range of personal differences alongside the more generally acknowledged ethnic origin, gender, physical and mental abilities, such as 'academic or vocational qualification, accent, age, caring responsibilities, learning difficulties, marital status, political affiliation, religion, sexual orientation, spent or irrelevant conviction, trade union or non trade union membership'.

Over time, all these definitions have been reworked in one way or another, with the United Nations' version (2000) regarded by Clements and Jones (2002:13) as all-embracing, at the same time demonstrating the complexity that needs to be addressed. Thus:

> Diversity takes many forms. It is usually thought of in terms of obvious attributes – age differences, race, gender, physical ability, sexual orientation, religion and language.

with an added dimension for today's world:

> Diversity in terms of background, professional experience, skill and specialization, values and culture, as well as social class, is a prevailing pattern.
>
> (UN, 2000)

More a kaleidoscope than a mosaic?

Rather than a 'mosaic', the IPD illustrates diversity with its own multicolour design in the form of a snowflake, each snowflake representing a unique form made up of many different but equal parts to symbolize diversity and equality.

As yet another analogy, the concept of diversity points to every single member of the organization as being a unique shape, as in a jigsaw, everyone together making up the picture that is the whole, and which is not complete if even one of the pieces is left out. But both the concept of a mosaic and the human jigsaw suggest an immutable and static whole, coloured and original as the total image may be. And snowflakes melt!

My own flight of fancy leads me more to the kaleidoscope, with its innumerable permutations of patterns depending on the way the shapes and colours re-form again and again. For those of us concerned with training and development, perhaps we should envisage diversity more within the kaleidoscope's vibrant and changing patterns, different pictures each time it is shaken up, but always combining from the same source – and that is the challenge!

Managing diversity – theory and practice

A simple model of good practice is provided by La Fasto (1992) from an American case study (The Baxter Healthcare Corporation) and is shown in Figure 14.1. This is a different sequence from Rosener above, who puts 'valuing' before 'managing'. Creating harmony at work calls for managing and developing people as individuals in order to ensure fairness and consistency, that is to say, being responsive to different needs.

Nevertheless, Harris and Foster (2004) suggested that 'it is easy to talk about managing diversity but difficult to do'. Their study of the way operational management handled diversity in practice was carried out in a large organization, with an online retail operation and retail stores across the country in both the USA and the UK. One of the significant findings was that in both, managers relied heavily on formal prescriptive employment procedures to ensure consistency of treatment for all employees. Harris and Foster saw this as opting for 'the tried and tested route of treating everyone the same', while in principle supporting the view that different people needed different treatment.

Figure 14.1 The diversity progression

In another extensive research project, Anderson and Metcalf (2003) from the National Institute of Economic and Social Research (NIESR), collected evidence on the impact of diversity policies from a wide selection of published research. Among the many more positive conclusions was the relatively negative one that organizational diversity carries with it the potential for conflict in the workplace through misunderstandings. These can be caused by cultural, educational and personality differences, among many others. This confirms Harris and Foster's findings above that some managers prefer to 'keep their head below the parapet', and suggests that central support for the practice of effective conflict management is part of the diversity equation.

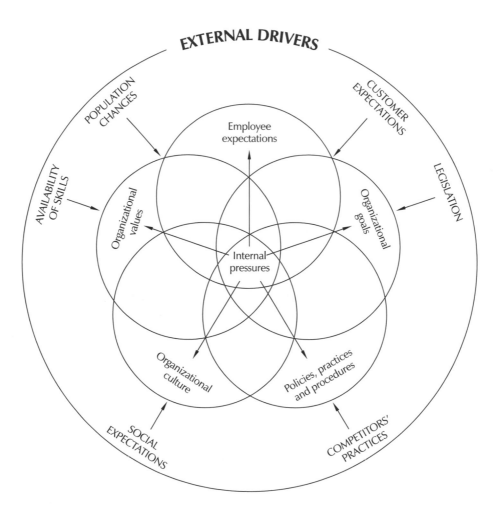

Figure 14.2   Managing diversity: pressures forcing action by employers

The business case

Worman (1996:8) points to the 'voluntary self-interest of adopting a diverse workforce'. Her model (1998) demonstrates the external as well as the internal pressures forcing action by employers (see Figure 14.2).

It is useful to take general lessons from the experience of the more progressive companies whose successes in managing diversity are reported worldwide. These include such US 'giants' as Procter and Gamble, Du Pont and McDonald's, as reported by Labich (1996), and Thomas's (1996) studies of Bell South Corporation, Hallmark Cards, Goodyear Tire and Rubber, and General Motors, among others.

In the UK, SmithKlineBeecham and Rank Xerox are two of the many examples singled out by Ford (1996) as publicly demonstrating commitment to equal opportunity and diversity in ways that suit their particular culture and operational objectives. For example, SmithKlineBeecham is reported as conducting a company-wide survey of some 8,000 employees, and among the gaps identified by the respondents were training opportunities, career guidance and communication.

Small and medium-sized enterprises (SMEs) are also responding to the call for diversity. As part of a management development strategy in what Booth (2004) describes as a 'High Tech World', with worldwide offices, Fluent (Europe) has developed guidelines to meet legislative requirements. These include diversity, harassment and paternity leave, and can be accessed by all employees through the HR intranet site. In 2004, Fluent was in the first 20 of the *Financial Times* Best Places to Work awards. Booth (2004) reports that the result was said to have been largely affected by a confidential online questionnaire completed by employees, which included questions on work–life balance, diversity issues and how fairly people are treated. As will be seen below, this company extends its diversity policy to include contractors as well as customers.

FLUENT EUROPE'S GUIDELINES

Note: The following are extracts only from the six-page document issued individually to all employees of the organization – and signed for, as received.

Equality & Diversity (Equal Opportunities)

Fluent Europe is wholly committed to the uncompromising principle and practice of Equal Opportunities in employment. We aim to promote a working environment free from discrimination, harassment and bullying and to provide equality of opportunity for all, in every area of employment and business. We have created a formal system to exclude discrimination from Fluent, but it is employees as individuals who can do the most to change or remove attitudes and assumptions that discriminate against other people ...

Under no circumstances will the Company tolerate any form of less favourable treatment being imposed upon employees, job applicants, contractors or customers.

Fluent strives to ensure that all employees, potential employees, customers and contractors are treated fairly and equally both at work, and during any connections with the Company. We believe all employees, potential employees, customers and contractors have the right to respect for private and family life, their home and correspondence. We expect all employees to promote equal opportunities in the workplace; if we all abide by the value of respecting others, then we can guarantee a sure Equal Opportunities climate exists and is preserved.

Failure to observe and respect the Equality and Diversity policy may result in disciplinary action being taken, up to and including dismissal for misconduct.

Reviews of the Policy

We will undertake regular reviews of our Equality & Diversity policy, along with all other existing policies and procedures, taking action to eliminate any form of unlawful discrimination, ensuring we maintain and encourage the highest standards of Equal Opportunities.

Application of the Equality & Diversity Principles

These principles apply to all stages of recruitment, selection, training, promotion, transfer, pay, benefits and rewards and the Personal Development Review procedures, in addition to all Terms and Conditions of employment.

What does this mean in practice?

In Recruitment & Selection

Our principles and practices of Diversity & Equality are implemented equally during all stages of recruitment and then once an individual joins the Company. For the duration of the recruitment process, all parties involved focus simply on the requirements for the job and on each individual applicant's suitability for the position, and ability to perform the role. No other factors come into play. Each role at Fluent has its own Job Description, which is regularly reviewed and is key in the recruitment process. When a position arises within the company, the placing of adverts is carefully planned to ensure that the opportunity to apply is made available to as many people as possible. In order to prevent discrimination at this early phase, throughout the interview and selection stages we follow paradigm procedures, and the process is recorded from start to finish.

In Training & Development

Within Fluent there are opportunities to continually develop. We ensure that our Performance Development Review (PDR) covers training that is both specific to the job, and also follows a

Training & Development plan that is focused to each individual's requirements. In order to prevent discrimination during the PDR process, a clear criterion is followed which involves the assessment of skills against the skills needed to achieve current and future objectives based on the individual's own career aspirations.

Tackling Discrimination – What to do if you feel the Diversity & Equality policy is being ignored

Firstly, should you feel comfortable with such approach, you should discuss any concerns with your line manager. However, if you feel at all unable to discuss such matters with your line manager, for whatever reason, you should raise the issue with a member of the Human Resources department.

Your concerns will always be dealt with seriously, and where possible, in absolute confidence. Confidentiality will be maintained where possible, however should some details need to be disclosed as part of the investigation process, care will be taken to protect both the interests of the complainant and any other individuals cited.

All allegations of breaching the Company's Equality & Diversity policy will be fully investigated. If you are the victim of a breach of this policy, we recognise the courage it takes to make an allegation. We are in every respect committed to treating such allegations sensitively and will take every precaution to ensure that if you bring a complaint of this nature to our attention, you will be protected from further discrimination, and any form of victimisation as a result of your complaint.

Any act of direct or indirect discrimination, sexual harassment, racial harassment, victimisation, and discrimination on the grounds of any of the categories on page 1 of this policy or breach of the company's Equal Opportunities policy will not be tolerated. It will not be regarded as a minor offence and further to a thorough investigation, should Fluent have reasonable grounds to believe that a breach of the Equality & Diversity policy has occurred then disciplinary action may follow, up to and including dismissal.

Dignity at Work

Fluent Europe endeavours to make sure that, as is their right, all employees work in an environment in which the dignity of each individual is respected and is free from threat or intimidation. **Bullying, Harassment and Victimisation** in any form is totally unacceptable to the company and treated with extreme seriousness, considered as misconduct and subject to the company's disciplinary procedures.

Harassment is recognized by the Company as unreasonable, unwelcome and offensive behaviour that may create an intimidating, hostile, degrading or offensive environment for an individual, which results in the violation of their dignity. Harassment fails to respect the rights, dignity and feelings of others and can relate to any personal characteristic; it may be intentional or unintentional.

Victimisation is treating someone less favourably than others are or would be treated in the same or similar circumstances, because they have made a complaint or allegation of harassment or discrimination or have acted as a witness or informant.

Bullying may be characterised as offensive, intimidating, malicious or insulting behaviour, any abuse or misuse of power through means intended to undermine, humiliate, denigrate or injure the recipient; it can be a single incident or persistent.

Harassment & Bullying

… in general terms, harassment is unwanted conduct which affects the individual's dignity, and any actions and comments that are viewed as demeaning and unacceptable to the individual. Behaviour that is considered bullying or harassment by one person may be considered firm management by another. Extreme cases of such are more easily identified, however it's the 'grey' areas that cause problems. For guidance purposes only, and by no means exhaustive or exclusive, examples of what Fluent consider unacceptable behaviour include:

- Spreading malicious rumours, or insulting someone (particularly on the grounds of race, sex, sexual orientation, religion or religious belief, age and disability).
- Copying memos that are critical about someone to others who do not need to know.
- Ridiculing or demeaning someone – picking on them or setting them up to fail.
- Exclusion or victimisation.
- Unfair treatment.
- Overbearing supervision or other misuse of power or position.
- Unwelcome sexual advances – touching, standing too close, display of offensive materials.
- Making threats or comments about job security without foundation.
- Deliberately undermining a competent worker by overloading and constant criticism.
- Preventing individuals progressing by intentionally blocking promotion or training opportunities.

Victimisation

Victimisation consists of treating someone less favourably than others are or would be treated in the same or similar circumstances, because they have made a complaint or allegation of harassment or discrimination or have acted as a witness or informant.

Unacceptable behaviour which includes bullying, harassment, victimisation, unwanted physical contact, unwanted verbal conduct, unwanted non-verbal conduct, and any other unwanted conduct will not be condoned or permitted by Fluent. Each employee carries the responsibility for their own behaviour at work and to uphold the Company value of respect and dignity for others.

I .... hereby confirm that I have read and understood the above Equal Opportunities policy.

Signed ....

Date ....
With acknowledgement to Fluent (Europe) Ltd, (2004).

The advantages of relating more to diverse customers has been highlighted by Donaldson (1994:6), who cites the BBC World Service as one of the early pioneers in management of diversity training, which is said to have 'helped achieve a workforce which more closely reflects the service's world wide audience'. Among a number of other UK employers similarly relating to external community patterns are Birmingham City Council, Littlewoods and Asda.

Proactive organizations have been wide-ranging and include Rolls-Royce Military Airlines Ltd, Scottish Hydro Electric, NSK-RHP Europe Ltd and Royal Mail South Wales.

Grand Met (IPD 1996:7) sums up the business case succinctly:

> Customers are increasingly looking through the front door of companies they buy from. If they do not like what they see in terms of social response, they will not go in.

Such international endorsement emerging in the 1990s of the business case for diversity by well-known and influential organizations has continued to be widely researched and reported. Numerous examples in both the public and private sector of small and large organizations have been cited as evidence of business success following on from a positive diversity policy. Nevertheless, despite many individual examples, there is said to be insufficient reliable evidence available for a general conclusion, overall, that the operation of such a policy in isolation from other considerations will necessarily lead to improved performance, or improved profitability. Worman (2003), in her foreword to the NIESR research project quoted above (Anderson and Metcalfe, 2003), advises that 'we are yet on the nursery slopes regarding the management of diversity. ... My view is that we need to be prepared to focus on developing different and appropriate management styles and systems in order to embrace diversity.'

Ethics

It might be more directly relevant for those of us responsible for training and development to remind ourselves of the ethical arguments supporting the notion of diversity. It has been said that fear, ignorance and the preservation of selfish interests are at the root of most discriminatory practices. Emerging now for the 21st century is a groundswell of opinion that businesses have an ethical obligation to widen their horizon and must cast aside the non-acceptance of divisions within our society. A model diversity programme is no substitute for evidence of commitment from senior management, and only proactive efforts will translate the rhetoric of equal opportunities for everyone into workplace reality.

Levi-Strauss & Co provides an example of focusing on workplace diversity as part of its company values. Its 'Aspirations Statement' (Glasenk, 1997:10) describes the kind of leadership required to value diversity:

> Leadership that values a diverse workforce (age, sex, ethnic group, etc.) at all levels of the organization, (and values) diversity in experience, and a diversity in perspectives.

And continues:

> We have committed to taking full advantage of the rich backgrounds and abilities of all our people and to promote a greater diversity in positions of influence ....

TRAINING FOR DIVERSITY

Although most published information on diversity training has tended to highlight individual organizations, in an UK survey on successfully managing diversity initiatives, reported by Kandola and Fullerton (1994), the 285 that responded represented a mix of small, medium and large organizations, with some 60 per cent in the private sector. From the responses, fair selection training to recruiters was said to be one of the 10 most successful initiatives, together with training trainers in equal opportunities. Introducing awareness training to staff, although taking place, appeared less likely to be evaluated for effectiveness, perhaps because it was more difficult to establish criteria. At that time, training in awareness and communication was seen by nearly half the organizations as a priority area for future action, although these two terms are too general for practical application, unless defined in terms of identified needs within a particular organization and for a specific group.

Various writers have continued to highlight training in recruitment practices which embrace, for example, placing advertisements where minority groups might see them, and where they will attract the attention of all the population. Equally, the question of retention and development of employees is recommended as a management training issue that is now being addressed more widely.

It is one thing to advocate more focused training in general and another to consider in practice what is the best fit. For as long as I can remember, communication(s) training has remained high on the list for managers' training needs – a subject that continues to be delivered universally in various forms, and still with a number of different organizational objectives. As for awareness training, this usually includes a necessary appreciation of the relevant employment legislation as well as a mix of behavioural studies. Training programmes may include case studies, role play and simulation. Enhancing management ability to carry out appraisals in a fair and equitable manner, an appreciation of recruitment and selection processes, without unfairly discriminating, even-handed grievance and disciplinary practices – these are all likely to be viewed just as extensions to what might have become institutionalized equal opportunities programmes, planned around statutory obligations. Small wonder, then, that training for workplace diversity receives comparatively little direct reporting, although more specialized literature on the subject is now emerging. Attention tends to focus more on new initiatives, which are generally as much about mission statements and objectives as specific practical examples.

The way forward

Certainly, training for diversity is likely to be influenced by senior management's perception of what is appropriate for the corporate image as well as the organization's public and private commitment to valuing people as individuals. Progressive organizations accept workplace diversity as covering diverse styles of working, thinking and communicating with others from a rich 'mix' of different people, and see it as a positive advantage. They no longer expect that everyone should end up conforming to some central and long-established 'norm'. Outmoded preconceptions of the 'norm' have been suggested by Ouseley (1994) as having the attributes of 'an able-bodied caucasian male', to which could be added, 'working full-time with no domestic responsibilities' – a stereotype from the past!

So far we have considered the training function in the light of winning the hearts and minds of those predisposed to question the value of a diverse workforce. Today's emphasis is on the importance of all employees having an equal chance to develop their full potential, and at the same time making a positive contribution to the undertaking. Development programmes aimed at achieving this will call more and more for ways of mutually exchanging the values and knowledge of culturally and socially diverse individuals, with a mutual recognition of similarities as well as differences.

Collin (2004:275–76) suggests that women and disabled people, together with cultural and social minorities who suffer from negative stereotyping, tend to reinforce this themselves by correspondingly low expectations and aspirations. Although this blanket assumption can be challenged by success stories from within these groups, in many organizations, trainers should still be wary of judging learning abilities solely on the dominant culture standards. Action learning might be an appropriate solution.

So how, as trainers, do we attempt to aid people at all levels in the organization to unblock their particular mindsets and to recognize what they really see and believe about different people? Perhaps the first step is to confront our own limitations. We all carry baggage which holds our beliefs and prejudices – our view of the world which has built up from childhood. And as Handy (1993:76ff) reminds us, it is only if we know people very well that we accept them as the kind of people they are, with whatever differences. When dealing with others we are likely to make assumptions about how they will behave and so on, and from these assumptions most of us then tend to categorize and predict. For example, 'older workers do not adapt easily to new ideas' is a form of stereotyping, with expectation of certain characteristics.

Torrington and Hall (1995) quote Ellis and Sonnenfield (1993) as being concerned that training for diversity carries some risk of reinforcing stereotypes. In my own experience amateur role play, for example, holds such underlying dangers of caricature performances which in themselves could inadvertently cause distress to others as well. Equally, not everyone enjoys playing a part in what is necessarily an unreal situation. Nevertheless, it can also be argued that being free to play a role may enable the individual to see another point of view, and there is growing recognition among trainers of the value of experiential learning when helping people confront their own, often unrecognized, prejudices. In their exploration of the learning process by 'suspending reality' – that is, through drama – Beard and Wilson (2002:76–78) contend that one of the benefits of role play is that it helps to promote awareness and understanding of those taking part. Clements and Jones (2002:117–18) evidence a new approach which is gaining ground, that of employing professional actors for verisimilitude.

Awareness programmes are seen as 'sensitizing workers and managers to the needs of a culturally diverse workforce', albeit realistically linking this to 'maximizing potential productivity'. Cooper and White (1995) reinforce Kandola and Fullerton's suggestion that all employees in an enterprise should feel reliant on one another for overall success, and this team spirit directs attention from individual differences towards similarities.

On the other hand, more than one writer has emphasized the inherent danger of targets or positive action, that is, singling out a particular group for special training and thus suggesting they are different. This could work either way: for example, men only for outdoor activity training, women only for assertiveness training (or the reverse). Although such segregation is occasionally appropriate, it is fast becoming less likely, and trainers are starting to reassess their programme content to suit heterogeneous groups. A mix of people with common workplace interests such as their team, or their section, can build on cultural and gender differences within a spread of age groups which may also include people with different characteristics or physical abilities, for example, female paraplegic, older Asian male, female young ex-offender, male carer, and many other permutations.

With the spotlight on amendments to the Disability Act, trainers should also be aware of an employer's responsibility to ensure that people with dyslexia are not denied opportunities. Another development to note is the provision of IT training by specialist advisers, which can present a future livelihood in the e-commerce age for people hitherto regarded unable to able to enter the employment field on equal terms. Leading-edge bodies such as the Royal National Institute of the Blind (RNIB) and parallel organizations advise on specialist technology to help with the recruitment and retention of, for example, visually impaired staff, those with hearing difficulties, and the sadly increasing number of people under the age of 35 who suffer spinal injuries resulting from accidents.

The challenge for training is to focus on the unique contribution from each individual, rather than an over-emphasis on stereotypical differences and social category. It could be said that even to differentiate between management 'development' and employee 'training' in itself has a discriminatory shade of meaning. Certainly, though, trainers should be looking at flexibility of venue – access for the handicapped, centrally located for carers with home responsibilities, and with some sensitivity towards dietary restrictions and customs – and timing of training events so as not to exclude those on part-time, shift or flexible working, and with due regard to religious observances such as fast days and prayer time.

IS THE EDUCATIONAL APPROACH ENOUGH?

Removing the main barriers to the cultivation of what amounts to a paradigm shift of attitude within an organization calls for more than what has been described as the educational approach: that is to say, information giving and examples of best practice such as examples by Clements and Jones (2002:36). Necessary as this remains, it is perhaps worthwhile to repeat what all experienced equal opportunities trainers already endorse. Within the wider context of diversity, instead of addressing single issues separately and thus reinforcing the 'difference' (and some trainers still need to be wary of going into autopilot on just three – gender, race and disability), effective diversity training is emphatically not only about instruction on legislation and best-practice processes. It is to do with the generation of particular experiences, and reflection, rather than exhortation to conform. Clements and Jones (2002:37) reflect the view that diversity training should be less directed to the blame culture and litigation, and more about facing up to hidden and generally unrecognized assumptions and prejudices.

One of the means of achieving this might be discussion on values, perception and attitudes through focus groups, with views from minorities on how they themselves perceive their position – a proactive role for training within the organization. Hunt's Chapter 13 of this book on Reflective Practice could usefully be revisited, while appropriate delivery methods are addressed in Chapters 16, 17 and 18. I am also indebted to Robertson (1994) for the following (unpublished) views. They were originally designed to cover training on racial awareness, and have been expanded here into good counsel for diversity awareness programmes:

- We are all members of the same species.
- Differences exist between cultures – we learn and acquire them.
- No one human culture is superior or inferior to any other; cultures do however differ, especially in their strengths and richness.
- Mental, physical and cultural differences do not cause sexism, racism, ageism and the like, but they are often used to justify and maintain the existence of discrimination.

And as Holmes (1987:50) points out, 'Nature confers different abilities on different people but a development approach for individual fulfilment comes from the premise that each person's growth centres upon the realization of whatever potential he or she might have.'

TRAINING CHECKLIST FOR DIVERSITY

The following checklist has been adapted for diversity training from one organization's example of good practice in equal opportunities training.*

Trainer's attitudes

- Inform yourself about workplace diversity – read, discuss, undertake training yourself.
- Check feedback mechanisms regarding your training work. Are they working? How do you know?

Training content – delivery and materials

- Have all audio-visual materials and handouts been checked for offending images and language?
- Are all your documents in a form that are readable for everyone (for example, in font size and colour)?
- Do your seating arrangements take account of the hard of hearing?
- Can diversity be built into case studies/exercises? How effective is role play? Ensure you are not illustrating people in stereotypical ways.

Access and participation

- Are those distributing information for you ensuring it is seen by all?
- Do you need to consider other channels for circulating information?
- What information do you ask for – disabled access? Dietary requirements?
- Can you ever provide child care?
- Is the make-up of your training events predominantly white male/female? Or segregated special groups? Check through the planning process and ask yourself why.

Tutors and training providers

- Are the people you use for training aware of your organization's diversity policy?
- Who do you usually use for training? Are they all white? Predominantly male heterosexual? Female for all-women groups?
- Does any trainer's approach to diversity give you cause for concern? Have you challenged him/her? How would you do so?

*With acknowledgements to NACRO original document (1987).

THE LAW

Many international and other large UK-based organizations, particularly those with European connections, are positively moving towards expansion of their existing equal opportunities policies into an all-embracing approach to diversity, if only for demographic reasons, including skills shortages. Nevertheless, evidence indicates that institutionalized discrimination still exists, and there continue to be perceived inequalities of opportunity and treatment of various minority groups. Indeed there is suggestion in some quarters that the growing emphasis on diversity and its link with organizational efficiency serves to mask the realities of discrimination.

Alongside what has been called 'the sophistication of equal opportunities' and the current emphasis on a holistic approach, amendments to the Race Relations Act (2000) impose a general duty on (listed) public authorities to promote racial equality in the areas of jobs and training. Compliance with the new Employment and Race Directives from the European Union (EU) in 2001 has further expanded statutory protection to minority groups. Regulations on direct and indirect discrimination on the basis of sexual orientation and on religion or belief came into force in 2003. There are further regulations on 'access' for people with disabilities; legislation is also in place on what is described as 'work/life balance' issues, such as paternity leave, statutory holiday entitlement and part-time working. Legal redress against ageism will come into force in 2006.

Employers committed to the management of diversity accept that some form of legal framework will always be necessary. When considering management training, it is useful to present what the law says as a backcloth to positive discussion on voluntarism versus legal penalties. It also helps to remove misconceptions (the 'I know for a fact ...' statements), while a judicious use of case studies will serve to demonstrate what the courts are saying about what is not good practice.

Historically, in the United Kingdom the very first statutory breakthrough for individual equal rights at work was with the Equal Pay Act in 1970, although of course the Disabled Persons Act and its quota requirements had been brought in towards the end of World War II (1944). In 1974 legislation founded on the principles of equal treatment for sex and race was later followed by Codes of Practice with the aim of promoting voluntary improvements in areas such as selection and promotion. The legislation does not provide for group action. Some positive action related to training is permissible by law, but in general 'quotas' and other proportional representation at the workplace have not been seen as the best way forward. Instead employers have been encouraged to analyse the composition of their workforce and takes steps to redress imbalances, and to make positive and public commitment to equality of treatment and opportunity. There are a number of government-backed initiatives to provide a platform for promoting such commitment, including a separate Employers' Forum for Disability, Gender Equality, and Age, together with the 'Leadership Challenge' from the Council for Racial Equality (CRE).

In the United States it is often said that the legislation on equal rights came about as a result of the original 1960s campaign for civil rights, and specifically, racial equality. Federal laws provide for positive selection of candidates from minority groups and women, associated with an obligation to meet statistical targets from workplace 'profiles'. This long-standing positive action policy has more recently been argued in some states to effectively demean women and minority groups, because of growing suggestions that in order to fulfil the legal obligations, it is not always the most qualified person selected for the job or promotion.

In Europe different countries have differing legislation, but those in the European Community (EC), including the UK, were signatories to the Treaty of Amsterdam, 1977. Directives adopted under the Social Chapter include equal treatment.

The law still has a place, in that statutory provisions underpin the ideology within a framework of rules that also provide safeguards against discriminatory practices related to disability, gender, race, religion or belief, or sexual orientation.

An overview of the main UK legislation relating to equal opportunities is appended to this chapter, although it is not intended to be a detailed account of all the relevant statutes.

TOWARDS A LEARNING ORGANIZATION?

We have seen that the drive towards organizational effectiveness and business success has led to the United Kingdom embracing an originally transatlantic notion of diversity, which emphasizes the contribution each individual employee can make to the overall impact of the organization, whether in profit-making or social terms. Leaders in industry and commerce are already coming forward to champion the cause publicly. The training function has a crucial role in reinforcing this increasingly wide view of equal opportunities, and in seeking the most appropriate ways for 'awareness' to be engendered and nurtured through appropriate learning opportunities for everyone. If the concept of diversity does indeed result in the paradigm shift envisaged, 'trainers' will find themselves entering even further into the role of change agents within the truly learning organization defined by Pedler, Boydell and Burgoyne (1989) as 'one which facilitates the learning of all its members and continually transforms itself'.

CONCLUSION

There is a compelling business case for encouraging a rich diversity within the workforce. Worldwide, we all tend to identify with others similar to ourselves in organizations with which we come into contact, as customers, clients or associates.

There is also an ethical argument, and this message has been adopted by leaders in the field of equal opportunities, as can be seen from the case studies and other examples. In spite of the advances that have occurred over the past 30 years or so, there remain a number of areas still to be addressed in an increasingly global marketplace. For many of these, training and development is in the forefront, holding the key to investing in people as the most important asset.

BT AND DIVERSITY

Then (1988)

A decade and a half ago (1988) the then-styled British Telecom issued a 'Guide for Managers and Supervisors', *Equality of Opportunity in Practice*. The basics covered at that time relating to 'Training and Education' are well worth reproducing for the purpose of today's management training, as they still go to the heart of the matter, in simple terms:

Training and Education

General

Make sure all your staff are told of training and education opportunities for which they are eligible to apply or which could meet their developments needs. Do not assume that any particular group will not be interested or suitable.

Residential Courses

Give as much notice as possible of residential courses so that those with young children or other dependants can make arrangements for their care.

Consider the use of alternatives to residential courses where domestic responsibilities make it impossible for staff to be away from home overnight; in some cases, distance learning might provide an answer.

Industrial Language Training

If communication difficulties are acting as a barrier to an individual's advancement, affecting efficiency or working relationships, industrial language training provided by, e.g. local authority units may be able to help.

Special Training Schemes

From time to time BT offers special training schemes for groups which have been under represented in particular areas of work e.g. engineering training for women. If you feel that locally organized training would benefit members of your staff from under represented groups, discuss it with the Equal Opportunity Adviser.

Now

As a leading player in global telecommunications, BT believes it is critical to harness the talents, skills and capabilities of its entire people to gain and retain competitive advantage. In doing so BT aims to create opportunities for everyone in the company to achieve their best in the interest of themselves and the company as a whole.

In BT, managing diversity embraces a range of key programmes from measuring employee attitudes and expectations, auditing behaviours and practices, to engaging in initiatives to raise the profile of individuals in minority groups. Examples include:

A Steering Group of senior operational managers
advising on high level strategy and policy for the management of diversity.

A Women's Development portfolio
providing opportunities for personal and professional development for women of all grades.

An Ethnic Minority Network
which is the voice of BT's ethnic minority employees. Amongst other functions it acts as sounding board for senior BT management to test ideas for new policies.

The Disability programme
includes forums at which disabled employees meet with senior managers to discuss BT's approach to disability issues and their work requirements.

With acknowledgement to BT Equal Opportunities Policy Unit.

THE DIFFERENCE STARTS WITH YOU

Extracts from Oxfam's Diversity Strategy

Definition of Diversity
Oxfam

- sees Diversity as a description of the visible and invisible differences that exist between people, such as, gender, race, ethnic origin, physical and mental ability, sexual orientation, age, economic class, language, religion, nationality, education, and family/marital status.
- recognises that these visible and non-visible differences between people can also lead to differences in experiences, values, attitudes, ways of thinking.

Diversity Principles

Oxfam wants to value diversity both by having a Diversity of people involved in the organisation and by utilising the differences that people bring with them (i.e. varied perspectives, experiences and approaches) as a resource in our ways of working.

For Oxfam, behaving in a way that values Diversity reinforces our organisational culture:

- being aware of others' perspectives and communicating in an appropriate way is **collaborative**
- considering different ways of doing things and not assuming the usual way is the only way is **innovative**
- taking responsibility for one's actions so that Oxfam is seen to be true to its values is **accountable**
- tapping the potential of a diverse group of people in pursuit of organizational goals contributes to **making a difference**
- making the best use of resources, including the experience and knowledge of others is **cost effective**.

Oxfam believes that valuing Diversity is not just an issue of awareness but is also about **Managing Diversity**. Managing Diversity is a strategically driven approach to:

- valuing and accepting the contribution of each individual
- increasing productivity and efficiency by creating a harassment free environment
- tapping the potential of a diverse group of people
- exercising fair and flexible management practices.

Oxfam recognises that whilst Diversity is about valuing the many sorts of differences that exist between people, there are also some groups who are particularly marginalised, socially excluded and denied equal rights. Therefore the strategy will be sensitive to the position of ethnic minorities, people with disabilities and women whilst seeking to create an environment where all differences are respected and cherished, as this brings benefits for everyone in the organisation.

Whilst Oxfam is committed to valuing Diversity there may be occasions when nationality or family situations have to be taken into account when recruiting or assigning staff, for example, during civil war or other war …

Objectives

Oxfam will begin to achieve the aims of the Diversity Strategy through the following strategic objectives:

1. Develop attitudes and behaviours that support valuing of Diversity. The focus will be on providing learning and development opportunities.
2. Increase the Diversity of volunteers and of staff at all levels. The focus will be on improving the recruitment process.

3. Develop staff from under represented groups into senior management positions. The focus will be on skills and career development.
4. Communicate commitment to valuing Diversity. The focus will be on demonstrating the commitment.
5. Increase the Diversity of supporters. The focus will be on reaching out to diverse communities.
6. Monitor progress on Diversity and use to reshape the strategy. The focus will be on establishing systems for measuring achievements ...

Reproduced with permission. For full text see oxfam.org.uk/aboutus/diversity.htm

APPENDIX: THE LEGAL FRAMEWORK

Equality Commissions

Equal Opportunities Commission
Council for Racial Equality
Disability Rights Commission
(Predicted to be merged into one before 2006.)

Equal Pay Act (EPA) 1970

This is amended by the Sex Discrimination Act 1975 and the Equal Pay (Amendment) Regulations 1983. The purpose of the Equal Pay legislation is to eliminate discrimination between men and women in pay and other terms of their contract of employment. It gives a woman the right to equality in terms of her contract when she is employed:

- on like work: that is, work of the same or broadly similar to that of a man;
- on work rated as equivalent: that is, on a job on which a job evaluation study has shown to have equal value to that of a man;
- on work of equal value: that is, in a job which is equal to that of a man in terms of the demands made on her under such headings as skill, effort and decision-making.

The Act applies to men and women although the term 'woman' is used throughout
    See also EOC Code of Practice.

Sex Discrimination Acts (SDA) 1975 and 1986

This covers sex discrimination in employment. The main points are:

- Employers cannot lawfully discriminate in the arrangements made for recruitment, selection, training, promotion or transfer.
- It is unlawful for an employer to discriminate in the benefits, facilities or services provided to employees.
- Discrimination is unlawful in dismissals or other favourable treatment of employees.
- It is unlawful to discriminate against a woman as regards age of retirement.
- Exceptions are made where gender is a genuine occupational qualification for the job.
- It is not unlawful to give different treatment to men and women in respect of pregnancy and childbirth.

See also Code of Practice.

Race Relations Act (RRA) 1975, Race Relations (Amendments) Act 2000

These cover racial discrimination in employment. The main points are:

- It is unlawful for employers to discriminate in the way arrangements are made for recruitment, selection, training, promotion or transfer.
- Exceptions are made where race is a genuine occupational qualification.

See also Code of Practice.

Disability Discrimination Act (DDA) 1995, DDA Amendment Regulations (2004)

These prohibit various forms of discrimination in employment:

- From October 2004 blanket exclusions of people with a certain type of disability are banned.
- Employers cannot lawfully discriminate against disabled workers in the arrangements made for recruitment, selection, training, promotion or transfer.
- It is unlawful to discriminate against disabled workers in relation to terms and conditions of employment.
- It is unlawful to discriminate against disabled workers in relation to employment benefits.
- It is unlawful to dismiss a person solely on the grounds of his/her disability.

Definition of 'a disability'

Generally speaking a 'disability' is a physical or mental impairment which has a substantial and long-term adverse effect on the ability to carry out normal day-to-day activities (Section 1(1). This section is amplified in Schedule 1 and includes 'progressive conditions'.

See also Code of Practice.

Employment Act 2002

This includes:

- Maternity, paternity and adoption leave rights,
- The right to request flexible working.
- Union learning representatives.

Employment Equality (Sexual Orientation) Regulations 2003 and Employment Equality (Religion or Belief) Regulations 2003

- Both apply from any point in the employment relationship from recruitment to dismissal.
- The regulations outlaw harassment and victimization.

See also Guidance published by ACAS.

Ageism

Legislation is due in 2006 to comply with the EU Employment Directive.

Bibliography

Anderson, T and Metcalf, H (2003) *Diversity: Stacking up the evidence*, London, CIPD

Beard, C and Wilson, J P (2002) *The Power of Experiential Learning*, London, Kogan Page

Booth, N (2004) 'Handling HR in the high tech world of applied computational fluid dynamics', *South Yorks and District Newsletter*, CIPD, **30**, September, pp 16–18

Clements, P and Jones, J (2002) *The Diversity Training Handbook*, London, Kogan Page

Collin, A (2004) 'Learning and development in human resource management', in I Beardwell, L Holden and T Claydon (eds), *Human Resource Management,* London, Pitman, pp 275–76

Cooper, G and White, B (1995) 'Organisational behaviour', in S Tyson (ed), *Strategic Proposals for HRM*, London, IPD

Dale, M (2003) *Recruitment and Selection*, London, Kogan Page

Donaldson, L (1994) The bottom line on diversity in the workplace, *Personnel Today Conference Daily*, IPD Harrogate Conference, 28 October

Ellis, C and Sonnenfield, J A (1993) 'Diverse approaches to managing diversity', *Human Resource Management*, **33**, 1, pp 79–109

Ford, V (1996) 'Partnership is the secret of success', *People Management*, **2**, 3, pp 34–36

Glasenk, N (1997) 'Diversity in the workplace', paper presented in a Plenary Session, IPD National Conference, Harrogate, 22 October

Handy, C (1993) *Understanding Organisations*, 4th edn, Harmondsworth, Penguin

Harris, L and Foster, C (2004) 'Diversity in the workplace', paper presented at the CIPD Professional Standards Conference, Keele University, 28–30 June

Holmes, R (1987) *The People's Kingdom*, London, Bodley Head

IPD (Institute of Personnel and Development) (1996) *Managing Diversity: A Position Paper*, London, IPD

Kandola, R and Fullerton, J (1994) *Managing the Mosaic: Diversity in Action*, London, IPD

La Fasto, F (1992) 'Baxter Healthcare Corporation', in B W Jackson, F La Fasto, H G Schmaltz and D Kelly, 'Diversity', *Human Resource Management*, **31**, 1 and 2

Labich, K (1996) 'Making diversity pay', *Fortune*, **134**, 5, pp 113–15

Moody, M (2003) 'Training in diversity', *Workplace Diversity and Discrimination*, Croner Briefing, 1, September, p 5

Newell, S (2002) *Creating the Healthy Organisation: Wellbeing, diversity and ethics at work*, London, Thomson Learning

Ouseley, H (1994) 'Facing up to the challenge of a diverse workforce', *Personnel Today Conference Daily*, 27 October, IPD Conference

Pedler, M, Boydell, T and Burgoyne, J (1989) 'Towards the learning company', *Management Education and Development*, **20**, 1, pp 1–88

Robertson, A (1994) Contribution to *Module 2: Human Resource Management and Equal Opportunities*, MEd in Training and Development programme, Division of Adult Continuing Education, University of Sheffield, unpublished

Thomas, R (1996) *Redefining Diversity*, New York, Amacom

Torrington, D and Hall, L (1995) *Personnel Management: HRM in action*, 3rd edn, Hemel Hempstead, Prentice Hall, pp 394–474

United Nations (2000) *UN Experts Group Meeting on Managing Diversity in the Civil Service* [Online] www.un.org

Worman, D (1996) 'Managing diversity', *People Management*, 2 May, p 8

Worman, D (1998) 'Managing diversity, pressures forcing action by employers', unpublished

Worman, D (2003) 'Foreword', in T Anderson and H Metcalfe, *Diversity: Stacking up the evidence*, London, CIPD, pp vii–viii

15

Multilingual and Multicultural HRD

Toni Ibarz

INTRODUCTION AND LEARNING OBJECTIVES

For most professionals words like 'globalization' or 'multinationalism' have ceased to be buzz words and have become inescapable realities. This is not only because motorways and aeroplanes have shortened travel or because capital can often ignore national boundaries, but also because technological developments have penetrated the world of work and our homes. Often, when buying off the screen via satellite, cable or internet, the place that provides the goods or the service may not be in our own country. Purchasing requests no longer have to be supplied from the country in which they were initiated. Data processing centres located in parts of the world where the costs are low can compete with more established centres. Similarly, when phoning companies like airlines, particularly out of hours, it is quite normal to hear an unusual accent at the other end of the line. In most cases it is not possible to know if the person who has satisfied our enquiry was a foreign national working in our country or if we have been transferred to a distant part of the world.

In today's marketplace competition comes from every corner of the globe and is forcing businesses to look at new ways of cutting costs. Successful trading nations have to go beyond simply exporting their products: they are also expected to establish their support services wherever they are engaged in economic activity. As a result of the trend towards internationalizing business and services, increasing numbers of people are working in multilingual and multicultural settings.

The literature on this subject points out that traders and business people have always been pioneers in establishing links and communicating with people from other nations. There are many historical examples of trade-sponsored initiatives leading to social and cultural change. Columbus is one such example, the main aim of his sponsors being to open cheaper trade routes to the East. What is new about the global economy, according to Seelye and Seelye-James (1995:xvii), is its scale. Everyone everywhere is affected, not just professional people. There have been large movements of people in search of opportunities for work and social improvements, within and between countries. As a result there is no need to link multiculturalism or multilingualism exclusively to international managers or to those who have access to the new technologies. They point out that: 'More than 100 languages are spoken in schools in New York City, Chicago, Los Angeles, etc.' They conclude by emphasizing the need to adapt to the new working and social environment: 'Dealing across cultures has gone from being a take-it-or-leave-it proposition to being a prerequisite for survival – your survival.'

Having read this chapter you will:

- be aware of the importance of linguistic understanding in international contexts;
- be able to operate successfully in cross-cultural situations;
- know some of the key factors in language learning;
- be able to relate some of the approaches to language learning to those of general training and development; and
- be able to use some of the key principles of cross-cultural training.

MULTILINGUAL TRAINING AND DEVELOPMENT

Monolingual and multilingual societies

The previous section contained statements that pointed to the need to acquire new skills and values as a result of relatively recent social and technical changes. However, this may be misleading, or at least before going into further considerations, the opportunity for reflection about the issues raised should not be missed. When discussing these issues, there is a danger of adopting a view of modern society which for want of a better term can be called 'Western', prevalent mainly in English-speaking developed countries, where the assumption is that monolingualism is the norm and where there is a single dominant culture and tradition.

In addition, we have often been led to believe that this situation has been stationary for many years or even centuries. But this is far from the truth. Even today there are around 5,000 languages in the world and there are approximately 200 countries. It follows, therefore, that bilingualism and multilingualism, to a greater or lesser degree, are much more the norm in most countries. If this is the case, it could be argued that the ability to live and work in multilingual/multicultural communities is not as new as we think and that perhaps, in Western societies, we should consider language learning as yet another human ability that has faded as societies have become more 'civilized'. As with many abilities, such as dancing, we now have to undertake sophisticated training programmes to regain what was once natural to most human beings.

The need for foreign language training

The intention of the reflection contained in the previous paragraph is to give perspective to the issues that will be discussed below. The reality for most organizations is that in order to maximize their market effectiveness they have to operate in multilingual and multicultural contexts. There are advantages for individual employees, for the enterprise, and for the customers. Many writers in the field confirm this view. Bloch (1995:15) states, 'High-level personnel with language skills are becoming more and more necessary to corporate efficiency and success in the global environment.' Others go further. Buorgoin (in Bloch, 1995:16) argues that, 'During the next ten years a foreign language may be more helpful than a college degree, given the rapidly rising internationalization of business.' But we can again look into the past to understand the present reason why foreign languages are given such prominence in some organizations. As early as the 16th century a commonly heard statement was, 'The best language is always the customer's.' Moreover, Willy Brandt, the former German Chancellor stated, 'If I sell to you I will speak English, but if you want to sell to me *dann mussen Sie Deutsch sprechen.*'

Here is a list indicating what employers look for when recruiting graduates:

- adaptability and flexibility;
- foreign languages;
- practical experience in industry;
- the quality of the programme studied;
- IT skills;
- academic marks gained;
- having lived and worked in foreign countries;
- the university at which the degree was taken;
- having a PhD;
- qualifications gained at foreign universities.

Source: *Deutsche Bundesamt – Institut der deutschen Wirtschaft* (in Bloch, 1995:16)

It is clear from the above that the Germans are aware of the importance of foreign languages. It would be interesting to ask employers in other countries whether they would establish a similar set of priorities. Also, it would be useful to think about what most employers mean when they refer to 'foreign languages'. It is likely that they do not refer to the language studies undertaken by 'pure linguists' (students from humanities degrees) but to those undertaken by students who combine linguistic skills with marketable training like accounting, engineering, etc.

LANGUAGE IN THE COMMUNICATION AGE

We have considered the need for foreign language training, although the adjective 'foreign' that has just been used may not always be appropriate. For example, is Spanish a 'foreign' language in the USA? It may be more desirable to use the term 'modern language training' instead, but this also could be too restrictive. What we are dealing with in this chapter is how to encourage effective communication in multicultural organizations and international markets and, therefore, a wider term that incorporates more than just speech may be more appropriate.

Language training should work at several levels of complexity, and this leads some authors to indicate that they feel the term 'training' is inappropriate. 'Training implies that there is a beginning and end to the process, while learning never ends – and this is certainly true of languages' (Little, 1994:15). Language is central to very complex developmental processes and, although training can develop the abilities of the individual and satisfy the needs of an organization at a given moment, it is often an important ingredient in an individual's lifelong education.

The preferred term is simply language learning (LL), because language often incorporates non-verbal signals such as gestures, facial expression, tone of voice, social etiquette, etc. To avoid possible confusion caused by using such a generic term, in the cases where there is a need to establish a clear difference between a first language or mother tongue, and a language learned (usually later in life) or second language, the abbreviations used will be L1 for the former and L2 for the latter.

The next few paragraphs offer further considerations on the place of language within the larger context of communication. The aim is to encourage thought about an aspect of our lives which, as Crystal (1997:2) says, 'belongs to everyone'. We all communicate using at least one language and we can all claim that we have some experience of LL. In practice, however, we are more or less competent communicators without giving much thought to the processes involved.

The media often remind us that we live in the 'communication age'. Communication is a term that can be interpreted in different ways and is often used to establish clearly the context in which an account or an argument is to unfold. Fiske (1990:1) describes the challenge presented to anyone attempting a definition: 'Communication is talking to one another, it is television, it is spreading information, it is our hair style, it is literary criticism: the list is endless.' Fortunately, he soon reaches a definition that is adequate for the purposes of this chapter: communication is 'social interaction through messages'.

Factors that influence effective communication

Figure 15.1 shows the multiplicity of factors influencing the process of communication. The upper part of the figure depicts the communicator deciding on a particular message, encoding this in a particular language and then emitting this as speech, written communication or body language. This is then received, decoded and interpreted by the receiver. A message from the communicator to the receiver is one-way communication (radio or television broadcasts, letters, e-mail, railway station announcements, etc). When a response is made, ie, the feedback loop, this then becomes two-way communication (discussions, negotiations, etc.). Two-way communication is generally more effective and more likely to ensure that both parties agree about the meaning of the interaction.

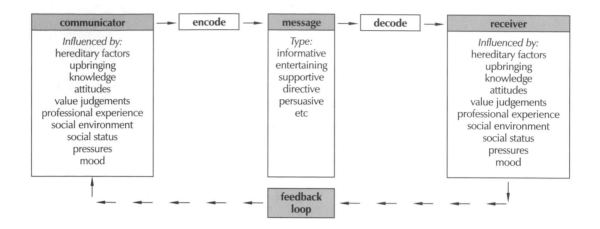

Figure 15.1 The communication process

Figure 15.2 highlights the additional factors that play an important part in communication between speakers who do not share their first language. The assumption in this case is that they are both communicating in the same language and one of them is an L1 speaker and the other an L2 speaker. If the dialogue is flowing all these elements are combined in a process of message encoding and decoding that takes place at considerable speed. One or both speakers may have to resort to a range of strategies that may include gestures, pointing, drawing, the use of a third language, etc.

LANGUAGE TRAINING IN HRD

It is clear that language learning is a complex but potentially rewarding experience and that it is a way of gaining access to other cultures. This last point should not be overlooked: the language learner develops cross-cultural empathy which may be put to good use in any multicultural environment and not just in relation to the one language studied. There are, as has already been indicated, clear benefits for the individual and there are also benefits for organizations. In this section the aim will be to focus very much on practical aspects of LL and on the potential impact it may have on the individual in terms of personal development.

Very recently I received a brochure from a very well-established recruitment consultancy agency which specializes in accountancy and from which I have taken the following paragraph:

> Thus we are seeing the rise of the multinational accountant, the UK-version of which, it seems, is let down only by his or her lack of second or third language skills. It's proving to be a big handicap in some cases, and while language studies require a rather different learning approach compared to technical accounting, it is worth persevering if full advantage is to be taken of the best international career moves. Simply believing that 'English is the business language of the world' could severely limit your options.

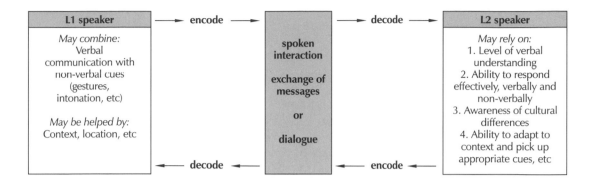

Figure 15.2 Factors that contribute to effective interaction between L1 and L2 speakers

This text is very appropriate to provoke thought around the more practical issues involved in LL. First of all, it comes from the 'real world'; it is not published for an academic audience. Second, it goes to the point by highlighting the potential 'handicap' of being a native English speaker. Third, it reinforces some of the points made earlier in relation to the nature of language learning: 'language studies require a rather different learning approach'.

How long does it take to learn a language?

Because there are many misconceptions of how long it takes to learn a language to an advanced level, it may be useful to consider the case below of Mike who was successfully trained to speak German. He is only one example; each success story differs and it would be wrong to assume that his is the only way.

A SUCCESSFUL LANGUAGE LEARNING EXPERIENCE

Mike describes his intensive course:

I learnt German in the USA, at the Defense Language Institute. The course was 46 weeks. I believe other courses such as Russian and Mandarin were longer than a year. Our class of 13 had two primary instructors (one Austrian and one American). Classes ran approximately six hours per day (8:30–3:30, one hour for lunch), five days a week. We had roughly one to two hours of homework per night, but some studied much less and some much more. We had classes with other instructors each day, usually for two or three class periods. The overwhelming majority – at least 90 per cent – of the faculty were native German speakers and were fluent in both German and English.

The first few weeks were spent learning phrases (listening and speaking) and developing an ear and tongue for the language. After the first few weeks, we began studying the grammar and vocabulary structures of the language for one or two periods per day. We had a language lab once per day in which we listened to radio broadcasts, news broadcasts, and radio serial programmes. We also studied the culture a significant amount. We occasionally watched newscasts, movies and television programmes. Near the end of the programme we began writing and delivering short speeches about controversial topics and then discussed them in class, and we were not able to speak in English.

We were required to speak only German during some class periods (even in the beginning), but in others, such as grammar lessons we could speak English if needed.

(I had been asking Mike questions via e-mail. My last question was about the impact of the course on his personal and professional life.)

As for your last question, I don't use my language skills very often in my work, though I have used both German and Spanish on a few legal matters I worked on. I think of it more as a personal achievement, and I use my languages more conversationally with friends than anything else. I do believe that studying foreign languages has increased my overall language and communication skills.

I should mention that I have been contacted on several occasions by headhunters trying to fill legal positions in Germany and Austria based on my language skills, so I suppose that it has provided opportunities that otherwise would not have been available.

Cheers,
Mike

ENGLISH AS THE LINGUA FRANCA

From the point of view of LL, a division between the English-speaking countries and the rest may help to throw further light on some of the issues hinted at above, when the word 'handicap' was used. A more extreme version of this view appeared on a sticker distributed by an association of language teachers: 'Monolingualism is a curable disease.' Because English is fast becoming the lingua franca of the modern world (Crystal, 2003), above all in such influential sectors as the new technologies, business, tourism and entertainment, and because geographically many English speakers are isolated from contact with other languages, those who are brought up and live in English-speaking countries tend to be less motivated to learn another language.

By contrast, speakers of most other languages are often, from an early age, encouraged to learn a second and third language for political, commercial or cultural reasons. The strong term 'disease' would be justified not just by the loss of professional opportunities at an individual level and the negative impact on exports and international relations, but also by the loss in terms of personal development (as Mike indicates in his answer to my last question) caused by the lack of exposure to a new mental discipline in terms of transferable skills, and to the missed opportunity of becoming more 'multiculturally' aware by having been in contact with at least one alternative culture in the course of the foreign language learning experience.

The global dominance of English encourages many speakers of other languages to gain at least a working use of the language in many fields. Browsing through sites on the use of the internet in education, I came across a paper in which a Spanish schoolteacher from a poor district of Madrid reported that his students in a geology class had become avid followers of NASA sites developed for schools in the USA. 'They are in English, of course, but the youngsters have come to terms with the fact that English is the lingua franca, and they use it with more familiarity than their teachers, which is an added advantage from a pedagogical point of view.'

We see therefore that the division between English speakers and the rest is useful in order to highlight the fact that motivation and the sociocultural context in which a learner engages in a process of LL are fundamental considerations. There is, however, another reason for spending time making this distinction. The result of this linguistic imbalance is that the teaching of English is a large industry with a very wide range of up-to-date teaching materials, while the learners of many other languages have to make do with very limited, outdated resources. In addition, most language teaching methods, methodologies and theories have been led by research based on learners of EFL (English as a foreign language) and then applied to or incorporated into the teaching of other languages.

THEORIES OF LANGUAGE LEARNING

The framework on which current thinking on L2 training is based requires a few theoretical considerations. In this section we consider issues related to language itself and to the fascinating and unique capacity for language learning that human beings have. Most of us find the way a child learns a language a total mystery, and the excitement that the parents express at every step of a child's linguistic development is witness to this amazing feat. There are several theories about how children learn their mother tongue. Below four of the main ones are very briefly explained:

1. *Imitation or behaviourist:* Children learn simply by imitation and habit formation. They receive positive reinforcement and continue to imitate and practise until they form habits of correct language use.
2. *Cognitive:* Based on Piaget's (1950) theories, language develops as concepts are formed. Linguistic structure will emerge only when there is an established cognitive foundation. For example, before children can use structures of comparison they need to have developed the conceptual ability to make judgements of size.
3. *Innatist:* Chomsky (1959) claimed that children are biologically programmed for language learning and that language develops in the same way as other biological functions.
4. *Interactionist:* A child makes linguistic progress according to biological ability and linguistic environment. The type of language used by adults, and their ability to adapt and simplify it to give the child a maximum opportunity to interact and learn, play a crucial part.

Most authors agree that it is possible to see several of the above theories and others as complementary, and useful to explain different aspects of a child's linguistic development, rather than seeing them as opposed and contradictory. Crystal (1997:237) in his informative *Cambridge Encyclopedia of Language* reflects such a view: 'Doubtless imitative skills, a general language-learning mechanism, cognitive awareness, and structured input all play their part in guiding the course of language acquisition.' Research in these areas is difficult and far from conclusive. Not surprisingly, theories of foreign or second language acquisition resonate with similar statements, although it is important not to carry any parallels too far, above all in the case of adult learners. The key differences for adults learning an L2 are as follows:

On the one hand adults:

- already have a language and this reduces their motivation to learn another;
- already have a language which 'interferes' with the learning of an L2;
- are more self-conscious of errors in pronunciation and grammar;
- are less able to assimilate cultural differences;
- are in most cases much less exposed to the L2 than a child to its mother tongue;
- usually learn or study in a context which is not authentic (the need to speak the L2 in a classroom situation is usually contrived);
- may choose to remain silent during a lesson.

On the other, adults:

- already have a language which may 'help' with the learning of an L2;
- can read and write;
- often have sophisticated learning strategies that can simplify the learning of some aspects of the L2;
- can respond more effectively to feedback.

These key differences have an important impact on the theories detailed above. Close parallels exist between language learning and learning in general; and research into language learning has informed our understanding of how we learn (see Pinker, 1995). Therefore when consideration is given to the main theories in L2 learning, we find that they are basically the same theories but that they have undergone important modifications:

1. *Behaviourist:* Learning by habit formation, the same as in the acquisition of L1 (mother tongue or first language). The difference here is that the learner confronts the learning of L2 with the habits learnt in L1, which, depending on the languages involved, may be a greater or lesser obstacle.
2. *Cognitive:* Learners use their already developed cognitive abilities in a creative way to produce hypotheses about the structure of L2. They construct rules, put them into practice, and alter them if they do not produce the expected result. At each stage learners have developed a language system to cope with communicating in the foreign language, which

Selinker (1972) called an 'interlanguage', an ever-evolving and dynamic system which shares elements of the L1 and L2.

3. *Innatist or 'the monitor model':* Similar to some of Chomsky's ideas on L1 learning and proposed by Krashen (1982). L2 follows a pre-set sequence of learning stages. The learner makes progress by taking part in communicative acts during which he or she is guided mainly by intuition much as a child would be. The process is 'monitored' by the formal learning of rules and information about the workings of the language. This is an influential theory in the development of the so-called communicative methods.

4. *Interactionist:* An adult makes linguistic progress when exposed to comprehensible input. The type of language used by teachers and interlocutors, and their ability to adapt and simplify it to give the learner a maximum opportunity to interact and learn, play a crucial part.

Theories are important because they are the foundation of the many methods that exist for language learning and because they help trainers and learners to make informed choices and take control of their training or learning programmes.

TEACHING AND TRAINING METHODS

The many different methods in existence are based on a particular view of language learning and usually recommend the use of a particular set of techniques and teaching materials. They all have advantages and disadvantages and some are better at achieving certain outcomes than others (Richards and Reynandya, 2002). Some authors claim that they all work provided motivation, perseverance and adequate support are present. These days most good courses tend to be flexible in their approach and are eclectic, instead of adhering to only one method. They will adopt the method appropriate to the needs of the learner and the circumstances in which the learning is taking place. The objectives of the course and often the individual objectives of the learner play a determining part in deciding on methods at each stage of the learning curve. The tendency is towards the tutor as adviser or facilitator and towards learner-centredness. Some of the most influential methods are described below.

The academic or grammar translation method

This is based on detailed analysis of the written language and includes translation exercises, the learning of grammar and the memorization of vocabulary as the main activities. After being the main method for many decades, if not centuries, it was almost universally rejected (outside literature-based university courses) in the 1960s and 1970s. However, in the last few years, some teachers have argued that some aspects of translation can play a part in reinforcing other skills.

The audiolingual method

The emphasis is on teaching the spoken language through dialogues and drills. A typical lesson starts with a controlled dialogue that introduces only a few new vocabulary items and includes examples of one or two new structures. The students listen to an audio-tape or CD, and repeat the sentences. They then do some drills connected with the dialogue. Finally they are allowed to incorporate the vocabulary and structures into more open activities. The homework is usually to go to the language laboratory to practise more dialogues and drills. Language is divided into the four skills of listening, speaking, reading and writing, which have to be taught in that order. This method in its pure form is hardly ever found in today's classroom but was once very influential. Above all we find that its emphasis on the spoken language, the division into four skills (listening, speaking, reading and writing), and the step-by-step approach are still in widespread use.

The direct method

This shares elements with the previous one. The aim is to involve the learner in speaking and listening to the L2 in realistic everyday situations. No use is made of the L1. Tutors often use drama techniques and simplified language in their presentations, and follow them by questions which the students have to answer in the L2. Learners are encouraged to think in the target language. The language is introduced via listening and learners often spend weeks without seeing the written form of the language. Formal grammatical rules are avoided. Pair and group work are often introduced. This is a very influential method, with many variations, and has been used especially in EFL teaching.

Communicative teaching

Also linked to the previous one but influenced by the theory of interlanguage. Learners are encouraged to communicate in their transitional language. The important thing is to get the message across regardless of accuracy. The tutor becomes a facilitator in creating situations in which the learners exchange messages. The main activities are information gap situations and guided role-plays. The courses are organized in terms of the meaning ('notions') required in order to communicate in particular functional contexts.

The last three methods share the criticism that they neglect the teaching of grammar and deprive students of the principles and rules that will allow them to generate new language, which is as error-free as can be expected from an L2 speaker. And in spite of the claims made to support the success of such methods, they are not universally accepted. Some see the success of classroom-based language teaching as limited and contrast it with the relative ease with which people in contact with a language in a real situation come to terms with the new language. They search for methods that can get closer to the natural experience of language learning and for ways of making learners more aware of their potential and their limitations, and more responsible for their own learning.

Some of the alternative approaches proposed represent very radical departures from the established methods. They tend to place more emphasis on individual than group learning, and several of them are often referred to as the 'humanistic approaches':

- *Suggestopedia* – based on the unused potential of the brain that can be released by reaching a state of total relaxation while being exposed to hearing the foreign language.
- *The Silent Way* – a method that avoids, as much as possible, tutor participation. A few very simple elements are introduced, usually with colours and pictures, and learners make up their own sentences whenever they want. The L1 is not used and the tutor remains as 'silent' as possible.
- *Community Language Learning* – uses the methods of counselling therapy. The tutor/counsellor develops strong personal links with the learners who speak in their L1 and are given L2 translations by the tutor. The learner then repeats what the tutor has said. The aim is not so much to learn the language as to allow the learner to come to terms with their emotions through the use of the L2. What is interesting about this method is that it is based on the type of messages, which are at the opposite end of the spectrum of the messages usually exchanged in most L2 classrooms, where the great majority are of no real interest to the person voicing them. This is often seen as reducing personal involvement and contributing to low motivation.

These three examples underscore the constant search for ways of improving the process of L2 acquisition and reinforce the point that there is a wide choice of methods. It should also follow that companies entering the field need to seek professional advice if they want to avoid making expensive mistakes and wasting precious resources.

As a form of summary of this section some of the buzz words and expressions are listed below. They may appear in most publicity and information related to good, up-to-date, LL courses. They are:

- teaching *in* rather than *about* the target language;
- interactive use of the language;
- focus mainly on listening and speaking during contact sessions;
- emphasis on *use* of the language as much as possible for real communication;
- manageable tasks;
- pair and group work;
- use of role-plays and simulations.

THE MANAGEMENT OF LANGUAGE TRAINING

Being aware of the complexities involved in the strong relationship between cross-cultural awareness and foreign language skills and some degree of familiarity with the theories of language acquisition are only a first step in the direction of creating or recognizing a high-quality programme in L2 training. It is, however, an important first step that should give some understanding of the issues involved.

One of the characteristics of any effective HRD strategy is having realistic aims. Because of the many existing misunderstandings that surround L2 training, professionals in the field often tell anecdotes about companies that approach them with formidable requests such as: 'Our sales manager (with no previous experience of L2 learning) has to chair a meeting in Italy in four weeks time, it is very important that she conducts the meeting in Italian ...'; 'We are going to visit our partners in Russia in the summer and would like to be able to communicate in Russian, unfortunately we are very busy at present and can only spare one hour a week ...' Once the realistic aims have been established, a key factor is a systematic approach to the management of the programme.

Britain is a good test bed for study of LL programme management. On the one hand, it is a country with a long tradition in the fields of both training and management. On the other, as indicated earlier, it has a very poor record in the learning of modern languages, with a population that lacks experience and motivation in this area. Many of its European counterparts give such programmes a very high priority and invest very large sums in them. By contrast a large number of British companies involved in export do not even have a LL strategy and simply respond to situations on an ad hoc basis. An additional challenge is that while most other countries focus mainly on the teaching of English, British companies have to train their staff in a variety of different languages. The final irony is that because of the high marketability of its own language, many of the positive developments and examples of good practice that have taken place in the field of LL in the last few decades have happened in the UK. One such example is reported by David Jackson of Knoll Pharmaceuticals (now part of Abbott Laboratories) in an article entitled 'A winning strategy' (Jackson, 1995).

KNOLL PHARMACEUTICALS

The scheme is part of an integrated human resource strategy to develop a truly international culture within the business, and is linked to another major initiative which has delivered global competences weighted by function, role and national culture, and cross-cultural awareness training.

This LL programme in French, Spanish, German and Italian was developed in partnership with Nottingham Clarendon College Languages Department and is run on site by native speakers from the college's tutorial staff. The driving philosophy behind the scheme is the maximization of shareholder value. This is achieved by ensuring that the assessment is measured against the requirements of the job, focusing on adding value. Particular benefits have been reported in:

- dealing with international phone calls;
- participation in international meetings;
- discussions with suppliers and customers;
- time saved in translation of documents.

One of the strengths of the programme is its flexibility. The scheme consists of a series of 12-week sessions of two hours per week held in the workplace at times designated to minimize disruption of work. There are nine stages that span the range from survival to near native. The scheme has been so successful that a training site has been developed which includes four dedicated LL rooms equipped with audio, video and satellite TV, and the introduction of Superhighway technology is being considered. This considerable investment was justified by the saving in administration costs that have accrued since the centre was established.

Not all companies, particularly small or medium-sized ones, could match such a model. It is interesting to note that Jackson's company chose to go into partnership with an experienced institution rather than going it alone and risk a period of trial and error. Jones (1993:91) suggests a list of questions that should be of assistance to businesses when looking for such a partner:

- What experience do you have of company LL?
- What methods of teaching do you use?
- What kind of teaching materials would you use?
- What are the qualifications of your tutorial staff?
- How long should my staff take to reach each of the agreed levels?
- Have you any clients similar to us who can recommend you?
- What extra costs are there on top of the tuition fees (for materials and equipment)?

A final and very important question is, how will the results be measured? This can be done by progress and diagnostic tests but often a better alternative are external assessments such as the ones provided by the Institute of Linguists and the London Chamber of Commerce and Industry. In the UK context, a government initiative based on the use of competences as the basis for a framework in National Vocational Qualifications and led by the Languages Lead Body also has a major contribution to make in this area. Similar bodies exist in other countries.

A systematic approach

The brochure from the recruitment consultants referred to earlier, hinted that the approach to language learning is different to the learning approaches most business people are used to: 'Language studies require a rather different learning approach compared to technical accounting.' Progress is non-linear and a multiplicity of skills are involved in most activities at even at the most basic levels. This is perhaps more reason why it is important to give an external structure to the learning process based on a systematic approach. Smith and Arkless (1993) give guidelines for good practice based on the recommendations of the Association of Language Excellence Centres, a professional body for public and private sector providers of LL and related services for business. They begin by emphasizing the importance of offering quality in all areas, including marketing and customer service and above all in programme management and product knowledge, in this case language teaching expertise.

A systematic approach would follow several stages:

1. An *enquiry form* as the basis for recording information which may be useful when formulating a training proposal.
2. A *language needs analysis* for each individual to be trained as part of a corporate programme, including job description, previous LL experience, company/personal aims. A large organization may require a language audit to determine the existing foreign language capability. Diagnostic tests are often used.
3. A *training proposal* based on the previous stage. It contains a summary of the course that has been designed for this particular company. It includes information such as the groups in which individuals will be placed, aims and objectives, materials, timing, location, evaluation procedures and cost.
4. A *trainer briefing*. Tutor or trainer effectiveness, together with learner motivation, is considered to be the most influential factor in the level of success of a LL programme. Unlike other kinds of training, LL is heavily dependent on the competence and even personality of the tutor who is often the only model that the learner can aim to imitate. They need to be fully briefed on the training model proposed.
5. *Evaluation.* Progress should be under regular review. The process is usually informal, often supported by tests and even examinations as has been indicated above. The process of formative feedback is often fundamental. At the end of the programme, individual and group reports should be presented. Trainees should also be consulted about their views.
6. *Trainer development.* Trainers should also benefit from the evaluation process and be offered appropriate professional development.
7. Ongoing *quality control* permeates all the stages that make up the process.

THE GOOD LANGUAGE LEARNER

Can anyone be trained? This is a good question, and since we all manage to learn an L1, it is theoretically possible. In practice, however, there are studies that suggest that there are cases where the resources that would need to be allocated may not justify the exercise. One such study based on middle managers by Koch (1996:25) suggests that previous academic excellence or business acumen are not the best predictors of performance in L2. One of the measurements he suggests is based on the psychological predisposition of the learner towards other cultures: 'It has been empirically suggested that such personality traits as empathy, open-mindedness, flexibility and tolerance are associated with cross-cultural success.' This would confirm some of the points made at the beginning of this chapter. However, it is worth noting that such characteristics would also be very valuable in coping with the 'humbling experience' that is involved in learning an L2, particularly at the early stages, when the trainee is corrected and/or 'exposed' in front of others (often members of staff with less seniority), deprived of the linguistic shield that the use of one's own language offers in everyday encounters.

Lightbown and Spada (1993:34) use a series of statements to define some of the characteristics involved. They should provide ample food for thought to anyone interested in this aspect of the process. A good L2 learner:

- is a willing and accurate guesser;
- tries to get the message across even if specific language knowledge is lacking;
- is willing to make mistakes;
- constantly looks for patterns in the language.

Factors such as risk taking, focusing on the message rather than the language, adaptability, lack of inhibitions and ability to detect patterns significantly influence the degree of success.

Crystal (1997:375) questions if there is a genuine aptitude for L2 training. With sufficient motivation, intelligence and opportunity, anyone should be able to succeed. He also adds another important dimension to the search for key defining characteristics: 'Of particular importance is an ability to detect phonetic differences (eg, of stress, melody, vowel quality) – something which can manifest itself in other domains, such as drama or music.'

Ideally each of us should have all these characteristics, and others like memory and even being eternally young. However, as in so many other areas of learning and training, the emphasis should not be so much on aptitude as on the ability to resort to learning strategies which good training and development should encourage and develop. They are closely linked to learner styles and to the need to tailor courses to the specific needs of individuals and of group as a whole.

THE NEW TECHNOLOGIES

This chapter began with references to the impact of the new technologies on our daily and professional life, and if we are to believe the hype it will be a lifelong learner's paradise. If there is an area in which the promises may become a reality, it is likely to be in LL. There are already many useful and well-established developments, for example satellite television. Computers are also making a major contribution, although the existing systems are still mainly text-based, which is not the main domain in which most L2 acquisition concentrates. Pictures, and above all the widespread use of sound, will bring about major changes in the area of modern language teaching methods.

The opportunities for exposure to the language of our choice will multiply. We may have many opportunities to communicate in the L2 and will be able to gain easy access to current resources and information online. That languages is one of the areas which will make the greatest gains is not surprising. The internet and the WWW are about communicating information, and about communications that are the kinds of fertile ground on which LL should thrive (Feyten, 2001; Warschauer, 2000).

There are already many opportunities offered in the area of computer-based learning. Although claims still have to be supported by adequate research, much is happening and both tutors and learners often report their latest discoveries with excitement. As has just been stated, text-based resources are widely available. For example, newspapers from most countries and in many languages are usually easy to access, as is information about many organizations, institutions and events that are very useful in developing the cross-cultural dimension, an area which classroom teaching often found difficult to come to terms with. There are also many interesting and informative sites that are developed with the language learner in mind. Some of the web-sites for trainers/learners of English are:

http://www.catesol.org
http://www.tesol.org
http://www.planetenglish.com/
http://www.eslcafe.com/
http://www.auralog.com/

Those interested in a wider overview of issues related to culture and language may want to visit the following sites as examples:

http://www.ecml.at/conf/flyer.asp
http://www.camsoftpartners.co.uk/index.htm
http://fis.ucalgary.ca/alle/
http://www.worldlanguage.com/
http://www.cilt.org.uk/
http://www.becta.org.uk/
http://www.lang.ox.ac.uk/library/call.html

Overwhelming complexity is one of the characteristics of the internet. From the point of view of LL there are some important pedagogical implications. First of all, what will be the future role of the trainer? Assistance will have to be offered so that time wasting and confusion do not overwhelm the learner. It is likely that training of trainers will become a major priority. There are also conceptual implications that have not yet been properly discussed. To what extent is the experience of surfing the Net (when looking at sites in a foreign language), with its emphasis on decision-making and constant evaluation of materials akin to, for example, a visit to a foreign city? Are the new technologies not just complementing what was already there and/or offering greater opportunity for practice, but also offering opportunities for developing new skills? Will the changes go beyond how we learn into what we learn?

E-mail is already being used for collaborative learning in modern languages. Tandem learning (students linked individually and in groups to speakers of the L2) is having a major influence in a few institutions (http://tandem.uni-trier.de/). The role of CALL (computer assisted language learning) is already well established and there are many useful CD ROMs. One of their strengths is that they are excellent at giving attention to sound, which is often one of the main challenges in L2 acquisition. Often melody or intonation and not so much pronunciation is the main obstacle in trying to get a message across.

All these developments may be seen as fragmented and complementary and all have their place in an eclectic approach. There are also already in existence projects that try to bring together all these experiences and use sound extensively. They call themselves 'virtual language centres'. One example is Auralog, a Paris-based company that combines multimedia activities with the support and feedback of an online tutor to create what is known as a 'blended learning' method. In this approach the learners are advised on how to make the most of the materials and are allowed to engage in real online communication.

MULTICULTURAL/CROSS-CULTURAL LEARNING

We can see, therefore, that while language contributes to the formation of meaning it is rarely the complete message. There are other factors, most of which can loosely be termed 'cultural', which include gestures, tone of voice to indicate emotion, social conventions, religious beliefs, etc. We refer to the problems experienced by travellers and international professionals as culture shock, not as language shock, although as we will see the two are related. Hofstede (1994:209) describes the experience:

> As illustrated over and over again in the earlier chapters, our mental software contains basic values. These have been acquired early in our lives, and they become so natural as to be unconscious. Based upon them are our conscious and more superficial manifestations of culture: rituals, heroes, and symbols. The inexperienced foreigner can make an effort to learn some of the symbols and rituals of the new environment (words to use, how to greet, when to bring presents) but it is unlikely that he or she can recognise, let alone feel the underlying values. In a way, the visitor in a foreign culture returns to the mental state of an infant, in which he or she has to learn the simplest things over again. This usually leads to feelings of distress, of helplessness, and hostility towards the new environment.

Perhaps he is overstating his case, but the points made are valid. This passage is trying to warn companies against the danger of having to terminate a placement abroad prematurely by being ignorant of the impact of the experience on the person involved. Hofstede also highlights the need for LL which incorporates cultural awareness, and not simply when travelling abroad, but when welcoming foreign visitors or when working and collaborating with ethnic minority people, businesses and organizations.

Harris and Moran (1989:271) state that employee development programmes would appear to have common objectives:

1. To encourage greater sensitivity and more astute observations of situations and people who are culturally different.
2. To foster greater understanding in dealing with representatives of micro-cultures within one's own country.
3. To improve customer and employee relations by creating awareness of cultural differences and their influence on behaviour.
4. To develop more cosmopolitan organizational representatives who not only understand the concepts of culture, but also can apply this knowledge to interpersonal relations and organizational culture.
5. To increase managerial effectiveness in international operations, especially with regard to cross-cultural control systems, negotiations, decision making, customer relations, and other vital administrative processes.
6. To improve cross-cultural skills of employees on overseas' assignment, or representatives of micro-cultures in our own country.

7. To reduce culture shock when on foreign deployment, and to enhance the intercultural experience of employees.
8. To apply the behavioural sciences to international business and management.
9. To increase job effectiveness through training in human behaviour, particularly in the area of managing cultural differences.
10. To improve employee skills as professional intercultural communicators.

More specific objectives can be seen in the Canadian International Development Agency (CIDA) cross-cultural training programme's focus on achieving seven skills:

1. Communicate respect.
2. Be non-judgmental.
3. Personalize knowledge and perceptions.
4. Display empathy.
5. Practise role flexibility.
6. Demonstrate reciprocal concern.
7. Tolerate ambiguity.

In the USA, Peace Corps training has the following objectives:

- Prepare the volunteer to accept and be tolerant of values, beliefs, attitudes, standards, behaviors, and a style of life that might be quite different from one's own.
- Provide the skills to communicate this acceptance to another person.
- Provide the sensitivity and understanding necessary to effectively interact with a person from another culture.
- Teach appropriate behaviour responses in situations where characteristics of the other culture prevail.
- Prepare the volunteer to understand, anticipate, and cope effectively with the possible reactions to him or her as a stranger or as a stereotype of his or her own culture.
- Provide an understanding of one's own culture and the problems cultural bias might create.
- Provide the adaptive skills to cope with one's own emotional reactions in the new and strange situation and to satisfy one's own culturally-conditioned behavior.
- Provide the skills needed for continued learning and adjustment in the other culture.
- Help develop an orientation toward the sojourn in the other culture as a potentially interesting, enjoyable, and broadening experience. (Harris and Moran, 1989:287)

CONCLUSION

The emphasis throughout this chapter has been on raising awareness of the implications for training and development within multilingual and multicultural areas. The aim has been to dispel misconceptions and to encourage consideration of the key theoretical and practical issues involved. The intention is to encourage greater participation by ensuring success based on realistic expectations of language and cross-cultural programmes. With this in mind, some of the main points are reiterated below:

- the link between language and communication;
- the interdependence of language and culture;
- the important role of geography and L1 in determining attitude towards L2 and opportunities for bilingualism and even multilingualism;
- the ways in which people have tried to make sense of language acquisition and the theories they have formulated;
- the ways in which the theories have been translated into practice in the form of teaching and training methods;
- the importance of a systematic approach to managing a programme;
- the role played by the individual and the personal characteristics that may contribute to effective training;
- the changing world of training and the opportunities offered by digital technologies.

Hopefully, several of the issues raised will provide food for thought for those involved in training and development. A few questions may help to stimulate the process:

- What could the role of LL and cross-cultural training be within an overall HRD strategy?
- How could an organization you are familiar with implement an LL or cross-cultural development strategy?
- What is your own experience of LL and cross-cultural training? What were the strengths and limitations?
- Which language would be of greatest use to you?
- How would you go about learning that language to a proficient level?
- What do you think would be the strengths and limitations of LL courses advertised in the press as self-study courses?
- What would be the advantages and disadvantages of a total-immersion language course?

Bibliography

Argyle, M (1988) *Bodily Communication,* New York, Routledge

Bloch, B (1995) 'Career enhancement through foreign language skills', *International Journal of Career Management,* **7**, 6, pp 15–26

Bullon, P (1997) 'Profesionales en la Red: Algunos web de escuelas', *iWorld,* 8 October

Cassany, D, Luna, M and Sanz, G (1993) *Ensenyar Llengua,* Barcelona, Editorial Grao

Chomsky, N (1959) 'Review of *Verbal Behaviour* by B F Skinner', *Language,* **35**, pp 26–58

Cook, V (1988) *Chomsky's Universal Grammar,* Oxford, Blackwell

Cook, V (1991) *Second Language Learning and Language Teaching,* London, Edward Arnold

Crystal, D (1997) *The Cambridge Encyclopedia of Language,* Cambridge, Cambridge University Press

Crystal, D (2003) *English as a Global Language,* Cambridge, Cambridge University Press

Ellis, R (1986) *Understanding Second Language Acquisition,* Oxford, Oxford University Press

English, L and Lynn, S (1995) *Business across Cultures,* New York, Longman

Feyten, C M *et al* (2001) *Teaching ESL/EFL with the Internet: Catching the wave,* New Jersey, Prentice Hall

Fiske, J (1990) *Introduction to Communication Studies,* New York, Routledge

Hancock, J (1994) 'Breaking the language barrier', *Training Technology and Human Resources*, **7**, 5, pp 5–7

Garcia, Guy (2004) *The New Mainstream: How the multicultural consumer is transforming American business*, New York, HarperCollins

Gardenswartz, L, Rowe, A, Digh, P and Bennett, M (2003) *The Global Diversity Desk Reference: Managing an international workforce*, Melbourne, Pfeiffer Wiley

Hampden-Turner, C M, Trompenaars, F, Lewis, D and Trompenaars, A (2000) *Building Cross-Cultural Competence: How to create wealth from conflicting values*, New Haven, CT, Yale University Press

Harris, P R and Moran R T (1989) *Managing Cultural Differences*, Houston, TX, Gulf Publishing

Harris, V (1997) *Teaching Learners How to Learn*, London, Centre for Language Teaching and Research

Hofstede, G (1994) *Cultures and Organizations*, London, HarperCollins

Ismail, A and Ganuza, J L (1997) 'Internet en la education', Madrid, Anaya Multimedia

Jackson, D (1995) 'A winning strategy', *Training Officer*, **31**, 5, pp 136–37

Jones, R (1993) *How to Master Languages*, Plymouth, How to Books

Koch, H L (1996) 'Middle managers targeted for second language training (Spanish) can be screened and educated more efficiently', *Journal of European Industrial Training*, **20**, 7, pp 24–28

Krashen, S (1982) *Principles and Practice in Second Language Acquisition*, Oxford, Pergamon

Languages Lead Body (1995) *Implementing the National Language Standards*, London, Languages Lead Body

Lieberman, S, Berardo, K, Simons, G (2003) *Putting Diversity to Work*, New York, Crisp

Lightbown, P M and Spada, N (1993) *How Languages are Learned*, Oxford, Oxford University Press

Little, B (1994) 'Language matters', *Training and Development*, **12**, 12, pp 15–16

Little, D and Brammerts, H (eds) (1996) *A Guide to Language Learning in Tandem via the Internet*, CLCS Occasional Paper No 46, Trinity College, Dublin

Maurais, J and Morris, M A (eds) (2003) *Languages in a Globalising World*, Cambridge, Cambridge University Press

Norton, B *et al* (eds) (2004) *Critical Pedagogies and Language Learning*, Cambridge, Cambridge University Press

Richards, J C and Renandya, W A (eds) (2002) *Methodology in Language Teaching: An anthology of current practice*, Cambridge, CUP

Piaget, J (1950) *The Psychology of Intelligence*, London, Routledge and Kegan Paul

Pinker, S (1984) *Language Learnability and Language Development*, Cambridge, MA, Harvard University Press

Pinker, S (1995) *The Language Instinct*, Harmondsworth, Penguin

Rees, J I and Rees, C J (1996) 'Lost for words … and losing business', *Industrial and Commercial Training*, **28**, 3, pp 8–13

Reid, M A and Barrington, H (1997) *Training Interventions*, London, Institute of Personnel and Development

Schofield, P (1996) 'Watch your language', *Human Resources*, **23**, pp 93–97

Seelye, H N and Seelye-James, A (1995) *Culture Clash*, Lincolnwood, IL, NIC Business Books

Selinker, L (1972) 'Interlanguage', *International Review of Applied Linguistics*, **10**, pp 209–31

Smith, J and Arkless, C (1993) 'Guidelines on good practice in foreign language training', *Journal of European Industrial Training*, **17**, 7, pp 14–17

Terceiro, J B (1997) *Socied@d Digit@l*, Madrid, Alianza Editorial

Trimnell, E (2003) *Why You Need a Foreign Language – And How to Learn One: English speaking professionals and the global challenge*, Bangor, Booklocker

Trompenaars, F and Hampden-Turner, C M (2004) *Managing People Across Cultures*, Mankato, Capstone

Trompenaars, F and Woolliams, P (2004) *Business Across Cultures*, Mankato, Capstone

Tudor, I (1996) *Learner Centredness as Language Education*, Cambridge, Cambridge University Press

Warschauer, M (2000) *Electronic Literacies: Language, culture, and power in online education*, Hawaii, Lea

Webber, S L (1997) *Trade Talks?*, London, Centre for Language Teaching and Research

Section Five:

Delivering Learning,
Training and Development

16

Open, Distance and Flexible Learning

Geoff Chivers

INTRODUCTION AND LEARNING OBJECTIVES

In this chapter we will consider the opportunities for formalized learning which have opened up in modern times through a wide variety of approaches aimed at minimizing the time teachers and trainers need to spend in direct classroom contact with learners (Rowntree, 1992).

Attempts to sum up all the approaches in one term have not really succeeded, and a widely used compromise is to refer to open, distance and flexible learning (ODFL). A major task of this chapter is to closely consider the terms open learning, distance learning and flexible learning, which are sometimes used in very specific ways and sometimes in very generalized, even vague ways, giving rise to confusion.

The chapter will clarify the strengths and limitations of conventional classroom-based teaching and learning, and demonstrate how newer approaches to formalized learning can complement these strengths and overcome some of the weaknesses.

The chapter moves on to consider the general issues which arise in developing systems not dependent on classroom interaction between teachers and learners as the main method of achieving effective learning. Managing ODFL systems is demanding, and a further key aim is to outline issues to be faced by managers of such systems.

The wide range of ODFL approaches now available through newer information technologies will be reviewed briefly, but these are taken up in much greater depth in the following two chapters. Here we will simply consider their main strengths and limitations in the context of effectively supporting learning in the affective, cognitive and skills domains.

Having read this chapter you will:

- understand the nature of open, distance and flexible learning;
- know the advantages and disadvantages of open and distance learning;
- understand the locus of control in the learning process between the tutor and student; and
- be familiar with the requirements of a corporate learning centre.

FROM TEACHING TO LEARNING

The development of ODFL is not just a story of technological interventions in teaching and learning, but also a story of changing relationships between teachers and learners. One of the most striking aspects of ODFL is its widespread utilization in adult education and training, but limited spread into the compulsory schooling system thus far. A fundamental aspect of formalized education and training is that historically it has been set in the context of a power relationship between teachers and learners. This reality is expressed as much by the use of the term 'discipline' to mean subject area of study (eg, physics, history, or French), as by the cane that was once wielded by most secondary school teachers in Britain.

The conventional approaches to formal teaching and learning have been set in a context with many important associated values, whether overt or covert. Through their lives adults learn a great deal by informal methods. However, this learning, mainly gained from life experience, but also from general reading, watching television, etc is not regarded as carrying much status (except perhaps in pub quizzes or when helping somebody to change a wheel on their car).

Learning which takes place in a classroom and institutional setting, and under the control of a teacher, has come to be regarded as the highest status, most important and most worthwhile type of learning.

There are many reasons for this. The teachers are clearly more expert than the learners in the area of learning in question, and this confers status. The whole process is highly visible, and we can accrue evidence of successful learning taking place by teacher-designed assessment procedures. Indeed, valued qualifications are awarded to successful learners following extended periods of learning and assessment. Formalized teaching taken forward in institutions by recognized teachers leads to both employment opportunities and the growth of professions (teacher, educational administrator, school secretary, and so on). All those employed by the formal education and training organizations have had a strong vested interest in promoting face-to-face teaching as the most important way to achieve learning.

However, because of the sheer variety of ways in which learning can occur, it has never been possible for the formalized teaching bodies to monopolize learning, and certainly not adult learning.

In Western society, the Christian Church controlled most of the formalized learning opportunities until the 15th century, when the introduction of the printing press opened the door to the possibility of encouraging learning outside the control of the Church. Indeed, the book has for hundreds of years been the forerunner of all that we now consider important in terms of learner control of learning.

As we go on to consider ODFL systems, we could do well to keep the book in mind as an example of a learning system covering all of these approaches. The benefits that we see in books in aiding learning alongside or instead of classroom lessons are much the same benefits which we can recognize in ODFL systems. The limitations of books in aiding learning can also exist in these more purposeful learning support systems, but much effort has gone into reducing the disadvantages and increasing the benefits.

Many limitations exist in a learning system based wholly on classroom teaching. Often we think of the poor quality of teaching offered, and we have all had bad experiences of this that we can readily quote. Even more fundamental than this as a disadvantage, however, is the requirement that the learner has to be in the classroom in time for the lesson, and must stay in the room and concentrate wholly on the lesson for its full duration.

We will all have had experiences of wishing ourselves to be almost anywhere than in the class, and this is hardly a good basis for learning. One of the fundamental advantages of ODFL systems is the opportunity for the learner to control the place and time of learning. These are vital concerns of adult learners, who are constrained in both respects by their personal circumstances (paid employment, caring responsibilities, etc).

The whole rationale for distance learning courses is to enable those who live and work at considerable distance from the learning providers to nevertheless take forward their studies without having to travel, with the cost and time implications. It is no surprise that correspondence courses established themselves soon after national and international postal systems were established, to meet the needs of learners spread out across North America and the British Empire for example.

Of course there are still many people who are constrained from any travelling to classes because of physical infirmity or disadvantage, because they are in prison, or because they work abroad (or at sea). Again, it is no surprise that ODFL approaches were introduced at an early stage for adults constrained from travelling to institutions for their studies.

Time constraints are often equally as difficult for adults to grapple with, in terms of regular classroom attendance. My own life is not only hectic, but has no regular pattern in terms of working hours and places, so that regular weekly class attendance is out of the question, and finding two or three consecutive days to attend an intensive course almost as difficult.

For many potential adult learners disadvantage is placed on disadvantage such that it is simply impossible for them to ever undertake formal study by attendance at conventional courses. This is one reason why so many adults go for years without undertaking any formal study. Even for those in employment, opportunities to undertake classroom-based study organized by their employer are limited by schedules and the number of course places available at any one time. Many workers are specialists in their field and therefore have to look outside their organization for training, or work for small firms that cannot organize training for them. One of the most important areas of growth within ODFL in recent years has been the provision of opportunities to learn in this way by larger employers. This is a topic taken up later in this chapter.

Let us move on to consider some definitions concerning ODFL, starting with distance learning.

DISTANCE LEARNING

Distance learning systems in their 'purest' form require no face-to-face interaction between the learner and those organizing and offering the learning. In principle, this means that not only does the learner have no face-to-face involvement with any teachers, but also that the learner can be registered to undertake the learning, begin and take forward the learning, complete the learning, be assessed on this learning, and, if appropriate, awarded a qualification, without ever being in the same building as anyone associated with the organization offering the learning. This has been, and is still in some cases, the situation with distance learning undertaken with correspondence colleges, or via the purchase of language learning packages for that matter.

Generally such distance learning systems involve registration for the course, or receipt of the learning package by post, followed by receipt of learning materials by post and submission of course work for assessment also by post. Communication also takes place by telephone in most cases, while the advent of fax and e-mail is opening up the possibility of transferring significant volumes of text by electronic means. The newer technologies offer communication at a distance from tutor to learner and learner to learner by a whole variety of approaches, from e-mail to video conferencing. These possibilities will be considered in the next chapters.

Any system of learning that aims to operate without any face-to-face contact with those organizing the system will probably have to be well thought out and structured if it is to succeed. Many matters related to the organization of the learning system, which may be little considered, or ignored, in a face-to-face learning system, will need to be explained clearly in writing in a purely distance learning system, where the learners do not have an opportunity to ask questions easily and quickly of the learning programme designers and deliverers.

Similarly, the learning material will have to be well designed and presented in a situation where learners are not in dialogue with teachers. It is also very important to note that the material will be open to general public scrutiny, while classroom processes are still a much more 'private' affair.

There are many advantages for the learner arising from a text-based distance learning system. At once all time constraints are relaxed, since the learning can in principle take place at any time, day or night, seven days a week. For sighted adult learners at least, text-based materials are familiar learning tools since all those who can read will have learned at some stage from books, course handouts, manuals, etc. Text-based materials are generally produced in sections, with each section being convenient to lift and carry about. In this way study can be undertaken almost anywhere which is lit, including doctors' waiting rooms, public transport, or the works canteen.

Distance learning systems may still impose time and place constraints on learners. For example, some distance learning courses require a certain amount of material to be delivered each week or each month, and may be 'paced' by delivering a package of materials weekly or monthly, with course work based on the study of the materials to be delivered at set intervals. On the other hand, the use of a package of distance learning materials, where the learning is not assessed in any way, may not involve any pacing of this type.

Many more modern distance learning systems go beyond the use of text-based materials, and may re-introduce time constraints. For example introducing radio or television broadcasts in support of text-based material, as the UK Open University did at its opening in 1970, requires learners to set aside time to receive such broadcasts, unless recording equipment is set up to allow 'time shifting'. Equipment will be needed to receive the broadcasts, and even more to record them.

TELEVISION AND TRAINING – BIG CHANGES FOR SMALL FIRMS

The introduction of digital broadcasting opens new possibilities for education and training on television. With the expansion of broadcasting airtime specialist channels become feasible, while the convergence of broadcasting and information technologies presents new and innovative opportunities for delivering training to companies and to individuals. At present training-related programmes have a very limited presence on TV. Sir John Harvey-Jones' 'Troubleshooter' series for the BBC showed how the expertise of an experienced manager could be disseminated to a general audience in an informative and entertaining way. Yet this example is very much television programmes as product, crafted to meet the interests of a general audience rather than to realize specific in-company training objectives.

Another approach is to integrate the production of television programmes into a training process which relates to issues such as managing change. A recent project initiated by the media production company AV Edge Ltd and funded in part through the EU programme Adapt, presents an interesting example of how the process of making programmes for television can be incorporated into a larger change management intervention. This project has resulted in a multimedia training package for use by SMEs. It includes six TV programmes, which document the experiences of a core group of SMEs (small and medium-sized enterprises) as they review their experiences and devise and implement strategies for change management. The participating companies are largely owner-managed or family-owned companies operating mainly in the service industry. All are successful at their present level but are aware that the uncertain nature of the environment means that they need to innovate if they are to continue this success in a rapidly changing marketplace.

The AV Edge team devised a strategy that involved the key managers in these companies in an experiential training programme. The more formal elements of this process involved meetings and discussions among the various managers at which they exchanged their views and experiences. These activities were documented on video and the material is used in the TV programmes. The managers were also interviewed on site to elaborate on the issues facing the companies and to provide a visual context for the discussions.

While these production strategies are similar to those used in conventional television production, AV Edge has also included a more innovative approach which involves the use of digital video cameras by the managers. These cameras are provided on request and are used by the managers to capture significant points in the development of the company as it meets new challenges and faces significant decisions. The managers use the video cameras as a means of capturing the reality that they are experiencing.

Later, by examining, reflecting and discussing the video presentation of their perceptions of this reality, they gain greater control over the situation and the issues that emerge. Even though the initial intention in the use of video cameras was to record material for a television programme it has become clear that video, as a medium, has a powerful potential as a means of examining the dynamics and processes within a company. By involving the managers and staff of a company in the production of video reports it is possible to generate a process of preparing and planning for change. With the advent of digital broadcasting and the introduction of specialist channels for education and training, video material generated in this way can be brought to a wide public.

With acknowledgement to John MacMahon, Editor of Educational Programmes, Television, at Radio Telefís Éireann, Dublin.

Newer technologies may introduce further constraints on time and place, for example video conferencing, while others such as computer conferencing may allow complex interactions between learners (and tutors) over considerable time periods on a very flexible basis. If these are the advantages of 'pure' distance learning, what are its limitations? To answer this question, perhaps we should come back to the issue of classroom-based learning. Despite my earlier strictures, this approach has been used by all kinds of societies over all of recorded history, so the approach must have something in its favour. Leaving aside for a moment the issue of cost-effectiveness in learning delivery, we must recognize that for learning to go forward there must be motivation to learn. Here the classroom-based approach to teaching and learning has much to offer.

The teacher can increase motivation in many ways through direct interaction with the learner. Teachers can be a source of inspiration, encouragement, friendly advice, positive criticism, and comradeship. For many learners fear of 'letting down' the teacher can be of itself a major source of motivation to learn, especially in difficult fields. While teachers and trainers can do their best to offer such support at a distance, by phone or text-based messages, it is much more difficult to do so than in a face-to-face situation (Evans, 1994).

While some of us may like to settle down with a good book from time to time, we are social animals and prefer to spend much of our time with others. This is especially so when faced with challenges we find stressful and worrying, which can often be the case for adult learners. The stress is less and the fun of learning greater, in general, when we meet and learn with others.

At its worst the distance learning system can isolate learners, create seemingly impenetrable barriers to learning part-way through learning programmes, with no immediate help in sight, and become an inhuman, inflexible, bureaucratic and dreary form of learning provision. This has doubtless been a major reason for the high dropout rate from earlier correspondence courses, 70–80 per cent being regarded as tolerable in some cases.

For this reason, even where a range of methods of contacting learners at a distance is available, very few purely distance learning courses have been introduced in modern times.

For example, even the UK Open University, which is seen as an outstandingly successful distance learning university, in fact includes significant elements of face-to-face contact with tutors and fellow learners in most of the courses. Despite the excellence of the learning materials developed by the Open University, many educationalists believe that its successful retention of students and higher pass rates relative to earlier correspondence courses lies with its very sensible retention of many of the benefits of face-to-face tuition, including the allocation of specific local tutors to particular groups of students over extended periods of learning (Bell, 1993).

The decision to include face-to-face learning sessions within a distance learning course, especially where these are obligatory, should not be taken lightly. We have already discussed the problems that arise for many adult learners when they are required to travel for classes. In many mixed-mode learning programmes, which strongly feature distance learning but include some face-to-face components, the bulk of the learning is delivered in distance learning form. The face-to-face sessions are used to motivate learners, and focus on learning which is difficult to achieve at a distance (for example the development of teamwork, or some practical skills). This is a matter to which we will return in the context of flexible learning developments. Birchall (1990) introduces the idea of third-generation distance learning, where video conferencing, e-mail, and voice mail reduce the need for face-to-face contact still further.

OPEN LEARNING

Open learning is by no means as easy to define as distance learning. Indeed, there are very many definitions of open learning, and it is often used as an umbrella term for any learning system that is not significantly based on face-to-face tuition.

Part of the confusion arises from the use of the word 'open' to mean entry onto a study programme without prior academic qualifications. The dominance of the Open University in the UK has not been helpful, since it does have open entry in this sense, but delivers its courses by distance learning methods.

Alternatively, 'open' can be used to imply a learning approach which is open to negotiation, which is not always tutor-led, and which offers possibilities for changes to course objectives, content and methods of learning and assessment, if relevant. The public library stands as one of the ultimate examples of an open learning institution in this sense, and many a working woman or man has gained her or his 'education' by public library membership. As the entry cost into the world of the internet reduces, the scope for access to information by this route is increasing.

Although access to information of itself does not provide an education, or even support learning in any depth, any system which empowers the learner is moving in the direction of an open learning system in my view. This takes us back to my own earlier comments about power relationships in learning, which are further explored by Edwards (1991).

From a power viewpoint, any learning system can be seen as sitting somewhere along a continuum, with the conventional institutional system at one end and completely independent learning at the other, as illustrated in Figure 16.1.

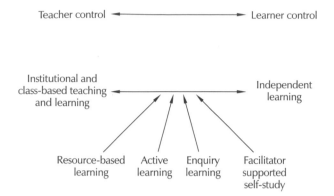

Figure 16.1 The teaching–learning system continuum

At the left-hand end of the spectrum the institutional teachers and managers control virtually everything:

- what courses to offer;
- who can come on them;
- what the courses will cover;
- how they will be structured and taught;
- how they will be assessed;
- how decisions will be made on successful course completion.

Learners can only influence the situation by not taking the course, dropping out, or criticizing the course (normally after completion of studies). In general adults seek at least some control of the system under which they are expected to learn. Enlightened adult educators and trainers make every effort to empower learners within the constraints under which they have to work.

Learning programmes leading to qualifications are subject to many institutional or awarding body constraints, but even here increased flexibility around the delivery of learning programmes is possible. Many qualification courses can be taken with little classroom attendance, and are often referred to as 'open learning courses'.

Where does distance learning fit into this continuum? Many distance learning courses do offer 'open' features, as the learner controls the time and place of study. However, many distance learning courses are very much controlled by the delivering institutions, the UK Open University being a case in point, and in this case fall towards the left-hand end of the continuum. This is not necessarily a criticism, since all institutions in effect set up contracts with their adult learners and attempt to act in their best interests. A completely 'open' system may sound ideal, but the fully independent learner is open to failure to learn, indeed often to not even engage in learning at all (Fox, 1991).

I believe that it is very important for educators to keep the issues of power and control to the front of their minds when developing learning programmes. Too much tutor control and learners can become antagonistic and drop out of learning programmes; too little and they can become apathetic!

Learners vary greatly in their capability to learn autonomously, which adds to the challenge of determining where to place a learning programme along the continuum. Older adults whose formative learning experiences were gained in traditional schools may not consider themselves able to cope with significant levels of self-direction in learning. Indeed they often regard themselves as short-changed when tutors refuse to teach, or offer only limited availability even to discuss their course work. Research has also identified that adults learning in physical isolation by online methods may well bemoan the lack of human and social contact (Selwyn, Gerard and Williams, 2002).

Many teachers and trainers are also threatened by being required to operate towards the right-hand end of the spectrum, where they are not able to fully demonstrate their undoubted classroom teaching skills or subject expertise. The loss of power to control the teaching and learning process may also be keenly felt, especially where the trainer is being held responsible for the achievement of specific learning by the learners.

Harper (1993) summarizes the case for open learning from the learner's perspective as follows; open learning:

- dispels the learner's common notion that classroom attendance is equivalent to effort and achievement;
- recognizes that different students learn at different speeds and in different ways;
- helps learners to learn how to learn;
- helps learners to accept responsibility for their own learning;
- encourages learners to be more active in their learning; and
- generates motivation and commitment and stimulates a sense of self-management.

While all this can be the case, poorly prepared open learning materials, poorly supported by uncommitted trainers, can lead to loss of confidence in learners and failure to learn. It is vital therefore to take forward the best interests of learners and trainers.

OFFSHORE OPEN LEARNING

A North Sea oil company needed to conduct training on safety for visitors to exploration and production platforms in the North Sea. There was particular concern that contractors should be aware of the hazards, the control measures in place, and the expected safe working practices.

There was also a need to train company staff on technical issues related to risk control. Each platform had a safety officer who could undertake some training. There was concern to standardize the training to meet both needs, and to ensure that day-to-day work did not stand in the way of everyone receiving training.

The answer was seen to lie with an open learning approach, especially given that workers could undertake open learning work in the time they had free from operational duties. The need was for self-paced learning, which would be highly interactive and draw in the learners to increase their motivation. The safety training field benefits from visual inputs, and requires checks that learning is taking place fully and effectively.

An interactive video approach was therefore considered most appropriate in both cases. Video material was shot on the oilrigs in line with the storyboards generated by experts in relevant aspects of risk management. Commentaries were added to give full video material. This was then edited to generate a high level of multiple-choice interactivity.

Feedback and evaluation records were built into each programme. The two programmes have been used extensively and have proved very effective in terms of learner acceptance and learner effectiveness.

FLEXIBLE LEARNING

The ambiguity about the meaning of open learning, and the move towards very flexible methods of accessing information and contacting members of the learning community have encouraged the wider use of the term 'flexible learning'. While flexible learning may be used in connection with both open and distance learning, it could well incorporate face-to-face tuition, tutor-less learning groups, indeed any appropriate continuation of learning methods where the learner's real needs and possibilities are to the fore.

The concept of flexible learning has been defined by the Further Education Unit of the UK Department for Education and Employment as:

> the adaptation of available learning opportunities to meet the needs of the learner in a way which optimises the autonomy of the learner as well as the effectiveness of the process of learning. (FEU, 1983:11)

As with open learning, the term 'flexible learning' is used by different people in different ways in different countries. Malone (1997:5) states that:

> This is not merely the result of different languages and cultures, but rather the outcome of different educational, training and vocational training systems and alternative applications of new technology.

As with open learning there are degrees of flexibility available to suit particular learning needs, but also the culture and customs of particular organizations providing learning opportunities (Waterhouse, 1990). A university will not expect its students to learn mainly in classrooms, and much encouragement is given to learning in the library, by study at home or in the hall of residence, from other students, and from practical experience. In contrast a secondary school will hold its students in classrooms for most of each school day, with school teachers controlling much of the learning process. Similarly, work organizations will vary greatly in the extent to which they allow or encourage flexibility in learning provision. Clearly young craft apprentices cannot be left to find out for themselves how to operate powerful and fast-moving machinery in the apprentice training school, or on the shop floor; nor can newly recruited soldiers be left to teach themselves from a manual how to fire a rifle.

In contrast many experienced workers are operating at the frontiers of knowledge and skill in their specialist fields. Within their work organizations such workers may not be able to turn to the training department to advise them on how to take their learning forward, let alone organize this for them (Johnston, 1993).

The mind shift from regarding learning as an activity largely directed by teachers and trainers within a classroom environment, to seeing it as an activity primarily of concern to learners, where they will be offered as much flexibility as possible to determine their best ways to learn, is difficult (Bailey, 1992). Once it has been made, there are many exciting options that open up. These retain an important place for face-to-face learning directed by teachers and trainers, and for learning in groups, but do not see these as an automatic requirement, nor as necessarily a major part of a learning programme.

Decisions about how to take learning forward rest substantially with the learners, and in this case some flexibly delivered programme will generally result. Unless geography makes it impossible, learners will generally favour undertaking demanding and longer study programmes that include some face-to-face teaching and some group learning. However, the onward march of learning technologies continues to open up ways to learn autonomously which were just not possible in the past.

ISSUES FOR THE LEARNER IN ODFL

Much of the current literature on ODFL considers the changed situation from the viewpoint of the providers of learning programmes and/or the companies for which the learners are working. This is because the developers of new technology-based learning programmes are selling to training providers in the first instance, and because companies see ODFL as a lever to achieve organizational change. However, it is the learner who has to achieve the learning, and many ODFL schemes have failed because the real needs and circumstances of the learners were not properly considered.

A spectacular example of this phenomenon has been the collapse of the UK's e-university (UKEU), which was set up with £62 million in investment, and only enrolled 900 students, missing the initial modest target of 5,600 (Johnston, 2004).

Learners will vary greatly in terms of their initial motivation to learn autonomously, or to plan their learning autonomously. They will also vary greatly in their ability to learn autonomously, either at all or by particular learning methods. Learning providers with experience in dealing with very heterogeneous groups of learners and a commitment to ODFL will tend to offer a range of face-to-face learning opportunities, but not insist that these are all taken up. They will also provide plentiful opportunities for potential learners to discuss their learning hopes and ideas with experienced learning guidance professionals. The UK Open University is a good example of this approach. From the outset some learners will not attend many classes and will not seek much contact with their tutors otherwise. In contrast, some learners will seek a great deal of advice on learning options, attend every class which is organized, and contact their tutors frequently.

Many learners will seek more or less general guidance and specific learning support from professionals, depending on how well their studies are going and how relevant they seem to future personal scenarios. In general, as time goes by and learners become more confident in their ability to learn by ODFL, so they will see less and less need for class contact and tutor support. The Open University takes account of this trend by offering many more classroom sessions for its foundation courses than for its more advanced courses which follow on from these.

It may well be argued that a major purpose of adult education is to develop learners' self-confidence in 'owning' their own learning, and the ability to take learning forward on a self-help basis. Malone (1997:14) argues that:

> Open learning is an ideal means of developing the necessary skills and attitudes of self-reliance and initiative precisely because they are exactly those that are acquired when doing open learning.

Laurillard (2002) has shown that when students are given freedom to work through computer-based learning material in their preferred way, they use a wide-ranging variety of routes. Differences in learning styles are also an important consideration in regard to learner options in the ODFL context. Text-based open and distance learning materials with limited scope for inter-action with the text via problem-solving exercises, or exercises that encourage creativity, are likely to be more suitable for those who learn best by starting from reflection and theory, rather than those who learn best from an action-oriented start. This relates to Honey and Mumford's (1992) learning styles (see Chapter 10), although this widely adopted concept has been challenged by Moseley (2004), whose research on learning-style instruments throws doubt on their validity.

However, today an enormous range of open learning materials is available to suit a wide variety of learning styles as well as learning topics and levels. Computer-based training (CBT) programmes, which encourage experimentation and a trial-and-error approach to learning, are available. Indeed the most sophisticated CBT packages will allow learners a variety of options in the way in which they learn from the package, according to their own preferred style. Research is in progress to develop CBT systems that will not only diagnose from learner interaction what each learner does or does not know, but also how the learner prefers to learn, and adjust the delivery of learning accordingly.

Recent research on the characteristics of university students learning by electronic means indicates that those who are risk-averse in learning do less well than those who seek new challenges in learning (Kickul and Kickul, 2004).

ODFL has been taken up substantially in the corporate world in recent years, for a whole variety of reasons which we will consider in the next section. Many errors have been made in this process, for many reasons. Fundamentally, however, these reasons come down to not taking sufficient account of the needs and circumstances of the learners. There is little point in setting up an open learning centre in the workplace if the packages available are of no relevance to the workforce, or if the level of learning involved is too high or too low. Nor will workers be able to benefit from the open learning centre if their work and general life demands never give them time to get access to it to do some studying. In some companies supervisors have been reluctant to allow workers to attend open learning centres during working hours. While there may be good reasons for this reluctance, there has to be accord across a work organization about how an open learning centre is supposed to work for it to be successful. If learners perceive discord at management level they will be very reluctant to involve themselves in ODFL at work, however much money is spent on centres, learning equipment and packages.

Worker motivation to learn needs to be very carefully considered if open learning centres are to be cost-effective, otherwise they may remain empty rooms, or worse, rooms full of workers gossiping for long periods during working hours. Stephenson (1992) found that the presence of a tutor improves performance. At the very least workers will want their learning achievements to be recognized, and known about by their superiors and peers. It is all too easy for this to be overlooked when ODFL methods are employed. The increasing trend towards assessment and accreditation of learning is a very real benefit here, since much ODFL has explicit learning objectives which are readily accessible. It is unsurprising that ODFL programmes leading to well-regarded qualifica tions are especially popular with workers, and learners generally (Thorpe, 1993).

ISSUES FOR ODFL PROVIDERS

Broadly considered there are three types of ODFL providers: those that sell services directly to learners; those that incorporate ODFL approaches into learning programmes offered in the public sector institutions; and those that offer ODFL opportunities within the context of work organizations. Consideration of the issues affecting those operating businesses based on offering ODFL, directly to learners or to organizations where learners are based, is beyond the scope of this chapter. The development and production of ODFL programmes and materials for open sale in this way is now a huge and expanding industry. The content and forms of ODFL involved depend primarily on marketing considerations. There are mass markets for packages on subjects as varied as foreign languages, great paintings or learning the guitar. Many employers base their ODFL provision largely or entirely on such 'off-the shelf' materials and equipment, with an increasing trend towards multimedia packages. Universities and colleges have tended to develop their own ODFL packages which are most commonly incorporated within more conventional courses, or offered on a stand-alone basis for qualifications.

It is the issues faced by organizations which have already been providers of conventional learning programmes in switching some of their provision to ODFL that I wish to focus upon now. The first question should always be, why change towards ODFL anyway? This change will cause upheavals of various kinds, and the benefits need to be clearly identified if the costs involved are to be justified:

- Are there potential learners that we can reach more readily by ODFL methods whom we would like to support?

- Do we have existing learners who could learn more readily through access to ODFL methods?
- Are there training needs that we cannot currently meet properly or at all by conventional methods?
- To what extent do we know that the ODFL approach will lead to more and better learning on a cost-effective basis, and that this learning will benefit the medium-term profitability of the organization?

While it may not be possible to fully answer these questions before going forward, by asking them across the organization a whole range of issues can be clarified. Once there is clarity on why a change toward ODFL is justified then it is easier to persuade teachers, trainers, line managers and learners alike that the effort to change their practices will pay off. All too often particular ODFL methods have been hurriedly introduced in organizations as varied as universities and international companies with no real justification beyond their trendiness in the eyes of one or two senior managers or trainers. The concerns of lower-level staff have been overridden and very substantial expenditure has been incurred, with no lasting benefit to the organization. Meanwhile the learners involved have been damaged, and the overall standing of ODFL diminished.

While there can be no recipe for success, long experience would suggest that for most organizations it is better to start small, and to grow ODFL systems gradually, learning by experience, rather than go for a blockbuster approach. While the introduction of top-down comprehensive change can look exciting, and theoretically efficient in time and money, in fact this approach has failed sufficiently, even in progressive organizations, for us to question its wisdom.

Where a training department exists in a company it is very undesirable to initiate an ODFL centre or ODFL course without involving the trainers located there. Even though these trainers may be informed that their existing work is valued, and that they will be just as busy as with face-to-face courses, the open learning centre or course will immediately be seen as a threat. While not all trainers will be willing to change role and learn new skills, there will usually be one or more who will consider doing so. These trainers should be identified and empowered to move into the ODFL field, undertaking whatever training is needed for their new roles. As far as possible these staff should be retained inside the training department and encouraged to take forward some of their pre-existing conventional training work. In this way ODFL is demystified, and no barriers are built up between dedicated ODFL staff and the other trainers.

Once the work grows to involve several ODFL programmes there will be a need to designate a manager for this work. At this stage, it may be worth considering an external appointment to bring in higher-level and novel expertise. However, any such appointment needs to be made carefully so that the ODFL manager is able to fit into the culture of the training function and the culture of the company overall. Otherwise there is a danger of the ODFL function becoming sidelined, and eventually being seen as a costly and unnecessary adjunct to the HRD function rather than a key driver of it.

Alternatively, a sympathetic and experienced company trainer could move into the ODFL management function. Nobody should be appointed who does not have experience of ODFL work, however. In this case new appointments could be considered to work under this manager, perhaps trainers with expertise in ODFL technologies that the company has identified as valuable.

The choice of which learning programmes to offer in ODFL format must be based on careful consideration of learner needs and company functional needs, not on the glamour of the new technologies involved. Ideally, the early choices should be of programmes which are clearly relevant to the learners and the company, are of high quality, and proven success in other places. Seeing is believing, and nothing succeeds like success.

So often the first ODFL programmes introduced into companies (or offered by colleges to their students) are based on unproven technological platforms, delivering study programmes which have only just been developed, in new fields, and offered to learners with no previous ODFL experience, by untrained trainers and teachers who also have no previous experience. It is no wonder that failure results, especially where the learners see no particular reason for the use of an ODFL approach in the first place. The literature increasingly offers reports covering the learner's experience in studying via ODFL methods, especially computer-based methods (Bird, 2004; Matikainen, 2002).

Learners need to learn how to benefit from ODFL in general, and from particular approaches for each learning need. Considerable attention needs to be given to how this is achieved, since the first experience of learning, or trying to learn, by ODFL is strongly formative in regard to attitudes towards the concepts involved. There is much sense in conducting face-to-face sessions initially to introduce the approach, and to take learners through issues around self-directed learning.

If following this stage well-proven delivery systems are used to support quality learning programmes on topics of real interest to learners, which are relevant to their needs, then success is most likely. The potential advantages and disadvantages of open and distance learning from the learner's viewpoint are summarized in Table 16.1.

THE CORPORATE OPEN LEARNING CENTRE

Corporate learning centres have grown rapidly in the past 20 years. Marx (1995) reported that 8 per cent of the 'Fortune 500' companies in the USA were using interactive media learning programmes. Kay (1995) reports that Target Stores uses computer-based training to ensure consistency in corporate training across its 600 stores. The UK is said to be the leader in computer-based training (Littlefield, 1994). The Rover Group has spent £2 million setting up its own learning enterprise, Rover Learning Business, to support specialized learning inside and outside the car industry.

Other UK companies which have set up corporate open learning centres include Lucas, British Steel, British Telecom and Norwich Union (Malone, 1997). This task is not necessarily without its challenges, as my own learners have reported in dissertations based on studies in organizations as varied as ones in the aerospace industry and the Singapore Armed Forces. Reasons for slow progress or outright failure include lack of senior management support, lack of consultation with learners, or a fixation on inappropriate technologies. The greatest success is usually achieved when the real needs of the learners, in line with company objectives, are fully considered.

Table 16.1 Potential advantages and disadvantages of open and distance learning from the learner's viewpoint

Potential Advantages	Potential Disadvantages
Access to learning materials and programmes may be easier.	There may be less guidance on the level, relevance and appropriateness of learning materials and programmes.
Learning may be achieved on a flexible basis in terms of time.	Lack of timetabled classes may lead to learning being neglected.
Learning can be carried out at a pace to suit the learner.	Lack of a clear timetable may lead to learning taking place too slowly, and ultimately petering out.
Learning may be achieved on a flexible basis in terms of place.	No suitable place for learning may be identifiable.
Learning can be carried out in one's own time.	No designated time is allowed (eg, by employers for work-related learning).
Learning programmes may be tailored to individual's needs.	Employer's needs may be inadequately covered without this being recognized by learners.
Cognitive learning at one's own pace may be very effective.	Learning in the affective and skills domains may be difficult to achieve.
ODL encourages autonomy in learning.	Lack of tutor support may lead to loss of motivation and failure to overcome learning blocks.
The absence of 'lessons' can make ODL less 'intimidatory'.	Lack of 'lessons' may lead to lack of discipline in study.
There is less chance of interpersonal conflict with tutors.	Informal mentoring relationships are unlikely to develop.
Lack of face-to-face involvement with tutors and learners may be helpful to introverts.	Lack of opportunity for comradeship, and peer learning may be demotivating.
Learning programmes and materials may be better structured and of high quality in terms of content and presentation.	Programmes and materials may be expensive, not tailored, out-of-date or even of poor quality. They may be over-dependent on one form of presentation.
Learning via new technologies can be exciting and motivating.	New technologies may involve high equipment or software costs, and can be daunting to learners.
Virtual reality systems can helpfully stimulate environments for learning which are difficult to achieve otherwise.	Such systems may be used as cheaper and poorer substitutes for experiential learning in real environments.
Assessment methods may be better thought out and more clearly explained.	Learners may still have difficulty determining what is required in assessments and less opportunity to negotiate these.

COMPUTER-BASED TRAINING IN ACCOUNTANCY

In October 1998 accountancy staff of the National Audit Office began studying Business Planning Techniques, a non-core subject in the syllabus of the Institute of Chartered Accountants of England and Wales (ICAEW), via computer-based training (Rogers, 1998). In doing so they made history as the first students to study the ICAEW syllabus by an open learning method, outside a classroom structure.

The course was created by EQL International following a policy decision by the ICAEW that its non-core subjects could be studied via open learning materials produced by other organizations, subject to ICAEW accreditation. EQL International produces CD ROMs covering the other four non-core subjects: professional practice, business and company law, economics, and management and marketing. The company had approximately 4,500 students taking one or more non-core subjects via these CD ROMs in the 1998–99 academic year.

The accountancy firm Mazors Neville Russell has had up to 140 students taking the ICAEW syllabus, and estimates that the cost per subject per student makes the CD ROM approach much cheaper than traditional methods, as well as offering flexibility in study.

A review of the outcomes at the National Audit Office revealed that students found the computer package easy to use and were impressed by the amount of interaction. They were able to work through the course at their own pace, and could repeat elements they were less confident about prior to the assessment. While training colleges have quoted one week as the time required to cover a subject, the CBT package enabled students to complete their studies and take the assessment in two and a half days.

It is further reported that 90 per cent of universities are using CBT packages on their accountancy courses, with banks also quoted as major users. The breakthrough into ICAEW syllabus usage is seen as very significant in the context of professional institutions' support for open learning.

Physical centres for company open learning

There is no need to set up a formal open learning centre before ODFL is introduced into a company. However, as the utilization of ODFL approaches increases, there is sense in considering whether a formal centre for open learning should be designated (Davies, 1989). Generally the setting aside of a room or rooms for this purpose, followed by equipping them with technological aids to open learning and open learning packages, points to the designation of one or more dedicated staff. Failure to take this step frequently leads to misuse of the centre, even to its despoilation. Further than this, the facility needs to be properly looked after by somebody who can support learners in using equipment and provide some basic guidance on what is available and its appropriateness for specific learning purposes.

There is a strong case for proper records to be kept on the utilization levels of the centre: which staff have visited, when, how long for and what learning programmes they have undertaken.

While this may seem somewhat intrusive, this data would be automatically available for attendance on any in-company training course. Such records are valuable in defending the work of the open learning centre if it is proving attractive, or at least alerting management to problems if it is being poorly utilized. Knowing when staff prefer to attend, what topics are of most interest, and which open learning packages are proving most valuable is very important in terms of managing the centre, and its growth, on a cost-effective basis (Dorrell, 1993).

Record-keeping is also valuable for staff utilizing the centre, in terms of proving that they are not wasting company time, and in terms of maintaining a central record of their learning achievement. As ODFL grows in work organizations the open learning centre may become a main source of in-company learning, which justifies locating learning guidance services, learning support services and learning assessment work within the centre. If such centres are to achieve their full potential they must be planned in the context of company and staff learning needs overall, and not in isolation from the face-to-face training provision and attendance on external courses.

Tailor-made programmes

As ODFL moves centre stage in an organization it is likely that there will be an increasing need for tailor-made ODFL programmes rather than only off-the-shelf packages. These can be commissioned from external vendors, or designed and developed by in-company staff. The issue of cost-effectiveness looms large here. Again there has been a tendency to commission very expensive high technology-based ODFL packages which have proved of limited value in use, merely because of their exciting 'bells and whistles'. The golden rule is to employ the lowest level of technology which will fully meet the learning needs, and to ensure that these needs are fully evaluated, involving potential learners as far as possible.

Reputable vendors of tailor-made ODFL programmes will never seek to offer packages based on technologies and costs beyond the needs of the learners and the best interest of the company. Package specification should be a matter of negotiation between the vendor and the company representatives and follow a full training needs analysis.

Moving to development of in-company expertise in the preparation of ODFL programmes often increases the involvement and motivation of everyone involved. Quality is a real concern and considerable staff training may be needed, followed by much practice and piloting of materials. However, quality improvement is then possible in-house, and by a process of iteration very good quality, relevant and effective ODFL programmes can be produced. Once internal staff have moved up to the level of producing strong ODFL materials, it may prove cost-effective to produce a great deal of such materials in-house. However, it is rarely cost-effective to reinvent the wheel, and the external providers of off-the-shelf materials should always be kept in focus, especially if their materials can be modified to meet learner needs more closely.

It is also essential to ensure that a fixation on ODFL, and especially particular approaches, is not allowed to override common sense. A short learning programme required for a small number of learners on a one-off basis is probably still best delivered by a face-to-face approach, both in terms of effectiveness and cost.

CONCLUSION

The most powerful learning programmes are often those which involve a careful mix of face-to-face classes, study of open learning materials, practice of skills and application of knowledge, followed by reflection, free-choice study of literature of personal interest and relevance, and assessment of learning by appropriate methods.

The most successful trainers and teachers of adults will be those who are confident in using a wide range of approaches to learning, who network with trainers offering complementary knowledge and skills, and who can tailor ODFL programmes to meet learning needs closely on a cost-effective basis.

The following chapters take us into consideration of the choices of specific ODFL systems and their strengths and limitations. To encourage the reader to consider these seriously, let me close with some reports concerning the sheer cost-effectiveness of ODFL programmes in larger companies:

- Fuller and Saunders (1990) report that British Telecom estimated that it would cost £40 million to train its 20,000 operators to use computerized telephone exchanges. However, instead of going down the face-to-face training route, BT bought a computer-based training system for £4 million to achieve the same learning outcome and saved £36 million.
- Littlefield (1994) reports that Rank Xerox claims to have saved millions of dollars as a result of heavy investment in interactive video and CD ROM in the training of service engineers, where otherwise real and expensive equipment would have to be taken out of service for practice sessions.
- Forlenza (1995) reports that the average initial cost of implementing a computer-based training system, including hardware, is $8 per employee per hour of training, compared to an average of $50 for the same amount of conventional classroom training.
- Johnston (1993) refers to estimates by the Learning Methods Branch of the Employment Department that the cost advantages of open and flexible learning over conventional methods ranged from 12 to 90 per cent in the training context.

Such comparisons should properly consider the nature and added value of the training, but nevertheless offer much food for thought to all involved in adult learning provision.

Bibliography

Bailey, D (1992) 'Facilitator not teacher: role changes for tutors in open learning nurse education', *Journal of Advanced Nursing*, **17**, 8, pp 983–91

Bell, R E (1993) *The Open University: Exciting innovation or disappointing revival?*, Occasional Papers: Policy and practice in continuing education and training for youth and adult studies, School of Education, Milton Keynes, Open University

Birchall, D (1990) Third generation distance learning', *Journal of European Industrial Training*, **14**, 7, pp 17–20

Bird, C M (2004) 'Sinking in a C–M sea: a graduate student's experience of learning through asynchronous computer-mediated communication', *Reflective Practice*, **5**, 2, pp 253–63

Bond, D (ed) (1988) *Developing Student Autonomy in Learning*, London, Kogan Page

Davies, W J K (1989) *Open and Flexible Learning Centre*, London, National College for Educational Technology

Dorrell, J (1993) *Resource-Based Learning: Using open and flexible learning resources for continuous development*, Maidenhead, McGraw-Hill Training Services

Edwards, R (1991) 'The politics of meeting learner needs: power, subject, subjugation', *Studies in the Education of Adults*, **23**, 1, pp 85–97

Evans, T D (1994) *Understanding Learners in Open and Distance Learning*, London, Kogan Page

Forlenza, D (1995) 'Computer–based training', *Professional Safety*, **40**, 5, pp 28–29

Fox, S (1991) 'The production and distribution of knowledge through open and distance learning', *Education and Training Technology International*, **26**, 3, pp 269–80

Fuller, A and Saunders, M (1990) 'The paradox in open learning at work', *Personnel Review*, **19**, 5, pp 29–33

Further Education Unit, Department for Education and Employment (1983) *Flexible Learning Opportunities*, London, FEU

Harper, K (1993) 'Why flexible learning?', *Banking World*, **11**, 8, pp 45–46

Honey, P and Mumford, A (1992) *Manual of Learning Styles*, 3rd edn, Maidenhead, Honey

Johnston, C (2004) 'MPs to probe e-uni collapse', *Times Higher Education Supplement*, 11 June, p 12

Johnston, R (1993) 'The role of distance learning in professional development', *Management Services*, **37**, 4, pp 24–26

Johnston, R (1997) 'Distance learning: medium or message', *Journal of Further and Higher Education*, **21**, 1, pp 107–22

Kay, A S (1995) 'The business case for multimedia', *Datamation*, **4**, 11, pp 55–56

Kickul, J and Kickul, G (2004) 'E-learning challenges and processes: understanding the role of student self-efficacy and learning goal orientation', *International Journal of Management Education*, **4**, 1, pp 29–38

Laurillard, D M (2002) *Rethinking University Teaching*, 2nd edn, London, RoutledgeFalmer

Littlefield, D (1994) 'Open learning by PC or paper?', *Personnel Management*, **25**, 9, p 55

Malone, S A (1997) *How to Set Up and Manage a Corporate Learning Centre*, Aldershot, Gower

Marx, W (1995) 'The new high tech training', *Management Review*, **84**, 2, pp 57–60

Matikainen, J (2002) 'Web-based learning environments – a scene of social interaction', *Lifelong Learning in Europe*, **7**, 4, pp 247–54

Moseley, D (2004) 'Out of style', *People Management*, July, p 44

Rogers, A (1998) 'Computers add up for accountants', *Sunday Times*, 4 October, pp 7–11

Rowntree, D (1992) *Exploring Open and Distance Learning*, London, Kogan Page

Selwyn, N, Gerard, S and Williams, S (2002) '"We are guinea pigs really": examining the realities of ICT-based adult learning', *Studies in the Education of Adults*, **34**, 1 pp 23–41

Stephenson, S D (1992) 'The role of the instructor in computer–based training', *Performance and Instruction*, **31**, 7, pp 23–26

Thorpe, M (1993) *Evaluating Open and Distance Learning*, Harlow, Longman

Waterhouse, P (1990) *Flexible Learning*, Bath, Network Educational Press

17

E-Learning: A Guide to Principles and Practice

Maggie McPherson

INTRODUCTION AND LEARNING OBJECTIVES

As a result of advances in information and communication technologies (ICT) over the past few decades, together with an increasingly competitive environment, employers and professional associations now need staff with communication, planning and networking skills, as well as problem-analysis and problem-solving abilities (Kakabadse and Korac-Kakabadse, 2000; McPherson and Nunes, 2004). The call for employees to become more flexible and self-confident professionals, and to engage in lifelong learning, has intensified. Broader access to a range of increasingly powerful, flexible, friendly and cost-effective IT systems, together with the advent of increased connectivity made available by the internet and the World Wide Web (WWW), has led numerous educational researchers, lecturers and training practitioners to investigate the implications and possibilities of technologies for teaching, learning and training. It is in that context that this chapter will discuss the potential of e-learning.

Having read this chapter, you will:

- be aware of what is meant by the term 'e-learning';
- be familiar with some advantages and disadvantages of this learning approach;
- appreciate the complexity of making the transition to a new learning culture;
- be able to identify a number of issues associated with the design, development and implementation of e-learning.

WHAT IS E-LEARNING?

According to the Department for Education and Skills (DfES) *E-Learning Strategy Consultation Document*, 'if someone is learning in a way that uses information and communication technologies (ICTs), they are using e-learning' (DfES, 2003). Other researchers, such as Igonor (2002), describe e-learning as teaching that is delivered electronically and place particular emphasis on making use of the World Wide Web (from hereon described as the web). Indeed, the term e-learning is often used in a variety of ways, often interchangeably with terms such as open learning, networked learning, virtual learning and online learning. The main characteristic linking these terms is the use of ICT as a delivery vehicle, and in fact the term 'e-learning' is frequently used to describe any learning taking place through the use of ICT-supported environments: that is, any courses that use computer mediated communication (CMC) and are not entirely delivered using traditional face-to-face (f2f) methods. Thus, e-learning can be described as the use of ICT to deliver a broad array of solutions that develop knowledge and improve performance. Therefore, for the remainder of this chapter, the term 'e-learning' will be used to summarize the overlapping approaches that make use of ICT for gaining skills and knowledge, and will be used as an umbrella term for all online and internet-based learning.

WHY IS E-LEARNING IMPORTANT?

The development of e-learning has provided greater opportunities for enabling interaction between individuals and groups and allowing learners to share information. Indeed, it can have a significant impact on teaching, learning and training by providing access to new information sources through the internet for educationalists, researchers and learners. As industry increasingly adopts technological solutions to make information available to employees through a broad set of internet-based collaborative technologies, businesses become virtual workplaces.

E-learning is already being used more widely in education and training, and this can be exploited in the home and in community centres, as well as in schools, colleges, universities and the workplace. Individuals are discovering that they can now access courses that were hitherto unavailable to them, making it easier for them to get involved in personal and professional learning. Furthermore, trainers are now able to make greater use of technology to incorporate various modes of ICT, such as e-mail, instant messaging, online meetings, bulletin board systems and video conferencing within web-based learning environments to support the learning process.

BENEFITS OF E-LEARNING

For many training professionals and educationalists, enthusiastic about seeking improved methods of facilitating the learning process, the answer to increasing quality within educational provision seems to lie in the use of e-learning. Daniel (1998) suggests that e-learning can be used in a flexible manner to suit the requirements of the individual students, based on asynchronous communication. According to French *et al* (1999), e-learning also offers the opportunity to gain requisite continuing professional development to professionals who might otherwise find it difficult to attend programmes of study or conferences.

> The web's communication protocol is supporting hypertext and hypermedia principles [thus enhancing] the application of many new didactic approaches or models.
>
> (Van Brakel, 1999:390)

Consequently the adoption of an e-learning solution is becoming increasingly attractive as a solution to provide flexibility and/or to widen participation (McPherson, 2003). Thus, benefits from e-learning for learners, tutors and organizations alike, which have also been discussed by a number of other authors such as Stamatis, Kefalas and Kargidis (1999), Nunes and Fowell (1996) and Eisenstadt and Vincent (1998), could be summarized as follows:

- electronic distribution of course material;
- flexibility for learners – when to study, at what pace;
- supporting different learning styles;
- accommodation of different ability levels;
- establishment of communication between learners and tutors;
- engendering contact between learners;
- greater access to information;
- greater flexibility in maintaining and up-dating course documentation.

Benjamin (1994), as cited by Salmon (2000:11), further qualified these benefits for the e-learner as being 'unlocked from the shackles of fixed and rigid schedules and from physical limitations' and 'released into an information world which reacts to his or her own pace of learning'. E-learning aims at providing these types of benefits through different ICT-based infrastructures. However, the introduction of educational technologies has not been without its critics.

DISADVANTAGES OF E-LEARNING

Although there is much literature advocating innovative uses of e-learning to enhance learning, according to the *Economist* Global Executive (2003), it still remains greatly under-utilized, despite its potential and some successes. Persistent concerns about the design and implementation of e-learning have formed the basis of one of the most controversial discussion topics in the educational community (Kapenieks *et al*, 2004; Taraman, 2004; Capuano, Gaeta and Pappacena, 2003). Many question why there is still a reluctance to make use of e-learning, and educationalists continue to debate the most appropriate use of technology in teaching and learning. Reeves and Hedberg (2003) believe that most e-learning environments remain mired in outmoded educational methods. Reeves feels that the effectiveness of technology in any learning environment depends upon the degree that it supports appropriate 'pedagogical' dimensions. Another problem is that although many educationalists are expert in their subject area, they are as yet relatively inexperienced in methods for online teaching and learning (McPherson, Nunes and Zafeiriou, 2003). Additionally, many students are as yet also ill-equipped for the demands of e-learning (Nunes, McPherson and Rico, 2000). This being the case, the question must be asked whether e-learning can be successful.

WHAT IS REQUIRED TO MAKE E-LEARNING SUCCESSFUL?

The development of good e-learning courses is complex. Both experience and the literature indicate that a holistic team approach is required to implement successful initiatives. For instance, unless attention is paid to changing teaching and learning practices, the introduction of e-learning initiatives risks becoming a mere panacea (Ausserhofer, 1999; Bowskill, 1998) rather than fulfilling a real need. One could go even further and say that it is not even enough that the courses are well designed or that the module delivery adopts appropriate pedagogical approaches, and that tutors are well versed in their subject matter areas and are able to facilitate online courses (McPherson and Nunes, 2004). In fact, many people may be involved in the process of e-learning development, and initiatives involving the implementation of e-learning must consider the various interests of multiple stakeholders.

The need for change management

The introduction of e-learning represents a significant change in practice that really needs to be managed carefully, and there are a number of important components at different levels that require alignment through the process of change management. Figure 17.1 is intended to illustrate some of the many layers that may be associated with e-learning, and it is considered important to discuss some of the most important issues, starting with the broadest level, associated with each of these levels.

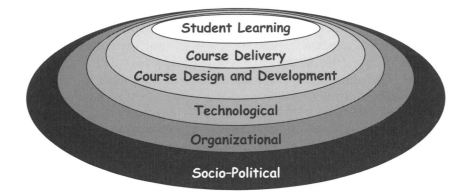

Figure 17.1 Identification of interested e-learning stakeholders at different levels

Socio-political issues

Society in the 21st century is being propelled into an unprecedented transformation, rivalling that of the Industrial Revolution. This is in no small part due to the speed of the ICT developments that have materialized from the convergence of computing and telecommunications over the last few decades. These advances created an exponential increase in the amount of new information and knowledge for all sectors of society. Faced with the phenomenon described as globalization, stakeholders such as government policy-makers, funding bodies, as well as managers and administrators have become concerned with issues related to the emergence of the 'e-society'. For example, e-learning is regarded as important by the UK government (DfES, 2003) because it believes it can contribute to objectives for education: raise standards; improve quality; remove barriers to learning and participation in learning; prepare individuals for employment; provide upskilling in the workplace; and ensure that every learner achieves his or her full potential.

Organizational issues

If implementation of e-learning is to be successful, there is a need for strategic alignment of institutional interests coupled with effective leadership. The change from face-to-face learning to e-learning needs careful management. Proposed goals need to be agreed through consensual debate by the various stakeholders that have an interest in organizational issues, such as senior management or board members, strategists and policy-makers, financial managers or administrators, evaluators, and possibly even shareholders in some cases.

However, before it is decided whether e-learning is a suitable approach, a business case needs to be established and the genuine learning needs of learners within the institution need to be identified. Before too much time and effort is committed to the project, it may be helpful to commission a feasibility study to determine this. All options for addressing the organization's training gap should be considered in order to decide which approach will produce outcomes that will best meet learners' needs. If it is decided that e-learning is a practical choice for meeting learning aims and objectives, the design and development process can be carefully deliberated, with an estimate of effort and associated costs made to assess the viability of the proposal. Once agreed upon, e-learning strategies need appropriate top-level support for realization through common commitment.

This view is supported by a consultation report by the Department for Education and Skills (DfES, 2004) on e-learning, which revealed that a majority of its respondents considered that it was the role of leadership to drive forward the e-learning strategy within their institutions. Several also suggested that a culture of change towards e-learning had to be promoted, yet some of those thought that it was very often the very same people who were in a position to influence and change who lacked sufficient IT skills to appreciate the benefits of e-learning. It is therefore suggested that in order to facilitate successful e-learning implementation, institutions need to work out how to achieve commitment, and need to be sufficiently flexible for all staff involved to be able to respond appropriately and to put into effect the changes that will be necessary at all levels.

Project management

There are too many vital decisions that must made to leave things to chance, so an appropriately skilled person must be appointed to take control of all key aspects of an e-learning project. Whether a small-scale project is being developed individually, or a larger initiative is being realized through team effort, it should be appreciated that the process is complicated. The project manager must identify and implement a proven, repeatable project management process that will work for the organization's strategy. As part of these activities, an intimate knowledge of educational processes and relevant development tools need to be acquired; appropriate resources need to be planned for and committed (which requires full support from above); there needs to be effective coordination of effort (depending on team size and roles); and appropriate communication procedures must be ensured.

Technological issues

E-learning technologies can be described as comprising the underlying infrastructure and software specifically adapted for learning, and it is obvious that unless attention is paid to such issues, the whole e-learning concept falls apart. Technologies for enabling e-learning generally fall into these main categories:

- underlying technical infrastructure;
- universal work stations (for learners and tutors, this usually means a multimedia PC equipped with a web browser);
- ICTs which enable widespread learner networking and access to the web;
- software tools which enable educationalists to author and deliver usable courses.

Those most likely to be concerned with issues in this area are IT managers, learning environment technologists and/or training support staff. It may be helpful to commission a full and realistic analysis of technical needs, specifications and a schedule of the proposal before fully committing to the project.

To design and develop a course around technology that is not readily available to those intended to use it is a waste of time and energy, and the whole initiative will be doomed to failure. It is therefore suggested that technologists become acquainted with the potential learning audience before recommending a particular learning environment. This will ensure that the course requires no more than is strictly necessary in terms of the available bandwidth, processing power, sound cards, audio and video plug-ins, browser generations, and local and network security settings. Only then will it be useful to proceed with designing courses to run in the environment. Unfortunately, many technical people enthusiastically build high-tech courses and then try to oblige learners to upgrade to the required technology specifications. However, this is not a recommended course of action (Parkin, 2001). Both learners and tutors must have the appropriate level of access. If this is not achieved, then regardless of the quality of the course content, it will not achieve the desired result.

It is recommended that a prototyping approach (developing trial versions of the application) be considered in order to enable iterative elicitation, definition, and communication of learner needs and user requirements (Smith, 1997). This will allow for appropriate testing and tracking. Finally, the e-learning application needs to be tested early and repeatedly, from both a user and a technical perspective!

COURSE DESIGN AND DEVELOPMENT ISSUES

The design of e-learning (which comprises establishment of the curriculum) and the development (which involves turning the curriculum into reality) are interdependent. Stakeholders associated with course design and development issues include educational specialists, educational systems designers, web developers, graphic artists, animators, audio-visual specialists, all of whom need to work closely with training managers and subject matter specialists.

Curriculum design can be described as a process that determines what knowledge, understanding, skills, abilities, values and attitudes a particular course is seeking to develop. The course design team needs to take the learning context and learners' needs into consideration: the prerequisites, aims, objectives, assessment methods and so on. Heinich *et al* (1996) proposed a useful six-step learner-centred model (ASSURE) to act as a guide for planning and delivering instruction utilizing electronic media; see Table 17.1.

Although the ASSURE model was not specifically intended for e-learning, it may provide a useful guide. However, it is suggested that EMAR (which stands for Educational Management for Action Research), as shown in Figure 17.2 (McPherson and Nunes, 2004), could be very useful as an appropriate action research framework.

In the EMAR framework, the first step is to decide on a suitable pedagogical model. This is initially determined by agreeing on an underlying educational philosophy of how learners

Table 17.1 The ASSURE model

A	Analyse learners
S	State objectives
S	Select methods, media and materials
U	Utilize materials
R	Require learner participation
E	Evaluate

Source: Heinich *et al* (1996)

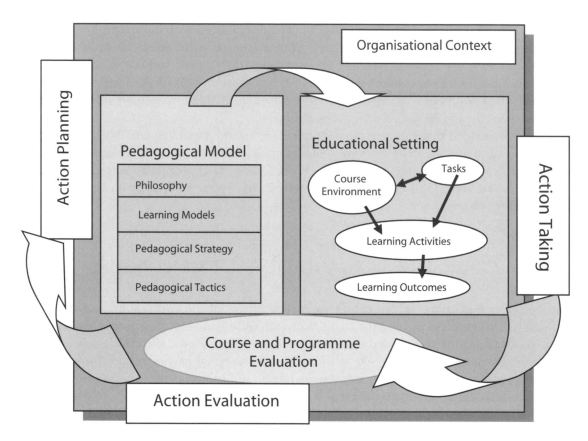

Figure 17.2 The EMAR model

learn. For instance, the behaviourist school of thought has strong connotations with transmission of knowledge (where learning involves listening or reading and remembering). The Cognition and Technology Group at Vanderbilt University (1991) criticized this approach and suggested that when learners simply memorize information, learning may well occur but the learner may not realize when it is applicable. On the other hand, the constructivist camp suggests that the learning of a concept must involve building on existing knowledge and active engagement with the skills to be acquired. Once the philosophy has been decided, appropriate learning models can be selected, and a particular pedagogical strategy and corresponding pedagogical tactics can be chosen.

After the pedagogical model has been established, a course environment, incorporating learning tasks and activities, can be designed in order to lead the learner towards the desired learning outcomes. Specific decisions about the course (such as content, level, activities, length, experience and ability required by the delivery team) need to be made in close collaboration with the development team (if different from the design team) in order to enable the appropriate selection of delivery modes. This shared knowledge facilitates decisions regarding the most appropriate educational systems design (ESD) to be developed and implemented (Nunes, 1999; Nunes and McPherson, 2003). An ESD (also referred to in the literature as instructional design) indicates the need for detailed specification of learning needs, materials, activities and delivery methods and needs. The various ICT components need to be blended to suit learning aims and follow coherent pedagogical approaches. ESD is based on frameworks comparable with those used in information systems (IS) design and development methodologies.

While all the levels discussed thus far influence a successful outcome, it should be noted that many experts feel the most effective e-learning requires student learning considerations to be at the core of the design, development and delivery process. For that reason, the next section will discuss delivery in the context of student learning.

Student learning and delivery issues

At the beginning of this chapter, it was pointed out that employers and professional associations need staff with a range of new skills. In this context, memorization of theory or definitions (associated with behaviourism) is of little value if learners are unable to use their new knowledge and ideas in diverse and unfamiliar situations. In fact, high-level skills (such as critical thinking, gathering of facts/concepts, effective communication, planning and networking skills, problem-analysis and problem-solving abilities), demand much greater learner participation in the learning process, and are best acquired through realistic and relevant contexts (situated learning).

It is suggested that a constructivist learning approach, which shares perspectives and tests ideas with others in a social context, allows learners to develop a much deeper understanding of the new concepts being explored. Although the key stakeholders are of course the learners themselves, there are other significant figures associated with the delivery process such as educational specialists, programme leaders, training staff, ICT specialists, course tutors, researchers and evaluators. Transferring course delivery into a more learner-centred e-learning environment requires a profound shift in learner and staff attitudes, as all these individuals are likely to have preconceived experiences and views (based on their own learning experiences) of how learning does or should take place.

From this it can be seen that the current learning culture needs to be assessed for a successful uptake of e-learning. If this represents a significant alteration in practice, then change management processes should be put into place to shift from one set of information management procedures, organisational behaviour and pedagogical approaches to another. It is also essential to deal with a host of learner and learner support issues, as well as pay attention to the tutorial team and staff development issues. As well as considering the effective and appropriate use of e-learning materials, some thought must be given to development of online learner skills. If tutors are inexperienced with e-learning, help will be needed to acquire the necessary skills to achieve learning aims and objectives in an unfamiliar environment. Thus, it is essential that tutor training should be made available to help them develop suitable teaching and learning strategies, to learn how to effectively facilitate learners' use of CMC tools for peer-to-tutor and peer-to-peer interaction, and to know how to provide appropriate student support.

Conclusion for implementation of e-learning solutions

The main advantage of using an e-learning approach is flexibility of time and place for both learners and providers, thus offering professionals the opportunity to gain requisite continuing professional development. The disadvantages include the complexity of making use of technology in teaching and learning, and inappropriate design, development or implementation because of inexperience with this new media. Successful e-learning requires a holistic view of the design, development and implementation of new initiatives, with due attention paid to managing the change in teaching practice and learning processes.

There are a number of issues for e-learning at different levels which require alignment through the process of change management. At the broadest level, there are socio-political pressures for e-learning to raise standards; improve quality; remove barriers to learning and participation in learning; prepare individuals for employment; provide upskilling in the workplace; and ensure that every learner achieves his or her full potential. Organizational concerns include cultural issues, organizational support, project management for new initiatives, communication issues, technical and resource issues, and staff training. Issues associated with the technology that are of significance are appropriateness, ease of use, support issues and access issues. With regard to the design and development of e-learning, it is felt that attention should be paid to doing proper needs analyses; underlying pedagogy; collaborative team development; consistency and standardization; attention to the delivery mode; expertise and training support; and design for ease of learning with the technical environment. Course delivery issues are generally pedagogical concerns; appropriateness of e-learning; contact issues; and support in terms of both tutor advice and technology.

Many of the concerns raised relate to areas such as involvement of all stakeholders; staff support within the organizational setting; teamwork and consistency within the area of curriculum development; and the educational systems design. These are areas which must not be ignored. Finally, if the e-learning initiative is to accomplish the aim of engendering high-level skills, it is recommended an active and learner-centred approach should be adopted in order to achieve the best results.

BLENDED LEARNING FOR A MASTER'S DEGREE IN TRAINING AND DEVELOPMENT

Some years ago technology-based learning methods were regarded as the solution to traditional forms of delivery, allowing the students to study at a time, place and pace which was suitable to them. (See Chapter 16 for a discussion on flexible learning.) There was no doubt that this freed students in some respects, but it also distanced them from close interaction with other students and tutors. The result was that many students were dissatisfied with the experience, and there were high levels of drop-out. The cost of developing materials was also high, and take-up of programmes was not at the levels required to sustain some organizations which failed, such as the Xebec and UK e-universities.

One solution that arose in response to the limitations of technology-based training was blended learning, which is normally used to describe a combination of delivery mechanisms including ICT, web and face-to-face. The Master's degree in Training and Development at the University of Bradford is an example of this. It is a part-time distance learning programme for those employed in the training and development field. As professionals in mostly full-time employment, the students need a flexible, part-time course that enables them to fit their studies around their work and family life. The students come from all over the United Kingdom, Europe and as far afield as Saudi Arabia. This means that regular attendance at university is not always an option. Many of the students view the course as a way of improving their prospects in their jobs, and as a vital part of their own continuing professional development.

Traditionally the course has been delivered as five weekend residential sessions held over two years and four large folders of written learning material. As Moore (1993:23) points out, 'The main weakness of many distance education programmes is their commitment to only one type of medium.' In this case, the medium is the static written material that students take away from each residential session. We set out to improve the learning on the course by focusing on solutions to the following issues:

- the sense of isolation associated with distance learning;
- flexible learning that is relevant to each individual's circumstances;
- keeping the material as up to date as possible;
- providing more than just 'learner-content interaction' in the periods between face-to-face contact. (Moore, 1993)

To achieve this we felt that adopting a blended learning approach would be the best solution. This would involve retaining the original residential face-to-face element and integrating the Blackboard virtual learning environment (VLE), which can be accessed by computer from anywhere in the world.

We have implemented five key changes:

- *Shared community*: we felt it crucial to develop a strong sense of shared community between students and tutors so that everyone could ask questions and feel that they were never far from help or advice. This was achieved by using discussion forums in the VLE. We used a general forum to discuss course-relevant material and a café forum for socializing.
- *Guided reading:* in order to keep the course up to date and flexible, we changed from using the written material to having course texts. However, instead of having a small number of core books that students had to read, we had three categories of reading material: Highly Recommended books or book chapters containing the material that would be most useful to cover the basics; Recommended books would extend the students' knowledge and allow them to look at their own areas of interest; and finally, Additional Reading would provide a starting point for extended reading into areas of personal interest.
- *Weekly tasks:* to support this reading, we introduced weekly tasks to the VLE. Each task consisted of finding out information, discussing what had been found with other students and then reflecting upon the discussions and thoughts generated.
- *Administrative support:* the VLE allowed us to provide easy access to the students for all course documents, such as the student handbook, assignments and extension forms.
- *Learning portal:* we gathered together a range of relevant and useful internet-based resources to help the students further their reading and research.

Overall, the aim has been to blend traditional distance learning with the opportunities offered by the internet and technology, while making the learning flexible and learner-centred. Davies (2003) points out that 'The first problem [of e-learning courses] was that students had come to expect certain things of a university.' One of those expectations is face-to-face contact with their tutors. By the nature of their jobs our students tend to be people-focused, and value that face-to-face contact.

Blended learning provides the opportunity to retain the strengths of traditional methods – in our case, the face-to-face contact of the residential sessions. It then incorporates the benefits of new technology, which is vital in distance learning courses to keep students interested, motivated and feeling part of a network of support.

Feedback collected so far has indicated that this innovative blended learning approach has been very successful for both students and tutors. The relationship between the residentials, VLE and course texts has provided a balanced approach to study.

With acknowledgement to Neil Currant, MEd in Training and Development tutor.

APPENDIX: THE A–Z OF TRAINING METHODS

Table 17.2 outlines a variety of learning and teaching methods that can be used in group-based and individual training.

Table 17.2 A–Z of training/system methods

	Trainer's perspective	Trainees' perspective
Action learning sets Involve a group of people convening to bring to the set real work problems. They act as comrades in adversity, supporting and challenging each other. Each participant works on his or her problem between set meetings and brings new information and solutions back to the group.	Degree of interdependence of group members. Trainer can help to establish learning set or act as learning set advisor. Advisor can offer support or helpline and guide process if needed.	Typically, the group meets once a month for half a day over a period of six to nine months. Learning through questioning is very powerful.
Action maze Similar to a case study, but uses printed instructions to guide a group through to a predetermined conclusion. It is called a maze because choices and options are offered at certain stages – rather like a pathway. Set situations will result from the choice of option. Discovery of preferred paths are the main outcome of this exercise.	Can be useful for problem-solving or decision-making. Requires careful design. Allows participant interdependence.	Incorrect decision-making can result in high levels of learning – learning from mistakes is good!
Brainstorming Creative ideas from participants. Group is allowed to submit ideas or suggestions and none are rejected. No discussion and no value judgements are made at this stage. All ideas can be rearranged and assessed later.	Allows trainer to quickly gather information on the levels of knowledge of the participants. Allows the generation of a lot of ideas in a short space of time and creates a climate of creativity. Exploration can produce exciting results!	Good fun and very creative, allowing a lot of participant input with no discussion. Most people can contribute without much effort. Participants feel a sense of ownership of the ideas.

Table 17.2 *continued*

	Trainer's perspective	Trainees' perspective
Bulletin board/newsgroups/ computer conferencing Bulletin boards and newsgroups provide specialist information. Computer conferencing allows discussion of specific topics.	Exchange of ideas can be carried out using this medium. Connection to the internet is required and the associated costs should be considered.	Newsgroup contributors tend to act as tutors and answer questions posted to the newsgroup quickly. One question posted can be responded to by many other people, providing a great variety of styles that a user can apply to specific situations.
Business game simulations Dynamic exercises or case studies – usually involving 'coming to terms' with a situation, then managing it via a set of imposed decisions. Computerized models offer complex data, and often decisions that interact.	Interactive element generates enthusiasm, notably when teams are in simulated competition. Can be linked with team development. Model can be challenged as unrealistic.	Offers practice in management – observation, analysis, judgement, decision making, etc. Can instil confidence.
Buzz groups Small groups, often formed after an input session, answer a set question or complete a set task and report back to the trainer or the rest of the group.	Avoid one group giving all the answers and leaving nothing for the other group to offer. Very participative and a large number of contributions can be offered in a short space of time.	Help rapid knowledge gain and starts trainee thought processes. Good group support engendered.
Case study Examination of events or situation (often real-life) usually aimed at learning by analysing the detailed material or posing, and defining solutions for problems.	Especially useful for analysis of existing/proposed systems. Can incorporate exercises. Simple cases may be unrealistic. Difficult to reproduce an exact duplicate of the working environment.	Opportunities exist for both exchange of views on 'what matters' and problem-solving.
CD ROM/CD writers CD ROM is now a well-known term that stands for 'Compact Disk Read Only Memory', and CD ROMs are limited to retrieval of stored data. CD writers are now also readily available, allowing training providers to press their own CDs.	CD ROMs and CD writers offer a means of delivery for computer-based training (CBT) programs, and are now more often than not built into modern computers. They have high-capacity optical data storage, offering a valuable reference source.	Use of keyboard seems to help motivation for many. Use of images can offer a variety of learning techniques in the learning process. Retrieval can be in form of text, picture and sound, making for a varied and interactive form of self-motivating learning.

Table 17.2   *continued*

	Trainer's perspective	Trainees' perspective
Computer-based training (CBT) Learner-managed coverage of programmed material, usually involving keyboard and screen, but compatible hardware and software are needed.	Many varied uses but good for presenting technical data. Present levels of technology make logic-based programmes most reliable. Care should be taken to ensure the material is appropriate (ie, evaluate before use). Screen material may be complex and tutorial help should be provided.	Learners use keyboard in line with screen instructions, calling forth information and responding to questions. CBT is able to offer work place simulations, incorporating sound, animation, and still or moving video clips, thus offering learners an insight to applications in practice.
Computer-supported collaborative learning (CSCL) Involves hands-on experiences for learners via a computer-supported environment.	Best practice for concept learning entails building on existing knowledge, and simulations can provide valuable hands-on interaction, where groups of learners can communicate and collaborate.	Simulation environments can be located anywhere on the internet, and users can experience active engagement with the skills, thus gaining a richer under standing through their shared dialogues.
Continuing professional development (CPD) Enables individuals to systematically build and improve their personal profile in a given profession.	A process of systematic, relevant, continuing and planned development within a particular profession. Expectations need to be clearly communicated to facilitate excellent practice within a given field.	Enables individuals to broaden their knowledge, skill and personal qualities necessary for carrying out professional and technical duties throughout their working life.
Discovery learning 'Learning without a teacher' – but usually in a controlled (pre-designed) set-up, and under supervision.	Considerable design work needed. Safety paramount – may need special adjustments, and so may be unrealistic. Best suited to tasks involving dismantling, checking, adjusting, rebuilding.	Offers challenges and builds confidence as learners master new skills. Helps understanding of principles. Time constraints do not affect learning process as with many other processes.

Table 17.2 *continued*

	Trainer's perspective	Trainees' perspective
Discussion Free exchange of information, opinions, etc. A 'controlled' discussion may follow a planned path, the leader controlling the agenda; an 'open' discussion may mirror members' priorities.	May be time-consuming – especially if discussion wanders or 'process problems' emerge. Attitudes may harden rather than adjust. Especially suitable for development or adjustment of attitudes and opinions.	Individual participation may be affected by group composition. Also offers feedback to trainer on learning achievement. Promotes group cohesion.
Distance education (DE) A well-known term, which has been used for many years to describe courses offered at a distance from the training/ education provider. They nowadays often make use of information and communication technology (ICT).	Involves creating a planned learning experience that will take place away from the provider. It may demand particular course designs, utilize a variety of communication methods, and require special organizational and administrative arrangements.	Particularly associated with course delivery environments that are not wholly provided using traditional face-to-face courses. Thus, it enables access to education for those unable to attend conventional courses.
Exercise Carrying out a particular task along prescribed lines. Often a test of knowledge earlier communicated.	Exercise must relate to the working environment, with attainable objectives. Some form of assessment can give an idea of how much has been learned by the end-user.	Highly active form of learning; satisfies needs for practice to apply knowledge or develop skill. Testing gives confidence.
Experiential learning This, as described by Kolb, is a cyclical process whereby learners first gain experience then reflect on it. Hopefully, new insights or learning emerge from this that can be reapplied.	This type of learning begins with a concrete experience, followed by reflection, which is then related to existing theory, and finally a reformulated hypothesis is tested in a new situation.	Individuals carry out tasks and then in small groups describe and recall their 'experiences' at the level of relationships, emotions and feelings. New ideas emerge that can be tested in other environments.
Films and videos 'Visual lectures' that are often presented in dramatized form. Bespoke products can be expensive although off-the-shelf products (eg, Open University or other mass-produced videos) can be cheaper and of high quality.	Care needed to ensure material (not just title) is relevant. Useful as a precursor to discussion; can be 'stopped' at key points for discussion.	As 'Lectures' – but addition of moving images and drama can significantly aid motivation. Possible to relate to relevant situation.

Table 17.2 *continued*

	Trainer's perspective	Trainees' perspective
Fish bowl exercises Particularly useful in behavioural exercises and analysis. An inner circle of people doing the task are observed by an outer circle – hence the term 'fish bowl'. Outer circle take no part in the actual activity but merely observe and analyse. Inner and outer circle then swap.	Can be set up to allow one group to demonstrate, or to allow practice to occur while other look on and learn through observation. Useful to allow trainer to focus on a small group while others observe. More effective when the inner group are unaware of what the outer group are looking for.	Allow observational skills to develop. Good to sit out for a while. If in inner circle, can feel under pressure.
Instruction Formula-based 'teaching' session: 1 Tell – how to do. 2 Show – how to do. 3 Do (supervised practice). 4 Review process and results.	For introducing skills, usually in line with a planned breakdown of small sequential practice stages. Skill may be best addressed as a whole, rather than in parts, but lengthy stages 1 and 2 yield memory problems. Typically, follows some other form of training, the skills to be learned being those of application.	Design/balance of session important. Confidence is built by mastery and link-up of stages. Provides a vehicle for feedback to instructor. Time constraints can be eliminated with reference to the learning process.
In-tray methods Often used in time management training. Uses a simulated in-tray with a just a few or many tasks, and the participant has to order tasks, allocate times, and explain reasoning behind decisions. After such exercises the results are analysed and discussed.	Requires very careful planning and thought. Appraisal can be time-consuming. Can be complex or simple, low theoretical base and very practical.	Participant has to decide priorities, make decisions, read items, decide which to delegate, interpret and carry out sets of instructions, all with interruptions and other distractions. Very participant-centred, with high levels of transfer.
Language laboratory Individual booths equipped with audio programmes and linked to a central tutor.	Allows learner-paced language tuition and practice, without 'speaking in public'. Machine management seems to promote motivation.	Good for early stages but cannot replace eventual need to practise in public. Gives confidence to individual learners as the embarrassment factor is less apparent.

Table 17.2 *continued*

	Trainer's perspective	Trainees' perspective
Lecture Structured, planned talk. Usually accompanied by visual aids, eg, overhead projector slides (OHPs), PowerPoint slides, flip chart.	Suitable for large audiences where participation is not needed. Content and timing can be planned in detail. However, audience input should be considered in the form of seminars.	A lively style is needed. Communication of material may be limited if no provision of feedback to lecturer. Unless structure is carefully planned and is animated, audience will tend to lose concentration.
Multimedia and video conferencing Although hardware and software can still be expensive, this allows contact between distributed sites where distance makes travel time and cost prohibitive.	CBT and video can be combined in multimedia programmes, which can offer both information, and practice in using the information to specific ends, eg, problem-solving.	Allows two-way interactive communication sessions between people who are not able to meet in the same location.
Networked learning A broad term that means learning through the medium of ICT.	Allows learners and facilitators to interact through ICT and offers opportunities to apply new pedagogies.	Focuses on information literacy and prepares individuals for lifelong learning through the medium of ICT.
Open forum Panel of experts. More balanced answers are forthcoming if the questions are seen beforehand.	Allows a team of expert people to support the learning, and enables a degree of free flow of questioning. With themed questions, momentum can be generated. List of questions can be built over a period of time in training sessions to put to an invited panel.	Allows participants access to outside experts as well as trainers and colleague expertise. Can deflect difficult questions away from trainers and facilitators.
Open learning Can be described as courses and training schemes that are intended to meet the individual educational needs of learners.	Focuses on providing wider access to educational opportunities, and can be defined as a learner-centred philosophy.	For participants, open learning makes access to education more flexible, and also provides a more equitable learning experience, ie, learners decide what, where, when and how to learn.

Table 17.2 *continued*

	Trainer's perspective	Trainees' perspective
Outdoor development programmes Dynamic open-air exercises that are usually carried out in teams. Traditionally composed of recreation pursuits; now markets are demanding new approaches such as real community or environmental projects as opposed to planks and drums.	Offers practice in management, in challenging circumstances. Also used to develop teamwork, communication and leadership, as well as self-analysis.	Physical challenge may be deselecting if tough. Some learners may not accept relevance of physical environment. Importance of teamwork often learned in such programmes.
Problem-based learning (PBL) Provides a stimulus for learning based on messy, complex real-world problems.	Challenges learners to increase skills for effective critical thinking and problem-solving.	Learners need to integrate and organize acquired knowledge to ensure its recall and use to solve future problems.
Project-based learning 'Large scale exercise', but leaving most of the process within learner discretion. Frequently involves collecting and reporting data, then offering conclusions and recommendations for improvement.	Like exercises, needs realism and attainability. If 'real life', must have support of those responsible for reality. Ideally recommendations will be 'actioned'.	Like exercises offers practice and simultaneously 'tests'. Stimulates analysis and creativity as well as reporting skills.
Prompt list List of 'questions to which a person should have answers'.	Can highlight interpersonal differences in terms of values – and hence stimulate debate. Can be used in conjunction with 'Exercise' category in form of assessment.	Good as a form of non-directed learning. Can give a good idea of how much the end-user has learned when used with some form of assessment.
Radio and television broadcasts Often linked with national courses and qualifications (eg, Open University).	Large potential audiences permit costly programmes. Satellite TV is likely to offer new and wider subjects.	Viewing times often unsociable but use of video equipment can overcome this. Can be linked to tutorial assistance by phone.
Real play Real-play actors can be used to display difficult employee behaviours or techniques of good management behaviour to help develop coaching and appraisal skills. [http://www.dramafortraining.com/how/workshops.htm]	Once briefed by the trainer, actors take on the full characteristics of the role to be demonstrated. Having undertaken theatre training enables actors to imitate particular personalities and behaviours and sustain a role far longer than a delegate role-player might be able to.	Familiar participant discomfort caused by role-playing is minimized by use of real-players. Real-playing actors can demonstrate awkward and strange customer behaviours, allowing reflective responses in customer-facing situations.

Table 17.2 *continued*

	Trainer's perspective	Trainees' perspective
Role-play Enactment of role(s) in protected environment. Participants are asked to suspend self-reality and adopt other roles.	Mainly used to practise face-to-face skills (eg, selling) combined with review critiques from trainers and/or other learners.	Unless disciplined, can cause embarrassment. Degree of reality of design is an important factor for participants. Can be good for video feedback.
Role reversal Enactment of reversed roles by two or more learners in simulated situation.	Mainly used to help those who operate in face-to-face situations to appreciate their contacts' needs and feelings.	As with role-play, needs discipline and realism.
Self-managed learning Learner-paced coverage of printed material, often augmented by audio and/or video tapes.	Can be implemented either with or without a basic learning plan. Knowledge retention can be good if learner motivation is high.	Motivation often declines if learning material is difficult or 'dull'. Tutorial help can be important.
Simulations Any large simulation exercise that attempts to represent a high degree of reality, often also termed business or management 'games'. Games often have rules, players and are competitive.	Need to be careful about possible unexpected outcomes due to the levels of reality in the simulation. High levels of . planning and preparation needed. Useful as an exercise towards the end of a programme to consolidate practice of previous narrow skills, thus developing complex high-level skills.	Permits more complex scenarios to develop that are close to real life, yet allows participants to practise and make mistakes in a safe environment. Can enable participants to generate a high degree of interdependence.
Study groups Task-briefed groups that also practise process review, aided by a process consultant, who does *not* operate outside this role.	Offers appreciation of need for both task and process management; also group learning processes.	Some learners dislike lack of structure. May generate stress.
Syndicate Larger tasks and exercises involving planning and preparation. Divides the main group into smaller groups with separate rooms. Groups are asked to discuss tasks and solve or identify a specific problem. Followed by a review.	Allow group sharing, exchange and support. Provides an opportunity for more in-depth work than buzz groups. There is greater opportunity for quieter members to contribute over time.	Allows group to develop its strength and identity due to larger complex project.

Table 17.2 *continued*

	Trainer's perspective	Trainees' perspective
T-group training 'T' stands for training. A form of process sensitivity training. No tasks are set and the group is required to examine and discuss the ongoing process within itself.	This is not an easy option! Requires trainers to face anxiety of not knowing or offering expertise or to be the expert.	Can be frustrating but is worth working through – very rewarding.
Virtual learning environment (VLE) Can be used to replace or supplement conventional classrooms, enabling learning to take place over the internet with different levels of face-to-face contact.	Can be used to run individualized, self-directed as well as interactive course components, but design needs care to match the needs of the students.	Learners are, to varying extents, able to undertake learning activities at convenient times and at their own pace.
Virtual reality training Enables creation of a simulated environment for training purposes.	Technological advances and reduced costs of processing power have allowed VR developments to become more cost-effective.	Users can learn by experience and 'explore' the environment they are trying to learn about without risk to health or safety, but feel reassured that making mistakes will not be costly.
Web-based learning Learning via the internet and the World Wide Web (WWW) – now a widely available resource. Although hardware and software has come down in price, connection fees and associated running costs (monthly fee to service provider and phone bill) should be considered.	Extensive research should be carried out to find appropriate websites. Evaluation of learning objectives should also be carried out. Codes of practice can be drawn up to discourage downloading of inappropriate information.	Allows users to learn at their own pace and in their own time. Exciting way to learn as the resources are extensive and tend to present information in a clear manner. However, internet information sources are not always reliable and should be verified before use.

Source: Maggie McPherson and Colin Beard

Bibliography

Ausserhofer, A (1999) 'Web based teaching and learning, a panacea?', *IEEE Communications Magazine*, **37**, 3

Benjamin, A (1994) 'Affordable, restructured education: a solution through information technology', *RSA Journal*, May, pp 45–49

Bowskill, N (1998) 'Networked learning: a review paper', in P Levy *et al* (eds), *NetLinkS Report* [Online] http://netways.shef.ac.uk/rbase/reports/chapter.htm (accessed 14 March 2003)

Capuano, N, Gaeta, M and Pappacena L (2003) 'An e-learning platform for SME manager upgrade and its evolution toward a distributed training environment', in *Proceedings of the 2nd International LeGE-WG Workshop on E-Learning and Grid Technologies: A Fundamental Challenge for Europe*, Paris, 3–4 March 2003

Cognition and Technology Group at Vanderbilt University (1991) 'Technology and the design of generative learning environments', in T Duffy and D Jonassen (eds), *Constructivism and the Technology of Instruction: A conversation*, New Jersey, Lawrence Erlbaum Associates, pp 77–89

Daniel, J (1998) 'Can you get my hard nose in focus? Universities, mass education and appropriate technology', in M Eisenstadt and T Vincent (eds), *The Knowledge Web: Learning and collaborating on the net*, London, Kogan Page

Davies, T (2003) 'Some personal thoughts from a "traditional" academic moving towards e-learning', [Online] http://elearningeuropa.info/doc.php?lng=1&id=1159&doclng=1 (accessed 3 September 2004)

DfES (Department of Education and Skills) (2003) *Towards a Unified E-Learning Strategy: Consultation Document*, London, DfES [Online] http://www.dfes.gov.uk/elearningstrategy/elearning.stm (accessed 28 August 2003)

DfES (2004) *Progress towards a Unified E-Learning Strategy*, London, DfES [Online] http://www.dfes.gov.uk/elearningstrategy/online.cfm (accessed 15 December 2004)

Economist Global Executive (2003) 'Lessons from afar', Economist Education Outlook, *Economist*, 8 May [Online] http://www.economist.com/globalExecutive/Education/executive/printerFriendly.cfm?story_id=1762562 (accessed 15 November 2003)

Eisenstadt, M and Vincent, T (eds) (1998) *The Knowledge Web: Learning and collaborating on the net*, London, Kogan Page

French, D (1999) 'Preparing for internet-based learning', in D French, C Hale, C Johnson and G Farr (eds), *Internet Based Learning: An introduction and framework for higher education and business*, London, Kogan Page

Heinich, R, Molenda, M, Russell, J D and Smaldino, S E (1996) *Instruction, Media and Technologies for Learning*, 5th edn, Englewood Cliffs, NJ, Prentice Hall

Igonor, A (2002) 'Success factors for development of knowledge management in e-learning in Gulf region institutions', *Journal of Knowledge Management Practice*, **3**

Kakabadse, A and Korac-Kakabadse, N (2000) 'Leading the pack: future role of IS/IT professionals', *Journal of Management Development*, **19**, 2, pp 97–155

Kapenieks, A, Zuga, B, Buligina, I, Gercane, L, Kulitane, I, Vucena, A, Rudzite, M and Trapenciere, I (2004) 'Innovative e-learning in regional development projects in Latvia', Report prepared within EU 5th Framework programme project Higher Education Reform Network (HERN), Seminar in Glasgow 'Key Features of Teaching and Learning in the University of Learning', 21–24 January 2004, Continuing Education Development Foundation, Latvia

McPherson, M A (2003) 'Planning for success in elearning in HE: a strategic view', in F Jakab and A Čižmár (eds), *Proceedings of the 2nd International Conference on Emerging Telecommunications Technologies and Applications and the 4th Conference on Virtual University (ICETA 2003)*, 11–13 September 2003, Košice, Slovak Republic, pp 449–52

McPherson, M A and Nunes, J M (2004) *Developing Innovation in Online Learning: An action research framework*, London, RoutledgeFalmer

McPherson, M A, Nunes, J M and Zafeiriou, G (2003) 'New tutoring skills for online learning: are e-tutors adequately prepared for e-learning delivery?', in A Szücs, E Wagner and C Tsolkidis (eds), *Proceedings of 12th European Distance Education Network Annual Conference on The Quality Dialogue; Integrating Quality Cultures in Flexible, Distance and eLearning (EDEN 2003), 15–18 June 2003, Rodos Palace Hotel, Rhodes, Greece*, pp 347–50

Moore, M (1993) 'Three types of interaction', in K Harry, M John and D Keegan (eds), *Distance Education: New perspectives*, London, Routledge

Nunes, J M (1999) *The Experiential Dual Layer Model (EDLM): A Conceptual Model Integrating a Constructivist Theoretical Approach to Academic Learning with the Process of Hypermedia Design*, PhD thesis, University of Sheffield

Nunes, J M and Fowell, S P (1996) 'Hypermedia as an experiential learning tool: a theoretical model', *Information Research*, **2**, 1, August [Online] http://informationr.net/ir/2–1/paper12.html (accessed 15 November 2003)

Nunes, J M and McPherson, M A (2003) 'Using an educational systems design (ESD) framework to support action research in continuing professional distance education', *Journal of Computer Assisted Learning*, **19**, 4, pp 429–37

Nunes, J M, McPherson, M A and Rico, M (2000) 'Design and development of a networked learning skills module for web-based collaborative distance learning', in *Proceedings of 1st ODL International Workshop, 2000, Universidad Politécnica de Valencia, Centro de Formación de Postgrado, Valencia, Spain, 19–21 July 2000*, pp 117–31

Parkin, G (2001) 'How do success factors for e-learning differ from success factors for classroom training?', *Learning Circuits*, November [Online] http://www.learningcircuits.org/2001/nov2001/geek2.html (accessed 17 August 2004)

Reeves, T and Hedberg, J (2003) *Interactive Learning Systems Evaluation*, Englewood Cliffs, NJ, Educational Technology Publications

Salmon, G (2000) *E-Moderating: The key to teaching and learning online*. London, Kogan Page

Smith, A (1997) *Human Computer Factors: A study of users and information systems*, London, McGraw-Hill

Stamatis, D, Kefalas, P and Kargidis, T (1999) 'A multi-agent framework to assist networked learning', *Journal of Computer Assisted Learning*, **15**, 3, pp 201–10

Taraman, S R (2004) 'An innovative e-learning approach for design education', *Proceedings of the 2004 International Conference on Engineering Education (ICEE): Global Excellence in Engineering Education*, October 17–21 2004, University of Florida, Gainesville, Florida.

Van Brakel, P (1999) 'Teaching information management via a web-based course', *Electronic Library*, **17**, 6, December, pp 389–94

18

The Design of Effective Group-based Training Methods

Colin Beard

INTRODUCTION AND LEARNING OBJECTIVES

In this chapter we will focus on the design, selection and use of group-based participative training methods that could be used in the *delivery* of traditional group-based training courses. The chapter will examine the definition of the frequently used term 'training methods' and explain the contextual setting of training methods with regard to their fit with learning objectives and teaching strategies. We will also examine the use of particular training techniques and the creative use of materials.

By *method* we simply mean *a known approach or procedure; an acknowledged practice by trainers as a way of teaching or promoting learning*. The term 'method' represents the basic 'how to' level of training as a sub-component of the learning objectives; method also embraces the use of *techniques* and *materials* (see Table 18.1). For example, a case study is often described as a training 'method', but within such a method, trainers can use 'techniques ' such as energizers, or hooks. While there is no hard and fast dividing line it is useful to recognize the sequencing as shown from left to right in Table 18.1.

Table 18.1 Methods as a basic teaching process

1. Examine learning needs of group, individuals, organization	2. Write learning objectives	3. Consider learner profiles and design approach strategies	4. Select methods	5. Design techniques	6. Prepare materials
	or performance criteria	Trainer-centred	Case study	Icebreakers	Envelopes
	or learning outcomes	Learner-centred	Buzz groups	Energizers	Masking tape
		Consider planned and emergent leaders	Syndicate	Dice games	Washable cards
		Consider needs of activist, pragmatist, reflector and theorist	Lecture	Attitude scales	Layered flip charts
			Film clip analysis	Role hats	Coloured pins
			Fish bowl	Deconstructing skills	Video cases
			Action maze	Closers	Post-it labels
			Outdoor management development	Road show	
			Coffee and papers	Marketplace	
				Card games	
				Score cards	

Having read this chapter you will:

- understand the principles upon which to select training methods;
- understand the necessity for sequencing and pacing training;
- be able to use an 11-point checklist for considering selection and design of training methods; and
- be aware of the stages of group development.

GROUP TRAINING METHODS

Underpinning trainer attitudes, knowledge and skills

The trainer role can be conducted by a manager, supervisor, specialist facilitator or developer and by 'role' we mean the part they play. This important role can involve the writing of training strategies and policy, design and production, delivery, and evaluation of learning programmes. For the purpose of this chapter we are going to concentrate on the delivery role.

One of the secrets to good training delivery lies with the tools the trainer uses – *the training methods*. Poor trainers can be patronizing and performance becomes an exaggerated ego trip; others can be clock-watchers, bored with doing the job. Rae (1995:xxv) refers to trainer types and trainer roles and offers a trainer grid using the three axes of teaching skills, concern and competence. This results in a complete range of trainer types from professional trainer, humble expert to endearing bumbler and arrogant charlatan! But good trainers cannot only communicate and impart knowledge; they can motivate, help people to learn, spark innovation and creativity and promote a hunger to learn. They should be open-minded and in touch with their own emotions, while letting participants explore, analyse and question within a 'safe learning environment'. Most importantly trainers manage the learning content and the learning process and so should be good questioners, careful listeners and observationally astute.

The choice and appropriate use of any training method will clearly be influenced and underpinned by the knowledge and skill of the trainer. Understanding many of the underlying theoretical concepts will help with the selection, design and use of training methods, for example:

- balancing participant challenge and support (Raw, 1991)
- learning cycle (Kolb, 1984)
- learning styles (Honey and Mumford, 1982)
- planned or emergent learning (Megginson, 1994)
- neuro-linguistic programming (Bandler and Grinder, 1975)
- reality (Binstead and Stuart, 1979)
- scheduling, sequencing and group dynamics (Randall and Southgate, 1980)

- serialists and holists (Phillips and Pugh, 1994)
- tutor dependency (Adler, 1975)
- understanding the role of emotion in learning (Fineman, 1997)
- multiple intelligence (MI) (Gardner, 1983)
- experiential learning (Beard and Wilson, 2002).

Challenging ideas can be found in this book and elsewhere about how training specialists can facilitate and support learning rather than just teaching it. These ideas have led to a fundamental questioning of some training, particularly that which is based on participant passivity, tutor dependency and over-simplified ideas of how humans behave at work. Controversial statements made back in the 1950s by Rogers (1993:302–3) often continue to stimulate us to challenge our own assumptions:

> It seems to me that anything that can be taught to another is relatively inconsequential and has little or no significant influence on behaviour. ... I find that one of the best but most difficult ways for me to learn is to drop my own defensiveness, at least temporarily, and to try to understand the way in which this experience seems and feels to the other person. ... I find that another way of learning for me is to state my own uncertainties, to try to clarify my puzzlement, and thus get closer to the meaning that my experience actually seems to have.

It is within this context that trainers continue to reflect upon their own practice, continue to read and study, and generally engage in the lifelong learning process. All trainers have their own delivery style, which is underpinned by their own values and beliefs about learning. These values and beliefs are often displayed through their voice and in their body language. But whatever the trainer style or role, it is the knowledge and understanding of the needs, wishes and experiences of the learners that is perhaps most central to the art of good training.

Many trainers use methods with which they are familiar, but in this chapter we aim to encourage you to try out your own new and original methods that will effectively support the transfer of knowledge, skills and attitudes to participants. This is often more satisfactory than relying on 'pre-packaged' activities; any one 'method' should not be seen as a quick-fix 'solution' to a particular training 'problem'. Flexibility is required in training and development. Those participants who arrive for their 'injection of solutions' are also not taking sufficient responsibility for their development. Designing stimulating and effective programmes, often under constraints of time, money or resources, is not easy. It is important for you as a trainer to be clear about the limits of your skills: some techniques do demand a high level of competence if they are to be used effectively and safely. It is for this reason that some techniques should perhaps carry a 'training health warning'. The CIPD (1998:1) for example has produced a 'Guide to Outdoor Training' because of concerns that if this 'method is not used carefully the results can be damaging to some employees – and hence their employers – with the accompanying risk of litigation'. This chapter aims to help trainers to become aware of the diverse range of training methods that currently exist, or that can be created by careful design.

SELECTING METHODS

Many textbooks on training methods have a section on choice and selection but rarely offer any substantive advice. There are actually few good guiding rules and so any advice usually discusses the basic variables that influence choice such as levels of understanding, objectives, time available and so on. The 'best fit' is likely to be chosen in the light of these factors, but the flow or sequence of the whole event is also a very important guide to selection.

The programme or course has a beginning, a middle and an end. The scene-setting often determines the relationship of the trainer and the participants, and thus influences what people will and will not be willing to do later on. Managing the emotional climate requires a great deal of skill (Mortiboys, 2002). The gradual building up of energy and inquisitiveness is a essential group process that influences method selection. The dynamics of individual and group development will need to be understood by trainers; for instance, Tuckman and Jenson's (1977) stages of group development: forming, storming, norming and performing. Understanding this learner dynamic is a key skill in trainer development. Balancing the control of what is learned, how it is learned, when, and where it is done can be subtly shifted so that greater control is given to the learner towards the middle or end of courses or programmes by the careful selection of the methods.

The characteristics of the training population will clearly influence the design process, and there are a number of basic matters that need to be considered early on. Getting hold of any training needs analysis (TNA) information is very important, and will inform the writing of the programme aims and objectives. It is essential to ensure, early on in the process, that a 'training solution' is appropriate. Learning outcomes, training objectives and performance criteria all have to be discussed and agreed by key stakeholders. They not only provide direction and focus for the training but they also set standards. In turn the objectives, learning outcomes or performance criteria will influence the choice of methods. Aims and objectives should be clearly defined and understood. It is really a joint process with the training designers and those requesting or purchasing the course or programme. The time available for the course or programme will also influence method selection. There is rarely enough time to cover everything that trainers want or need to cover, but it is very important not to over- or underestimate the amount of material that can be covered in the time slot.

Some methods will require the availability of more tutors, and tutor ratios and gender mix are generally important considerations in the delivery of training. Teams of tutors need to plan the mix of female–male where possible unless circumstances dictate otherwise. A ratio of one tutor to four trainees is recommended in the excellent *Training Skills for Women* produced by the Commonwealth Secretariat in 1984. In our experience numbers as high as 12 can be easily accommodated in some courses but discussion in such situations needs very skilled trainers to sense many of the needs of participants. Another rule of thumb is that often a minimum of one day of design and planning is needed for each day of training. Some trainers suggest there should be a ratio of 5:1 preparation time versus delivery time.

When delivering training programmes to groups of people the layout of the room and the vertical and horizontal closeness of the trainer in relation to the participants are vital factors in group dynamics. Standing up in front of the seated group means the trainer is positioned higher and apart, thus horizontally and vertically 'distanced'. This can be counter-productive if in-depth group discussion is needed. Good physical learning environments enable people and information to move around the room in a flexible way.

The group culture should also be considered. In our travels around the world we have found that in parts of Asia there is a reluctance to be critical, while people in Prague told us that the older generations have been used to suppressing their emotions. The increasing internationalization of training programmes means that we all need to consider our audience very carefully. Trainers and developers can use international assignments to help to understand the broad range of cultural issues that will influence design and the selection of methods. Some people also suggest that senior managers, for example, do not want too much of 'that participative stuff'. However, when such sessions are carefully planned managers are easily encouraged to participate in productive process work. On one occasion, we remember well-dressed, very senior people willingly falling to their hands and knees to reorganize our masking tape version of their organizational management matrix, which had been designed on the carpet! Age, experience, group homogeneity, and many other factors are clearly going to influence the selection and design of methods.

In these days of pressure to demonstrate good returns on training investment we must be very careful about our choice of resources. Buying in expensive materials as we shall see later is not always an effective way to proceed. It is also important to avoid over-concern with your available 'resources' too early in the design or selection of training methods. In the past some outdoor providers have provided management activities based on the recreational skills of their instructors and the materials and resources available, such as canoes, ropes and rafts. Many trainers admit to cobbling together a programme using a combination of challenging tasks and activities, using existing resources in exciting locations, and these, mixed with good facilitation skills, can sometimes produce memorable development events. However, sometimes this is by luck rather than design and with repetition these can become less fulfilling – when this happens it is the time to take a fresh look at method design. The essential ingredients that give rise to successful courses or programmes should be a matter of great research interest to any good trainer.

Some methods will be more appropriate for the development of skill formation; knowledge acquisition; the changing of individual attitudes; and the broader company culture (psychomotor, cognitive or affective learning domains – Bloom *et al*, 1956). Lecture methods can quickly convey information as well as concepts and models. It is clear that teaching our children to swim is best carried out in a swimming pool: watching a video can have limitations. But leaving our children to their own devices, allowing learning of swimming through exploration and discovery would not be a good idea. The teaching of trampolining is now carefully designed so that individual moves are broken down into their basic constituent parts or building blocks, so that they can be tried before building the whole move. This idea of *deconstructing* basic skills or knowledge can help with the design and selection of methods, an idea that is further explored in the examples below.

'Experiential' learning could be said to be using the old adage 'I hear, I forget; I see, I remember; I do, I understand', which is a simple version of Dewey's concept of experiential learning (Dewey, 1938). But in the process of designing 'doing' methods we can move through different levels of reality and simulation. It may not always be feasible to use the 'real thing'. Van Matre (1979) has for many years helped children to understand photosynthesis by getting them inside a leaf-shaped tent, with ping-pong balls as cells so that they can manufacture sugars. The principles are easy to grasp and the experience often memorable. For a more advanced approach to experiential training and development see Beard and Wilson (2002).

'I do, I understand' should be considered with caution, for example in the training of tree-felling – it is dangerous for both the tutor and the trainee. This *can* be taught indoors first, using methods to gain basic narrow skills and to test understanding before trying the real thing with gradually increased levels of risk. Flying aeroplanes and coping with emergencies, for example, are taught using 'simulation'. How else would you teach people such as fire-fighters to perform their duties in large-scale disasters?

There are also times when participation is not the best method, such as when the information to be learned is highly technical or when information has to be put across very quickly. Much of the computer skills training that takes place today is available on the computer itself in step-by-step, on-screen programmes. Sequences and offering feedback at intervals are crucial. The reading of the manual in this case is no longer an easy and efficient way to learn.

Design checklists can be used to get started and to set the selection of methods within the broader context. The following is an 11-point simple checklist for consideration in the selection and design of training methods:

1. Consider carefully all the information from any assessment of training needs.
2. Examine in detail the aims and objectives – break them down into their constituent parts. Ask, 'What do people need to be able to do or know by the end of the course?'
3. Decide on specific content – and themes.
4. Consider any constraints and opportunities and make it *in keeping* with the group.
5. Consider the creation a of good learning atmosphere – the physical and psychological space.
6. Choose, modify or create learning methods.
7. Organize and check the sequence of all the methods/activities.
8. Consider all the things that might go wrong or not work and plan for contingencies.
9. Consider methods that help the programme review, and support the transfer of learning.
10. Evaluate everything – make notes on your laptop about training methods improvements while they are fresh in your mind.
11. Feedback into future course design.

Beard and Wilson (see Chapter 11) offer a much more complex 'Learning Combination Lock' as a more advanced approach. There are of course a whole range of learning methods and techniques based on the basic learning process of trial and error, observation, thinking, conceptualizing and imitation. These might include lectures, demonstrations, instruction, tutor-guided experience, case studies, role-play, simulations, guided experiment, problem-solving exercises and learner-directed enquiry. Table 18.1 at the beginning of this chapter illustrates a range of training methods and techniques. If possible, consider taking a degree of risk and break out of your own comfort zone and design new methods to meet the very specific needs of the people you are working with, thus avoiding the over-use of set materials taken off the shelf. While a disciplined approach, using well-known underlying principles, is essential in the delivery of training, the introduction of elements of creativity and originality to the design of training methods can produce events that will maximize participant learning; and they can create opportunities to help people unlearn old habits too! Some flexibility is needed: an ability to vary delivery according to people's needs and the ability to change methods as and when required allow trainers to be sensitive, thus responding to participant signals.

Sequencing and pacing

A useful framework to use in the analysis of the sequence of methods chosen is a modified version of an outdoor management development evaluation framework offered by Dainty and Lucas (1992). On the vertical axis in Figure 18.1, the task structure is 'tight' when the skill is very specific such as rope or knot work or abseiling, and it is 'loose' when the task is broad and less structured, such as a rescue exercise. Low process intensity occurs when there is a low personal focus, where self-reflection and feedback remain low. The opposite end of the lower axis involves methods where the opposite is the case and considerable self or group reflection and discussion take place. This creates a potential generic design for the learner 'journey'.

The framework thus suggests that appropriate methods are needed for each quadrant: also that the methods, in many courses, actually move through the sequence from quadrants one to four. For example, in a negotiating course the trainer might use relaxing exercises to start such as icebreakers, followed by focused skills analysis such as listening, paraphrasing or questioning, followed by tactics such as opening and closing, eventually aggregating these skills and proceeding on to broad negotiation skills. The course might then continue to look at the

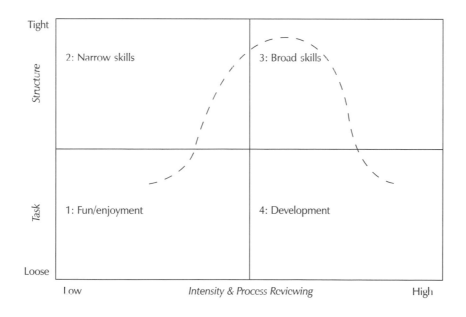

Figure 18.1 Design and sequencing of training methods: the learner journey

personal development aspects of the learning that has taken place, focusing more deeply on process work, and so on. The case study on negotiating public access to the countryside below illustrates one example of how to use this sequencing model.

The following is an activity design checklist that can help trainers to achieve correct sequencing. Decide when to choose methods that:

- set the scene and establish climate;
- start from participant levels of skill, knowledge and attitudes;
- introduce subsidiary essential skills and knowledge;
- allow regular practice after input;
- allow student-directed enquiry and study;
- regularly review the key learning or principles;
- introduce composite/complex skills and knowledge;
- relate/apply the learning to other situations and focus on transfer.

Sequencing and pacing are also considered in Tracey (1992), and Cornell's 'flow learning' (1989) allows training methods to build up group energy:

1. *Awaken participant enthusiasm* – use activities that induce playfulness and alertness.
2. *Focus participant attention* – use activities that focus the enthusiasm developed in stage 1 in ways that help prepare for the experience, absorption and exploration in stage 3.
3. *Direct participant experience* – use activities that allow opportunities for absorption and personal discovery.
4. *Share participant inspiration* – use activities that reinforce and congratulate new awareness and learning, and inspire further action.

Other patterns to consider are those of participant energy levels that are often familiar to experienced trainers. Waves of activity and participation energy are often interspersed with lulls; understanding these can be helpful for both the learner and the trainer. No one can operate at full speed all the time. After lunch, for example, is a time when the lecture method is unlikely to be productive. Trainers also learn to predict the ebb and flow of participants over, say, a week-long event, and some even have explicit 'temperature charts' for people to fill in during the course of the week to write notes on personal or group energy levels. It can then be considered acceptable to have low and high points. Mortlock (1987) talks of *Adventure Waves* where adventurous periods are followed by a time for reviewing and briefing before the next wave. This same pattern can equally be applied to intellectual stimulation, practical work and group energy levels; thus trainers need to be able to read the group energy levels and create or influence the course rhythm. Pace-changing methods are therefore very important. Good trainers will try to get everyone to catch a wave! Rodwell (1994) outlines a range of 'icebreakers' 'energizers' and 'closers'.

Another dimension which trainers should consider when selecting and sequencing training methods is the degree to which reality is introduced into the training methods. The sequencing of simulation or real scenarios is a skill to develop. Some 25 years ago Binstead and Stuart (1979) explored the role and use of 'reality' strategies in learning. They suggest that if the participants see learning as having a high degree of reality to them or their work it will be approached more positively than low reality methods. But low reality strategies can be useful, allowing risk or experimentation by participants, as the scenarios are not perceived as real and thus are not threatening. Raising elements of reality towards the end of training sessions can also facilitate higher transfer of behaviours to the workplace environment. There are three elements of reality that Binstead and Stuart consider:

1. the *environment* in which the learning is located;
2. the extent of the reality of the *tasks* that have been designed; and
3. the extent to which the *processing* is real.

To illustrate this skill, the case study on negotiating access shows a practical example of how participant skills and knowledge can be gradually developed as the methods embrace greater elements of reality over time. The case study on negotiating not only illustrates some of these principles, but it also demonstrates how the level of reality can be altered at the sub-ingredient level, such as the people involved, the equipment used, the information, the rewards offered and the feedback techniques used. Binstead and Stuart did not consider these factors in their research.

NEGOTIATING PUBLIC ACCESS TO THE UK COUNTRYSIDE: SKILLS PRACTICE SECTION OF A THREE-DAY TRAINING COURSE

The early part of the course uses a 'narrow skills' practice (see the Dainty and Lucas framework). Here we deconstructed 'negotiating' into its many sub-skills such as influencing, questioning, persuasion, listening, tactics, entry, developing rapport, closing and so on. The latter part of the course used broad skills practice, but with varying levels of reality or simulation.

From low content reality ...

Exercise A: Redecorating the office

The material was taken from a standard loose-leaf package on negotiating. It is a paper exercise. There is no incentive. It concerns a contract price to decorate an office suite. Content reality is low. The written case material on decorating contains a review sheet that looks at the forces in use in negotiating and the approaches that can be used by the two sides. People are asked to identify opening gambits and write their answers on paper.

Exercise B: Driving a bargain

A written exercise about cars – people are told that this is a warm-up for a real car exercise when people can pit their wits against real negotiators! This adds to the incentive to concentrate on all exercises. Here the content reality is again low – these people do not negotiate car prices in their jobs.

Exercise C: Buying a new car

Real cars are used. Real log-books are used. Real car prices are offered. Car book prices are available. Cars can be inspected and faults found, both inside and outside, as they are located in the car park. The keys are made available. One vehicle is an uncleaned 4-wheel drive and the other is a nicely valeted VW Polo. The brief informs people that 'You have moved to the National Park and need a 4-wheel drive for bad weather and to tow your new caravan.' False money is used but a prize is offered. The people that the participants negotiate with are real, trained negotiators and they are located in an office where the deals will take place. Final agreements are written in sealed envelopes so that the winners can be decided later. Content reality is again low, process reality is high.

... to high content reality

Exercise D: Negotiating access to UK land on behalf of the public

Here we use high content reality and high process reality. Real negotiators are again present. Real information, eg, facts and figures on sheep headage payments, ranger support offered, wall damage payments, litter arrangements, is provided. Real participants are access officers or public rights-of-way officers. They are observed on video by the rest of the group. The incentive is to try to do a good job in front of their peers, to try to put all the skills and knowledge acquired on the course into practice and try to meet their own preset prices and subsidy targets decided in their negotiating plans. They argue their case with real negotiators and are debriefed afterwards. The video is then replayed with self and peer assessment taking place.

EMOTION AND LEARNING

The gradual shifting of the elements of reality requires careful attention. Over the last few years fire-fighters and other rescue services have had the benefit of using computer simulations, intelligent systems and virtual reality, which create emergency scenarios that are very close to reality thus enabling very exacting and demanding training to take place before participants enter the highly emotional reality of real emergency (see for example www.coltvr.com/vector).

Some training methods use drama therapy or theatrical style role-plays that also enable the balance of reality and simulation to be altered. One example is described in the UK CIPD journal, *People Management,* where the hypothetical and the actual became accidentally blurred for the Hereford Hospital Trust training programme (Merrick, 1998). Complex training programmes have also been recently designed to use methods of role-play and simulation to help the police and social workers deal more effectively with child abuse; but for some people the simulations can come too close to their own life experiences. Professional actors have often been brought in to ensure that their skilled abilities enhance the simulation while reducing the emotional risk to course participants. The design of training methods in emotionally laden areas or in the field of emergency service work is exacting and requires considerable trainer skill. Here we recommend a cautious approach.

Fascinating articles have appeared in journals (eg, Fineman, 1997) and in textbooks (Boler, 1999) addressing such areas as the role of emotion and risk in learning. Method selection sometimes needs to ensure that people are more in touch with their emotions so that they may learn more effectively. What and how learning takes place is clearly inextricably connected to participant motivations and emotions. Boler (1999) examines many of the ethical issues that arise in the training and development of 'emotional work', often found in the service industries. Alongside the dangers outlined above we now consider the role of fun, play, risk and emotion in the choice and design of learning methods.

Trainers do need to know when to encourage learners to 'let go' of their obsession with success, performance or grades, and when to enable learners to relax and make greater connections with their emotions and feelings. How many times have we failed in an interview because we were nervous, or not performed well in a sport because we were too tense, or not delivered a very good speech because we were not relaxed? How then do trainers connect participants to these feelings? It is certainly crucial for trainers to be in touch with their own emotions and feelings, and those of the people they are working with, whether it be anger, humour, anxiety and so on. Carefully designed methods can help to tune into these feelings when it is required or appropriate to do so.

Humour in learner–tutor correspondence on distance learning programmes also gives us ideas about how people are able to gently expose some of their true feelings about their work. The following extracts are interesting:

> This presentation is a vast improvement on your first assignment from which my optic nerves are still recovering. (Said my tutor on reading my second attempt, as a mature student, at using a draft standard dot-matrix printer some years ago.)

> Positively my last fling! You asked for 'lots of comments' – and I have surpassed myself and I am now off to immerse myself in an extremely large gin and tonic. Not to drown my sorrows but merely to recuperate. (Said my tutor on reading the last edition of my 'draft' dissertation!)

Some student humour during the stressful last leg in the period of doing a research dissertation in training and development:

> Would it be better to lump the data together? What do you think? Does it make sense? (Sounds like a song!) The razor blades are in a safe place (but I can't help noticing that length of rope in the garage!!!!) I will phone you soon for some quality psychotherapy. Regards …

P.S. someone told me you can buy these (dissertations) on the world-wide web?' (Extracts from a letter to me as a tutor, from a senior training and development officer at a major UK hospital studying for a Master's degree.)

Well, it's now 12.30 in the morning and I think I should go to bed. This has been a useful exercise for me, even if tedious for you. I look forward to any pearls of wisdom you may wish to cast in my direction. Goodnight! (A senior training manager, London Underground.)

Dear Colin, I have added to my draft in the past two weeks but still feel frustrated by a lack of real headway, combined with a growing feeling that I'm not really sure what I'm doing!! (Training Manager, Magistrates Courts.)

It can be important for participants to be in touch with these emotional responses and to pass on these stories and tales, and myths and legends to other students to set a positive agenda and culture for future groups. Mortiboys (2002) has produced an excellent guidance booklet for the 'Emotionally intelligent leader'. What role does emotion play in the development of innovation and risk-taking in learning for example? Raab (1997:161) from Melbourne University examines the anxiety problems that occur when the trainer avoids becoming the expert. In her article,'Becoming an expert in not knowing – reframing teacher as a consultant', she begins with a story that:

> alerts us to the terrible anxiety experienced by both clients and consultants (students and teachers) when forced to stay in the present and face their unknowingness. Traditional models of teaching operate without acknowledging the extent of this anxiety.

Working with difficult subjects

In the IPD's *People Management,* Pickard (1996:28) noted that, 'Innovation is experiencing a renaissance.' The article went on to comment that the UK Department of Trade and Industry has an Innovation Unit; there are now MBAs in innovation; two-thirds of secondary schools in Singapore teach 'constructive thinking'; and in New Zealand children as young as two are being taught to think creatively. Trainers can of course use training methods to create a climate of creativity, fun or play, thus generating risk-taking or innovation. The following are practical examples that highlight the use of creative training methods to teach difficult subjects.

CREATIVE TRAINING DESIGN: RESEARCH METHODOLOGY TRAINING

This method uses popular images or fictional characters to help participants to understand the complex world of 'research methodology'. Careful selection of popular images that are well known to most of the participants can be helpful: the use of Shakespearean quotations can sometimes be risky! Many learners have found that when embarking on a piece of research,

research methodology is difficult to understand. Thorpe and Moscarola (1991:127) in an article that inspired this experiment, comment that: 'they see research as following elaborate rules and procedures and see it as something that is both complex and difficult'.

I first tested out my new method with overseas students in Singapore. I was charged with delivering a session to Master's students who were human resource managers operating in Singapore, Malaysia and China. Methodology was full of academic, unknown language – deduction, validity, reliability, triangulation, ontology, epistemology, hermeneutics, ethnography – all very confusing.

Stage 1: Start with the known and the simple – and make it fun

The approach I have now developed involves starting from notions of four consulting role models – detective, doctor, travel agent and salesperson. The 'consulting styles' are described in Margerison (1988) who said that: 'We all have an approach to giving advice based upon a consulting model. It may not be written down, but it reflects itself in the way in which we consult and give advice.'

Having read about the four roles the key words associated with each are written out by participants on washable cards and then examined and discussed. Students describe how such people conduct their work as follows:

The medical analogy: the doctor

- client/organizational illness to be cured;
- looking for good/normal health, or unhealthy organization;
- symptoms;
- diagnosis;
- medicine is prescribed;
- operation – cut out unhealthy bit.

The travel agent

- assumes client is on a journey;
- go through their objectives and work out best way to destination;
- question-based – how much money are you going to spend?
- client-focused;
- suggest other destinations.

Stage 2: Engagement

Students then examine the four consulting styles and discuss their *own* consulting styles.

Stage 3: Take a step closer to the unknown – using popular fiction

Students then move on to focus on the art of detecting or *investigation* – investigation is essentially what research is about. They examine five detectives, described in Thorpe and Moscorola (1991): Hercule Poirot, Sherlock Holmes, Maigret, Columbo and Dirty Harry. All five detectives have their different approaches and the students relate well to 'research as detection'. This approach is, however, being supplemented as all the characters are male. Overseas students know a great deal about famous global detectives – for me the risk paid off. A profile is provided for each detective and key words are extracted based on their reading small profiles and their own knowledge:

- science and microscopes (Sherlock Holmes);
- proven fact;
- listens and tries to understand;
- prods and pushes (Dirty Harry);
- unconventional;
- deductive reasoning;
- chemical testing;
- facial observations (Columbo);
- intuition.

The creator of Sherlock Holmes was Sir Arthur Conan Doyle who studied medicine at Edinburgh University, where the methods of diagnosis of one of the professors are said to have provided the ideas for the methods of 'deduction' used by Holmes. Medicine and detectives had common links. All of these words associated with detecting can, with care, relate to recognized research perspectives. Research is a form of investigation.

Stage 4: Slowly move into the unknown: research perspectives and language

The participants then move on to consider two fictitious dissertations and the appropriate methods of investigation:

1. The effect of height on performance in high-rise towers in Singapore.
2. Myths and legends in training and development.

Participants compare the research approach for the two investigations. One clearly lends itself to quantitative studies, perhaps using scientific approaches, focusing on statistics, proof, evidence; has some degree of neutrality towards the research objects ... and so on. The other study is qualitative in nature, uses people's perception, attempts to describe and understand meaningful social action; is subjective, and where no group values are wrong ... many other key words are present on plastic cards and the group sort the words and allocate them to one or the other type of investigation.

Moving on from polarized dichotomies, students consider the complex mosaic of research perspectives. The methodology debate unfolds in front of the students without them realizing they have acquired some of the language of methodology. They argue and discuss the meaning of truth and the nature of what can be known or what is real.

Stage 5: Developing a kit

Eventually this was designed as a whole 'kit' involving a plastic briefcase, a video containing Dirty Harry and Poirot film extracts, pre-prepared instructions, washable cards – some blank and some with key words printed on them. Empty old video cases were used to house the sets of cards per kit. Labels were designed and printed on A4 paper to insert into the video cases. The principal journal articles were also included in the black plastic portfolio case.

Metaphors

> Once upon a time Martians and Venusians met, fell in love, and had happy relationships together because they respected and accepted their differences. Then they came to Earth and amnesia set in: they forgot they were from different planets. Using this metaphor to illustrate the commonly occurring conflicts between men and women, Dr. John Gray explains how these differences can come between the sexes and prohibit mutually fulfilling loving relationships.

This extract is from a popular book which hit the headlines in 1993. It was called *Men are from Mars – Women are from Venus*. In this classic case the metaphors of planets was used to convey meaning; to describe the reasoning behind the difference between men and women. Such metaphors provide another way of reflecting and focusing on particular experiences, and so allow us to gain new insights. A metaphor is a figure of speech. Something is spoken of as if it *is* something that it only resembles. A metaphor transfers meaning, and the word itself is derived from the Greek *meta* (trans) and *pherein* (to carry).

Beard and Wilson (2002), building on the work of Gass (1995), create six techniques that can be used by trainers.

Before the training activities

- *Prior* to the activity taking place the facilitator asks questions that focus the learning that might occur. The facilitator *directly frontloads* the experience.
- *Prior* to the activity the facilitator sets the scene or context of the activity, so as to *relate it* to the specific learning (that is, to the work conditions of participants, such as the problems of

loading in a warehouse environment, or the problems of the reception desk team). The facilitator *frames* the experience.

- *Prior* to the activity the facilitator might deliberately but indirectly make reference to fictitious events, to try to prevent certain behaviours occurring. For example, 'We had a group last week that did this and failed, because all the men put their "Mr. Fix-it hat" on and moved straight into solutions mode, preventing discussion from …' The facilitator can *indirectly frontload* the experience.

After the training activities

- *After* the activity the facilitator might not make any insightful comment about the experience. *The experience speaks for itself.*
- *After* the activity the facilitator might provide the group with feedback about their general behaviour, such as what they did well, what they might need to work on, or what they learned. *The facilitator speaks for the experience.*
- *After* the activity the facilitator might use questions to foster a group discussion about the activity. *The facilitator debriefs the experience.*
  (adapted from *Book of Metaphors*, Gass, 1995)

Frontloading, framing and other techniques can be developed much further, and can include appropriate famous film clips, video footage of previous groups, television soap extracts or cartoon images to send powerful messages. They often work well with young people. These media can reinforce key points, especially if they are seen as coming from other known or respected sources. Such media can be potent when the medium and message speak for themselves, thus providing excellent techniques that remove the scepticism associated with the facilitator who provides instant expert solutions. Beard and Rhodes (2002) have written on the use of newspapers and comic strips for adults and kids as reflective techniques. While picture-based metaphors help with a way of seeing, thought-based metaphors illustrate a way of thinking, sound metaphors guide a way of hearing, emotional metaphors access a way of feeling, and activity metaphors can illustrate a way of doing things.

Metaphors present for example a powerful tool to access and explore feelings, enabling entry into emotionally sensitive areas. Feelings about work are so often expressed in metaphorical terms. 'I am just a small cog in a big machine.' 'I'm in a new team creating a work of art!' Many of these techniques are discussed in detail in the book *The Power of Experiential Learning* (Beard and Wilson, 2002), and a key chapter for understanding metaphors is that on altering reality. The experience–person match is thus a complex process, and there are many methods to consider and choose from to help people interpret their experience. This imaginative use of myth, metaphor, allegory, fable and story to convey meaning is a key skill of good facilitators.

Corporate metaphors are likely to be different. Specialized high-rope courses are popular in many parts of the world, and the rope challenges can represent the challenges of real life. Cliffs can represent the challenges of a giant project or a daunting life change an individual might have to make. Benson (1987:204) suggests that instead of coming at problems from rational deliberation and logic, which can lead to protectionism and defence, metaphors can be more intuitive and spontaneous:

> Every method, exercise, or technique then as I use it, is a metaphor: a way of shifting perception and creating meaning. I am not interested in any medium or technique as an end in itself but as a means of engaging people and providing a context for work, which is directly related to the members' level of ability and willingness to act. From this perspective the value of any technique lies not in its skill or knowledge base but in what it points to, its ability to act as a signpost, open up dialogue, and encapsulate meaning.

Storytelling

Considerable skill is called for to develop good psychological settings for training and development programmes. Stories can be a good way to relax participants on a programme, and they can be told for many reasons, sometimes just for light relief. They can also re-engage people after lunch, for example. They are as important to adults as they are to children. I often like to tell stories when the mood is right; of the day I missed the helicopter for an interview on the Scilly Islands; the time when my frog died on me in my zoology exams and my subsequent failure to resuscitate it!

Storytelling has revived in popularity and many people have recently experienced the wonderful stories told by North American indigenous people now living in Britain. Stories and metaphors can also be used by trainers with a message to get across, and Parkin (1998) in her book on storytelling for trainers tells how they can be powerful training tools. Gathering groups of learners to tell stories and to find meaning in them is becoming an important tool in personal and organizational learning.

PLAY AND FUN

A storytelling approach to the *evaluation and review* of training methods is very easy to construct and has many applications. It consists of a booklet of strips of paper, cut from an A4 sheet that has typed statements on it. The strips are then stapled together to form a booklet. In pairs each partner reads out and finishes off the sentence with a personal comment and then passes it back to the other partner. It can be used for process work, and is good for personal development programmes. The statements could include:

The session I *enjoyed* most on this development programme was ...
The things that *stimulated me to learn more* were ...
The most *productive* ...
The positive part of *working as a team* on this assignment was when ...
The contribution *I valued most from you* as a group member was when ...
Something I *learned about myself* was ...

Good learner-centred reviewing techniques allow people to:

> express themselves and their experiences, examine issues and concerns, explore new ideas and thoughts, gain emotional understanding and enjoy themselves. (Greenaway, 1993:17)

PLAY AND FUN: COFFEE AND SUNDAY PAPERS – 'PLAYING WITH THE LITERATURE'

At a weekend at the residential training centre of the Department for Employment in the UK in April 1997, 30 mature students (who were training managers studying for a Master's degree in Education, Training and Development) were part of a very simple experiment. I decided to offer a session that was designed to allow students to *play* with their ideas and concepts following a period of quiet reading and sharing of thoughts over early morning coffee and biscuits. We used the idea of lounging about reading the Sunday papers – but used journal material from a range of well-known sources: *People Management, Management Learning, Management Education and Development, People and Organizations, Training and Development, Industrial and Commercial Training, Sloan Management Review, Harvard Business Review*, and many others. Included in the material were articles that encouraged students to be aware of themselves as learners or their uncritical reception of 'material', such as the article by Tony Watson (1996) on 'Motivation: that's Maslow, isn't it?' We were encouraging students to become more relaxed about the 'literature' associated with their subject, to encourage them to share, become fascinated, get copies of lots of material and communicate their findings to each other.

As a tutor I acted merely as a scribe and facilitator – letting go of my concerns about my expertise and as a result the sessions produced much debate. The evaluation of the session subsequently showed that students wanted more time in future to repeat such an exploration of a broad range of literature and to play with concepts and ideas in this way. This is of interest as participative techniques are often said to be very time-consuming and lack depth of content. This perhaps is a short-term view – depth and content have to be considered in relation to medium- and long-term student learning.

By 2004 this technique had been used all over the world, including trainers in China, students in Hong Kong and Singapore, engineers in Finland, and with 300 senior managers undertaking 'Organizational development' courses in the United Kingdom. The overwhelming response has been that the technique is powerful, especially the quiet time followed by the collaborate learning of chatting, telling, sharing, selling.

A funny video tape for seven-year-olds from the international children's store, the Early Learning Centre, was designed to improve counting skills. Children do the voices with wonderful effect. It is called *Cecil was a caterpillar*. Cecil grew and grew by two centimetres every time he ate a fellow caterpillar. He became enormous. But then he shrank to two centimetres – 'What have you done,' cried a girlfriend. 'I've been sick!' exclaimed Cecil. It seemed a really good medium to introduce feeding and trophic levels, biomass and energy waste to undergraduates. Trivial? It is extremely funny and seems to get the lecture off to a good start, and the concentration levels continue to be high. But why? This is known as the 'hook'. Is it fun, play, relaxation? Why does a simple tape of just three or four minutes extend student concentration levels well beyond the 15–20 minutes norm? This 'hook' engages the majority of people at the start of the session.

Garratt (1987) refers to the fact that intellectual property is a key tradable commodity; and that nurturing, harnessing and capturing this will be the key to future success. Participants can of course be useful in the design of training methods and materials. One database was collected over many years by simply designing training programmes to find out what the audience knowledge levels were. They collected facts by researching pre-prepared material that was presented in large envelopes with specially designed covers. The information that participants researched was written up on cards and these were all collected up each year and new information was continually added to a computer database. The latest result, 15 years on, is a book of facts and figures about the environment in the UK for a period of some 300 years. This method uses the notion 'participant intellectual property development' (PIPD) as a vital tool in the development of training materials. In training in the use of feedback and criticism, trainers can collect live anonymous material such as letters of complaint to and from firms, letters of apology, or memos collected from within the workplace. In delivering sessions on evaluation, trainers can collect real samples from all over the world over many years, and participants can gauge which are best and why, and form a spectrum of good and not-so-good evaluation methods and forms.

VISUALIZATION, REALITY AND SIMULATION IN LEARNING – TREE-FELLING INDOORS!

One participant on a training-the-trainer course decided not to do a training session on day three of a five-day programme. After some discussion it transpired that he lacked the confidence to 'stand up front and deliver a session'. His session, however, turned out to be very creative and it resulted in the best peer review. He took tree-felling and safety as his preferred theme – difficult, but he knew lots about it and felt he could pass on a lot of knowledge, and because the outdoors was where he felt comfortable. I explained that he could not really have time to conduct a real session in the outdoors in 20 minutes. So he brought the woodland indoors!

The session used paper and card, together with other real props, rolled up flip-chart paper and masking tape. Real saws were used to demonstrate ideas and most of the techniques were taught by participants imagining what they would do next. They were encouraged to look up into the imaginary tree and think about and comment on the wind direction, the places where the heavier branches were, etc and to try to work out the direction the tree would be best felled. Tape was used to show the direction of fall, the safety zones, the danger zones and so on. Most of the group came out to the front (the middle of the floor space) to have a go at something.

USING MATERIALS CREATIVELY

The effectiveness of training methods can often be considerably enhanced by using support materials in a creative way. Masking tape and pre-prepared cards can be used to help participants recreate conceptual models, or design organizational charts or company reporting structures. We have already looked at the use of popular images, recycled video boxes and washable cards. Television programmes and advertising footage contain a wealth of material that can easily be put on video. Paper booklets can easily be created; flip charts can be cut to form layers with pre-prepared information on each layer; instructions for participants can be placed in specially designed envelopes or plastic cases; trainers can put pencil outlines on flip charts as reminders – no one can see them in the audience and coloured sticky markers are useful to mark flip chart sheets so that trainers are not fumbling to find the right sheet.

Training methods can also incorporate card games, eg, in communication exercises, allocated cards can allow participants so many slots to speak. Dice exercises, score cards, 'behavioural hats' (see for example de Bono's 'hats' in Rodwell, 1994:136–39) or road shows can also be incorporated. The possibilities are endless, and trainers can develop a whole toolkit of materials and resources that can be ready to support the delivery of their training methods and create a more professional approach. David Leigh (1996) suggests a basic survival kit list for trainers to carry, as well as lists of tips for trainers. In my Master classes on experiential learning, I demonstrate the complex 'Learning Combination Lock' by giving everyone six polystyrene cups, one inside the other, to construct and deconstruct the model (Beard and Wilson, 2002).

CONCLUSION: THE FUTURE OF TRAINING METHODS

The world is changing and, in his crystal ball gazing, Megginson (1994) was supposed to look into the future. He anticipated tree of knowledge briefcases (TOK cases), cyborg technology, learning techneurology and other virtual and fictitious ideas. However, within a few years of writing the article, many of his deliberately controversial ideas had already materialized! While the company induction brain chip implant is not yet available – thank goodness – the video/TV/telephone wristwatch is here, and companies now offer 'greater learning through relaxation'. Lifetools, for example, offer special effects of hypnotic light and sound pulses to help people to relax, or to energize, and visualize. Arthur C Clarke is said to have predicted in 1945 that orbital satellites would revolutionize communications, but his ideas were regarded as too far-fetched and not worthy of consideration! The future is going to be exciting for trainers and developers. Death by PowerPoint bullet points may be a thing of the past!

Bibliography

Adler, P S (1975) 'The transitional experience', *Journal of Humanistic Psychology*, **15**, 4, pp 13–23

Bandler, R and Grinder, J (1975) *The Structure of Magic: A book about language and therapy*, Palo Alto, CA, Science and Behavior Books

Beard, C M (1996a) 'Environmental training: emerging products', *Journal of Industrial and Commercial Training*, **28**, 5, pp 18–23

Beard, C M (1996b) 'Environmental awareness training – three ideas for change', *Eco-Management and Auditing*, **3**, 3, pp 139–46

Beard, C and Rhodes, T (2002) 'Experiential Learning: Using comic strips as "reflective tools" in adult learning', *Australian Journal of Outdoor Education*, **6**, 2

Beard, C and Wilson, J (2002) *The Power of Experiential Learning*, London, Kogan Page

Benson, J F (1987) *Working More Creatively with Groups*, London, Routledge

Binstead, D and Stuart, R (1979) 'Designing reality into management learning events', *Personnel Review*, **8**, 3

Bloom, B S, Engelhart, M D, Furst, E J, Hill, W H and Krathwohl, D R (1956) *Taxonomy of Educational Objectives: The classification of educational objectives, Handbook 1: Cognitive domain*, London, Longmans, Green

Boler, M (1999) *Feeling Power: Emotions and education*, London, Routledge

Commonwealth Secretariat (1984) *Training Skills for Women*, London, Commonwealth Secretariat

Cornell, J (1989) *Sharing the Joy of Nature*, Nevada City, CA, Dawn Publications

Dainty, P and Lucas, D (1992) 'Clarifying the confusion: a practical framework for evaluating outdoor management development programmes for managers', *Management Education and Development*, **23**, 2, pp 106–22

Dewey, J (1938) *Education and Experience*, New York, Collier Macmillan

Fineman, S (1997) 'Emotion and management learning', *Management Learning*, **28**, 1, pp 13–25

Gardner, H (1983) *Frames of Mind: The theory of multiple intelligences*, New York, Basic Books

Garratt, B (1987) *The Learning Organization*, London, Fontana

Gass, M A (1995) *Book of Metaphors*, Dubuque, IA, Kendall Hunt

Greenaway, R (1993) *Playback: A guide to reviewing activities*, London, Employment Department, and Endeavour, Scotland

Havergal, M and Edmonstone, J (2003) *The Facilitators Toolkit*, 2nd edn, Aldershot, Gower

Honey, P and Mumford, A (1982) *The Manual of Learning Styles*, Maidenhead, Peter Honey

IPD (1998) *A Guide to Outdoor Training*, London, IPD

Kolb, D A, (1984) *Experiential Learning: Experience as the source of learning and development*, Englewood Cliffs, NJ, Prentice Hall

Krathwohl, D R, Bloom, B S and Masia, B B (1964) *Taxonomy of Educational Objectives: The classification of educational goals, Handbook 2: Affective domain*, London, Longmans, Green

Leigh, D (1996) *Designing and Delivering Training for Groups*, London, Kogan Page

Margerison, C (1988) *Managerial Consulting Styles*, Aldershot, Gower

Megginson, D (1994) 'Planned and emergent learning: a framework and a method', *Executive Development*, **7**, 6, pp 29–32

Merrick, N (1998) 'Theatrical treatment', *People Management*, 22 January, pp 44–46

Mortiboys, A. (2002) *The Emotionally Intelligent Lecturer*, Birmingham, SEDA Publications

Mortlock, C (1987) *The Adventure Alternative*, Cumbria, Cicerone Press

Parkin, M (1998) *Tales for Trainers*, London, Kogan Page

Phillips, E M and Pugh, D S (1994) *How to Get a PhD*, 2nd edn, Buckingham, Open University Press

Pickard, J (1996) 'A fertile grounding', *People Management*, **2**, 21, pp 28–37

Raab, N (1997) 'Becoming an expert in not knowing – retraining teacher as consultant', *Management Learning*, **28**, 2, pp 161–75

Rae, L (1995) *Techniques of Training*, 3rd edn, Aldershot, Gower

Randall, R and Southgate, J (1980) *Cooperative and Community Group Dynamics*, London, Barefoot Books

Raw, T (1991) 'Using the outdoors as a learning medium for young people', *Transition*, pp 13–14

Rodwell, J (1994) *Participative Training Skills*, Aldershot, Gower

Rogers, C (1993) *The Carl Rogers Reader*, London, Constable

Sieberman, M (1990) *Active Training: A handbook of techniques, designs, case examples and topics*, San Diego, CA, Lexington Books

Thompson, J and McGivern, J (1996) 'Parody, process and practice – perspectives for management education', *Management Learning*, **27**, 1, pp 21–35

Thorpe, R and Moscarola, J (1991) 'Detecting your research strategy', *Management Education and Development*, **22**, 2, pp 127–33

Tracey, W R (1992) *Designing Training and Development Systems*, 3rd edn, New York, Amacom

Tuckman, B W and Jenson, M A C (1977) 'Stages of small group development revisited', *Group and Organizational Studies*, **2**, pp 419–27

Van Matre, S (1979) *Sunship Earth*, Martinsville, IN, American Camping Association

Watson, T (1996) 'Motivation: that's Maslow, isn't it?', *Management Learning*, **27**, 4, pp 447–64

19

Problem-Based Learning (PBL)

John Blewitt

INTRODUCTION AND LEARNING OBJECTIVES

Problem-based learning (PBL) has at its core a concern for development – of the individual, of the group, of a community of practice and ultimately, by extension, the organization. PBL, like human resource development (HRD) itself, anticipates and enables qualitative change to occur by facilitating the emergence of skills, knowledge, understanding, and above all the individual and organization capabilities that can conceive of, initiate and implement change. As Ulrich and Smallwood (2004:119) say, these capabilities 'are the outcome of investments in staffing, training, compensation, communication, and other human resource areas'. Organizations generate new ideas and activities through learning, continuous improvement and innovation across time, space, department and division. Learning means finding ways of making connections, developing new practices, generating new knowledge and understanding, benefiting from rather than repeating past mistakes and failures.

> A study of more than 150 new products concluded that 'the knowledge gained from failures [is] often instrumental in achieving subsequent successes. ... In the simplest terms, failure is the ultimate teacher.' IBM's 360 computer series, for example, one of the most popular and profitable ever built, was based on the technology of the failed Stretch computer that preceded it. In this case, as in many others, learning occurred by chance rather than careful planning. A few companies, however, have established processes that require their managers to periodically think about the past and learn from their mistakes.
>
> (Garvin, 1993:85)

PBL has an important contribution to make in formalizing creative learning processes that turn mistakes into significant opportunities for personal, professional and organizational development.

Having read this chapter you will:

- understand the key principles informing PBL;
- understand the relationship between PBL and the development of a learner's capability;
- understand the significance of process in PBL;
- be aware of the possibilities and potential of PBL to HRD.

ORIGINS AND PRINCIPLES

PBL emerged from developments in medical education in the 1960s and 1970s, particularly at McMaster University in Canada and a little later at the University of Limburg at Maastricht in the Netherlands, the University of Newcastle in Australia and the University of New Mexico in the United States. Reflecting on some years of curriculum development experience, Barrows and Tamblyn (1980) argue that PBL essentially rests on two key assumptions. They are, first, that learning through a problem situation produces a far more effective and usable body of knowledge than learning acquired through more conventional memory based means such as a lecture course or reading a book; and second, that skills used in treating patients were in most instances problem-solving skills. So PBL mirrors real-world experiences.

The work at McMaster did not focus simply on individual students acquiring the skills and knowledge necessary to practise, but rather the learning undertaken was exploratory, occurring in small groups operating collaboratively and cooperatively, with the tutor acting as facilitator and guide rather than instructor. Additionally, learning was not abstracted from the real world but rooted in it. The emphasis was placed on the relevance and transferability of learning from the formal education organization to the clinic or hospital. Learning was, therefore, if not exactly situated in a real-life setting, placed in a vivid and recognizably authentic context. Much of the critical academic literature on PBL emanates from the medical or broadly health-related spheres, but the axial principles and practices that have emerged from this experience have been applied to many other areas of higher education and professional learning – business, management, engineering, social work, accountancy, architecture, construction, legal training, and so on (Boud and Feletti, 1997).

In some institutions there has been an almost evangelical enthusiasm for PBL that has simultaneously generated impressive claims and some scepticism over the method's effectiveness, perceived faddishness and overall significance. One reason for the enthusiasm was tutors' belief that PBL addressed the 'whole' student, facilitated interdisciplinarity and nurtured positive attitudes to learning. Consequently, the 1980s and 1990s saw curriculum developments and professional applications multiply. Barrows and Tamblyn (1980) argue that PBL offered what teachers, trainers and students really needed, namely:

- the development of reasoning skills;
- contextual or situated group inquiry or learning;
- vocationally and/or practically relevant activity;
- self-directed learning.

PBL was also seen as focused and practical rather than theoretical, or pejoratively academic, but as with many other dynamic and heuristic learning stratagems, clear, precise and stable definitions, or indeed practices elude those who wish to contain either meaning or action within a relatively static framework. Savin-Baden (2000:16) states that PBL is inevitably and properly multifaceted. It comes in many guises, forms and differences which 'stem from the discipline or professional knowledge base into which it is introduced'. She goes on to suggest that in many ways it is an ideology 'rooted in the experiential learning tradition' articulating a set of values, principles and assumptions about the nature of learning and the learner, who is neither an information processor nor an empty vessel waiting to be filled.

One useful distinction offered by Bereiter and Scardamalia (2000) is that between PBL (uppercase) and pbl (lowercase). PBL is the now well-documented approach to learning, and pbl is the more indefinite collection of learning activities that give problems an important role, but act mainly as a stimulus device. Therefore, it would be mistaken to view PBL as being simply about problem-solving, or indeed problem posing, although the latter, as Stephenson and Galloway (2004) remark in their discussion of empowering adult education, is very much about the analysis of underlying (political) causes and (power) relationships and the identification of group (or other) actions necessary to effect personal, social or institutional change. This is central to Boud (1985; Boud and Feletti, 1997), who sees student-centredness as being of principal importance. He highlights the following:

- the social and professional experience of the learners;
- the recognition that learners must take responsibility for their own learning;
- that real-life learning or PBL cannot be confined neatly to discrete academic boundaries or disciplines;
- that theory is not and cannot be separated from professional practice or action;
- the process of acquiring new knowledge is as important as its content, perhaps more so;
- that teachers, lecturers, tutors, mentors, managers are most properly conceptualized as facilitators or enablers rather than instructors;
- that assessment of outcomes is the responsibility of the individual learner, his/her colleagues and the facilitator;
- that to effectively communicate new learning to others, learners need to concentrate on developing their communication and interpersonal skills.

PBL draws on developments in other fields, particularly reflective practice and professional learning (Eraut, 1994), emotional intelligence (Goleman, 1996), performativity and Mode 2 Knowledge Production (Gibbons *et al*, 1994), which is heterogeneous, trans-disciplinary and located essentially in its context of application and the reflexivity of modern life, consisting 'in the fact that social practices are constantly examined and reformed in the light of incoming information about those very practices, thus constitutively altering their character' (Giddens, 1990:38). These macro theories mark out the contexts shaping the theories and practices of PBL, and the view of professional workers as knowledge managers, workplace innovators, creators of learning opportunities that engage with 'problems' in our increasingly complex and connected environment.

PBL: A WAY OF PROFESSIONAL AND LIFELONG LEARNING

PBL is a way of learning. It does more than focus people's attentions on solving problems, for it enables individuals, groups and organizations to improve, change and grow. Engel (1997) suggests that PBL enables learners to become capable in a set of generalized competences which may also be identified as a specific set of objectives. These include:

- adapting to and participating in change;
- dealing with problems, making reasoned decisions in unfamiliar situations;
- reasoning critically and creatively;
- adapting a more universal or holistic approach to issues;
- empathy, appreciating the other person's point of view;
- collaborating productively in groups or teams;
- identifying individual strengths and weaknesses and undertaking appropriate remediation, for example through continuing self-directed learning (or CPD).

Following Senge's (1990) conceptualization of 'the learning organization', PBL may also be conceived as a way of learning that nurtures conditions, enabling creativity and flexibility to emerge through the adaptation and generation of new knowledge, understandings, products and practices. Given this, PBL permits adult professional learning to be effective, because it requires learning to be:

- active;
- integrated;
- cumulative;
- constructive;
- meaningful;
- adaptive;
- generative.

Generative learning requires new ways of looking at the world, of overseeing working relationships, developing human resources, creating new products and product concepts, of managing knowledge in competitive environments and being (commercially) successful. Knowledge creation, product development and the growing of professional capabilities (and competences) are frequently motivated by problems such as poor communication, inefficient working practices,

Table 19.1 Defining characteristics of PBL

What	How	Why
Learner-centred and experiential	Authentic tasks from the discipline or professional field. Learners are responsible for locating and evaluating the various resources required.	Relevance is one of the primary motivators in becoming a more self-directed learner.
Inductive	Content is introduced through the process of problem-solving.	*Deeper* learning takes place when information is introduced within a meaningful context.
Builds on/challenges prior learning	If the case is relevant, learners can call on what they already know or think they know. They can then test assumptions, prior learning strategies and facts.	Learning takes place when there is a conflict between prior learning and new information or situation – a 'disorienting dilemma'.
Context-specific	PBL content is grounded in the kinds of challenges faced by practitioners in the field.	Context-specific information tends to be learned at a deeper level and retained longer.
Problems are complex and ambiguous, and require meta-cognition	Real-life problems require students to analyse their own problem-solving and learning strategies.	PBL develops the capability to use higher-order thinking skills such as analysis, synthesis, evaluation, and creation of new knowledge.
Creates a disorienting dilemma	Good PBL cases present information that makes simple solutions difficult: while the solution may address one problem, it may create others.	Learning takes place when there is a conflict between prior learning and new information.
Collaborative and interdependent	Learners work collaboratively and cooperatively in small groups in order to address the presented case or 'problem'.	By collaborating, learners see other kinds of problem-solving strategies used, discuss the case using their collective information, and learn to take responsibility for their own and others' learning.

Source: adapted from *What is Problem Based Learning?*, University of California, Irvine [Online] http://www.pbl.uci.edu/whatispbl.html

decline in market share, unhelpful personality clashes, obsolete ideas, technologies, skills or knowledge(s). What are needed to overcome these problems are learning, critical reflection, and time and space in which interactions can occur to organize and shape the creation of new information, ideas and action. In doing this, the workforce itself becomes empowered, motivated and committed, and as such is the key to efficient and effective human resource development. Nonaka and Toyama (2004) call the phenomenological time and space where new knowledge is created and by extension where new learning occurs, problems posed and solved, *ba* (literally 'place', and when combined with the Chinese script for numbers it becomes 'experience'). They write:

> *Ba* can emerge in individuals, working groups, project teams, informal circles, temporary meetings, virtual spaces such as email groups, and at the front line contact with the customer. *Ba* is an existential place where participants share their contexts and create new meanings through interactions. Participants of *ba* bring in their own contexts, and through interactions with others and the environment, the contexts of *ba*, participants, and environment change.
>
> (Nonaka and Toyama, 2004:102)

By applying ideas and concepts from those researching and theorizing the management, creation and emergence of knowledge, the notion of the learning environment, usually associated with the institutional contexts of schools, colleges and universities, can be transposed to the workplace, business, professional association or community group. So for *ba* read learning environment, and for interactions read collaborative and cooperative learning (PBL and pbl). The capacity to manipulate knowledge, information and understanding and the management of human, financial and material resources in a complex, uncertain and changing environment are now familiar constants in the lifeworlds of professional people. Knowledge is crucial to their continuing development and to their continuing efficient performance, so much so that frequently we see the entwining of concepts – the 'knowledge economy', the information or 'knowledge society' with the necessity of life-wide and 'lifelong learning'. Knowledge and learning is everywhere. It is with us throughout our personal and professional lives.

KNOWLEDGE AND PBL

Educational philosophers argue that knowledge can be divided into distinct categories, for example, knowledge that proposes that such and such is the case, which in an organizational setting is sometimes referred to as explicit knowledge, codified in rules, artefacts, policy documents, routines and so on, and knowledge that refers to knowing how to do something, which is invariably tacit and embedded, and basically resides in expertise and experience. (See Chapter 7, 'Knowledge Management'.) People in professional settings need to develop their knowledge, understandings and expertise that recognize the validity and pertinence of both. Discussing this, Margetson writes:

> Expertise is an ability to make sound judgements as to what is problematic about a situation, to identify the most important problems, and to know how to go about solving or at least ameliorating them. ... Problem based learning places emphasis on what is needed, on the ability to gain prepositional knowledge as required, and to put it to the most valuable use in a given situation. ... [It] requires a much greater integration of knowing that and knowing how [than content based study].
>
> (Margetson, 1997:38)

PBL enables, indeed requires, the discovery of skills, competences, capabilities, relationships, interactions, knowledge, concepts and practices that are at least new to the individual learner or learning group. It may involve learning how to make tacit knowledge more explicit, and explicit knowledge tacit: that is, how we simply do things. In this way, PBL has a close affinity to action research/learning, and it is possible to effectively combine the two (Cockerill *et al*, 1996). Although wheels should not be continuously reinvented, in some cases they need to be if the knowledge and experience of process is to be fully valued. In this context, the notion of process (and process knowledge) refers to those understandings necessary to perform and apply the methods, procedures and practices that contribute to professional action. Process is what professionals do and how they learn.

Margetson (1997:39–40) goes on to state that the PBL process:

- encourages open-minded, reflective, critical and active learning;
- pays due respect to learner and facilitator, as persons with knowledge, understanding, feelings and interests who come together to share a learning experience;
- reflects the complex, reflexive and changing nature of knowledge – that is, knowledge is complex and changes as a result of responses by communities of practitioners to problems perceived and acted upon.

PBL: THEORETICAL UNDERPINNING

What has become known in education circles as constructivism underpins PBL. Savery and Duffey (1995) and Schmidt (1995), Hendry (1996) and Hendry, Frommer and Walker (1999) argue that PBL expresses in practice major constructivist values and principles. For Hendry, Frommer and Walker (1999:361–62), these include:

- Knowledge exists in the minds of people: it is a pattern in space and time. Ideas or perceptions are spatio-temporal patterns that develop when a person interprets a situation or remembers something.
- The meanings or interpretations people give to things depend on their prior knowledge.
- Perceptual and ideational knowledge together with processes of reasoning are constructed from within, in relation with the world.
- Common knowledge derives from a common brain and body – perceptual knowledge (for example visual, audio, tactile) and actions (bodily movements).
- Knowledge is created through perception and action.
- A person's knowledge may become untenable, or combine to produce a 'conceptual conflict' in his/her interrelation with the world.
- The creation of knowledge constitutes reattainment of an integrated or tenable form, which is qualitatively different from any previous knowledge.
- Creation or the reattainment of tenable knowledge is active and requires energy, or correlated mental effort and time.
- Knowledge creation is pleasurable and satisfying.

(I have substituted the synonyms 'tenable' and 'untenable' for 'sustainable' and 'unsustainable', as the latter terms are used quite differently in debates around Education for Sustainability.)

Learners and new learning frequently require some sort of conceptual conflict, or what Mezirow (1991) has termed a 'disorientating dilemma'. New experiences, new ideas, new practices may disturb the current ways we understand things, and as a result we attempt to accommodate or perhaps alter our new perceptions and understandings. In a workplace context, knowledge and understanding are constantly being altered, constructed, from our encounters with a range of personal, social, technical, technological, operational, managerial, social and psychological influences. Indeed, this constructive interplay of conflicting or challenging experiences disturbing our social, and cognitive equilibrium may be conceived as a dialectic of creativity, where disturbance is ultimately replaced by a new, if short-lived, equilibrium. However, too much conflict, too much arousal or disorientation may increase individual or group anxiety and lower the sense of group or self-efficacy, leading to withdrawal, feelings of powerlessness, apathy or fatalism. Neither learning nor development will take place in this context.

Although real-life problems are often dressed up euphemistically as challenges rather than problems, there is a need to manage the PBL environment so that it nurtures and sustains development, leading to significant learning and productive change. Consequently, groups and teams need to clearly understand the nature of the problem and its various implications. Following Weick and Van Orden (1990), problems may be usefully classified as being either *problems of uncertainty* – that is, problems of ignorance solved by gathering additional information – or *problems of equivocation* – that is, problems where there are many conflicting interpretations of what is taking place.

Problems of equivocation such as how to manage culturally diverse teams, complicated working relationships and functions, may require not simply more information, but rather information that is qualitatively richer. These problems will also require skills of analysis, synthesis and evaluation which involve and stimulate complex thinking. Given this, a number of variables influence the effectiveness of PBL, including:

- the nature of the learner's knowledge, particularly as it impacts upon the problem and the identification of what it is considered needs to be learned;
- the nature of the problem – its complexity or otherwise;
- the adeptness of the group facilitator in helping to promote effective and productive learning experiences;
- the interest, engagement, focus and commitment of the participants to the task or problem at hand;
- the capacity to generate and reflect upon new knowledge, capabilities and skills before applying them;
- the sense of achievement and its possibility.

When faced with a PBL situation, Hmelo and Lin (2004) argue that learners must use 'metacognitive' strategies to identify what they don't know and what they need to learn more about. This includes the capacity for self-directed learning, which has applications in formal and non-formal learning environments, in universities and business environments.

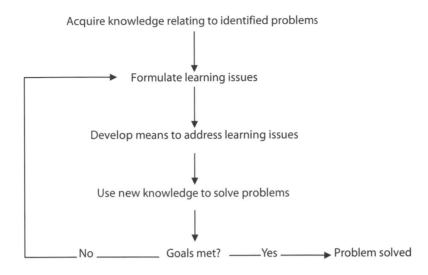

Figure 19.1   PBL: a model for self-directed learning (adapted from Hmelo and Lin, 2004)

Good self-directed learners set their learning goals, proactively select information, and self-evaluate the effectiveness of their learning, deciding whether or not to repeat the learning process. This requires being capable of continuously learning from experience by reflecting on the actions undertaken during the learning process. Inevitably in a PBL context such reflection involves a considerable degree of critical thinking if the learning experience is to be fully developmental for the individual, the group and the organization.

Critical reflection and criticality generally has received considerable attention in discussions of the future direction of management education (Dehler, Welsh and Lewis, 2001; Gosling and Mintzberg, 2004). Reynolds (1999:173) suggests that employing critical thinking as 'a disciplined approach to problem solving' mistakenly presumes that problems are fairly simple to resolve. They frequently are not unless the embedded nature of power relationships in the organization and the wider socio-political context are fully appreciated. This echoes Stephenson and Galloway (2004), and similarly, Fenwick and Parsons (1998) argue that given the interconnected and interrelated nature of the world it is also mistaken to conceptualize our engagement with it as merely a series of problems to be overcome. It is far more complex, complicated, embodied and relational than that. Referring to Lave and Wenger's (1991) work on situated learning, they argue that the way we apprehend problems and choose actions is intimately intertwined with the network of people, objects and meaning creations of the particular moment. Each learner therefore develops understanding in relation to context and situation. Quoting Thrift and Pile's (1995) theoretical approach to everyday choice-making they suggest a number of resonant areas important for both professional and problem-based learning:

● Understanding (and therefore any learning strategy) is created within conduct itself which flows ceaselessly, is adaptable, is future-oriented but not always intentional.

- Understanding is often beyond the realm of what can be stated explicitly.
- Understanding is worked out in joint action, always binding the individual to others in shared understandings of what is real, what is moral, what is actual.
- Understanding is situated and cannot be abstracted from its constituting time and place.

Finally, with reference to Varela's enactivist perspective of cognition, Fenwick and Parsons write:

> Enactivism suggests that life is an emerging dynamic, a network of actors and objects that is interrelated in particular socio-cultural-historical interactions. Problems or possibilities are 'enacted' within this dynamic network. The perceiver-knower is implicated as an active, creative agent who embodies knowledge while generating intentions that guide choices for subsequent action from this embodied knowledge. Perception unfolds continually in 'perceptually guided action'. Thus, problem-perception and response is embedded in and revealed through emergent networks of activity.
>
> (Fenwick and Parsons, 1998:62)

Much PBL activity will generate new ideas, theories, inquiries and approaches which construct knowledge and capabilities around a particular task, issue or problem, but the PBL process needs to go beyond the immediate and immanent. Effective HRD needs to foster a capacity to perceive problems that connects to both obstacles and possibilities of creative overcoming. This will inevitably need a critical and reflexive mode of thinking and acting, drawing strength from complexity, uncertainty and risk. In this way, it will be possible to move beyond the familiar refrains of 'It can't be done', 'We've always done it that way', 'I don't know how to do that' or 'I don't what to do/learn …' which predispose people to deny change.

FACILITATING PBL

In PBL environments the role of the facilitator is important because he or she enables learning by supporting or scaffolding development, as individuals and groups become more fully engaged. Learners must acquire a sense of responsibility and a confidence to manage problem-solving tasks holistically, because invariably PBL situations require of people the capacity to consider multiple perspectives, influences, consequences, practices and possibilities. This will mean being able to ask appropriate questions to stimulate and foster ongoing action and learning. In writing about environmental science education, Dahlgren and Oberg (2001) identify five types of questions that accomplish this purpose. They are:

- *encyclopaedic questions* – requiring fairly straightforward answers;
- *meaning-oriented questions* – requiring the search for the phenomenological meaning of terms and concepts;
- *relational questions* – requiring the search for connections and interrelationships;
- *value-oriented* – evaluative and often comparative in nature;
- *solution-oriented* – practical and management focused.

In addition, Greening (1998) writes of the need to nurture effective group dynamics, ensuring that:

- Each individual contributes to the group goal by offering proposals, critiques and summaries.
- Individuals operate in a supportive manner, attending to and recognizing the contribution of others.
- Group cohesiveness is best maintained through clarifying, organizing and facilitating individual contribution to the group process.
- Negative energies and actions – freeriding – is minimized or eliminated or dwarfed by more positive actions and energies.

Referring to a study of teacher education stressing the importance of group functioning, Hendry, Frommer and Walker write:

> Group functioning is important because students must feel comfortable in recalling and expressing their ideas; they should not be made to feel anxious by other group members, or have their self-efficacy undermined. A group in which there is co-operation and people feel accepted is more likely to have higher rates of learning and identify a greater range of learning issues than one characterized by competitiveness. This claim is supported by a recent review of research on problems in cooperative environments ... which shows that in cooperative conditions, 'the average person ... solved problems better than 72.5% of the participants in the competitive condition'.
>
> (Hendry, Frommer and Walker, 1999:367)

Effective facilitation is central to successful PBL activity, but as Savin-Baden (2003) clearly argues, 'facilitation is context-bound' and rooted in specific 'ecologies of practice': that is, those experiences, beliefs and practices that professionals develop in their particular fields of operation and responsibility. Human resource development together with any attendant learning helps constitute that practice. However, researchers on facilitation have identified general issues that may serve as useful guidance to the facilitator new to PBL. The ability to trust your own judgement and those of others within the group needs to be promoted by establishing a framework that enables people to comfortably and effectively reflect. Savin-Baden (2003:25) outlines three components to facilitating this:

- *support* – must be constructive and empowering;
- *direction* – must involve encouragement and respect individual autonomy;
- *structure* – must be stable and relatively predictable.

Heron (1989, 1993) suggests there are three modes of facilitation that could be investigated, applied and later evaluated:

- *The hierarchical mode* – facilitators take a controlling and directive role, setting objectives, challenging opposition and so on.
- *The cooperative mode* – facilitators share power with the team in order to enable them to be self-directed learners.
- *The autonomous mode* – the autonomy of the PBL team is fully respected with the facilitator simply setting the conditions in which learning will take place.

WORK RELATIONS AND HUMAN RESOURCE DEVELOPMENT: A PBL SCENARIO

Two relatively autonomous teams within an organization that prides itself on its capacity to learn need to cooperate more effectively in order for them to function efficiently. Relations between the two teams have deteriorated over time, leading to an unnecessary duplication of roles, a failure to communicate meaningfully and a culture of mutual blame and recrimination. How can this situation be improved?

The PBL task is for key members of the two teams to review working practices, clarify perceptions of problems and seek effective and practical solutions. This may be accomplished in dialogue facilitated by the line or HRD manager. S/he must ensure opposing and contradictory views are fully explored and new ways of anticipating future problems and operating collaboratively and cooperatively are identified, supported, piloted and evaluated.

What knowledge, skills, capacities and relationships need to be developed to affect this?
How could PBL be made to work to improve the situation?

THE EFFECTIVENESS OF PBL

It should be self-evident that any way of learning adopted by an organization or HRD manager is effective if it leads to improvements in professional practice, knowledge, skills and understanding. To date there have been a large number of PBL evaluations, particularly in higher education, and although these are by no means consistent (Newman, 2003) in their findings and conclusions, PBL is increasingly being adopted in new areas. There are sometimes, as Newman states, exaggerated claims for PBL, but as Albanese suggests, 'perhaps it is a more humane learning environment that promotes collegial interactions which is the ultimate outcome of PBL' (2000:736). Others have argued that PBL proves very effective in securing longer knowledge retention, better reasoning processes, more self-directedness in learning and higher motivation and commitment.

If it is adopted within an HRD context, evaluations need to address issues of knowledge gains in areas relating to both the what and the how, to process as well as product, to outcome as well as output, the capacity to grow and continue learning as well as the identification and implementation of particular solutions to particular problems in one particular moment of time. Evaluation may also need to explore whether the learning undertaken has been deep, strategic or surface, or a combination of all three. To adapt Moon's (1999:122) summary of categories, it may be valuable to consider the following.

Deep approach

- Relating of ideas to previous knowledge and experience.
- Looking for patterns and underlying principles.

- Checking of evidence and relating it to conclusions or solutions.
- Examining of logic, argument, reason in a careful and critical manner.

Surface approach

- Learning without reflecting on either purpose or strategy.
- Not making connections between related bits of knowledge.
- Following set procedures or memorizing facts in a routine and uncritical manner.
- Finding difficulty in tackling new ideas, issues or problems.
- Feeling unduly pressured by the need to operate differently.

Strategic approach

- Putting consistent effort into the PBL activity.
- Finding the appropriate conditions and material for successfully resolving the PBL activity.
- Managing time and effort effectively.
- Being alert to the perceived or identified criteria for success and achievement.

Kanet and Barut, writing about PBL for productions and operations management, conclude:

> because students are challenged to apply theory to a practical setting, they in fact learn it more deeply. They respond to the method by thinking and acting independently, and demonstrate their abilities to be self-learners. The biggest reward is to see them develop their self-confidence to clearly define problems from unstructured situations and apply knowledge competently.
>
> (Kanet and Barut, 2003:112)

Changing the way learning or even problems are conceived, is a complex process and it may be the case that in some instances a combination of deep and surface learning is required to ensure an optimal or effective outcome.

CONCLUSION

PBL offers human resource development a way of learning that aids collaboration and team working, autonomy and responsibility, critical and creative thinking, innovation and connectivity, and the capacity to move beyond the constraints of the immediate and the particular. The time is therefore ripe for extending the range of PBL activities from the simulated environments often found in formal education to the real and existentially authentic worlds of continuing professional development and workplace learning.

Bibliography

Albanese, M (2000) 'Problem-based learning: why curricula are likely to show little effect on knowledge and clinical skills', *Medical Education*, 34, pp 729–38

Barrows, H S and Tamblyn, R M (1980) *Problem-Based Learning: An approach to medical education*, New York, Springer

Bereiter, C and Scardamalia, M (2000) 'Process and product in problem-based learning (PBL) research', in D H Evensen and C E Hmelo (eds), *Problem-Based Learning: A research perspective on learning interactions*, New Jersey, Lawrence Erlbaum Associates

Boud, D (1985) *Problem-Based Learning in Education for the Professions*, Sydney, Higher Education Research and Development Society for Australasia

Boud, D and Feletti, G (eds) (1997) *The Challenge of Problem Based Learning*, 2nd edn, London, Kogan Page

Cockerill, S, Stewart, G, Hamilton, L, Douglas, J and Gold, J (1996) 'The international management of change: a problem-based learning/case study approach', *Education and Training*, **38**, 2, pp 14–17

Dahlgren, MA and Oberg, G (2001) 'Questioning to learn and learning to question: Structure and function of problem-based learning scenarios in environmental science education', *Higher Education*, **41**, pp 263–82

Dehler, G E, Welsh, M A and Lewis, M W (2001) 'Critical pedagogy in the "New Paradigm"', *Management Learning*, CE,4, pp 493–511

Engel, C E (1997) 'Not Just a method but a way of learning', in D Boud and G Feletti (eds), *The Challenge of Problem Based Learning*, 2nd edn, London, Kogan Page

Eraut, M (1994) *Developing Professional Knowledge and Competence*, London, Falmer Press

Fenwick, T and Parsons, J (1998) 'Boldly solving the world: a critical analysis of problem-based learning as a method of professional education', *Studies in the Education of Adults*, **30**, 1, pp 53–66

Garvin, D A (1993) 'Building a learning organisation', *Harvard Business Review*, **71**, 4, pp 78–91

Gibbons, M, Limoges, C, Nowotny, H, Schwartzman, S, Scott, P, and Trow, M (1994) *The New Production of Knowledge*, London, Sage

Giddens, A (1990) *The Consequences of Modernity*, Cambridge, Polity Press

Goleman, D (1996) *Emotional Intelligence*, London, Bloomsbury

Gosling, J and Mintzberg, H (2004) 'The education of practical managers', *MIT Sloan Management Review*, **5**, 4 pp 19–22

Greening, T (1998) 'Scaffolding for success in problem-based learning', *Med Educ Online* [Online] http://www.Med-Ed-Online.org. (accessed 26 September 2004)

Hendry, G D (1996) 'Constructivism and education practice', *Australian Journal of Education*, **40**, pp 19–45

Hendry, G D, Frommer, M and Walker, R A (1999) 'Constructivism and problem-based learning', *Journal of Further and Higher Education*, **23**, 3, pp 359–71

Heron, J (1989) *The Facilitator's Handbook*, London, Kogan Page

Heron, J (1993) *Group Facilitation*, London, Kogan Page

Hmelo, C E and Lin, X (2004) 'Becoming self-directed learners: strategy development in problem-based learning', in D H Evensen and C E Hmelo (eds), *Problem-Based Learning: A research perspective on learning interactions*, New Jersey, Lawrence Erlbaum Associates

Kanet, J J and Barut, M (2003) 'Problem-based learning for production and operations management', *Decision Sciences Journal of Innovative Education*, **1**, 1 pp 99–118

Lave, J and Wenger, E (1991) *Situated Learning: Legitimate peripheral participation*, Cambridge, Cambridge University Press

Margetson, D (1997) 'Why is problem-based learning a challenge?', in D Boud and G Feletti (eds), *The Challenge of Problem Based Learning*, 2nd edn, London, Kogan Page

Mezirow, J (1991) *Transformative Dimensions of Adult Learning*, San Francisco, CA, Jossey-Bass

Moon, J A (1999) *Reflection in Learning and Professional Development*, London, Kogan Page

Newman, M (2003) *A Systematic Review and Meta-analysis on the Effectiveness of Problem Based Learning LTSN* [Online] http://www.regard.ac.uk/research_findings/L139251097/report.pdf

Nonaka, I and Toyama, R (2004)'Knowledge creation as a synthesizing process', in H Takeuchi and I Nonaka (eds), *Hitotsubashi on Knowledge Management*, Singapore, Wiley Asia

Reynolds, M (1999) 'Grasping the nettle: possibilities and pitfalls of a critical management pedagogy', *British Journal of Management*, **9**, pp 171–84

Savery, J R and Duffy, T M (1995) 'Problem based learning: instructional model and its constructivist framework', *Educational Technology*, September–October

Savin-Baden, M (2000) *Problem-Based Learning in Higher Education: Untold stories*, Buckingham, Open University Press

Savin-Baden, M (2003) *Facilitating Problem-Based Learning: Illuminating perspectives*, Buckingham, Open University Press

Schmidt, H G (1995) 'Problem-based learning: an introduction', *Instructional Science*, **22**, pp 247–50

Senge, P (1990) *The Fifth Discipline: The art and practice of the learning organization*, London, Random House

Stephenson, P and Galloway, V (2004) 'Problem-based learning', in G Foley (ed), *Dimensions of Adult Learning: Adult education and training in a global era*, Maidenhead, Open University Press/McGraw-Hill

Thrift, N and Pile, S (eds) (1995) *Mapping the Subject: Geographies of cultural transformation*, London, Routledge

Ulrich, D and Smallwood, N (2004) 'Capitalizing on capabilities', *Harvard Business Review*, **82**, 6

Varela, F J, Thompson, E and Rosch, E (1993) *The Embodied Mind: Cognitive science and human experience*, Boston, MA, MIT Press

Weick, K and Van Orden, P (1990) 'Organizing on a global scale: a research and teaching agenda', *Human Resource Management*, **29**, 1, pp 49–61

20

Management Training and Development: Problems, Paradoxes and Perspectives

Colin Beard and Dominic Irvine

INTRODUCTION AND LEARNING OBJECTIVES

The UK has about 2.75 million people who exercise managerial roles. About 1.1 million are in middle and senior management positions. About 90,000 people enter management roles each year. The great majority of these have no prior formal management education and training. (Constable and McCormick, 1987: Executive summary)

Constable and McCormick (1987) and Handy (1987) in their seminal reports both identified the need for formal, coherent training and development programmes for managers in response to the shortcomings of British management education in the context of international competition. In 1997, the UK Institute of Personnel and Development published its first guide on international management development (IPD, 1997). This reflects the increasing use of strategic alliances (Gugler, 1992) and cross-border trade (Daniels and Radebaugh, 1995) as a consequence of globalization (Harris and Moran, 1996; Julien, 1996). In the UK, there is an ever-growing assortment of training and development opportunities for managers. These range from MBAs to outdoor management development programmes in remote parts of the countryside. All purport to develop the manager, resulting in them being better suited to the challenges of the future.

In this chapter, we explore various problems, paradoxes and perspectives of management development. The aim of the chapter is to examine the fundamental issues that affect management training and development (MTD). Reference is made to literature dealing with specific tools and techniques of MTD. We start by examining the nature of management. Then we investigate briefly the nature of development. Third, we explore the differing perceptions as to the purpose of management development. We then list the many and varied techniques of MTD. Fifth, we examine the difficulties of determining the effectiveness of MTD. Finally we conclude with a review of issues that ought to be taken into account when approaching the task of training and developing managers.

Having read this chapter you will:

- understand the difficulty in accurately defining 'management';
- know the main roles of a manager;
- know the essential principles of continuing professional development; and
- be able to evaluate management training and development.

WHAT DO WE MEAN BY MANAGEMENT?

According to Drucker (1974:45) 'Effectiveness is the foundation of success – efficiency is concerned with doing things right. Effectiveness is doing the right things.' To measure, as Drucker suggests, the effectiveness of a given MTD programme it is necessary first to establish what is the desired outcome. Without this, measuring success is somewhat imprecise. To paraphrase Levitt (1991), 'unless you know where you are going, any road will take you there'. A clear idea of management enables those individuals involved in MTD to:

- assess the management development requirements of an individual;
- evaluate management development courses;
- measure the success of such management development programmes.

Herein lies the fundamental difficulty in MTD: 'What do we mean by management?' A 'lack of understanding of the concepts, principles and techniques of management makes it difficult ... to train managers' (Koontz et al, 1984:11). Defining management is not as simple as it might appear. Many authors have attempted definitions of management (eg, Killen, 1977; Stoner and Wankel, 1986; Torrington et al, 1989) to name a few, with varying degrees of success. In contrast some authors (eg, Drucker, 1974) argue that management cannot be defined and suggest that a description of management is all that is possible. To illustrate the difficulties this creates for MTD, some examples of definitions and descriptions are considered next. The examples cited are but a few of the many that abound. For a review of the distinction between training, education and development, see Chapter 1.

Definitions of management

A specific feature must be exclusive to an activity in order to define it according to Geach (1956). Handy (1993:361) suggests that trying to work out what are the defining elements of management is extremely difficult:

> It has never been easy to define what a manager is, or what he (sic) does. It is a useful concept, 'management', the missing 'X', the exact qualities that are important, this tends to shift from equation to equation. Definitions of the manager, or the manager's role, tend therefore to be so broad that they are meaningless, or so stereotyped that they become part of the background. 'Yes, of course', we say and take no further notice.

To illustrate the breadth of definitions in use consider that offered by Torrington *et al* (1989:4):

> management is not just a job done by people called 'managers'; it is an aspect of the job done by all those who have to cope with the problems and opportunities of organization: social workers, editors, ward sisters, chefs, housewives, and engineers, school teachers, and clergyman, the administrators, and many more.

Definitions such as this are almost suggesting that 'to live is to manage'. This may be the case: everybody has to manage to a greater or lesser extent whether it be pocket money, or a multi-billion pound business. However, a definition this broad is of little value to MTD as it validates almost any form of training on the grounds that it will involve management to varying degrees.

What do managers do?

A commonly adopted solution that avoids the need to embrace the thorny issue of defining management is to describe the management process instead. By 'management process' what is meant is 'what managers do' (eg, Koontz *et al*, 1984). Indeed, Drucker (1974:37) argues that a description of management is all that is possible:

> Management ... cannot be defined or understood – let alone practised – except in terms of its performance dimensions and of the demands of performance on it. The tasks of management are the reason for its existence, the determinants of its work, and the grounds of its authority and legitimacy.

This initially seems sensible reasoning. However, it can be applied to any activity. For example: '*Music* ... cannot be defined or understood – let alone practised – except in terms of its performance dimensions ...' A *musician* is unable to make music without an instrument just as a manager without a situation to manage is unable to manage. The problem has shifted from defining the nature of management to defining what constitutes a management task, but the uncertainty remains.

Managers' roles

Mintzberg (1973) is one of the few writers in this area to have attempted a systematic evaluation of what constitutes management. Mintzberg proposed 10 interrelated working roles performed by all managers. These are divided into three interpersonal roles, three informational roles and four decisional roles:

Interpersonal roles:

- figurehead;
- leader;
- liaison.

Informational roles:

- monitor;
- disseminator;
- spokesman.

Decisional roles:

- entrepreneur;
- disturbance handler;
- resource allocator;
- negotiator.

Like Mintzberg, Stoner and Wankel (1986) described the roles of a manager. Stoner and Wankel's implication is that management requires an individual to be many things. The key headings of Stoner and Wankel's (1986:6–8) description have been listed below to illustrate this point:

- Managers work with and through people.
- Managers balance competing goals and set priorities.
- Managers must think analytically and conceptually.
- Managers are mediators.
- Managers are politicians.
- Managers are diplomats.
- Managers are symbols.
- Managers make difficult decisions.

The implications for management development are somewhat demanding. A person going into management would seem to require experience in the diplomatic service, a seat in parliament, an ability to mediate, and proven leadership – to name but a few. A tall order for the training department of an organization! This example illustrates the complexity in creating a basis and direction for management development.

Descriptions of management that preceded Mintzberg (1973) contain similar elements but not in such detail. For example: in the early part of the century, the French industrialist, Henri Fayol, wrote that all managers perform five management functions: 'they plan, organize, command, coordinate and control' (Robbins, 1991:4). Robbins adds that 'today, we've condensed these down to four: planning, organizing, leading and controlling' (1991:4). Once again these definitions are extremely broad. The teacher undertakes the four activities described by Robbins. The teacher plans, organizes, leads and controls the lesson. It could be argued that a teacher satisfied the 10 roles that Mintzberg describes as well as those of Fayol and Robbins in which instance the word 'teacher' is synonymous with 'manager'. While management is an aspect of the teacher's role, just as teaching may be part of a manager's role, neither is the core aspect of the other's job.

Placing these broad, abstract concepts into the tangible realistic development training for managers is problematic. At what stage is a manager deemed satisfactorily competent at managing uncertainty? The concept does not enable a management trainer, citing the criteria identified earlier to easily:

- assess the management development needs of an individual;
- provide a template for management development;
- measure the success of such management development programmes.

Clearly a functional approach to management, which requires an improvement in organizational and individual performance, can be carried out with differing management styles and strategies. In a era of hierarchical flattening, and the de-layering of middle management, 'management' might manifest itself in a different form. Modern approaches might interpret the manager role as one of service to the internal customers – that is, staff (Whitaker, 1994).

The National Occupation Standards for management and leadership (Figure 20.1) describe the expected performance levels and can also be used for:

- auditing management capability;
- benchmarking organizational performance;
- developing organizational structures;
- improving the performance of individual managers;
- defining job roles and job descriptions;
- recruiting and selecting personnel;
- identifying training and development needs;
- defining personal development and continuing professional development programmes;
- developing training programmes;
- developing vocational and academic qualifications;
- managing and assessing performance;
- coaching and mentoring;
- planning for succession and developing promotion criteria;
- defining pay and reward schemes;
- counselling managers for redeployment and redundancy.

While the Management Standards Centre standards may be very useful, they are still a description and not a definition. In describing what a manager does, they fail to explain what is required to be a manager – the factor 'X' (Handy, 1985). The defining feature of management enabling distinction from other activities such as teaching, without having to rely on descriptions, is absent. It may be that management is analogous to Wittgenstein's example of the aroma of coffee (cited in Mounce, 1988), or Nagel's (1979) example of what it is to be a bat – impossible to define.

Where does this leave MTD? How can MTD proceed if it is not possible to overcome the first hurdle, deciding what management is? Hospers (1990:122) argues that it is quite possible to understand what is meant without being entirely clear as to the precise constitution of a term:

> Among a definite set of characteristics, no one characteristic has to be present as long as all or even some of the others are present; but it cannot do without them all. This might as well be called the quorum feature of definitions. A quorum of Senators must be present before the Senate is officially in session, but no particular senator has to be there.

This is not to imply that an acceptable definition of management will be ambiguous but that the edges of the application of the definition may be unclear. In some situations the definition is clearly applicable and others not, but that there is an area where the applicability and usefulness of the theory is not clear cut. Guba (1990:17) in this instance discussing the use of the term 'paradigm', notes that there are great many ways in which the word is used, and argues that rather than those being a weakness, they can be considered a strength. Perhaps the same could be said of management:

> I believe that it is important to leave the term in such a problematic limbo, because it is then possible to reshape it as our understanding of its many implications improves. Having the term not cast in stone is intellectually useful.

It is sufficient to note here that management is not a clear and precise term on which MTD can be based. Before embarking upon a training programme it is first necessary to satisfy oneself that the outcomes of the programme relate to the concept of management as understood not only by the training organization, be it internal or external, but also by the organization for whom the training is being delivered. These are issues of culture and beliefs and are discussed in more detail later.

WHAT DO WE MEAN BY DEVELOPMENT?

Development can be likened to 'growth', except that the latter is often associated with getting bigger and the former is associated with getting better or wiser. The ever-changing nature of work necessitates a process of continual management development. As Fahey and Narayanan (cited in Segal-Horn, 1994:28) suggest, 'Without a willingness to consider alternative futures, an organization is likely to find itself constrained and victimized by its implicit presumption that the future is going to be largely a replication of the past.' It is perhaps for this reason that the IPD

The new standards for
management and leadership
consist of the following units:

A   Managing self and personal skills

A1   Manage your own resources

A2   Manage your own resources and professional
      development

A3   Develop your personal networks

B   Providing direction

B1   Develop and implement operational plans for
      your area of responsibility

B2   Map the environment in which your
      organisation operates

B3   Develop a strategic business plan for your
      organisation

B4   Put the strategic business plan into action

B5   Provide leadership for your team

B6   Provide leadership in your area of
      responsibility

B7   Provide leadership for your organisation

B8   Ensure compliance with legal, regulatory,
      ethical and social requirements

B9   Develop the culture of your organisation

B10   Manage risk

B11   Promote equality of opportunity and diversity
      in your area of responsibility

B12   Promote equality of opportunity and diversity
      in your organisation

C   Facilitating change

C1   Encourage innovation in your team

C2   Encourage innovation in your area of
      responsibility

C3   Encourage innovation in your organisation

C4   Lead change

C5   Plan change

C6   Implement change

D   Working with people

D1   Develop productive working relationships
      with colleagues

D2   Develop productive working relationships with
      colleagues and stakeholders

D3   Recruit, select and keep colleagues

D4   Plan the workforce

D5   Allocate and check work in your team

D6   Allocate and monitor the progress and quality
      of work in your area of responsibility

D7   Provide learning opportunities for colleagues

E   Using resources

E1   Manage a budget

E2   Manage finance for your area of responsibility

E3   Obtain additional finance for the organisation

E4   Promote the use of technology within your
      organisation

E5   Ensure your own actions reduce risks to
      health and safety

E6   Ensure health and safety requirements are
      met in your area of responsibility

E7   Ensure an effective organisational approach
      to health and safety

F   Achieving results

F1   Manage a project

F2   Manage a programme of complementary projects

F3   Manage business processes

F4   Develop and review a framework for marketing

F5   Resolve customer service problems

F6   Monitor and solve customer service problems

F7   Support customer service improvements

F8   Work with others to improve customer service

F9   Build your organisation's understanding
      of its market and customers

F10   Develop a customer focussed organisation

F11   Manage the achievement of customer
      satisfaction

F12   Improve organisational performance

Figure 20.1 The Management Standards Centre Management and Leadership units (with acknowledgement to the Management Standards Centre, www.management-standards.org.uk)

Providing direction
Provide leadership for your team

B5

UNIT SUMMARY

What is the unit about?

This unit is about providing direction to the members of your team and motivating and supporting them to achieve the objectives of the team and their personal work objectives.

Who is the unit for?

The unit is recommended for team leaders.

Links with other units

This unit is linked to units D1 Develop productive working relationships with colleagues, B6 Provide leadership in your area of responsibility and D5 Allocate and check work in your team in the overall suite of National Occupational Standards for management and leadership.

Skills

Listed below are the main generic skills which need to be applied in providing leadership for your team. These skills are explicit/implicit in the detailed content of the unit and are listed here as additional information.

- Communicating
- Planning
- Team building
- Leading by example
- Providing feedback
- Setting objectives
- Motivating
- Consulting
- Problem solving
- Valuing and supporting others
- Monitoring
- Managing conflict
- Decision making
- Following

Figure 20.2   MSC Unit 5: Providing direction: provide leadership for your team

Providing direction
Provide leadership for your team

B5

OUTCOMES OF EFFECTIVE PERFORMANCE

You must be able to do the following:

1 Set out and positively communicate the purpose and objectives of the team to all members.

2 Involve members in planning how the team will achieve its objectives.

3 Ensure that each member of the team has personal work objectives and understands how achieving these will contribute to achievement of the team's objectives.

4 Encourage and support team members to achieve their personal work objectives and those of the team and provide recognition when objectives have been achieved.

5 Win, through your performance, the trust and support of the team for your leadership.

6 Steer the team successfully through difficulties and challenges, including conflict within the team.

7 Encourage and recognise creativity and innovation within the team.

8 Give team members support and advice when they need it especially during periods of setback and change.

9 Motivate team members to present their own ideas and listen to what they say.

10 Encourage team members to take the lead when they have the knowledge and expertise and show willingness to follow this lead.

11 Monitor activities and progress across the team without interfering.

BEHAVIOURS WHICH UNDERPIN EFFECTIVE PERFORMANCE

1 You create a sense of common purpose.

2 You take personal responsibility for making things happen.

3 You encourage and support others to take decisions autonomously.

4 You act within the limits of your authority.

5 You make time available to support others.

6 You show integrity, fairness and consistency in decision making.

7 You seek to understand people's needs and motivations.

8 You model behaviour that shows respect, helpfulness and co-operation.

Figure 20.2   MSC Unit 5: Providing direction: provide leadership for your team *continued*

Providing direction

Provide leadership for your team

B5

KNOWLEDGE AND UNDERSTANDING

You need to know and understand the following:

General knowledge and understanding

1 Different ways of communicating effectively with members of a team.

2 How to set objectives which are SMART (Specific, Measurable, Achievable, Realistic and Time-bound).

3 How to plan the achievement of team objectives and the importance of involving team members in this process.

4 The importance of and being able to show team members how personal work objectives contribute to achievement of team objectives.

5 That different styles of leadership exist.

6 How to select and successfully apply a limited range of different methods for motivating, supporting and encouraging team members and recognising their achievements.

7 Types of difficulties and challenges that may arise, including conflict within the team, and ways of identifying and overcoming them.

8 The importance of encouraging others to take the lead and ways in which this can be achieved.

9 The benefits of and how to encourage and recognise creativity and innovation within a team.

Industry/sector specific knowledge and understanding

1 Legal, regulatory and ethical requirements in the industry/sector.

Context specific knowledge and understanding

1 The members, purpose, objectives and plans of your team.

2 The personal work objectives of members of your team.

3 The types of support and advice that team members are likely to need and how to respond to these.

4 Standards of performance for the work of your team.

Figure 20.2 MSC Unit 5: Providing direction: provide leadership for your team *continued*

advocates 'continuous professional development' (CPD), the essence of which is continually developing managerial competence. This requires self-direction, self-management and responsiveness to the development opportunities, be they generated through work or outside of the workplace. The essential principles of CPD (adapted from IPD, undated:3) are:

- Development should be continuous in the sense that the professional should always be actively seeking to improve performance.
- Development should be owned and managed by the individual learner.
- CPD is a personal matter and the effective learner knows best what he or she needs to learn.
- Development should begin from the individual's current learning state.
- Learning objectives should be clear and wherever possible should serve organizational or client needs as well as individual goals.
- Regular investment of time in learning should be seen as an essential part of professional life, not an optional extra.

The process is one of self-development. The key to self-development is that learners take responsibility for their own learning: what they learn, when they learn, with whom they learn, where they learn and how they learn. In so doing, the learner accepts the consequences of choosing a programme or programmes of self-development.

Over the years the self-development approach has moved from periphery to centre stage and there are few training programmes in organizations today that do not include self-development elements in the design and delivery (Stansfield, 1996). While this can be seen as placing the power and control in the hands of the learner, a process typically referred to as 'empowerment', it can sometimes be used as a means of abdicating responsibility by the organization for the learner. It can also be used as a means of reducing expenditure on training programmes as coaching and developing staff is often time-consuming, demanding and expensive. Two sources that provide detailed and informative discussion of self-development are Pedler (1990) and Megginson and Whitaker (1996).

Current evidence from many companies suggests that as pressures increase on a managers' time and resourcefulness, more organizations are focusing on the facilitation of self-development. According to Megginson and Whitaker (1996) the reasons for the increasing popularity of self-development are as follows:

- society ebbs and flows between individual choice on the one hand and social and organizational definitions of what is needed on the other; currently we seem to be approaching the end of a trend towards individualization;
- the increase in the 'unprogrammability' of jobs which makes teaching and course-based training design much less relevant to the work of organizations;
- a move from role cultures to achievement cultures;
- the removal of layers of management has meant that people have had to fend for themselves and use their own best judgement more. The knowledge explosion and the proliferation of specialisms implies that bosses, trainers and experts of all sorts find it harder than before to know as much about jobs as the people doing them. Organization capability is decreasingly

located in the plant, finance and systems of the firm, and increasingly in people's heads, so these staff need to be in charge of their own development;

- people doing skilled and professional work are less likely than before to be actually employed by the organization, and more likely to work as consultants, contractors or suppliers – the flexible firm; and, in the extreme, the virtual firm: companies with huge turnover but only a handful of actual employees;
- learning at the start of a career that lasts a lifetime applies to nobody's job nowadays: continuous learning is the norm;
- as organizations federalize or fragment into business units, new forms of organizational 'glue' are needed to keep the enterprise together. The networking involved in self-development provides a powerful bond between people who may not work directly together.

The historical precedent for self-development pre-dates modern changes in business practice. Successive Indian civilizations have for thousands of years developed methodologies for self-discovery, self-improvement and self-development (Parikh, 1991:10):

> The relevance becomes even more clear when you reflect on the evolution of management over time. The initial focus was on 'how to get more and better work done through machines'. The next step was 'how to get more and better work done through people'. Now the emerging interest is in 'how to develop people through work'. The thrust of management now is more towards 'mobilizing' rather than just 'organizing'. This implies creating an environment that makes better people out of your employees, rather than just better employees out of your people. Unless the people are developed to their maximum potential, corporations cannot achieve their best, reach their peak performance level, and maintain it. This is what managing yourself is all about.

Valuable lessons can be learned from other cultures, not least the opportunity to challenge widely held beliefs on the way management should be conducted. A cautionary note is offered by Ackers and Preston (1997) who argue that the differences between cultures means that it is rarely an easy process of transplanting a differing approach in full. For a discussion on the differences between cultures and the way in which they affect business, see Daniels and Radebaugh (1995), Franke *et al* (1991) and Harris and Moran (1996).

Given the importance of self-development, the lack of time allocated by managers for self-development, management development or the coaching and development of staff is of concern. If Parikh's (1991) argument is accepted, everything a manager does is an opportunity for self-development and time taken to realize this potential should be encouraged. There are numerous tools and techniques available to help with self-development, for example: life lines, life planning, career development, self-awareness, action learning sets, learning logs and personal portfolios. The benefits of maintaining a personal portfolio incorporating a record of work done and knowledge and skills acquired are:

- a personal portfolio provides a record of work done – useful when seeking a new appointment;
- it assists in career development;
- it provides evidence of performance and development;
- it helps in determining the direction and focus for self-development;

- it can provide evidence of both corporate and team portfolios;
- it can be used to illustrate the benefits of tasks done;
- it can assist in appraising performance in the absence of a formal process.

A personal portfolio might include:

- a work file and/or box in which information is stored;
- cross-referenced achievements detailing learning outcomes, experience and skills acquired;
- materials such as copies of reports produced, publications and products;
- certificates for academic, vocational and non-vocational qualifications;
- details of ongoing studies;
- job specifications of previous and current posts including original advertisements;
- newspaper or newsletter cuttings, reports, photographs, video and audio tape footage;
- professional links with other organizations;
- learning logs.

The process of self-development is as much an issue of personal development as it is management development. It could be argued that to treat management development as a separate issue distinct from developing the person is akin to the mind/body fallacy of Cartesian Dualism (Hospers, 1990). That is to say the two cannot be viewed separately. If you develop the manager, you develop the person; if you develop the person you develop the manager. The issue then for management development is in terms of how to ensure that a skill learned in one environment, for example managing the risk in outdoor activities, can be transferred and utilized in another setting such as managing a business. It is not a failing of the definition of management in that it is not possible to distinguish between a teacher and a manager, but that a teacher *is* a manager. On this basis, it could be argued that it is an issue of relatives, although not in a nihilistic sense (MacIntyre, 1994). For the teacher, more of the workload is dedicated to teaching than managing and for the manager, more time is dedicated to administrative or strategic tasks than teaching. Both are inherently managerial by nature.

PERCEPTIONS OF MANAGEMENT TRAINING AND DEVELOPMENT

The third issue facing those working in MTD (the first being the problem of defining management, the second being the nature of development) is the validity of the various theories. Increasingly within the literature, concepts which have been considered almost *a priori* knowledge in MTD are being critically scrutinized, for example Holman *et al's* (1997) review of Kolb's theory of experiential learning and Reynolds' (1997) critical examination of learning styles. MacIntyre (1994:107) for example, takes a critical look at the research evidence on which contemporary management is based and describes from an alternative paradigm a very different way of viewing research into management:

the social world of everyday, hard-headed, practical, pragmatic, no-nonsense realism which is the environment of management is one which depends for its sustained existence on the systematic perpetuation of misunderstanding and of belief in fictions ... the realm of managerial expertise is one in which what purport to be objectively-grounded claims function in fact as expressions of arbitrary, but disguised will and preference.

The problematic nature of management and the increasing number of challenges to core concepts mean that it is necessary to understand the implicit assumptions inherent within the various MTD approaches. These different approaches are referred to here as paradigms, using the broad definition offered by Guba (1990:17): 'A paradigm is a basic set of beliefs that guides action, whether of the everyday garden variety or action taken in connection with a disciplined inquiry.' While this is the definition used here, Goodman (1997) discusses the various other ways in which the term is used.

Issues of paradigm are not questions of absolutes in that one paradigm is better than the others. They represent instead the perspective taken. If it were possible to determine which paradigm was categorically right or wrong,

There would be no doubt how to practise inquiry. But all such belief systems or paradigms are human constructions, and hence subjected to all the errors and foibles that inevitably accompany human endeavours. (Guba, 1990:18–19)

Thus, the choice of MTD programme will reflect the perspective of the individual, the trainer and/or organization. For example, it is important for the individual concerned with the selection of MTD programmes to be wary of 'coffee table book' promises that offer for example 'common sense' approaches to management development. The hard-headed world of management (MacIntyre, 1994) that depends upon a common sense approach may have much appeal to the practitioner. However, the notion of common sense as justification has mythical validity. Common sense is not, as it would sometimes appear to be seen, *a priori* knowledge. Common sense is the 'unquestioned delimitation of the terrain of relevance from that of irrelevance' (Grey and Mitlev, 1995:79). To be guided by common sense may in fact be to entrap 'oneself in the current "traditions" or "fads" dominant among the social groups to which we belong, at work or elsewhere' (Gill and Johnson, 1991:28). Common sense may be a little more than a convenient label under which to hide unresolved issues. Moreover, *common sense* is not always *common practice*!

The power of a commonly understood concept can be phenomenal. Consider the problems associated with persuading others that the world was round, or the difficulties experienced by Darwin when presenting his treatise. Thus caution must be exercised when employing a particular MTD approach to ensure that the technique has some validity and is appropriate. What is being argued here is not that one particular approach is necessarily better than another but to foster an awareness that while one approach may appear the obvious and the most logical approach it may do so not as a function of a carefully considered set of beliefs, values, morals and ethics but because of other variables which provide an illusion of credibility such as common sense. For example, consider the different ways in which management development is viewed. According to Ackers and Preston (1997:687):

One perspective sees management development as a form of help and argues that it is necessary for managers to learn about the organizational culture for their own benefit and well being. The sense of confusion associated with a change of organization or job is intended to be lessened by senior management providing enough information to managers, so that they know what is expected of them and are able to feel part of their new place of work. Promotion opportunities and attendance on management training courses should not only provide the individual with additional knowledge and skills, but also result in improved job satisfaction and enjoyment overall. In this unitarist view, business needs and personal self-development happily coincide.

In contrast, alternative views of MTD do not see the relationship between the manager and the organization as quite so cosy. Höpfl and Dawes (1995) refer to management development not just in terms of the realization of potential but also in terms of regulation and control. As Ackers and Preston (1997:687) illustrate, 'Critics of MD (management development), on the other hand, argue that it occurs purely for the benefit of senior management and manipulates the individual managers involved.' In this view management development is perceived more in terms of the power of senior management over those in lesser positions. This is best exemplified by the unlikely event that a participant will criticize the MTD process in which he or she is involved because in so doing they are making a statement about the person who selected the methods in the first place. To criticize and destroy the training method upon which a company's strategy rests is to call into question those who have advocated its use. It is, in effect, making a statement as to their competence in choosing such a method. An alternative way of knowing that seeks not to develop and better understand the MTD methods in use but fundamentally destroys the credibility upon which the method rests is hardly likely to find favour with those who have chosen the initial strategy (Ackers and Preston, 1997).

We have first-hand experience of working as consultants to organizations where individuals have challenged the perceived wisdom of the training methods to which they are being subjected. Unfortunately, in many such instances, rather than this being taken as an opportunity to review the validity of the technique used, those raising their concerns have been seen as either 'not part of the team', or 'of the wrong stuff' by the employing organization. Höpfl and Dawes (1995:26) illustrate the power of the relationship between those who have control over MTD programmes and those who do not. They suggest that:

> The pursuit of an appropriate management paradigm of managerial practice leads to a partial acknowledgement of the person and a partial extension of power. This fundamental and underlying paradox resides at the heart of management development.

The point being made is that while on the one hand MTD takes into account the need of the individual and provides appropriate resources, be it training or otherwise to meet those needs, it is still within the context of control of those who are in charge within the organization. Dispenza (1996:245) applies this line of reasoning to the notion of empowerment and concludes that:

> Those who do the empowering allow those who are being empowered a defined locus of power. I would argue that the term 'empowerment' involves the depoliticization of control. … Control is the underlying outcome, but the meaning of the relationship is managed … in such a way as to

make the exercising of that control a less contentious issue: the idea of being empowered is a more comfortable prospect than being controlled (both for those doing the empowering and those being empowered), but the outcome may be the same.

Views such as those expressed by Dispenza (1996) and Höpfl and Dawes (1995) illustrate the careful way in which seemingly well-understood terms, when scrutinized, turn out to be contradictory.

The world of management is a constantly changing environment, not just in terms of the greater opportunities brought about through changes in technology but also in terms of the way in which people work together. Increasingly there is an emphasis away from motivating and controlling staff in a mechanistic way to where responsibility is being divested more widely in the organization. The implications for MTD are that the approach taken needs to reflect the paradigm on which it is based. It should be able to reflect the changing culture of modern management and if necessary facilitate the change.

The difficulty is not only that there are differing perspectives about the purpose of MTD but also a change in the beliefs that underpin the way an organization is managed. To complicate the matter further, these changes vary from industry to industry, culture to culture and from one country to another. In the telecommunications market, the shift from state-owned organization to private company has resulted in a blurring of the boundaries between public and private sector MTD (Beard and Hartman, 1999). With some private sector managers taking 'time out' to work in voluntary organizations, elements of corporate MTD are transmogrifying the nature of voluntary sector MTD and vice versa (Paton and Hooker, 1990). Changes such as this are reflected in managerial behaviour often evidenced by a change in the language used, for example, from *control* to *empowerment* (Dispenza, 1996).

TECHNIQUES OF MANAGEMENT TRAINING AND DEVELOPMENT

In assessing the various tools that can be used in MTD the assumption being made is that it is possible to train and develop managers. As Smith (1993) noted, the nature/nurture argument, the influences of childhood and other experiences, may all play a part in the debate on how managers can or should be trained and developed. Wickens (1992:3) goes as far as to ask whether 'management development is dead'. He argues for a more holistic approach, an idea with which Doyle (1995) in his article on reforming management development appears to agree.

It is unsurprising given the conceptual problems described earlier that there are a great many tools and techniques offered. The cultural influences of other working styles, in particular the Japanese, mean that the range of techniques can be bewildering. For example, Collis (1993) drawing on Chinese philosophy, has no doubt that the secret lies in Confucianism. Parikh (1991) argues it is to Indian traditions that we should turn. Ackers and Preston (1997) argue that Japanese approaches might suit the Japanese culture but not that of the UK. In another ongoing debate, Ibbetson and Newell (1996) argue that 'adventure-based experiential learning' provides the key to effective management development. Again, it is possible to find those who disagree;

for example Irvine and Wilson (1994) are more cautious in their support of what they term 'outdoor management development'.

A common theme throughout all the activities is an experiential element that reflects the pragmatic nature of management. Both Stoner and Wankel (1986) and Mintzberg (1973) argue that activities in MTD are essential. As Mintzberg (1973:188) somewhat esoterically described the process:

> One cannot learn to swim by reading about it. One must get into the water, splash around, and practise various techniques with advice from someone who knows what skills swimming requires. Eventually, with sufficient feedback, he (sic) learns to swim. The same holds true for management skills. The student must be immersed in the milieu; he must practise the skill; and he must receive constructive feedback on his performance from someone who understands the skill.

This would seem to make sense. It is hard to imagine that any amount of study will adequately equip a manager for the experience of having to inform an employee that his or her services are no longer required. As a nurse once said to one of us, 'You don't have to have had a baby to be a midwife – but it helps.'

The various approaches are described in more detail in Chapters 16, 17 and 18. Listed below is a sample of the many and varied tools and techniques available:

- attending short courses, seminars, workshops, conferences;
- being coached by a more experienced colleague;
- forming a learning agreement;
- establishing a mentorship relationship;
- participating in a learning/support group;
- team working;
- undertaking a special project, assignment or consultancy;
- taking on a new area of responsibility;
- changing work practices or systems;
- a variety of on-the-job methods such as focused staff meetings, reading, discussion, reflection, observation and maintenance of a learning log;
- undertaking a research contract;
- seeking and receiving feedback;
- engaging in action research;
- action learning sets;
- qualification courses – educational, eg, MBA, Master's degrees, or vocational programmes, for example, the MCI;
- outdoor management development (OMD) programmes – see the OMD case study;
- development portfolios;
- a secondment or exchange;
- critical incident techniques;
- SWOT analysis – strengths, weaknesses, opportunities and threats;
- specialist development consultants;
- providing cover, deputizing, shadowing.

OUTDOOR MANAGEMENT DEVELOPMENT PROGRAMMES

OMD has become increasingly popular as a method of developing managerial effectiveness. It relies on the use of a combination of classroom and outdoor activities to create an environment conducive to changing behaviour. It primarily focuses on personal development.

Outdoor Management Development continues to evolve and change, taking on new dimensions as trainers reconsider the amount of physical recreational activity in the programmes which occurred as a result of instructor expertise in this area in many of the outdoor centres located in the National Parks in the UK. Such recreational activities which translate into teamwork or leadership courses have been criticized for their potential for deselecting or dis-interesting some participants, relying to some extent on physical strength or good psychomotor skills. CMD programmes increasingly employ specialists who are skilled in the design and facilitation of such programmes, and they have begun to incorporate community projects or environmental projects into the management development activities. This offers a greater sense of reality to the project, unlike the traditional 'planks and drums' exercises, as well as providing a sense of giving; which appears to enhance a participant's energy and possibly, the degree of transfer of learning (Beard, 1996). See Irvine and Wilson (1994) and Ibbetson and Newell (1996) for information.

DEVELOPING THE EMOTIONALLY INTELLIGENT MANAGER

Marketing material for emotional intelligence courses for managers suggests that there are many benefits to the development of emotional intelligent managers: it is said for example that emotionally intelligent managers contribute to improved team morale, more collaborative working, less energy waste on politicking and game play, and reduced loss of client goodwill through poor attitudes or indifference. Understanding and managing emotional intelligence, emotional effectiveness, motivation, enjoyment and satisfaction is said to be a good investment. Emotional intelligence (EI) has been popularized by Daniel Goleman is his work *Emotional Intelligence: Why it can matter more than IQ* (1996), and in turn this has spawned a proliferation of management programmes focusing on this subject.

Dyke, Martin and Woollard (2000) explore why emotional intelligence is important to the training and development of managers. They make reference to Senge, who wrote that 'working with personal mastery means entering the realm of matters of the heart' (1994:29), and Edgar Schein (1978), who noted that the distinguishing feature of a top executive is not skill or ability but emotional competence. Dyke *et al* say that:

> in management development the barriers to learning are often emotional blocks, rather than those of inadequate IQ. For example, an executive undertaking a business strategy course needs to not only understand the concepts and techniques but also to be motivated and confident in applying what he or she has learned. Learning needs to speak to whole brain, not just the 'thinking' brain'.
>
> (Dyke, Martin and Woollard, 2000:31)

Emotional intelligence does mean that managers should have a wide understanding and appreciation of 'self'. All managers have their own personal drivers that affect how they work with others. Dyke *et al* noted that when they were working with a group of management consultants, all of them successful, bright, attractive people, they discussed some of the drivers that lay beneath their hard-working professionalism. They did not dig too deeply, but noted the managers identified their own need to:

- be competitive, and always know the right answers;
- be responsible for others, and do the right thing for them;
- be perfect and never fail;
- always try harder and do better.

Such behaviours can be destructive to managers: working against them, developing a self-criticism, a self-punishment, encouraging dissatisfaction so that when these managers arrive at their goal, and achieve good performance, it is not good enough, and so leads to dysfunctional behaviours. The article describes a significant issue, the development of emotional managers: that is, the psychology of perfection and neurosis. (See also the work on neurosis by therapists Jeanette De Wyze and Allan Mallinger in their book *Too Perfect* (1995).)

Fineman notes that the rules of emotional expression are organizationally defined, and there can be significant differences between individual's privately held feelings and the emotion he or she displays at work. He has written extensively about emotional intelligence in managers (1997) and in organizations (1993). He lists the work of many influential writers on the subject of the debilitating nature of anxiety, fear and stress, and notes that emotions have been seen as 'unwanted' and 'undesirable' in the rational, logical workplace. Managers learn to survive, how to adapt and 'play the game', avoid blame, operate in a political climate, and learn when to be deferential. These, according to Salaman and Butler (1996), are emotional behaviours that appear in order that managers can avoid the painful experience of being singled out, of being blamed, and because they need allies. It is suggested however that such strategies are essentially 'fear-based' management and as such are likely to be ineffective and undesirable.

A significant theme emerging in management development is the use of 'emotional labour' and 'emotional engineering' in the workplace. Emotional labour was a term originally coined by Hochschild (1983) in reference to stewardesses working in the airline industry, where the women's emotions are commodified into a 'product'. Such emotional work is now prevalent, and typified by work for Disney and McDonald's. Boler (1999) considers how these corporately defined emotions represent an important conceptual opening between public and private spaces. Boler cautions against the development of an emotional intelligence movement, and suggests that it might be interpreted as a re-emergence of the mental hygiene movement, revived more recently in a postmodern form. Boler devotes much of her work to gender issues, and devotes a whole chapter to a critique of Daniel Goleman's work, referring to his book as reading like a 'blueprint for male CEO success'.

Words of wisdom on management development

Gerard Egan in *The Skilled Helper* (2002:19) talks about the commonsense wisdom in the helping professions, and says: 'Helpers need to be wise, and part of their job is to impart some of their wisdom, however indirectly, to their clients.' He then says that wisdom can be defined 'an expertise in the conduct and meaning of life' or 'an expert knowledge system concerning the fundamental pragmatics of life'. He then asks what the characteristics of wisdom might be, and offers some possibilities:

- self-knowledge and maturity;
- knowledge of life's obligations and goals;
- an understanding of cultural conditioning;
- the guts to admit mistakes and the sense to learn from them;
- a psychological and a human understanding of others; insight into human interactions;
- the ability to 'see through' situations; the ability to understand the meaning of events;
- tolerance for ambiguity and the ability to work with it;
- being comfortable with messy and ill-structured cases;
- an understanding of the messiness of human beings;
- openness to events that don't fit comfortably into logical or traditional categories;
- the ability to frame a problem so that it is workable; the ability to reframe information;
- avoidance of stereotypes;
- holistic thinking; open mindedness; open-endedness; contextual thinking;
- meta-thinking, or the ability to think about thinking and become aware about being aware;
- the ability to see relationships among diverse factors; the ability to spot flaws in reasoning; intuition, the ability to synthesize;
- the refusal to let experience become a liability through the creation of blind spots;
- the ability to take a long view of the problem;
- the ability to blend seemingly antithetical helping roles, being one who cares and understands while being also the one who challenges and 'frustrates';
- an understanding of the spiritual dimensions of life.

These seem to offer a very generic set of skills as good advice to any manager!

EVALUATING THE EFFECTIVENESS OF MANAGEMENT TRAINING AND DEVELOPMENT

The other part of Levitt's (1983) suggestion about knowing where to go is not just that we know the starting point, but that we also know at what stage we are on the journey and when we have reached the destination. This is achieved through evaluation. Evaluating MTD is a challenging task. As Douglas (1983) noted, managing at any one time is a complex blend of skills. Determining whether the action of the manager is attributable to a particular programme of training or whether it a function of some other unknown variable can be difficult. A brief recollection of Elton Mayo's classic experiment (cited in Brown, 1988) illustrates the difficulty of determining what is or are the causal variable(s). Evaluation of MTD is subject to the same well-documented difficulties as experienced in social science research in general. To take the process of conducting interviews for example; there are difficulties with the translation of meaning (eg, Deutscher, 1984), differences in culture (eg, Daniels and Radebaugh, 1995) and problems of interpretation (eg, Emory, 1985). There is also the difficulty of determining whom to evaluate. Smith and Piper (1990:9) have identified four groups of people directly involved in MTD who should be involved in its evaluation:

1.   the purchaser of training;
2.   the training agency;
3.   the trainee; and
4.   the independent contracted assessor or researcher.

Consider the perspective identified earlier that an individual is unlikely to criticize a course because in so doing he or she is making a statement about those who organized the course. Given this, asking for an unbiased evaluation from a participant is perhaps optimistic. If the participant's evaluation is considered along with that of all the parties identified thus far as having a stake in the process – an evaluation by the organization which delivered the training or development; the colleagues of the individual, who should be asked whether they think the manager has improved in the areas for which the training was prescribed; possibly an independent review – then the perspective is likely to be more balanced. Too often, as Smith and Piper (1990:9) suggest, the 'potential value of these informed views is seldom realized'. More commonly an end-of-course questionnaire is distributed to the participant to be completed prior to their departure. This 'happy sheet' evaluation as it is known, because it is completed during the euphoria often associated with the end of a course, serves only to provide information as to whether the participants *think* they have changed rather than whether they *have* changed. Such an evaluation should be avoided. Information as to the effectiveness of a programme can only be known some time after an MTD programme has finished and the person has settled back into the working environment. The nature of the evaluation should take into account the difficulties associated with research into the social sciences. Texts such as Gill and Johnson (1991), de Vaus (1993) and Denzin and Lincoln (1994) give some idea of the many issues and variables involved.

KEY ISSUES TO CONSIDER

Before deciding on the appropriate MTD tool, it is first necessary to ask:

● What do I mean by management? That is to say, what are the skills required for the post of manager within the organization?
● What is the culture of the organization? The preferred method of MTD varies from one organization to another. For example, an organization dependent on volunteers will need to

develop a different set of skills to those serving the public sector. (See the case study on BTCV illustrating their strategy for management development.) The public sector has different requirements to those of commercial businesses (see Sanderson and Foreman, 1996). In addition to the types of organization there are international variations in culture.

- What MTD tools are best suited to equipping the individual with the required skills, given the culture of the organization?
- How will the MTD intervention be evaluated both in terms of auditing the need and determining the effectiveness?

CONCLUSION

The complexity of variables which constitute the MTD environment provide a rewarding and challenging sphere of work. Successful MTD interventions depend on ensuring that there is a 'best fit' between the needs of the individual, the organization and those responsible for the delivery of the programme. Lewis (1991) provides a useful framework for achieving the latter objective. What has been argued in this chapter is that because the process of MTD is fraught with a great many variables, it is essential that time is spent determining in the first instance what is meant by management. It is only when this is achieved that an assessment of the skills of managers can be undertaken to determine the type of MTD intervention required in order to furnish participants with the desired skills and knowledge. Determining the desired management style also enables effective evaluation. These strategies will ensure that a situation does not arise whereby managers are equipped with skills which conflict with the nature of the business. For example, if the culture of the business is based on a rigid hierarchy, advocating empowerment may cause frustration and conflict and ultimately loss of staff, or business, or both. Similarly, equipping managers with skills based on an American culture of business will not help when conducting business with Asian countries.

Given the immense complexity of management, it is easy to take any MTD intervention and find faults and criticize. This is an essential part of the process by which the tools and techniques used are developed to ever improve their effectiveness. Critics should note that while it is easy to find fault, attempting to improve the way in which we manage is a worthy quest and is better than not developing managers at all.

Bibliography

Ackers, P and Preston, D (1997) 'Born again? The ethics and efficacy of the conversion experience in contemporary management development', *Journal of Management Studies*, **34**, 5, pp 677–701

Beard, C (1996) 'Environmental training: emerging products', *Journal of Industrial and Commercial Training*, **28**, 5, pp 18–23

Beard, C and Hartman, R (1999) 'European and Asian Telecoms – a new role in global sustainable development, *European Business Review*, **99**, 1, pp 42–54

Bowler, M (1999) *Reflective Practice Writing and Professional Development*, London, Routledge

Brown, R (1988) *Group Processes*, Oxford, Blackwell

Collis, R (1993) 'The people factor', *Business Life*, February, pp 57–65

Constable, J and McCormick, R (1987) *The Making of British Managers*, London, British Institute of Management/Confederation of British Industry

Daniels, J D and Radebaugh, L H (1995) *International Business Environments and Operations*, 7th edn, Wokingham, Addison Wesley

de Vaus, D A (1993) *Surveys in Social Research*, London, UCL Press

Denzin, N K and Lincoln, Y S (eds) (1994) *Handbook of Qualitative Research*, Thousand Oaks, CA, Sage

Deutscher, I (1984) 'Asking questions (and listening to answers)', in M Bulmer (ed), *Sociological Research Methods*, 3rd edn, Homewood, IL, Irwin

Dispenza, V (1996) 'Empowering students: a pragmatic philosophical approach to management education', *Management Learning*, **27**, 2, pp 239–51

Douglas, T (1983) *Understanding People Gathered Together*, London, Routledge

Doyle, M (1995) 'Organizational transformation and renewal – a case for refraining management development?', *Personnel Review*, **24**, 6, pp 6–18

Drucker, P F (1974) *Management Tasks, Responsibilities, Practices*, Oxford, Heinemann

Dyke, C, Martin, J and Woollard, J (2000) 'Why EQ matters for consultants and developers', *Organisation and People*, **7**, 1, February, pp 29–34

Emory, C W (1985) *Business Research Methods*, 3rd edn, Homewood, IL, Irwin

Franke, R H, Hofstede, G and Bond, M H (1991) 'Cultural roots of economic performance: a research note', *Strategic Management Journal*, **12**, pp 165–73

Geach, P T (1956) 'Good and evil', in P Foot (ed), (1967) *Theories of Morals*, Oxford, Oxford University Press

Gill, J and Johnson, P (1991) *Research Methods for Managers*, London, Paul Chapman

Goleman, D (1996) *Emotional Intelligence: Why it can matter more than IQ*, Bantam, London

Goleman, D (1998) *Working with Emotional Intelligence*, Bloomsbury, London

Goodman, N W (1997) 'Paradigm, parameter, paralysis of mind', *British Medical Journal*, **307**, pp 1627–29

Grey, C and Mitlev, N (1995) 'Management education – a polemic', *Management Learning*, **26**, 1, pp 73–90

Guba, E G (ed) (1990) *The Paradigm Dialog*, Newbury Park, CA, Sage

Gugler, P (1992) 'Building transnational alliances to create competitive advantage', *Long Range Planning*, **25**, 1, pp 90–99

Handy, C (1987) *The Making of Managers: A report on management education, training and development in the United States, West Germany, France, Japan and the UK*, London, National Economic Development Office

Handy, C (1993) *Understanding Organizations*, 3rd edn, Harmondsworth, Penguin

Harris, P R and Moran, R T (1996) 'European leadership in globalization', *European Business Review*, pp 32–41

Holman, D, Pavlica, K and Thorpe, R (1997) 'Rethinking Kolb's theory of experiential learning in management education', *Management Learning*, **28**, 2, pp 135–48

Höpfl, H and Dawes, F (1995) 'A whole can of worms! The contested frontiers of management development and learning', *Personnel Review*, **24**, 6, pp 19–28

Hospers, J (1990) *An Introduction to Philosophical Analysis*, London, Routledge

Ibbetson, A and Newell, S (1996) 'Winner takes all. An evaluation of adventure based experiential learning', *Management Learning*, **27**, 2, pp 163–85

IPD (Institute for Personnel and Development) (1997) *The IPD Guide On International Management Development*, London, IPD

IPD (undated) *Continuing Professional Development*, London, IPD

Irvine, D and Wilson, J P (1994) 'Outdoor management development – reality or illusion?', *Journal of Management Development*, **13**, 5, pp 25–37

Julien, P A (1996) 'Globalization: different types of small business behaviour', *Entrepreneurship and Regional Development*, **8**, 1, pp 57–74

Killen, K H (1977) *Management*, Boston, MA, Houghton Mifflin

Koontz, H, O'Donnell, C and Weihrich, H (1984) *Management*, 8th edn, Maidenhead, McGraw-Hill

Levitt, T (1983) 'The globalization of markets', *Harvard Business Review*, May/June, pp 92–102

Levitt, T (1991) 'Marketing myopia', *The Best of the Harvard Business Review*, Boston, MA, Harvard Business School

Lewis, P (1991) 'Eight steps to the successful appointment of a training consultant', *Journal of European and Industrial Training*, **15**, 6, pp 25–29

MacIntyre, A (1994) *After Virtue*, 2nd edn, London, Duckworth

Mallinger, A E and De Wyze, J (1995) *Too Perfect: When Being in Control Gets out of Control*, New York, Fawcett Books

Management Charter Initiative (1997) *Management Standards: Key role A – Manage activities*, London, (For further details contact: MCI, Russell Square House, 10–12 Russell Square, London WC1B Tel 020 7872 9000; website: www.management–charter–initiative.org.uk)

Mintzberg, H (1973) *The Nature of Managerial Work*, New York, Harper & Row

Mintzberg, H (1991) 'The manager's job: folklore and fact', *The Best of the Harvard Business Review*, Boston, MA, Harvard Business School

Mounce, H O (1988) The aroma of coffee', *Philosophy*, **64**, pp 159–73

Nagel, T (1979) 'What it is like to be a bat', *Mortal Questions*, Cambridge, Cambridge University Press

Parikh, J (1991) *Managing Yourself – Management by detached involvement*, Oxford, Blackwell

Paton, R and Hooker, C (1990) *Developing Managers in Voluntary Organizations – A handbook*, Sheffield, Employment Department

Pedler, M (1990) *Self-development in Organizations*, New York, McGraw-Hill

Reynolds, M (1990) 'A biography of self-development', in M Pedler, J Burgoyne, T Boydel and G Welshman (eds), *Self-development in Organizations*, Maidenhead, McGraw-Hill, pp 3–19

Reynolds, M (1997) 'Learning styles: a critique', *Management Learning*, **28**, 2, pp 115–33

Robbins, S P (1991) *Organizational Behaviour*, 5th edn, Englewood Cliffs, NJ, Prentice Hall

Sanderson, I and Foreman, A (1996) 'Towards pluralism and partnership in management development in local government', *Local Government Studies*, **22**, 1, pp 59–77

Segal-Horn, S (ed) (1994) *The Challenge of International Business*, London, Kogan Page

Smith, A J and Piper, J A (1990) 'The tailor-made training maze: a practitioner's guide to evaluation', *Journal of European and Industrial Training*, **14**, 8, pp 1–24

Smith, R (1993) 'Born to be boss', *Health Service Journal*, 8 April

Stansfield, L M (1996) 'Is self-development the key to the future?', *Management Learning*, **27**, 4, pp 429–45

Stoner, J A F and Wankel, C (1986) *Management*, 3rd edn, Englewood Cliffs, NJ, Prentice Hall

Torrington, D, Weightman, J and Johns, K (1989) *Effective Management – People and organization*, Hemel Hempstead, Prentice Hall

Whittaker, V (1994) *Managing People*, London, HarperCollins

Whittaker, V and Megginson, D (1996) *Cultivating Self-development*, IPD Guide, London, IPD

Wickens, P (1992) 'Management development is dead!', *Management Development Review*, **5**, 5, pp 3–7

Wills, S (1993) 'MCI and the competency movement: the case so far', *Journal of European Industrial Training*, **17**, 1, pp 9–11

Section Six:

Assessment and Evaluation of Learning, Training and Development

21

Evaluation and Assessment

Catherine Edwards Zara

INTRODUCTION AND LEARNING OBJECTIVES

Our preoccupation with evaluation and assessment springs from an age-old desire or compulsion to 'understand and improve our lot' (Pawson and Tilley, 1997:xi). This endeavour involves our setting out to discover all that we can, or all that we can use, about how effective we are. We may do this to comprehend or to justify past actions or we may do it to become more successful in the future achievement of identified goals and aspirations. Any exploration of current scope and parameters of evaluation and assessment needs to acknowledge our normal daily experiences of mulling over and muddling through.

Methods of evaluation and assessment can offer us the illusion of being able to measure the unmeasurable anomalies of human experience. They can help us make judgements within hierarchical frameworks about how well we are doing by comparison with others. They can help us give an account of our own and others' contributions to particular projects and ventures. They can give us some insight into our own growth, progress and development. By and large we devise and seek them in order to exert a sense of rigorous control in an unpredictable and uncertain world.

What kind of control and how, why, where, when and with whom, are guided in the first instance by the concept at the heart of the term evaluation – to value. If one accepts that, essentially, evaluation is a process for establishing the value or worth of something (Bramley, 1996:4) then this chapter is specifically concerned with the value or worth of those changes that take place through the process of learning. More precisely still, it focuses on learning related to employment, the workplace, continuing employability and professional development.

Because values are at the heart of evaluation and of assessment, they are activities that may attract controversy and disagreement, particularly where there are underlying conflicts of interest in the world of work. Different stakeholders in any evaluative exercise may be looking for different things from the process and outcomes. They may want to tackle a problem that had not been tackled by other means. Methods of evaluation and assessment are therefore sometimes deployed to help stakeholders make better decisions. They are also deployed to justify decisions or courses of action already taken (Pawson and Tilley, 1997:xii). People may want to protect their investment, or promote a particular image. Even when these differences have been taken in to account and common ground negotiated, the values of individuals involved in the evaluation process still make it a subjective endeavour. People may have different criteria by which they are making their judgement, or different ways of interpreting agreed criteria.

Evaluation and assessment in many areas of our lives surround those of us living in post-industrial economies. Children are continually tested for achievement and progress; their schools are publicly held to account through league tables indicating how 'well' pupils perform. The extent to which different schools can genuinely be compared with one another through these mechanisms and the cost to the self-esteem of children and staff being judged have been much reported. Customer care feedback sheets proliferate in hotels, restaurants, fast food chains and modes of public transport. The promotion of customer care and consumer power has become a dominant reason for justifying such evaluations. But the extent to which this data is subsequently analysed and acted upon effectively can vary enormously.

Assessment of an individual's work performance and of learning related to it is also frequently justified in relation to the customer base of a particular industry or service. For instance, staff recruitment assessment processes act as gatekeeping mechanisms that restrict entry into a particular workplace or profession. This should help protect the public from poor practitioners. But it can also prohibit entry by members of diverse groups who differ from the incumbents, with the resultant loss of new and important contributions to the workplace. So staff recruiters in large organizations monitor the effectiveness of equal opportunity policies by evaluating data collected from interviewees. Again, what happens to this data and the extent to which it informs future practice, in turn become the subjects of higher education evaluative research projects, and so it goes.

This exponentially growing trend towards accountability (Phillips, 1994a, 1994b) has, at the extreme edges, become an obsession no longer producing or pointing towards better practice. The demonstration and production of evidence that assessment or evaluation has taken place has in some respects, become an end in itself. Power (1997:3) calls this the 'audit explosion' in a 'society engaged in constant checking and verification, an audit society in which a particular style of formalized accountability is the ruling principle'. At the other extreme, there are still workplaces and areas of public activity where a total lack of concern for either suggests considerable arrogance or uncertain reputation.

This chapter concentrates, in the main, on areas that appear to be most topical and most likely to be of value to readers who wish to discriminate between different approaches they intend to use, or that might be used on them. It offers examples by way of illustration of some of these different approaches, but it does not to offer a comprehensive array of detailed examples. These can be sought by reference to the texts drawn upon to arrive at this overview.

Having read this chapter you will be able to:

- explain key terms associated with evaluation and assessment;
- critically analyse approaches to evaluation and assessment;
- identify different methods of evaluation and assessment.

KEY TERMS

Many of the terms in this field are used interchangeably, notably evaluation and assessment themselves. Meanings and usage certainly overlap, although you might read authors who use them as if they are discrete. In this chapter I propose to use the term 'evaluation' to refer to a structured analysis of learning, training and development, by stakeholders. The evaluation could be of an event, a process or an 'outcome'. The stakeholders could be learners, employers, designers, trainers, managers, owners, consultants or researchers. Evaluation might be located at individual, group, project, organizational, corporate or community level. I will use 'assessment' more specifically in relation to the learning or performance of an individual learner. Much of this literature aligns itself in this way, although it is important to stress again that this is simply a convention, and you should not be too concerned where you find this otherwise. Evaluation and assessment in these senses are located in the broader societal and institutional frameworks of audit, monitoring and inspection. The purpose of all of these is to enable people to make informed judgements.

The term 'evaluation' tends to be employed to encompass all activities undertaken to help educators, trainers and learners decide what aspect of teaching and learning design and methodology worked and what did not, what should be kept and what changed. This is to arrive at a judgement about the intrinsic value and worthwhileness of an approach to learning. Evaluation can be top-down, bottom-up, or collaborative and negotiated.

Those aiming at greater rigour might employ the term and techniques of 'validation'. The key question here is, 'Is this the most appropriate way for this kind of learning to be achieved?' Tools of validation attempt to measure accurately whether specific learning objectives or prescribed outcomes have definitely been achieved or not (Newby, 1992). An example is the appropriate design of a multiple choice test, in which participants on a health and safety course have to record the correct sequences of a number of essential actions and procedures. With both of these terms it is the learning event, process or intervention that is under scrutiny rather than the learners themselves. The design of the test itself can be 'measured' or judged by comparison with others of a similar nature and with close reference to the original objectives. Those concerned with very refined methods have distinguished different types of validity. Clarke (1999), for example, discusses construct (p 117), content (p 137), convergent (p 89), external (p 88), internal (p 42) and face (p 137) validity.

A sister concept to validity is 'reliability'. Testing for reliability means being concerned to demonstrate that a particular approach or method is likely to stand the tests of time and place, producing consistent results in all manner of contexts and circumstances regardless of the individuality of trainers or learners.

The term 'assessment' by contrast tends to be employed to encompass activities which help decide what the individual learner has learned. The emphasis here is on that individual's capacity and ability rather than the means by which he or she achieved the learning. Terms such as 'test' and 'measurement' here apply to the learner's demonstration of acquired learning. It can be important to distinguish between the assessment of ability, performance and learning. For example, the competence movements in the United Kingdom, the United States and Australia were initially developed on the premise that it was more important to assess work performance than the learning required for its maintenance or improvement. However, this changed rapidly in the UK as the promotion of National Vocational Qualifications (NVQs) became a new marketing opportunity for the post-compulsory education and training sector, and NVQs became options within secondary school curricula. For examples of current approaches to assessment in this sector see Wallace (2001:63), and Fawbert (2003:245). The 'standards and competence' approaches to the assessment of work-related learning and worker ability (performance) came under intense scrutiny because of a number of developments. The two most influential were the rapid growth of, and access to, information technology, and the quality assurance movement. Despite this or maybe because of it, they have if anything become even more robust, and have had considerable impact on the shaping and presentation of more traditional academic curricula.

Another assessment-related term is staff appraisal. Staff appraisal can be perceived as somewhat ineffective when conducted on an annual or biannual basis. However, where it is aligned with more regular staff supervision it can prove more popular with employees and employers alike. Staff appraisal is increasingly, though not systematically, being linked to the evaluation of the effectiveness of staff development and the assessment of individual learning in the workplace, as organizations attempt to negotiate the boundaries between employers' and employees' responsibility for individuals' contribution to the viability and competitiveness of the workplace.

Two more key terms associated with evaluation and assessment are accreditation and certification of learning. 'Accreditation' literally refers to the attribution of publicly recognized units of credit for attainment of a particular course of study, or demonstration of evidence of achievement or ability. 'Certification' refers to the awarding of a named certificate, usually representing a number of units of credit. In the workplace these might take place through NVQs as discussed above for a range of semi-skilled, skilled and sub-professional groups. For more senior occupations accreditation and certification will be organized in conjunction with professional bodies representing those specific occupational interests. Much work-related accreditation and certification takes place through educational institutions, as employees demand external evidence of transferable skills in a marketplace where they will want or be required to change jobs and/or careers much more frequently. The processes of accreditation and certification of learning or competence are also in turn submitted to the further evaluative processes of quality assurance and standardization. So internal or external examiners and verifiers are trained and appointed to moderate and verify assessment and examination procedures. The purpose of moderation is to ensure parity between assessed candidates, especially where different assessors are involved and their interpretation of set assessment criteria might differ. The purpose of verification is to ensure that the criteria for assessment are being applied appropriately to the assessment process.

The evaluative and assessment processes above are by and large predicated on negotiations between individuals in organizations, in the context of broad organizational policies and procedures such as boards of examination or staff development and appraisal policies. There is also a tradition of alternative approaches to evaluation and assessment, based on the notion that the groups within which an individual works and is learning are influential in that learning process, and therefore responsibility for learning, achievement and success should be located at a group rather than individual level. Teamwork, collaborative evaluation, peer review audit (Heron, 2004:129; Boud,1992) and group assessment and review, all stem from this perspective that assessing the individual in isolation from the group misses essential aspects of the broader issues affecting workplace learning and competitiveness.

CONTEMPORARY APPROACHES TO EVALUATION

The specific purpose in evaluating a training intervention will influence the choice of method and approach. The effectiveness of that choice will be determined by the appropriateness of the approach and methods, how well it is carried out, what other stakeholders contribute to or detract from the process, and of course, what is being evaluated. The purpose might be to gauge the impact of training on learners' understanding, behaviour or attitudes (Bloom, 1964) as it affects their workplace performance. It might be to justify the cost of the training staff salaries and budget. It might be to stimulate creative thinking and problem-solving in a turbulent or stagnating environment. It might be to look at links between staff development and organizational effectiveness or profitability, employee satisfaction or organizational survival. In these contexts evaluation is best placed within a cycle of training and development of people and organizations, as shown in the training wheel in Figure 21.1.

Here evaluation is conceived in parallel with training needs analysis and design. It is not something that is tacked on to the end of the process as an afterthought. The premise here is that you cannot know if you have arrived if you did not know where you were bound. This concep-

Figure 21.1 The training wheel

tualization applies fairly comfortably where specific skills or quantifiable knowledge are the subject of the training, where discrete objectives can be set. It is less applicable or should held more loosely where the aim of professional development or learning experiences is to provoke creative thinking, new perceptions of self and others or the challenging of attitudes.

Evaluation of a planned learning or training event or intervention is notoriously difficult to carry out in ways that are valid and verifiable. Few courses or developments take place these days without some kind of feedback sheet being handed out or feedback discussions being tabled, but these procedures run the risk of appearing superficial. There are some complex reasons for the difficulties entailed, which are not just to do with a genuine desire, or lack of it, to be flexible, responsive and creative.

Kirkpatrick's (1967, 1994) now classic model of four levels of training evaluation is probably still the most robust. It widely used both in research into training effectiveness and in human resource development (HRD) practice, and is still cited in contemporary texts (see for instance Buckley and Caple 2004:299; Joy-Matthews, Megginson and Surtees 2004:223; Gibb 2002). Kirkpatrick's evaluation levels are Reaction, Learning, Behaviour and Result.

- Level 1: What is the initial *reaction* of participants to the training? (This is often elicited from oral discussions and feedback checklists at the end of specific events.)
- Level 2: What have participants actually *learned* from the training?
  (This is often not measured at all. When it is, it can be through tests, contributions to portfolios, more detailed oral or written feedback.)
- Level 3: Are participants *behaving* differently as a result of the training?
  (Assessment through observation is sometimes used to determine this. It can be notoriously prone to bias, and difficult though not impossible, to verify.)
- Level 4: Has the training of these participants has the desired *result* in the workplace?
  (Measures here are considered the hardest to apply or to attribute specifically to the training.)

This has been derived and adapted from Kirkpatrick's original and numerous subsequent sources. You may want to compare it with others including Warr, Bird and Rackham's CIRO approach (1970). This has tended to be used more widely in Europe. The acronym CIRO refers to the evaluation of context, input, reaction and outcome. A succinct explanation can be found in Phillips (1991:46). Further applications can be found in Bramley (1996); Barrington and Reid (1997), Gibb (2002) Buckley and Capel (2004), and Joy-Matthews *et al* (2004).

The longer it takes to evaluate any aspect of a training course and track its link to workplace performance, the more unrelated factors may intervene (Parry, 1997:4). There might, for instance, be aspects of organizational policy and practice where it is vital that the effectiveness of training is evaluated, for the well-being of staff. Nevertheless, the possibilities of undertaking this effectively might vary enormously. A nuclear processing plant might require safety checks to be understood by all staff and rigorously applied. In this instance it would be conceivable to pre-test, train, and re-test levels of employee knowledge in relation to fixed procedures.

One could also test for retention of learning after a certain period of time. This could give very accurate indicators of the effectiveness of training at individual level, with additional information regarding the impact on the organization (not to mention the world at large!) gleaned from comparative accident and incident statistics. One then also has to take into account the additional effect of raised awareness on those statistics. Actual numbers of incidents might have gone down, while reported incidents go up due to increased awareness and sense of responsibility. There might be no accurate way of gauging the real figures, but this does not mean it is not worth trying. It depends what is at stake and how much is invested in the desired 'outcomes'.

Equally important for the aforementioned nuclear processing plant might be the requirement to monitor the effectiveness of anti-discrimination at work training. The pre-testing and re-testing of attitudes and behaviours could still prove worthwhile indicators of change and progress. The numbers of people from diverse groups represented at senior management level, or the number of harassment incidents reported, might offer some indication of effectiveness of training at organizational level. But over what period of time might one expect to have to monitor change before it can be deemed to have taken place or not? The effect of other factors and variables might be even less easy to identify and monitor. Again, however, this does not mean one should decide to abandon evaluation. It means one should take care to make tentative or modest claims unless one has clear evidence.

Evaluative methods

At whichever level you are evaluating there are always basic questions you need to ask:

- Why are you undertaking the evaluation?
- Who are the stakeholders?
- How will you gather information?
- Who will have access to it?
- How will it be analysed?
- How will it be used and why?
- Is there a predesigned or standard instrument available? (This might be particularly relevant for computer-based training.)
- Have you got the time and resources to pilot your methods?
- Can you anticipate the time and resources needed to complete the evaluation?
- How accurate does the information need to be, and if very accurate, how are you going to deal with error and bias?
- When, how often and over what period of time will it be undertaken?

You then need to look at the types of evaluative method or instrument you think are most suitable or available. These might include:

- personal inventories;
- attitudinal diagnostic questionnaires;
- factual written tests;
- observations of practice or of interpersonal skill;
- group brainstorming or analysis;

- focus groups;
- observation of work performance;
- analysis of documentation according to predefined or open criteria;
- portfolios of evidence;
- individual or group interviews.

EVALUATION OF TRAINING INCLUDING USE OF FOCUS GROUP METHOD USING A COMBINATION OF KIRKPATRICK'S FOUR LEVELS AND THE CIRO FRAMEWORK

Evaluator: Training Officer
Organizational context: Training Department, Radio Telefís Éireann (RTÉ) Dublin, Ireland

Training needs analysis has identified a need for more effective and creative way of training television directors, camera crew and production assistants. RTE is the sole provider but is susceptible to public ratings of programmes.

Input: Training in the use of storyboarding.

Evaluative methods used: observation and description; focus groups and discussion; questionnaire.

Reaction – immediate: Increased capability in the use of and enthusiasm for storyboarding in the case study group. Limited use in control group indicating little change.

Learning: Evidence of learning taking place can be inferred from subsequent changes in behaviour.

Behaviour: clear evidence that group were able to use the technique effectively in programme production.

Outcomes – longer term: The impact of the 'Hawthorne' effect was considered as future groups not subject to such rich research and evaluative processes used the storyboarding technique much less subsequently.

In his discussion around the various methods used in this case study, Ryan placed particular emphasis on the effectiveness of the focus group not only as an evaluative tool but as a means of reinforcing motivation and commitment to the original learning aims. The method was chosen because its perceived strengths are that it encourages group behaviours involving creative exchange of ideas and the opportunity to express feelings. The group discussion was facilitated rather than ad hoc. This was to maximize diversity of opinion sharing while keeping to the topic under consideration. Ryan considered that the principal perceived weakness of this method was the hazard of leaving participants disappointed if the 'wish list' created as a result of creative thinking is not fulfilled. He dealt with this by discussing the issue with the participants.

Further information on the use of focus groups is in Patton (1990:336), and the details of this fascinating study can be found in the unpublished MEd thesis of Thomas Ryan in the University of Sheffield Library.

With acknowledgements to Tom Ryan, Radio Telefis Eireann, Dublin.

Evaluating reactions to training

In some circles it has become fashionable to talk in a rather derogatory way about end of course feedback as 'happy' sheets. However, where evaluation of even this brief nature is not entered into cynically but as a part of a genuine dialogue between learners, learning facilitators and learning media, the explicit expression of feelings and ideas immediately after an event, experience or incident has an absolutely essential and significant role to play. Like any aspect of reflection it enables learners to begin to communicate not only with others but just as important, with themselves. The more complex issue is what status the data collected in this way should have in relation to future planning of learning for others, or further learning for the person or group giving the feedback. There are no formulae which can guide this part of the process. 'Bad' feedback, and 'painful feelings' do not necessarily indicate that there was no useful learning. Nor do they always indicate that the design or content of an event needs radically changing. Likewise 'good' feedback does not imply everything was relevant and appropriate at all times. There may be much more complex and subtle human reasons. This will always be a matter of subjective judgement, an art and not a science.

Formats for evaluations at this level can vary from open oral discussion to individual conversation, from a simple blank sheet to a list of topics. Sometimes negotiation of criteria for feedback takes place at the beginning of a learning event, enhancing ownership of the whole process. Sometimes organizers have particular data they are required to collect which relate to organizational policy. Common criteria include:

- *content* – level, relevance, interest, quality, quantity;
- *style* – pace, format, accessibility of language, flexibility, interactivity;
- *media* – readability, variety, clarity, user-friendly, familiar or innovative, stimulating;
- *personnel* – motivation, presentation, commitment, professionalism;
- *location* – comfort, fit-for-purpose, refreshments, access, facilities;
- *timing* – in relation to external and internal events;
- and finally, *congruence* of all the above with the overall aims and objectives.

Evaluating cognitive learning from training

It is generally acknowledged that a high percentage of activities designed to train people are not subsequently followed by a specific evaluation of what participants have learned. The extent to which people know more, or better, is often only traced through occasional anecdotal evidence. Indeed the interface between the evaluation of effective training and the assessment of individual learning is always problematic. To state the obvious, it is easiest to test simpler learning objectives, for example, the acquisition of procedures for using a new piece of IT software. On the other hand, the extent to which someone understands what becoming anti-racist or a more flexible manager of people means is much harder to test with the same kind of certainty, because we have intrinsic problems agreeing definitions of these things in the first place.

Evaluating affective learning through training

This is perhaps the most highly contested area of human resource development to evaluate, and indeed to conduct. There are subtle and complex factors that come into play within the domains of feelings, attitudes, values and ethics. It can be very difficult to agree what constitutes hard evidence of learning outcomes being experienced or demonstrated. And there can be a wide variation in the value base of participants in the evaluative process. Power relationships between different stakeholders can be paramount in the submergence or foregrounding of particular learning issues and incidents. However, in some areas of professional practice, training in these areas is deemed essential to improve practice and adhere to professional standards. An obvious example is counselling, but any interpersonal skills training aimed at improving communications must take serious account of the affective domain. One excellent and comprehensive approach can be found in Heron's book on facilitation (2004).

Evaluating changes in practice and behaviour after training

Where we are talking about the acquisition of new skills that are demonstrated and then tried out in training, learners require time and the appropriate occasion to practise new learning over a period of time before new skills become habitual. Paramedics (albeit more thoroughly trained in the first place) are much more likely to retain first aid training (because they get lots of opportunities to practise it) than is a college lecturer doing a three-hour workshop on first aid to fulfil basic college requirements. Methods associated with evaluating behaviour change are mainly based on observation, either in a simulated environment or in the workplace itself. They might also be based on performance or production results. In order to evaluate the changes in behaviour we need to assess the trainee against certain specific measures. These behavioural measure require careful specification and writing. Mager's (1991) informative advice on preparing instructional objectives is strongly recommended.

Evaluating how an organization benefits from training

One of the current trends in organizational evaluation of training is the desire to measure 'return on investment'. This has become highly relevant in some sectors where budgets and sponsorship are increasingly competitive, and where it is necessary to justify expenditure or devise strategic plans at operational level. There are those who have attempted to devise ways of predicting the monetary value of training, that is to say, the extent to which training can enhance profitability, increase productivity, develop new markets or create business opportunities (Phillips, 1994a). An example of the kind of outfit that markets itself using this approach is a creative writing correspondence course that guarantees to return a student's fee if he or she has not earned that much and more through publication within the first 18 months after the course.

While it is acknowledged that 'the relationship of input to output can almost never be established without considerable effort' (Phillips, 1994a:3), the point here is to attain a level of confidence in what can be attributed to what, to an extent which will satisfy stakeholders, be they senior management, sponsors, or in the instance cited above, student/customers. Phillips attributes the increased pressure to demonstrate return on investment in the USA, at least, to the emergence and convergence of five factors. These are the increase in training and development budgets; the linking of HRD to competitive business strategies; the perception of HRD as critical to total quality management; the need for return on investment information by senior executives, and the general trend towards accountability which has already been discussed in this chapter's introduction (Phillips, 1994a:5–6).

Once again, the biggest issue at stake in attempting to measure return on investment of training is the level of accuracy of that measurement. One has to judge whether the extra time and rigour taken to produce criteria for valid and reliable data, to gather data and analyse it according to those criteria, and to communicate and disseminate the results, will achieve more than approximations and estimates. However, the work that Phillips has done and the number of case studies he cites are worthy of further study for anyone wishing to investigate his specific techniques and formulae in greater detail.

Note also that organizational change has itself become so continual that any data analysed might be more use in justifying past investment than it can be in predicting and forward planning. For those with the resources and a certain level of organizational stability, the analysis is well worth investigating. In many cases the assurance of certainty these quantitative methods seek to achieve can be illusory.

In summary, the easier it is to gather evaluation data, particularly at the individual reactive level, the more often we tend to do it, and the less likely it is to be seriously convincing or powerful. Conversely the harder it is to gather evaluative data, particularly at the level of organizational effectiveness, the less we tend to do it but the more valuable and powerful it is for us when we do.

CONTEMPORARY APPROACHES TO ASSESSMENT

Contemporary approaches to the assessment of the learning of individuals and of workplace performance have been influenced by two essentially countervailing philosophies. The first is the competence movement and the second is the concept of continuing professional development. The key difference between them relates to the locus of control, responsibility and accountability around what it is considered important to know (or for some, what knowledge is), and what it is considered important to be able to apply effectively in the workplace. This of course raises the controversial question, effective for whom?

Abstract generalizations around these issues become problematic, and perhaps the easiest way of illustrating the debate is by caricaturing an organizational philosophy and management structure in which these different approaches might seem desirable. A very hierarchical organization, say a biscuit factory, where role demarcation is clear-cut, might choose to take a competency approach to staff development. A 'flatter' organization, such as a small public relations agency, or an owner/manager organization such as a GP practice, might embrace continuous development with a high degree of self-responsibility for learning and for keeping up to date with current techniques and research.

Part of the controversy includes different perceptions and conflicts of interest around the notion of standards, both of education and training provision and of workplace performance. In the UK, the 1997 Dearing Report made a clear (but elsewhere strongly disputed) case for the establishment of a coherent national qualification framework at every level, congruent with the national curriculum in schools and with national vocational qualifications in the workplace. There was vociferous opposition to these developments in many quarters, with an alternative case being made for peer review and for a rich and diverse mix of provision and approaches. At the heart of the controversy lay different perceptions of the nature and value of learning, and conflicts of interests around issues such as freedom, responsibility and independence on the one hand, and guaranteed standards and accountability on the other.

Whether assessment is related to a certificated and accredited qualification or local workplace performance criteria, there are perennial dilemmas associated with any assessment process. These include:

- the assessor as advocate for the person being assessed;
- anxiety around the implications of failure;
- leniency or strictness in the application of criteria;
- interpretations of criteria;
- rigid adherence to 'objective' criteria undermining creativity and originality;
- the assessor as gatekeeper for entry into a professional body or academic community;
- consistency between assessors;
- consistency of assessment over a period of time;
- consistency of assessment in different locations and between different cohorts;
- the impact of the environment and context of assessment – the notion of the 'competent workplace';

- the 'halo' effect of previous performance of the assessed person or of his or her power position in the profession or organization;
- the ownership of learning and of assessment.

These and associated concerns have led to various assessment approaches designed to overcome the worst defect. None of these ultimately remains unchallengeable.

Diagnostic assessment

Diagnostic assessment has returned to centre stage with the current emphasis on the Skills for Life agenda. Individual learning and skills audits are becoming increasingly popular as a way of locating ownership of the learning process with the individual, who can use it as a negotiating 'tool' with learning providers around agreed outcomes. Design models increasingly cover academic, personal and professional learning needs. Fawbert (2004:39–40), for example, covers practical skills, intellectual skills, interpersonal skills and intrapersonal skills.

Formative and summative assessment

Concerns about the role of assessment either in enhancing or inhibiting learning have led to a distinction between formative and summative assessment. Formative assessment offers feedback to learners while their programme or period of learning is still taking place, so that they can act on and improve their performance. Summative assessment marks the arrival (or not) of the learner at a specific stage or level of learning. At its simplest, formative assessment includes the assessor's detailed and overall comments on a piece of written work, which the learner can use to improve either that piece or the next one. An example of a summative assessment is the grade given for the final piece of work, or the percentage achieved in an exam.

Norm referencing and criteria referencing

Norm referencing entails the comparing and contrasting of standards reached by groups of students being assessed during the same period. This is sometimes called benchmarking. Consistency is apparently achieved by organizing results around clusters of grades or percentages: a certain proportion of A grades, a certain proportion of Bs and so on. This method is criticized for not taking into account the different levels of ability and achievement of groups. The alternative of criteria-referenced assessment aims at the production of set criteria to which assessors are meant to adhere, offering greater consistency within and between groups. In practice even when these are conscientiously used, it is claimed that benchmarking is still in operation, and that assessors subconsciously weight criteria according to their educational background, personal experience and preferences. The other problem with criteria is that over time, knowledge in and across disciplines grows and criteria may need to be constantly updated to account for this, thus undermining any claims for consistency or universal standards.

Self and peer assessment

Arguments in favour of self-assessment are made on two main counts. The first is that self-assessment approaches encourage individual responsibility for and commitment to learning to a much greater degree. Hence learning is deeper, richer and more relevant for that individual. The second is that the learner is best placed to judge what learning has taken place, and the authority of that knowledge should be recognized. Is it through positional power only, within the assessing organization, is it through external credibility, the actual knowledge and understanding of the learner, or the 'body of knowledge' in the subject being assessed? Obvious criticisms of self-assessment include the degree to which learners are too hard or too soft on themselves in relation to their perception of the standard required. Also problematic can be the learners' ability to locate their achieved understanding within a much broader spectrum of knowledge.

Peer assessment helps to deal with some of this dilemma by the moderating effect that several different perspectives bring to that of the individual. This can also be beneficial where ownership of and motivation for learning is vested within a group of learners, as in the focus group in the case study above, especially when the learners also share the same status in relation to the process and the task of assessment. However, other factors influencing group dynamics, including power games and trade-offs, can create equal if different problems for fair and equitable assessment processes.

Competence-based assessment

Frameworks for competencies have been devised along somewhat different principles in Australia, the United States and Britain, with several other countries now beginning to look at what they might adopt or adapt. The impetus for NVQs in Britain gathered momentum in the 1980s, with the government's response to indicators that Britain was lagging behind other European countries, with higher unemployment figures, and lower-skilled and more poorly qualified workers. Concerns expressed in the Manpower Services Commission's *New Training Initiative: An Agenda for Action* (MSC, 1981) culminated in the 1996 White Paper *Working Together, Education and Training* (DoE, 1986). The core idea was that each industry would set up a lead body with overall responsibility for the development of standards.

The assessors of NVQ candidates are either their own workplace supervisors, where they have one, or an equivalent person from another workplace. The advantage of the former is that assessment formally or informally already forms part and parcel of the normal supervisory and management functions within organizations. A supervisor should have an in-depth knowledge of a person's work performance, and be best placed to ensure that appropriate evidence is gathered. The disadvantages are that personal bias or knowledge of the person, unrelated to what is being assessed, will result in the misuse of power and position in relation to the assessment.

One of the great strengths of the competency approach is also its greatest weakness. Taking time to gather evidence of different and corroborating kinds can result in deeper learning, if the candidate evidently needs to learn aspects of the job in order to demonstrate competence, and is afforded the time to do this well. It can strengthen the case for a candidate's competence, and result in the production of a portfolio of evidence which is far more meaningful than a piece of 'writing about' produced via an exam or test. However, the gathering of such evidence and its assessment have become notoriously time-consuming. There are huge problems around the availability of opportunities to demonstrate some of the competencies required for completing a qualification. The number of obstacles to successful completion can lead to corner-cutting, and a corruption of the assessment process. Assessors collude with candidates over incomplete areas of evidence in order to complete an otherwise seemingly endless process.

CONCLUSION

The aim of this chapter was to offer an overview of contemporary approaches to evaluation and assessment in the workplace. It also offers an insight into some of the controversies and anomalies surrounding any systematic attempt to account for learning and performance, while acknowledging the importance and value of our attempts to do so. In fact we can no longer opt out of this growing trend towards accountability. The best we can do is to be as clear as possible why we are evaluating or assessing something or someone. Where we have power we can leave room for challenge by others, and be pragmatic about the percentage of resources we invest in these endeavours. Where we are at the mercy of others' criteria and processes, we can use our insights to get the maximum learning and value out of them for ourselves.

Bibliography

Barrington, H and Reid, M (1997) *Training Interventions*, London, IPD

Bee, F and R, (1994) *Training Needs Analysis and Evaluation*, London, IPD

Bloom, B (1964) *Taxonomy of Educational Objectives*, New York, Longmans and Green

Boud, D (1992) 'The use of self-assessment schedules in negotiated learning', *Studies in Higher Education*, **17**, 2, pp 185–200

Bramley, P (1996) *Evaluating Training*, London, IPD

Brown, S and Knight, P (1994) *Assessing Learners in Higher Education*, London, Kogan Page

Buckley, R and Caple, J (2004) *The Theory and Practice of Training*, London, Kogan Page

Carter, C (1980) *Why and How to Examine*, Oxford, Blackwell

Clarke, A (1999) *Evaluation Research: An introduction to principles, methods and practice*, London, Sage

Coates, H and Wright, J (1991) *The Integration of Work Based Learning with Academic Assessment*, Coventry, Coventry Polytechnic

Dearing, R (1997) *Higher Education in the Learning Society: Report of the National Committee of Enquiry in Higher Education*, London, HMSO

DoE (Department of Education) (1986) *Working Together, Education and Training, Government White Paper Cmnd 9823*, London, HMSO

Fawbert, F (2003) *Teaching in Post-Compulsory Education: Learning, skills and standards*, London, Continuum

Fletcher, S (1991) *NVQs Standards and Competence*, London, Kogan Page

Garavan, T Costine, P and Heraty, N (1995) *Training and Development in Ireland: Context, policy and practice*, Dublin, Oak Tree Press

Gibb, S (2002) *Learning and Development: Processes, practices and perspectives at work*, Basingstoke, Palgrave Macmillan

Gibbs, G (1989) *Dimensions of Assessment*, Oxford Centre for Staff Development

Harrison, R (2002) *Employee Development,* 3rd edn, London, CIPD

Heron, J (2004) *The Complete Facilitator's Handbook,* London, Kogan Page

Holyfield, J and Moloney, K (1996) *Using National Standards to Improve Performance*, London, Kogan Page

Joy-Matthews, J, Megginson, D and Surtees, M (2004) *Human Resource Development*, 3rd edn, London, Kogan Page

Kirkpatrick, D (1967 and 1994) *Evaluating Training Programmes*, San Francisco, CA, Berrett-Koehler

Lee, R (1996) 'What makes training pay?', *Issues in People Management,* 11, London, IPD

Mager, R F (1991) *Preparing Instructional Objectives*, 2nd edn, London, Kogan Page

MSC (Manpower Services Commission) (1981) *A New Training Initiative: Agenda for action.* Sheffield

Newby, T (1992) *Validating Your Training*, London, Kogan Page

Otter, S (1992) *Learning Outcomes in Higher Education*, London, Employment Department FEU

Patton, M Q (1990) *Qualitative Evaluation and Research Methods*, London, Sage

Parry, S B (1997) *Evaluating the Impact of Training*, Alexandria, VA, American Society for Training and Development

Pawson, R and Tilley, N (1997) *Realistic Evaluation*, London, Sage

Phillips, J J (1991) *Handbook of Training Evaluation and Measurement Methods*, 2nd edn, London, Kogan Page

Phillips, J J (1994a) *Measuring Return on Investment, Volume 1*, Alexandria, VA, American Society for Training and Development

Phillips, J J (1994b) *Measuring Return on Investment, Volume 2*, Alexandria, VA, American Society for Training and Development

Plant, R and Ryan, R (1992) 'Training evaluation: a procedure for validating an organization's investment in training,' *Journal of European Industrial Training*, **16**, 10, pp 22–38

Power, M (1997) *The Audit Society: Rituals of verification*, Oxford, Oxford University Press

Reid M and H Barrington (1997) *Training Interventions*, 5th edn, London, IPD

Shapiro, L (1995) *Training Effectiveness Handbook*, New York, McGraw-Hill

Talbot, C (1992) 'Evaluation and validation: a mixed approach', *Journal of European Industrial Training*, **16**, 5, pp 26–32

Tight, M (1996) *Key Concepts in Adult Education and Training*, London, Routledge

Wallace, S (2001) *Teaching and Supporting Learning in Further Education: Meeting the FENTO standards*, Exeter, Learning Matters

Warr, P B, Bird, M and Rackham, N (1970) *Evaluation of Management Training*, Aldershot, Gower Press

22

Accounting for the Human Resource Development Function

Chris Wiltsher

INTRODUCTION AND LEARNING OBJECTIVES

Training and development is costly. It is necessary for any successful organization but it adds to the costs of the organization, and anything which adds to costs must be justified. Successful organizations survive by being cost-effective. Successful Human Resource Development (HRD) professionals supply cost-effective training and development programmes which help organizations become and remain successful.

But what is 'cost-effective training and development'? How do we assess programmes in monetary terms? How do we determine costs and benefits? What measures shall we use? What information do we need? The aim of this chapter is to look briefly at some of the issues relevant to accounting for HRD.

The chapter is about accounting in a double sense. We are concerned first with accounting in the sense of giving an account of income and expenditure, assessing costs and benefits, showing gains or losses. Second we are concerned with accounting in the sense of presenting HRD to management. Underlying this chapter is the view that money spent on training and development is part of an organization's investment. Just as organizations invest in plant and machinery, so they must invest in people. Part of our concern with accounting is the need to show that investment in training and development is worthwhile.

Viewing training and development as investment has important implications for accounting. The appraisal of investment is different from the assessment of, say, productivity, and the relationship between costs and benefits is treated differently. It is helpful for HRD managers to recognize these differences and tailor their accounting accordingly.

Even if HRD is viewed as investment, financial accounting is necessary. The HRD function must work within the financial parameters set for it. It will have a budget. Senior management will not be happy if the budget is exceeded, which is very likely to happen if a watch is not kept on costs. If the HRD function is expected to survive by being a service provider and charging its customers for services rendered, then accurate costing is needed to decide how much the customer should pay, and audit is needed to decide whether the customer was charged enough.

Audit is also needed to show that HRD programmes are cost-effective. As we noted above, any additions to an organization's costs must be justified. The HRD function is increasingly expected to show it does deliver the training and development required by the organization and its managers, and that it uses resources efficiently and effectively. This means that the HRD function must be subject to audit like any other section of the organization, even though auditing the HRD function may not be as straightforward as auditing other sections of the organization.

In this chapter we shall look at factors affecting costing and auditing the HRD function and some ways of approaching these tasks. There are many books on accounting that offer detailed descriptions of costing and auditing methodologies. Here we are more interested in principles and issues than detailed methodologies.

Having read this chapter you should understand:

- why costing and auditing are important;
- factors affecting costing of the HRD function;
- factors affecting auditing of the HRD function; and
- ways of addressing the problems raised.

THE NEED FOR FORMAL ACCOUNTING

As we have already suggested, HRD professionals need to pay attention to accounting, to costing and auditing, in order to operate professionally and to justify their work and even their very existence in an organization.

We live in very competitive times, dominated by 'the bottom line', the financial results of the organization's activities. At the end of the financial year, is the organization in surplus or deficit, showing a profit or a loss? No organization can survive if it consistently makes losses, even in the not-for-profit sectors.

Consequently in most organizations any and every activity is judged by its contribution to the financial health of the organization. Activities that do not help to improve organizational health are a liability. Activities that consume large amounts of resource with very little outcome are a liability. And liabilities are shed. Sometimes the activity is simply stopped, as when a factory closes; sometimes the in-house supplier is replaced by an external provider, as when catering, cleaning or data-input services are contracted out.

HRD functions are no exception to the general rule. They consume resources, and they produce outcomes. Clearly some training and development is necessary in any organization. What is not clear, what must be demonstrated, is that the training and development provided is a good use of resources.

This means that HRD professionals must show that they are providing the training and development required to meet the organization's objectives. They must also show that they are using resources effectively. In other words, they must show that what they are providing delivers the right results for the lowest cost. They must show that the job could not be done better by an external consultant – and in most organizations, better means 'more cheaply'.

It is this last factor that forces HRD professionals to pay attention to financial costing and auditing. The HRD function will be examined alongside other functions of the organization, and will be judged by comparison with them. The common denominator in all the judgements will be financial: what does it cost, what do we get out of it? The HRD function must be able to withstand scrutiny in these terms.

HRD professionals should be grateful for at least some of this pressure. The need to examine their own costs and results is also a spur to develop programmes that produce the required results in a satisfactory manner. That means focusing on the aims and objectives of the programmes offered, and ensuring that they are realistic, appropriate and met. As professionals we should welcome the opportunity to justify our programmes. What we also need to do is make sure that the complexity of the HRD function is appreciated by those making judgements.

Problems in costing and auditing the HRD function

The main problem we have already noted: the measures that are used to justify a function are primarily financial. Usually they involve some form of cost-benefit analysis. In this the costs of an activity are calculated, and the benefits of that activity for the organization are also calculated. Then the two are compared, to see whether the benefits outweigh the costs.

For example, on a production line making screws, the costs will include the costs of raw materials, labour, machinery, space, quality control, packaging and delivery; the benefit is the money paid by customers in buying the screws. If not enough money comes in, the process cannot continue.

This is a very simple case. Cost-benefit analysis has become very sophisticated, in order to cope with the great variety of activities in the modern world. Models exist to allow analysis of costs and benefits in production environments, service environments, mixed environments, and so on. However, all cost-benefit analysis in the end relies on the same principles: everything is translated into money or a money equivalent so that comparisons can be made.

It is here that problems arise for the HRD function. It is very rarely possible to translate the outcomes of training and development programmes immediately into monetary terms. Often the results of a programme do not become evident until some time later, and there is rarely a direct link between a training programme and increases in output, for example.

This is where treating training and development as an investment becomes significant. Any investment involves the outlay of money now in pursuit of future benefits; and any investment carries with it a degree of risk, that the benefits may be less than expected, and may not justify, or even cover, the outlay. In deciding whether or not to take the risk, organizations appraise their proposed investments. To do this they find ways of stating the anticipated benefits in monetary terms, and then examining the projected returns in relation to the expected outlay.

Investment appraisal has become sophisticated, with different methods adopted for different forms of investment and different forms of company policy. Accounting textbooks such as McLaney (1991) provide details. Here we need only to be aware of the principles used and some of the terminology.

An outline of investment appraisal

Investment appraisal is concerned with making a reasoned estimate of the costs and benefits of a particular investment project, in order to decide whether or not the investment is worthwhile.

It is important to note that investment analysts make estimates. They recognize that they are concerned with future benefits, and that it is impossible to predict the future completely.

In investment appraisal, costs and benefits are expressed in monetary terms, but it is recognized that both costs and benefits may include intangibles. For example, if we introduce a new IT system, we have among other things the tangible costs of the hardware and software and the intangible costs of the disruption to the organization during the changeover from the old system to the new. Tangible benefits might include more accurate and up-to-date performance statistics, while intangible benefits might include better decision-making by managers armed with better information. Investment analysts have developed methods of including intangibles in their estimates.

The main way of doing this is to concentrate attention on cash flows, rather than actual values. Cash flow is simply a measurement of money coming in and going out, designed to show whether we are gaining or losing money. As a simple example, suppose I wish to invest £1,000 for five years. At the end of five years I should like to have more than £1,000. I can assess different ways of investing my money by looking at the flow of money in and out of my account of the period of five years: which method creates the greatest net income at the end of the period? From this perspective it does not matter whether I am investing £1,000 or £100,000: the cash-flow calculations can be done in the same way.

Since the value of money changes over time, through factors like inflation, investment analysts often try to estimate the present value of future cash flows using a method known as discounting. In normal circumstances, discounting is only useful when the period of interest is measured in years, and so will not be greatly used in accounting for HRD. However, where long-term investment in training and development is under discussion, discounting may be valuable. Again, accounting textbooks will supply the necessary detail.

Of more significance for HRD accounting is the method used in a particular organization to assess the worthwhileness of an investment. There are four main methods in general use: net present value, payback, accounting rate of return and internal rate of return. We can state the essence of each method briefly as follows:

- *Net present value:* the net present value of a sum S is the sum we need to invest now in order to have S at the specified time in the future. Using this method of analysis, we try to calculate the net present value of the expected return on our investment, taking account of all costs and benefits.
- *Payback:* this method of analysis tries to answer the question, 'How long will it take for the investment to pay for itself'?
- *Accounting rate of return:* sometimes known as rate of return on investment, this method involves calculating the annual rate of return on the investment by comparing the annual rate of return on the investment with the initial outlay.
- *Internal rate of return:* this method uses discounting techniques to discover the rate of return on the investment which would give a net present value of zero.

Each of these methods has strengths and weaknesses, which are explored in detail in textbooks such as McLaney (1991). We cannot go into further detail here. For our present purposes there are two important things to note. The first is that the different methods can produce very different answers to the question of whether or not an investment is worthwhile. If you are going to argue that training and development is an investment, it is vital to know which method of appraisal will be applied by your organization.

The other thing to note is that all four methods depend on the accurate identification of costs and benefits and cash flows. We have already noted that this is not as simple in the case of HRD as in some other parts of an organization. But it must be done, and it will be done: if the HRD function does not do it, the accountants will. Thus it is in the interest of the HRD function to find ways of measuring costs and outcomes that offer possible translation into monetary terms. We shall now look at how this might be done, beginning with the costs.

COSTING

Costing is in some ways a purely mechanical exercise; the sort of task for which a computer spreadsheet is ideal. However, it must be done with great care, so that the figures are correct and the correct figures are used. That is, not only must we ensure that we include accurate amounts or good estimates, we must also ensure that we include all items which should be included and, just as important, exclude all items which should be left out. Decisions about what to include and what to exclude can make a significant difference to our costings.

The costs of the HRD function can be divided into two broad groups:

1. costs associated with specific HRD activities; and
2. other costs.

We shall look at each group separately, and then see how they are related.

First we should note that costing has a cost: the collection of information required to allocate costs itself takes time and therefore has a cost. It is important that we concentrate on those costs that can be economically assessed.

Particular activities

Every specific HRD activity – a training day, a concentrated course, a development programme spread over months – has costs associated with it. Some of these are direct costs, some indirect:

- *direct costs* are costs that can be easily traced to the particular activity, for example the cost of speakers;
- *indirect costs* are costs that cannot be identified easily or economically with a particular activity.

An example of an indirect cost might be the cost of staff time devoted to setting up an activity: it is often difficult to say exactly how much time has been spent on this, partly because most HRD staff are involved in several activities at once, and it would be uneconomic to keep a detailed record of time spent on each.

Often indirect costs must be estimated. Depending on the operating and accounting policies of the organization, indirect costs may be counted as overheads. In that case they may be counted as a departmental overhead, and ignored in the costing of particular activities. Alternatively, indirect costs might be included in the costing of particular activities by some formula, such as dividing the overhead cost by the number of events, or the number of course participants, in a given period.

It is worth noting also the difference between fixed and variable costs:

- *fixed costs* are costs that are incurred however many people participate in the activity, for example the cost of space in which to hold the activity;
- *variable costs* are costs that change according to the number of participants, for example the cost of photocopying material to be handed out to participants.

We can now list the main headings for costing:

Direct costs

- publicity and recruitment;
- space for the activity;
- equipment;
- materials;
- reception;
- fees and expenses (external staff);
- time of internal staff;
- participants' time and expenses;
- catering;
- feedback.

Indirect costs

- development;
- planning;
- follow-up.

Let us look more closely at each item in the lists.

Direct costs

- *Publicity and recruitment:* most training activities will need some form of publicity and there will be costs associated with recruitment, such as receiving and recording enrolments and cancellations.
- *Space for the activity:* the HRD function may have its own dedicated space for its activities, but on occasions even that may be unsuitable; whether the space used is dedicated or not, it carries costs.
- *Equipment:* the HRD function may have its own equipment, such as OHP and slide projectors; if not, such equipment must be provided. Again, equipment is costly, whether owned or not.
- *Materials:* under this heading we put the cost of handouts for the participants, including the cost of photocopying; we must also take into account the cost of consumables such as pens, paper, flip-chart pads and OHP acetates.
- *Reception:* someone needs to receive the participants, record their presence, hand out initial papers and name badges and answer the questions about parking and the programme that accompany training activities; staff time given to this is not available for other duties, and is a cost.
- *Fees and expenses (external staff):* if external speakers, trainers or tutors are used they will require payment, which is a cost; further costs are incurred in processing their claims, and in ensuring that they arrive and depart.
- *Time of internal staff:* HRD staff or other personnel from the organization involved in staffing the activity are giving time which is taken from other duties, and that is a cost, which can be quantified as a proportion of annual staff costs.
- *Participants' time and expenses:* those who take part in a training activity are also taking time away from other duties and tasks; their work may be covered, or they may be expected to work harder to make up the time, but their absence is a cost to someone.
- *Catering:* tea, coffee, juice, biscuits, lunch, even drinking water for a hot day: all these are costly to provide and should be included in the costing of the activity.
- *Feedback:* every training activity should give opportunity for evaluation and feedback, and providing the necessary questionnaires or other instruments is a cost, as is the time taken to analyse the results.

Indirect costs

- *Development:* this includes needs analysis and the development of appropriate ideas; it also includes liaison with the customers, that is, those who will participate in the activity or those who will send the participants.
- *Planning:* this includes staff time to prepare the event, booking space, arranging speakers and other staff, ensuring availability of equipment, materials and catering, producing a detailed programme (and making last-minute adjustments).
- *Follow-up:* gathering information and carrying out evaluation and audit.

In connection with indirect costs, it is worth noting that the Institute of Personnel and Development reckons that 'a useful and generally accepted rule of thumb' is that each hour of learning activity on a face-to-face course requires five hours of development time (Beaton and Richards, 1997: section 2, p 49).

As one might expect, in practice the items do not divide up as neatly as this schema suggests. For example, it may be possible to use a publicity opportunity to cover more than one activity. If the HRD function owns and maintains equipment such as overhead projectors, the cost of such equipment becomes an indirect cost (but do not forget to write the equipment off over the appropriate period for your organization). Participants' time might be allocated by the organization as a cost to the participants' department, and not included in the costing of the HRD activity.

When all the local rules have been applied, we can use the item headings above to draw up a chart of the kind shown in Table 22.1 for each activity.

From this exercise we can work out the total cost of the activity. It is then simple to work out a break-even point, that is, how many participants are needed to make the exercise worthwhile. This may be a function of whether or not participants – or their managers – are paying for the activity. If so, the costing allows us to decide how much to charge. It is here that the fixed and variable costs become important.

Fixed costs must be met no matter how many people attend. These therefore are commitments which are entered into as soon as the activity is arranged. They may bring with them a cancellation cost: for example, if a room is hired and then the activity is cancelled, you may still have to pay a proportion of the room hire charge. Cancellation costs must be taken into account when decisions are made about whether or not an activity is to go ahead, for it may be more cost-effective to proceed with a small number of participants than cancel completely.

Variable costs may also involve commitments, for example to caterers about minimum or maximum numbers. Generally there is more flexibility with variable costs. However, their very flexibility can cause problems, as expected participant numbers can change very rapidly, and we may have to allow for those who do not turn up on the day or turn up unexpectedly, assuming there will be space for them.

Table 22.1 Costing HRD activity

	Development	Planning	Publicity and Recruitment	Delivery	Evaluation	Follow-up
internal accommodation						
external accommodation						
equipment						
materials						
consumables						
reception						
external staff fees						
external staff expenses						
internal staff time						
participants' time						
participants' expenses						
catering						
Total						

HRD function

The costs of particular activities taken together form part of the costs of the HRD function as a whole, and will usually be the major part. We have already noted that some of the costs of the HRD function as a whole might be included in the costs of particular activities by some formula for the allocation of overhead costs. Examples might be the cost of dedicated training space or equipment owned and maintained by the HRD function. However, not all overhead costs can be easily or economically distributed.

The overhead costs of the HRD function might include:

- staff costs;
- staff development;
- course development;
- space;
- administration.

We can look at these in more detail:

- *Staff costs:* these are the costs of the HRD staff , including salaries and related costs such as insurance, and not forgetting the costs of temporary help at particular times.
- *Staff development:* HRD staff need training and development too! If the organization wishes to have good HRD it must pay the price.
- *Course development:* in addition to the development of particular activities, the HRD function will be constantly on the watch for training and development needs and opportunities. Is new equipment on order for part of the organization? Is legislation appearing which will demand training? Do individual managers have plans which will require staff development programmes? Discovering the answers to questions like these is time-consuming and costly – but necessary.
- *Space:* the HRD function needs office space, at least.
- *Administration:* this covers the cost of stationery, postage, telephones, computer equipment, and everything else necessary to allow the HRD function to function.

Opportunity costs

Opportunity costs are the costs of ignoring a possible course of action. For the HRD function, opportunity costs are significant in that they represent the cost to the organization of not adopting HRD solutions.

Suppose a company is faced with increased demand for its products, which means increased production. Increased production might mean employing more staff, or having existing staff work longer hours; or it might mean offering existing staff training to improve individual productivity and so achieve the increase without extra staff or longer hours. If the company ignores the possibility of training, there is an opportunity cost. The opportunity cost is the difference between the cost of the training and the cost of the extra hours or employees. For audit purposes, opportunity costs are significant, because they represent in some way what can be done with resources.

All costing information is necessary for audit purposes, because audit is in part about the cost-effectiveness of activity. It is therefore worth taking the time and trouble to make sure that the figures are correct, and that costing estimates are realistic. Overly optimistic costings and overly pessimistic costings are equally bad. Both lead to the view that the HRD function is not able to manage its affairs properly. Accurate costing is the basis for good performance in audit.

Accurate costing is also necessary for identifying cash flows to use in the appraisal of training and development as investment. For example, in a cash-flow analysis, the capital cost of equipment will usually be shown as depreciating over a fixed period, so the contribution of equipment cost to the costs of particular courses or the HRD function as a whole will be different in different years. This can make a difference to whether or not a particular course is regarded as viable.

AUDITING

We turn now to the next part of our concern: auditing the HRD function.

There are two main purposes of audit:

1. to check that resources have been used properly, for the intended purpose;
2. to check that resources have been used to the best advantage.

Audit is often said to be about 'value for money', because resources are usually expressed in terms of their monetary value. However, not all resources can be expressed easily in monetary terms, nor is it always easy, or even possible, to express outcomes in monetary terms. So 'value for money' is too simple. A better description of the concerns of auditors might be 'value for input': in other words, audit is supposed to show whether or not scarce resources are being used to the best advantage for the organization.

Another way of putting this, in terms familiar to management accountants and those they advise in senior management, is to say that audit is concerned with the return on investment. Having invested a certain amount of resource in a particular function, we ask: what do we get back, and when? We recall that these questions are important in investment appraisal. Audit provides some of the information required to answer them.

The emphasis here on the organization points us to a significant difference between evaluation and audit. Evaluation is about the effectiveness in delivery; audit is about contribution to an organization.

For the HRD function, evaluation is concerned with the outcomes of training and development activities. In evaluation we ask questions such as: how much did participants learn? Were the training methods appropriate? Questions such as these are important for assessing the effectiveness of the HRD function in delivering training and development.

In audit the effectiveness of the HRD function is set in the context of the organization's goals. The key question is: could the same, or better results, have been achieved more cheaply? For the HRD function this becomes: can the organization's training and development needs be met more efficiently and cheaply in other ways?

In answering this kind of question, two comparisons must be made. First, there is a comparison with other methods of delivering training and development, such as using external contractors. Second, there is a comparison with other possible uses of the resources: what else could the organization have done with the resources devoted to HRD? If we keep these underlying questions in mind, the process of audit becomes clearer.

There are two levels at which audit can operate in the HRD function. We can audit particular activities, and we can audit the function as a whole. In both cases, auditors will need to know what resources have been used and what effects have been achieved.

Particular activities

We look first at the audit of particular activities. These might be single events or programmes lasting days or even months.

The questions we are asking are about the use of resources. We must therefore be able to say what resources have been used for the activity. Some of this information will be given to us by the costing exercise for the activity, following the lines of the previous section.

However, we must also take account of the costs to others of our provision. Each person who participates in an activity is a cost to someone. Cover must be provided for that person, or their work must be carried out in some other way. That cost is part of the resource of the activity. Clearly this information can only be obtained from the participant's manager, and it may be hard to come by. It may be that the participant is simply expected to work harder to compensate for time spent on a training activity, in which case the participant is paying the cost, not the organization.

One result of such an exercise might be a cost per participant for the activity, expressing what it cost the organization for each person who attended. This is a useful measure of comparison with other ways of providing the same training.

On the other side of the account, we are concerned with the outcomes of the activity. Naturally we shall have carried out some form of evaluation of the activity. This will tell us something about what the participants have learnt and their level of satisfaction with the activity.

We might also measure the effectiveness of training by the qualifications gained by participants. This should not be neglected as it provides an objective criterion for the success of an activity. However, not all training leads to qualifications, and not all qualifications lead to improved performance on the job. For audit purposes we need to assess the impact of the activity on participants' performance in their daily work.

To do this we need to obtain information about their performance before and after the activity. There are several possible sources of this information:

- *Participants* themselves may have noticed improvements in their performance, and may be able to quantify the improvement.
- *Participants' managers* should be able to offer an assessment of improvements in performance.
- *Participants' colleagues* also may notice improvement, especially if their own work depends in some way on the performance.

Information in all these cases might be collected by interview or questionnaire or a combination of these. In some cases it might also be possible to have an objective measurement, for example, the increase in speed of a data-input clerk after training.

However the information is collected, it is important to ensure that there is some comparability across activities. This implies that the questions used to collect information must be carefully phrased. A question like, 'Has John's telephone manner improved?' is very specific and does not allow for comparison with other training activities (although it might allow comparison with others doing the same job). Comparison with other training activities would be better served by a question like, 'Have you noticed any change in the way Mary carries out her duties?'

It is important that the information sought on changed job performance should relate to the training activity. We are interested in the effect of the training activity on performance, and the training activity may relate only to a small part of the task. It may be also that there are other factors that will prevent improved performance however effective the training. Beaton and Richards (1997: section 2, p 3) quote the case of a production line supervisor who,

> noted an increasing number of substandard goods being passed as perfect and asked for a training programme in identifying defects. However, a more in-depth analysis of the problem revealed that it was caused by poor lighting conditions. Staff were fully aware of what constituted defects, but were unable to see them.

All this shows that assessing changes in performance is not easy. We should notice too how subjective the assessment is bound to be: it is rarely that one can directly link training with increased performance. Of course in the case of new machines, it is easy – but that is the exception rather than the rule.

Note that for the assessment of improvement, it is necessary to know what the starting point was. There are formulae for trying to assess improvement which can be found in the books noted at the end of this chapter. It is important to realize that even where a formula is used, the assessment of improvement is subjective, because the formulae all require data derived from the subjective assessments of participants or their managers.

It is also important to note the time factor in assessing improvement. Not all improvement in performance can be measured immediately. While training in customer relations may result in more satisfied customers, it may be months before their return demonstrates the level of satisfaction. Moreover, some of the benefits of training, such as improved staff morale or a change of organizational culture, may not show themselves clearly for a long time.

We should also note that we do not always have to show that a training activity was a success. In order to improve our training and development programmes we must acknowledge mistakes and learn from them, and involve others in helping us to see and correct the deficiencies.

Finally, we must note that this kind of audit is related to the objectives of the participants' employers: they need training that meets their requirements.

Accounting for People

The Accounting for People Task Force was instituted because of the growing importance of human capital management. Its remit was to investigate performance measures used to assess investment in human capital; champion the business case for these reports; produce an advisory report; and make recommendations. The final recommendations suggested that reports on human capital management should:

1. have a strategic focus:
    communicating clearly, fairly and unambiguously the Board's current understanding of the links between the HCM policies and practices, its business strategy and its performance; and including information on:

- the size and composition of the workforce;
- retention and motivation of employees;
- the skills and competences necessary for success, and training to achieve these;
- remuneration and fair employment practices;
- leadership and succession planning;

2. be balanced and objective, following a process that is susceptible to review by auditors;
3. provide information in a form that enables comparisons over time and uses commonly accepted definitions where available and appropriate.

(AFP, 2003:4)

This chapter describes some of the advantages and challenges in accounting for HRD. Furthermore, not every firm wants to or is able to provide this information publicly. Foong and Yorsten identified a number of obstacles which made reporting difficult:

Not something that can be shared externally.
Measurement not first priority for the company.
Not enough time and resources.
HR professionals unaware of value/No clear return on investment.
Lack of clear guidance and universal practice.
Global and Group issues.
Little support from senior management/Low status of HR.

(Foong and Yorsten, 2003:31–32)

Return on investment

The return on investment (ROI) model for training has been championed by Phillips (1997). It is based on the four steps of Kirkpatrick's evaluation model: response, learning, behaviour and results. To these Phillips adds the additional step of ROI, which provides a monetary valuation of the training impact.

Philips (2002) suggests that many organizations spend less than 1 per cent of their budget on evaluation and measurement of training. Using the ROI approach she suggests that incorporating accountability throughout the programme will cost approximately 4–5 per cent. However, she argues that this cost will be offset by savings identified by the ROI. She also recommends that the ROI method is not applied to all programmes but to between 5–10 per cent of all training for reasons of cost; however, this makes it more suitable for large organizations than small ones.

The ROI method converts qualitative issues into quantitative measures and uses a conservative approach to the estimation of the figures. These are then given a monetary value, so the benefit can be reasonably assessed. Phillips (2002) maintains that it is normally only calculated for the first year, because if the benefits are not quickly realized then it is unlikely that they ever will.

In the presentation of results not all intangibles should be included in the figures because they may undermine the credibility of the more accurate ones. Instead Phillips recommends that these are listed separately. They include for example reduced stress, image of the organization, and absenteeism.

HRD function

This last point becomes even more significant when we turn from particular activities to the audit of the HRD function as a whole. Here we need to show that the HRD function is contributing effectively and efficiently to the objectives of the organization.

The problem for the HRD function is to demonstrate the contribution of training and development to the organization. One method clearly is to use the audit of particular activities to build up a picture. But this must then be taken a step further: it must be shown that the overall contribution is valuable.

An important element in this will be the costs of the HRD function. We have already looked at some of the factors affecting costing of the HRD function. One factor not so far discussed is the way in which the costs of the HRD function are allocated by the organization. In some organizations the costs of departments with an organization-wide remit, such as the HRD function, are treated as organizational overheads and allocated across all departments according to some formula. In other organizations, HRD costs are carried on individual managers' budgets. In some organizations the HRD function is expected to recover its costs from its customers, that is, other parts of the organization; in other cases the cost of HRD is treated as an organizational investment.

Each organization has its own way of dealing with the costs of functions such as HRD, and the method is usually decided without reference to those affected. However, it is important to be aware of how costs are allocated in your organization, since this has an effect on how the case for cost-effectiveness is presented.

In addition to costing information, there are several sources of information to assist in showing the value and effectiveness of the HRD function:

- *Investment appraisals* carried out for or by other parts of the organization should take account of the associated investment in training. This information can be used both to show that the HRD function is performing effectively in relation to that investment, and to see how training and development contributes to the cash-flow analysis of the organization.
- *The organization's mission statement* will give objectives. How do training and development programmes contribute to meeting those objectives? For example, in an organization whose mission statement includes references to customer care, what development and training is offered to staff to help improve customer care?
- *Statistics may help.* For example, an organization may keep a record of customer complaints. Has the volume of complaints gone down after staff training?
- *Opportunity costing* has been discussed already. If not spent on HRD, what else would the money have been spent on? Would these other activities have had a beneficial effect on the organization? Can we compare the effects in any way?
- *Competition:* there are always other ways of providing the training and development needed in an organization, but those alternative ways may not be as cost-effective as an in-house HRD function. It is important here to compare like with like, and ensure that an alternative form of training would do the same job. Sometimes what seems to be a cheaper way of doing things turns out to be more expensive because it does not do the whole job.

We can see from this very brief overview that auditing the HRD function is a complex operation. Often the audit will be carried out by those with little knowledge of HRD, and often the major focus will be financial. By being aware of the background to audit, and able to offer constructive ideas about how effective audit can be done, HRD professionals will be better able to convince management of the value and cost-effectiveness of their work.

CONCLUSION

Accounting is a large and complex area, which has only been touched on in this chapter. However, the main principles of costing and auditing are simple. With just a little care and attention to detail, HRD professionals can ensure that accounting becomes a useful management tool which helps in the provision of quality HRD. That is the justification of costing and auditing the HRD function, and it is too important for the task to be left to those who do not understand HRD.

Bibliography

Accounting for People (2003) *Accounting for People: Report of the task force on human capital management*, www.accountingforpeople.gov.uk

Beaton, L and Richards, S (1997) *Making Training Pay*, London, IPD

Blackwood, A (1995) *Accounting for Business*, Sunderland, Business Education Publishers

Foong, K and Yorsten, R (2003) *Human Capital Measurement and Reporting: A British perspective* [Online] www.accountingforpeople.gov.uk (accessed 3 November 2004)

Hall, N (1976) *Cost Benefit Analysis in Industrial Training*, Manchester, Manchester University Department of Adult Education

Head, G E (1994) *Training Cost Analysis: A how to guide for trainers and managers*, rev edn, Alexandria, VA, ASTD

Lumby, S (1995) *Investment Appraisal and Financial Decisions*, 5th edn, London, Chapman Hall

McLaney, E J (1991) *Business Finance for Decision Makers*, London, Pitman

Newby, A (1992) *Cost Effective Training: A manager's guide*, London, Kogan Page

Parsons, J G (1997) 'Values as a vital supplement to the use of financial analysis in HRD', *Human Resource Development Quarterly*, 8, 1, pp 5–13

Philips, J J (1994) *Measuring Return on Investment*, Alexandria, VA, ASTD

Phillips, J J (1997) *Handbook of Training Evaluation and Measurement Methods: Proven models and methods for evaluating any HRD programme*, Houston, TX, Gulf Publishing

Phillips, P P (2002) *Understanding the Basics of Return on Investment in Training: Assessing the tangible and intangible benefits*, London, Kogan Page

Spencer, L M (1986) *Calculating Human Resource Costs and Benefits*, New York, Wiley

Stevens, B (1973) *Measuring the Return on Management Training*, London, Industrial Society

Watts, J (1996) *Accounting in the Business Environment*, 2nd edn, London, Pitman

23

Intellectual Capital

Alan Cattell

INTRODUCTION AND LEARNING OBJECTIVES

An important consideration for organizations in the 21st century is their ability to understand the nature of, and realize the value of their 'intangible and invisible assets' or 'intellectual capital'. Brinker states:

> Intellectual capital has been in existence for as long as companies have had customers, it's what makes a company worth more than the sum of its countable parts. As an asset, it has been (inadequately) covered for years by the blanket term of goodwill. Unlike accounting goodwill, intellectual capital appreciates.
>
> Brinker (2004:1)

During 1995 Netscape, with 50 employees and a value of US $17 million, went public. After the first day of trading Netscape's stock market value was US $3 billion. However, it was not only the company's physical and financial capital that investors were buying into. What they really bought were the people who had built up Netscape as a company, along with their knowledge, skills, abilities, ideas and talent. Investment was also being made in Netscape's ability to innovate and be creative in terms of bringing a differentiated and timely product to a market which was ready for it. What investors really bought was the *intellectual capital* of the firm.

It is becoming accepted by an increasing number of companies that future success depends on their ability to utilize their intellectual resources and to appreciate the inherent value of these. However many firms spend less time and effort in evaluating and tracking these than they do for financial and physical assets.

Much of the thinking around intellectual capital is still confined to frameworks and working practices that are part of industrial-age thinking and reinforce existing thinking and mindsets (Allee, 2000). The term 'capital' should no longer be confined to tangible monetary or material assets, but should also include intangible assets.

Relating intellectual capital and intangible assets to organizational perspectives, Gu and Lev (2001:2) suggest that intangible (knowledge or intellectual) assets are the main drivers of corporate value and growth.

Within this context a view of HRM and HRD as an added-value resource rather than cost to the organization will be developed within this chapter, along with identification of human and social capital (as elements of intellectual capital) in particular as an opportunity rather than a threat for HR in general.

Stiles and Kulvisaechana (2003:3) set the scene for the chapter when they state:

> There is a large and growing body of evidence that demonstrates a positive linkage between development of human capital and organisational performance. The emphasis on human capital in organisations reflects the view that market value depends less on tangible resources, but rather on intangible ones, particularly human resources. Recruiting and retaining the best employees, however is only part of the equation. The organisation also has to leverage the skills and capabilities of its employees by encouraging individual and organisational learning and creating a supportive environment in which knowledge can be created, shared and applied.

Having read this chapter you will:

- understand the main components of intellectual capital;
- understand the difference between tangible, intangible and invisible assets;
- be aware of some of the methods of quantifying and measuring these;
- be aware of the implications for HRM and HRD professionals.

MAIN COMPONENTS OF INTELLECTUAL CAPITAL

Literature suggests that intellectual capital is made up of a number of facets, all of which have asset value if tapped into by an organization. Kaplan and Norton (1993), Svieby (1997) Stewart (1997) and Harvey and Lusch (1999) propose that intellectual capital is a broad term which includes internal dimensions like patents, concepts and human capabilities, and external dimensions such as brands, reputation and trademarks.

Garavan *et al* (2001) identify that a common theme is the distinction between external, internal and human capital dimensions. They note Haanes and Lowendahl's (1997) view that intellectual capital consists of two elements, namely tangible and intangible. The intangible category consists of competence and relational resources. Competence is defined at two levels, *individual* knowledge, skill and aptitude, and *organizational* knowledge in the form of databases, technology, processes and procedures.

Wright, Dunford and Snell (2001) propose that intellectual capital includes human, social and organizational (structural) capital:

> Intellectual capital is embedded in both people and systems ... the stock of human capital consists of human (knowledge, skills and abilities of people), social (valuable relationships among people) and organisational (the processes and routines within a firm).
>
> (Wright *et al*, 2001:716)

Customer (external) capital is also included by both Mayo (2000) and Allee (2000) as a key element of intellectual capital. Stiles and Kulvisaechana (2003) suggest that if competitive advantage is to be achieved, integration between human, social and organizational capital is required. To achieve this, the customer perspective also needs to be included.

Combining input from a number of authors as shown in Table 23.1, Table 23.2 offers some pointers towards the content of the various elements.

Human capital

While the main purpose of human capital is to realize the talent potential of individuals, the accumulation of and investment in talented employees by organizations may not be enough. There must also be motivation and desire on the part of individuals to contribute and invest their skills and experience in the organization. Without such a commitment or engagement, effective utilization of human capital will not happen. Links between human and organizational/structural capital are therefore key.

Organizational/structural capital

In creating work processes that leverage competitiveness, organizations need to find a balance between possessing efficient technology, systems and procedures, and the needs of employees as regards participation and management/rewarding of talent. This requires that companies consider the ways that performance management, incentive and reward systems impact on the motivation of the workforce to develop and use their skills and knowledge. The prevailing culture of an organization has a direct correlation with recruitment and retention, in addition to creating a climate of employee commitment and development.

Dess and Picken (1999:11) suggest that the key role of organizational capital is to link the resources of the organization through processes that create value for customers and sustainable competitive advantage for the company.

Table 23.1 Notable authors on the various forms of capital

Theorist	Year	Consists of
Becker Drucker	1975 1985	**Human capital**: knowledge, expertise, education. **Intangible**: resides in individuals, complementary to other forms of capital. Difficult to measure. Differentiates mental effort from physical labour and enables learning to be taken into account.
Bourdieu Coleman Burt	1986 1988 1992	**Social capital**: **intangible**: resides in networks and relationships and is collectively owned. Difficult to measure but enables the added value of organizational skills to be taken into account.
Kaplan and Norton	1992	Customers, internal business processes, learning and growth.
Brooking	1996	Market assets, human-centred assets, intellectual property and infrastructural assets.
Svieby	1997	Invisible assets of the organisation including: employee competence, skills, education and experience and their ability to act in a variety of situations. **Internal structure**: management, structure, patents, models, R&D capability, software. **External structure**: image, brands, customers and supplier relations.
Bradley	1997	Innovation. Tradeable, cheap to reproduce, appreciates rather than depreciates with use. Multiple and potentially simultaneous application.
Roos *et al*	1997	**Human capital, organizational capital and relational capital**: thinking and non-thinking assets where the distinction is made because human capital requires management in a different way. Relational capital includes relationships between internal and external stakeholders.
Stewart	1997	**Human capital, structural capital and customer capital:** intellectual material: knowledge, information, intellectual property and experience which can be utilized to create wealth. Customer capital includes relationships between customers and suppliers.
Haanes and Lowendahl	1997	Suggest a distinction between intangible resources of **competence**: the ability to perform at individual and organizational levels and **relationship**: company reputation and customer loyalty. Both of these exist individually and collectively.
Edvinnson and Malone	1997	**Human capital**: employees and managers and what they can do individually and collectively. **Systems**: which represent the knowledge in the company as regards patents, contracts, databases, information and production technology. **Market**: relationships between the organization and external bodies, suppliers, distributors and customers.
Bontis	1997	**Human capital, structural capital, relational capital, intellectual property:** unlike intellectual capital, intellectual property is a protected asset with a legal definition.
Ulrich	1998	**Competence and commitment of employees**: knowledge, skill or ability is applied to meeting the organization's goals and purposes.
Nahapiet and Ghoshal	1998	**Individual and social tacit and explicit knowledge**

Table 23.1 *continued*

Theorist	Year	Consists of
Granstrand	1999	**Immaterial resources: intellectual property, goodwill** and power in internal/external relationships, **relational and organizational capital, human competence.** Ownership is key. Capitalized value can be attributed only if it is possible to exploit intellectual assets.
Sullivan	1999	Knowledge that can be converted into profits. **Human capital**: individual employees who possess skills, knowledge, and know-how. Each employee possesses **tacit** knowledge (uncodified) that the organization should seek to utilize, and **intellectual assets** are created whenever human capital is codified. When this occurs the firm can move the intellectual asset rather than the individual to wherever it is needed.
Teece	2000	**Intangible assets:** knowledge, competence, brands, reputation, customer relationships, intellectual property.
Mayo	2000	**Human capital**: capability, knowledge, skill, experience and networking, with the ability to achieve results and the potential for growth. **Individual motivation**: aspirations, ambition, drives, work motivation and productivity. **Work group effectiveness**: support, mutual respect, sharing and values. **Leadership**: clarity of vision and ability to communicate that vision. **Organizational climate**: culture, freedom to innovate, openness, flexibility and respect for the individual.
Dzinkowski	2000	**Intellectual assets and knowledge assets** made up of **human capital, organizational (structural capital) and customer (relational) capital.** Fixed or flexible, and both the input and the output of the value creation process. The end-product of knowledge transformation.

Adapted from Garavan *et al* (2001) and Dean and Kretschmer (2002)

Customer/relational capital

Svieby (2004) suggests that individual competence and the professional/technical ability and expertise of knowledge workers to deal directly and efficiently with customers may directly influence the customers' view of an organization. It is these intangible relationships that form perceptions of the firm, its reputation and image. In the process the value of such assets is primarily influenced by how well the company solves its customers' problems. Additional to customer focus, customer/relational capital should also consider the needs of all external stakeholders: investors, creditors and suppliers, and their perception of the company.

Social capital

The concept of social capital highlights the asset value of human relationships which are based on mutual concern, support and trust. Cohen and Prusak (2001) observe that low social capital organizations tend to have higher turnover rates, and that knowledge

Table 23.2 Areas of capital

Human capital	Individual education, know-how, competence, ability to act in a variety of situations, experience, judgement, wisdom, knowledge, skill, motivation and attitude. *Having individual talent.*
Organizational/structural capital (internal)	*Infrastructure assets* such as reporting structures, operating systems, databases, methodologies, routines, codified knowledge, documents, technology, information and communications infrastructure, processes, procedures, concepts, models of how the business operates, incentives, performance measurement systems, culture, corporate values, clear vision, leadership. *Intellectual property* such as patents, copyrights, design rights, trade marks and trade secrets. *Having work processes that leverage competitiveness.*
Customer/relational capital (external)	Customer contracts, distribution channels, licensing agreements, relationships, reputation, image, loyalty, satisfaction, market share, alliances with customers, strategic partners, suppliers and investors; includes brand, recognition and goodwill. *Understanding the value chain and knowing stakeholder and customer wants/needs in order to meet and deliver these rapidly and efficiently.*
Social capital (internal and external)	Shared norms and social relationships, shared values, support, cooperative action, networks, trust, mutual understanding, asset value of human relationships, linkages between individuals. *Having the capability to leverage individual talent and ability to meet organizational, customer and community needs.*

management travels effectively through organizations along existing social pathways which have been built up between people on the basis of trust and understanding. In working on a project for Zurich Financial Services, Cunningham, Dawes and Bennett (2004) observed that the project was not solely about learning new skills: that is, a human-capital focus. It also involved learning to collaborate across different cultures in order to enhance the profitability of the business.

With its stress on linkages between individuals, social capital has the potential to create conditions and learning that are tacit, unique and durable.

LINKS BETWEEN THE DIFFERENT FORMS OF CAPITAL

In this section the links between how the various forms of capital interact with one another are examined. Research carried out by Bontis, Chong Keow and Richardson (2000:85–100) with MBA students working in both the service and non-service sectors in Malaysia sought to establish links between human, structural and customer capital. Social capital was not included in the study, and the key findings were as follows.

Human and organizational/ structural capital

Much effort is expended in the non-service sector in absorbing large capital outlays on plant and machinery, to the detriment of investment in human capital. In the service sector the implications are that there is a real challenge for knowledge-intensive firms to codify or externalize much of the tacit knowledge that resides in employees' minds.

Human and customer capital

The study showed that regardless of sector there is a positive relationship between human and customer capital. The conclusion drawn is that the more competent an organization's employees are, the better they will understand customers' needs and wants. Additionally they are more capable of developing customer capital to retain customer loyalty.

Customer and organizational/structural capital

The research by Bontis *et al* also highlighted the fact that regardless of sector, organizations that invest heavily in becoming customer focused and market driven will automatically create efficient organizational routines and processes that will service their clientele well.

Relationship between organizational/structural capital and business performance

This element of the study showed that any organization's efforts to codify (make explicit) organizational knowledge and thus further develop structural capital does ultimately yield competitive advantage.

Overall the research confirmed that besides hiring, developing and promoting the brightest individuals that they can attract, organizations must also support individuals in sharing their human capital through organizational learning and externalization into information systems.

TANGIBLE, INTANGIBLE AND INVISIBLE ASSETS

This section of the chapter explores the different types of asset that have an impact on capital. Fahy (2000:94–104) identifies three groups, tangible, intangible and invisible, the main features of which are described below.

Tangible

These have the properties of ownership and are fixed, current assets. They are generally measured at a moment in time. They include such features as land, plant, equipment, stocks, debtors and bank deposits. Their value is reasonably easy to measure. The book value of these assets is measured through conventional accounting procedures, and is generally reflected in the balance sheet evaluation of companies.

Intangible

These are assets that have a relatively unlimited capacity. Firms can exploit their value by using them in-house, renting them (in licences and franchises) or selling them as brands. They include features such as intellectual property, trade marks, patents, company reputation, and networks and databases. The presence of intangible assets accounts for the significant differences between the balance sheet valuation and market valuation of public companies.

These significant differences were highlighted during the so-called dot.com boom of the 1990s. Here intangible and *invisible* assets accounted for the high stock market value of many of the firms involved. Essentially the only assets of many of the companies involved were the skills and creativity of a group of young and able professionals who were thought to have business acumen and an understanding of the internet.

In the majority of organizations today intangible and invisible assets play a greater role than tangible assets.

Capabilities (invisible assets)

These are very difficult to value. They have a limited capacity in the short term, as it takes time to develop the learning and skill updating necessitated by change. However, once this is done they have relatively unlimited capacity in the longer term. They include features such as skills of individuals and groups, organizational routines and interactions through which company resources are coordinated, successful teamwork, supportive organizational culture, and trust between management, employees, strategic partners and allies. A plus for the organization is that individual skills can be highly tacit, inimitable and non-substitutable. A minus is that they can be sought after and hired away by competitors.

Figure 23.1 shows the relationship of the features highlighted so far in this chapter, plus the distinctions between tacit and explicit knowledge which are further covered in Chapter 7 on 'Knowledge Management'.

METHODS OF QUANTIFICATION AND MEASUREMENT

Svieby (2004) provides a regular update and brief overview of a number of approaches (currently 28) for measuring intangible assets. This is a useful reference point for those wishing to gain deeper insights into the subject. Additionally, two Swedish companies, Skandia (2004; see also Edvinsson and Malone, 1997) and Celemi (2004) also have considerable experience in the area. Both have websites explaining their approaches.

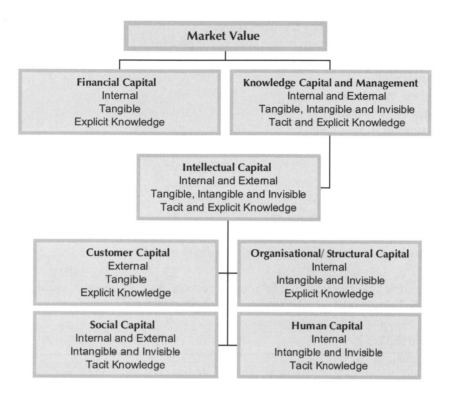

Figure 23.1   Forms of capital contributing to market value
Source: adapted from Skandia (1997)

Measures of people are more difficult to specify than those of financial aspects. However, the intention of the next element of the chapter is to highlight some useful pointers to measuring intangible and invisible assets.

Measurement dimensions

The main and simplest dimensions of measurement are: time, quantity, cost and quality. Mayo (2000: 521–33) suggests that there are a number of quantification choices of value (either added or lost) that can be measured, based on outputs. Three of these are shown below, while the fourth, levels of competence and expertise, will be shown later in the chapter:

1.   Financial measures of value:
     –   patents with revenue streams;
     –   customer contracts and contacts;
     –   licences;
     –   franchises;

   – added value produced by teams of people;
   – replacement costs of knowledge, systems or people.
2. Bottom-line contributory figures:
   – volume of sales;
   – numbers of customers;
   – productivity measures;
   – measures of innovation;
   – efficiency measures;
   – ratios.
3. Perceptions of others:
   – employee satisfaction and motivation surveys;
   – decisions on levels of potential;
   – customer satisfaction surveys;
   – performance reviews and 360-degree feedback.

Mayo also suggests that the negative financial effects of poor intellectual capital management can be calculated in terms of quantifying the effects of:

- loss of key people;
- loss of key customers;
- lost revenues due to lack of capability or inadequate response.

In measuring such effects, human capital (headcount, turnover figures, identification of key knowledge workers), customer capital (identification of key customers, customer feedback) and financial capital implications can be calculated. To do so, organizational/structural and social capital in the form of collaboration between HR, Business, Marketing and Finance in generating and consolidating such information also needs to be employed.

Besides measuring the negative effects of poor intellectual capital management, an alternative approach is to take a more positive stance. Here measurement could be used to identify possible value creation opportunities or to uncover costs not revealed by traditional accounting methods.

Measurement implications

Human capital dimensions are at the heart of intellectual capital, as their negative effects can have a knock-on effect across the other areas of capital.

High turnover for instance can result in higher recruitment and training and development costs, less customer continuity and satisfaction, resulting in more mistakes, increased workload and consequently low morale. It is therefore important for companies to recognize the linkages between and across areas of measurement, and the strategic impact of these.

Research carried out by Bontis and Fitz-enz (2002) within the financial services industry in the USA sought to establish the consequences of effective human capital management within organizations'. The research showed that:

- Development of senior management leadership capabilities is the key starting point for the reduction of turnover rates and retention of key employees.
- Effective management of intellectual capital assets yields higher financial results per employee. The development of human capital is positively influenced by employee educational levels and overall employee satisfaction.
- Employee satisfaction, motivation and commitment have positive and also long-term impacts on intellectual capital management, knowledge management and therefore business performance.
- Knowledge management initiatives can decrease turnover rates and support business performance if they are aligned to HR policies and strategy.
- Business performance is positively influenced by the attitudes of organizational employees and their ability to generate new knowledge. This favourable level of performance acts as a deterrent to turnover, which in turn positively affects human capital management.

The survey instrument used in the research asked respondents to comment on employee satisfaction, employee motivation, human capital, management/leadership, knowledge sharing, employee commitment, value alignment, structural capital, process effectiveness, knowledge integration, training, retention of key people, customer capital, knowledge generation and business performance.

To complement the survey instrument areas used by Bontis and Fitz-enz, Figure 23.2 illustrates a range (not an exhaustive list) of measurement possibilities and choices which the reader may find it useful to consider.

To ensure integration of measurement across all areas of capital, an increasing number of organizations are adopting *stakeholder* or *scorecard* approaches. These are intended to weigh the interests of a variety of stakeholders, both internal and external, to an organization. Guest *et al* (2000:4) favour such approaches in terms of emphasizing outcomes that are of concern or interest to a range of stakeholders. They contend that these should 'reflect employee attitudes and behaviour, internal performance, such as productivity and quality of goods and services; and external indicators such as sales and financial performance'.

Among the 28 measurement and reporting approaches identified by Svieby (2004) and mentioned earlier in this chapter, at least 10 adopt such scorecard approaches. Perhaps the best known of these are Kaplan and Norton's Balanced Scorecard (1992) and the Skandia Navigator (1994).

IMPLICATIONS FOR HR PRACTITIONERS

Huselid (2003) suggests that besides having just one scorecard, it may be useful to have other 'nested' scorecards which make up part of the overall process. These could include a workforce scorecard focused on workforce behaviours and outputs, complemented by an HR scorecard. To have any meaning, these need to be owned corporately but developed as part of an integrated scorecard process, to stop them being taken forward in isolation from each other.

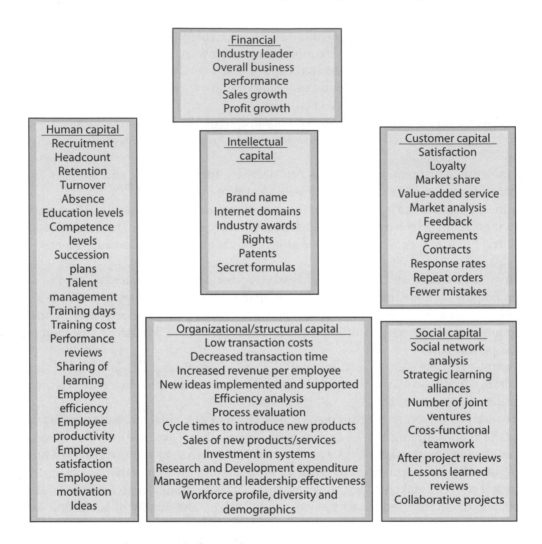

Figure 23.2 Metrics for sources of capital

A model of an HR scorecard utilizing a combination of Mayo's (2000) levels of competence and expertise and appropriate headcount, turnover and financial figures and information is shown in Figure 23.3.

Kaplan and Norton (2000) and Becker et al (2001) have also proposed models of HR score-cards as useful frameworks. Evans (2003:31) outlines a useful questionnaire approach for HR professionals which was developed from the work of Becker *et al* (2001).

In seeking to measure and quantify value, Mayo states:

> By understanding who is adding the different kinds of value, and who has the potential to add the value we need for the future, our investments in people development can be planned and managed intelligently. ... There is a risk that we spend an immense amount of effort in diagnosis

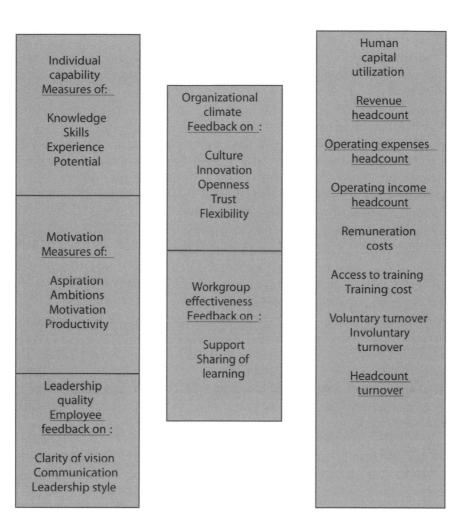

Levels of competence and expertise   Other indicators

Individual
capability
Measures of:

Knowledge
Skills
Experience
Potential

Motivation
Measures of:

Aspiration
Ambitions
Motivation
Productivity

Leadership
quality
Employee
feedback on :

Clarity of vision
Communication
Leadership style

Organizational
climate
Feedback on :

Culture
Innovation
Openness
Trust
Flexibility

Workgroup
effectiveness
Feedback on :

Support
Sharing of
learning

Human
capital
utilization

Revenue
headcount

Operating expenses
headcount

Operating income
headcount

Remuneration
costs

Access to training
Training cost

Voluntary turnover
Involuntary
turnover

Headcount
turnover

Figure 23.3   An example of an HR scorecard

and analysis and go to great lengths to prove what is obvious and already known. However, such effort is likely to lead to an embedded methodology that becomes as important an indicator of performance as any financial ones. Inherent within most organizations are systems of performance review, feedback, agreement of performance objectives, derivation and tracking of individual and organizational competencies. HRM departments generate recruitment, turnover, retention, head-count and workforce profile statistics. Additionally employee satisfaction and customer satisfaction surveys and evaluation of training and quality management initiatives have the potential to reveal much of the information which is required for the effective measurement and reporting of capital.

Mayo (2000:521:533)

A key challenge for HRD professionals is to consider how best we utilize the information that we generate, in order to both measure and report on human capital and also to influence the strategic agenda of the organizations we work for. Evaluation of training and learning interventions is only part of the story.

Foong and Yorsten (2003) suggest that HR departments need to measure human capital to ascertain the cost of investment in human capital and the return from those investments. Here the emphasis is on human capital as an investment not a cost. In doing so they also argue that measurement of human capital provides a framework for human resources to move from a 'soft' skill business to a 'hard' one.

In the past Ulrich (1998b) has proposed that human resources, in the sense of both labour and a business function, have been considered as a cost to be reduced and minimized. The increased interest by organizations in the concepts of human capital, core competencies, and resource-based value over the last decade mean that there is a prime opportunity for HR in general to be seen as a potential source of value creation.

Baker and Aldrich (1996) suggest a move away from employer-sponsored training towards learning taking place in the work context itself. The European Commission's White Paper *Teaching and Learning: Towards a learning society* (1997), in considering investment in human and intellectual capital, argues that investment in formal HRD and work-based learning strategies should be considered on an equal basis to investment in physical capital.

Sloman (2003) and Harrison and Kessels (2004) propose that there has been a transition from training to learning, and also point towards a closer relationship between learning and performance. This perhaps confirms the need identified by Foong and Yorsten (2003) for HRD to become that bit more hard – but within limits.

The CIPD report *Performance through People: The new people management* (2001) points towards turning rhetoric into reality by putting people management at the centre of business concerns. It states:

> As with any paradigm shift, the main obstacles to change aren't physical. They lie in traditional comfort zones: mindsets that are happier with 'hard' quantifications of physical capacities and utlizations than 'soft' measurement of intangibles. … Although progress is being made in areas such as brand valuation, markets have been slow to develop convincing metrics for valuing intangibles, and most senior managers have no experience of using them to manage internally.
>
> (CIPD, 2001:12–13)

REPORTING OF CAPITAL

A number of organizations, notably Skandia in Sweden, have successfully utilized human capital approaches and evaluation to gain sustainable competitive advantage. However, it would appear that despite theory and rhetoric regarding intellectual capital (particularly human capital), reporting of intangible/invisible assets is spasmodic and difficult to say the least. In the USA legal considerations, competitive sensitivity and concern for the practical difficulties of collecting information form some of the reasons for this. Research by Scarborough and Elias

(2002) in the UK highlights the fact that of the 10 organizations involved in their study, all were involved in measurement but were doing so for internal purposes only. None of the results were published in company reports or other external documents.

According to Stiles and Kulvisaechana (2003:20) and Huselid (2003) there are two major issues that lead to difficulty in reporting intangibles. First, there is no common framework for reporting that goes beyond historical information (such as cost of selection, or training) to 'more detailed' information on workforce quality. Second, many firms lack databases and audited information that can give strong and relevant information to investors.

The creation and development of consistent and coherent internal mechanisms and HR architecture is suggested by Stiles and Kulvisaechana (2003) as a necessary condition for effective external reporting.

CHALLENGES FOR HRD

From an HRD point of view there is a need to convince internal and external stakeholders of the value that can be added through business-driven learning, training and development interventions. Comment from a number of sources points towards such a need:

> There is a need for HRD professionals to ensure the development of a strategic role, to clarify their functional role, develop the new skills required … and more clearly state their value and contribution to organizational success.

> (Sambrook and Stewart, 2002:187)

Research into developing corporate learning strategy by Luton University highlighted the fact that training and development interventions were not leading to an output of intellectual capital (Coulson-Thomas, 2001).

In 2004 Mercer HR Consulting reported on research into change carried out with a sample population of 1,057 worldwide HR professionals. This revealed that the main driver for change was not in saving costs, but the fact that HR needed to add more value but was not currently perceived to be doing so.

In developing metrics and reporting mechanisms for intellectual capital, HRD practitioners have an opportunity to address some of the concerns above.

CONCLUSION

This chapter has identified the various forms that intellectual capital can take, and considered the differences between tangible, intangible and invisible assets. Measures of quantifying and measuring these have been discussed and some of the implications for HRM and HRD identified.

In considering the various elements of intellectual capital there is an opportunity for HRD professionals to see the bigger strategic picture of an organization from the perspective of a range of stakeholders. Included within this are potential approaches for linking individual, organizational and networked learning to the notion of adding value and thus competitive advantage.

However, a health warning is suggested by Gratton (2004:20) when she states:

> I don't know about you, but I always have rather complicated and mixed feelings about HR metrics. It is right and sensible to create metrics around what you believe to be important to organizations, but in creating metrics we make fundamental assumptions, some of which may well be incorrect.
>
> In HR we are particularly prone to 'metric-itus'; in part I guess, because our inferiority complex about Big Brother the finance department, with its array of sexy and unimaginably complicated financial metrics. So being able to measure what we do is a good thing.
>
> (Gratton, 2004:20)

In her article, Gratton highlights the fact that while it may be believed by many that remuneration and promotion are the key to retention of employees, this might not be the case. Research by Pittinsky and Shih (2004) showed two levers to be crucial to employee commitment to an organization: first, opportunities for formal and informal learning and the degree of alignment between these opportunities and the employee's commitment to their career; and second, employees were more attached to their companies when they felt that they were part of small work groups.

As regards the field of intellectual capital management there is an obvious need for more research, particularly in identifying best practice rather than solely theory. The intention of this chapter has been to stimulate the reader to find out more about the area, and in doing so to encourage development of his/her own intellectual capital.

Bibliography

Allee, V (2000) 'The value evolution: addressing larger implications of an intellectual capital and intangibles perspective', *Journal of Intellectual Capital*, 1, 1, pp 17–32

Baker, T and Aldrich, T E (1996) 'Prometheus stretches building identity and cumulative knowledge in multi employer careers', in M B Arthur and D M Rousseau (eds), *The Boundaryless Career: A new employment principle for a new organisational era*, New York, Oxford University Press

Becker, B E, Huselid, M A and Ulrich, D (2001) *The HR Scorecard: Linking people, strategy and performance*, Boston, MA, Harvard Business School Press

Becker, G. S (1975) *Human Capital: A theoretical and empirical analysis*, 2nd edn, New York, National Bureau of Economic Research

Bontis, N (1998) *Intellectual Capital Questionnaire*, Hamilton, Canada, Institute for Intellectual Capital Research

Bontis, N, Chong Keow, W C and Richardson, S (2000) 'Intellectual capital and business performance in Malaysian industries', *Journal of Intellectual Capital*, 1, 1, pp 85–100

Bontis, N and Fitz-enz, J (2002) 'Intellectual capital ROI: a causal map of human capital antecedents and consequents', *Journal of Intellectual Capital*, 3, 3, pp 223–47

Bourdieu, P (1986) 'The forms of capital', in J G Richardson (ed), *Handbook of Theory and Research for the Sociology of Education*, New York, Greenwood

Bradley, K (1997) 'Intellectual capital and the new wealth of nations 1 and 11', *Business Strategy Review*, 8, 1, pp 53–62

Brinker, B (2004) *Intellectual Capital: Tomorrow's asset, today's challenge* [Online] www.cpavision.org (accessed July 2004)

Brooking, A (1996) *Intellectual Capital: Core asset for the third millennium enterprise*, London, International Thomson Business Press

Burt, R S (1992) *Structural Holes: The social structure of competition*, Boston, MA, Harvard University Press

CIPD (Chartered Institute of Personnel and Development) (2001) *Performance through People: The new people management – the change agenda*, London, CIPD

Cohen, D and Prusak, L (2001) *In Good Company: How social capital makes organizations work*, Cambridge, MA, Harvard Business School Press

Coleman, J S (1988) 'Social capital in the creation of human capital', *American Journal of Sociology*, **94**, Supp pp S95–S120

Cunningham, I, Dawes, G. and Bennett, B (2004) *The Handbook of Work Based Learning*, Aldershot, Gower

Coulson-Thomas, C (2001) 'Fashion victim', *People Management*, **7**, 17, p 51

Dean, A and Kretschmer, M (2002) 'Can ideas be capital? Factors of production in the post-industrial economy: a review and critique', *Academy of Management Review*, December

Dess, G G and Picken, J C (1999) *Beyond Productivity: How leading companies achieve superior performance by leveraging their human capital*, New York, American Management Association

Drucker, P (1985) *Managing in Turbulent Times*, New York, Harper and Row

Edvinsson, L and Malone, M (1997) *Intellectual Capital: Realising your company's true value by finding its hidden roots*, New York, HarperCollins

EEC (European Economic Community) (1997) *Teaching and Learning: Towards a learning society*, White Paper, EEC

Evans, C (2003) *Managing for Knowledge: HR's strategic role*, Oxford, Butterworth-Heinemann

Fahy, J (2000) 'The resource-based view of the firm: some stumbling blocks on the road to understanding sustainable competitive advantage', *Journal of European Industrial Training*, **24**, 2/3/4, pp 94–104

Foong, K and Yorsten, R (2003) *Human Capital Measurement and Reporting: A British perspective* [Online] www.accountingforpeople.gov.uk (accessed 3 November 2004)

Garavan, T N, Morley, M, Gunnigle, P and Collins, E (2001) 'Human capital accumulation: the role of human resource development', *Journal of European Industrial Training*, **25**, 2/3/4, pp 48–68

Gratton, L (2004) 'Means to an end: are we measuring the right things?', *People Management*, **9**, 17, 2 September

Gu, F and Lev, B (2001) *Intangible Assets: Measurement, drivers, usefulness*, Stern Business School, New York University [Online] www.stern.nyu.edu (accessed December 2001)

Guest, D, Michie, J, Sheehan, M and Conway, N (2000) *Effective People Management*, London, CIPD

Haanes, K and Lowendahl, B (1997) *The Unit of Activity: Towards an alternative to the theories of the firm, structure and style*, ed H Thomas, Copenhagen, Wiley

Harrison, R and Kessels, J (2004) *Human Resource Development on a Knowledge Economy: An organisational view*, Basingstoke, Palgrave Macmillan

Harvey, M G and Lusch, R F (1999) 'Balancing the intellectual capital books: intangible liabilities', *European Management Journal*, **17**, pp 29–41

Huselid, M A (2003) Presentation to DTI Accounting for People seminar, London, 18 July

Kaplan, R S and Norton, D P (1992) 'The Balanced Scorecard measures that drive performance', *Harvard Business Review*, **70**, 1, January–February, pp 71–79

Kaplan, R S and Norton, D P (1993) 'Putting the Balanced Scorecard to Work', *Harvard Business Review*, September–October

Kaplan, R S and Norton, D P (2000) 'Having trouble with your strategy? Then map it', *Harvard Business Review*, September–October, p 169

Mayo, A (2000) 'The role of employee development in the growth of intellectual capital', *Personnel Review*, **29**, 4, pp 521–33

Mercer Consulting (2004) quoted in 'Partnership drives worldwide change', *People Management*, **9**, 17, p 12

Nahapiet, J and Ghoshal, S (1998) 'Social capital, intellectual capital and the organizational advantage', *Academy of Management Review*, **22**, 2, pp 242–68

Pittinsky, T and Shih, M (2004) 'Retention as a lead HR measure of commitment?', *American Behavioral Scientist*, February

Roos, G, Roos, J, Edvinsson, L and Dragonetti, N C (1997) *Intellectual Capital: Navigating in the new business landscape*, New York, New York University Press

Sambrook, S and Stewart, J (2002) 'Reflections and discussion', in J Tjepkema, J Stewart, S Sambrook, M Mulder, H ter Horst and J Scheerens (eds), *HRD and Learning Organisations in Europe*, London, Routledge

Scarborough, H and Elias, J (2002) *Evaluating Human Capital*, London, CIPD

Sloman, M (2003) *Training in the Age of the Learner*, London, CIPD

Stewart, T A (1997) *Intellectual Capital: The new wealth of organizations*, New York, Doubleday

Stiles, P and Kulvisaechana, S (2003) *Human Capital and Performance* [Online] www.accountingforpeople.gov.uk (accessed July 2004)

Svieby, K E (1997) *The New Organisational Wealth: Managing and measuring knowledge-based assets*, San Francisco, CA, Berret-Koehler

Svieby, K E (2004) *Methods for Measuring Intangible Assets* [Online] www.svieby.com (accessed July 2004)

Ulrich, D (1998a) 'Intellectual capital = competence × commitment', *Sloan Management Review*, **39**, 2, Winter, pp 15–27

Ulrich, D (1998b) 'A new mandate for human resources', *Harvard Business Review*, **76**, 1, January/February, pp 124–34

Wright, P M, Dunford, B B and Snell, S A (2001) 'Human resources and the resource based view of the firm', *Journal of Management*, **27**, pp 701–21

Useful websites

Skandia: www.skandia.se/hem/hem.jsp (accessed September 2004)
Celemi: www.celemi.com (accessed September 2004)

Section Seven:

Managing the Human Resource Function

24

Total Quality Training and Human Resource Development

John P Wilson and Ron Chapman

INTRODUCTION AND LEARNING OBJECTIVES

In this chapter we will be considering two main dimensions. The first addresses how training and development can contribute to the introduction, development and ongoing support of the total quality management (TQM) process. Training and development play a critical role in the achievement of TQM; this is strongly endorsed by Thomas (1992:xvi) who stated that, 'Training and development have a central – arguably *the* central – role to play in making quality a reality.' Furthermore, it is in the Human Resource Development (HRD) department where the organizational change consultants normally reside; thus it is personnel from this department who are frequently the main drivers and maintainers of TQM throughout the organization.

The second dimension addresses how we can ensure that the training and development we provide is quality training. Training and development specialists must not only be able to deliver the training and support required for TQM; they must also do so in a quality manner. In other words, they must walk the talk.

The two dimensions of training for quality and quality training are very closely related and therefore we will use the term Total Quality Training to cover both of them.

Having read this chapter you will:

- be able to define quality;
- understand some of the principles of the quality gurus;
- be aware of the main quality standards;
- be able to apply the European Foundation for Quality Management model to the training and development process; and
- understand the principles and approach of Investors in People.

QUALITY

What is quality?

In common with many words that are in daily use, and which we think we understand until we inspect them closely, 'quality' is much more complex than first appears. Defining quality has proved to be a relatively elusive concept as the following quotations reveal:

Crosby (1979) 'Conformance to requirements.'
Deming (1982) 'Quality should be aimed at the needs of the consumer, present and future.'
Juran (1989) 'Fitness for purpose.'
'The totality of features and characteristics of a product or service that bear on its ability to satisfy stated or implied needs.' (ISO 8402, 1986)

And total quality management is defined by the British Standards Institution (1991:2) as:

A management philosophy embracing all activities through which the needs and expectations of the customer and the community, and the objectives of the organization are satisfied in the most efficient and cost-effective way by maximizing the potential of all employees in a continuing drive for improvement.

The business case for quality

At the end of World War II manufacturing output was relatively low and demand exceeded supply. For this reason manufacturers were able to sell all they produced almost regardless of quality. Moreover, there was little competition, which encouraged a complacent attitude among suppliers of products.

One country in particular, Japan, had a major influence on manufacturing quality in the West. At the end of the war its industry was devastated but, through attention to quality, it ultimately succeeded in capturing large slices of many industries. This caused concern among many

Western companies who had seen their market share decline and therefore they decided to adopt many of the production techniques employed in Japan. The irony of this was that one of the main figures contributing to the renaissance of Japanese industry was Dr W E Deming from the USA who lectured on quality procedures.

This changing scenario affecting industry in the West was described by Mortiboys (1991:3), in a guide to chief executives, who stated that:

Our traditional management style has been based upon:

- short term profitability (businesses);
- clamping down on costs, but tolerating high levels of waste;
- a take-it-or-leave-it attitude to customers;
- treating employees as productive robots;
- competing on price (businesses);
- buying at the lowest price;
- discouraging change – but changing arbitrarily when forced to change;
- macho-management – the troubleshooter.

This management style was successful only as long as:

- employees would do as they were told;
- demand exceeded supply;
- customers' expectations increased only slowly;
- the worldwide situation didn't change.

But after World War II the situation *did* change, slowly at first, but then faster and faster, until we reached the current worldwide situation that is characterized by:

- more competitors than ever;
- fiercely competitive strategies;
- fluid and unpredictable financial systems;
- customers' expectations increased;
- investors' expectations increased;
- everything changing;
- businesses and service organizations fighting to survive in this environment.

Standards

In Britain production standards had existed for a long period and had been driven by the armed forces in their requirements for reliable equipment. The Engineering Standards Association was founded in 1901 to ensure levels of quality and subsequently was renamed the British Standards Institution (BSI). The standards detailed by BSI were generally for specific areas; however, it recognized the need for an encompassing standard that addressed the whole process of design, manufacture and delivery. In 1979 it introduced BS 5750 to improve the quality of management and this has since led to the European EN 29000 and the more internationally recognized ISO 9000 standards.

The quality gurus

A number of people have been influential in the development of quality within organizations. Another source for the quality movement can be traced back to the 1920s when Walter Shewhart, a business executive at AT&T's Hawthorne Plant in Chicago, utilized statistics to control the quality of telephones manufactured at the plant.

Building on Shewart's work, Dr W E Deming worked in the US Department of Agriculture and the Bureau of the Census in statistical sampling techniques. His main impact on quality occurred not in the USA but in Japan where in the late 1940s and early 1950s he spent much time lecturing on statistical quality control to various groups including The Union of Japanese Scientists and Engineers (JUSE). As a result of Deming's influence on Japanese manufacturing production he was awarded Japan's highest honour, The Second Order of the Sacred Temple.

Deming devised a checklist of 14 points to help achieve quality:

1. *Create constancy of purpose* to improve product and service.
2. *Adopt new philosophy* for new economic age by management learning responsibilities and taking leadership for change.
3. *Cease dependence on inspection* to achieve quality; eliminate the need for mass inspection by building quality into the product.
4. *End awarding business on price:* instead minimize total cost and move towards single suppliers for items.
5. *Improve constantly and forever the system of production and service* to improve quality.
6. *Institute training on the job.*
7. *Institute leadership:* supervision should help do a better job; overhaul supervision of management and production workers.
8. *Drive out fear* so that all may work effectively for the organization.
9. *Break down barriers between departments:* research, design, sales and production must work together to foresee problems in production and use.
10. *Eliminate slogans, exhortations and numerical targets* for the workforce, such as 'zero defects' or new productivity levels. Such exhortations are divisive as the bulk of the problems belong to the system and are beyond the power of the workforce.
11. *Eliminate quotas or work standards, and management by objectives or numerical goals:* substitute leadership.
12. *Remove barriers that rob people of their right to pride of workmanship*: hourly workers, management and engineering; eliminate annual or merit ratings and management by objectives.
13. *Institute a vigorous education and self-improvement programme.*
14. *Put everyone in the company to work to accomplish the transformation.* (Bendell, 1991:6)

Not all of Deming's points are accepted by other commentators, in particular the elimination of slogans and quotas. However, many of these points can be applied to the HRD department. Similarly, the points made by another guru, Juran (1989), also have applicability to the delivery of Total Quality Training. Juran advocated a 'quality trilogy' of quality planning, quality control, and quality improvement and developed a 'Quality Planning Road Map' which is as follows:

1. Identify who are the customers.
2. Determine the needs of the customers.
3. Translate those needs into our language.
4. Develop a product that can respond to those needs.
5. Optimize the product features so as to meet our needs as well as customers' needs.
6. Develop a process which is able to produce the product.
7. Optimize the process.
8. Prove that the process can produce the product under operating conditions.
9. Transfer the process to Operations. (Bendell, 1991:9)

Juran (1989) provides powerful ammunition for the HRD specialist when interacting with senior management on quality issues. He maintains that most quality defects are caused by poor management rather than poor workmanship, and that 80 per cent of quality problems arise from management control. He maintained that training to address quality issues should begin at the top of the organization. Unfortunately, management is often very reluctant to address this and mistakenly believes that it knows what is required:

> The instinctive belief is that upper managers already know what needs to be done, and that training is for others – the workforce, the supervision, the engineers. It is time to re-examine this belief. (Juran, quoted in Bendell, 1991:10)

Crosby (1979:111–12) insists that there are absolutes of quality management:

> Quality means conformance, not elegance.
> There is no such thing as a quality problem.
> There is no such thing as the economics of quality; it is always cheaper to do the job right the first time.
> The only performance measurement is the cost of quality.
> The only performance standard is Zero Defects.

Juran criticizes Crosby's 'zero defects' because he believed that it was based on the notion that the majority of quality problems are a result of careless and unmotivated workers. Crosby (1979:112–19), however, maintained that 'quality is free' and detailed 14 steps to achieve it:

1. Management Commitment
2. Quality Improvement Team
3. Quality Measurement
4. Cost of Quality Evaluation
5. Quality Awareness

6. Corrective Action
7. Establish an ad hoc Committee for the Zero Defects Programme
8. Supervisor Training
9. Zero Defects Day
10. Goal Setting
11. Error Cause Removal
12. Recognition
13. Quality Councils
14. Do it Over Again

A further influential writer on quality and customer care was Claus Moller who invented the Time Manager system personal organizer and, in the mid-1980s, developed the customer care programme 'Putting People First' for Scandinavian Airline Services and British Airways. This programme was held to be largely responsible for the improved performance of both airlines. The company Time Manager International provided training for a variety of organizations including the 16,000 employees of the European Commission.

Moller emphasized the value of training and wrote a 10-point training philosophy:

1. Training should bring about change.
2. Training is a process.
3. Training is an integral part of the company's strategy.
4. Training requires management commitment.
5. Training must be inspirational.
6. Training is for everyone in the company.
7. Training should be easily understood.
8. Training should include tools and written material.
9. Training should be geared to the target group.
10. Training should be holistic. (Bendell, 1991:23)

BEST PRACTICE BENCHMARKING

If we accept that quality means 'conformance to specifications' then quality means whatever we define it to mean. Thus, we may define the specification so low that in fact the product or service we produce may be so completely lacking in quality that people will not purchase it.

McDonald's produce burgers consistently to an exacting standard millions of times per day; however, that standard will not be the same as that required for a five-star Egon Ronay restaurant where customers will expect food of a different calibre. This is not to say that food produced in one restaurant is necessarily inferior, only that it is designed for different markets and has its own standards. Likewise, if we consider automobiles; the quality of a BMW has a significantly higher specification compared with the cars produced in the former communist countries of Eastern Europe.

Thus quality on its own is of limited value since it can be specified at any level. There is no ultimate measure of quality; it is all relative and for this reason services and products need to be compared with others in order to produce some form of hierarchy. This is done by benchmarking, which involves comparing your organization with the best in the field in order to assess how good, bad or indifferent your performance is.

Best Practice Benchmarking (BPB) essentially involves:

- establishing what makes the difference, in their customers' eyes, between an ordinary supplier and an excellent supplier;
- setting standards in each of those things, according to the best practice they can find;
- finding out how the best companies meet those challenging standards;
- applying both other people's experience and their own ideas to meet the new standards – and, if possible, to exceed them. (DTI, 1991:1)

The reason for companies undertaking BPB is that there are numerous advantages, including:

- better understanding of their customers and their competition;
- fewer complaints and more satisfied customers;
- reduction in waste, quality problems and reworking;
- faster awareness of important innovations and how they can be applied profitably;
- a stronger reputation within their markets;
- and as a result of all these, *increased profits and sales turnover.* (DTI, 1991:1)

In order to undertake BPB there are five steps in the process that can be taken. These apply not only to the organization but also to the HRD department and provide a useful template for the enhancement of training and development provision.

Step 1. What are we going to benchmark?

The main factors in deciding which areas to benchmark are to consider those that are of most importance to the customer or stakeholders and which will have the main impact on the profitability or cost-effectiveness of the organization.

Benchmarks that might be considered for customers of training and development include:

- availability of courses;
- support for line managers;
- speed of response to enquiries;
- consistency of quality of delivery;
- accuracy of training records, etc.

The best way to find out what is of importance to your customers and stakeholders is to ask them, using questionnaires, interviews, focus groups, course evaluation forms, etc.

There is a view among many managers that what gets measured gets done. Thus, if specific performance indicators are identified for a department or the whole organization they will provide a focus for attention. Benchmarking factors that assess and enable the evaluation of the HRD department's performance compared to others include:

- number of courses delivered;
- number of training days delivered by each trainer per year;
- the cost of delivering training courses;
- the level of income per trainer;
- the level of client and delegate satisfaction;
- the number of repeat purchases of training, etc.

Step 2. Who are we going to benchmark against?

There are four main types of approach with which an organization can benchmark itself: internal, competitive, parallel, and generic (Bramham, 1997).

First, there is the opportunity to assess performance against other parts of the same organization (*internal*). This will provide some general indicators but there will be no direct comparison of like-for-like information. To do this the HRD department will need to compare itself against other HRD departments in the same organization if there are multiple sites. Equally, if the organization has operations in other countries then this too provides the basis for comparison. This internal benchmarking is probably the easiest form to undertake and because the operations are similar it provides the same principles for comparison. On the other hand, it is rather introspective and does not provide an external basis for comparison. For smaller HRD departments these options are unlikely to be available.

The second form of benchmarking is *competitive* and is undertaken through comparison with direct competitors. In this way clear evidence may be provided against which to assess the extent to which the organization is performing within its particular industry or field. There are a number of difficulties involved in obtaining this information, since the other organizations may not willingly reveal commercially confidential information. However, there are industry monitors that provide market information reports and standard guidelines of industry practice.

The third type of benchmarking involves the comparison of one organization with one or more organizations which operate in *parallel* industries. For example, a bus operator might compare its operating standards with those of an airline. Or, a university might compare its student record handling with that of a credit card company.

Lastly, organizations can look for information and comparisons with those in totally different organizations – *generic*. For example, Marks & Spencer, the retailer, decided to produce sandwiches and learned how to butter bread by studying the practices of screen printing in the textile industry.

VALUE STREAM MAPPING TO MEET THE 40-DAY ENGINE TARGET FOR ROLLS-ROYCE PLC, USING DMAIC

Rolls-Royce operates in the civil and defence aerospace, marine and energy markets, and employs 35,000 people. Its engines are used by 500 airlines, 4,000 corporate aircraft and helicopter operators, 160 armed forces, 50 navies, and energy customers in almost 120 countries. To be competitive, the 40-day engine is the focus for all Rolls-Royce supply chain improvement, reflected within the on-time delivery, quality and lead time measures cascaded to suppliers. The reason for 40 days is that Rolls-Royce does not have any part that is worked on for more than 20 days, and world-class companies have lead times that are only double their process time.

One aspect of the strategy to improve supplier performance to Rolls-Royce is through the deployment of Supplier Development Leaders (SDLs). These personnel are strong in lean tools and techniques, and are deployed throughout the supply chain to improve performance and maintain focus to achieve on-time delivery, quality and lead-time measures through support and training. An example of this training was to carry out a value stream mapping activity on a small lock plate which locks the turbine blade in place within the aero engine, using the define, measure, analyse, improve, control approach to continuous improvement (DMAIC).

Defining the project

Step one was to establish a representative part on which to carry out the activity. In this instance the decision was taken on the most problematic part; however it can be against value, volume, material type or anything similar.

Step two was to gather data on the representative part. Data maintained on the factory operating system is not always a true reflection of reality, and therefore data is collected at each point throughout the process of manufacture: set-up time, operating time, batch quantity, scrap rate and so on. This is not always an easy task, as operators can be very suspicious of why people want them to collect the data, and the SDLs can come up against resistance. If they take time and patience to explain the reasons for collecting the data and what the outcome will be, the operators are more accepting. Never tell somebody, always sell the idea to them.

Measuring the project

Step three was to plot a flat-line profile of the part based on several data sheets. The reason for this is to gain a 'regular' picture of the part. If only one lot of data is used there may be special cause; however, using the average over several data sheets gives a clearer picture. The flat-line profile defines non-value-added time (waste) against value-added time (changing/modifying the metal). The profile indicates the delays (flat lines) in the process: delays to which lean tools and techniques can be applied to eliminate the waste. See Figure 24.1.

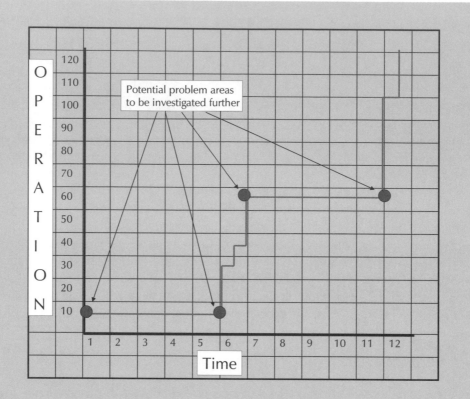

Figure 24.1 An example of a flat-line profile

Step four was to create a team to work the value stream activity. Value streams look at the whole process from raw material to finished parts delivered to the customer. It is necessary to include key personnel, with the right knowledge, from the various stages throughout the process, but the team could be unwieldy if everyone who touches the part is included. Also, while staff are in the value stream mapping event, which can take two or three days, parts are not being produced and therefore profit is not being gained. It is a balance for the company to weigh up profit versus time off the job that might produce a long-term benefit. The collated value stream map data also provides a variety of information such as lead time of the part and inventory cost.

Step five was to carry out the event. This means walking the process, collecting data, then drawing it up into a representative picture, which is known as the current state. It gives all attendees a good overview of the process and lots of discussions take place, often with good ideas for improvement, which can be captured for the second stage, which is known as the future state.

Analysing the project

For step six, once the current state has been mapped, a brainstorming activity can take place. 'Off the wall ideas' should not be ruled out: all ideas should be considered. A review of the map will also reveal many opportunities for removing waste from the process, which brings about improvement too.

Step seven is to assess those suggestions and start looking at what is realistic in the timescale. As these suggestions are made, a future-state map can be drawn, taking these opportunities into account. The future state will also show new measures regarding inventory costs, lead time and so on.

Implementing the project

Step eight is the plan to move from the current state to the future state, the owner of each activity, the timescale and so on.

Control the project

Step nine is often omitted when coming to the end of a project. This is where the activities are reviewed to see how the project could have been improved, and those changes are adopted ready for next time. It is the opportunity to ensure that procedures and processes implemented are robust and stable, to check all relevant personnel are fully trained and understand the changes, and to ensure there is a feedback process in place to identify possible improvements in the future. This is a very valuable activity to gain lessons learned, but it takes discipline to make it happen.

It is very easy to do the activity and even agree a plan, but the hardest thing is to make the changes happen to achieve the benefits predicted. In this instance the company was able to reduce inventory costs from £23,000 to £1,900 and reduce the lead time from 240 days to 20 days. That represents a significant benefit to any company, I am sure you will agree.

With acknowledgement to Stephanie Warren, Supplier Development Leader, Rolls-Royce plc.

Step 3. How will we get the information?

We have already mentioned that finding clear information which allows benchmarking is not an easy task. Indeed, the applications for assessment for the UK Quality Awards state that, 'The British Quality Foundation will take all reasonable action to ensure that applications and information therein are treated in strict confidence' (British Quality Foundation, 1994:7). While some information may not be immediately available there are numerous sources where benchmarking details can be found, including trade organizations, industry and financial publications, government reports, etc.

Two detailed delivery specifications or standards for the provision of management development are provided for buyers and suppliers (DfEE, 1997). These criteria may help reduce the following responses to management development training:

> I sent two people on a management course – the brochure made it sound ideal. From their comments and what happened afterwards I suspected we had been taken in by the publicity material.
>
> This young manager was very excited by the course content, but a lot of it was not relevant to the way we do things here and he tended to annoy colleagues with the jargon he had picked up.
>
> The managers who went on the programme started off very enthusiastic, but then it started to go a bit flat and I lost touch with what they were up to. I wouldn't use that course again. (DfEE, 1997:3)

Step 4. How will we analyse the information?

It is the customers and stakeholders who will provide the main sources of what should be the primary benchmarks. Then, when the information has been gathered it is necessary to quantify the details where possible and ensure that like is compared with like. Managers and other employees in the organization should be consulted as to the relevance and applicability of the findings.

Step 5. How will we use the information?

It is insufficient to only gather the information: it must be acted upon even if the findings reveal that the organization is operating in an excellent manner. The company needs to retain its pre-eminent position and this means that it cannot rest on its laurels. New standards should be continually introduced which are realistic and attainable. The best practice of today very rapidly becomes the common practice of tomorrow.

BPB does not require massive investments of energy to have significant results, although the degree of commitment will have a direct bearing on its impact. The time and effort invested can be repaid very quickly. The DTI (1991:2) reports that the main requirements for BPB are:

- a strong commitment from top management to act on any major opportunities for improvement that are revealed;
- a small amount of training and guidance for employees who will have to gather the information needed to identify and analyse best practice;
- authorization for employees to spend some of their time on benchmarking activities.

QUALITY CONTROL AND QUALITY ASSURANCE

Quality control involves checking the quality of the products or services on a regular basis; where large volumes are involved this may be frequently undertaken through statistical sampling procedures. Oakland (1997:13) states that quality control is:

essentially the activities and techniques employed to achieve and maintain the quality of a product, process, or service. It includes a monitoring activity, but is also concerned with finding and elimi-nating causes of quality problems so that the requirements of the customer are continually met.

However, this is insufficient to ensure that quality is achieved – this can only be done through ensuring that quality is built into every stage of the process. This is known as quality assurance and is defined by Nielsen and Visser (1997:6) as follows:

> quality assurance can be regarded as the whole range of activities intended to integrate and control factors that influence the output and outcomes in such a way that the envisaged quality output is permanently guaranteed. This definition comprises both quality maintenance and permanent quality improvement.

In a study of quality in initial vocational education in the Netherlands and Denmark, Nielsen and Visser (1997:5) maintain that there should be a minimum of four dimensions of quality indicators:

1. input: the qualifications and motivation of those admitted and the resources provided by the training institutions;
2. process: the aim, structure and content of the course, the planning and execution of teaching, the physical framework, the teachers, the learning environment, and the management of training institutions;
3. product: passed examinations, school leavers' vocational, personal and general compe-tences, course completion and drop-out rates;
4. effect: employment, productivity, innovative capacity, competitiveness, societal engagement and personal *joie de vivre* as well as intellectual resources.

With regard to the above points, Nielsen and Visser (1997:5) state that 'Quality in education must be related to the values, aims and objectives of the three user groups: pupils/students, labour market purchasers, and society in general.' It is clear that these three stakeholder groups have different expectations and therefore quality can only be assessed when related to the objectives specified for each field. In Denmark and the Netherlands (Nielsen and Visser, 1997:3) initial vocational education objectives are described in policy statements and legislation:

> This means that the system of vocational education and training will:
>
> 1. motivate young people to train and ensure that all young people who want vocational training have genuine opportunities to obtain it and to choose from a number of training schemes (or programmes);
> 2. give young people and adults training which provides a basis for future working life and contributes to their personal development and to their understanding of society and its development;
> 3. satisfy the needs of the labour market for the occupational and general qualifications required to develop trade and industry, including the development of trade and industry, labour market conditions, workplace organizations and technology;
> 4. provide training that will serve as a basis for further training.

WHAT IS SIX SIGMA?

Motorola was probably the first company in the world to set Six Sigma as its quality goal. In the increasing complexity of technology, an approach based on parts per hundred (percentages) was no longer relevant. It was in 1989 that Motorola set out to achieve a defect rate of not more than 3.4 parts per million within five years. The Sigma ranges from two to six (see the table below, in which 'σ' denotes sigma). It is based on an established statistical approach that shows how much product or process normal distribution is contained within specification. The figures below take into account the fact that the mean might vary by up to 1.5σ about the nominal target:

$2\sigma = 308770$
$3\sigma = 66810$
$4\sigma = 6210$
$5\sigma = 233$
$6\sigma = 3.4$ defects per million opportunities or 99.99966 per cent yield!

Obviously the higher the Sigma value, the less likely it is that a defect will occur. Six Sigma is much more than just a scale as far as Motorola is concerned. Its view is that Six Sigma is a long-term business strategy, with the objective being focused process improvement and variation reduction. Six Sigma improvement projects are the most likely path taken by companies, but the Six Sigma concept can also be applied during the design stage of a product or process.

Why are companies doing Six Sigma?

It was not long before many of the US giants – Xerox, Boeing, GE and Kodak – followed Motorola down the Six Sigma path. In 1987 GE announced that it would save US $500 million that year because of Six Sigma, and by 1998 the programme savings had risen to US $1.2 billion. The bottom line is that corporations moving towards Six Sigma levels of performance have saved billions of dollars and boosted their stock values.

How can you implement it?

Six Sigma requires top-level management commitment with a long-term vision. The other key ingredient is training. The training equips the designated staff with the appropriate tools and techniques, and enables them to manage the programme and guide improvement projects. Six Sigma practitioners are commonly known as master black belts, black belts and green belts. A typical black belt spends 20–25 days in training (making green belt in 10–15 days) and carries out an improvement project over a three- to six-month period. Black belts normally then work full time on improvement projects, and green belts spend around 20 per cent of their time on improvements.

With acknowledgment to Brian Harvey, Clamonta Ltd.

QUALITY AWARDS

There are numerous awards that have been established worldwide to recognize quality excellence. The existence of these prestigious awards would appear to encourage excellence and provide an opportunity to promote the organization and to benefit from potential new business and enhanced customer perception. The Deming Award, instituted in 1951 in Japan, is the world's oldest. A checklist indicates the main areas of focus:

1. Policy and objectives
2. Organization and its operation
3. Education and its dissemination
4. Assembling and dissembling information and its utilization
5. Analysis
6. Standardization
7. Control
8. Quality assurance
9. Effects
10. Future plans (Ainger *et al*, 1995:120)

In the USA the Malcolm Baldridge Award, instituted in 1987, is named after a US Commerce Secretary. It is the highest honour for quality achievements and its purpose is to encourage quality awareness in American business. The checklist for the award is as follows (Ainger *et al*, 1995:122):

	Points
Management of process quality	140
Senior executive leadership	90
Human resource development and management	150
Strategic quality planning	60
Information and analysis	80
Customer focus and satisfaction	300
Quality and operational results	180

Inspired by the lead of Japan and the USA a number of European companies established the European Foundation for Quality Management (EFQM) in 1988 for the purpose of encouraging quality and excellence. The EFQM (www.efqm.org) and the British Quality Foundation (BQF) use the model and points weightings shown in Figure 24.2.

In order to apply for the UK quality award, which began in 1994, the applicant organization first conducts a self-assessment of the degree of total quality and level of maturity for each category in the assessment model. The benefits of undertaking this process are that it helps to provide an objective evaluation of the organization's strengths and weaknesses. It is often the HRD department that has the responsibility for conducting this assessment.

On having completed the self-assessment a formal application is made of no more than 75 sides of A4, which is considered by a team of five to seven assessors. Subsequently, an award jury consisting of senior managers and academics then makes a decision on which applicants to visit.

Figure 24.2 consists of enablers and results, both of which carry a weighting of 50 per cent. The enablers criteria address *how* results are achieved; and the results criteria address *what* the organization has achieved. The processes of the organization allow the abilities of the people to be channelled to produce the results. The BQF (1994:9) states that:

> CUSTOMER SATISFACTION, PEOPLE (employee) SATISFACTION and IMPACT ON SOCIETY are achieved through LEADERSHIP driving POLICY AND STRATEGY, PEOPLE MANAGEMENT, RESOURCES and PROCESSES, leading ultimately to excellence in BUSINESS RESULTS.

In order to benchmark the performance of the organization, details about the enablers and results need to be provided. Information about results criteria needs to be provided as follows:

1. the key parameters your organisation uses to measure results and achievements;
2. for each key parameter, data is required. Ideally this will be in the form of trends over three years or more; The trends should highlight:
   a. – your organisation's actual performance;
   b. – your organisation's own targets, and, wherever possible;
   c. – the performance of competitors;
   d. – the performance of 'best in class' organisations.
3. the extent to which the parameters presented reasonably cover the range of your organisation's activities; the scope of the results is an important consideration for the assessors;
4. for each of the results criteria evidence is required of the relative importance of the parameters presented. (BQF, 1994:10)

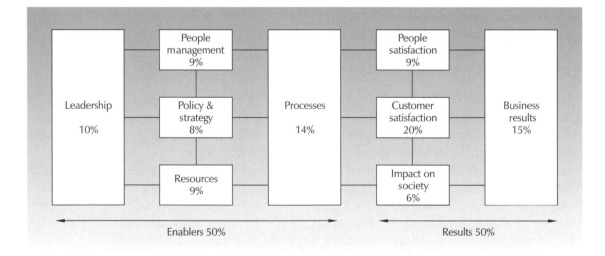

Figure 24.2 The EFQM/BQF award assessment model: people, processes and results

Specific details of the nine enablers and results should be supplied to the BQF. Training and development professionals would normally provide input into all these areas in the course of their work, in particular number 3. The main areas of the UK quality award (BQF, 1994:12–15) are:

1. *Leadership*
    The behaviour of all managers in driving the organization towards Total Quality.
    How the executive team and all the other managers inspire and drive Total Quality as the organisation's fundamental process for continuous improvement.
2. *Policy and strategy*
    The organisation's mission, values, vision and strategic direction and the manner in which it achieves them.
    How the organisation's policy and strategy reflects the concept of Total Quality and how the principles of Total Quality are used in the formulation, deployment, review and improvement of policy and strategy.
3. *The management of the organisation's people*
    How the organisation releases the full potential of its people to improve its business or service continuously.
    Evidence is needed of how:
    people resources are planned and improved;
    the skills and capabilities of the people are preserved and developed through recruitment, training and career progression;
    people and teams agree targets and continuously review performance;
    the involvement of everyone in continuous improvement is promoted and people are empowered to take appropriate action;
    effective top-down and bottom-up communication is achieved.
4. *Resources*
    The management, utilisation and preservation of resources.
    How the organisation's resources are effectively deployed in support of policy and strategy.
5. *Processes*
    The management of all value-adding activities within the organisation.
    How processes are identified, reviewed and, if necessary, revised to ensure continuous improvement of the organisation's business/service.
6. *Customer satisfaction*
    What the organisation is achieving in relation to the satisfaction of its external customers.
7. *People satisfaction*
    What the organisation is achieving in relation to the satisfaction of its people.
8. *Impact on society*
    What the organisation is achieving in satisfying the needs and the expectations of the community at large. This includes perception of the organisation's approach to quality of life, the environment and to the preservation of global resources and the organisation's own internal resources.

9. *Business results*
    What the organisation is achieving in relation to its planned performance and in satisfying the needs and expectations of everyone with an interest in the organisation, and in achieving its planned business/service objectives.

TOTAL QUALITY TRAINING AND DEVELOPMENT

It is clear from the guidelines provided by the quality gurus and the awards that training and development contribute significantly to TQM. A brief resume of the role education, training and development play demonstrates this:

● Training and development have a central – arguably *the* central – role to play in making quality a reality – Thomas.
● Institute training on the job – Deming.
● Training for quality should begin at the top – Juran.
● Supervisor training – Crosby.
● Training is an integral part of the company's strategy – Moller.
● Education and its dissemination – Deming Award.
● Human resource development and management – Malcolm Baldridge Award.
● The skills and capabilities of the people are preserved and developed through recruitment, training and career progression – UK Quality Award.

From the above endorsements of the role of training and development it becomes essential not only that the HRD department supports the whole TQM process, but also that it provides a quality service to its customers. Oakland (1997:109) asserts that this includes:

> For *all* staff, written procedures should be established and maintained for:
>
> ● identifying and reviewing individual training needs;
> ● carrying out the training;
> ● keeping records of training, including qualifications.

Where does Total Quality Training start? Ideally, it should be part of the mission statement of an organization. If it is part of that mission statement, then it states from the outset that the organization is serious about quality and training. This then feeds down throughout the organization and becomes an almost invisible, but critically essential, dimension of the organizational culture (Caroselli, 1996).

Investors in People

Investors in People (IiP) is a quality award related to training and development provided by an organization for all its employees. This national standard was designed in 1990 to support British business by ensuring the development of employees so that they could respond to the demanding competitive environment. The standard was developed by the National Training Task Force in partnership with major business organizations and professional and employer organizations. The development was supported by the Employment Department and, in 1991, was tested by Training and Enterprise Councils and Local Enterprise Councils.

The IiP standard is based on business-located research which demonstrates that effective investment in people can result in enhanced business performance in areas such as: increased production, improved quality, reduced costs, and greater customer satisfaction. The standard has been successfully introduced in many organizations and has encouraged a focus on training and development activities as they relate to the overall business needs of the organization. It has also been introduced in Australia and a number of other countries. A variation has been developed in Ireland called Excellence Through People.

The standard was revised in 2000 and again in 2005, see Figure 24.3.

The Investors in People Standard

Principles	Indicators	Evidence requirements
Developing strategies to improve the performance of the organisation An Investor in People develops effective strategies to improve the performance of the organisation through its people.	**1 A strategy for improving the performance of the organisation is clearly defined and understood.**	1 Top managers make sure the organisation has a clear purpose and vision supported by a strategy for improving its performance. 2 Top managers make sure the organisation has a business plan with measurable performance objectives. 3 Top managers make sure there are constructive relationships with representative groups (where they exist) and the groups are consulted when developing the organisation's business plan. 4 Managers can describe how they involve people when developing the organisation's business plan and when agreeing team and individual objectives. 5 People who are members of representative groups can confirm that top managers make sure there are constructive relationships with the groups and they are consulted when developing the organisation's business plan. 6 People can explain the objectives of their team and the organisation at a level that is appropriate to their role, and can describe how they are expected to contribute to developing and achieving them.
	2 Learning and development is planned to achieve the organisation's objectives.	1 Top managers can explain the organisation's learning and development needs, the plans and resources in place to meet them, how these link to achieving specific objectives and how the impact will be evaluated. 2 Managers can explain team learning and development needs, the activities planned to meet them, how these link to achieving specific team objectives and how the impact will be evaluated. 3 People can describe how they are involved in identifying their learning and development needs and the activities planned to meet them. 4 People can explain what their learning and development activities should achieve for them, their team and the organisation.
	3 Strategies for managing people are designed to promote equality of opportunity in the development of the organisation's people.	1 Top managers can describe strategies they have in place to create an environment where everyone is encouraged to contribute ideas to improve their own and other people's performance. 2 Top managers recognise the different needs of people and can describe strategies they have in place to make sure everyone has appropriate and fair access to the support they need and there is equality of opportunity for people to learn and develop which will improve their performance. 3 Managers recognise the different needs of people and can describe how they make sure everyone has appropriate and fair access to the support they need and there is equality of opportunity for people to learn and develop which will improve their performance. 4 People believe managers are genuinely committed to making sure everyone has appropriate and fair access to the support they need and there is equality of opportunity for them to learn and develop which will improve their performance. 5 People can give examples of how they have been encouraged to contribute ideas to improve their own and other people's performance.
	4 The capabilities managers need to lead, manage and develop people effectively are clearly defined and understood.	1 Top managers can describe the knowledge, skills and behaviours managers need to lead, manage and develop people effectively, and the plans they have in place to make sure managers have these capabilities. 2 Managers can describe the knowledge, skills and behaviours they need to lead, manage and develop people effectively. 3 People can describe what their manager should be doing to lead, manage and develop them effectively.

Plain English Campaign's Crystal Mark does not apply to Indicator 3.

Figure 24.3   An overview of the Investors in People Standard framework (with acknowledgement to Investors in People, www.iipuk.co.uk)

Principles	Indicators	Evidence requirements
Taking action to improve the performance of the organisation An Investor in People takes effective action to improve the performance of the organisation through its people.	**5 Managers are effective in leading, managing and developing people.**	1 Managers can explain how they are effective in leading, managing and developing people. 2 Managers can give examples of how they give people constructive feedback on their performance regularly and when appropriate. 3 People can explain how their managers are effective in leading, managing and developing them. 4 People can give examples of how they receive constructive feedback on their performance regularly and when appropriate.
	6 People's contribution to the organisation is recognised and valued.	1 Managers can give examples of how they recognise and value people's individual contribution to the organisation. 2 People can describe how they contribute to the organisation and believe they make a positive difference to its performance. 3 People can describe how their contribution to the organisation is recognised and valued.
	7 People are encouraged to take ownership and responsibility by being involved in decision-making.	1 Managers can describe how they promote a sense of ownership and responsibility by encouraging people to be involved in decision-making, both individually and through representative groups, where they exist. 2 People can describe how they are encouraged to be involved in decision-making that affects the performance of individuals, teams and the organisation, at a level that is appropriate to their role. 3 People can describe how they are encouraged to take ownership and responsibility for decisions that affect the performance of individuals, teams and the organisation, at a level that is appropriate to their role.
	8 People learn and develop effectively.	1 Managers can describe how they make sure people's learning and development needs are met. 2 People can describe how their learning and development needs have been met, what they have learnt and how they have applied this in their role. 3 People who are new to the organisation, and those new to a role, can describe how their induction has helped them to perform effectively.
Principles	Indicators	Evidence requirements
Evaluating the impact on the performance of the organisation An Investor in People can demonstrate the impact of its investment in people on the performance of the organisation.	**9 Investment in people improves the performance of the organisation.**	1 Top managers can describe the organisation's overall investment of time, money and resources in learning and development. 2 Top managers can explain, and quantify where appropriate, how learning and development has improved the performance of the organisation. 3 Top managers can describe how the evaluation of their investment in people is used to develop their strategy for improving the performance of the organisation. 4 Managers can give examples of how learning and development has improved the performance of their team and the organisation. 5 People can give examples of how learning and development has improved their performance, the performance of their team and that of the organisation.
	10 Improvements are continually made to the way people are managed and developed.	1 Top managers can give examples of how the evaluation of their investment in people has resulted in improvements in the organisation's strategy for managing and developing people. 2 Managers can give examples of improvements they have made to the way they manage and develop people. 3 People can give examples of improvements that have been made to the way the organisation manages and develops its people.

Figure 24.3 *continued*

Glossary

Words can mean different things to different people. This glossary explains what certain words mean as they appear in the Investors in People Standard.

Business plan
This is a plan that sets out the organisation's objectives. It may also be known as an or ganisational plan, corporate plan, strategic plan, development plan or improvement plan.

Capabilities
These are the knowledge, skills and behaviours the organisation's leaders and managers need.

Constructive feedback
This is information provided to an individual that allows them to understand their particular strengths and their areas for improvement in relation to their performance.

Constructive relationships
This refers to positive working relationships between managers and representative groups.

Consult
This means managers and representative groups regularly examining issues of mutual concern together so that they can take account of the views of employees when making decisions that are likely to affect their interests.

Continually
This means happening often but with breaks in between each event.

Contribution
This is the ideas, time and ef fort that people give to an organisation to help it achieve its objectives.

Equality
This means recognising that while people are different and need to be treated as individuals, ever yone is the same in terms of having equal value, equal rights as human beings and a need to be treated with dignity and respect. In terms of the opportunity to learn and develop, equality means preventing and removing discrimination because of someone's race, sex, disability, sexuality, religion or belief, age, marital status or other personal characteristics. It makes sure that all groups have appropriate and fair access to learning and development opportunities.

Evaluation
This means reviewing the results of learning and development activities and identifying whether they have achieved their intended objectives and how this has had an impact on performance.

Impact
This means the results achieved and the effect this has had on performance.

Lear ning and development
This is any activity that develops skills, knowledge or attitude. Activities may range from formal training courses run internally or externally to informal on-the-job training or coaching.

Manager
This is anyone who is responsible for managing or developing people. This includes top managers.

Objectives
These ar e the results the organisation aims for to achieve its vision. To know if the objectives have been achieved, they need to be specific, measurable and time-bound. Specific means identifying exactly what needs to be achieved. Measurable means knowing how much has been achieved (for example, 5% up, £100 more or five people more). Time-bound means setting a deadline for achieving the objectives (for example, by the end of this three-month period or within one year).

Organisation
This is the body that is working with the Investors in People Standard. It can be profit-making or non-profit-making, a charity, a subsidiar y or a business unit.

Ownership
This means people playing a greater role in the success of the organisation, and being willing to own a decision and be accountable for its outcome.

People
This is anyone who helps the organisation to achieve its objectives – whatever role they play. It includes par t-time workers, voluntary workers, people on renewable short-term contracts, and regular, casual employees. Where an indicator refers to 'people', it means everyone in the organisation (including managers and top managers). The only exception to this is where the assessor decides, based on evidence collected, that they will accept nearly everyone.

People who are members of representative groups
This r efers to people who act as official representatives, rather than ordinary members.

Purpose
This describes why an organisation exists and what its business is. This could be expr essed thr ough a mission statement.

Quantify
This means explaining, in measurable terms, the results achieved through learning and development activities.

Regularly
This means at least once a year, but it could be more often. It is up to the organisation to define what is appropriate.

Repr esentative groups
These are groups like trade unions, other workplace representatives, staff associations, works councils and partnership councils.

Strategy
This is the way an organisation aims to achieve its vision.

Team
This is a small or large group of people who come together to work towards a shared goal - for example, a project team, a branch or department. In small organisations, a team may be the whole organisation. As a result, where an evidence requirement refers to team, this will mean the whole organisation if there ar e no smaller teams.

Top managers
These ar e the most senior people in the organisation who ar e likely to be responsible for developing strategies and approving major investments. This could be the owners, the board of directors, partners or senior managers.

Vision
This describes wher e an organisation wants to be in the future and what it wants its people and its customers to say about it.

For more information contact us:

INVESTORS IN PEOPLE UK

Published by

TSO

www.tso.co.uk

Crystal Mark
Clarity
approved by
Plain English Campaign

Investors in People UK
7–10 Chandos Street
London W1G 9DQ

T. +44 (0)20 7467 1900
F. +44 (0)20 7636 2386

ISBN 0 11 706167 0

E. information@iipuk.co.uk

© Investors in People 2004

www.investorsinpeople.co.uk

Figure 24.3 *continued*

A TQM process

For any TQM initiative to be successful there needs to be impetus to the organization. This may come from a variety of sources but it is frequently the HRD department that is responsible for the implementation of the process. (The TQM process is shown in Figure 24.4.) This energy influences the balance of the status quo and encourages commitment to the process of introducing change. This will occur in the areas of training, communication, systems and teams, which leads to a culture change. This change in culture towards one which values quality throughout the organization will then translate into improved organizational performance. Palmer and Wilson (1995:10) state that, 'Training is one of the key factors which influences the success or otherwise of TQM initiatives.'

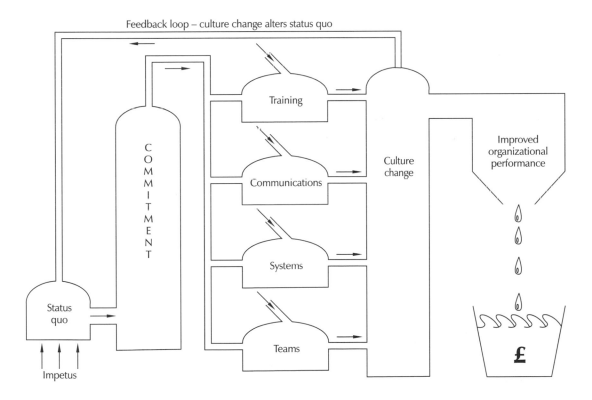

© R.Palmer

Figure 24.4 The TQM process

CONCLUSION

Training is an essential component of the TQM process. Moreover, quality training is essential in order that the HRD department is valued and highly respected. Oakland (1997:318) sums up these points by maintaining that:

It's Monday – it must be training
- Training is the single most important factor in improving quality, once commitment is present. Quality training must be objectively, systematically, and continuously performed.
- All training should occur in an improvement cycle of ensuring training is part of quality procedure, allocating responsibilities, defining objectives, establishing training organisations, specifying needs, preparing programmes and materials, implementing and monitoring, assessing results, and reviewing effectiveness.

A systematic approach to quality training
- Responsibility for quality training of employees rests with management at all levels. The main elements should include error/defect/problem prevention, reporting and analysis, investigation and review.
- Training procedures and records should be established. These should show how job competence is demonstrated.

Total Quality Training, or learning, is therefore an all-embracing system that applies from chairman to cleaner. An illustration of this is the man who was seen 'pushing a broom' by a visiting Senate committee to the NASA plant where the Apollo space rocket was being assembled. When asked by one of the committee what he was doing, he replied, 'I help to put men on the Moon!'

He obviously had an instilled perception that cleanliness was as important as any other function that was carried out within the plant, and the person who had explained the importance of his job function had left an indelible mark as to his importance within the NASA plant and operation. That encouragement about the value of people in achieving quality was probably facilitated by a member of the training and development staff.

Bibliography

Ainger, A, Kaura, R and Ennals, R (1995) *An Executive Guide to Business Success through Human Centred Systems*, London, Springer Verlag

Basu, R and Wright, J N (2003) *Quality Beyond Six Sigma*, Oxford, Butterworth-Heinemann

Bendell, T (1991) *The Quality Gurus: What can they do for your company?*, London, DTI

Bramham, J (1997) *Benchmarking for People Managers*, London, IPD

BQF (British Quality Foundation) (1994) *The 1995 UK Quality Award: Application brochure*, London, British Quality Foundation (British Quality Foundation, 32–34 Great Peter Street, London, SW1P 2QX; Tel 020 7654 5000)

BSI (British Standards Institution) (1991) *BS 4788:2, Quality Vocabulary*, London, BSI

Caroselli M (1996) *Quality Games for Trainers: 101 playful lessons in quality and continuous improvement*, London, McGraw-Hill

Crosby, P B (1979) *Quality is Free*, New York, Mentor Books

Deming, W E (1982) *Out of the Crisis*, Cambridge, MA, MIT Press

DfEE (Department for Education and Employment) (1997) *Quality Counts. A standard for the delivery of management development – for buyers of management development*, London, HMSO. Copies available from MCI, Russell Square House, 10–12 Russell Square, London WC1B 5BZ. Tel 020 7872 9000

DTI (Department of Trade and Industry) (1991) *Best Practice Benchmarking*, London, DTI

IiP (Investors in People) (1991) *The National Standard: Links to assessment indicators*, Sheffield, Employment Department (Investors in People UK, 4th Floor, 7–10 Chandos Street, London W1G 9DQ. Tel 020 7467 1900; website www.investorsinpeople.co.uk)

IiP (2000) *The National Standard*, London, IiP

Juran, J M (1989) *Juran on Leadership for Quality: An executive handbook*, New York, Free Press

Mortiboys, R J (1991) *Leadership and Quality Management: A guide for chief executives*, London, DTI

Nielsen, S P and Visser, K (1997) *Quality Debate in Initial Vocational Education: School-based quality measures at intermediate level: A Danish–Dutch comparison*, Thessaloniki, CEDEFOP

Oakland, J S (1997) *Total Quality Management*, Oxford, Butterworth-Heinemann

Palmer, R and Wilson, J P (1995) 'Maintaining the energy for commitment to quality', *Training for Quality*, 3, 2, pp 9–13

Taylor, P and Thackwray, B (2001) *Investors in People Explained*, 4th edn, London, Kogan Page

Thomas B (1992) *Total Quality Training: The quality culture and quality training*, Maidenhead, McGraw-Hill

25

Marketing Human Resource Development

Jennifer Joy-Matthews

INTRODUCTION AND LEARNING OBJECTIVES

Many people associate the word 'marketing' with advertisements and selling and none of the rest of the marketing process. There might also be an image of all that unsolicited junk mail that arrives on one's desk. Consequently, there is the possibility of resistance to the idea of marketing Human Resource Development (HRD) within an organization.

The perceived lack of focus on the issue of marketing HRD might be one of the reasons why training and development are not always given the credence they deserve:

> The situation in many companies is that there is not a meaningful tradition of valuing and developing their staff. Consequently there are real difficulties in embracing new ideas and practices that inevitably mean change, and challenge existing ways of thinking and acting. (Megginson *et al*, 1999:13)

Staying ahead of the competition and coping with the increasingly turbulent environment are issues that challenge most managers, thus, focusing on the development of themselves and their staff has to be of major importance. Attracting or locating those organizations and individuals who are extremely successful at employee development is also critical. Furthermore, those individuals and organizations who are good at being noticed and obtaining the business either in their own organization or as an external agent are also necessary in order survive in this competitive environment. Arising from this need to attract business is the marketing process, which is about matching the person with the need to the person with the solution.

HRD specialists are involved in two main forms of marketing, internal and external. The HRD specialists who are employed by and work within an organization will have one set of needs: raising their visibility by being seen as successful and the natural choice for providing development opportunities. Far more development is being outsourced, and internal developers need to remain a viable choice.

External HRD specialists need to find a way to gain entry into an organization so that they are seen as a viable choice. Consequently there is now a degree of competition between the internal and the external provider. However, in either case the specialist needs to be seen as adding value to the organization.

In discussing current leading ideas Joy-Matthews, Megginson and Surtees (2004:46) say, 'The Chartered Institute of Personnel and Development (CIPD) uses the phrase "business partner" as a central plank of its professional development programme. Business partners must add value to the organization and collaborate in supporting the goals and projects of others.'

This relatively new concept of 'business partners' can be part of the internal or external HRD professionals' way to gain acceptance at a strategic level within the organization. Talking the language of senior managers and directors can give the HRD function an entry into higher corporate life. By aligning HRD and strategic organizational outcomes it should be possible to market training, development and learning more successfully within an organization.

This chapter will be of interest to a wide range of people. Whether you are an internal trainer or developer, line manager, external consultant or freelance trainer, whether you work as a sole trader or for a large multinational, marketing ideas are offered for your consideration.

Having read this chapter you will:

- understand the need to market training and development;
- understand the marketing process;
- be able to identify it within your organization or consultancy;
- be able to evaluate the strengths and weaknesses of the marketing process; and,
- be able to take action to improve the process by using a variety of tools and techniques.

WHY MARKET?

Moorby (1991:152–3), talking about the internal marketing of employee development, says: 'With the acceleration of change ... employee development in many organizations has adopted a positive approach to marketing its contribution.'

What is meant by the term 'marketing'? Frank (1994:4) offers two definitions, the first from The Institute of Marketing, UK: 'Marketing is the management process that enables clients' needs to be identified, anticipated and satisfied.' The second is from the American Marketing Association: 'Marketing is both an art and a science which enables the optimum conditions for the interaction of supply and demand to be created.'

A combination of the two definitions covers the issues that are important. It is a management activity; it is about a whole process from identification to satisfaction that involves analytical, scientific techniques; and there is a considerable art in being able to create supply and demand!

In his book *Imaginization,* Gareth Morgan (1997:45–49) recounts the tale of George the termite. George is the director of training and development for a large organization. He works with a few consultants and provides the service the other managers want. He networks both inside the organization and externally. He searches for people who will want to make use of his service. He does a good job and his reputation gains him respect and repeat business. He does not have a department, highly detailed training plan or a large budget but he does have a clear idea of what he wants to achieve. He focuses on adding value and builds on success.

So some element of marketing the function and process of HRD is necessary, although it may not be of the overt nature that is often associated with marketing products. As Harrison (1997:198) says:

> It is not to do with glossy brochures or expensive selling efforts. It is to do with finding out the kind of service or product that best meets the needs of internal customers as well as those outside the organization for whom planned learning events provided or initiated by the company also have important value – those other stakeholders ... 'non-employees'.

In this case study some issues that confront anyone attempting to market their product or service are explored.

DAVID MATTHEWS, FREELANCE OUTDOOR PURSUITS INSTRUCTOR AND TRAINER

The business: David is a freelance outdoor instructor/trainer.

The clients: come from a variety of groups: schools, youth clubs, college and university students, hen nights and stag parties, managers, disabled groups and families. He also works with individuals and a large percentage of his work comes from supply teaching.

The product/service: he offers includes hill walking, orienteering, caving, climbing, abseiling and development games and exercises.

The costs: the equipment required for these activities is expensive and needs to be kept in good repair. The insurance is costly and as a trainer who works with under-18-year-olds he has to hold a licence from the Adventure Activities Licensing Authority. He also needs to pay himself a reasonable daily rate for instructing.

The constraints: the season when most people want to be involved in outdoor activities is in the warm weather, which in Britain means April to October. This means that for five months of the year there is little work, so consistent income generation is problematic. However, there are opportunities for marketing.

Marketing: currently consists of repeat trade, a leaflet and two advertisements in a local publication and a London-based outdoor activity magazine.

Exercise:

- What would you identify as David's main marketing issues?
- What would you suggest are some possible solutions? (Some solutions are offered in the final part of this chapter.)

With acknowledgement to David Matthews, outdoor pursuits instructor and trainer.

Let's continue by considering who the customers for HRD are and where they might be found, either in the HRD person's own organization or externally, and the issue of what they need.

WHO AND WHERE ARE THE CUSTOMERS AND HOW DO YOU KNOW WHAT THEY NEED?

Customers within the context of HRD are not always the individuals experiencing the development intervention. In addition to meeting their learning needs, the HRD function should also take into account 'buyer' behaviour.

The marketing of HRD is important; however, Harrison (1997) highlights just how little academics have commented on it. Currently there is a desire to see HRD in a strategic context and with this comes the links between HRD and marketing theory. Some of the reason for the past oversight by academics is that HRD is classed as a service, rather than a product (Linton, 1997) and this alone makes the task of marketing it more difficult. The problems are familiar in that most of the results and benefits of HRD are intangible. It may not be considered vital and even if it is viewed as an investment, it has to compete with other investments, like new equipment, premises or new staff. However, without taking a lead from some of the basic principles of marketing, HRD will struggle to add value.

In most commercial business transactions a customer receives goods or a service and hands over his or her cash. However, the exchange is often more complex with HRD. For example, in an ideal case a manager may contact the HRD function, because a new computer is being installed and she feels that her secretary needs some word-processing skills. Not having an 'in-house' IT trainer, a brochure is pulled out of the file and the secretary is booked onto an external course. (A survey by The Industrial Society pointed to the fact that it is often the secretaries who know that they need training and that their line manager will not support it!)

Who is the customer?

The manager needs the secretary to work the computer. The secretary needs the skills. The HRD manager needs to find a training supplier. The training supplier needs the work. A very complex arrangement of needs and services and customers exists and in many cases the individual consuming the development intervention is not always the customer or client. A secretary might feel that the line manager also needs the training! When marketing HRD, selling the benefits to the wrong person in the supply chain may be an unproductive activity.

Wilson *et al* (1992) suggest that customers can be grouped together according to their specific needs, not just their development needs but a range of needs that become important when trying to satisfy customers. Analysing the market with these questions can help:

- What service is on offer:
    Personal development
    Management development
    Organizational development
- At what price or cost:
    High (lengthy accredited courses)
    Low (resource centres)
- How to contact the customer:
    Direct mail
    Selling
    Consultancy
- Where to deliver it:
    Classrooms
    Open learning
    On the job
    Web-based

Whether the market is the human resource population of an organization or the international community, customers will have very different and specific needs. Kotler and Armstrong (1994) refer to this as 'buyer behaviour', or the factors customers take into account when deciding what to purchase. If a development need has been identified and there are choices as to how that need can be satisfied, then the HRD function will be in competition with other suppliers. The likely issues of competition for HRD practitioners will be:

- trends and fashion – on/off the job;
- resources and technology – intranets, etc, trainers, budgets;
- suppliers and materials – brochures, handouts, video, etc;
- new entrants – competitors, customer perception.

A key part of the job of managing the HRD function is to address this issue of competition. Peters (1989:50) recommends 'niche marketing'. This would involve emphasizing the expert or specialist HRD function as opposed to the mass or volume approach. This means paying particular attention to the less obvious attributes of the service. Unfortunately this kind of customer care can be at odds with professional HRD practitioners who believe learning is the sole reason for their interventions and activity. This may be true, but learners have expectations.

If they expect free coffee and biscuits when they arrive at a morning workshop and do not get them, it may interfere with the whole learning experience. As Moorby (1991:152–3) points out: 'Creation of physical facilities that meet customer expectations. For example, if four-star residential quality is what is expected and will be paid for – provide it'.

Being clear about what you offer, and ensuring that you deliver, are important; if you fail you will have created a negative image in the eyes of your customers from which it is very difficult to recover.

Ideally these customer expectations or the softer side of HRD activity could be checked out along with the harder issues surrounding the training-needs analysis. If a range of individual learning preferences are incorporated within the design of a tailor-made programme the costs may become so high that it becomes unaffordable. It will become far more efficient and practicable to segment customers.

By segmenting the market you enable the HRD service to be packaged according to the expectations of a particular customer group. Linton (1997) recommends segmenting any HRD market into four groups of decision-makers:

- Directors – who need their corporation to perform.
- Department managers – who seek efficiency.
- Training professionals – who rate cost-effectiveness highly.
- Trainees – who are concerned with personal performance.

In order to market the HRD function effectively to these groups, an analysis should be undertaken using the questions described earlier. What should become clear from this are the very different learning needs, preferences and expectations that originate from the different segments.

It will be at this point that the HRD function should consider what its target market or preferred customer segment is. Strategic decisions of this kind may have been taken by the HRD function's host organization. It may be written into the training manager's job description and objectives. For commercial HRD businesses it may be specific segments that generate profit or high-volume activity. Marketing the function to individuals demands a very different strategy to marketing to a board of directors. The suggestion here is that the HRD function cannot excel at both and to create a quality learning experience as perceived by the customer, priority should be given to one or the other.

By specializing and targeting the service in this way, the ability to become more effective increases. The profile and reputation of the service grow and one of Peters' (1989) preferred marketing tactics occurs by word of mouth. It would seem that an attractive market to be in is director development. If this group is convinced HRD can make a difference, they will send their entire workforce through the HRD function. No, it is not quite like that! To equip the HRD function in order to compete with other executive development programmes would take a large investment in premises, expertise, facilities, catering and probably accreditation. None the less, a high price could be asked, and even paid, for the HRD function's expertise. However, high overheads might make the HRD function too expensive to train the entire workforce.

PINDERFIELDS & PONTEFRACT HOSPITALS NHS TRUST

The Trust is a provider of regional and district-wide acute healthcare. Situated in West Yorkshire, England, it operates from five geographical sites. Being a large Trust its HRD needs are considerable. It has, due to its diverse service profile, professional staff and history, inherited four functions active in training, education and developing employees. In addition, contracts with universities are agreed through a local Education and Training Consortium. The Centre for Learning and Development has more than doubled in size since being created and works with approximately 80 per cent of the 2,500 organizational staff each year. It consists of:

Learning and Development Manager;
Professional Development Manager;
Learning and Development Facilitator;
Training Officer;
Centre Administrator;
Secretary;
Youth Trainee; and
Project Nurse.

The purpose of the function is to help the organization achieve its goals by enhancing the performance and professionalism of the workforce. It has classrooms and expertise that enable learning to be facilitated across the generic management and professional areas. Being the only HRD function within the organization that can currently offer an integrated approach to development (that is, all development except medical/clinical skills) it could be described as having a competitive and differential advantage over the others. It still, however, targets supervisors, ward and/or general managers with its marketing strategy. In doing so it offers accredited management development programmes and generates income by selling places on these to managers outside the organization. This income then supports other development at the personal level by equipping a learning centre and at higher levels by funding organizational and professional development.

By concentrating its marketing efforts towards management development and creating a quality learning experience for this particular customer group, the Trust's HRD function claims the following benefits:

- Influencing a target group who have the sanctioning power to allow others to develop personally.
- Generating income that supports personal, organizational and professional development.
- Promoting the function's services and activities through 'word of mouth' referrals (manager to manager, and manager to staff).
- It bypasses senior managers who tend to look elsewhere for their own needs.
- Adding more value to all services year-on-year due to the income generated.

With acknowledgement to Richard Firth, Learning and Development Manager.

This case study illustrates how important it is to consider HRD customer needs, as well as individual learning needs. There is no suggestion here that one is more important than the other but they are difficult to separate. By understanding what customers and consumers expect from the HRD function, there is a greater chance of providing what they need.

It also demonstrates that targeting a specialized customer segment and offering a quality service to this group can lead to spin-off activity. Other industries do this through 'branding' for example, Virgin Cola or Virgin Railways. Why not HRD?

HOW DO YOU REACH THE CUSTOMERS?

The purpose of reaching training and development customers in a marketing context is to inform them of:

- the service provided;
- the benefits of those services;
- the next steps needed to turn interest into business.

For the communication from HRD organization to customer to be successful three key points need to be considered:

1. Use a medium that the customer uses.
2. Use a language and style that matches the customer's needs.
3. Make contact when it is timely for the customer.

Use a medium that the customer uses

There is little point using costly advertising in a magazine or journal that is read by a very small percentage of your potential market, or sending a mailshot to managers who are not in a position to purchase your services. Use market research techniques to establish the best medium for your particular market, for example telephone interviews, postal surveys or focus groups. For a range of mediums see the section on 'Core techniques for communicating with customers'.

Use a language and style that matches the customer's needs

The customer is more likely to buy when the benefits described closely match his or her particular needs. It is useful to remember that those needs will not just be about HRD outcomes but also about the way that you convey the benefits in your promotional materials. Some people prefer great detail, theoretical models, techniques, etc, while others are less interested in your processes and more concerned whether you are credible and have a proven track record or are accredited. To discover a suitable format ask a sample of customers and review materials from other suppliers.

Make contact when it is timely for the customer

The best time to contact a potential customer is when they have a specific training or development need that can be addressed using your services. This relies on having access to accurate information on potential customers or being fortunate with good timing! An example of a seasonal influence on demand for training and development is the need of some line managers to spend any unused training budget just before their financial year ends. This is so that they can argue for at least an equal training budget for the following year.

Keeping a record of all existing customers and their past buying patterns means you can contact them at opportune times. To attempt to contact customers who are in a known busy period, for example accountancy firms leading up to the usual financial year ends of 31 December and 31 March, or gas companies during the winter, will probably result in your information being ignored. It is better to send it when your target is likely to have the time to read and respond to it.

Core techniques for communicating with customers

Start with effective market research to identify how best to reach your customers. This way, resources are not wasted on ineffective communication.

There are many ways of communicating with customers and potential customers. Finding ways that are appropriate for your style and your potential customers is essential. Examples of marketing communication include:

- direct mailing;
- telephone sales;
- brochures and inserts;
- HRD newsletters;
- corporate newsletters;
- Internet and intranet;
- seminars and conferences;
- focus groups;
- media:
  advertisements on television and radio;
  advertisements in journals and newspapers;
  articles or case studies;
- customer visits and consultancy;
- word of mouth.

Direct mailing

Sending unsolicited information in the post to potential customers usually gives a poor success rate. If you know that the recipient is in need of your type of services then you can expect a much higher success rate. There is a high probability that the person you send your information to feels inundated with similar information from other suppliers. It is not unusual for some line managers to throw away unsolicited marketing materials before reading them. (See the case study about David Matthews, the outdoor pursuits instructor and trainer, who targets copies of his brochure to tourists boards and local accommodation providers.)

Telephone sales

Many organizations try to get leads through telephone sales. This can be when there is no prior contact and no knowledge of a particular need for your product at the target organization. This requires a particular set of combined selling and telephone skills. In the case of training products this often requires the seller to be able to answer questions on training. This can be a difficult problem especially if the product supplied is not off-the-shelf but tailor-made.

Brochures and inserts

There are companies that specialize in producing brochures. A training organization could employ them using their specialists to produce the artwork and write the script. Although this can be expensive it can be worthwhile if the image portrayed by the brochure is critical to marketing success. Many organizations have access to computer publishing packages that allow them to design and produce their own brochures. This reduces the outsourced costs, but will incur in-house costs, particularly as it can be time-consuming. Inserting brochures or leaflets into appropriate publications is another method that is used. (See the case study about the IYHF who produced a simple two-sided A4 sheet that sells the benefits of the Hostel 2000 programme.)

HRD newsletter

This provides a regular opportunity to promote your services to your customer base. To encourage busy customers to read it, it must contain interesting material. Perhaps it could cover a summary of a new concept in HRD or a review of successful high-profile courses so that the reader will see that similar benefits could possibly be repeated for them. (See the case study on BBSRC who produce a newsletter called *Spectrum*.)

Corporate newsletters

Having regular HRD features in a corporate newsletter will be cheaper than producing a separate one for HRD. If it has a wide circulation, probably due to its contents appealing to a wider audience, it can be a very cost-effective way of promoting the HRD function to all levels of the organization.

Internet and intranet

An ever-increasing number of businesses are advertising their products on the internet. This leads to the problem of encouraging a potential customer to find and open up your particular web pages. It is likely that your information is lost in the mass of HRD information on the Net.

Larger organizations have their own intranet. The HRD function has the opportunity to promote its intranet website address to all employees, increasing the chances of people with HRD needs opening up its pages and seeing its promotional material. There are specialist companies that design and set up websites if you are unable to do so yourself.

Seminars and conferences

Seminars can be used as a vehicle for promoting your services to key budget holders. To encourage line managers to take time out from their usual work activities and attend a seminar, you will probably need to offer something that they will perceive as adding value to their working life.

Training organizations often have a representative as a speaker at conferences. The key to this is to promote your organization while giving interesting information to the audience. This often takes the form of a case study of a successful HRD intervention, even better if it is on a topical issue. A benefit of this approach is the ability to target the type of conference that will have an audience suited to your needs. The Chartered Institute for Personnel and Development's Harrogate and London conferences, and The American Society for Training and Development's conference, are prime examples.

Focus groups

Gathering together a group of people, at random or specifically chosen, to discuss a particular topic is one way to raise awareness about an issue. It enables the HRD practitioner to refine his or her own ideas and consequently design a product or service that is appropriate to the customer's needs.

Media – advertisements on television and radio

In the UK there is very little HRD promotion on television or radio except for government-funded schemes such as NVQs and training schemes for the unemployed. This is probably due to a combination of the high cost and the difficulty in targeting an HRD audience.

Media – advertisements in journals and newspapers

Advertising in professional HR and management journals will aim your promotion at a known target audience. Newspapers will give a wider circulation. Both are expensive. Your advertisement is likely to be compared to others and you therefore need to ask the following questions. Can I afford the expense and resources to make it compare favourably? If not, is there better value in investing in other marketing mediums?

Media – articles or case studies

Writing an interesting article or case study that promotes your organization is a much cheaper alternative to advertising. The time spent writing it can be costly and often professional ghost-writers are used to give a polished edge to the article.

Customer visits and consultancy

It is an important skill of HRD professionals to be able to promote their services when opportunities occur during visits with potential customers. A key skill taken from consultancy is to be able to spot the possible benefits your services can provide for potential customers. This is particularly useful when they themselves have not identified the need. Some HRD organizations link themselves to consultancies which recommend them as part of a possible solution to various business change strategies.

Word of mouth

A number of HRD organizations rely on referrals from satisfied customers to promote their work. If this works sufficiently well it can help reduce expensive investments in marketing.

THE BIOTECHNOLOGICAL AND BIOLOGICAL SCIENCES RESEARCH COUNCIL (BBSRC)

Matching with customers' language and technology

The BBSRC is a UK government-funded body whose principal remit is to fund 'blue sky' research in the fields of biological science and biotechnology. To complete this task it has an annual budget in the order of £150 million. It is also charged with developing world-class researchers and raising public awareness and understanding of science. The Council employs about 3,500 staff, the majority of whom are actively involved in research projects, including the highly public investigation into BSE and the cloning of Dolly the sheep.

The BBSRC has a small, centralized training team based in Swindon. The team is supported by, and in turn supports, training officers at institute sites across the country, providing a wide range of activities and facilities for staff and organizational development. Success with in-house training activity has led to increasing requests from universities for the team to run programmes for university-based researchers.

Reaching their customers

The training team sends a training brochure to every employee at the beginning of the year. Training notice boards display key information at each site. However, they believe that the most effective high-profile promotion seems to be through the organization's regular HR newsletter, *Spectrum*. Much effort is made by the central team to give the training officers, who are closer to the customers, the skills and knowledge to promote training. This includes using external suppliers to develop their marketing and influencing skills.

The training team's own market research has indicated that their customers, particularly the scientists, use IT in their work and are proactive in using the organization's own intranet. The team have training pages on the Intranet but realize that without the knowledge or will to find them among the thousands of other pages they are ineffective as a marketing tool. To overcome this, they are developing a house style for their literature that mimics web pages with a list of information links to the internet. This will better integrate training information into the medium and language used by their customers and therefore increase its effectiveness as a marketing tool.

This is a good example of a training function using innovative thinking to help respond to the changes in technology and language used by its customer base.

With acknowledgement to John Scott, Training Consultant, BBSRC and Ian Andrews, Consultant.

HOW DO WE KEEP THE CUSTOMERS?

It is important to keep customers! Marketing campaigns can be expensive if they are not geared to give a good return on investment. Targeting existing or past customers offers a safer return on investment, as you are aiming your products at people with a proven ability to buy your services. If you keep your customers satisfied, you are likely to be the first people asked when a new need arises or may be recommended to others.

Factors leading to a potential loss of existing customers are:

- They are dissatisfied with the product you supply.
- They can make significant cost savings from another supplier.
- There is political pressure to try another supplier.
- There is a company policy to use another supplier and/or go out to tender after a set period.

Here are some ways to improve customer loyalty:

- Exceed customer expectations.
- Relationship marketing.
- Growing the business within a customer organization.

Exceed customer expectations

This can be done in:

- pre-course information;
- course delivery outcomes;
- post-course follow up.

The ability to achieve this is often dependent on the level of customer expectation and the investment in resources you feel able to apply to a customer.

Relationship marketing

HRD services are purchased by people. By working on the relationship between those people and yourself it is possible to gain customer loyalty. This can be achieved by:

- ensuring that they perceive that they are important to you;
- building rapport with them;
- giving them opportunities to gain prestige with their peers and in particular their boss;
- taking time to understand their needs more specifically;
- encouraging them to take ownership for the service that you provide;
- offering rewards or incentives for repeat business.

Growing the business within a customer organization

Once having gained access to an organization, if you have a reasonable rapport with your contact you should use them to gain information on who else in their organization is likely to want your products. The contact may be encouraged to make referrals and even introductions on your behalf. This requires good judgement as to how far you can push one customer to help provide another. If you get this wrong you may damage your relationship with the existing customer who then may take his or her business elsewhere.

If you get the relationship right and your contact has confidence in your ability to improve their own status if they recommend you, then they become a champion for you and your products. This is a very cost-effective way to market your services.

EVALUATING THE WHOLE MARKETING PROCESS

As has been demonstrated earlier, the whole process of marketing is complex and time-consuming. As a result of this it is also expensive, so it is critical to attempt to assess the return on investment.

A sensible place to start would be by remembering just what the original issue/problem was: has it been addressed satisfactorily? Can you place a value on this?

The following case study shows how a small idea has grown over a number of years into a worldwide initiative. It has gained support from a variety of people at all levels within numerous organizations. Some attempt has been made to assess the take up of the training.

Exercise: What would you do to assess how successful the marketing of this initiative has been?

INTERNATIONAL YOUTH HOSTEL FEDERATION (IYHF) – HOSTEL 2000

The IYHF is a secretariat for national associations that run youth hostels. The Youth Hostel Association of England and Wales (YHA) is one of these national associations and has been involved in training and development activities for many years. The YHA's Personnel Director and a lecturer from High Peak College have been working with a steering group from 14 European associations; this work resulted in an acknowledgement of a need for training. Funding provided by the European Union has so far enabled a training needs analysis (TNA) and the design and delivery of a series of courses to be undertaken on behalf of the steering group. The process is described below.

Hostel 2000

Stage 1

European Force funding enabled a TNA across participating associations to be undertaken. It raised awareness and helped with the product specification. The following key areas were identified as needing a training input:

- managing customers;
- managing operations;
- managing people;
- managing finance and resources;
- managing information;
- managing environment;
- managing quality.

Stage 2

European Leonardo funding enabled the steering group to design a course, a handbook, and for a training programme to be delivered in English and German with common training manuals, acetates and videos. Participating countries included Denmark, England, France, Germany, Portugal, the Republic of Ireland, Scotland, Spain, Sweden and Wales.

The concept was to train a team of trainers who would be licensed to deliver courses they had experienced as participants. 'Training the Trainer' was the first course followed by training those trainers in customer care.

The cascading approach means that there are now about 30 trainers, recruited by invitation, and 693 trainees who have experienced the course. The individual associations incorporated these courses into their own training programmes.

Stage 3

Another two years' funding was obtained from Leonardo and further courses were designed and delivered to support the TNA undertaken in Stage 1:

- Working with Young People
- Quality Management
- History, Philosophy and Ideals of the Youth Hostel Movement with Selling Techniques
- Managing Staff through Change.

With acknowledgements to Terry Rollinson, Personnel Director, YHA, and Kay Price, High Peak College.

A key issue that arises from this case study is how to evaluate the success of the initiative. Remembering the original need is important – in this case it was to raise the level of provision in all associations. In this instance we are interested in how successful the marketing of the programme has been. We can assess this in two main ways:

1.   Collecting data to demonstrate the number of courses run, the number of trainees involved and which countries they represent.
2.   Attempting to find a measure, or measures, of improvements within the hostelling network would demonstrate the ultimate worth of the initiative.

The primary evaluation of the programmes to date shows:

- The ability to undertake translations has improved and the trainers can have confidence in the training pack they receive.
- Some trainers are more assiduous than others at going back to their own associations and running courses.
- There is still a need to convince the General Secretaries of the national associations to take ownership of the courses rather than pass it to the trainers.

Some of the solutions to the identified problems are:

- Try 'double-handed' delivery to ensure and increase the quality and quantity of courses run. It is crucial to spread the message.
- Arrange more 'Training the Trainer' courses to ensure the team can cope with cascading courses into other countries around the world.
- Sell the benefits to General Secretaries to engage them more in the process.
- Use word of mouth – as the courses cascade and success becomes known, more associations will want to become involved, so the next step is to go beyond Europe.

THE WAY FORWARD, OR WHAT YOU CAN DO

Theories and case studies are very useful. However, what really matters is how you apply the information in your own work.

It seems that one of the main methods you can employ is a SWOT analysis. What are the *strengths* and *weaknesses* of the way you currently market your services? Do you actively market, or are you waiting for the work to come to you and wondering why it does not? A wonderful trainer at Guardian Business Services once said, 'Trainers should strap on a backbone.' He went on to explain that many trainers do not plead their case effectively or blow their own trumpets! Knowing what you have done well and telling people about it are essential. Being aware of areas where you need to develop and improve is also essential. Benchmarking against other organizations, not necessarily just training and development ones, is a great way to identify relative strengths and weaknesses.

Where are the *opportunities* for you to grow? Try working on consolidating relationships with existing clients and accessing new clients (see earlier parts of this chapter for practical ideas). The world is changing at an ever-increasing pace and, while this can be discomforting, it also provides opportunities of new markets and products.

What are the *threats* that face you? It seems to be a fact of life that training and development are cut in lean times. Taking steps to be really useful to a client while working with them is essential. Some organizations are starting to see that in lean times undertaking training and development is a great use of time.

Thomson (2004:23) raises the issue of branding within HRD. He says, 'A brand was once little more than the public face a company gave its products or services. But today's powerful brands encompass much more than that. They represent the whole business, including its people.' Thomson continues by asking, 'How many organisations have internal marketing budgets? How many have internal communications budgets that form part of the external marketing spend?'

It seems to me that any person engaged in HRD, whether a generalist or specialist, should give consideration to his or her 'brand'. External consultants and trainers are quite likely to do this as a part of their marketing strategy. How many internal training/development departments or functions have a brand that is well known throughout the organization (for positive reasons)?

As a final exercise for this chapter ask yourself:

- What are you currently doing to market yourself?
- How do you know you are being successful?
- What could you do in the future?
- What is your 'brand' and how many people would recognize it?

CASE STUDY REVISITED: DAVID MATTHEWS, FREELANCE OUTDOOR PURSUITS INSTRUCTOR AND TRAINER

At the start of the chapter we asked what you would do to increase David's trade. Here are some of our ideas.

Constraints

There is a low budget for marketing and a lack of expertise in marketing. There are several markets and therefore David needs to consider market segmentation, dealing with each of the segments separately or combining them into manageable groups:

- *Supply teaching in outdoor centres:* delivering what the centres require and being professional and supportive with the groups and permanent members of staff is probably the best strategy. However, this work relies on external factors over which he can have little control, eg, the number of school groups making bookings and the health of permanent members of staff. He should consider how he might gain access to centres that he does not currently work for, researching where those centres are and then undertaking a targeted mailshot. However, as this work pays less well than other work he needs to keep it to a reasonable percentage.
- *Schools:* the same strategy as for supply teaching, with the addition of relationship marketing, building a relationship with the client; perhaps sending New Year cards to the teachers. Christmas cards are often lost in the general melee and are not appropriate in all schools where the dominant religion is not Christian. Keeping a record of notable incidents that occurred on the last visit to personalize the card is also a way of building the relationship.
- *Youth clubs:* some local authorities have magazines and mailing lists for youth clubs in their area. Getting his name known on a wider scale will be useful.
- *College and university students:* accessing 'freshers' weeks' where students are choosing to join a society, and making contact with lecturers who have a need for outdoor pursuits.
- *Hen nights and stag parties*: this is likely to be word-of-mouth marketing. So telling participants, such as teachers and youth leaders, on other courses that this is an option is one way to attract more business.
- *Managers:* at the moment this is very much a reactive process. Working on designing a new brochure and identifying likely contacts is sound use of the winter months.
- *Groups with disabilities:* many instructors are not experienced with such groups, so capitalizing on this strength and ensuring that all publicity contains reference to working with disabled groups and individuals is essential.
- *Families:* brainstorming contact points and then placing brochures there is one way, for example, contacting Youth Hostels, bed and breakfast establishments and other holiday accommodation, and building the relationship with the owners/managers so that they will promote him.

- *Individuals:* considering whether it is possible to run an open course and in that way cut the cost to each participant. Quite often individuals have no one to come with but do need or want individual tuition, so forming them into a group is one option.
- Building and using a website is a way to market all his activities: www.dm-adventure.co.uk

These are ideas for a sole trader working outside an organization. However, much of the process of brainstorming and benchmarking are equally as appropriate for an in-house operation. The other case studies give examples of how the organizations have changed or shaped their product and processes and in doing so have been in a much stronger position to market themselves.

Bibliography

Frank, E (1994) 'Marketing HRD – an overview', *Journal of European Industrial Training,* **18**, 10, pp 4–9

Gilley, J W and Eggland, S (1982) *Marketing HRD within Organizations: Enhancing the visibility, effectiveness and credibility of programs,* New York, Jossey-Bass Wiley

Harrison, R (1997) *Employee Development,* London, Institute of Personnel and Development

Joy-Matthews, J, Megginson, D and Surtees, M (2004) *Human Resource Development*, 3rd edn, London, Kogan Page

Kotler, P and Armstrong, G (1994) *Principles of Marketing,* 6th edn, Englewood Cliffs, NJ, Prentice Hall

Linton, I (1997) *Marketing Training Services,* Aldershot, Gower

Megginson, D, Joy-Matthews, J and Banfield, P (1999) *Human Resource Development,* London, Kogan Page

Moorby, E (1991) *How to Succeed in Employee Development,* Maidenhead, McGraw-Hill

Morgan, G (1997) *Imaginization: New mindsets for seeing, organizing, and managing,* San Francisco, CA, Sage

Peters, T (1989) *Thriving on Chaos,* London, Pan

Thomson, K (2004) 'Brand of gold', *People Management,* **10**, 7, 8 April, p 23

Wilson, R, Gilligan, C and Pearson, D (1992) *Strategic Marketing Management,* Oxford, Butterworth-Heinemann

Acknowledgement

Acknowledgement is due to Ian Andrew and Richard Firth who contributed to this chapter in the first edition.

26

Managing the Human Resource Development Function

Pete Sayers

INTRODUCTION AND LEARNING OBJECTIVES

This chapter is about the day-to-day management and leadership of the Human Resource Development (HRD) function within an organization. It will look at issues affecting the management of HRD practitioners but, predominantly, look at issues affecting the management of HRD as a function. It will look at HRD as something that affects individuals, teams and the organization as a whole. It will assume that the person with responsibility for the HRD function is also part of the organization, though many of the issues discussed would also be relevant for an external consultant advising an organization that has outsourced HRD.

Exactly what we call the person managing the HRD function can be problematic. Responsibility for HRD is not the same as being in charge of the HRD function. The person responsible for HRD within any organization is (or should be) its chief executive. The person responsible for any individual's development on a day-to-day basis is (or should be) that person's line manager. Megginson *et al* (1999) argue strongly that the line manager's role is crucial both in the development of individuals and in the linking of HRD to the organization's objectives. The extent to which line managers do this, or are able to do this in practice, is problematic. How they can be helped in this role by appropriate leadership from an HRD function is a theme that runs through this chapter.

Moves to flatten organizational structures, as advocated by Peters (1993), have led many organizations to decrease the size of central training departments. In many organizations responsibility for training and the appropriate training budget have been delegated to production units. These can then choose to purchase training provision from outside the organization, or, in many cases, from elsewhere within the organization. They may choose to employ a training manager within their department to advise and help other managers diagnose and meet the training needs of their staff or they may use external consultants for this purpose. They may also be able to call upon the services of a central HRD function.

Where an organization retains a central training department or unit, it is most probable that it will have had to become, a) more market-oriented in its provision, and, b) more advisory or strategic in its thinking. Such moves often accompany a change of name from 'training' to 'development'. Another route, noted by Harrison (1997) is for training departments to consolidate their position within the organization by generating external income through the provision of NVQs and similar qualifications for people outside the organization.

Many possible scenarios exist, and there is considerable variation in how arrangements for training and development are set up, even when considering similar types of organizations. In this chapter the term 'HRD function' will be used as a generic term to cover all of these. Hopefully, the variety of HRD functions retain enough in common for most, if not all, of what follows to be of relevance or interest.

The management of an HRD function has a number of interesting facets to it. These can be looked at from two main perspectives:

1. managing the HRD role within an organization; and
2. managing a team of HRD professionals and support staff.

The first perspective will apply irrespective of the size of the HRD function, and is the basis of most of the issues explored below. In many organizations the number of HRD professionals employed is very small; in which case the second, how to manage the training and development team, may seem of little relevance, or even wishful thinking. There is, however, an interesting possibility here: if the number of people directly employed within the HRD function is small, then others in the organization may be encouraged to develop the skills and insights of the HRD specialist, in order to act as catalysts within their own work areas or even as part-time trainers. In this case, the manager of the HRD function may well have a substantial team, though not a large department.

Managing the HRD role within an organization can be further subdivided into:

- *how to manage* – leadership style, issues of power and control, principles and values; and
- *what to manage* – content and structural considerations for the HRD function.

Having read this chapter you will:

- be able to distinguish between management and leadership;
- know the five leadership roles;
- be able to use 'role' power and 'personal' power to lead and manage; and
- be able to apply Blanchard *et al*'s (1986) situational leadership model to the HRD function.

MANAGEMENT AND LEADERSHIP OF THE HRD FUNCTION

The objective here is to examine ways in which a number of theoretical models of leadership and related ideas can be used and adapted to help the manager of the HRD function.

Leadership is both an essential part of management development and a quality that is often seen as separate from management. Lowe and Lewis (1994:47) illustrate the distinction by pointing out that 'no one ever *managed* an army into battle'. The distinction between *managing change* and *leading change* is more subtle and it is the former term that is more commonly used. There are different ways of defining leadership, and differing ways in which people in organizations describe the behaviours of their managers as good leadership or not. There is, in popular language, considerable overlap in usage of the two terms (see Figure 26.1), but leadership is usually seen as more proactive than management.

Lowe and Lewis (1994) suggest that leadership is more inspirational and more emotionally engaging than the more rational activity usually referred to as management. A successful HRD function will need to demonstrate a balance between proactivity and reactivity.

Leadership, itself, is a term that can be used in different ways. It can be applied to the qualities and behaviour of a unique leader or to those that any member of a team may demonstrate. The former lends itself to the popular definition that sees leadership as a quality certain great individuals are born with. It can also apply to the type of leadership that a professional expert is called upon to use. The second sees leadership as a quality that any person can develop and learn under the right circumstances. Adair's (1973) model of 'action-centred leadership' uses this second definition. It is the kind of leadership that members of teams use selectively to enable the team to progress. As trainers who run leadership courses know, the individual providing the leadership is frequently not the nominated leader.

Both of the above definitions of leadership will be of use to the manager of the HRD function. There are five leadership roles that are of particular interest here:

- the professional expert;
- the provider of vision;

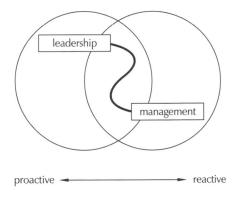

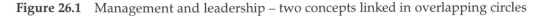

Figure 26.1 Management and leadership – two concepts linked in overlapping circles

- the modeller of the process;
- the internal consultant;
- the organizational politician.

The professional expert

The most obvious way they can show leadership is through keeping up with developments in their field – maintaining a level of professional expertise and a body of knowledge relating to training opportunities and appropriate qualifications. HRD experts will be able to identify trends in training and development and explore new ways of developing their practice in line with innovations in HRD theory and practice. There are, however, problems if the only kind of leadership the manager of the HRD function demonstrates is that of the expert. Managers will also need, equally, to be facilitators of learning. More of this below in the section on control and facilitation.

The provider of vision

Another aspect of leadership is to provide vision – both for the HRD team and for the role of HRD within the organization. As the HRD manager is unlikely to be the organization's chief executive it will not be up to the manager of the HRD function to provide the vision for the business as a whole. It may well be, however, up to the manager of the HRD function to contribute to it, by providing a vision of how people need to interrelate and develop themselves, in order to achieve the organization's mission and strategic aims.

The modeller of the process

Another way of demonstrating leadership in relation to HRD is to be a good role model – to be an illustration of the leadership qualities required to achieve the vision, and to be an embodiment of good practice. Nevis (1987) has worked with an approach to organizational consultancy based on Gestalt therapy. One of a number of techniques he recommends is *modelling the process.*

The starting point is for the consultant (or in this case, the manager of the HRD function) to increase his or her awareness of what is present and what is missing in what Nevis calls 'the client system'. The client system can be a small group or the whole organization. For example, the HRD manager might notice that in meetings of departmental managers people really don't listen well to each other. Listening is, then, what is missing. To model the process, the HRD manager demonstrates good listening skills as often as possible. The others present have the opportunity to learn something about listening skills from the HRD manager modelling the process during their meeting. This will be more effective than other ways of dealing with the problem, which might include complaining in the meeting, or talking critically about it outside the meeting. Modelling the process is safer, in so far as it doesn't involve criticizing others, and can be used in the presence of both senior and junior colleagues equally effectively. In an organization where the dominant management style is 'Do as I say', rather than 'Do as I do', modelling the process will be an effective technique for the HRD manager to use to facilitate organizational learning.

The internal consultant

The manager of the HRD function is in a very good position to do a needs analysis on the organization and to help senior managers solve problems. In more complex cases, this may also involve collaborating with outside consultants. The advantage the internal consultant has is his or her intimate knowledge and understanding of the organization and its culture. It is a role that has the potential to both increase the influence of the HRD function and the job satisfaction of its manager. To show leadership in this area is to be proactive as well as reactive, and to be able to judge what kind of contribution is appropriate at any one time. Blanchard *et al's* (1986) situational leadership can offer useful guidance (see below in the section on control and facilitation).

The internal consultant may be called upon to work with individuals, established teams, and sometimes with the whole organization (more on this below in the section on large-scale interventions). In any of these cases, but more demandingly in the latter two, the manager of the HRD function may notice various forms of resistance to change. The resistance may appear to be located in individuals, or it may be a feature of the organizational culture. In either case the trick will be to understand the resistance before attempting to work with it, through it or against it. Argyris (1990) offers consultants (internal or external) a route through typical organizational behaviours, explains their purpose (ie, what they appear to achieve for the perpetrator, however dysfunctional they are for the wider mission of the organization), and ways of working with them.

The manager of the HRD function operating as internal consultant is in an interesting position here. He or she, as part of the organization, may well be prone to the very behaviour patterns Argyris comments on. The disadvantage is that these patterns may not be something the manager is fully aware of. In other words it may be an organizational blindspot that the HRD manager shares. On the other hand, the advantage is that an internal consultant may find it easier to build common ground with others in the organization and, with the heightened awareness that comes from learning about one's own behaviour as well as that of others, may be able to facilitate good learning in others.

The problem with behaviour patterns (especially one's own) is that they are often out of awareness. Increasingly organizations are using diagnostic instruments to describe behaviours or personality types. Many of these form the basis of 360-degree feedback by comparing perceptions of self with perceptions from a range of others. Organizational culture surveys measure the gap between 'current' and 'ideal' behaviour. The results from these instruments make the process of describing behaviour patterns more objective, and enable desirable behaviour changes to be discussed more rationally. The manager of the HRD function can use these instruments on the HRD team. This increases confidence in using these instruments and provides useful insights into the manager's and the team's behaviour.

The organizational politician

The problem with managing the HRD function is that it requires an ability to operate within the internal politics of the organization. This might require the HRD manager to compete with other managers for influence or resources, and to defend the HRD budget against contraction in times of recession. In this arena there might be a tendency to resort to the lowest common denominator of managerial behaviour demonstrated in the organization as a whole, rather than to maintain the ideals of the HRD professional.

The question for the manager of the HRD function is how to be an effective operator within the organization at the same time as being a role model and showing leadership as a human resource developer. One answer to this is to be a good team player. The team is the organization's management team, whether or not the individual managers in the organization perceive themselves as operating as a team. The kind of leadership the manager of the HRD function can demonstrate most effectively is the kind of leadership required of the good team player.

Katzenbach and Smith (1993) provide an overview of the difficulties encountered in building senior teams. Collins (2001) analyses leadership in a number of US companies and concludes that great companies establish strong senior teams by 'first getting the right people on the bus, then working out where to drive it'. The HRD manager may not be able to, or want to, influence a wholesale replacement of the organization's senior team. He or she should be able to persuade senior managers of the importance of effective teams, and effective leadership, and the link between the two. Goleman, Boyatzis and McKee (2002) explain the need for leaders to have and use emotional intelligence. An effective leadership style will be equally important for the HRD function itself. Both Collins and Goldman advocate a style of leadership that is self-aware, humble and team-focused.

How to play this team role effectively can also be guided by other models of communication. Transactional analysis (TA) (Stewart and Jones, 1987) offers some useful insights into the psychology of interpersonal communication that can be used for organizational problem-solving. Techniques for facilitating training groups can be deployed to facilitate organization problem-solving as well as individual learning. Heron (1993) examines some of the psychological issues affecting personal development in the workplace, as an information base for group facilitation techniques. These are techniques which the manager of the HRD function can use from the position of 'expert' and 'facilitator'. They can be used by the HRD professional in training groups, and they can equally well be used by the manager of the HRD function as a member of the organization's management team.

CONTROL AND FACILITATION – COACHING AND SUPPORTIVENESS

In an organization where the responsibility for developing individuals resides with line management, a lot of the leadership required in this area is outside the control of the HRD professional. It might be, then, difficult for the managers of HRD functions to see how they can show leadership if they are unable to exercise control. In the scenario where HRD is a line management responsibility and training budgets are delegated to operating units, it may be difficult for the manager of the HRD function to see how to be anything other than reactive. Other managers decide what training and development is required and where and when training needs will be met.

Adair's model, on the other hand, says that any member of a team can demonstrate leadership. It therefore follows that any member of a team, not just the one who controls the budget, can be proactive. The manager of the HRD function can show leadership in the context of both operational units and the organization as a whole without having to have that control.

The issue of power and control is an interesting one. Sayers and Matthew (1997) make a distinction between 'role' power and 'personal' power. Role power can be used to control others, but in a way that is more likely to achieve compliance than commitment and in a way that if used inappropriately can cause resentment and resistance. Role power comes with the job title, position within the hierarchy and the ability to control budgets. Personal power, on the other hand, comes from clarity of purpose, strength of character and the respect that earns, and leads individuals to feel in control. This distinction between 'controlling' and 'feeling in control' is a subtle, important and paradoxical distinction. Individuals who feel in control will talk about being in control of their lives, their time, their relationships, etc. Individuals who control using role power are more likely to talk about being in control of other people, places and resources.

The manager of the HRD function may have some role power deriving from his or her position within the organization and professional expertise, but it is more likely that the HRD manager's influence within the organization will be on the basis of personal power. Leadership will not be on the basis of control but of facilitation.

Sayers and Matthew (1997) present two continuums to illustrate the distinction between role and personal power and between the power that derives from being the 'expert' and that which derives from being the 'facilitator' (see Figure 26.2). When a larger amount of personal power is deployed, there is a corresponding decrease in the influence of role power.

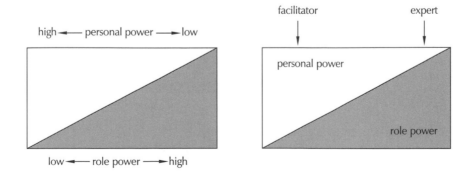

Figure 26.2 The relationship between role power and personal power

A third model of leadership, which is useful in this context, is Blanchard *et al*'s (1986) 'situational leadership' (see Figure 26.3), which is used here to illustrate when and where different kinds of leadership are required. There are four quadrants: directing, coaching, supporting and delegating. In the normal course of supervising staff, Blanchard *et al* suggest a manager will need to move through the quadrants in that order – from bottom right to bottom left. Sayers and Matthew (1997) are most interested in the kind of power that facilitators need to use in the coaching and supporting quadrants when a high level of supportiveness is required to create the right learning environment for others.

Where the day-to-day decision-making about training and development has been delegated to line managers, one of the key roles of a central HRD function will be to assist the organization in creating the overall environment for learning required to develop staff to meet agreed objectives. The manager of the HRD function will be most valued if he or she is able to operate effectively in a supportive capacity. This requires a higher level of personal power, rather than role power. Leadership here will be more facilitative than expert. There will be occasions, in the coaching quadrant, when HRD expertise will make the greater contribution, but the expertise will be most effectively deployed when line managers feel sufficient personal support from the HRD expert to implement the idea for themselves. When this happens, the HRD expert will be able to move into the delegating quadrant and trust that the line managers will be able to fulfil their HRD roles with only minimal support. Delegation will only be effective if line managers know that the central support will be there if needed.

To be an effective internal consultant the manager of the HRD function will need to be able to play this kind of coaching and supporting role within the organization as a whole, and within its senior management team in particular.

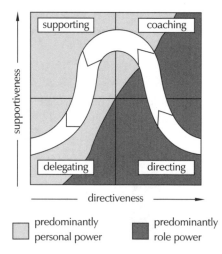

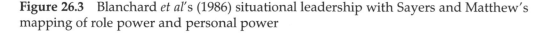

Figure 26.3 Blanchard *et al*'s (1986) situational leadership with Sayers and Matthew's mapping of role power and personal power

Coaching (and mentoring)

Coaching is being done in two separate ways within organizations. Senior managers often use an executive coach, someone outside the organization who helps them think through situations arising at work. HRD managers may well be in a position to recommend this form of coaching to senior management, and may even benefit from some external coaching themselves. The other choice is for line managers to coach their staff. This becomes part of the way line managers take responsibility for the development of their staff. Some managers coach easily as part of their natural style, but most need some training and support to become good coaches for their staff. The managers of the HRD function may well find themselves falling between these two different ways of coaching by providing informal coaching to other managers within the organization. They are not the coachee's line managers but neither are they someone external with whom the coachees have a coaching contract. Some HRD managers are redefining their role to become explicitly recognized as internal coaches for other managers. In other words they are ensuring that the role of HRD professional as coach forms part of a professional, learning contract.

A good coach will be able to work on both the 'outer game' and the 'inner game' (Galwey 1974, 2000), getting at emotional issues (doubts, anxieties and so on) within the individual that prevent effective problem solving and inhibit the energy and commitment needed to implement solutions. An external coach may know little about the manager's business but be very effective at helping improve management performance.

The key difference between a coach and a mentor is business expertise and knowledge. Mentors are usually chosen because they can offer advice based on relevant experience. Clutterbuck (2004) describes the difference on his website as:

> Coaching is primarily about performance and the development of specific skills. Mentoring is much more broadly based and intuitive, focusing on developing capability and often includes longer term help in career self-management.

Many organizations are now introducing mentoring schemes which are performance related and hence blur this distinction. Parsloe and Wray (2000) wisely avoid getting stuck in attempts to define the difference. Coaching and mentoring are both sources of expertise, influence and learning. The manager of the HRD function might choose a mentor as a source of advice and help. That mentor may well end up coaching: that is, helping the manager do some inside-out, rather than outside-in, learning. People tend to find it easier to recognize the need for a mentor, when what they really need is coaching.

PRINCIPLES AND VALUES

What underpins the HRD function? Is it structural, financial or ethical considerations? Reid and Barrington (1997) look at the training function within organizations as a structural issue concerned primarily with the content and organization of training programmes and the best location in the organizational structure for decisions about training. Harrison (1997) spends some time examining budgetary issues, especially those related to outsourcing training and development. The issue of greater interest in this chapter is the underpinning ethics of the HRD function that guide managers of the HRD function in deciding how to play their role.

A theoretical model that maps a potentially useful relationship between leadership style and the management of HRD has been produced by Covey (1992). Covey's contribution has links to a variety of sources, from theories and techniques of communication and personal development (many examples of which are referenced elsewhere in this chapter) and to individual values and attitudes in the 'learning organization' (as developed in, for example, Senge, 1992). The key word for Covey is 'principle'. Principles are fixed and non-negotiable. They are not subject to the vagaries of organizational politics, but can determine a pragmatic route through them. As Covey (1992:25) puts it:

> Principle-centred leaders are men and women of character who work with competence . . . on the basis of natural principles and build those principles into the centre of their lives, into the centre of their relationships with others, in their management processes, and into their mission statements.

Covey's approach is driven by personal insights and metaphors as a way of understanding models of leadership, and he identifies four management paradigms, shown in Table 26.1.

The first paradigm can be seen as one where training would be done primarily as a way of helping individuals perform the tasks necessary for the job. The second starts with benign paternalism and can also be the basis of the model many employers have used to motivate their staff and help manage change, by allowing employees to choose training and learning opportunities up to an agreed amount but not necessarily job-related. The third is the model most closely associated with the title HRD and one which forms the basis of many current models of training and development, including Investors in People. In this paradigm training and development are seen as effective when individual development needs are linked to the achievement of business objectives in a planned way. How this model can be used further is explored later, in the section on strategic and operational decision making.

The fourth paradigm is the one Covey is interested in promoting. A whole-person approach to HRD is not likely to prove problematic for the HRD professional but may be problematic for the manager of the HRD function if the organization's senior executives are working with a different

Table 26.1 Covey's (1992) four management paradigms

Need	Metaphor	Paradigm	Principle
Physical/economic	Stomach	Scientific, authoritarian	Fairness
Social/economic	Heart	Human relations (benevolent authoritarian)	Kindness
Psychological	Mind	Human resource	Use and development of talent
Spiritual	Spirit (whole person)	Principle-centred leadership	Meaning

paradigm. The strongest argument in favour of the fourth paradigm is the recognition that for many organizations people are the most expensive and most valuable asset. As Peters (1993) has passionately put it, the success of companies such as Microsoft is built on the creativity and motivation of its staff, not just their physical presence at work for a set number of hours. He quotes evidence of companies failing to recognize or realize the potential of their workforce. In order to tap this energy and creativity the HRD function has to develop the whole person.

In the fields of both personal development and leadership development there is increasing interest in 'spiritual intelligence'. Zohar and Marshall (2000) believe that spiritual intelligence is a way people solve problems of meaning and value and goes beyond emotional intelligence (Goleman, 1996). Covey uses the term 'spiritual' to underpin a whole-person approach, and offers a number of practical ways in which the manager of the HRD function can model the process.

STRATEGIC VS OPERATIONAL DECISION-MAKING

Establishing a balance between individual, team and/or organizational HRD

Harrison (1997) suggests four levels at which HRD can operate within a business. She raises these in the form of questions for managers of the HRD function when considering the business goals or strategic objectives that HRD is meant to serve within their organizations:

- No systematic training or longer-term development?
- Isolated tactical training at operational level?
- Focused HRD at the business unit level?
- Strategic HRD at the corporate level?

The first of these describes the situation, hopefully, before the HRD function is up and running. The subsequent three can be seen as stages of development for the HRD function. This could imply that if there is strategic HRD at the corporate level, then neither focused HRD at the business unit level nor isolated tactical training at operational level are required any longer. These might be seen as tiers of development for the HRD function (see Figure 26.4) which operate in a similar way to Maslow's hierarchy of needs (1954) – ie, you cannot effectively work at tier 2 unless tier 1 is well established.

In order for there to be focused HRD at the business unit level, line managers will need to be confident that if they identify an individual training need, it will be met. They will want assurance that the HRD function can help them deliver the easy things before they entrust it with something more complex or risky such as team development or implementing the training implications of a business plan. Line managers in business units are more likely to accept the effort required to implement the training implications of the business plan if they know that similar efforts are going on at the corporate level. They are more likely to engage with the HRD function if they see senior management doing the same.

If all three tiers are operational, training for individuals at tier 1 will not be 'isolated'. However, one way that line managers can test the flexibility and responsiveness of the HRD function is to see how they respond to an isolated request for assistance.

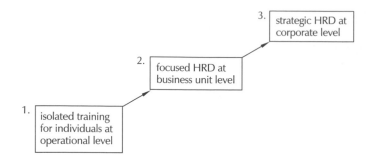

Figure 26.4 Three tiers of operation for HRD

The manager of the HRD function will need to ensure that the HRD professionals are deploying their skills at each of the three levels – and are providing:

    a. training and development opportunities to meet individual needs (tier 1);
    b. team development and training to achieve specific objectives at business unit level (tier 2);
    c. HRD involvement in strategic planning and development at senior management level (tier 3).

Tier 1

To achieve (a) the manager of the HRD function will need knowledge of a wide range of training and development opportunities, including a wide range of qualifications that individuals can work towards for both individual, career and business development. Qualifications will include certificated status for first-aiders (and similar specialisms), nationally recognized vocational qualifications (generic and transferable), and academic qualifications such as MBAs. Individuals may go on courses (often uncertificated) to learn counselling and other interpersonal skills, the results of which can be applied at work and elsewhere in people's lives. The extent to which this kind of self-development for individuals is encouraged within the organization will depend on quite where its management culture is in Covey's paradigm chart discussed earlier.

The HRD manager will need to ensure that there are sufficient resources available to meet individual training needs. This might come in the form of fees for courses run outside the organization, availability of suitable expertise (eg, external training consultants) to bring into the organization, or equally suitable and expert colleagues within the organization.

One of the choices the manager of the HRD function has to make is what staff to employ for this purpose and how to develop them further once appointed. It is usually easier to make the case to senior management to appoint new staff to the HRD function when there is a new specific training need to be met, and for which there is sufficient demand to warrant employing someone full- or part-time within the organization. A good example is IT training. Once the IT (or any other specialist) trainer is in post, though, other considerations may arise.

Harrison (1997) points to cases where organizations have found it easier to cut training departments in times of recession and to outsource a reduced quantity of specialist training demand. This becomes a more acceptable solution where the HRD function is a collection of individual trainers each doing their own specialism and working only at tier 1 of Figure 22.4.

One way of minimizing this is for the HRD manager to ensure a team approach to training and development. Harrison (1997) and Reid and Barrington (1997) stress the value of appropriate qualifications in training and development for HRD professionals. Such qualifications are generic, rather than specific, and equip the HRD professional for a wide variety of work.

Tier 2

If the HRD function within the organization is to operate well at tier 2 (focused HRD at business unit level), the HRD manager will need a team of equally able staff to meet demand – people who can perform a supportive, internal consultant role. As mentioned earlier, this may come from within the HRD department; it may involve external consultants; and it may involve staff from other departments who have an interest in training and development. Whoever it involves, in order to deliver team development, the HRD function will need to operate well as a team itself, and attend to its own team development. If the major activity at business unit level is the implementation of the training and development implications of a business plan, individual HRD professionals will need to be able to turn their hand to a variety of facilitation functions – problem solving, interpersonal communication, etc.

At the business unit level, and at the higher corporate level, the manager of the HRD function will benefit from having a structure to work to. In the UK a government initiative, 'Investors in People' (IiP) provides a standard for organizations to achieve in the way they organize and manage HRD. IiP is now well-established in the UK and being introduced or considered by a number of other countries. To gain recognition as an 'Investor in People' an organization is assessed against a set of 'indicators' by a regional or local assessment centre. The standard and the list of assessment indicators provide a very useful model for HRD managers. In many organizations it is easier for the HRD manager to promote a national standard than his or her own model. Equally advantageous is when the initiative comes externally to the chief executive – for example, from a government agency – and is linked to an offer of partial funding for the initial costs. Central to IiP is the linking of training and development activity to the business planning process. Whether or not the business unit is part of an organization that has achieved or is committed to achieving the Investors in People standard, the linking of a training and development plan to the overall business plan will be an essential first step. In addition to this, mechanisms will be required to link business objectives with individual goals – usually a personal appraisal scheme. Training and development needs to be effectively delivered and, more importantly, its effectiveness evaluated in the context of achieving business objectives, and senior management needs to demonstrate its commitment to, and involvement in, the developmental process. Continuous improvement is a cornerstone of the IiP process. Formal recognition lasts for just three years before re-assessment. See Chapter 20, and Gilliland (1996) for further details.

Investors in People neatly fits into Covey's third paradigm, in which individual needs are linked to business objectives. However, this may not be quite so at home in his fourth paradigm which emphasizes a whole-person approach. Team development that is designed to align the values that guide management attitudes and behaviour and determine organizational culture will be more at home in Covey's fourth paradigm. A principled approach to management development is consistent with being an Investor in People. The aim is to ensure that the values are appropriate to the most effective long-term achievement of the mission.

Values can be described and the prevalence of one value can be measured using psychometric testing. Such measurements can help specify the extent to which the process that is being modelled by senior management in an organization is the process that is going to lead to long-term business success.

Tier 3

Working effectively at tier 3 of Figure 22.4 – strategic HRD at corporate level – will be the greatest challenge to the manager of the HRD function. One of the goals of the HRD manager will be to ensure that an appropriate model of both individual and organizational learning and development has a central place in senior management thinking.

Reid and Barrington (1997:180) list three conditions that have to be satisfied if the training function is to secure a relatively stable place within an organization:

1.   the management team should accept responsibility for training;
2.   the training function should be appropriately structured within the organization;
3.   specialist training staff should be seen as professionals – trained, with clearly defined roles.

To this a fourth needs to be added:

4.   the HRD function must set a good example of the values it advocates and the principles that drive it. To be good listeners, it must demonstrate good listening. 'You cannot talk yourselves out of what you behave yourself into', as Covey (1992) has put it.

Harrison (1997) points out that the delegation of training (and other budgets) to operational units can lead to fragmentation of the HR policy and overall organizational mission. Given control over budgets and the power that goes with it, managers of operational units have been observed to go their own way. If this occurs, a central HRD function may be able to provide a coordinating role, but only if the individual HRD professionals collaborate in a way that is acceptable to the operational unit. The mission of the HRD function is 'to be heard' and the strategy 'to listen'.

Where delegation of budgets has led to a lack of cohesion, the manager of the HRD function will need to be able to offer cohesion. Employees of the organization will see in-house training and development events as offering one of the best opportunities to meet and share ideas with colleagues in other units, and perhaps in that way regain a sense of corporate identity and mission. On the other hand, where there is considerable central control exercised in the organization, the HR function may be one of the few advocates of individual learning, self-development and 'taking responsibility' for oneself.

In some organizations both these stratagems may, paradoxically, be required.

Dealing with chaos

Stacey (1991) examines the way that the fractal patterns of chaos theory offer a metaphor for managers in how to manage the unpredictable and the paradoxical. Managers may claim to manage by objectives but, given that it is impossible to predict the future, will, in reality, need to resort to a form of creative improvisation.

In times of rapid change the need for creative improvisation increases. It is at this point that the manager of the HRD function may no longer know exactly what to do, or what to advise senior managers. It may, however, be a good time to re-evaluate strategy in the light of circumstances.

The beautiful fractal patterns of chaos theory occur at places in the graphical representation of a certain type of mathematical formulae. They occur at those places where there is slowest progression towards either zero or infinity. There is a tendency in Western society to look for a right answer that can be seen as the opposite of the wrong answer. Chaos theory suggests that steering a route between opposite poles might produce the more elegant solution. This is no revolutionary insight as liberal (in the broadest sense of the word) politicians have been seeking the middle road for years. Within the politics of teaching and learning (in which training and HRD can be included) though, there is a tendency to respond to new ideas in the same way as the clothes-conscious respond to fashion: in with the new and out with the old.

Research into the effectiveness of teaching methodologies consistently points to the learner's relationship with the teacher as the strongest factor determining the quality of the learning. It seems, then, that good, collaborative working relationships are more likely to lead to the success of an HRD strategy than adherence to the current, preferred orthodoxy.

The manager of the HRD function will have her or his own preferred paradigm, but success in implementing it will, paradoxically, mean having to work effectively with directors and operational managers who are working with other paradigms.

Learning from feedback

People can learn from feedback. However, most people also get defensive and resistant if feedback is not given well, or if they fear that accepting feedback is linked to blame. They need to work in an organizational culture that values feedback – not a blame culture. Neuro-linguisitic programming (NLP) offers a useful set of techniques and principles for helping individuals at work to learn how to use feedback. Andreas and Faulkner (1996) lists the set of presuppositions that form a foundation to learning NLP techniques and which are also useful for the manager of the HRD function operating at the strategic, corporate level. One is, 'The meaning of your communication is the response you get.' Another is 'Underlying every behaviour is a positive intention.' Any HRD manager having a difficult time in the organizational politics and struggling to be heard or valued, may find such slogans from NLP lack immediate attractiveness. However, on reflection, it can be seen that the essence of good feedback is the separation of intentions from effects. If people feel that their (good) intentions have been understood, they are more likely to listen to unintended (bad) effects.

For any HRD professional operating at the strategic, corporate level, work soon gets unpredictable. It may be the actions of senior managers that produce the unexpected or it may be the interventions of the HRD professional. Small actions in a chaotic environment soon produce large unpredictable effects. Even the best devised plans produce unwanted side effects. This has greater risks for the manager of the HRD function than it does for an external consultant. After all, if things go wrong, the external consultant can leave and seek future business elsewhere. The manager of the HRD function will need to be able to continue working within the organization and this is likely to mean being able to deal with any feedback that needs to be given or received in the light of unexpected negative effects.

Large-scale interventions

A major challenge to the manager of the HRD function is to evaluate trends in HRD theory and practice. One emerging field for HRD worth mentioning at this point is the 'large-group intervention'. In this context a large group could be more than 2000 people. Bunker and Alban (1997) give an overview of 12 methods of large-group interventions currently in practice. Increasingly organizations, especially large organizations, are recognizing that their current dominant culture cannot adapt fast enough to the changes that their business must accommodate if they are to survive in the marketplace. To make a significant change across an organization within a short time-scale requires all members of the organization to participate in collective debate and decision-making. Such events may also include other stakeholders and customers.

Most of the methods used to achieve this rely on someone (an internal or external consultant) organizing venues, catering, and information flows to ensure that a lot of people attend a lot of meetings within a short period. Venues can be anything from a conference hall to an aircraft hangar. Events designed to facilitate whole organization change require the senior management team to interact with the rest of the organization in a way that enables each group to talk among themselves and to each other.

Such events require a large amount of planning and organization and will be a huge challenge to the manager of the HRD function. Working with large numbers can be scary, to say the least, but the benefits of success are also huge. If HRD is to be seen as a prime strategic mover within the organization and the manager of the HRD function is to be seen as the person who can be relied upon to effect strategic change at corporate level, then the large-scale intervention will be one way to make a considerable mark.

FURTHER POINTS FOR MANAGERS OF A TEAM OF HRD PROFESSIONALS

Throughout this chapter there have been parallels drawn between the qualities required of the manager of the HRD function and the manager of a team of HRD professionals. It is of value to remember that cloning individuals is unlikely to benefit the HRD team. It is far healthier if there is a mix of individuals, perhaps along the lines of Belbin's (1993) team roles. All will benefit from a leadership style that provides vision, models the process and works effectively within the politics of the organization. Blanchard *et al*'s (1986) situational leadership applies equally well to the management of the HRD team and issues of power and control are equally problematic. Sayers and Matthew (1997) describe some of the paradoxical situations that people can get into if they attempt to use role power where personal power would be more effective. If the manager of the HRD function is over-controlling (using role power) he or she is unlikely to feel in control of a team of HRD professionals. HRD professionals don't usually want to be told what to do. Megginson *et al* (1999) have a chapter on 'managing the HRD specialist' and their suggestions are intended for managers using internal or external HRD professionals. One of the messages is, 'Know what you want', which is about clarity of vision, not instructions. The manager of the HRD function is much more likely to feel in control if there is a shared vision for the HRD function and if working relationships within the team are good.

Techniques and ideas from counselling and therapy are increasingly influencing HRD practice. Lowe and Lewis (1994) note that 'organizational development and individual development go hand in hand'. HRD professionals engage emotionally with what they do, and benefit from techniques that have been developed by other professionals who need to manage the emotional effects of their work as well as the practical ones. Social workers and therapists have 'supervision' sessions where practitioners can talk through the issues and the emotional stresses involved in their work. Managers of HRD functions may well need to have similar supervision sessions with their staff. These can be linked to coaching sessions. Supervision and coaching as activities have a lot in common. Both are means of reflecting on experience and emotional engagement, with a view to learning and development.

Another technique increasingly being used by training consultants is the 'awayday' – a day away from the office where staff can review their work and talk through future plans. Again, topics of discussion will be about both practical issues and the emotional stresses of the work. A good awayday will contain a mix of serious content and relaxation. A lot can be achieved by an after-lunch walk with colleagues.

CONCLUSION

This chapter has presented a number of ideas about the management of the HRD function. It has looked at models of leadership that can be applied to the management of the HRD function and how issues of control and facilitation impinge on those models. Principles and values that underlie the practice of HRD underpin how HRD professionals work at a number of levels. Three tiers of activity – working with individuals, working at business unit level and working at the strategic, corporate level – require different approaches, both from the HRD professional in general and the manager of the HRD function in particular. Steering a course through the politics of the organization benefits from an insight into chaos theory and techniques for giving and taking feedback. Effecting a significant change in the organization over a short period presents one of the greatest challenges to the manager of the HRD function.

Bibliography

Adair, J (1973) *Action Centred Leadership*, Maidenhead, McGraw-Hill

Andreas, S and Faulkner, C (1996) *NLP: The new technology of achievement*, London, Nicholas Brierley

Argyris, C (1990) *Overcoming Organizational Defenses*, Englewood Cliffs, NJ, Prentice Hall

Belbin, R M (1993) *Management Teams: Why they succeed or fail*, Oxford, Butterworth-Heinemann

Blanchard, K, Zigarmi, P and Zigarmi, D (1986) *Leadership and the One Minute Manager*, London, Collins

Bunker, B B and Alban, B T (1997) *Large Group Interventions*, San Francisco, CA, Jossey-Bass

Clutterbuck, D (2004) [Online] http://www.clutterbuckassociates.com/mentoring

Collins, J (2001) *From Good to Great*, New York, Random House

Covey, S R (1992) *Principle-Centred Leadership*, London, Simon & Schuster

Galwey, T (1974) *Inner Game of Tennis*, New York, Random House

Galwey, T (2000) *Inner Game of Work*, New York, Texere

Gilliland, N (1996) *Developing Your People through Investors in People*, Aldershot, Gower (Investors in People UK, 4th Floor, 7–10 Chandos Street, London, W1M 9DE. Tel 0171 467 1900. http://www.iipuk.co.uk)

Goleman, D (1996) *Emotional Intelligence: Why it can matter*, London, Bloomsbury

Goleman, D, Boyatzis, R E and McKee, A (2002) *The New Leaders*, Boston, MA, Harvard Business School Press

Harrison, R (1997) *Employee Development*, London, IPD

Heron, J (1993) *Group Facilitation*, London, Kogan Page

Katzenbach, J R and Smith, D K (1993) *The Wisdom of Teams*, New York, HarperCollins

Lowe, P and Lewis, R (1994) *Management Development Beyond the Fringe*, London, Kogan Page

Maslow, A H (1954) *Motivation and Personality*, New York, Harper

Megginson, D, Joy-Matthews, J and Banfield, P (1999) *Human Resource Development*, London, Kogan Page

Nevis, E C (1987) *Organizational Consulting: A gestalt approach*, New York, Gardner Press

Parsloe, E and Wray, M (2000) *Coaching and Mentoring*, London, Kogan Page

Peters, T (1993) *Liberation Management*, London, Pan

Reid, M A and Barrington, H A (1997) *Training Interventions*, 5th edn, London, IPD

Sayers, P L and Matthew, R G S (1997) 'Issues of power and control: moving from "expert" to "facilitator"', in S Armstrong, G Thompson and S Brown (eds), *Facing up to Radical Changes in Universities and Colleges*, London, Kogan Page

Senge, P M (1992) *The Fifth Discipline*, London, Century Business

Stacey, R (1991) *Chaos Frontier*, Oxford, Butterworth-Heinemann

Stewart, S and Jones, V (1987) *TA Today – A new introduction to transactional analysis*, Nottingham, Lifespace

Tannenbaum, R and Schmidt, W H (1958) 'How to choose a leadership pattern', *Harvard Business Review*, March/April, pp 95–101

Zohar, D and Marshall, I (2000) *Spiritual Intelligence*, London, Bloomsbury

Bibliography

Abbot, J (1994) *Learning Makes Sense: Recreating education for a changing future*, Letchworth, Hertfordshire Education 2000

ACACE (1982) *Continuing Education: From policies to practice*, Leicester, ACACE

Ackers, P and Preston, D (1997) 'Born again? The ethics and efficacy of the conversion experience in contemporary management development', *Journal of Management Studies*, **34**, 5, pp 677–701

Adair, J (1973) *Action Centred Leadership*, Maidenhead, McGraw-Hill

Adler, P S (1975) 'The transitional experience', *Journal of Humanistic Psychology*, **15**, 4, pp 13–23

Adorno, T W (1973) *Negative Dialectics*, New York, Seabury Press

Ainger, A, Kaura, R and Ennals, R (1995) *An Executive Guide to Business Success through Human Centred Systems*, London, Springer Verlag

Albanese, M (2000) 'Problem-based learning: why curricula are likely to show little effect on knowledge and clinical skills', *Medical Education*, **34**, pp 729–38

Allee, V (2000) 'The value evolution: addressing larger implications of an intellectual capital and intangibles perspective', *Journal of Intellectual Capital*, **1**, 1, pp 17–32

Anderson, T and Metcalf, H (2003) *Diversity: Stacking up the evidence*, London, CIPD

Andreas, S and Faulkner, C (1996) *NLP: The new technology of achievement*, London, Nicholas Brealey

Andrews, K A (1994) *The Concept of Corporate Strategy*, Irwin, McGraw-Hill

Ansoff, H I (1987) *Corporate Strategy*, Maidenhead, McGraw-Hill

Applebaum, E, Bailey, T, Berg, P and Kallenberg, A L (2000) *Manufacturing Advantage: Why high performance work systems pay off*, London, Cornell University Press

Argyris, C (1990) *Overcoming Organizational Defenses*, Englewood Cliffs, NJ, Prentice Hall

Argyris, C (1991) 'Teaching smart people how to learn', *Harvard Business Review*, May/June, pp 99–109

Argyris, C (1992) *On Organisational Learning*, Oxford, Blackwell

Argyris, C (1994) 'Good communication that blocks learning', *Harvard Business Review*, July–August, pp 77–85

Argyris, C and Schön, D A (1978) *Organizational Learning: A theory of action perspective*, Reading, MA, Addison-Wesley

Argyris, C and Schön, D A (1974) *Theory in Practice: Increasing professional effectiveness*, San Francisco, CA, Jossey-Bass

Armstrong, M (1987) 'HRM: a case of the emperor's new clothes?', *Personnel Management*, **19**, 8, pp 30–35

Armstrong, M (1992) *Human Resource Management: Strategy and action*, London, Kogan Page

Armstrong, M (1996) *Performance Management Survey*, IPD press release, London

Armstrong, M (2002) *Employee Reward*, London, CIPD

Armstrong, M and Long, P (1994) *The Reality of Strategic HRM*, London, IPD

Ashton, D and Green, F (1996) *Education and the Global Economy*, Cheltenham, Edward Elgar

Ashton, D and Sung, J (2002) *Supporting Workplace Learning for High Performance Working*, Geneva, International Labour Organization (ILO)

Atkins, S and Murphy, K (1993) 'Reflection: a review of the literature', *Journal of Advanced Nursing*, **18**, pp 1188–92

Atkinson, J (1984) 'Manpower strategies for flexible organisations', *Personnel Management*, August, pp 28–31

Atkinson, R L, Atkinson, R C, Smith, E E and Benn, D J (1993) *Introduction to Psychology*, 11th edn, New York, Harcourt, Brace, Jovanovich

Ausserhofer, A (1999) 'Web based teaching and learning, a panacea?', *IEEE Communications Magazine*, **37**, 3

Bailey, D (1992) 'Facilitator not teacher: role changes for tutors in open learning nurse education', *Journal of Advanced Nursing*, **17**, 8, pp 983–91

Bailey, D (2000) 'Learning needs analysis by another name', *Training Journal*, April, pp 26–29

Bailey, D and Sproston, C (1993) *Choosing and Using a Consultant*, Aldershot, Gower

Baker, T and Aldrich, T E (1996) 'Prometheus stretches building identity and cumulative knowledge in multi employer careers', in M B Arthur and D M Rousseau (eds), *The Boundaryless Career: A new employment principle for a new organisational era*, New York, Oxford University Press

Bandler, R and Grinder, J (1975) *The Structure of Magic: A book about language and therapy*, Palo Alto, CA, Science and Behavior Books

Barham, K, Fraser, J and Heath, L (1988) *Management of the Future*, Berkhamsted, Ashridge Management College

Barney, J B (1991) 'Firm resources and sustained competitive advantage', *Journal of Management*, **17**, pp 99–120

Barrington, H and Reid, M (1997) *Training Interventions*, London, IPD

Barron, A (2004) 'Getting to know those in the know', *People Management*, 15 July, p 25

Barrows, H S and Tamblyn, R M (1980) *Problem-Based Learning: An Approach to Medical Education*, New York, Springer

Bassi, L J, Benson, G and Cheney, S (1996) 'Top ten trends', *Training and Development*, November, p 28

Birchall, D and Tovstiga, G (1999) 'The strategic potential of a firm's knowledge portfolio', *Journal of Management*, **17**, pp 99–120

Basu, R and Wright, J N (2003) *Quality Beyond Six Sigma*, Oxford, Butterworth-Heinemann

Beard, C M (1996a) 'Environmental training: emerging products', *Journal of Industrial and Commercial Training*, **28**, 5, pp 18–23

Beard, C M (1996b) 'Environmental awareness training – three ideas for change', *Eco-Management and Auditing*, **3**, 3, pp 139–46

Beard, C and Hartman, R (1999) 'European and Asian Telecoms – a new role in global sustainable development', *European Business Review*, **99**, 1, pp 42–54

Beard, C and Rhodes, T (2002) 'Experiential learning: using comic strips as "reflective tools" in adult learning', *Australian Journal of Outdoor Education*, **6**, 2

Beard, C and Wilson, J P (2001) *The Power of Experiential Learning: A handbook for educators and trainers*, London, Kogan Page

Beardwell, I, Holden, L and Claydon, T (2004) *Human Resource Management: A contemporary approach*, London, FT/Prentice Hall

Beaton, L and Richards, S (1997) *Making Training Pay*, London, IPD

Beaumont, P B (1992) 'The US human resource literature: a review', in G Salaman (ed), *Human Resource Strategies*, London, Sage

Beck, A and Jones, T (1988) 'From training manager to human resource manager – not a rose by any other name!', *Industrial and Commercial Training*, May/June, pp 7–12

Becker, B E and Huselid, M A (1998) 'High performance work systems and firm performance: a synthesis of research and managerial implications', *Research in Personnel and Human Resource Management*, **16**, pp 53–101

Becker, B E, Huselid, M A and Ulrich, D (2001) *The HR Scorecard: Linking people, strategy and performance*, Boston, MA, Harvard Business School Press

Becker, G. S (1975) *Human Capital: A theoretical and empirical analysis*, 2nd edn, New York, National Bureau of Economic Research

Beckman, T J (1999) 'The current state of knowledge management', in J Liebowitz (ed), *Knowledge Management Handbook*, Boca Raton, FL, CRC Press, pp 1.1–1.22

Bee, F and Bee, R (1994) *Training Needs Analysis and Evaluation*, London, IPD

Beer, M and Nohria, N (eds) (2000) *Breaking the Code of Change*, Boston, MA, HBS Press

Beer, M and Spector, B (1989) 'Corporate wide transformations in human resource management', in R E Walton and P R Lawrence (eds), *Human Resource Management: Trends and challenges*, Boston, MA, Harvard University School Press

Belbin, R M (1993) *Management Teams: Why they succeed or fail*, Oxford, Butterworth-Heinemann

Bell, R E (1993) *The Open University: Exciting innovation or disappointing revival?*, Occasional Papers: Policy and practice in continuing education and training for youth and adult studies, School of Education, Milton Keynes, Open University

Bendell, T (1991) *The Quality Gurus: What can they do for your company?*, London, Department of Trade and Industry (DTI)

Bengtsson, J (1991) 'Human resource development: educatinoeducation, training and labour market development', *Futures*, December, pp 1085–1106

Benjamin, A (1994) 'Affordable, restructured education: a solution through information technology', *RSA Journal*, May, pp 45–49

Benner, P (1984) *From Novice to Expert*, London, Addison-Wesley

Bennis, W (1989) *On Becoming a Leader*, London, Century Business Books

Bennis, W (1993) *An Invented Life: Reflection on leadership and change*, Reading, MA, Addison-Wesley

Benson, J F (1987) *Working More Creatively with Groups*, London, Routledge

Bereiter, C and Scardamalia, M (2000) 'Process and product in problem-based learning (PBL) research', in D H Evensen and C E Hmelo (eds), *Problem-Based Learning: A research perspective on learning interactions*, New Jersey, Lawrence Erlbaum Associates

Bertels, T and Savage, C M (1998) 'Tough questions on knowledge management', in G von Krogh, J Roos and D Kleine (eds), *Knowing in Firms: Understanding, managing and measuring knowledge*, London, Sage, pp 7–25

Betcherman, G, Leckie, N and McMullen, L (1997) *Developing Skills in the Canadian Workplace*, Ottawa, Canadian Policy Research Networks

Binstead, D and Stuart, R (1979) 'Designing reality into management learning events', *Personnel Review*, **8**, 3

Birchall, D (1990) 'Third generation distance learning', *Journal of European Industrial Training*, **14**, 7, pp 17–20

Bird, C M (2004) 'Sinking in a C–M sea: a graduate student's experience of learning through asynchronous computer-mediated communication', *Reflective Practice*, **5**, 2, pp 253–63

Blackler, F, Crump, N and McDonald, S (1998) 'Knowledge, organizations and competition', in G von Krogh, J Roos and D Kleine (eds), *Knowing in Firms: Understanding, managing and measuring knowledge*, London, Sage, pp 67–86

Blackwood, A (1995) *Accounting for Business*, Sunderland, Business Education Publishers

Blanchard, K, Zigarmi, P and Zigarmi, D (1986) *Leadership and the One Minute Manager*, London, Collins

Blantern, C (1997) 'Dialogue and organizational learning', in M Pedler, J Burgoyne and T Boydell (eds), *The Learning Company*, 2nd edn, Maidenhead, McGraw-Hill

Bloom, B (1964/5) *Taxonomy of Educational Objectives*, New York/Harlow, Longmans and Green

Bloom, B S (1965) *Taxonomy of Educational Objectives*, Harlow, Longman

Bloom, B S, Englehart, M D, Hill, W H and Krathwohl, D R (1956) *Taxonomy of Educational Objectives*, London, Longman, Green

Bloom, B S, Engelhart, M D, Furst, E J, Hill, W H and Krathwohl, D R (1956) *Taxonomy of Educational Objectives: The classification of educational objectives, Handbook 1: Cognitive domain*, London, Longmans, Green

Boler, M (1999) *Feeling Power: Emotions and education*, London, Routledge

Bolton, G (2001) *Reflective Practice Writing and Professional Development*, London, Paul Chapman

Bolton, M (1995) *Assessment and Development in Europe: Adding value to individuals and organisations*, Maidenhead, McGraw-Hill

Bond, D (ed) (1988) *Developing Student Autonomy in Learning*, London, Kogan Page

Bontis, N (1998) *Intellectual Capital Questionnaire*, Hamilton, Canada, Institute for Intellectual Capital Research

Bontis, N, Chong Keow, W C and Richardson, S (2000) 'Intellectual capital and business performance in Malaysian industries', *Journal of Intellectual Capital*, **1**, 1, pp 85–100

Bontis, N and Fitz-enz, J (2002) 'Intellectual capital ROI: a causal map of human capital antecedents and consequents', *Journal of Intellectual Capital*, **3**, 3, pp 223–47

Booth, N (2004) 'Handling HR in the high tech world of applied computational fluid dynamics', *South Yorks and District Newsletter*, CIPD, **30**, September, pp 16–18

Boselie, P, Paauwe, J and Richardson, R (2003) 'HRM, institutionalisation and organisational performance', *International Journal of Human Resource Management*, **14**, 8, pp 1407–29

Boud, D (1985) *Problem-Based Learning in Education for the Professions*, Sydney, Higher Education Research and Development Society for Australasia

Boud, D (1992) 'The use of self-assessment schedules in negotiated learning', *Studies in Higher Education*, **17**, 2, pp 185–200

Boud, D and Feletti, G (eds) (1997) *The Challenge of Problem Based Learning*, 2nd edn, London, Kogan Page

Boud, D and Miller, N (eds) (1996) *Working With Experience: Animating learning*, London, Routledge

Boud, D, Cohen, R and Walker, D (1993) 'Understanding learning from experience', in D Boud, R Cohen and D Walker (eds), *Using Experience for Learning*, Buckingham, SRHE and Open University Press

Boud, D, Keogh, R and Walker, D (eds) (1985) *Reflection: Turning experience into learning*, London, Kogan Page

Bourdieau, P (1986) 'The forms of capital', in J G Richardson (ed), *Handbook of Theory and Research for the Sociology of Education*, New York, Greenwood

Bourget, L (1996) 'The changing face of power: how can consultants prepare to help managers through the power shift?', in J W Pfeiffer (ed), *The 1996 Annual Vol 2, Consulting*, San Diego, CA, Pfeiffer

Bowles, S and Gintis, H (1976) *Schooling in Capitalist America*, London, Routledge and Kegan Paul

Bowskill, N (1998) 'Networked learning: a review paper', in P Levy *et al* (eds), *NetLinkS Report* [Online] http://netways.shef.ac.uk/rbase/reports/chapter.htm (accessed 14 March 2003)

Boyd, E M and Fales, A (1983) 'Reflective learning: key to learning from experience', *Journal of Humanistic Psychology*, **23**, 2, pp 99–117

Boydell, T (1971) *The Identification of Training Needs*, London, BACIE

Boydell, T H (1983) *Identification of Training Needs*, London, BACIE

Bradley, K (1997) 'Intellectual capital and the new wealth of nations 1 and 11', *Business Strategy Review*, **8**, 1, pp 53–62

Bramham, J (1997) *Benchmarking for People Managers*, London, IPD

Bramley, P (1996) *Evaluating Training*, London, IPD

Bright, B (1996) 'Reflecting on "reflective practice"', *Studies in the Education of Adults*, **28**, 2, pp 162–84

Brinker, B (2000) 'Intellectual capital: tomorrow's asset, today's challenge', [Online] http://www.cpavision. org/vision/wpaper05b.cfm (accessed July 2004)

British Council (1996) *Education and Training Market Plan*, London, New Leaf

British Quality Foundation (1994) *The 1995 UK Quality Award: Application brochure*, London, British Quality Foundation (British Quality Foundation, 32–34 Great Peter Street, London SW1P 2QX; Tel 020 7654 5000)

British Standards Institution (BSI) (1991) *BS 4788:2, Quality Vocabulary*, London, BSI

Britton, C and Baxter, A (1994) 'Gender and access to higher education: biographies of mature students', paper presented at the BSA Annual Conference, University of Central Lancashire

Brockbank, A and McGill, I (1998) *Facilitating Reflective Learning in Higher Education*, Buckingham, SRHE and Open University Press

Brockbank, A and McGill, I (2004) *The Action Learning Handbook: Powerful techniques for education, professional development and training*, London, RoutledgeFalmer

Brockbank, A, McGill, I and Beech, N (2002) *Reflective Learning in Practice*, London, Gower

Brookfield, S (1991) *Understanding and Facilitating Adult Learning*, Buckingham, Open University Press (first published 1986)

Brookfield, S D (1995) *Becoming a Critically Reflective Teacher*, San Francisco, CA, Jossey-Bass

Brooking, A (1996) *Intellectual Capital: Core asset for the third millennium enterprise*, London, International Thomson Business Press

Brown, A (1984) *Consultation*, Oxford, Heinemann

Brown, D and Armstrong, M (1997) 'Terms of enrichment', *People Management*, 11 September, pp 36–38

Brown, R (1988) *Group Processes*, Oxford, Blackwell

Brown, S and Knight, P (1994) *Assessing Learners in Higher Education*, London, Kogan Page

Browning, D (1990) 'Beyond GCSE: real choices for adults', *Adults Learning*, **1**, 3, pp 147–48

Brunner, D D (1994) *Inquiry and Reflection: Framing narrative and practice in education*, Albany, State University of New York Press

Bryant, R (1995) 'Why does being a mature student have to be so painful?', *Adults Learning*, May, pp 270–71

Buckley, R and Caple, J (2004) *The Theory and Practice of Training*, London, Kogan Page

Bullon, P (1997) 'Profesionales en la Red: Algunos web de escuelas', *iWorld*, 8 October

Bunker, B B and Alban, B T (1997) *Large Group Interventions*, San Francisco, CA, Jossey-Bass

Burke, W W (1982) *Organizational Development: Principles and practices*, Boston, MA, Little, Brown

Burnes, B (2004) *Managing Change*, London, Prentice Hall

Burt, R S (1992) *Structural Holes: The social structure of competition*, Boston, MA, Harvard University Press

Burton-Jones, A (2001) *Knowledge Capitalism: Business, work, and learning in the new economy*, Oxford, Oxford University Press

Buzan, T (1995) *The MindMap Book*, London, BBC Books

Cabinet Office, Training and Development Division (1988) *A Guide on How to Do a Training Needs Analysis*, London, Cabinet Office (OMCS)

Capuano, N, Gaeta, M and Pappacena L (2003) 'An e-learning platform for SME manager upgrade and its evolution toward a distributed training environment', in *Proceedings of the 2nd International LeGE-WG Workshop on E-Learning and Grid Technologies: A Fundamental Challenge for Europe*, Paris, 3–4 March 2003

Carkhuff, R (1983) *The Art of Helping*, Amherst, MA, Human Resources Development

Caroselli M (1996) *Quality Games for Trainers: 101 playful lessons in quality and continuous improvement*, London, McGraw-Hill

Carr, W (1995) *For Education: Towards critical educational inquiry*, Buckingham, Open University Press

Carter, C (1980) *Why and How to Examine*, Oxford, Blackwell

Cassany, D, Luna, M and Sanz, G (1993) *Ensenyar Llengua*, Barcelona, Editorial Grao

CEDEFOP (1996) *Glossorium: Vocational training*, Luxembourg, Office for Official Publications of the European Communities

CEDEFOP (1995a) *Teachers and Trainers in Vocational Education: Vol I: Germany, Spain, France and the United Kingdom*, Luxembourg, Office for Official Publications of the European Communities

CEDEFOP (1995b) *Teachers and Trainers in Vocational Education: Vol 2: Italy, Ireland and Portugal*, Luxembourg, Office for Official Publications of the European Communities

CEDEFOP (1997) *Teachers and Trainers in Vocational Education: Vol 3: Austria, Belgium, Greece, Luxembourg, and the Netherlands*, Luxembourg, Office for Official Publications of the European Communities

CEDEFOP (1998) *Teachers and Trainers in Vocational Education: Vol. 4 Denmark, Finland, Iceland, Norway and Sweden*, Luxembourg, Office for Official Publications of the European Communities

CEDEFOP (2004) 'Belgium: Conclusions of the 2003 Conference on Employment'' *cedefopinfo*, 1

CERI (Centre for Educational Research and Innovation) (1996) *Education at a Glance: Analysis*, Paris, OECD

CERI (1997) *Education at a Glance: OECD indicators 1997*, Paris, OECD

Chalofsky, N (1992) 'A unifying definition for the human resource profession', *Human Resource Development Quarterly*, 3, 2, pp 175–82

Chalofsky, N and Lincoln, C (1983) *Up the HRD Ladder*, Reading, MA, Addison-Wesley

Chandler, A D (1962) *Strategy and Structure*, Cambridge, MA, MIT Press

Chartered Institute of Personnel and Development (CIPD) (2001) *Performance through People: The new people management*, London, CIPD

CIPD (2004a) *High Performance Working Factsheet*, London, CIPD

CIPD (2004b) *Reward Management Survey*, London, CIPD

CIPD/Engineering Employers Federation (EEF) (2003) *Maximising Employee Potential and Business Performance: The role of high performance working*, London, EEF

Chomsky, N (1959) 'Review of verbal behaviour by B F Skinner', *Language*, 35, pp 26–58

Clark, D (1992) 'Education for community in the 1990s: A Christian perspective', in G Allen, G and I Martin, (eds), *Education and Community: The politics of practice*, London, Cassell

Clarke, A (1999) *Evaluation Research: An introduction to principles, methods and practice*, London, Sage

Clements, P and Jones, J (2002) *The Diversity Training Handbook*, London, Kogan Page

Cleverley, G (1971) *Managers and Magic*, Harmondsworth, Pelican

Clift, R T, Houston, W R and Pugach, M C (eds) (1990) *Encouraging Reflective Practice in Education: An analysis of issues and programs*, Columbia University, Teachers College Press

Clutterbuck, D (2004) [Online] http://www.clutterbuckassociates.com/mentoring

Coates, H and Wright, J (1991) *The Integration of Work Based Learning with Academic Assessment*, Coventry, Coventry Polytechnic

Cockerill, S *et al* (1996) 'The international management of change: a problem-based learning/case study approach', *Education and Training*, **38**, 2, pp 14–17

Cognition and Technology Group at Vanderbilt University (1991) 'Technology and the design of generative learning environments', in T Duffy and D Jonassen (eds), *Constructivism and the Technology of Instruction: A conversation*, New Jersey, Lawrence Erlbaum Associates, pp 77–89

Cohen, D and Prusak, L (2001) *In Good Company: How social capital makes organizations work*, Cambridge, MA, Harvard Business School Press

Coleman, J S (1988) 'Social capital in the creation of human capital', *American Journal of Sociology*, **94**, Supp pp S95–S120

Collin, A (2004) 'Learning and development in human resource management', in I Beardwell, L Holden and T Claydon (eds), *Human Resource Management*, London, Pitman, pp 275–76

Collins, J (2001) *From Good to Great*, New York, Random House

Collis, R (1993) 'The people factor', *Business Life*, February. pp 57–65

Commission of the European Communities (1991) *Structures of the Education and Initial Training Systems, ELIRIDICE and CEDEFOP project*, Luxembourg, Office for Official Publications of the European Communities

Commonwealth Secretariat (1984) *Training Skills for Women*, London, Commonwealth Secretariat

Constable, J and McCormick, R (1987) *The Making of British Managers*, London, British Institute of Management/Confederation of British Industry

Contu, A, Grey, C and Örtenblad, A (2003) 'Against learning', *Human Relations*, **56**, 8, pp 931–52

Cook, M (1990) *Personnel Selection and Productivity*, Chichester, Wiley

Cook, V (1988) *Chomsky's Universal Grammar*, Oxford, Blackwell

Cook, V (1991) *Second Language Learning and Language Teaching*, London, Edward Arnold

Cooper, G and White, B (1995) 'Organisational behaviour', in S Tyson (ed), *Strategic Proposals for HRM*, London, IPD

Cornell, J (1989) *Sharing the Joy of Nature*, USA, Dawn Publications

Cosh, A, Hughes, A and Weeks, M (2000) *The Relationship Between Training and Employment Growth in Small and Medium Enterprises*, Nottingham, DfEE Publications

Coulson-Thomas, C (2001) 'Fashion victim', *People Management*, **7**, 17, p 51

Council on Competitiveness (1987) 'Analysis of US competitiveness problems', *America's Competitive Crisis: Confronting the new reality*, April, pp 121–26

Covey, S R (1992) *Principle-Centred Leadership*, London, Simon & Schuster

Crosby, P B (1979) *Quality is Free*, Mentor Books, New York

Crystal, D (1997) *The Cambridge Encyclopedia of Language*, Cambridge, Cambridge University Press

Crystal, D (2003) *English as a Global Language*, Cambridge, Cambridge University Press

Cuba, E G (ed) (1990) *The Paradigm Dialog*, Newbury Park, CA, Sage

Cunningham, I, Dawes, G. and Bennett, B (2004) *The Handbook of Work Based Learning*, Aldershot, Gower

Dahlgren, MA and Oberg, G (2001) 'Questioning to learn and learning to question: structure and function of problem-based learning scenarios in environmental science education', *Higher Education*, **41**, pp 263–82

Dainty, P and Lucas, D (1992) 'Clarifying the confusion: a practical framework for evaluating outdoor management development programmes for managers', *Management Education and Development*, **23**, 2, pp 106–22

Dale, M (2003) *Recruitment and Selection*, London, Kogan Page

Daniel, J (1998) 'Can you get my hard nose in focus? Universities, mass education and appropriate technology', in M Eisenstadt and T Vincent (eds), *The Knowledge Web: Learning and collaborating on the net*, London, Kogan Page

Daniels, J D and Radebaugh, L H (1995) *International Business Environments and Operations*, 7th edn, Wokingham, Addison Wesley

Dato' Seri, M M (1991) 'The way forward – Vision 2020', Prime Minister's Department, working paper presented at the Malaysian Business Council

Dauphinais, B, Price, C and Pederson, P (The Price Waterhouse Change Integration Team) (1996) *The Paradox Principles*, Chicago, IL, Irwin

D'Aveni, R A (1995) *Hyper-Competitive Rivalries: Competing in highly dynamic environments*, New York, Free Press

Davenport, T, De Long, D and Beers, M (1998) 'Successful knowledge management projects', *Sloan Management Review*, **39**, 2, pp 43–57

Davenport, T H and Probst, G (eds) (2000) *Knowledge Management Casebook: Siemens best practices*, Munich, Publicis MCD Verlag/Wiley

Davenport, T H and Prusak, L (1998:5) *Working Knowledge: How organizations manage what they know*, Boston, MA, Harvard Business School Press

Davies, T (2003) 'Some personal thoughts from a "traditional" academic moving towards e-learning', [Online] http://elearningeuropa.info/doc.php?lng=1&id=1159&doclng=1 (accessed 3 September 2004)

Davies, W J K (1989) *Open and Flexible Learning Centre*, London, National College for Educational Technology

Dearden, R (1991) 'Education and Training', in G Esland (ed), *Education, Training and Employment, Vol. 2, The educational response*, Wokingham, Addison-Wesley, pp 84–95

Dean, A and Kretschmer, ? M (2002) 'Can ideas be capital? Factors of production in the post-industrial economy: a review and critique', *Academy of Management Review*, December

Dearden, R (1991) 'Education and Training', in G Esland (ed), *Education, Training and Employment: Vol. 2, The educational response*, Wokingham, Addison-Wesley in association with Open University, pp 84–95

Dearing, R (1997) *Higher Education in the Learning Society: Report of the National Committee of Enquiry in Higher Education*, London, HMSO

De Geus, A P (1989) 'Planning as learning', *Harvard Business Review*, March/April, pp 70–74

Dehler, G E, Welsh, M A and Lewis, M W (2001) 'Critical pedagogy in the "New Paradigm"', *Management Learning*, CE, **4**, pp 493–511

Deming, W E (1982) *Out of the Crisis*, Cambridge, MA, MIT Press

Denzin, N K and Lincoln, Y S (eds) (1994) *Handbook of Qualitative Research*, Thousand Oaks, CA, Sage

DfEE (Department for Education and Employment) (1997) *Quality Counts. A standard for the delivery of management development – for buyers of management development*, London, HMSO. Copies available from MCI, Russell Square House, 10–12 Russell Square, London WC1B 5BZ. Tel 020 872 9000

DfES (Department for Education and Skills) (2003) *Towards a Unified E-Learning Strategy: Consultation Document*, London, DfES[Online] http://www.dfes.gov.uk/elearningstrategy/elearning.stm (accessed 28 August 2003)

DfES (2004) *Progress towards a Unified E-Learning Strategy*, London, Department for Education and Skills [Online]http://www.dfes.gov.uk/ elearningstrategy/online.cfm (accessed 15 December 2004)

DoE (Department of Employment) (1986) *Working Together, Education and Training, Government White Paper Cmnd 9823*, London, HMSO

DTI (Department of Trade and Industry) (1991) *Best Practice Benchmarking*, London, DTI

Dess, G G and Picken, J C (1999) *Beyond Productivity: How leading companies achieve superior performance by leveraging their human capital*, New York, American Management Association

Deutscher, I (1984) 'Asking questions (and listening to answers)', in M Bulmer (ed), *Sociological Research Methods*, 3rd edn, Homewood, IL, Irwin

De Vaus, D A (1993) *Surveys in Social Research*, London, UCL Press

Dewey, J (1933) *How We Think*, Boston, MA, Heath

Dewey, J (1938) *Education and Experience*, New York, Collier and Macmillan

Dewey, J (1939) *Freedom and Culture*, New York, Putman

Dispenza, V (1996) 'Empowering students: a pragmatic philosophical approach to management education', *Management Learning*, **27**, 2, pp 239–51

Dixon, N (1994) *The Organizational Learning Cycle*, Maidenhead, McGraw-Hill

Donaldson, L (1994) 'The bottom line on diversity in the workplace', *Personnel Today Conference Daily*, IPD Harrogate Conference, 28 October

Dorrell, J (1993) *Resource-Based Learning: Using open and flexible learning resources for continuous development*, Maidenhead, McGraw-Hill Training Services

Douglas, T (1983) *Understanding People Gathered Together*, London, Routledge

Doyle, M (1995) 'Organizational transformation and renewal – a case for refraining retraining management development?', *Personnel Review*, **24**, 6, pp 6–18

Drucker, P (1954) *The Practice of Management*, Maidenhead, McGraw-Hill

Drucker, P F (1974) *Management Tasks, Responsibilities, Practices*, Oxford, Heinemann

Drucker, P (1985) *Managing in Turbulent Times*, New York, Harper and Row

Drucker, P (1998) 'The coming of the new organization', *Harvard Business Review on Knowledge Management*, Boston, MA, Harvard Business School Press, pp 1–19

Drucker, P F (1992) 'The new society of organizations', *Harvard Business Review*, September/October, pp 95–104

Drucker, P (1993) *Post-Capitalist Society*, Oxford, Butterworth-Heinemann

Dubin, P (1962) *Human Relations in Administration*, Englewood Cliffs NJ, Prentice Hall

Dyke, C, Martin, J, and Woollard, J (2000) 'Why EQ matters for consultants and developers', *Organisation and People*, **7**, 1, February, pp 29–34

Easterby-Smith, M and Graca, M (2004) 'Self service: can your organisation make rapid strategic changes when necessary, even to core competences?' *People Management*, **10**, 3, February, pp 37–38

Ecclestone, K (1996) 'The reflective practitioner: mantra or a model for emancipation?', *Studies in the Education of Adults*, **28**, 2, pp 146–61

Economist Global Executive (2003) 'Lessons from afar', Economist Education Outlook, *Economist*, 8 May [Online] http://www.economist.com/globalExecutive/Education/executive/printerFriendly.cfm?story_id=1762562 (accessed 15 November 2003)

Edis, M (1995) *Performance Management and Appraisal in Health Services*, London, Kogan Page

Edvinsson, L and Malone, M (1997) *Intellectual Capital: Realising your company's true value by finding its hidden roots*, New York, HarperCollins

Edwards, R (1991) 'The politics of meeting learner needs: power, subject, subjugation', *Studies in the Education of Adults*, **23**, 1, pp 85–97

Edwards, R (1993) *Mature Women Students*, London, Taylor & Francis

Egan, G (1962) *The Skilled Helper*, Monterey, CA, Brooks/Cole

Egan, G (1995) A clear path to peak performance', *People Management*, 18 May, p 35

Eisenstadt, M and Vincent, T (eds) (1998) *The Knowledge Web: Learning and collaborating on the net*, London, Kogan Page

Ellis, C and Sonnenfield, J A (1993) 'Diverse approaches to managing diversity', *Human Resource Management*, **33**, 1, pp 79–109

Ellis, R (1986) *Understanding Second Language Acquisition*, Oxford, Oxford University Press

Emory, C W (1985) *Business Research Methods*, 3rd edn, Homewood, IL, Irwin

Employment NTO (2000) *National Standards for Training and Development: Training and Development: Strategy*, Leicester, Employment NTO. (For further details contact: Employment NTO, Kimberley House, 47 Vaughan Way, Leicester LEI 4SG; Tel: 0116 251 7979, Website: www.empnto.co.uk)

Engel, C E (1997) 'Not just a method but a way of learning', in D Boud and G Feletti (eds), *The Challenge of Problem Based Learning*, 2nd edn, London, Kogan Page

English, L and Lynn, S (1995) *Business across Cultures*, New York, Longman

Ento (2002) *Standards in Learning and Development*, London, Ento

Eraut, M (1994) *Developing Professional Knowledge and Competence*, London, Falmer Press

Eraut, M (1995) 'Schön shock: a case for reframing reflection-in-action?', *Teachers and Teaching: Theory and Practice*, 1, 1, pp 9–22

Esland, G (1991) *Education, Training and Employment, Vol. 1, Educated labour – the changing basis of industrial demand*, Wokingham, Addison-Wesley

European Commission (1996) *White Paper on Education and Training: Teaching and learning: Towards the learning society*, Luxemburg, Office for Official Publications of the European Communities

European Commission (1997a) *Key Data on Education in the European Union '97*, Luxembourg, Office for Official Publications of the European Communities

European Commission (1997b) *Continuing Vocational Training: Europe, Japan and United States of America*, Luxembourg, Office for Official Publications of the European Communities

European Training Foundation (1997) *Report on the Vocational Education and Training System: Czech Republic*, Luxembourg, Office for Official Publications of the European Communities

Eurydice/CEDEFOP (1991) *Structures of the Educational and Initial Training Systems in the Member States of the European Community*, Luxembourg, Office for Official Publications of the European Communities

Evans, T D (1994) *Understanding Learners in Open and Distance Learning*, London, Kogan Page

Fahy, J (2000) 'The resource-based view of the firm: some stumbling blocks on the road to understanding sustainable competitive advantage', *Journal of European Industrial Training*, 24, 2/3/4, pp 94–104

Farnham, D (1997) *Employee Relations in Context*, London, IPD

Faulkner, D and Johnson, G (1992) *The Challenge of Strategic Management*, London, Kogan Page

Fawbert, F (2003) *Teaching in Post-Compulsory Education: Learning, Skills and Standards*, London, Continuum

Fenwick, T and Parsons, J (1998) 'Boldly solving the world: a critical analysis of problem-based learning as a method of professional education', *Studies in the Education of Adults*, 30, 1, pp 53–66

Feyten, C M *et al* (2001) *Teaching ESL/EFL with the Internet: Catching the wave*, New Jersey, Prentice Hall

Fineman, S (1997) 'Emotion and management learning', *Management Learning*, 28, 1, pp 13–25

Fiske, J (1990) *Introduction to Communication Studies*, New York, Routledge

Flanagan, J C (1954) The critical incident technique', *Psychological Bulletin*, 51, pp 327–58

Fletcher C (1997) *Appraisal: Routes to improved performance*, 2nd edn, London, IPD

Fletcher, S (1991) *NVQs Standards and Competence*, London, Kogan Page

Foong, K and Yorsten, R (2003) *Human Capital Measurement and Reporting: A British perspective* [Online] www.accountingforpeople.gov.uk (accessed 3 November 2004)

Ford, V (1996) 'Partnership is the secret of success', *People Management*, 2, 3, pp 34–36

Forlenza, D (1995) 'Computer-based training', *Professional Safety*, 40, 5, pp 28–29

Fowler, A (1990) 'Performance management: the MBO of the 1990s', *Personnel Management*, 22, 7, pp 47–51

Fox, S (1991) 'The production and distribution of knowledge through open and distance learning', *Education and Training Technology International*, 26, 3, pp 269–80

Frank, E (1988) 'An attempt at a definition of HRD', *Journal of European Industrial Training*, 12, 5, pp 4–5

Frank, E (1994) 'Marketing HRD – an overview', *Journal of European Industrial Training*, 18, 10, pp 4–9

Frank Press (1990) 'The role of education in technological competitiveness', *Siemens Review*, February

Franke, R H, Hofstede, G and Bond, M H (1991) 'Cultural roots of economic performance: a research note', *Strategic Management Journal*, 12, pp 165–73

Freire, P (1994) *Pedagogy of Hope: Reliving pedagogy of the oppressed*, New York, Continuum

French, D (1999) 'Preparing for internet-based learning', in D French, C Hale, C Johnson and G Farr (eds), *Internet Based Learning: An introduction and framework for higher education and business*, London, Kogan Page

Fulghum, R (1989) *All I Really Need to Know I Learned in Kindergarten*, London, Grafton Books

Fuller, A and Saunders, M (1990) 'The paradox in open learning at work', *Personnel Review*, **19**, 5, pp 29–33

Further Education Unit (1983) *Flexible Learning Opportunities*, London, FEU

Gael, S (1988) *The Job Analysis Handbook for Business, Industry and Government*, New York, Wiley

Gagné, R M (1967) *Learning and Individual Differences*, Columbus, OH, Merrill

Gagné, R M (1972) 'Domains of learning', *Interchange*, **3**, 1, pp 1–8

Galagan, P (1986) 'Editorial', *Training and Development Journal*, **40**, 3, p 4

Gallwey, W T (1974) *Inner Game of Tennis*, New York, Random House

Gallwey, W T (1996) *The Inner Game of Tennis*, London, Pan Books (also: *The Inner Game of Golf*)

Gallwey, W T (2000) *Inner Game of Work*, New York, Texere

Garavan, T N (1991) 'Strategic human resource development', *Journal of European Industrial Training*, 15, 1, pp 17–30

Garavan, T N (1997) 'Training, development, education and learning: different or the same?', *Journal of European Industrial Training*, **21**, pp 39–50

Garavan, T Costine, P and Heraty, N (1995) *Training and Development in Ireland: Context, policy and practice*, Dublin, Oak Tree Press

Garavan, T N, Costine, P and Heraty, N (1995) 'The emergence of strategic human resource development', *Journal of European Industrial Training*, **19**, 10, pp 4–10

Garavan, T N, Gunnigle, P and Morely, M (2000) 'Contemporary HRD research: a triarchy of theoretical perspectives and their prescriptions for HRD', *Journal of European Industrial Training*, **24**, 2/3/4, pp 65–104

Garavan, T N, Morley, M, Gunnigle, P and Collins, E (2001) 'Human capital accumulation: the role of human resource development', *Journal of European Industrial Training*, **25**, 2/3/4, pp 48–68

Garcia, Guy G (2004) *The New Mainstream: How the multicultural consumer is transforming American business*, New York, HarperCollins

Gardenswartz, L, Rowe, A, Digh, P and Bennett, M (2003) *The Global Diversity Desk Reference: Managing an international workforce*, Melbourne, Pfeiffer Wiley

Gardner, H (1983) *Frames of Mind: The theory of multiple intelligences*, New York, Basic Books

Gardner, H (1984) *Frames of Mind. Place: The theory of multiple intelligences*, London, Fontana

Garratt, B (1987) *The Learning Organization*, London, Fontana

Garratt, B (1995) 'An old idea that has come of age', *People Management*, **1**, 19, pp 25–29

Garratt, T (1997) *The Effective Delivery of Training Using NLP*, London, Kogan Page

Garvey, B and Williamson, B (2002) *Beyond Knowledge Management*, Harlow, Pearson Education

Garvin, D A (1993) 'Building a learning organisation', *Harvard Business Review*, **71**, 4, pp 78–91

Garvin, D A (1994) 'Building a learning organisation', *Business Credit*, **96**, 1, January, pp 19–28

Geach, P T (1956) 'Good and evil', in P Foot, (ed), (1967) *Theories of Morals*, Oxford, Oxford University Press

Geirland, J and Maniker-Leiter, M (1996) 'Five lessons for internal OD consultants', in J W Pfeiffer (ed), *The 1996 Annual Vol 2: Consulting*, San Diego, CA, Pfeiffer, pp 295–304

Gibb, S (2002) *Learning and Development: Processes, practices and perspectives at work*, Basingstoke, Palgrave Macmillan

Gibbert, M, Jonczyk, C and Völpel, S (2000) 'ShareNet – the next generation knowledge management', in T H Davenport and G Probst (eds), *Knowledge Management Casebook: Siemens best practices*, Munich, Publicis MCD Verlag/Wiley, pp 22–39

Gibbert, M and Krause, H (2000) 'Practice exchange in a best practice marketplace', in T H Davenport and G Probst (eds), *Knowledge Management Casebook: Siemens best practices*, Munich, Publicis MCD Verlag/Wiley, pp 68–84

Gibbons, M *et al* (1994) *The New Production of Knowledge*, London, Sage

Gibbs, G (1989) *Dimensions of Assessment*, Oxford Centre for Staff Development

Giddens, A (1990) *The Consequences of Modernity*, Cambridge, Polity Press

Giddens, A (1994) 'Jürgen Habermas', in Q Skinner (ed), *The Return of Grand Theory in the Human Sciences*, Cambridge, Cambridge University Press, pp 123–39

Gill, J and Johnson, P (1991) *Research Methods for Managers*, London, Paul Chapman

Gilliland, N (1996) *Developing Your People through Investors in People*, Aldershot, Gower (Investors in People UK, 4th Floor, 7–10 Chandos Street, London W1G 9DQ. Tel 020 7467 1900. http://www.iipuk.co.uk)

Gilroy, P (1993) 'Reflections on Schön: an epistemological critique and a practical alternative', in P Gilroy and M Smith (eds), *International Analyses of Teacher Education*, Oxford, Carfax, pp 125–42

Giroux, H A (1992) *Border Crossings: Cultural workers and the politics of education*, New York, Routledge

Gladstone, B (2000) *From Know-How to Knowledge*, London, Industrial Society

Glasenk, N (1997) 'Diversity in the workplace', paper presented in a Plenary Session, IPD National Conference, Harrogate, 22 October

Goleman, D (1996) *Emotional Intelligence: Why it can matter*, London, Bloomsbury

Goleman, D (1998) *Working with Emotional Intelligence*, Bloomsbury, London

Goleman, D, Boyatzis, R E and McKee, A (2002) *The New Leaders*, Boston, MA, Harvard Business School Press

Goodman, N W (1997) 'Paradigm, parameter, paralysis of mind', *British Medical Journal*, **307**, pp 1627–29

Gosling, J and Mintzberg, H (2004) 'The education of practical managers', *MIT Sloan Management Review*, **5**, 4 pp 19–22

Graham, G (1994) 'Lack of training shuts out poor', *Financial Times*, 14 March, p 4

Gramsci, A (1978) *Selections from the Prison Notebooks*, London, Lawrence and Wishart

Gratton, L (1997) 'Tomorrow people', *People Management*, 24 July, pp 25–26

Gratton, L (2004) 'Means to an end: are we measuring the right things?', *People Management*, **9**, 17, 2 September

Greenaway, R (1993) *Playback: A guide to reviewing activities*, London, Employment Department, and Endeavour, Scotland

Greening, T (1998) 'Scaffolding for success in problem-based learning', *Med Educ Online* [Online] http://www.Med-Ed-Online.org. (accessed 26 September 2004)

Greenwood, J (1993) 'Reflective practice: a critique of the work of Argyris and Schön', *Journal of Advanced Nursing*, **17**, pp 1183–87

Grey, C and Mitlev, N (1995) 'Management education – a polemic', *Management Learning*, **26**, 1, pp 73–90

Grimmet, P P, Mackinnon, A M, Erickson, G L and Riecken, T J (1990) 'Reflective practice in teacher education', in R T Clift *et al* (eds), *Encouraging Reflective Practice in Education: An analysis of issues and programs*, Columbia University, Teachers College Press, pp 20–38

Gu, F and Lev, B (2001) *Intangible Assets: Measurement, drivers, usefulness*, Stern Business School, New York University [Online] www.stern.nyu.edu (accessed December 2001)

Guest, D (1995) 'Human Resource Management, trade unions and industrial relations', in J Storey (ed), *Human Resource Management: A critical text*, London, Routledge, pp 110–41

Guest, D (1996) 'The psychological contract', paper presented to IPD National Conference, Harrogate

Guest, D, Michie, J, Sheehan, M and Conway, N (2000) *Effective People Management*, London, CIPD

Gugler, P (1992) 'Building transnational alliances to create competitive advantage', *Long Range Planning*, **25**, 1, pp 90–99

Guthrie, J P (2001) 'High involvement work practices, turnover and productivity: evidence from New Zealand', *Academy of Management Journal*, **44**, 1, pp 180–90

Haanes, K and Lowendahl, B (1997) *The Unit of Activity: Towards an alternative to the theories of the firm, structure and style*, ed H Thomas, Copenhagen, Wiley

Hall, N (1976) *Cost Benefit Analysis in Industrial Training*, Manchester, Manchester University Department of Adult Education

Hamel, G and Prahalad, C K (1994) *Competing for the Future*, Cambridge, MA, Harvard Business School Press

Hampden-Turner, C M, Trompenaars, F, Lewis, D and Trompenaars, A (2000) *Building Cross-Cultural Competence: How to create wealth from conflicting values*, New Haven, CT, Yale University Press

Hancock, J (1994) 'Breaking the language barrier', *Training Technology and Human Resources*, **7**, 5, pp 5–7

Handy, C B (1985) *Understanding Organizations*, 3rd edn, Harmondsworth, Penguin

Handy, C (1987) *The Making of Managers: A report on management education, training and development in the United States, West Germany, France, Japan and the UK*, London, National Economic Development Office

Handy, C (1990) *The Age of Unreason*, London, Arrow

Handy, C (1993) *Understanding Organisations*, 4th edn, Harmondsworth, Penguin

Handy, C (1985) *The Future of Work*, Oxford, Blackwell

Handy, C (1997) *The Hungry Spirit*, London, Hutchinson

Hansen, C D and Brooks, A K (1994) 'A review of cross-cultural research on human resource development', *Human Resource Development Quarterly*, **5**, 1, pp 55–74

Harper, K (1993) 'Why flexible learning?', *Banking World*, **11**, 8, pp 45–46

Harris, F R, Johnston, M K, Kelley, C S and Wolf, M M (1965) 'Effects of positive social reinforcement on regressed crawling of a nursery school child', in L Ullmann and L Krasner (eds), *Case Studies in Behaviour Modification*, New York, Holt, Rinehart and Winston

Harris, L and Foster, C (2004) 'Diversity in the workplace', paper presented at the CIPD Professional Standards Conference, Keele University, 28–30 June

Harris, P R and Moran R T (1989) *Managing Cultural Differences*, Houston, TX, Gulf Publishing

Harris, P R and Moran, R T (1996) 'European leadership in globalization', *European Business Review*, pp 32–41

Harris, V (1997) *Teaching Learners How to Learn*, London, Centre for Language Teaching and Research

Harrison, R (1995) *Consultants Journey*, Maidenhead, McGraw-Hill

Harrison, R (1997) *Employee Development*, London, IPD

Harrison, R (2002) *Employee Development*, 3rd edn, London, CIPD

Harrison, R and Kessels, J (2004) *Human Resource Development in a Knowledge Economy: An organisational view*, Basingstoke, Palgrave Macmillan

Harvey, M G and Lusch, R F (1999) 'Balancing the intellectual capital books: intangible liabilities', *European Management Journal*, **17**, pp 29–41

Havergal, M and Edmonstone, J (2003) *The Facilitators Toolkit*, 2nd edn, Aldershot, Gower

Head, G E (1994) *Training Cost Analysis: A how to guide for trainers and managers*, rev edn, Alexandria, VA, ASTD

Heilbroner, R L (ed) (1986) *The Essential Adam Smith*, Oxford, Oxford University Press

Heinich, R, Molenda, M, Russell, J D and Smaldino, S E (1996) *Instruction, Media and Technologies for Learning*, 5th edn, Englewood Cliffs, NJ, Prentice Hall

Hendry, C (1995) *Human Resource Management: A strategic approach to employment*, Oxford, Butterworth-Heinemann

Hendry, C, Bradley, P and Perkins, S (1997) 'Missed a motivator', *People Management*, 15 May, p 20

Hendry, G D (1996) 'Constructivism and education practice', *Australian Journal of Education*, **40**, pp 19–45

Hendry, G D, Frommer, M and Walker, R A (1999) 'Constructivism and problem-based learning', *Journal of Further and Higher Education*, **23**, 3, pp 359–71

Heron, J (1989) *The Facilitator's Handbook*, London, Kogan Page

Heron, J (1993) *Group Facilitation*, London, Kogan Page

Heron, J (1996) 'Helping whole people learn', in D Boud and N Miller (eds), *Working With Experience: Animating learning*, London, Routledge, pp 73–91

Heron, J (2004) *The Complete Facilitator's Handbook*, London, Kogan Page

Herriot, P (1992) *The Career Management Challenge: Balancing individual and organizational needs*, London, Sage

Herriott, P and Pemberton, C (1997) 'Facilitating new deals', *Human Resources Management*, **7**, 1, pp 45–46

Higgs, M and Rowland, D (2003) 'Is change changing?', Henley Working Paper HWP 0313, Henley, Henley Management College

Hill, W (1997) *Learning: A survey of psychological interpretations*, 6th edn, New York, Longman

Hiltrop, J (1996) 'Managing the changing psychological contract', *Employee Relations*, **18**, 1, pp 36–49

Hirsch, W and Jackson, C (1995) *Careers in Organizations: Issues for the future report*, London, Institute of Employment Studies

Hmelo, C E and Lin, X (2004) 'Becoming self-directed learners: strategy development in problem-based learning', in D H Evensen and C E Hmelo (eds), *Problem-Based Learning: A research perspective on learning interactions*, New Jersey, Lawrence Erlbaum Associates

Hodgkinson, M (2000) 'Managerial perceptions of barriers to becoming a "learning organization"', *The Learning Organization*, **7**, 3–4, pp 156–66

Hodgkinson, M (2002) 'A shared strategic vision: dream or reality?', *The Learning Organization*, **9**, 2, pp 89–95

Hodkinson, R (1997) 'Japanese forced into HR strategy rethink', report by Arthur Andersen, London, *People Management*, 23 October, p 16

Hofstede, G (1994) *Cultures and Organizations*, London, HarperCollins

Holbeche, L (1997) *Motivating People in Lean Organizations*, Oxford, Butterworth-Heinemann

Holbeche, L (ed) *High Performance Organisation Checklist*, Horsham, Roffey Park Institute

Holdaway, K and Saunders, M (1996) *The In-house Trainer as Consultant*, 2nd edn, London, Kogan Page

Holden, L and Livian, Y (1992) 'Does strategic training policy exist? Some evidence from ten European countries'. *Personnel Review*, **21**, 1, pp 12–23

Holly, M L (1989) 'Reflective writing and the spirit of inquiry', *Cambridge Journal of Education*, **19**, 1, pp 71–80

Holman, D, Pavlica, K and Thorpe, R (1997) 'Rethinking Kolb's theory of experiential learning in management education', *Management Learning*, **28**,2, pp 135–48

Holmes, R (1987) *The People's Kingdom*, London, Bodley Head

Holyfield, J and Moloney, K (1996) *Using National Standards to Improve Performance*, London, Kogan Page

Homans, G (1951) *The Human Group*, London, Routledge and Kegan Paul

Honey, P (1994) *101 Ways to Develop Your People Without Really Trying*, Maidenhead, Honey

Honey, P (1997) *Improve Your People Skills*, 2nd edn, London, IPD

Honey, P and Mumford, A (1986) *Manual of Learning Styles*, London, Peter Honey

Honey, P and Mumford, A (1992) *Manual of Learning Styles*, 3rd edn, Maidenhead, Honey

Höpfl, H and Dawes, F (1995) 'A whole can of worms! The contested frontiers of management development and learning', *Personnel Review*, **24**, 6, pp 19–28

Horkheimer, M (1947) *Eclipse of Reason*, Oxford, Oxford University Press

Hospers, J (1990) *An Introduction to Philosophical Analysis*, London, Routledge

Huang, Tung-Chun (1997) 'The effect of participative management on organizational performance: the case of Taiwan', *International Journal of Human Resource Management*, **8**, 5, pp 677–89

Hunt, C (1998) 'Learning from Lerner: reflections on facilitating reflective practice', *Journal of Further and Higher Education*, **22**, 1, pp 25–31

Hunt, C (2001) 'Shifting shadows: metaphors and maps for facilitating reflective practice', *Reflective Practice*, **2**, 3, pp 275–87

Huselid, M A (2003) Presentation to DTI Accounting for People seminar, London, 18 July

Husert, T (ed) (1967) *International Study of Attainments in Mathematics*, Stockholm, Almqvist & Wiksell

Ibbetson, A and Newell, S (1996) 'Winner takes all. An evaluation of adventure based experiential learning', *Management Learning*, **27**, 2, pp 163–85

Ichijo, K, von Krogh, G and Nonaka, I (1998) 'Knowledge enablers', in G von Krogh, J Roos and D Kleine (eds), *Knowing in Firms: Understanding, managing and measuring knowledge*, London, Sage, pp 173–203

Ichniowski, C, Shaw, K and Prenushi, G (1997) 'The effects of human resource practices on productivity: a study of steel finishing lines', *American Economic Review*, **87**, 3, pp 291–313

Igonor, A (2002) 'Success factors for development of knowledge management in e-learning in Gulf region institutions', *Journal of Knowledge Management Practice*, **3**

Incomes Data Services (1997) *Recruitment, Training and Development*, London, Institute of Personnel and. Development

International Labour Organization (ILO) (1977) *Meeting Basic Needs*, Geneva, ILO

International Labour Organisation and International Federation of Training and Development (2002) [Online] http://www.ilo.org

Institute of Personnel and Development (IPD) (1996) *Managing Diversity: A Position Paper*, London, IPD

IPD (1997a) *Reward Management Portfolio*, London, IPD, p 7

IPD (1997b) *Issues in People Management No. 22, Impact of people management practices on business performance*, London, IPD, p 16

IPD (1997c) *Consultative Document: Opportunity through people*, London, IPD

IPD (1997d) *The IPD Guide On on International Management Development*, London, IPD

IPD (1998) *A Guide to Outdoor Training*, London, IPD

IPD (undated) *Continuing Professional Development*, London, IPD

Investors in People (IiP) (1991) *The National Standard: Links to assessment indicators*, Sheffield, Employment Department (Investors in People UK, 4th Floor, 7–10 Chandos Street, London W1M 9DE. Tel 020 7467 1900; website www.investorsinpeople.co.uk)

IiP (2000) *The National Standard*, London, Investors in People

Irvine, D and Wilson, J P (1994) 'Outdoor management development – reality or illusion?', *Journal of Management Development*, **13**, 5, pp 25–37

Ismail, A and Ganuza, J L (1997) 'Internet en la education', Madrid, Anaya Multimedia

Jackson, D (1995) 'A winning strategy', *Training Officer*, **31**, 5, pp 136–37

Jacobs, R (1990) 'Human resource development as an interdisciplinary body of knowledge', *Human Resource Development Quarterly*, **1**, 1, pp 65–71

Jacobs, R L and Jones, M J (1995) *Structured On-the-job Training: Unleashing employee expertise in the workplace*, San Francisco, CA, Berrett-Koehler

Johnson, G (1987) *Strategic Change and the Management Process*, Oxford, Blackwell

Johnson, G and Scholes, K (2002) *Exploring Corporate Strategy*, 6th edn, Hemel Hempstead, Prentice Hall

Johnston, C (2004) 'MPs to probe e-uni collapse', *Times Higher Education Supplement*, 11 June, p 12

Johnston, R (1993) 'The role of distance learning in professional development', *Management Services*, **37**, 4, pp 24–26

Johnston, R (1997) 'Distance learning: medium or message', *Journal of Further and Higher Education*, **21**, 1, p 107–22

Johnston, R and Badley, G (1996) 'The competent reflective practitioner', *Innovation and Learning in Education*, **2**, 1, pp 4–10

Jones, M and Mann, P (1992) *International Perspectives on Development and Learning*, West Hartford, CT, Kumarian Press

Jones, R (1993) *How to Master Languages*, Plymouth, How to Books

Joy-Matthews, J, Megginson, D and Surtees, M (2004) *Human Resource Development*, London, Kogan Page

Julien, P A (1996) 'Globalization: different types of small business behaviour', *Entrepreneurship and Regional Development*, **8**, 1, pp 57–74

Juran, J M (1989) *Juran on Leadership for Quality: An executive handbook*, New York, Free Press

Kakabadse, A and Korac-Kakabadse, N (2000) 'Leading the pack: future role of IS/IT professionals', *Journal of Management Development*, **19**, 2, pp 97–155

Kandola, R and Fullerton, J (1994) *Managing the Mosaic: Diversity in action*, London, IPD

Kanet, J J and Barut, M (2003) 'Problem-based learning for production and operations management', *Decision Sciences Journal of Innovative Education*, **1**, 1 pp 99–118

Kapenieks, A, Zuga, B, Buligina, I, Gercane, L, Kulitane, I, Vucena, A, Rudzite, M and Trapenciere, I (2004) 'Innovative e-learning in regional development projects in Latvia', Report prepared within EU 5th Framework programme project Higher Education Reform Network (HERN), Seminar in Glasgow 'Key Features of Teaching and Learning in the University of Learning', 21–24 January 2004, Continuing Education Development Foundation, Latvia

Kaplan, R S (1996) 'Using the Balanced Scorecard as a strategic management system', *Harvard Business Review* (January–February), pp 75–85

Kaplan, R S and Norton, D P (1992) 'The balanced scorecard measures that drive performance', *Harvard Business Review*, **70**, 1, January–February, pp 71–79

Kaplan, R S and Norton, D P (1993) 'Putting the balanced scorecard to work" *Harvard Business Review*, September–October

Kaplan, R S and Norton, D P (2000) 'Having trouble with your strategy? Then map it', *Harvard Business Review*, September–October, p 169

Katz, H C, Kochan, T A and Keefe, J H (1987) 'Industrial relations and productivity in the US automobile industry', *Brookings Papers on Economic Activity*, **3**, pp 688–715

Katzenbach, J R and Smith, D K (1993) *The Wisdom of Teams*, New York, HarperCollins

Kay, A S (1995) 'The business case for multimedia', *Datamation*, **4**, 11, pp 55–56

Keep, E and Mayhew, K (1991) 'The assessment: education, training and economic performance', in G Esland (ed), *Education, Training and Employment, Vol. I, Educated Labour – The changing basis of industrial demand*, Wokingham, Addison-Wesley, pp 193–213

Kelly, G (1955) *The Psychology of Personal Constructs*, New York, Norton

Kenney, J and Reid, M (1986) *Training Interventions*, London, IPM

Kickul, J and Kickul, G (2004) 'E-learning challenges and processes: understanding the role of student self-efficacy and learning goal orientation', *International Journal of Management Education*, **4**, 1, pp 29–38

Kidd, J R (1983) *How Adults Learn*, revised edn, New York, Associated Press

Kilcourse, T (1996) 'Human resource development –a contingency function? (Whatever happened to theory Y?)', *Journal of European Industrial Training*, **20**, 9, pp 3–8

Killen, K H (1977) *Management*, Boston, MA, Houghton Mifflin

Kirkpatrick, D (1967 and 1994) *Evaluating Training Programmes*, San Francisco, CA, Berrett-Koehler

Kleiner, A and Roth, G (1998) 'How to make experience your company's best teacher', *Harvard Business Review on Knowledge Management*, Boston, MA, Harvard Business School Press, pp 137–51

Kling, J (1995) 'High performance work systems and firm performance', *Monthly Labour Review*, May, pp 29–36

Kluge, J, Stein, W and Licht, T (2001) *Knowledge Unplugged: The McKinsey & Company global survey on knowledge management*, Basingstoke, Palgrave

Knights, K and Sampson, J (1995) 'Reflection in the context of team-teaching'' *Studies in Education*, **17**, 1, pp 58–69

Knowles, M (1990) *The Adult Learner: A neglected species*, Houston, TX, Gulf Publishing (first published 1973)

Koch, H L (1996) 'Middle managers targeted for second language training (Spanish) can be screened and educated more efficiently', *Journal of European Industrial Training*, **20**, 7, pp 24–28

Kochan, T A and Barocci, T A (1985) *Human Resource Management and Industrial Relations*, Boston, MA, Little, Brown

Kogal, B and Zander U (1999) 'Knowledge of the firm and the evolutionary theory of the multinational corporation', *Journal of Intellectual Business Studies*, **24**, pp 625–45

Kohler, W I (1925) *The Mentality of Apes*, New York, Brace and World

Kohn, A (1993) 'Challenging behaviourist dogma: myths about money and motivation', *Compensation and Benefits Review*, March–April, pp 35–37

Kolb, D A 1984) *Experiential Learning: Experience as the source of learning and development*, Englewood Cliffs, NJ, Prentice Hall

Kolb, D A, Rubin, I M and McIntyre, J M (1974) *Organizational Psychology: An experiential approach*, Englewood Cliffs, NJ, Prentice-Hall

Koontz, H, O'Donnell, C and Weihrich, H (1984) *Management*, 8th edn, Maidenhead, McGraw-Hill

Kotler, P and Armstrong, G (1994) *Principles of Marketing*, 6th edn, Englewood Cliffs, NJ, Prentice Hall

Krashen, S (1982) *Principles and Practice in Second Language Acquisition*, Oxford, Pergamon

Krathwold, D R, Bloom, B S and Masis, B B (1964) *Taxonomy of Educational Objectives: The classification of educational goals, Handbook 2: Affective domain*, London, Longmans, Green

Kubr, M (1986) *Management Consulting: A guide to the profession*, Geneva, ILO

Kubr, M (1993) *How to Select and Use Consultants*, Managing Development Series 31, Geneva, ILO

La Fasto, F (1992) 'Baxter Healthcare Corporation', in B W Jackson, F La Fasto, H G Schmaltz and D Kelly, 'Diversity', *Human Resource Management*, **31**, 1 and 2

Labich, K (1996) 'Making diversity pay', *Fortune*, **134**, 5, pp 113–15

Languages Lead Body (1995) *Implementing the National Language Standards*, London, Languages Lead Body

Laurillard, D M (2002) *Rethinking University Teaching*, 2nd edn, London, RoutledgeFalmer

Lave, J, and Wenger, E (1991) *Situated Learning: Legitimate peripheral participation*, New York/Cambridge, Cambridge University Press

Lawler, E E (1995) 'The new pay: a strategic approach', *Compensation and Benefits Review*, July–August, pp 14–22

Lee, R (1996) 'What makes training pay?', *Issues in People Management*, **11**, London, IPD

Legge, K (1995) 'HRM: rhetoric, reality and hidden agendas', in J Storey, J (ed), *Human Resource Management: A critical text*, London, Routledge, pp 33–59

Leigh, D (1996) *Designing and Delivering Training for Groups*, London, Kogan Page

Levitt, T (1983) 'The globalization of markets', *Harvard Business Review*, May/June, pp 92–102

Levitt, T (1991) 'Marketing myopia', *The Best of the Harvard Business Review*, Boston, MA, Harvard Business School

Lewin, K (1951) *Field Theory in Social Science*, London, Tavistock

Lewis, P (1991) 'Eight steps to the successful appointment of a training consultant', *Journal of European and Industrial Training*, **15**, 6, pp 25–29

Lewis, P (2001) 'Reward management', in T Redman and A Wilkinson (eds), *Contemporary Human Resource Management: Text and cases*, Harlow, FT/Prentice Hall, Pearson Education

Lieberman, S, Berardo, K, Simons, G (2003) *Putting Diversity to Work*, New York, Crisp

Liebowitz, J (1999) *Knowledge Management Handbook*, Boca Raton, FL, CRC Press

Lightbown, P M and Spada, N (1993) *How Languages are Learned*, Oxford, Oxford University Press

Likert, R (1961) *New Patterns of Management*, New York, McGraw-Hill

Linton, I (1997) *Marketing Training Services*, Aldershot, Gower

Little, B (1994) 'Language matters', *Training and Development*, **12**, 12, pp 15–16

Little, D and Brammerts, H (eds) (1996) *A Guide to Language Learning in Tandem via the Internet*, CLCS Occasional Paper No 46, Trinity College, Dublin

Littlefield, D (1994) 'Open learning by PC or paper?', *Personnel Management*, **25**, 9, p 55

Long, P (1986) *Performance Appraisal Revisited: Third IPM survey*, London, IPM

Losey, M R (1999) 'Mastering the competencies of HR managers', *Human Resource Management*, **38**, 2, pp 99–111

Lowe, P and Lewis, R (1994) *Management Development Beyond the Fringe*, London, Kogan Page

Luecke, R (2003) *Managing Change and Transition*, Boston, MA, HBS Press

Lumby, S (1995) *Investment Appraisal and Financial Decisions*, 5th edn, London, Chapman Hall

Lupton, T (1971) *Management and the Social Sciences*, Harmondsworth, Penguin

Mabey, C and Salaman, G (1995) *Strategic Human Resource Management*, Oxford, Blackwell

MacDuffie, J P (1995) 'Human resource bundles and manufacturing performance: organizational logic and flexible production systems in the world auto industry', *Industrial Labour Relations Review*, **48**, pp 197–221

MacIntyre, A (1994) *After Virtue*, 2nd edn, London, Duckworth

Mager, R F (1991) *Preparing Instructional Objectives*, 2nd edn, London, Kogan Page

Maister, D (1989) 'Professional service firm management', in M Kubr (ed), *How to Select and Use Consultants*, Managing Development Series 31, Geneva, ILO

Malaysia: The Seventh Malaysia Plan 1996–2000 (1996) Prime Minister's Department, May, Percetakan Nasional Malaysia Berhad

Malone, S A (1997) *How to Set Up and Manage a Corporate Learning Centre*, Aldershot, Gower

Management Charter Initiative (1997) *Management Standards: Key role A – Manage activities*, London, (For further details contact: MCI, Russell Square House, 10–12 Russell Square, London WC1B 5BZ Tel 020 7872 9000; website: www.mci.org.uk)

Manpower Services Commission (MSC) (1981) *Glossary of Training Terms*, 3rd edn, London, HMSO

MSC (1981) *A New Training Initiative: Agenda for action.* Sheffield, Manpower Services Commission

MSC (1985) *A Glossary of Terms Used in Education and Training*, Sheffield, Training Division, MSC

Marchand, D A (1998) 'Competing with intellectual capital', in G von Krogh, J Roos and D Kleine (eds), *Knowing in Firms: Understanding, managing and measuring knowledge*, London, Sage, pp 253–68

Marchington, M (1995) 'Fairy tales and magic wands: new employment practices in perspective', *Employee Relations*, **17**, 1, pp 51–66

Margerison, C (1988) *Managerial Consulting Styles*, Aldershot, Gower

Margerison, C J (1995) *Managerial Consulting Skills*, Aldershot, Gower

Margetson, D (1997) 'Why is problem-based learning a challenge?', in D Boud and G Feletti (eds), *The Challenge of Problem Based Learning*, 2nd edn, London, Kogan Page

Marginson, P *et al* (1993) *The Control of Industrial Relations in Large Companies*, Research Paper No 45, Industrial Relations Research Unit, University of Warwick

Marx, W (1995) 'The new high tech training', *Management Review*, **84**, 2, pp 57–60

Maslow, A H (1954) *Motivation and Personality*, New York, Harper

Maslow, A H (1965) *Eupsychian Management*, Homewood, IL, Irwin/Dorsey

Massachusetts Institute of Technology (MIT) (1989) *Made in America*, Cambridge, MA, MIT Press

Matikainen, J (2002) 'Web-based learning environments – a scene of social interaction', *Lifelong Learning in Europe*, **7**, 4, pp 247–54

Maurais, J and Morris, M A (eds) (2003) *Languages in a Globalising World*, Cambridge, Cambridge University Press

Mayfield, E C and Carlson, R E (1966) 'Selection interview decisions: first results from a long-term research project', *Personnel Psychology*, **19**, pp 41–53

Mayo, A (2000) 'The role of employee development in the growth of intellectual capital', *Personnel Review*, **29**, 4, pp 521–33

Mayo, A and Pickard, J (1998) 'Memory bankers', *People Management*, 22 January, pp 34–38

McBeath, G (1990) *Practical Management Development: Strategies for management resourcing and development in the 1990s*, Oxford, Blackwell

McCalman, J and Paton, R A (1992) *Change Management: A guide to effective implementation*, London, Paul Chapman

McCarthy, D (1997) 'A critical analysis of the learning organisation concept with a view to establishing a framework for assessment and action', MEd dissertation, University of Sheffield

McDermott, R (1999) 'Knowledge management: why information technology inspired but cannot deliver knowledge management', *California Management Review*, **41**, 4, pp 103–17

McDrury, J and Alterio, M (2003) *Learning Through Storytelling in Higher Education: Using reflection and experience to improve learning*, London, Kogan Page

McGill, I and Beaty, L (1992) *Action Learning: A practitioner's guide*, London, Kogan Page

McGoldrick, J and Stewart, J (1996) 'The HRM–HRD nexus', in J Stewart and J McGoldrick (eds), *Human Resource Development: Perspectives, strategies and practice*, London, Pitman, pp 9–27

McGregor, D (1954) 'An uneasy look at performance appraisal', *Harvard Business Review*, **35**, 3, pp 89–94

McLagan, P A and Suhadolnik, D (1989) *Models for HRD Practice: The research report*, Alexandria, VA, ASTD Press

McLaney, E J (1991) *Business Finance for Decision Makers*, London, Pitman

McPherson, M A (2003) 'Planning for success in elearning in HE: a strategic view', in F Jakab and A Čižmár (eds), *Proceedings of the 2nd International Conference on Emerging Telecommunications Technologies and Applications and the 4th Conference on Virtual University (ICETA 2003)*, 11–13 September 2003, Košice, Slovak Republic, pp 449–52

McPherson, M A and Nunes, J M (2004) *Developing Innovation in Online Learning: An action research framework*, London, RoutledgeFalmer

McPherson, M A, Nunes, J M and Zafeiriou, G (2003) 'New tutoring skills for online learning: are e-tutors adequately prepared for e-learning delivery?', in A Szücs, E Wagner and C Tsolkidis (eds), *Proceedings of 12th European Distance Education Network Annual Conference on The Quality Dialogue; Integrating Quality Cultures in Flexible, Distance and eLearning (EDEN 2003)*, 15–18 June 2003, Rodos Palace Hotel, Rhodes, Greece, pp 347–50

Megginson, D (1994) 'Planned and emergent learning: a framework and a method', *Executive Development*, **7**, 6, pp 29–32

Megginson, D, Joy-Matthews, J and Banfield, P (1999) *Human Resource Development*, London, Kogan Page

Megginson, D and Whittaker, V (1996) *Cultivating Self-Development*, IPD Guide, London, IPD

Mercer Consulting (2004) quoted in 'Partnership drives worldwide change', *People Management*, **9**, 17, p 12

Merrick, N (1998) 'Theatrical treatment', *People Management*, 22 January, pp 44–46

Mezirow, J (1978) 'Perspective transformation', *Adult Education*, **28**, 2, pp 100–10

Mezirow, J (1981) 'Critical theory of adult learning and education', *Adult Education*, **32**, 1, pp 3–24

Mezirow, J (1991) *Transformative Dimensions of Adult Learning*, San Francisco, CA, Jossey-Bass

Mezirow, J and Associates (1990) *Fostering Critical Reflection in Adulthood: A guide to transformative and emancipatory learning*, Albany, State University of New York Press

Mills, C W (1967) *The Sociological Imagination*, Oxford, Oxford University Press

Millward, N (1993) 'Industrial relations in transition: the findings of the Third Workplace Industrial Relations Survey', paper presented to BUIRA, York, July

Milsome, S, Holmes, R and Suff, P (2003) *Creating High Performance Workplaces*, London, Work Foundation

Mintzberg, H (1973) *The Nature of Managerial Work*, New York, Harper & Row

Mintzberg, H (1979) *The Structuring of Organizations*, Englewood Cliffs, NJ, Prentice-Hall

Minzberg, H (1983) *Structure in Fives: Designing effective organizations*, Englewood Cliffs, NJ, Prentice Hall

Minzberg, H (1987) 'Grafting strategy', *Harvard Business Review*, July–August, pp 66–75

Mintzberg, H (1991) 'The manager's job: folklore and fact', *The Best of the Harvard Business Review*, Boston, MA, Harvard Business School

Mohrman, A M and Mohrman, S A (1995) *Performance Management is Running the Business: The new pay tool*, New York, American Management Association, p 2

Mohrman, S A and Lawler, E E III (1999) 'The new human resources management: creating the strategic business partnership', in R S Schuler and S E Jackson (eds), *Strategic Human Resource Management*, Oxford, Blackwell

Mokyr, J (1990) *The Lever of Riches: Technological creativity and economic progress*, New York, Oxford University Press

Mon, J A (1999) *Reflection in Learning and Professional Development: Theory and practice*, London, Kogan Page

Moody, M (2003) 'Training in diversity', *Workplace Diversity and Discrimination*, Croner Briefing, 1, September, p 5

Moon, J A (1999) *Reflection in Learning and Professional Development*, London, Kogan Page

Moorby, E (1991) *How to Succeed in Employee Development*, Maidenhead, McGraw-Hill

Morgan, G (1997) *Imaginization: New mindsets for seeing, organizing, and managing*, San Francisco, CA, Sage

Moore, M (1993) 'Three types of interaction', in K Harry, M John and D Keegan (eds), *Distance Education: New perspectives*, London, Routledge

Morrison, K (1996) 'Developing reflective practice in higher degree students through a learning journal', *Studies in Higher Education*, **21**, 3, pp 317–32

Mortiboys, A. (2002) *The Emotionally Intelligent Lecturer*, Birmingham, SEDA Publications

Mortiboys, R J (1991) *Leadership and Quality Management: A guide for chief executives*, London, Department of Trade and Industry

Mortlock, C (1987) *The Adventure Alternative*, Cumbria, Cicerone Press

Moseley, D (2004) 'Out of style', *People Management*, July, p 44

Mounce, H O (1988) 'The aroma of coffee', *Philosophy*, **64**, pp 159–73

Mumford, A (1995) *Learning at the Top*, London, McGraw-Hill

Mumford, A (2001) 'A learning approach to strategy', *Journal of Workplace Learning*, **12**, 2, pp 265–71

Murphy, J (1972) *The Education Act 1870: Text and commentary*, Newton Abbot, David and Charles

Nadler, L and Nadler, Z (eds) (1990) *The Handbook of Human Resource Development*, 2nd edn, New York, Wiley

Nagel, T (1979) 'What it is like to be a bat', *Mortal Questions*, Cambridge, Cambridge University Press

Nahapiet, J and Ghoshal, S (1998) 'Social capital, intellectual capital and the organizational advantage', *Academy of Management Review*, **22**, 2, pp 242–68

Nato, T (1988) 'The basis of life–innovator economies', in M A Choudary (ed), *Policy: Theoretical Foundations of Ethico-Economics*, Sydney, Nova Scotia, Centre of Humanomics, pp 83–96

Nemiroff, G H (1992) *Reconstructing Education: Toward a pedagogy of critical humanism*, Westport, CT, Bergin and Garvey/Greenwood Press

Nevis, E C (1987) *Organizational Consulting: A gestalt approach*, New York, Gardner Press

Newby, A (1992) *Cost Effective Training: A manager's guide*, London, Kogan Page

Newby, T (1992) *Validating Your Training*, London, Kogan Page

Newell, S (2002) *Creating the Healthy Organisation: Wellbeing, diversity and ethics at work*, London, Thomson Learning

Newman, M (2004) *A Systematic Review and Meta-analysis on the Effectiveness of Problem Based Learning LTSN* [Online] http://www.regard.ac.uk/research_findings/L139251097/report.pdf

Nielsen, S P and Visser, K (1997) *Quality Debate in Initial Vocational Education: School-based quality measures at intermediate level: A Danish–Dutch comparison*, Thessaloniki, CEDEFOP

Nonaka, I (1998) 'The knowledge creating company', *Harvard Business Review on Knowledge Management*, Boston, MA, Harvard Business School Press, pp 21–45

Nonaka, I, and Takeuchi, H (1995) *The Knowledge-Creating Company: How Japanese companies create the dynamics of innovation*, Oxford, Oxford University Press

Nonaka, I and Toyama, R (2004) 'Knowledge creation as a synthesizing process', in H Takeuchi and I Nonaka (eds), *Hitotsubashi on Knowledge Management*, Singapore, Wiley Asia

Norton, B *et al.* (eds) (2004) *Critical Pedagogies and Language Learning*, Cambridge, Cambridge University Press

Nunes, J M (1999) 'The experiential dual layer model (EDLM): a conceptual model integrating a constructivist theoretical approach to academic learning with the process of hypermedia design', PhD thesis, University of Sheffield

Nunes, J M and Fowell, S P (1996) 'Hypermedia as an experiential learning tool: a theoretical model', *Information Research*, **2**, 1, August [Online] http://informationr.net/ir/2–1/paper12.html (accessed 15 November 2003)

Nunes, J M and McPherson, M A (2003) 'Using an educational systems design (ESD) framework to support action research in continuing professional distance education', *Journal of Computer Assisted Learning*, **19**, 4, pp 429–37

Nunes, J M, McPherson, M A and Rico, M (2000) 'Design and development of a networked learning skills module for web-based collaborative distance learning', in *Proceedings of 1st ODL International Workshop, 2000*, Universidad Politécnica de Valencia, Centro de Formación de Postgrado, Valencia, Spain, 19–21 July 2000, pp 117–31

Oakland, J S (1997) *Total Quality Management*, Oxford, Butterworth-Heinemann

Ohmae, K (1991) *The Mind of the Strategist: The art of Japanese business*, New York, McGraw-Hill Educational

Organization for Economic Cooperation and Development (OECD) (1989a) *New Technologies in the 1990s: A socio-economic strategy*, Paris, OECD

OECD (1989b) *Education and the Economy in a Changing Society*, Paris, OECD

OECD (1990) *Human Resource and New Technology: Main trends and issues*, Centre for Educational Research and Innovation, Paris, OECD

OECD (1994) *Jobs Study*, Paris, OECD

Örtenblad, A (2001) 'On differences between organizational learning and learning organization', *The Learning Organization*, **8**, 3–4, pp 125–33

Örtenblad, A (2004) 'Toward a contingency model of how to choose the right type of learning organization', *Human Resource Development Quarterly*, **15**, 3, pp 347–50

Ortigas, C D (1994) *Human Resource Development: The Philippine experience, readings for the practitioner*, Manila, Ateneo de Manila University Press

Otter, S (1992) *Learning Outcomes in Higher Education*, London, Employment Department FEU

Ouseley, H (1994) 'Facing up to the challenge of a diverse workforce', *Personnel Today Conference Daily*, 27 October, IPD Conference

Palmer, R (2002) *Training with the Midas Touch: Developing your organization's greatest asset*, London, Kogan Page

Palmer, R and Wilson, J P (1995) 'Maintaining the energy for commitment to quality', *Training for Quality*, **3**, 2, pp 9–13

Parikh, J (1991) *Managing Yourself – Management by detached involvement*, Oxford, Blackwell

Parkin, G (2001) 'How do success factors for e-learning differ from success factors for classroom training?', *Learning Circuits*, November [Online] http://www.learningcircuits.org/2001/nov2001/geek2.html (accessed 17 August 2004)

Parkin, M (1998) *Tales for Trainers*, London, Kogan Page

Parry, S B (1997) *Evaluating the Impact of Training*, Alexandria, VA, American Society for Training and Development

Parsloe, E and Wray, M (2000) *Coaching and Mentoring*, London, Kogan Page

Parsons, J G (1997) 'Values as a vital supplement to the use of financial analysis in HRD', *Human Resource Development Quarterly*, **8**, 1, pp 5–13

Pascale, R (1995) 'In search of the new "employment contract"', *Human Resources*, November/December, pp 21–26

Paton, R and Hooker, C (1990) *Developing Managers in Voluntary Organizations – A handbook*, Sheffield, Employment Department

Patterson, M G, West, M A, Lawthom, R and Nickell, S (1997) 'Impact of people management practices on business performance', *Issues in People Management*, No. 22, London, IPD

Patton, M Q (1990) *Qualitative Evaluation and Research Methods*, London, Sage

Pavlov, J P (1927) *Conditioned Reflexes*, Oxford, Oxford University Press

Pawson, R and Tilley, N (1997) *Realistic Evaluation*, London, Sage

Pearn, M and Kandola, R (1988/90) *Job Analysis: A practical guide for managers*, London, IPM

Pearn, M and Kandola, R (1990) *Job Analysis: A practical guide for managers*, London, IPM

Pedler, M (1990) *Self-development in Organisations*, New York, McGraw-Hill

Pedler, M, and Aspinwall, K (1996) *'Perfect plc'? The purpose and practice of organizational learning*, London, McGraw-Hill

Pedler, M, Burgoyne, J, and Boydell, T (1989) 'Towards the learning company', *Management Education and Development*, **20**, 1, pp 1–8

Pedler, M, Burgoyne, J and Boydell, T (1991/97) *The Learning Company: A strategy for sustainable development*, London, McGraw-Hill, 2nd edn, Maidenhead, McGraw-Hill

Pepper, A D (1984) *Managing the Training and Development Function*, Aldershot, Gower

Peters, T (1989) *Thriving on Chaos*, London, Pan

Peters, T (1993) *Liberation Management*, London, Pan

Peters, T and Waterman, R (1982) *In Search of Excellence*, New York, Harper and Row

Pettigrew, A, Sparrow, P and Hendry, C (1988) 'The forces that trigger training', *Personnel Management*, December, pp 28–32

Phillips, E M and Pugh, D S (1994) *How to Get a PhD*, 2nd edn, Buckingham, Open University Press

Phillips, J J (1991) *Handbook of Training Evaluation and Measurement Methods*, 2nd edn, London, Kogan Page

Phillips, J J (1994a) *Measuring Return on Investment, Volume 1*, Alexandria, VA, American Society for Training and Development

Phillips, J J (1994b) *Measuring Return on Investment, Volume 2*, Alexandria, VA, American Society for Training and Development

Phillips, J J (1997) *Handbook of Training Evaluation and Measurement Methods: Proven models and methods for evaluating any HRD programe*, Houston, TX, Gulf Publishing

Phillips, K and Shaw, P (1996) *A Consultancy Approach for Trainers*, Aldershot, Gower

Phillips, P P (2002) *Understanding the Basics of Return on Investment in Training: Assessing the tangible and intangible benefits*, London, Kogan Page

Piaget, J (1950) *The Psychology of Intelligence*, London, Routledge and Kegan Paul

Pickard, J (1996) 'A fertile grounding', *People Management*, **2**, 21, pp 28–37

Pickard, J (2004) 'One step beyond', *People Management*, 30 June

Pinker, S (1984) *Language Learnability and Language Development*, Cambridge, MA, Harvard University Press

Pinker, S (1995) *The Language Instinct*, Harmondsworth, Penguin

Pinker, S (1997) *How the Mind Works*, London, Allen Lane

Pisano, G, Teece, D and Shuen, A (1997) 'Dynamic capabilities and strategic management', *Strategic Management Journal*, **18**

Pittinsky, T and Shih, M (2004) 'Retention as a lead HR measure of commitment?', *American Behavioral Scientist*, February

Plant, R and Ryan, R (1992) 'Training evaluation: a procedure for validating an organization's investment in training,' *Journal of European Industrial Training*, **16**, 10, pp 22–38

Poell, R F (1998) 'Organizing work-related learning projects: a network approach', PhD thesis, University of Nijmegen, Netherlands

Poell, R F and Tijmensen, E C M (1998) 'Using learning projects to work towards a learning organisation: two cases from professional work', in R F Poell and G E Chivers (eds), *Continuing Professional Development in Europe: Theoretical views, fields of application, and national policies*, Sheffield, University of Sheffield, pp 43–57

Poell, R F, Tijmensen, E C M and Van der Krogt, F J (1997) 'Can learning projects contribute to develop a learning organisation?', *Lifelong Learning in Europe*, **2**, 2, pp 67–75

Polanyi, M (1967) *The Tacit Dimension*, London, Routledge and Kegan Paul

Pollet, I (1992) 'Training and employment of the underprivileged: the role of social partners', *Journal of European Industrial Training*, **16**, 9, pp 23–28

Pont, T (1995) *Investing in Training and Development*, London, Kogan Page

Porter, M E (1980) *Competitive Strategy*, New York, Free Press

Porter, M E (1990) *The Competitive Advantage of Nations*, New York, Free Press

Porter, M E (2004) *Competitive Advantage*, New York, Free Press

Power, M (1997) *The Audit Society: Rituals of verification*, Oxford, Oxford University Press

Prais, S J (1995) *Productivity, Education and Training: An international perspective*, Cambridge, Cambridge University Press

Prahalad, C K and Hamel, G (1990) 'The core competence of the corporation', *Harvard Business Review*, May/June, pp 79–91

Purcell, J (1992) 'The impact of corporate strategy', in M Armstrong (ed), *Strategy and Action*, London, Kogan Page

Raab, N (1997) 'Becoming an expert in not knowing – retraining teacher as consultant', *Management Learning*, **28**, 2, pp 161–75

Radford, A (1995) *Managing People in Professional Practices*, London, IPD

Rae, L (1995) *Techniques of Training*, 3rd edn, Aldershot, Gower

Ralphs, L and Stephan, E (1986) 'HRD in the Fortune 500', *Training and Development Journal*, **40**, 10, pp 69–76

Ramhorst, D (2000) 'A guided tour through the Siemens Business Services knowledge management framework', in T H Davenport and G Probst (eds), *Knowledge Management Casebook: Siemens best practices*, Munich, Publicis MCD Verlag/Wiley, pp 126–40

Randall, R and Southgate, J (1980) *Cooperative and Community Group Dynamics*, London, Barefoot Books

Raw, T (1991) 'Using the outdoors as a learning medium for young people', *Transition*, pp 13–14

Rees, J I and Rees, C J (1996) 'Lost for words … and losing business', *Industrial and Commercial Training*, **28**, 3, pp 8–13

Reeves, T and Hedberg, J (2003) *Interactive Learning Systems Evaluation*, Englewood Cliffs, NJ, Educational Technology Publications

Reid, M A and Barrington, H (1997) *Training Interventions*, 5th edn, London, IPD

Revans, R W (1982) *The Origins and Growth of Action Learning*, Bromley, Chartwell-Bratt

Reynolds, M (1990) 'A biography of self-development', in M Pedler, J Burgoyne, T Boydel and G Welshman (eds), *Self-Development in Organizations*, Maidenhead, McGraw-Hill, pp 3–19

Reynolds, M (1997) 'Learning styles: a critique', *Management Learning*, **28**, 2, pp 115–33

Reynolds, M (1999) 'Grasping the nettle: possibilities and pitfalls of a critical management pedagogy', *British Journal of Management*, **9**, pp 171–84

Richards, J C and Renandya, W A (eds) (2002) *Methodology in Language Teaching: An anthology of current practice*, Cambridge, CUP

Robbins, S P (1991/3) *Organizational Behavior*, 5th/6th edns, Englewood Cliffs, NJ, Prentice Hall

Roberts, G (1997) *Recruitment and Selection: A competency approach*, London, IPD

Robertson, A (1994) Contribution to *Module 2: Human Resource Management and Equal Opportunities*, MEd in Training and Development programme, Division of Adult Continuing Education, University of Sheffield, unpublished

Rodwell, J (1994) *Participative Training Skills*, Aldershot, Gower

Rogers, A (1986) *Teaching Adults*, Buckingham, Open University Press

Rogers, A (1998) 'Computers add up for accountants', *Sunday Times*, 4 October, pp 7–11

Rogers, C (1974) *On Becoming a Person*, London, BBC Publications

Rogers, C (1993) *The Carl Rogers Reader*, London, Constable

Roos, G, Roos, J, Edvinsson, L and Dragonetti, N C (1997) *Intellectual Capital: Navigating in the new business landscape*, New York, New York University Press

Ross, M B (1982) 'Coping with conflict', in J W Pfeiffer (ed), *The 1982 Annual for Facilitators, Trainers and Consultants*, San Diego, CA, Pfeiffer

Rowntree, D (1992) *Exploring Open and Distance Learning*, London, Kogan Page

Ryan, P (1991) *International Comparisons of Vocational Education and Training for Intermediate Skills*, London, Palmer Press

Salaman, G (ed) (1992) *Human Resource Strategies*, London, Sage

Salmon, G (2000) *E-Moderating: The key to teaching and learning online*, London, Kogan Page

Sambrook, S and Stewart, J (2002) 'Reflections and discussion', in J Tjepkema, J Stewart, S Sambrook, M Mulder, H ter Horst and J Scheerens (eds), *HRD and Learning Organisations in Europe*, London, Routledge

Sanderson, I and Foreman, A (1996) 'Towards pluralism and partnership in management development in local government', *Local Government Studies*, **22**, 1, pp 59–77

Savery, J R and Duffy, T M (1995) 'Problem based learning: instructional model and its constructivist framework', *Educational Technology*, September–October

Saville and Holdsworth (1997) '1997 Appraisal survey', *Saville and Holdsworth Newsline*, October

Savin-Baden, M (2000) *Problem-Based Learning in Higher Education: Untold stories*, Buckingham, Open University Press

Savin-Baden, M (2003) *Facilitating Problem-Based Learning: Illuminating perspectives*, Buckingham, Open University Press

Sayers, P L and Matthew, R G S (1997) 'Issues of power and control: moving from "expert" to "facilitator"', in S Armstrong, G Thompson and S Brown (eds), *Facing up to Radical Changes in Universities and Colleges*, London, Kogan Page

Scarborough, H and Elias, J (2002) *Evaluating Human Capital*, London, CIPD

Scarborough, H and Swan, J (1999) *Case Studies in Knowledge Management*, London, IPD

Scarborough, H and Swan, J (2001) 'Explaining the diffusion of knowledge management: the role of fashion', *British Journal of Management*, **12**, 1, pp 3–12

Schein, E (1964) *Organizational Psychology*, 2nd edn, Hemel Hempstead, Prentice Hall

Schmidt, H G (1995) 'Problem-based learning: an introduction', *Instructional Science*, **22**, pp 247–50

Schofield, P (1996) 'Watch your language', *Human Resources*, **23**, pp 93–97

Schön, D A (1983) *The Reflective Practitioner: How professionals think in action*, New York, Basic Books

Schön, D A (1987) *Educating the Reflective Practitioner: Toward a new design for teaching and learning in the professions*, San Francisco, CA, Jossey-Bass

Schön, D A (ed) (1991) *The Reflective Turn: Case studies in and on educational practice*, New York, Teachers College Press

Schuler, R S and Jackson, S E (1987) 'Organisational strategy and organisational level as determinants of human resource management practices', *Human Resource Planning*, **10**, 3

Seelye, H N and Seelye-James, A (1995) *Culture Clash*, Lincolnwood, IL, NIC Business Books

Segal-Horn, S (ed) (1994) *The Challenge of International Business*, London, Kogan Page

Selinker, L (1972) 'Interlanguage', *International Review of Applied Linguistics*, **10**, pp 209–31

Selwyn, N, Gerard, S and Williams, S (2002) '"We are guinea pigs really": examining the realities of ICT-based adult learning', *Studies in the Education of Adults*, **34**, 1 pp 23–41

Senge, P (1990) *The Fifth Discipline: The art and practice of the learning organization*, London, Century

Shanks, D (ed) (1997) *Human Memory: A reader*, London, Arnold

Shapiro, L (1995) *Training Effectiveness Handbook*, New York, McGraw-Hill

Sharkie, R (2003) 'Knowledge creation and its place in the development of sustainable competitive advantage', *Journal of Knowledge Management*, **7**, 1, pp 20–31

Sieberman, M (1990) *Active Training: A handbook of techniques, designs, case examples and topics*, San Diego, CA, Lexington Books

Sinclair, J and Collins, D (1992) 'Viewpoint: training and development's worst enemies – you and management', *Journal of European Industrial Training*, **16**, 5, pp 21–25

Singapore Institute of Management and Development Dimensions International (1994) *Singapore*, Singapore, SIM/DDI

Singh, A (1979) 'The "basic needs" approach to development vs the new international economic order: the significance of Third World industrialisation', *World Development*, **7**, pp 585–606

Skinner, B F (1974) *Adult Behaviour*, London, Jonathan Cape

Skryme, D (1997) 'Knowledge management: making sense of oxymoron', *Management Insight*, 2nd Series, No 2 [Online] http://www.skryme.com/insights/22km.htm

Sloman, M (2003) *Training in the Age of the Learner*, London, CIPD

Smethurst, S and Hardy, R (2004) 'The allure of online', *People Management*, 29 July

Smircich, L and Calas, M (1987) 'Organizational culture: a critical assessment', in F M Jablin *et al* (eds), *Handbook of Organizational Communication*, Newbury Park, CA, Sage, pp 228–63

Smith, A (1997) *Human Computer Factors: A study of users and information systems*, London, McGraw-Hill

Smith, A J and Piper, J A (1990) 'The tailor-made training maze: a practitioner's guide to evaluation', *Journal of European and Industrial Training*, **14**, 8, pp 1–24

Smith, J and Arkless, C (1993) 'Guidelines on good practice in foreign language training', *Journal of European Industrial Training*, **17**, 7, pp 14–17

Smith, R (1993) 'Born to be boss', *Health Service Journal*, 8 April

Sonesh-Kedor, E and Geirland, J (1995) 'Developing more creative organizations', in J W Pfeiffer (ed), *The Annual*, vol. 2, San Diego, CA, Pfeiffer

Spangenburg, H H, Schroder, H M and Duvenge, A (1999) 'A leadership competence utilisation questionnaire for South African managers', *South African Journal of Psychology*, **29**, 3, pp 117–29

Sparrow, P (1996) 'Transitions in the psychological contract in the UK banking sector: implications for HRM', *Human Resources Management Journal*, **6**, 4, pp 75–92

Spencer, L M (1986) *Calculating Human Resource Costs and Benefits*, New York, Wiley

Stacey, R (1991) *Chaos Frontier*, Oxford, Butterworth-Heinemann

Stacey, R (1992) *Managing Chaos*, London, Kogan Page

Stamatis, D, Kefalas, P and Kargidis, T (1999) 'A multi-agent framework to assist networked learning', *Journal of Computer Assisted Learning*, **15**, 3, pp 201–10

Stammer, R and Patrick, J (1975) *The Psychology of Training*, London, Methuen

Stansfield, L M (1996) 'Is self-development the key to the future?', *Management Learning*, **27**, 4, pp 429–45

Steinberg, D (1989) *Interprofessional Consultation*, Oxford, Blackwell

Stephenson, P and Galloway, V (2004) 'Problem-based learning', in G Foley (ed), *Dimensions of Adult Learning: Adult education and training in a global era*, Maidenhead, Open University Press/McGraw-Hill

Stephenson, S D (1992) The role of the instructor in computer-based training', *Performance and Instruction*, **31**, 7, pp 23–26

Stevens, B (1973) *Measuring the Return on Management Training*, London, Industrial Society

Stevens, J (2000) *High Performance Working is for Everyone*, London, CIPD

Stewart, J and McGoldrick, J (eds) (1996) *Human Resource Development: Perspectives, strategies and practice*, London, Pitman

Stewart, S and Jones, V (1987) *TA Today – A new introduction to transactional analysis*, Nottingham, Lifespace

Stewart, T A (1997) *Intellectual Capital: The new wealth of organizations*, New York, Doubleday

Stiles, P, Gratton, L, Truss, C, Hope-Hailey, V and Mc Govern, P (1997) 'Performance management and the psychological contract', *Human Resource Management Journal*, **7**, 1, pp 38–66

Stiles, P and Kulvisaechana, S (2003) *Human Capital and Performance* [Online] www.accountingforpeople. gov.uk (accessed July 2004)

Stoner, J A F and Wankel, C (1986) *Management*, 3rd edn, Englewood Cliffs, NJ, Prentice Hall

Storey, J (ed) (1991) *New Perspectives on Human Resource Management*, London, Routledge

Storey, J (1992) *Developments in the Management of Human Resources*, Oxford, Blackwell

Storey, J (1995) *Human Resource Management: A critical text*, London, Routledge

Storey, J and Wright, M (2001) 'Recruitment and selection', in I Beardwell and L Holden (eds), *Human Resource Management: A contemporary approach*, Harlow, Pearson Education

Sumison, J and Fleet, A (1996) 'Reflection: can we assess it? Should we assess it?', *Assessment and Evaluation in Higher Education*, **21**, 2 pp 121–29

Sun, Li-Teh (1986) 'Confucianism and the economic order of Taiwan', *International Journal of Social Economics*, 13, 6, pp 3–53

Sun, Li-Teh (1997) 'Mean value, government and human development', *International Journal of Social Economics*, **24**, 4, pp 383–92

Sutherland, P (ed.) (1997) *Adult Learning: A reader*, London, Kogan Page

Svieby, K E (1997) *The New Organisational Wealth: Managing and measuring knowledge-based assets*, San Francisco, CA, Berret-Koehler

Svieby, K E (2004) *Methods for Measuring Intangible Assets* [Online] www.svieby.com (accessed July 2004)

Swartz, D H (1975) 'Similarities and differences of internal and external consultants', *Journal of European Industrial Training*, **4**, 5

Swieringa, J and Wierdsma, A (1994) *Becoming a Learning Organization: Beyond the learning curve*, Wokingham, Addison-Wesley

Talbot, C (1992) 'Evaluation and validation: a mixed approach', *Journal of European Industrial Training*, **16**, 5, pp 26–32

Tan, C H (1989) 'Confucianism and nation building in Singapore', *International Journal of Social Economics*, **16**, 8, pp 5–16

Tannenbaum, R and Schmidt, W H (1958) 'How to choose a leadership pattern', *Harvard Business Review*, March/April, pp 95–101

Taraman, S R (2004) 'An innovative e-learning approach for design education', *Proceedings of the 2004 International Conference on Engineering Education (ICEE): Global Excellence in Engineering Education*, October 17–21 2004, University of Florida, Gainesville, Florida

Taylor, F W (1911) *Scientific Management: The principles of scientific management*, New York, Harper and Row, reprinted 1947

Taylor, P and Thackwray, B (2001) *Investors in People Explained*, 4th edn, London, Kogan Page

Terceiro, J B (1997) *Socied@d Digit@l*, Madrid, Alianza Editorial

Thomas B (1992) *Total Quality Training: The quality culture and quality training*, Maidenhead, McGraw-Hill

Thomas, R (1996) *Redefining Diversity*, New York, Amacom

Thompson, J and McGivern, J (1996) 'Parody, process and practice – perspectives for management education', *Management Learning*, **27**, 1, pp 21–35

Thompson, M (2002) *High Performance Work Organisation in UK Aerospace*, The Society of British Aerospace Companies Human Capital Audit 2002, London, SBAC

Thompson, R F (1993) *The Brain: A neuroscience primer*, 2nd edn, New York, W H Freeman

Thomson, K (2004) 'Brand of gold', *People Management*, **10**, 7, 8 April, p 23

Thorpe, M (1993) *Evaluating Open and Distance Learning*, Harlow, Longman

Thorpe, R and Beasley, T (2004) 'The characteristics of performance management research', *International Journal of Productivity and Performance Management*, **53**, 4, pp 334–44

Thorpe, R and Moscarola, J (1991) 'Detecting your research strategy', *Management Education and Development*, **22**, 2, pp 127–33

Thrift, N and Pile, S (eds) (1995) *Mapping the Subject: Geographies of cultural transformation*, London, Routledge

Tight, M (1996) *Key Concepts in Adult Education and Training*, London, Routledge

Tjepkema, S (2003) 'The learning infrastructure of self-managing work teams', PhD thesis, Twente University, Netherlands

Torraco, R J and Swanson, R A (1995) 'The strategic roles of human resource development', *Human Resource Planning*, **18**, 4, pp 10–21

Torrington, D and Hall, L (1995) *Personnel Management: HRM in action*, Hemel Hempstead, Prentice-Hall

Torrington, D, Hall, L and Taylor, S (2002) *Human Resource Management*, Harlow, FT/Prentice Hall

Torrington, D, Weightman, J and Johns, K (1989) *Effective Management: People and organization*, Hemel Hempstead, Prentice Hall

Towers Perrin (1996) *Learning from the Past – Changing for the Future*, London, Towers Perrin

Townley, B (1989) 'Selection and appraisal: reconstituting social relations?', in J Storey (ed), *New Perspectives in Human Resources Management*, London, Routledge

Tracey, W R (1992) *Designing Training and Development Systems*, 3rd edn, New York, Amacom

Trimnell, E (2003) *Why You Need a Foreign Language – And How to Learn One: English speaking professionals and the global challenge*, Bangor, Booklocker

Trist, E L, Higgin, G W, Murray, H and Pollock, A B (1963) *Organizational Choice*, London, Tavistock

Trompenaars, F (1995) 'Worldwide vision in the workplace', *People Management*, 18 May, pp 25–26

Trompenaars, F and Hampden-Turner, C M (2004) *Managing People Across Cultures*, Mankato, Capstone

Trompenaars, F and Woolliams, P (2004) *Business Across Cultures*, Mankato, Capstone

Truss, C (20010 'Complexities and controversies in linking HRM with organizational outcomes', *Journal of Management Studies*, **38**, 8, pp 1121–49

Tuckman, B W and Jenson, M A C (1977) 'Stages of small group development revisited', *Group and Organizational Studies*, **2**, pp 419–27

Tudor, I (1996) *Learner Centredness as Language Education*, Cambridge, Cambridge University Press

Ulrich, D (1997) *Human Resource Champions, The next agenda for adding value and delivering results*, Boston, MA, Harvard Business School Press

Ulrich, D (1998) 'Intellectual capital = competence × commitment', *Sloan Management Review*, **39**, 2, Winter, pp 15–27

Ulrich, D (1998) 'A new mandate for human resources', *Harvard Business Review*, **76**, 1, January/February, pp 124–34

Ulrich, D and Smallwood, N (2004) 'Capitalizing on capabilities', *Harvard Business Review*, **82**, 6

United Nations (2000) *UN Experts Group Meeting on Managing Diversity in the Civil Service* [Online] www.un.org

United Nations Development Programme (1996) *Human Development Report*, New York, Oxford University Press

UNESCO (1995) *World Education Report*, New York, UNESCO

Usher, R S and Bryant, I P (1989) *Adult Education as Theory, Practice and Research: The captive triangle*, London, Routledge

Van Brakel, P (1999) 'Teaching information management via a web-based course', *Electronic Library*, **17**, 6, December, pp 389–94

Van der Krogt, F J (1998) 'Learning network theory: the tension between learning systems and work systems in organizations', *Human Resource Development Quarterly*, **9**, 2, pp 157–77

Van Manen, M (1977) 'Linking ways of knowing with ways of being practical', *Curriculum Inquiry*, **6**, 3, pp 205–08

Van Matre, S (1979) *Sunship Earth*, Martinsville, IN, American Camping Association

Van Wart, M, Cayer, N J and Cork, S (1993) *Handbook of Training and Development for the Public Sector*, San Francisco, CA, Jossey-Bass

Varela, F J, Thompson, E and Rosch, E (1993) *The Embodied Mind: Cognitive science and human experience*, Boston, MA, MIT Press

Ventris, G (2004) *Successful Change Management: The fifty key facts*, London, Continuum

Venzin, M, von Krogh, G and Roos, J (1998) 'Future research into knowledge management', in G von Krogh, J Roos and D Kleine (eds), *Knowing in Firms: Understanding, managing and measuring knowledge*, London, Sage, pp 26–66

von Krogh, G, Ichijo, K and Nonaka, I (2000) *Enabling Knowledge Creation: How to unlock the mystery of tacit knowledge and release the power of innovation*, New York, Oxford University Press

von Krogh, G, Roos, J and Kleine, D (1998) *Knowing in Firms: Understanding, managing and measuring knowledge*, London, Sage

Vroom, V (1965) *Work and Motivation*, Chichester, Wiley

Wallace, S (2001) *Teaching and Supporting Learning in Further Education: Meeting the FENTO standards*, Exeter, Learning Matters

Walton, J (1999) *Strategic Human Resource Development*, London, Pearson

Warr, P B, Bird, M and Rackham, N (1970) *Evaluation of Management Training*, Aldershot, Gower Press

Warschauer, M (2000) *Electronic Literacies: Language, culture, and power in online education*, Hawaii, Lea

Waterhouse, P (1990) *Flexible Learning*, Bath, Network Educational Press

Watkins, K (1989) 'Business and industry', in S Merriam and P Cunningham (eds), *Handbook of Adult and Continuing Education*, San Francisco, CA, Jossey-Bass

Watkins, K E and Marsick, V J (1993) *Sculpting the Learning Organisation: Lessons in the art and science of systemic change*, San Francisco, CA, Jossey-Bass

Watson, T (1996) 'Motivation: that's Maslow, isn't it?', *Management Learning*, **27**, 4, pp 447–64

Watts, J (1996) *Accounting in the Business Environment*, 2nd edn, London, Pitman

Webber, S L (1997) *Trade Talks?*, London, Centre for Language Teaching and Research

Webster, B (1990) 'Beyond the mechanics of HRD', *Personnel Management*, March, pp 44–47

Weick, K and Van Orden, P (1990) 'Organizing on a global scale: a research and teaching agenda', *Human Resource Management*, **29**, 1 pp 49–61

Wellens, J (1970) 'An approach to management training', *Industrial and Commercial Training*, **8**, 7

Wellington, B and Austin, P (1996) 'Orientations to reflective practice', *Educational Research*, **38**, 3, pp 307–16

Wenger, E (1998) *Communities of Practice: Learning, meaning, and identity*, Cambridge, Cambridge University Press

Wenger, E, McDermott, R and Snyder, W (2002) *Cultivating Communities of Practice*, Boston, MA, Harvard Business School Press

White, M, Hill, S, Mills, C and Smeaton, D (2004) *Managing to Change? British Workplaces and the Future of Work*, London, Palgrave Macmillan

Whitaker, V (1994) *Managing People*, London, HarperCollins

Wickens, P (1992) 'Management development is dead!', *Management Development Review*, **5**, 5, pp 3–7

Wiig, K (1990) *Expert Systems: A manager's guide*, Geneva, International Labour Organization

Wiig, K (1997) 'Knowledge management: where did it come from and where will it go?', *Journal of Expert Systems with Applications*, **13**, Fall, pp 1–14

Williams, T (1996) 'New technology, human resources and competitiveness in developing countries: the role of technology transfer', *International Journal of Human Resource Management*, 7, 4, pp 832–45

Wills, S (1993) 'MCI and the competency movement: the case so far', *Journal of European Industrial Training*, **17**, 1, pp 9–11

Wilson, J P (1997) 'An evaluation of the Management Charter Initiative M11 Standards as the basis for the development of a competence-based language syllabus', unpublished PhD thesis, University of Sheffield

Wilson, R, Gilligan, C and Pearson, D (1992) *Strategic Marketing Management*, Oxford, Butterworth-Heinemann

Winter, R (1995) 'An integrated approach to training and development', in S Truelove (ed), *The Handbook of Training and Development*, Oxford, Blackwell

Wolf, A (2002) *Does Education Matter? Myths about education and economic development*, London, Penguin

Wood, S, de Menezes, L and Lasoasa, A (2001) 'High involvement management and performance', paper delivered at Centre for Labour Market Studies, University of Leicester, May

Woodward, J (1965) *Industrial Organization*, Oxford, Oxford University Press

Worman, D (1996) 'Managing diversity', *People Management*, 2 May, p 8

Worman, D (1998) 'Managing diversity, pressures forcing action by employers', unpublished

Worman, D (2003) 'Foreword', in T Anderson and H Metcalfe (eds), *Diversity: Stacking up the evidence*, London, CIPD, pp vii–viii

Wright, P M, Dunford, B B and Snell, S A (2001) 'Human resources and the resource based view of the firm', *Journal of Management*, **27**, pp 701–21

Wurman, R S (2001) *Information Anxiety 2*, Berkeley, CA, New Riders

Zhou, S Z and Fink, D (2003) 'Intellectual capital web: a systematic linking of intellectual capital and knowledge management', *Journal of Intellectual Capital*, **4**, 1, pp 34–48

Zohar, D and Marshall, I (2000) *Spiritual Intelligence*, London, Bloomsbury

Useful websites

Skandia: www.skandia.se/hem/hem.jsp (accessed September 2004)

Celemi: www.celemi.com (accessed September 2004)

Index

NB: pages in *italic* indicate figures or tables

accounting for HRD function   423–38
  auditing   433–38
    human capital management: APF
        recommendations   435–36
    HRD function   437–38
    particular activities   434–35
    return on investment (ROI)   436
  bibliography   438
  conclusion   438
  costing *see* accounting for HRD function:
      costing   427–32
  formal accounting   424–27
    cost-benefit analysis   425
    costing and auditing HRD function, problems
        in   425–26
    investment appraisal   426–27
  introduction and learning objectives   423–24
accounting for HRD function: costing   427–32,
    437
  HRD function   431–32
  opportunity costs   432
  particular activities   428–31, *431*
    direct costs   428, 429

fixed costs   428, 430
indirect costs   429, 430
variable costs   428, 430
Accounting for People (APF)   435–36
Acts of Parliament and Regulations
  DDA Amendment Regulations (2004)
      273–74
  Disability   264
  Disability Discrimination (DDA) (1995)   273
  Disabled Persons (1944)   267
  Education (1871)   60
  Employment (2002)   274
  Employment Equality (Religion or Belief)
      Regulations (2003)   274
  Employment Equality (Sexual Orientation)
      Regulations (2003)   274
  Equal Pay (1970)   267, 272
    amended by Equal Pay (Amendment)
        Regulations (1983)   272
    amended by Sex Discrimination (1975)   272
  Race Relations (RRA) (1975)   273
  Race Relations (Amendments) (2000)   267, 273
  Sex Discrimination (SDA) (1975, 1986)   273

adult learner: theory into practice 220–33
  adult learning 221–22
    interpretation of learning 221
    knowledge and skills, links between 221–22
  andragogy 223–24
    consequences for learning 223–24
    pedagogy 223
  barriers to learning 229–32
    financial concerns 231
    institutional barriers 230–31
    perceived barriers 232
    personal and social factors 231–32
    practical issues 230
    psychological issues 229
  bibliography 233
  conclusion 232
  humanist theories 224–29
    experiential learning and the learning cycle 227, *227*, 228–29
    hierarchy of needs 225, *225*, 226
    learning spiral 228, *228*
    personal factors and learning 226–27
  introduction and learning objectives 220–21
  motivation and learning 222–23
adult learners 210–11
  and informed choices 211
  and responsibility 211
  experiences of 211
  maturity of 210
adult learning, styles of 211–14
  behaviourist theories 212
  cognitivist theories 212–13
  humanist theories 213–14
adult learning 201–19
  adults and adulthood 209–11
    adult, categories of 209
    adulthood 210–11 *see also* adult learners
    definitions 210 *see also main entry*
  bibliography 219
  case study: negotiation training 217–18
  competence, levels of 206–09
    learning and time 207
    learning as interactive process 207–09
    learning as iterative process 208, *208*, 209
  conclusion 218
  introduction and learning objectives 201

learning 202 *see also* definitions
learning process, the 202–06
  assimilating 204
  experiential learning 205, *205*, *206*, 206, *208*
  receiving 203
  storing 204–05
  taking in 203–04
  using 205
reasons for learning and practice 217–18
styles 211–16 *see also* adult learning, styles of
  how people want to learn 216
  intelligence, seven forms of 216
  reasons for wanting to learn 212–14
  what people want to learn 214–15, *215*, 216
appraisal
  investment 426–27
  performance 173–82
  staff 410
assessment 418–21
  competence-based 420–21
  diagnostic 419
  dilemmas associated with 418–19
  formative and summative 419
  norm referencing and criteria referencing 419
  of improvement and time factor 435
  self and peer 420

balanced scorecard 84, 96–97, 449, 450
benchmarking, best practice (BPB) 465–70 *see also* total quality training and HRD
  areas for benchmarking 465–66
  comparison with parallel industries 467
  competitive 466
  generic 467
  information, acquiring 469–70
  information, analysing 470
  information, using 470
  internal 466
behaviourist learning 212, 283, 284, 326
Blind, Royal National Institute for (RNIB) 264
Bloom, B S 6, 24, 205, 215, *215*, 219, 347, 411
  taxonomy of learning 215, *215*
British Quality Foundation (BQF) 469, 473, *474*, 474
British Standards Institution 460, 461

Burnes, B   46, 49–52, 57
  nine-element model: organizational change
    49–52

cognitive learning   212–13
communication/communication techniques
    279–80, 492–95
  brochures and inserts   493
  corporate newsletters   493
  customer visits and consultancy   495
  direct mailing   492–93
  focus groups   494
  HRD newsletter   493
  internet and intranet   493–94
  media
    articles or case studies   494
    journals/newspaper advertising   494
    television/radio advertising   494
  seminars and conferences   494
  telephone sales   493
  word of mouth   495
competence(s)   4, 20, 144–45, 169, 171–73, 368
  as basis for NVQ framework   289
  competence-based assessment   420–21
  competency approaches   169
  core competences   87, 88, 171
  definition   441
  key competences   171
  levels of   206–09
  review   175
competencies and HRD in USA   4, 18–19
  business competencies   19
  intellectual competencies   19
  interpersonal competencies   19
  technical competencies   18–19
competitive advantage   115–17, 159–60
computer mediated communication (CMC)
    320
constructivism/constructivist model   326–27, 371
consultancy: perspectives on partnership   187–98
  see also definitions
  bibliography   197–98
  introduction and learning objectives   187–88
  partnership   195–97
    collaboration and conflict   195–96
    openness   197

perceptions and needs   189–91
  case study: consulting in a healthcare
    environment   190
  internal and external consultants   190–91,
    191
  trainers: developmental paths   191
  training and consultancy, approaches to   191
process and power   192–93, *194*, 195
  case study: post-traumatic stress disorder
    192–93
  consultancy role models   193
  facilitation/politics of learning   192, 193 *see*
    also definitions
  five lessons for internal OD consultants   195
purpose and meaning   188–89

definitions   4–5
  adulthood   209
  competence   441
  consultation/consultant   188–189
  development   6, 138
  disability   274
  diversity   253–54
  e-learning   320
  education   5
  evaluation   409
  facilitation, modes of   192
  flexible learning   308
  human resource development   9–10, 84
  intellectual capital   440–41
  knowledge management   113, 114
  leadership   505
  learning, formal   202
  learning, informal   202
  learning   7
  learning organization   100–01
  learning system elements   102–03
  management   381–85
  marketing   485–86
  maturity   209
  PBL and pbl   367
  performance management   158
  quality   460
  quality assurance   471
  quality control   470–71
  reliability   409

strategy   86
total quality management   460
training   4–5, 138
vocational training   5
wisdom   399
workplace diversity   253–54
Deming, W E   460, 461, 462, 466, 476, 483
   Deming Award   476
design of effective group-based training methods
   see effective group-based training methods
Drucker, P   11, 24, 115, 130, 132, 161, 381, 382, 402,
   442, 455

e-learning: a guide to principles and practice
   319–42
   A-Z of training methods (appendix)   331, *331–39*
   benefits of e-learning   321
   bibliography   340–41
   case study: blended learning   329–30
   course design/development issues *see* e-
      learning: course design/development issues
   development of good courses   322–25
      change management   322, *323*
      organizational issues   323–24
      project management   324
      socio-political issues   323
      technological issues   324–25
   disadvantages of e-learning   322
   e-learning described   320
   importance of e-learning   320–21
   introduction and learning objectives   319–20
e-learning: course design/development issues
   325–28
   ASSURE learner-centred model   325, *326*
   conclusion for implementation of e-learning
      solutions   328
   EMAR model   325, *326*, 326–27
   student learning and delivery issues   327–28
E-Learning Strategy Consultation Document (DfES)
   320
Economic Co-operation and Development,
   Organisation for (OECD)   64, 68, 70, 80
   Convention (1960)   65–66
   economic development research   64
Education and Employment, Department for
   (DfEE)   67, 420, 470

Education and Skills, Department for (DfES)   320,
   323, 324
Educational Management for Action Research
   (EMAR) model   325, *326*, 326
Educational Research and Innovation, Centre for
   (CERI)   66, 67, 68, 70, 71, 79
effective group-based training methods   342, *343*,
   344–64
   bibliography   363–64
   conclusion: the future of training methods   362
   emotion and learning   352–59
      case study: research methodology training
         354–57
      computer simulations   352
      drama and role-play   353
      humour   353–54
      innovation   354
      metaphors   357–59
      storytelling   359
      training techniques   357–58
      working with difficult subjects   354
   group training methods   344–45
      underpinning trainer attitudes, knowledge
         and skills   344–46
   introduction and learning objectives   342–44
   play and fun   359–61
      case study: playing with the literature   360
      case study: visualization, reality and
         simulation   361
      learner-centred reviewing techniques   360
      participant intellectual property development
         (PIPD)   361
   selecting methods   346–52
      design checklists   348
      experiential learning   347–48
      flexibility   348–49
      group culture   347
      group dynamics   346–47
      resources   347
      training needs analysis (TNA) information
         346
   sequencing and pacing   349, *349*, 350–52
      activity design checklist   350
      case study: negotiating access   351–52
      participant energy levels   350
      reality, elements of   350–51

using materials creatively 362
emotional intelligence (EI) 367, 397–99, 513
  emotional engineering 398
  emotional labour 398
  importance of 397
  marketing material for courses 397
Emotional Intelligence: Why it can matter more than IQ 397
employee development/cross-cultural training programmes 293–94
  Canadian International Development Agency (CIDA) 294
  Peace Corps (USA) 294
Employers' Forum for Disability, Gender Equality and Age 267
Employment, Department of (DoE) 67, 420
  Technical and Vocational Education Initiative (TVEI) 67
Employment National Training Organisation 20
Engineering Standards Association 461
English as a foreign language (EFL) 283, 286
Enlightenment, the 242, 243
  John Dewey and C Wright Mills 243
equal opportunities and managing diversity 253–61
  business case, the 257, 261
  case study: Fluent Europe's guidelines 257–61
  differences between 253
  diversity defined 253–54 *see also* definitions
  ethics 261–62
  kaleidoscope or mosaic 255
  managing diversity – theory and practice 255, *255*, 256, *256*
ethics 261–62
European Centre for the Development of Vocational Training, The (CEDEFOP) 4, 5, 24, 37, 41, 71, 79
European Commission 60, 100
European Community (EC) 268
  Treaty of Amsterdam (1977) 268
European Foundation for Quality Management (EFQM) 473, *474*
European Union 111
  ageism directive (due 2006) 274
  compulsory education 60
  Employment and Race Directives (2001) 267

  European Social Charter 72
  vocational training 72
  White Paper on Education and Training (1996) 100, 102
evaluation and assessment 407–22
  bibliography 421–22
  case study: evaluation of training 414–15
  conclusion 421
  contemporary approaches to assessment 418–21 *see also* assessment
  contemporary approaches to evaluation 411, *411*, 412–17
    evaluative methods 413–14
    reaction, learning, behaviour and result 412
    retention of learning 412–13
  evaluating
    affective learning through training 416
    changes in practice and behaviour after training 416
    cognitive learning from training 416
    how an organization benefits from training 417
    reactions to training 415
  introduction and learning objectives 407–09
  key terms 409–11
    accreditation 410
    assessment 410
    certification 410
    reliability 409
    staff appraisal 410
    validation 409
Evaluation of Educational Achievement, the International Association for the 71
experiential learning and the learning cycle 227, *227*, 228–29, 396
  Kolb's learning cycle 208, *208*, 209, 215, 392

facilitation 192, 193, 375, 508–11
Financial Times Best Places to Work awards 257
Fortune 500 companies 10, 313
fundamentals of adult learning *see* adult learning

Glossarium (CEDEFOP) 4
Glossary of Training Terms 4
Group of Seven Economic Conference (1994) 66

Habermas, Jurgen   243–44
Handy, C   7, 24, 47, 49, 57, 153, 164, 181, 253, 263,
     380, 382, 385, 402
Heron, J   375, 378, 411, 416, 422, 508, 520
hierarchy of needs   225, *225*, 226 *see also* Maslow,
     A H
Honey, P and Mumford, A   171, 216, 219, 310,
     318, 344
human resource development   3–25 *see also*
     definitions
   bibliography   23–25
   conclusion   23
   definitions: training, education, development,
        learning, HRD   4–10
      education   5
      human resource development (HRD)   8–10
      learning   7–8
      training   4–5
   HRD roles   18–23
      competences in the UK   20
      competencies and HRD in USA   18–19 *see*
         also main entry
      standards in learning and development
         (Ento,   2002) 20–23
   human resources compass   14, *15*, 15–18
      HRD sector   15–16
      HRM and HRD sector   16–17
      HRM sector   17–18
   introduction and learning objectives   3–4
   operating environment of the human resource
        department   12–13, *13*, 14
      competitive strategy: potential entrants,
         buyers, suppliers and substitutes   14
   strategic HRD   10–12
      dimensions of strategy   10
      factors discouraging HRD   12
      pressures   11
human resource management   26–43
   bibliography   41–43
   case study: Managing People   33–34
   conclusion   40–41
   hard HRM: link with business strategy   30–32
      flexibility: functional and numerical   31
   high-performance work practices   38–40, *40*
   ideal types of personnel management and HRM
        28, *29*
   implications for action   34–38
      culture   37–38
      performance management   36
      reward management   36–37, *37*
      selection   35–36
      training and development   37
   introduction and learning objectives   26
   meaning, the search for   28–29
   origins and development of   27–28
   radical framework   30
   soft HRM   32–33
   unities and pluralities   29–30
Human Rights, Universal Declaration of (1948)
     73
humanist learning/theories   213–14, 224–29 *see*
     also Rogers, C
   community language learning   287
   language teaching   287
   silent way, the   287
   suggestopedia   287

identification of learning needs *see* learning needs
Imaginization   486
'Impact of people management practices on
     business performance' (IPD)   182
*Inquiry into the Nature and Causes of the Wealth of
     Nations, An*   59
intellectual capital   439–56
   bibliography   454–56
   challenges for HRD   453
   conclusion   453–54
   implications for HR practitioners   449–52, *451*
   introduction and learning objectives   439–40
   links between different forms of capital   444–45
      customer and organizational/structural   445
      human and customer   445
      human and organizational/structural   445
      relationship between organizational/
         structural capital and business
         performance   445
   main components of   440–41, *442–43*, *443–44*,
        444
      customer/relational capital   443
      human capital   441
      organizational/structural capital   441
      social capital   444–45

quantification and measurement methods
446–49, *500*
    measurement dimensions   447–48
    measurement implications   448–49
    scorecard/stakeholder approaches   449
reporting of capital   452–53
tangible, intangible and invisible assets
445–46, *447*
    capabilities (invisible)   446
    intangible   446
    tangible   445–446
International Labour Organisation (ILO)   75, 79
Investors in People (IiP)   84, 91, 477, *478–80*, 512,
515, 516

Japan   61, 75, 169
and Deming Award   473
economic output   64, 66
influence on manufacturing quality   460–61
quality control   462
Union of Japanese Scientists and Engineers
(JUSE)   462
Johnson, G and Scholes, K   10, 24, 86, 87, 89, 98
Juran, J M   460, 462–63, 483
planning road map   463

Kaplan, R S   84, 96, 98, *440*, *442*, 450, 455 *see also*
balanced scorecard
Kirkpatrick, D   412, 422, 436
levels of training evaluation   412, 414–15, 436
knowledge, tacit   117, 118–19, *119*, 239–40, 371
knowledge management   102, 111–33
and information technology   115
and learning   127–28, *128*
bibliography   131–33
competitive advantage   115–17
    attributes providing sustainable advantage
117
    external protection of knowledge   116
    internal protection of knowledge   116
conclusion   131
definitions   113–14 *see also main entry*
data, information, knowledge and wisdom
112, *113*, 113–14
dimensions of knowledge   119–20
    economies of scale   120

knowledge types   120
explicit and tacit knowledge   118–19, *119*
implementing knowledge management   128–30
    framework   129
    systems   130
introduction and learning objectives   111–12
knowledge management process, the   120–27
    see also main entry
knowledge workers   130–31
tacit knowledge   117, 118–19, *119*
knowledge management process, the   120, *121*,
121–22, *123*, 123–27
capture   127
generating knowledge   121–23
    culture   123
    diversity   123
    employees as source of knowledge   122
    research and development (R&D)   121–22
    suppliers and customers   122
    systematic creativity   122
knowledge acquisition   124
knowledge transfer   124–27
    application   127
    communities of practice   126
    levels of   125
    trust   126–27
transformation   124
vision and search   121
Kolb, D   208–09, 216, 219, 227, 234, 245, 344, 392,
403
experiential learning cycle   208, *208*, 209, 215,
392

Language Excellence Centres, Association of   289
language learning, computer-assisted (CALL)   292
language learning, theories of   283–85
adults learning second language (L2), key
differences for   284
cognitive   283, 284–85
imitation/behaviourist   283, 284
innatist/monitor model   283, 285
interactionist   283, 285
language learning: teaching and training methods
285–87
academic or grammar translation   285
audiolingual   286

buzz words/expressions   287
  direct   286
  communicative teaching   286
  humanistic approaches   287
Languages Lead Body   289
learning, face-to-face (f2f)   320
learning, taxonomy of   215, *215 see also* Bloom, B S
Learning Combination Lock   205, *207*, 348, 362
learning needs   137–55
  bibliography   155
  conclusion   154
  defining training priorities   143–54
    costing   154
    three-stage prioritizing process   154
  defining training and development   138–39 *see also* definitions
    cultural context   138
    learning needs and training needs   139
  introduction and learning objectives   137–38
  learning needs analysis (LNA)   137
  needs at departmental level   146–48
    problem-solving groups   146–48
    skills matrix   147–48, *148*
    SWOT analysis   146–47, *147*
  needs at individual level   150–53
    case study: Ford Motor Company's EDAP   151–52
    development opportunities   151
    training gap   150
  needs at occupational levels   148–49
    job analysis   148–49
    principles of job analysis   149
  needs at organizational level   141–45
    business objectives   141
    case study: LNA and competences in the Prison Service   144–45
    human resource planning   145
    new implementations   142
    performance gap   142–43, *143*
    performance measures   142
    problem-solving groups   143–44
  undertaking an LNA   139–40
    case study: broadening scope of LNAs in NGOs in Mali   140
    data collection   139
    levels of training needs   139

learning organizations and communities of practice   99–110
  bibliography   109–10
  case study: improvement teams   104–05
  case study: work-based learning projects   105–06
  communities of practice   103
  conclusion   108–09
  criticism of concept of the learning organization   106–07
    alternative view of learning organization   107
    learning and work, restricted view of   106–07
    neglect of power issues   106
  definition and characteristics   100–06 *see also* definitions
    background of concept   100
    individual and organizational learning   101
    knowledge management   102
    Pedler's five disciplines   101
    recurring themes in the literature   102
  introduction and learning objectives   99–100
Linguists, Institute of   289

making the most of consultancy *see* consultancy: perspectives on partnership
management by objectives (MBO)   161–62
Management Chart Initiative (UK)   169
management training and development (MTD)   380–403
  bibliography   401–03
  conclusion   401
  defining management   381–85, *386–89 see also* definitions
    management process   382
    managers' roles   383
    performance levels   384
    standards for management and leadership   *386–89*
  development, meaning of   385, 390–92
    continuous professional development (CPD)   390
    personal portfolio   391–92
    self-development   390–92
  emotional intelligence (EI) and managers   397–99
    benefits   397
    emotional labour/engineering   398

rules of emotional expression   398
evaluating the effectiveness of MTD   399–400
introduction and learning objectives   380–81
key issues to consider   400–01
perceptions of MTD   392–95
    choice of programme   393–94
    control and empowerment   394–95
    paradigm, issues of   393
    research into management   392–93
    validity of theories/techniques   392, 394
techniques of MTD   395–97
    available tools/techniques   396
    case study: outdoor management
        development programmes   397
wisdom, characteristics of   399
managing the HRD function   503–20
bibliography   520
conclusion   519
control and facilitation – coaching and
        supportiveness   508–11
    coaching and mentoring   511
    facilitative leadership   510
    leadership models   509–10
    role power and personal power   509, 509,
        510
    situational leadership   510, 510
HRD professionals, further points for managers
        of   518–19
    awaydays   519
    counselling and therapy techniques   519
introduction and learning objectives   503–04
management and leadership of HRD function
        505, 505, 506–08 see also definitions
    internal consultant   507
    modeller of process   506–07
    organizational politician   508
    professional expert   506
    provider of vision   506
principles and values   511–13
    management paradigms   512–13, 512
    spiritual intelligence   513
strategic vs operational decision-making   513–18
    balance between individual, team and/or
        organizational HRD   513
    chaos theory   517
    feedback, learning from   517–18

large-scale interventions   518
    tiers of operation for HRD 514,   514–16
Manpower Services Commission   4, 5, 6, 25, 420
    New Training Intiative: An Agenda for Action   420
marketing human resource development
        484–502 see also definitions
    applying information in own work   500–02
        branding   500
        opportunities and threats   500
        SWOT analysis   500
    bibliography   402
    case study: BBSRC – communication with
        customers   495–96
    case study: freelance outdoor instructor/trainer
        486–87, 501–02
    case study: NHS Trust   490–91
    customers and customer needs   487–91
        analysing market   488
        competition issues   488
        identifying customers/needs   488
        niche marketing   488–89
        segmenting market   489
    evaluating the whole marketing process
        497–99
        case study: IYHF Hostel (2000)   498–99
        issues/solutions arising from case study
            499
    introduction and learning objectives   484–85
    keeping customers   496–97
        exceed customer expectations   496 97
        growing your business within customer
            organization   497
        relationship marketing   497
    reaching customers   491–96
        appropriate medium   491
        communication techniques see
            communication/communication
            techniques
        language and style   491
        timing contact   492
    reasons for marketing   485–87
Maslow, A H   27, 41, 42, 225, 225, 226, 513, 520
    hierarchy of needs   225, 225
Megginson, D   344, 362, 390, 403 , 412, 422, 484,
        485, 502, 503, 520
mentoring   511

metaphors   357–59
  corporate metaphors   358–59
Mintzberg, H   16, 25, 101, 102, 109, 373, 378, 383,
    384, 396, 403
Moller, C   464
  training philosophy   464
multilingual and multicultural HRD   276–96
  bibliography   295–96
  conclusion   294–95
  English as the lingua franca   282–83
  good language learner, the   290–91
    characteristics of   291
    phonetic differences   291
  introduction and learning objectives   276–77
  language in the communication age   279–80
    effective communication, factors influencing
        279, *279*, *280*, 280
  language learning, theories of   283–85 *see also*
      main entry
  language training, management of   287–90
    case study: Knoll Pharmaceuticals   288–89
    measuring results   289
    systematic approach   289
    stages of systematic approach   290
  language training in HRD   280–82
    case study: successful LL experience   281–82
    time taken learning a language   281
  multicultural/cross-cultural learning   293–94
    employee development programmes:
        common objectives   293–94
      specific objectives   294
  multilingual training and development   277–78
    foreign language training, need for   278
    monolingual and multilingual societies   277–78
  new technologies   291–93
    computer-assisted language learning (CALL)
        292
    tandem learning   292
    useful websites   292
    virtual language centres   292–93
  teaching and training methods *see* language
      learning: teaching and training methods

national economic development and human
    resource development   58–80
  bibliography   78–80

  conclusion   78
  developing a nation's human resources *see*
      national human resource development
  human development   73–78
    case study: development in Malaysia   76–78
    case study: local NGOs in West Africa   74
    education and training for peace   73, 75
  Human Development Index   75
  introduction and learning objectives   58–59
national human resource development   59–73
  benchmarking national performance   70–71
    comparing standards   71
    lifelong learning commitment   70
    literacy and numeracy skills   71
  case study: Bahrain model   61–63
  demand and supply in the labour market   68,
      69
  demographic factors   60–61
  enforcement/encouragement of HRD   72–73
    training: European Social Charter   72
    wage bill levies   72
  flexibility in the workplace   69–70
  integrating education and training   67–68
    human resources intensive strategy   67
    mobility strategy   68
    polarization strategy   67
  national economic competition   63–64, *64*, 65
    knowledge-intensive societies   65
  national strategies   65–67
  OECD Convention   65–66
neuro-linguistic-programming (NLP)   239, 517
Norton, D P   84, 96, 98, 440, 442, 449, 450, 455 *see*
    also balanced scorecard

open, distance and flexible learning (ODFL)
    297–403
  bibliography   317–18
  conclusion   317
  corporate open learning centre   313–16
    case study: computer-based training   315
    physical centres   315–16
    record-keeping   316
    tailor-made programmes   316
  distance learning   302–05
    case study: television and training   303–04
    constraints on time and place   304

face-to-face learning sessions 305
motivation 304
third-generation 305
flexible learning 308–09 *see also* definitions
degrees of flexibility 308
from teaching to learning 300–01
introduction and learning objectives 299–300
issues for ODFL providers 311–13
advantages/disadvantages for learners 313,
314
choice of programmes 313
involving company trainers 312
management of programmes 312
issues for the learner in ODFL 309–11
computer-based training (CBT) 310
developing self-confidence 310
ODFL in workplace 310–11
variances in motivation and learning ability
309
worker motivation 311
open learning 305, *306*, 306–08
case study: offshore open learning 307–08
summary of case for 307
Open University (UK) 302, 305, 306
Opportunity through People (IPD) 164
organizational change 44–57
bibliography 57
case study: human resource issues – higher
education 53–55
conclusion 56–57
failure/incomplete success, reasons for 52–55
introduction and learning objectives 44–45
nature of change 46–47
economic approach theory (E) 47
elements of change 46–47
organizational capabilities approach theory
(O) 47
seven-S framework 47
two-dimensional diagram 47
paradox of change 45–46
paradox principles 46
role of HRD 55–56
process roles 56
task roles 56
transition methods 47–51
Field/Field Force Theory (Lewin) 47–48

injunctions to managers (Lupton) 48
Handy's schema 49
nine-element model (Burnes) 49–52
organizational trust 181

Pedler, M 100, 101, 109, 268, 390, 403
five disciplines 101
People Management 353, 354 (CIPD Journal) 353
performance management, effectiveness of
162–73
added value 163
competence and competence-related pay 169
competence-based/related pay 171, *172*, 172–73
control or empowerment 167, *167*, 168
integrated systems 163–64
motivation 164–66
balance and trust 165–66
case study: psychological contract 166
expectancy theory 164
psychological contracts 165–66
pay and rewards 168–69
performance and reward 169, *170*, 171
performance management 36, 157–62, *162*
definitions 158 *see also main entry*
shared vision 160–61
strategic goals: gaining competitive advantage
159–60
systematic approaches 161–62
performance management and human resource
development 156–86
bibliography 184–86
conclusion 182–84
effectiveness *see* performance management,
effectiveness of
implications for HRD professionals and
practitioners 183–84
implications for organizations, managers and
individuals 182–83
introduction and learning objectives 156–57
performance appraisal 173–82
case study: appraisal and training 174–75
forms of appraisal 175–76, *176*, *177*, 177,
178–80
ownership of appraisal 177, 181
purpose of 173–74
trust 181–82

performance management   157–62 *see also main entry*
'Performance management – the MBO of the 1990s' 161
Performance through People: The new people management   156, 452
Personnel and Development, Chartered Institute of (CIPD)   156, 173, 452, 485
   and Engineering Employers Federation Report (2003)   39, 163
Personnel and Development, Institute of (IPD, now CIPD)   158, 168, 182, 254, 255
Porter, M E   14, 25, 66, 78, 80, 84, 92, 98
Power of Experiential Learning, The   358
PricewaterhouseCoopers   46, 50, 51, 52
   Change Integration Team   46
problem-based learning (PBL)   365–79
   as way of professional and lifelong learning 368–70
      characteristics of PBL *369*
      competences   368
      generative learning   368–69
   bibliography   378–79
   case study: work relations and HRD   376
   conclusion   377
   effectiveness of PBL   367–77
      deep approach   376–77
      strategic approach   377
      surface approach   377
   facilitating PBL   374–75
      appropriate questions   374
      group functioning   375
      modes of facilitation   375
   introduction and learning objectives   365–66
   knowledge and PBL   370–71
      action research/learning   371
      expertise   370
      PBL process   371
   origins and principles   366–68
      PBL and pbl   367, 370
      student-centredness   367
   PBL: theoretical underpinning   371–72, *373*, 373–74
      constructivism   371
      critical reflection and criticality   373
      equivocation, problems of   372

metacognitive strategies   372
understanding, development of   373–74

Quality Awards, UK   469

Racial Equality, Council for (CRE)   267
   Leadership Challenge   267
reflective practice   234–51, 367
   bibliography   249–51
   introduction and learning objectives   234–36
   models and loops   237–39
      behaviour patterns: models I and II   237–38
      learning loops   238, *238, 239,* 239
   personal experience   247–49
      structured writing   248–49
   reflection into practice   245–47
      problems and approaches   245–47
      references   246
   reflection-in-action   239–42
      critiques   241–42
      points to note   240–41
      questions for reflection   241
      tacit knowledge   239–40
   social context   242–45
      critical reflective practice: beyond Schön 244–45
      critical social science: Jurgen Habermas 243–44
      influential authors   245
      the Enlightenment: John Dewey and C Wright Mills   243
      the reflective practitioner: Donald Schön 236–37
research   157, 160
   education (CERI)   67, 68, 70, 71
   Institute of Personnel and Development   168
   intellectual capital management   452–54
reward management   36–37, *37*
Reward Management Survey (CIPD)   172
Rogers, C   213–14, 219, 221–22, 224–25, 227–28, 345

scorecard/stakeholder approaches   449 *see also* balanced scorecard
Senge, P   50, 57, 100, 101, 102, 109, 368, 379, 397, 403

seven-S framework (strategy, structure, systems, staff, style, shared values, skills) 47
Singapore Institute of Management and Development Dimensions International 160
Singapore National Productivity Award 160–61
skills matrix 147–48, *148*
standards
    European (EN 29000) 461
Standardization, International Organization for 460
    ISO 9000 461
strategic goals: gaining competitive advantage 159–60
strategy and human resource development 83–98
    balanced scorecard, the 96–97, *97*
    bibliography 97–98
    case for strategic HRD (SHRD) 84, *84, 85,* 85–86
        organizations, types of 85–86
    conclusion 97
    introduction and learning objectives 83–84
    strategic analysis and HRD 92–93, *94*
        value chain analysis 92–93
    strategy, the problem with 89–90
    strategy and HRD *90*
    strategy and HRD – an historical context 91, *91*
    strategy and strategic HRD 86–89
        link with business life cycle stages 88–89
        strategic analysis 87–88
        strategic choice 87
        strategic decision-making, levels of 86–87
        strategy implementation 87
    Unipart: case study 95–96
    value chain for Unipart Group of companies 93–94, *94*
sustainable competitive advantage 156
SWOT analysis 146–47, *147,* 500

Teaching and Learning: towards a learning society (EC white paper) 452
total quality training and HRD 459–83
    best practice benchmarking (BPB) *see* benchmarking, best practice (BPB)
    bibliography 428–83
    case study: Six Sigma 472

case study: value stream mapping 467, *468,* 468–69
    conclusion 482
    introduction and learning objectives 459–60
    quality 460–64 *see also* definitions
        business case for 460–61
        Deming's checklist 462
        gurus 462–63
        Juran's planning road map 463
        management absolutes 463
        Moller's training philosophy 464
        standards 461
    quality awards 437–76
        areas of UK quality award (BQF) 475–76
        Deming Award and checklist 473
        EFQM/BQF award assessment model 474
        Malcolm Baldridge Award and checklist 473
    quality control and quality assurance 470–72
        quality indicators, four dimensions of 471
    total quality training and development 476–81
        Investors in People (IiP) 477, *478–80*
        TQM process 481, *481*
Trade and Industry, Department of
    Innovation Unit 354
Training Needs for Women 346
transactional analysis 508

United Nations 254
    Development Programme (UNDP) 66, 75, 80
    Human Development Index 75
United Nations Educational, Scientific and Cultural Organization (UNESCO)
    constitution 73
    education survey 60
United States of America (USA) 18–20
    Competitiveness, Council on (USA) 64
    competitiveness of economy: MIT research 64
    labour market and business process re-engineering 71
    legislation on equal rights 267–68
    reporting of capital: legal considerations 452
    Training and Development, American Society for 18, 181
    vocational and technical education 69

value chain/value chain analysis 92–94, *94*

Work Foundation 163
Working Together, Education and Training 420
workplace diversity and training 252–75
  bibliography 274–75
  case study: BT and diversity 269–70
  case study: Oxfam's diversity strategy 270–72
  checklist for diversity training 266
  conclusion 268–72
  educational approach 265–66
  equal opportunities and managing diversity
      253–61 *see also main entry*
  introduction and learning objectives 252

legal framework and issues 267–68 *see also* Acts
      of Parliament and Regulations
legal framework (appendix) 272–74 *see also*
      Acts of Parliament and Regulations
  equality commissions 272
  towards a learning organization 268
  training for diversity 262–64
    awareness programmes 264
    the way forward 263–64
Workplace Employee Relations Survey (UK) 38, 41
Workplace Industrial Relations survey 41
World Employment Conference 75